International Law of Human Rights

The Library of Essays in International Law
General Editor: Robert McCorquodale

Titles in the Series

International Law of Human Rights
Michael K. Addo

International Law and Indigenous Peoples
S. James Anaya

The International Criminal Court
Olympia Bekou and Robert Cryer

Democracy and International Law
Richard Burchill

Law of the Sea
Hugo Caminos

The Law of Treaties
Scott Davidson

Humanitarian Law
Judith Gardam

International Economic Regulation
Jane Kelsey

International Organizations
Jan Klabbers

International Peacekeeping
Boris Kondoch

Sources of International Law
Martti Koskenniemi

Space Law
Francis Lyall and Paul B. Larsen

Self-Determination in International Law
Robert McCorquodale

International Dispute Settlement
Mary Ellen O'Connell

International Crimes
Nikos Passas

International Environmental Law
Volumes I and II
Paula M. Pevato

State Responsibility in International Law
René Provost

Jurisdiction in International Law
Michael Reisman

Title to Territory
Malcolm N. Shaw

The Nature of International Law
Gerry Simpson

Collective Security Law
Nigel D. White

International Law of Human Rights

Edited by

Michael K. Addo

University of Exeter, UK

ASHGATE
DARTMOUTH

Published by
Dartmouth Publishing Company
Ashgate Publishing Limited
Gower House
Croft Road
Aldershot
Hants GU11 3HR
England

Ashgate Publishing Company
Suite 420
101 Cherry Street
Burlington, VT 05401-4405
USA

Ashgate website: http://www.ashgate.com

British Library Cataloguing in Publication Data
International law of human rights. – (The library of essays in international law)
1. Human rights
I. Addo, Michael K.
341.4'8

Library of Congress Control Number: 2004104910

ISBN 0 7546 2158 8

Printed and bound in Great Britain by TJ International Ltd, Padstow, Cornwall

Contents

PART V CHALLENGES

Acknowledgements

The editor and publishers wish to thank the following for permission to use copyright material.

Columbia Law Review for the essays: Anthony D'Amato (1982), 'The Concept of Human Rights in International Law', *Columbia Law Review*, **82**, pp. 1110–59; Dianne Otto (1997), 'Rethinking the "Universality" of Human Rights Law', *Columbia Human Rights Law Review*, **29**, pp. 1–46.

Fordham Law Review for the essay: Ruti Teitel (1997), 'Human Rights Genealogy', *Fordham Law Review*, **66**, pp. 301–17. Copyright © 1997 Fordham Law Review.

Harold Honju Koh for the essay: Harold Hongju Koh (1999), 'How is International Human Rights Law Enforced?', *Indiana Law Journal*, **74**, pp. 1397–417.

The Johns Hopkins University Press for the essays: Jack Donnelly (1984), 'Cultural Relativism and Universal Human Rights', *Human Rights Quarterly*, **6**, pp. 400–419. Copyright © 1984 The Johns Hopkins University Press. Reprinted with permission of The Johns Hopkins University Press; Robert McCorquodale with Richard Fairbrother (1999), 'Globalization and Human Rights', *Human Rights Quarterly*, **21**, pp. 735–66. Copyright © 1999 The Johns Hopkins University Press. Reprinted with permission of The Johns Hopkins University Press.

Oxford University Press for the essay: Matthew Craven (2000), 'Legal Differentiation and the Concept of the Human Rights Treaty in International Law', *European Journal of International Law*, **11**, pp. 489–519.

Virginia Journal of International Law for the essays: Fernando R. Tesón (1985), 'International Human Rights and Cultural Relativism', *Virginia Journal of International Law*, **25**, pp. 869–98; Makau wa Mutua (1996), 'The Ideology of Human Rights', *Virginia Journal of International Law*, **36**, pp. 589–657.

The Yale Law Journal for the essay: Laurence R. Helfer and Anne-Marie Slaughter (1997), 'Toward a Theory of Effective Supranational Adjudication', *Yale Law Journal*, **107**, pp. 273–391. Reprinted with permission of the Yale Law Journal Company and William S. Hein Company.

Every effort has been made to trace all the copyright holders, but if any have been inadvertently overlooked the publishers will be pleased to make the necessary arrangement at the first opportunity.

Series Preface

Open a newspaper, listen to the radio or watch television any day of the week and you will read or hear of some matter concerning international law. The range of matters include the extent to which issues of trade and human rights should be linked, concerns about refugees and labour conditions, negotiations of treaties and the settlement of disputes, and decisions by the United Nations Security Council concerning actions to ensure compliance with international law. International legal issues have impact on governments, corporations, organisations and people around the world and the process of globalisation has increased this impact. In the global legal environment, knowledge of international law is an indispensable tool for all scholars, legal practitioners, decision-makers and citizens of the 21st century.

The Library of Essays in International Law is designed to provide the essential elements for the development of this knowledge. Each volume contains essays of central importance in the development of international law in a subject area. The proliferation of legal and other specialist journals, the increase in international materials and the use of the internet, has meant that it is increasingly difficult for legal scholars to have access to all the relevant articles on international law and many valuable older articles are now unable to be obtained readily. These problems are addressed by this series, which makes available an extensive range of materials in a manner that is of immeasurable value for both teaching and research at all levels.

Each volume is written by a leading authority in the subject area who selects the articles and provides an informative introduction, which analyses the context of the articles and comments on their significance within the developments in that area. The volumes complement each other to give a clear view of the burgeoning area of international law. It is not an easy task to select, order and place in context essays from the enormous quantity of academic legal writing published in journals – in many languages – throughout the world. This task requires professional scholarly judgment and difficult choices. The editors in this series have done an excellent job, for which I thank and congratulate them. It has been a pleasure working with them.

ROBERT McCORQUODALE
General Series Editor
School of Law
University of Nottingham

Introduction

International Law of Human Rights: An Introduction

The inherently political nature of modern international law as a system largely hinged on the interests of state actors with a focus on territorial separation would seem an unlikely host for the idea of human rights, with its emphasis on the individual. Yet the idea and practice of rights has always been a part of, and in fact today flourishes in, this rugged environment of interstate politics. This blossoming of the idea of rights in international law may be largely attributed to the successful reconciliation of the objective ambitions of human rights with entrenched practices relating to national sovereignty and interstate competition for hegemony. In fact, these contradictions are structural in character and so run deeper than a mere effort at reconciliation, especially when one acknowledges the fact that the national authorities – on whose goodwill international law depends to make any difference to the human rights enterprise – are the primary violators of human rights. It has become a legitimately persistent source of frustration to human rights idealists and victims of violations that, in this field, international law promises so much and yet delivers very little.

To be fair, the reality of the international law of human rights is one of an extremely complicated and delicate puzzle that relies on the sensitivity of all actors and also the dexterity of its managers to reveal its true character. The visible, and in many ways tangible, successes of international law that we observe and experience today in the field of human rights are the product of centuries of slow and gradual evolution of a dynamic subject that has successfully adjusted to changing priorities and visions of the international community. What may have began as an unstructured, incoherent and ad hoc representation of a self-interested practice among states to acknowledge and respect the rights of aliens has now evolved into a comprehensive body of normative standards, processes and institutions that confirm the entitlement of *everyone* to human rights regardless of race, nationality, age or sex.

A diverse range of actors, including international organizations,[1] non-governmental organizations (Steiner, 1991; Willets, 1997; Brett, 1999, p. 399; Clapham, 2000, p. 175; Weiss and Gordenker, 1996) and national institutions acting individually and collectively, have contributed to the growth of international law of human rights. To these conventional actors may be added the unsung contribution of academic scholarship to the exposure, elaboration and debate concerning human rights matters in international law. Today, this field boasts a healthy body of academic scholarship that provides sufficient inspiration and focus for a selection of essays in a volume such as this. In truth, however, academic scholarship is inextricably linked to the contribution from the other well-known actors.[2] As a body of knowledge, the scholarship, in its inevitable diversity, has revealed and explained the intricate web of relationships between international law and national law, the relevance of human rights to conventional international law doctrines and the associations between international law of human rights, on the one hand, and established disciplines of politics, philosophy, sociology and economics on the other. However, the scholarship is not always descriptive; because international law is by no means a perfect discipline, there is also a body of critical scholarship focused on the inevitable shortcomings and problems of the subject. Most of this critical scholarship is constructive in its aims, focused on analyses, explanations and suggestions for an improved understanding and a more refined and effective working strategy. This particular dimension of the academic scholarship provides the more specific and direct inspiration for the selection of essays in this volume.

The Thematic Focus of the Essays

At the best of times, the realization of a purposeful cohesion in any collection of essays, often written at different times to different themes, is a success in itself. A remit to gather essays within a limited space that encapsulate the nature of a subject so diverse and so influential as the international law of human rights is truly impossible. Such a task would be more appropriately reflected in a less ambitious exercise in selection rather than a collection, and the essays in this volume are of that character. Nevertheless, it is possible to glean a thematic essence from the vast cornucopia of thoughts that have been represented in the essays selected for this volume. One of the essays' thematic distinctions is their primary focus on the international law of human rights, although unavoidably this also relates to the established regime of structured standards, processes and institutions that have collectively come to be referred to as international human rights law. Similarly, while the aim of the series of the International Library of Essays, of which this volume forms a part, is to develop a doctrinal (rather than a practical) overview, the essays understandably do not directly address matters relating to case law at either the national or international levels. In addition, the essays seek to target the contribution of critical scholarship that challenges some of the established, and in certain instances, unsettled wisdom in this field of international law.

This constructive critical scholarship of international law highlights important conflicts, inconsistencies and paradoxes generated by the subject. Some of these are structural, and so would require a radical rethink of the ethos of the subject, to redress, while others are largely superficial and may be confronted with relative ease. The 12 essays in this volume have been selected for their relevance to this constructive critical perspective of human rights scholarship. The articulation of the shortcomings and paradoxes, as well as any explanations and suggestions, are not meant to represent the ultimate and final word on the matter. Indeed, each of these essays was not only written at a different time and in a different context but also, and above all, written to its own agenda which may be different from that of the present volume. However, together they encapsulate a particular character of the international law in this field. For a subject whose full and comprehensive exposé cannot be undertaken in the limited space available here, such a narrow focus is legitimate.

Taking a critical perspective is a valuable exercise for a variety of good reasons. Either as a consequence of its nature or as a result of its successes, the law of human rights has attained a more revered status than the general international law of which it forms a part. It has come to be associated with good deeds and what is right. It is also a process by which wrongs may be rectified and a standard by which despotic governments are openly challenged. Although a part of international law, it has (relatively successfully) challenged the impervious norms of international law, such as sovereignty and non-intervention, and has consequently attained the status of untouchability: as it can appear to do no wrong, its shortcomings are, by and large, overlooked. Despite its widespread appeal, the international law of human rights remains a specialized discipline whose true character is alien and unknown to many and thus misunderstood. To challenge, object or criticize human rights law is considered an unfriendly and anti-democratic act. Yet, like any discipline, the international law of human rights is not a perfect system. It is riddled with both normative and practical shortcomings, not all of which are unavoidable but persist nonetheless. Some of the problems of the law of human rights are basic, but foundational, and it is valuable to confront some of these failures directly and openly if the future of the disciple is not to be compromised. Yet, in view of the deference with which scholars and policy-makers tend to approach human rights, such a critical approach is unlikely to come from sources external to the discipline itself. Effective confrontation of the shortcomings of the international law of human rights law can only come from within the discipline itself.

The international law of human rights, founded on a Westphalian substructure of sovereign independent states, makes a legitimate claim to legal certainty and objectivity that is normally associated with the rule of law; yet its strong political associations and implications, built around a specific historical and philosophical narrative, situates it in that delicate space between the unscrupulous instability of international politics, the subjectivity of historical narrative and the imprecision of philosophical thought. This is intellectually, as well as in reality, a pretty tough space to occupy, as the cynicism and distrust of the political sphere and the high expectations of the majesty of the law do not always blend successfully. The disorderly effects of the interface between politics and law tend to be much more evident in this field of international law, perhaps because of the direct and tangible implications of its shortcomings on the individual and on community groups. The consequences of failure in the human rights field are far more difficult to ignore or overlook than with any dimension of international law. With no fewer than 6 billion individuals looking up at one time or another to the promises held up by its ideals, human rights law not only carries a heavy and complex burden, but also an increased risk of failure and disappointment. In such a sensitive and unstable environment, a self-critical perspective is always valuable in seeking to limit the potential for abuse.

A Brief Overview

The role of international law in human rights matters during its formative years was unstructured, opportunistic and directly dependent on the convenience of national authorities. It was the extraterritorial challenges to the presumption that the guarantee – and so the protection – of individual rights was a matter of exclusive national competence that created the initial opportunities for a more engaging role for international law (Sohn and Buergenthal, 1973, ch. 2). In relation to aliens, the strategic response to this challenge of extraterritoriality in terms of the law of diplomatic protection was sufficiently specific and exceptional in its scope so as not to undermine the control exercised by national authorities (Amerasinghe, 1967; Borchard, 1915; Garcia Amador, 1958). Although it marginalized the individual victim, it represented an important acknowledgement of a facilitative role of international law in matters of individual welfare. As a crucial wedge in the door of *domaine reservé*, the law of diplomatic protection marked the humble beginnings of the slow and gradual process of empowering international law in matters relating to human rights.

Further challenges arising from the protection of victims of armed conflict, the slave trade and the protection of religious and other minorities, introduced new perspectives on the role of international law in the human rights field (Sohn and Buergenthal, 1973, p. 7 and ch. 4). Viewed in isolation, these individual instances for the expansion of the role of international law may seem insignificant but, together, they constitute the foundations of today's integrated regime of norms, processes and institutional structures devoted to the promotion of human rights. The origins of the international law of human rights would therefore seem to lie far beyond the formal evolutionary reorganization initiated by the Charter of the United Nations.

By 1945, so much had happened in international affairs as to alter noticeably the turf on which the law engaged with society. The marginalization of victims of human rights violations by national authorities had become manifestly objectionable, as had the military and political aggression among states that gravely undermined the Westphalian edifice on which international law stood. In addition, it had also become evident that states, on their own and amongst themselves, could not resolve the pressing problems of the time. Non-state entities, such as international organizations and non-governmental organizations, had emerged as important contributors and facilitators of the international process. The Charter of the United Nations became the formal embodiment of the outcome of the critical and essential reality check to inject certainty and predictability into international affairs based on the rule of law and cooperation among states.[3]

The Charter marked a fundamental departure from the usual practice of occasional and ad hoc resort to international law as the alternative of choice for redressing problems that exceeded the capabilities of individual states. It envisaged a wide-scale and integrated empowerment of international law in fields such as international security (Chapters I, VI and VII), economic development (Chapter I), decolonization (Chapters I and XII) and human rights (Chapters I and X). In these fields of partnership between international law and national regimes, the new international legal order envisaged a regime of policies and institutional structures for the effective realization of the aims and ambitions of the international community.[4] The actions and policies across the organization, but especially those of the Trusteeship Council, the General Assembly and the Economic and Social Council (ECOSOC) and its subsidiary Commission and Sub-Commission on Human Rights, contributed to the success of the human rights ideals set out in the Charter. However, the successful record in the specialized field of international human rights law masks the initial unpreparedness of international law to engage fully with the challenges thrust upon it by the new international order.[5] Still heavily under the influence of the Westphalian norms of sovereignty and non-intervention, it is hardly surprising that progress has been slow and largely opportunistic.

To the extent that the Charter did not prescribe a human rights programme of action, it is arguable that the legitimacy and constitutionality of a substantial part of *ex post* Charter human rights activity is inherently flawed or at least suspect. Such a conclusion rests on an exaggerated relevance of the Westphalian structure of international law that had already conceded to the new challenges set out in the Charter. The search for the constitutional legitimacy of human rights actions must therefore focus on the Charter itself, and a teleological perspective of its provisions reveals a sound and secure authorization of further action aimed at the effective realization of the ideals it sets out. First, and indeed most significant, is the identification of human rights ambitions among its purposes (Article 1(3)), which presupposes the need and reason to realize human rights ideals and also a need for further action. In addition, the empowerment of institutions, including the principal organs, to take action in the field of human rights – especially the express directive to the ECOSOC to establish specialized commissions (Article 68) to implement human rights goals – was a further indication of the consensus to move forward. A further indication of action appears in Chapter XII which directly and categorically launches the human rights programme by establishing and facilitating a programme of action for decolonization.

The Charter's authorization of human rights action was not unregulated. Indeed, the realization of all the purposes set out in the Charter was subject to the normative guidance of the principles of international law in Article 2. These principles reiterated the Westphalian norms of sovereignty (Article 2(1)), non-intervention (Article 2(7)) and, from these, the predictable endorsement of state consent, reciprocity, self-interest, territorialism and so on. From the perspective of the human rights ambitions, the insistence on the state-oriented norms in the Charter's principles was a source of contradiction and conflict. The challenge has always been one of defining a strategy to reconcile the human rights ambitions with the principles of international law. The legitimacy of the human rights programme depends on how successfully this balance was struck.

Another pillar of legitimacy of all action in the new international legal order was the symbiotic dependence between national and international regimes. This was represented in terms of the undertakings to cooperate (UN Charter, Articles 1 and 56). For purposes of its human rights ambitions, this required a separation between national and international responsibilities. The primary responsibility for the realization of human rights lay with national authorities, supported by international action. In this sense, international action was in a subsidiary, but nevertheless important, relationship with national responsibilities. This principle of subsidiarity has been a double-edged guiding light in the subsequent evolution of international human rights law and action (Corazza, 2003; Jackson, 2003; Petzold, 1993; Shelton, 1993).

This mindset of seeking to maintain a balance between the principles and purposes of the new international legal order informed the decision of the Commission on Human Rights to undertake a programme of standard-setting ahead of a scheme for responding to petitions against individual governments (ECOSOC Resolution 5 (I) of 1946). In seeking to reconcile the ostensible contradiction between principles and purposes of the Charter, this decision may be explained from two perspectives: a subjective perspective and an objective one. The subjective explanation recalls the temporal context (1947–1967) in which a strategy premised on the congenial accommodation of the interests of national authorities in the hope of securing their confidence and support was judged to be a valid end in itself. At the same time, from an objective perspective, it was fairly evident that the credibility and the wider success of the human rights programme depended on the definition and identification of a clear set of human rights standards that would provide the critical point of reference for international action. Such a point of reference was indispensable in the increasingly culturally diverse and politically polarized international community. To the extent that any agreement on the applicable standards would also represent a regime of 'higher consensus', it provided a more realistic springboard for the effective evolution of the modern law of human rights law. As the product of negotiation and interaction involving all the key actors, but especially states, it is unlikely to be denounced. In addition, the definition of standards predictably focused minds on their implementation and so established the next link in the chain of realization. Above all, it was not entirely insignificant that this strategy coincided with comparable plans in the European and American contexts where the preferences of some of the most powerful member states were articulated.

The products of the standard-setting enterprise, including the Universal Declaration of Human Rights and the long list of other human rights declarations and treaties (Brownlie and Goodwin-Gill, 2002), proved a remarkable success in view of the level and complexity of the political charge in the whole atmosphere. Indeed, in reality, the success of this enterprise exceeded the mere articulation of the standards. Cast in terms of the rule of law, the international human rights regime commanded far higher levels of respectability that enabled the launch of further and more daring policies. Charter-based institutions, such as the General Assembly, the Security Council and, more directly, the Economic and Social Council (ECOSOC), took advantage of the legal characterization of human rights to challenge governmental abuses. In the General Assembly and the Security Council there was always a tinge of political undercurrent but less so in ECOSOC where the renewed confidence in human rights was directed at reasserting the authority to redress petitions. Two decades of the Commission's denial of the authority to confront the petitions may seem an awfully long time from the perspective of modern human rights practice, but the competing interests and norms made this inevitable. The flagship ECOSOC Resolution 1235 (XLII) and 1503 (XLVIII) procedures,[6] as well as the political processes in the General Assembly (Cassese, 1992, p. 25, Quinn, 1992, p. 55) and the Security Council (Bailey, 1992, p. 304), are by no means the most rigorous of international procedures but they serve important complementary roles to the treaty-based supervision (Alston, 1992a). These international processes, together with national and regional regimes, represent the system of international protection.

The integration of disparate strategies may well be one of the great strengths of international law of human rights. Based on a complementary interdependence between national and regional regimes, as well as global structures, the international law of human rights has succeeded in transposing rhetorical political ideals into real outcomes. In the process it has made the act of challenging established Wesphalian wisdom a commonplace event. Represented as contestable ends in themselves, individual rights and freedoms are exposed as not the exclusive attribute of a social contract with governments but as an inherent part of human character. That national authorities now look to international law for inspiration and direction in human rights matters is truly an outstanding accomplishment.

Overall, the successes and achievements of the new international legal order have been remarkable. The Charter launched, and in that sense authorized, a radical reconsideration of the weaknesses of the Westphalian framework of international law. Through its human rights ambitions it cast a platform not merely for the 'internationalization of human rights', but also for the 'humanization of international law' (Buergenthal, 1978, p. 28). This adjustment of the perspective of international law elevated it from its secondary and largely peripheral relationship with national regimes to a respectable partnership that draws heavily on the pragmatic outcome orientation of international law. This empowerment of international law liberated it from its abstract shell of so-called 'state' sovereignty, territorial compartments and unrelated human communities into a world of tangible reality in which the involvement of individuals, groups and non-governmental organizations was no longer sacrilegious. This was nothing short of a direct challenge to the Westphalian mindset, confirmed further by the outcomes of the United Nations human rights standard-setting project. The revelation and restatement in these resolutions, declarations and treaties *inter alia* that rights were universal entitlements and, as such, ends in themselves, was essentially a denial of the territorial and social contract representation within the Westphalian model of international law. Even more challenging to this model was the formal recognition of the role of the individual in international law, as well as the unequivocal identification of national authorities as the fulcrum of human rights violations.

All of this advance in the international law of human rights is confronted with the unfortunate reality, of course, that change may only come about with the cooperation of the same national authorities that precipitated the human rights crisis in the first place. The whole edifice of international law in this field therefore remains rather insecure. This is a constrained working environment in which, unsurprisingly, it is neither possible nor realistic to deliver the expectations either quickly or sufficiently. As a result, the law's credibility has always been perched on an unforgiving knife-edge. Furthermore, this credibility depends on the law's ability to hold on to its gains, as well as to adapt to new challenges without losing its core ideals. Various aspects of the politics of international law remain fairly entrenched, unpredictable and unyielding challenges for human rights. The jostling for power and hegemony among states generates difficult problems concerning the universality and the objectivity of human rights. The passionate disagreement and debate between the different political alignments of states on the human rights dimensions of culture, development, the environment and so on are only typical of the challenges that remain unaddressed. The Cold War may have ended, but the fresh and bleeding human rights wounds it left behind on both sides cannot be avoided. There is also the problem of poverty and the marginalization of the world's poor. This is as much a challenge for the international law of human rights as is the need for swift and effective response to threats of genocide, ethnic cleansing, human trafficking and the proliferation of arms. That every one of these handicaps and challenges is attributable to the entrenchment or fetishization of aspects of the Westphalian structure of international law defines a truly uphill challenge for the international law of human rights.

The arena has been complicated further by entirely different challenges posed by the globalization of world economies in which the role of non-state actors, such as international intergovernmental institutions and transnational enterprises, has prominently eclipsed that of the state. So far, the international law of human rights has not clearly demonstrated an imaginative and flexible response to these new challenges in its application of its established standards.

Nature

For a subject with such widespread influence, it is rather ironic that basic and fundamental issues, such as the character of the international law of human rights, remain unresolved. In general, much is taken for granted without a coherent and secure explanation. In addition, the international law of human rights generates high expectations that it is unable to deliver. That the specialized field of international human rights law is a late development in the wider field of international law is confirmed by the identification of the Charter of the United Nations as the marker for the start of the era of an integrated and purposive system of international human rights law. However, the political and legal logistics of this era are far more complex. Through the Charter of the United Nations, international law has, in essence, been handed a poisoned chalice of human rights with the exaggerated expectation of delivering the most impossible of undertakings. The achievement of the Charter's human rights ambitions depends on a continual delivery of tangible outcomes based on a partisan commitment to the needs of individuals on a renewed culture of trust for government authorities. The most cursory of assessments would normally reveal irreconcilable paradigmatic contradictions between international law, in its devotion to servicing the state, and an adoration of sovereignty, non-intervention and territorialism, on the one hand, and human rights law with a commitment to the individual on the other. Without an independent identity, human rights law can only be conducted within the wider, even if often contradictory, priorities of state-centred international law, thus robbing it of the freedom and autonomy to determine and drive its own progress. For as long as states and national authorities seek and retain control over the direction of the international law of human rights, effective and genuine progress, other than that sanctioned by the state, can only come with unpredictable changes in time and circumstances. Yet time and circumstances are neither predictable nor tangible. That this stands as the key facilitator of the international law of human rights is a clear indication of its precarious nature.

So the international law of human rights turns out to be a not so perfect enterprise despite its visible and tangible successes. It is, in many ways, a bundle of paradoxes and contradictions affecting its character and effectiveness which decades of fantastic progress have been unable to unshackle. Some of its shortcomings are structural and thus run deep into its personality. Others are transient and superficial. Together, these present live and lively challenges. Ironically, some of the most pressing structural difficulties confronting human rights law lie in the same characteristics that guarantee its progress and success, including its heritage as a separate and specialized discourse of international law. Yet it is through being part of international law – which conceptually underwrites its independence – that human rights law has inherited some of the intractable problems, paradoxes and contradictions faced by the parent subject over the centuries. The absence of both an overall purposeful theory and a lack of doctrinal guidelines that determine its directions, ambitions and relationship with other disciplines are an inevitable legacy of the opportunistic evolution of international law as a tool of convenience in the hands of national authorities (Alston, 1996, p. xiii). International human rights law is as much everyone's friend as well as foe, with little or no inherent defences against abuse and misuse. Riddled with internal confusion about its character and purpose, it has developed into a largely dysfunctional enterprise with ambitions to universality and objectivity. There are no ready answers to some of these structural handicaps of this field of international law, but understanding the nature and effect of some of the problems bequeathed to human rights by mainstream international law gives a more realistic appreciation of the potential and expectations of the subject.

Despite the handicaps, the international law of human rights has gained the confidence and earned the respect of all the actors at the national and international levels, including national authorities, international organizations and non-governmental organizations, as well as most individuals. It is an indication of its success that no culture or governmental policy openly objects to the idea of human rights. That all have committed to the promotion and protection of human rights has turned the discipline into the standard norms of behaviour rather than the exception. Admittedly, the level of commitment and practice is variable. This is inevitable and, hopefully, time and circumstances will gradually level the commitment to a common standard of practice. The prognosis for the future looks reassuring. The enterprise can therefore only advance and, in this sense, even a little progress has an incremental impact and so is valuable.

The essay by Ruti Teitel on 'Human Rights Genealogy' (Chapter 1) focuses on the problem of the origins of human rights in international law. It highlights the shortcomings of internal dysfunctionality within international human rights itself, when Teitel's assessment of the implications of the widely accepted view that the founding of international human rights 'is one that is said to be *sua sponte*, a radical birthing, a discontinuous affair with only an ambivalent relation to preexisting rights theory' (p. 11) highlights the shortcomings of internal dysfunctionality within international human rights itself. The inevitable inference from this perspective of the international human rights law movement, which is founded in post-war Europe and birthed in the Second World War, is that human rights in international law are new, discontinuous (that is, bearing little or no relation to the past) and represent a judicialized reaction to the problems of the war. With the state as a source of human rights evil in this paradigm, the social contract basis of human rights is discredited and abandoned, and accordingly rights protection has moved from the domestic framework to 'alternative sites and systems' in international human rights conventions, mechanisms and processes (p. 5).

Time and practice have revealed a trail of unfulfilled, or indeed unfulfillable, promises from a judicialized model of the international law of human rights. It reflects high expectations in theory and delivers rather little in practice. Its claims to objectivity, universality and a special status are either exaggerated or plain unjustified. In a genealogical review, Teitel lays a substantial portion of the blame for the internal dysfunctionality of the international law of human rights at the door of the revolutionary model of the sudden emergence of a judicialized paradigm of international human rights law arising from post-war Europe. The inconsistency and contradiction that he documents as challenging the legitimacy of international human rights law are not original but his explanation is certainly interesting and unexplored. Whatever one's view of his explanation, it would be difficult to deny the compelling force of his conclusions that:

> After half a century, the foundational concepts of the reigning postwar model reveal growing slippage. The passage of time and change, both in the relevant circumstances and in theories of knowledge generally, have put increasing pressure on the paradigmatic rights model. The mounting claim of incoherence in the received international human rights account has had profound consequences for the theory's positive and normative force. (p. 14)

While Teitel cannot claim an objective and empirically uncontentious starting point, his concerns echo well-established angst that cannot be ignored. The essay raises implications that go to the normative roots and the practical credibility of international human rights law – both now and in the future. At this stage in the evolution of the international law of human rights, the idea of radical birthing after the Second World War is either shocking or taken for granted. The general preference for the latter could be nothing less than a shortsighted prescription for self-imposed intellectual disorder that is bound to return to haunt future generations of international human rights activists and scholars.

For the moment, the reasons for the wholesale endorsement of this – the radical post-war founding perspective of international human rights law – are uncertain and remain unexplored. The general indifference to the origins of modern international human rights law may speculatively be attributed to a variety of possible explanations, including the argument that the past is insignificant to a subject that is so contemporary, forward-looking and dynamic. However, such an explanation, in denying the unequivocal virtues of lessons from the past, cannot be sustainable. To misrepresent, underestimate or ignore links and lessons from the past is to sow seeds for potential misunderstanding and chaos.

Equally possible as an explanation is that the post-war judicialized paradigm of international human rights law, although unjustifiable or unsustainable on account of its disengagement from the past, is nevertheless attractive and indeed valuable. It creates a good platform on which to confront some of the impenetrable barriers to effective human rights protection arising from the Wesphalian model of international law in which international human rights law has had the misfortune to have situated itself. This is to exaggerate the character of international human rights law in order to move the discipline forward. This is to tell a noble lie for an effective outcome or to take the Machiavellian option in which the end justifies the means. Yet one cannot ignore the indiscipline and irresponsibility of this approach for wishing away or ignoring the potential consequences in the future when the whole enterprise could collapse like a deck of cards when its foundations are challenged and removed. This approach represents an unnecessary gamble with the future of the international law of human rights.

All of this reveals an unequivocal need for a coherent grand theory for the international law of human rights. Such a theory would provide a better indication of the nature of the subject and its ambitions, as well as help to clarify the expectations and misunderstandings surrounding the subject. A credible theory of the international law of human rights may remove, or at least explain, its dysfunctional relationships. But how should such a theory be crafted or revealed? Unfortunately, no such theory has been convincingly advanced. Perhaps a grand overall theory of the international law of human rights is a utopian ambition considering its unstable and unpredictable character. There could, however, be micro-theories on various aspects of international law of human rights, which together may represent a coherent grand theory. Teitel maintains a predictably pragmatic perspective with his suggestion that a credible theory can only emerge by assessing human rights practices and conventions. This is a backward, or *ex post facto*, theorization. It is an unconventional approach to theorizing, but international human rights presents unconventional challenges. Theorizing for a pragmatic and results-oriented discipline such as the international law of human rights is unlikely to be effective if it is primarily based on abstract ideas. It is critical that any theory identifies with the reality of the discipline and its context.

It is in the tradition of micro-theories that Anthony D'Amato's essay on 'The Concept of Human Rights in International Law' (Chapter 2) is written and should be seen. D'Amato's effort in defining the concept of human rights in international law is a valuable contribution to the wider enterprise of crafting a grand theory. His entitlement-retaliation theory is controversial in many respects and unconvincing in others. Its central ambition in seeking to situate and justify human rights law as part of a conventional Wesphalian model of international law misses the point of the dynamic relationship between international law and human rights law in its underlying assumption that such a Westphalian approach is necessary to legitimize human rights law. In the process, the theory omits or fails to appreciate how much international law itself needs, and indeed over time, has had to adjust in response to, the evolution of human rights law. A state-centred focus of human rights law is, in essence, one of the key factors in the dysfunctional relationship between international law and the law of human rights law. In this regard, D'Amato's theory may not have been at its most valuable.

Furthermore, founding human rights as 'entitlements' (the term D'Amato uses to refer to higher-order norms that bind all states and cannot be changed unilaterally) in customary international law, especially as derived from generalized treaty provisions, would be a source of some discomfort to human rights activists. Custom, as D'Amato himself acknowledges and others have strongly argued, is a notoriously unmanageable legal minefield (Koskenniemi, 1990). It lacks the certainty one would expect for a subject whose impact on individuals can be direct and tangible. Human rights deserves a far more secure base than in the vagaries and contradictions of traditional customary international law. The seeming inevitability of uncertainty about custom is a source of concern rather than an assurance to D'Amato and so he prefers to found his customary international human rights law on treaty practice rather than on the vagaries of traditional processes of action, reaction and consensus. This approach to the subject carries far greater promise, because it echoes the suggestion (also put forward by Teitel) to craft a theory of international human rights law by looking backwards over national and international practice rather than taking an abstract perspective. In a related way, the interest in treaties lends some support to the inquiry about the origins of human rights law. One may infer from this approach a more credible and gradual evolution of human rights in international law across the evolution of international law itself rather than its fantastic representation as a sudden post-United Nations Charter phenomenon.

A credible attempt at reconciling the dysfunctional relationship between international law and its human rights specialism must, at the very least, concede this reciprocal dynamic between the two disciplines. Human rights law, although a part of international law, is, however, not entirely dependent on its traditional standards of sovereignty, non-intervention and the objectivization of non-state actors. How far this suggestion of recognizing and appreciating an autonomous discipline of human rights in international law with its own priorities, processes and outcomes may be carried remains an open question.

Politics

The international law of human rights before the Charter of the United Nations was limited in many ways, but its grounding in social contract in particular crippled it into a matter of exclusive domestic jurisdiction and also largely into an inseparable part of the political system of individual states. All the while the subject rested entirely at the discretion of governments and was therefore in practice largely rhetorical and unrewarding for the individuals whose rights are meant to be secured, it lacked an objective basis. This predominantly political regime was transformed by the UN Charter's preference for a regime grounded in the rule of law. This departure from the political to the legal injected a sense of certainty and predictability that had been missing from the discipline and also reversed the focus of attention from governments to the needs of the individual. In the international context, where political concerns are not so easily separated from legal ones, the effort to ground human rights in the rule of law has not been entirely easy or successful. The image and ambition of an apolitical, objective and universal discipline has proved impractical and unworkable, partly because of the inevitability of competing interests at the national and international levels. In practice, international human rights law has been a continuing effort to reconcile the objectivity of legal ideals with the politics of entrenched privileges and practices at the national and international levels. As part of the tradition of dynamic evolution of human rights law, the importance of the political and the partisan has continued to diminish inversely with the gradual entrenchment of legal principles. Overall, and so far, the accounting record on this matter has proved extremely favourable to the law at both the national and international levels. In other words, the representation of human rights as legal standards has been accepted as the general norm with political concerns as the exception.

Even as an exceptional footnote to an increasingly structured legal regime, the political concerns that remain a part of the international law of human rights suggest critical weaknesses in the establishment of legal normativity and therefore an insecure and unbalanced accounting record between the law and politics. That there are areas of the corpus of the international law of human rights not based on a realistic and workable affirmation of the rule of law remains a matter of concern and discomfort for human rights scholarship. Thankfully, these hot spots of instability in the international law of human rights are restricted to concerns of political preferences and cultural differences. In certain sections of the scholarship these preferences and differences that have been manifested in highly partisan and reductionist debates relating to the objectivity, hierarchy and universality of human rights (Donnelly, 1982; Pollis and Schwab, 1979, p. 1; Bayefsky, 1996; Howard, 1992), are, in reality, not so readily transposed into legal standards. As these are areas that continue to witness continuing disagreement among actors, as well as reflecting flashpoints of inconsistent and dysfunctional practice among states, it should be understood that the nature and basis of the conflict and disagreement in these unsettled areas of international human rights practice is less about the relevance of political choices or the applicability of the law and more about the definition of the appropriate and acceptable balance between law and politics in international human rights. In any case, the inherently political nature of international law makes the outcomes of this balancing process less a matter of scientific legal method and more a matter of interaction between the diverse international actors including states, international organizations, non-governmental organizations and academic scholars. The appropriate balance is therefore as much a political standard as a legal one.

The four essays in Part II illustrate just one issue among the various issues involved in seeking to define a workable balance between legal standards and political concerns. On the subject of the universality of human rights within a disparate international cultural community, the scholarship is confused, unsettled and occasionally misleading, largely because of its deep entanglement with the many political disagreements, such as the Cold War, that have become an undeniable part of international law. Although the political handicap of international law is well known, astonishingly this crucial fact is ignored by some scholars in their portrayal of the international law of human rights as a pristine, objective and verifiable truth unsoiled by the corruption and infamy of politics. The naive and hypocritical denial of the relevance of political concerns and preferences in the development and processes of international law of human rights has undermined the credibility and effective representation of important legal norms and practices in this field.

Culture and its diversity has become a notorious battleground on which different political perspectives on human rights in international law continues to be fought. At the international level, a substantial part of the scholarship on culture and human rights has turned into an ideological engagement between so-called 'universalists' and 'relativists' focused on political finger-pointing at the failures and shortcomings of opposing political ideologies (Bayefsky, 1996; Tesón, Chapter 3; Mutua, Chapter 4). This is by no means an objective engagement to reconcile differences or to canvass and scrutinize a realistic perspective of the cultural implications of human rights. Rather, it is a concerted effort to discredit and undermine the other perspective. While the contradictions and inconsistencies of conventional ideological disagreements in themselves are no surprise, the employment of human rights and academic scholarship as weapons in this essentially partisan enterprise has not been well received. The subjective posturing, exaggeration and misrepresentation that may be taken for granted in normal ideological engagement is a source of confusion and discomfort for a subject such as human rights that is premised on its conceptual neutrality. Unfortunately, the same worthy attribute of neutrality has, in practice, exposed the vulnerability of the idea of human rights to abuse by partisan advocates.

In its ideological representation, the scholarship on the cultural implications for the international law of human rights has singularly failed to deliver any tangible and constructive outcomes, mainly because it has been so polarized and confrontational. The primary ambition in this, as in any ideological confrontation, is not the advancement of human rights but, rather, a dogmatic and inflexible outlook, devoid of tolerance or compromise. Ironically, neither side in this ideological clash challenges the importance of clarity and the need for clarification of a variety of issues in the international law of human rights, but both argue strongly that their narrow partisan perspective reflects the best and most appropriate statement of clarification. In the effort to secure their perspective, each is unashamed about misrepresenting or caricaturing the other or confusing the subject matter by an unnecessary mixture of issues that should in fact be separated. Not surprisingly, the confrontational representation of culture in human rights has received only little, if any, support in the international human rights practice of independent supervisory institutions founded on the accommodation and management of cultural practices, using imaginative interpretation of treaty texts (Prouvez, 2003/4, pp. 489–93).[7]

In Chapter 3, Fernando Tesón, in 'International Human Rights and Cultural Relativism', illustrates ideologically loaded scholarship on the subject of culture as part of the international law of human rights, and demonstrating key characteristics of polemicism, confrontation, caricature and misrepresentation. The strategy of accusation and blame that he employs in this essay leaves little or no room for the objective assessment of the role of cultural matters or the reconciliation of any differences generated by cultural diversity. In truth, the scholars for whom the conviction that universalism and relativism as incompatible moral alternatives has become a settled article of faith, the merits of alternative perspectives are unattractive. It is not an uncommon practice to discredit the other perspective on less than empirically verified grounds. For these scholars, this could, after all, be an intellectual 'declaration of war' in which the ruin of the opposite view justifies the cause by default. The outcomes of such a partisan 'war' to discredit and undermine, rather than to expose the merits of each perspective to scrutiny, only rarely, if ever, turn out to be constructive.

For Fernando Tesón, as with most ideologically motivated advocates of universalism, cultural relativism is an indefensible blot on the human rights landscape that enables despots and demagogues to abuse power (Bayefski, 1996). However, this is a conclusion premised on the characterization of culture as an extrinsic standard that cannot be reconciled with the idea and reality of human rights, a term restricted to civil and political rights (p. 74). This separation has been developed and sustained by a selective delimitation of human rights and cultural norms. That this is, in practice, an artificial separation devoid of the holistic perspective required for a credible human rights regime does not deter its employment in the campaign to discredit cultural relativism. Tesón develops further a discreditable image of cultural relativity by the conflation of fairly legitimate and wholly indefensible claims to cultural relativism. It is interesting to note that some of the claims he attributes to cultural relativists include 'arguments [that] may not yet have been articulated by relativist scholars or governments' (p. 74). As an instructive example in this essay, a (wholly indefensible) claim, attributed to relativists, that cultural traditions determine the existence of civil and political rights is conflated with a perfectly legitimate claim that cultural traditions may affect the scope of rights (pp. 74–75). This is a serious confusion between the existence of human rights based on the inherent entitlement of every individual to rights and the recognition of the different ways (often, but not always, driven by cultural differences) to their realization. The principles of subsidiarity and the margin of appreciation (see Macdonald *et al.*, 1993, p. 83) as well as the practice relating to permissible limitations, balancing competing claims and reservations in the practice of international human rights supervisory organs, confirm the legitimacy of potential differences in the scope of rights. How much of this is deliberate and strategic or is a matter of sheer reckless representation is uncertain but the caricature of extremism and improbability is easily depicted.

Similarly, the preference in Makau wa Mutua's essay on 'The Ideology of Human Rights' (Chapter 4) for labels other than the conventional dichotomy between universalists and relativists[8] to describe his preferences in the culture and human rights discourse does not alter the polemical and confrontational course he sets with the universalists. He seeks not merely to deconstruct the doctrines and practices of the international law of human rights but also to reconstruct them on his preferred terms. The deconstruction of the body of modern human rights reveals less of an objective and political discourse and more of an attempt to universalize partisan and imperfect Western liberal democratic ideology. That this characterization may undermine its legitimacy as universal morality is true. Similarly, there is considerable merit in the author's suggestion of reconstructing the corpus of human rights to 'allow diverse stakeholders to reflect on their meaning and the policy issues they raise' (p. 109) for, after all, cross-cultural referencing is indeed a useful variable in the creation of a universal corpus of human rights (p. 112). In the determination of 'genuine' universal normative standards, the author perceives little or no compromises.

In his proposals for reconstruction, Mutua seeks to distance himself from a root-and-branch transformation of human rights philosophy (pp. 154–55), and instead, advocates no more than an 'opportunity for all major cultural blocs of the world to negotiate the normative content of human rights law and the purposes for which the discourse should be legitimately employed' (p. 158). Yet he rejects one of the most viable opportunities to infuse cultural diversity into human rights thinking through the involvement and participation, *inter alia*, with the major international human rights instruments as 'positivistic' and therefore inadequate to endow the human rights corpus with multicultural universality. For him:

> There are fundamental defects in presenting the state as the reservoir of cultural heritage. Many states have been alien to their populations and it is questionable whether they represent those populations or whether they are little more than internationally recognized cartels organized for the sake of keeping power and access to resources. (p. 155)

Although this view may carry considerable academic merit, Mutua either misses the point of the reality of multiculturalism in an imperfect society or is adamantly determined to press his point of the illegitimacy of normative compromises developed around the Western conception of human rights. Indeed, in an international law system premised on the Westphalian paradigm it is unclear how else he proposes to realize a multicultural normative strategy without the modern state apparatus.

For Mutua, normative compromises developed on discredited Western conceptions appear to be no more than veiled attempts to transplant Western notions of political democracy and negative rights to African states. The emphasis in the Western conception of human rights on both the individual and civil and political rights undermines its amenability to genuinely fair compromises with other cultures. In the African context Mutua prefers a concept of multiculturalism based on the call (with which he sympathizes):

> ... for reconnection with certain human rights ideals from Africa's pre-colonial past to address social problems and to attempt to arrest political disintegration. The reconstruction of the ancient duty-rights dialectic, which was essential to the validity of Africa's social and political fabric, has been advanced as a critical starting point in the redefinition of the relationship between individual and the community, and individual and state. (p. 159)

Ironically, the ultimate outcome of such a multicultural representation of human rights may resemble a Western style democracy in certain respects, which is seen as insignificant or irrelevant as long as this fact is not predetermined by the Western-based human rights corpus. In reality, as this perspective of multiculturalism admits no compromises, it stands as an alternative to Western ideology.

Fortunately, the ideological representation of culture and cultural diversity does not reflect all the scholarship in this field. There are other scholars who have devoted attention to seeking a constructive reconciliation of genuine uncertainties (An-Na'im, 1992, p. 1; An-Na'im, 1987; Preis, 1996; Donoho, 1991; Mahoney, 1998). This category of scholarship contrasts with the polemical and confrontational engagement referred to above in its realism and open-mindedness. It is often critical of the extremism and inflexibility of the ideological approaches and, instead, advocates a balanced debate that draws on the strengths, and cautions against the shortcomings, of both relativist and universalist perspectives. Many of the strategies found in this line of scholarship have been endorsed and vindicated by the international human rights practice.[9]

Jack Donnelly in his essay, 'Cultural Relativism and Universal Human Rights' (Chapter 5), makes a fairly good effort at a balanced assessment of the issues by acknowledging the inevitability, and indeed the importance, of cultural diversity in a world of converging morality. From this premise he concludes, rightly, that the critical challenge in this exercise is the reconciliation of these competing normative preferences. That he ultimately advocates a weak cultural relativist standard that permits limited deviations from 'universal' human rights standards does not detract from the refreshing candour with which he approaches the subject. He not only enables the reader to appreciate the unreasonableness of the intolerance and posturing of extreme perspectives, but also highlights the complexity of factors involved in defining a credible balance.

Donnelly's theoretical framework is fairly simple but effective. For him, the realization of human rights can be represented on a continuum with relativism and universalism at opposite ends. He labels the extreme stations on this continuum, which he defines as 'ideal types', as radical. 'Radical cultural relativism' would hold that culture is the sole source of the validity of a moral right or rule and 'radical universalism' would hold that culture is irrelevant to the validity of moral rights and rules, which are universally valid' (p. 174). In between the extremes lie varying mixes of relativism and universalism which, depending on how close a particular balance is to the extreme ideal station, would be strong or weak (relativism or universalism). In practice, the definition of an effective balance along this continuum hinges on a wide and complex variety of factors relating to time, context, history and circumstances. Each situation may therefore have to be treated on its merits, bearing in mind the diversity of peoples, culture, interpretation and so on in a world of increasing moral convergence based on the internationalization of human rights standards (p. 190). One need not agree with Donnelly's conclusion that weak cultural relativity is a definitive final point on which to settle all competition between universal standards in a diverse cultural context but one can acknowledge that he certainly provides a formula with which fairminded scholars may work.

The indeterminacy and uncertainty that characterize the politics of the international law of human rights are not resolved by the voluminous and engaging scholarship focused on the closer look at the specific matter of culture. In her post-modernist and post-structuralist critique, 'Rethinking the Universality of Human Rights', Diane Otto (Chapter 6) offers an interesting insight as to why this is so. For Otto, the current polarized engagement between universalism and relativism is an outward gloss over an entrenched problem about power. The key handicap, according to Otto, in the mainstream scholarship is its failure to recognize and appreciate the power dynamic of which the culture debate is a consequential reflection. In its Cold War representation, the culture debate was driven by the competition between capitalist and socialist ideological emphasis in human rights law. The détente of this power struggle led to the separation of the civil and political rights, on the one hand, and the economic, social and cultural rights on the other. The post-Cold War consensus between socialism and capitalism has today moved the centre of the universality–relativity debate to the engagement between the developed states of the North and the underdeveloped states of the South. In this, as in its original power dialectic during the Cold War, the struggle for prominence between European and Third-World (African or Asian) cultures, Otto argues, is a marginal reflection of the competition between different versions of capitalism rather than a desire to address issues of cultural diversity:

> The opposition constructed between universality and cultural relativity is politically coded to advance the interests of competing claims to 'genuine' universal knowledge. The debate diverts attention from pressing issues like those of challenging masculinist domination, of realizing the interdependence and indivisibility of the Cold War-inspired generations of human rights, of implementing the right to development as something more than opening state borders to transnational capital, and of achieving global economic and social justice. The debate functions as a means of obscuring the issues of power and depoliticizing the struggle for economic dominance that is taking place. Understood in this way, the universalists are defending Europe's dominance and the relativists are seeking to reverse the duality that presently constitutes the South as Europe's Other. (p. 207)

Indeed, as the superintendents of the current relativist knowledge endorse the Cold War consensus that proposed a modernist (European) representation of human rights law as stated, *inter alia*, in the Universal Declaration on Human Rights (1948), the Vienna (1993) and Beijing (1995) Declarations there is no room or reason for transformative alternatives. The critique by relativists, and confirmed by conventional scholarship, is egalitarian and based on the same foundational philosophy of modernist human rights orthodoxy.

For change to be meaningful, it has to be structural – the sort that revises the foundational premises of modernist knowledge of human rights. Otto argues that this requires a full appreciation of the power dynamics involved in the debate about culture so as to construct effective responses, such as a commitment to depart from the excessive dependence on the mainstream knowledge that secures elite privileges. Similarly, the central position of the nation-state as a key pillar upon which Europe's hegemony is built may require reconsideration in any effective transformative strategy so as to enhance the diversity of local cultures that has come to be replaced by a superficial and artificial concept of 'national' culture. The avoidance of the artificial knowledge necessarily leads the strategist to reconsider the role of the law in human rights generally, and especially in cultural matters, because the law is the key instrument for legitimation of power and control. An effective transformative strategy must therefore confront and challenge the conventional narrative of law as an objective and detached regime devoid of political, social or economic counterknowledges. Only a realistic representation of the law can confirm its limitations as an effective instrument of change.

In the international law of human rights, culture has ceased to be a simple and predictable subject. Its straightforward anthropological representation in which diversity is a standard character (Preis, 1995) has not survived the combined onslaught of the Cold War and the branding of human rights as a legal standard. The former has corrupted culture as a factual concern into a part of a complicated power game, while the latter sought to afford culture an objective character. Neither perspective has been much use to an effective characterization of culture as part of human rights. Between them, the power outlook and the legal characterization have generated conflicting and irreconcilable demands of the idea and practice of culture within human rights. The conspiratorial subtext of the power paradigm is not only intangible but also indefinable, making it extremely difficult to inform policy. The legal standard, on the other hand, has fostered an abstract and unworkable notion of transcendental normativity that has failed to draw the support of different cultures. Yet, surprisingly, each representation has a contribution to make towards an effective understanding of the relevance of culture in the international law of human rights.

The endorsement of the legal characterization in the mainstream scholarship on this matter is not entirely surprising considering the preference for a predictable legal regime in the political order launched by the Charter of the United Nations. However, this emphasis, which is also reflected in the approach of the international human rights implementation processes and those of many non-governmental advocates, tilts the body of knowledge towards the abstract and conceptual concerns and further away from the reality. The commendable ambition of this enterprise to employ the law as the main, if not the sole, point of reference in the definition of an objective place of culture in the international law of human rights set itself a tough, if not impossible, task. It cannot, and must not, ignore the reality of international law as a system inextricably entwined with the politics of power and self-interest in which national elites consistently seek to secure parochial interests. The acknowledgement of this reality is a key to the construction of a workable legal policy in this matter.

The Paradox of Implementation

Implementation

The true value of the human rights strategy set out in the Charter of the United Nations lies in its effective implementation. In the absence of implementation, human rights remain little more than rhetorical promises. The point of implementation of human rights standards therefore marks a critical interface, between doctrine and reality, between rhetoric and action and between the priorities of national and international regimes. This is the stage at which the promises of human rights ideals mature into the reality of action and outcomes, and, therefore, the point of accountability. Effective implementation, however, requires a minimum level of institutional sophistication, founded upon a genuine commitment to act transparently, independently and professionally. Unfortunately, this can often challenge the partisan interests and privileges of national elite, as well as expose the inadequacy of national and international institutions. A viable and workable scheme for the implementation of the human rights standards set out in the various sources of international law is therefore indispensable to the genuine transformation of essentially political ideals into tangible legal entitlements. This subject can be both sensitive and complex. These divergent priorities that call for reconciliation as a part of the diverse processes of implementation are not untypical in the wider scheme of international law. Over the centuries, these have been settled on account of principles and guidelines, some of which are based on Westphalian ideals as foundational, while others have emerged in direct response to challenges posed by the slow and gradual empowerment of international law in human rights matters.

The conceptual differences between the enforcement and implementation of human rights are often ignored because both refer to the common purpose of converting human rights ideals into reality. This interchangeable usage may have contributed to an obfuscation of the expectations and outcomes of the human rights regime in international law. The transformation of human rights ideals into outcomes is hinged upon a long list of tasks to be performed at both national and international contexts by different actors. While all of the tasks may contribute to the implementation of the wider human rights policy or strategy, not all amount to its enforcement. Similarly, different actors contribute or perform different tasks at national and international levels. Some of the tasks are exclusive to a particular domain while others may be shared. The enforcement of human rights is a national responsibility directed at solving specific problems, whereas implementation, on the other hand, entails a broader spectrum of processes of which enforcement is a part. Implementation involves a general plan of action – often applicable to more than one jurisdiction – for turning an ideal into reality.

The implementation regime set up around the ECOSOC cements the view that the primary responsibility for the protection of human rights rests with national authorities, a principle that has since become entrenched. This principle of subsidiarity (Corazza, 2003; Jackson, 2003), apart from endorsing the sovereignty of national authorities (Petzold, 1993, p. 41; Mahoney, 1997; Shelton, 1993) also makes common sense in so far as implementation is, in essence, an exercise in the internalization of 'external' international law standards. As such, it requires the goodwill of national authorities but also the institutional structures at the national level in order to be effective. With subsidiarity, the implementation of international law standards in the field of human rights is no more than an enterprise in self-regulation, subject only to the secondary supervision of international procedure. From this perspective, it is evident that any serious expectations of objectivity and radical change may be exaggerated as long as states retain the freedom of choice of means as to how to transform international standards into domestic legal entitlements.

Another important practice of international law that may guide the implementation of its human rights strategy is one of complementarity and symbiosis. In the definition of the relationship between national and international regimes in human rights matters, international law has no ambition to replace domestic regimes but rather to complement them in aspects and dimensions in which the national system is unable to respond effectively. It is therefore not unusual for international law to rely and depend on national procedures and institutions for the realization of its standards. Conversely, the identification and definition of converging norms or the changing standards of international morality is most suitable for the international and, in particular, the multilateral scheme of law. The relevance of complementarity exceeds its vertical representation between national and international regimes. It is also relevant in a horizontal context between national regimes, as well as between international regimes or regional regimes. For example, the various supervisory bodies within the United Nations – the Charter-based and treaty-based institutions – complement each other in a whole variety of ways. Similarly, there is a symbiotic relationship between United Nations bodies and the diverse body of regional supervisory institutions. The true picture regarding the implementation of the international human rights strategy is one that perceives activities and processes at the national and international levels, as well as at the regional intergovernmental levels, as part of one single holistic totality, with the individual components complementing each other like cogs in a working machine. Consequently, the inefficient functioning of any one part impinges on the effectiveness of the whole system.

The numerous processes for the implementation of standards of international law of human rights fall under two broad categorisations of the political and the legal. The political processes encompass state-centred interactions based, *inter alia*, on *realpolotik* power-play, self-interest and political identity (Koh, 1997). Although their potential for effective human rights protection is largely opportunistic, they mark the entry point to a long implementation continuum that ends up in the structured refinements for a regime of international legal protection. In other words, it may be true that, in practice, each stage or approach to implementation has its central emphasis in terms of actors, aims and expectations, but the two broad approaches (the political and the legal) are inextricably linked. In fact, they are best perceived as parts of a single implementation strategy aimed at internalizing the norms and standards set out in international law (Koh, 1997; Mutua, 1998, p. 212). Sadly, the terms of this relationship between the political and legal implementation regimes are undefined and unstructured. Indeed each – but especially the political processes – is little more than an *ex post facto* rationalization of ad hoc and opportunistic responses to specific circumstances. Therefore the attempt to rationalize what are, in essence, sporadic and disparate reactions into a structured strategy carries a real risk of incoherence and unworkability.

In its deference to the Westphalian ideals of sovereignty and the autonomy of individual state authority, the political processes are weakest and most uncertain in terms of implementation outcomes, as exemplified by the well-documented handicaps and failings of the political processes (Alston, 1992a, p. 126; Farer and Gaer, 1993, p. 59), such as the procedures under ECOSOC Resolutions 1235 (XLII) and 1503 (XLVIII). It is significant, however, that these procedures represent the point of interface between the legal and the political processes in the long implementation continuum. At the entry point of the political processes, the unpredictable and often partisan priorities of the General Assembly or the Security Council in matters such as decolonization and anti-apartheid often lacked the doctrinal certainty and fairness that is associated with processes based on the rule of law. There have, no doubt, been some successes in the use of some political processes, most notably under the Helsinki Accord (Buergenthal, 1977; Estébanez, 1999, p. 329) and in the network of ad hoc and permanent working groups, special, country and thematic rapporteurs, committees, special envoys or representatives that continue to work in an integrated relationship with the UN Sub-Commission and Commission on Human Rights, the ECOSOC, the General Assembly and the Security Council (Alston, 1992, p. 1; Rodley and Weissbrodt, 2004). These bodies, at a minimum, set secure foundations for political debate on international human rights standards (Jernow, 1996; Flinterman, 1999, p. 125). The achievements of these political processes within the United Nations are an integral part of a wider framework touching on similar activities in the context of regional initiatives in Europe (see Coppel and O'Neil, 1992; Woods, 1992, p. 329; Estébanez, 1999, p. 35), the Americas (Harris and Livingstone, 1998; Davidson, 1992; Buergenthal, 1988; Pasqualucci, 2003; Cerna, 1992) and Africa (Murray 2000; Evans and Murray, 2002, Gittleman, 1982). All of these processes, however, share common characteristics, including the overwhelming role of the state and its agents as well as the marginalization of the individual. The internalization of human rights norms through the horizontal processes is largely at the discretion of the state, using the public law framework.

In contrast, and yet complementary to the political initiatives for the implementation of international human rights strategy is a body of implementation strategies grounded in the rule of law. Legal processes do not necessarily defer to the choices and priorities of national sovereignty, although they unavoidably recognize them. Rather, they seek to draw legitimacy from legal principles and standards that are often set apart from the control and manipulation of national authorities. These processes tend to be hinged on the perspective of a relatively higher degree of international law autonomy with its own priorities and its accommodation of non-state entities as legitimate participants. In practice, a substantial part of the legal standard for the implementation of international law of human rights coincides with the principles and mechanisms for the internalization of international human rights standards into domestic law (Koh, 1998). Ultimately, however, it must be conceded that the separation between the legal and political processes is justified more on account of academic clarity than on any realistic understanding of the practical expediency of the workings of international law where politics and law are inextricably fused. At the same time, there is a credibly arguable case for the *sui generis* representation of the international law of human rights hinged on an objective application of the rule of law. This dependence on an autonomous conception of the rule of law has not always been self-evident in this field of international law as it has been seen as the product of the gradual evolution and revelation (Sohn and Buergenthal, 1973; Sohn, 1982). Although the outcomes of this dynamic process remain uncertain, there is enough evidence to support a correlation between the diminishing influence of national authorities on the one hand and the increasing importance of independent processes and institutions based on the rule of law.

Enforcement

Harold Koh (1997, 1998, Chapter 7, this volume) must take credit for the structured representation of the diverse and disparate implementation processes that is here classed under the broad headings of the political and the legal. In his research into why states obey international law he highlights not only the relevance and relationships between the political and the legal but also those between the national and international regimes. In his writings he is at pains to emphasize the complementary and holistic interaction of these factors, some of which are classed as predominantly political and others as based largely on an autonomous concept of the rule of law. In his essay on 'How is International Human Rights Law Enforced?' (Chapter 7), Koh draws on the wider studies of why states obey international law. It is useful here to point out that why nations obey international law of human rights and how this law is enforced are two separate, albeit related, concerns. Why states obey international law is a justificatory inquiry whereas the enforcement of the law is often a structured process. In addition, obedience of international law is a political decision with a predominantly external perspective, whereas its enforcement is a legal process with domestic implications. The two concerns are, however, related to the extent that enforcement presupposes one or more of the justifications underpinning why states obey. In other words, without the commitment to obey the law, the issue of enforcement does not arise at all, and a qualitatively good reason for obeying the law correspondingly affects the effectiveness of enforcement. Also, the politics of obedience and the law of enforcement together form a core part of the implementation strategy for the international law of human rights. It is, in any case, important that this relationship is not exaggerated by using the two terms interchangeably.

Harold Koh is correct in his conclusion that while there may be diverse reasons for obeying international law, only a coherent and structured process – such as the legal processes identified in his essay – may be employed in its enforcement. Although the focus of his essay is on the legal processes for the enforcement of the international law of human rights, it is appropriate not to be detained here by the extent to which these processes also provide a credible justification as to why states obey the law. Both the 'horizontal' (international) and the 'vertical' (transnational) processes that he identifies form part of the legal framework on the implementation continuum referred to previously, with the important difference that the horizontal processes affect the international environment while the transnational processes integrate the international domain with the domestic forum. It is the transnantional processes that make the critical connection between the international and the domestic, as well as drawing on the contribution of all the actors who are normally marginalized in the implementation of the international law strategy for human rights.

All three dimensions of the transnantional process – interaction, interpretation and internalization – are equally and complementarily important to the effectiveness of the enforcement process, but it is the direct link between the interpretation and internalization of standards, on the one hand, and the tangible outcomes that individuals may claim as a matter of law, on the other, that cements their attraction. However, the fact that the effectiveness of all stages of enforcement, including the interaction of the diverse actors, may depend on the support and endorsement of national authorities is a lingering reminder of the precarious character of the entire process. Unfortunately, such is the turf upon which the game must be played – at least for the time being, until an autonomous regime of international protection is established. The expectation that a credible regime of international protection of human rights that is not based on the indulgence of national authorities may emerge sometime in the future cannot be taken for granted from the little evidence that may be gleaned from the structure of international criminal law (Cassese, Gaeta and Jones, 2002; Kittichaisaree, 2001; Broomhall, 2003). The future of human rights in international law rests squarely with the imaginative interpretation adopted by international agencies invested with that responsibility.

As Koh demonstrates, the treaties and declarations that have emerged as outcomes of the interpretation of the preferences of the norm entrepreneurs and their sponsors have proved valuable. However, the full potential of these instruments rests in the manner in which they are applied. In general, these instruments empower international institutions to define broad guidelines for application – internalization – by national authorities. The success of this enterprise, however, depends on the terms of their engagement, the commitment and expectations of the various actors (especially state actors) and the imagination applied by the collective membership of these institutions. In the wider scheme of things, the fantastic opportunity that interpretation offers to international law to capture the commanding heights of human rights law has not been used for a variety of reasons, including obstacles posed by national authorities. These challenges are not entirely unexpected if one considers not only the potentially transformative effect of radical interpretation but also the direct expectation that the outcomes of such interpretation may have to be internalized into domestic law and practice. It is rewarding to note that some institutions, such as the European Court of Human Rights, have moved beyond the foundational stages of debating the scope of their powers and so have accomplished notable successes (see Helfer and Slaughter, Chapter 8, this volume). At present, interpretation is perceived as a limited allocated task, endorsed by states to serve the valuable purpose of managing converging values in an extremely dynamic field of international law.

Internalization, the third stage in Harold Koh's calibration of enforcement, is by far the most critical to the entire enterprise. It represents the pivotal point of the transformation of human rights from rhetorical ideals into tangible outcomes. However, there is no prescribed manner for this important process: it is based squarely on the principle of subsidiarity by the terms of which national authorities retain the freedom of choice of means. Koh notes that the control exercised by national authorities over internalization – in its political, social but especially legal guise – can determine the effectiveness of the entire enforcement process. Enforcement, and especially the stage of internalization, is therefore an internal and practical undertaking subject to supervision by international law.

Supervision

The supervision of national enforcement regimes by international law forms yet another stage in the broader implementation strategy of the international law of human rights. Consistent with the structure for implementation, supervision is made up of complementary political and transnational processes. The scope of the political processes that form part of the conventional interaction between states on a horizontal basis has been discussed. The transnational processes for the supervision of national regimes revolve around the examination of states' reports,[10] the adjudication of interstate complaints,[11] individual complaints[12] and, in the case of the Torture Convention, the institution of investigations into allegations of systematic practice of torture (Article 20) have been the subject of continuing academic scrutiny (Mutua, 1998; Steiner, 2000; Higgins, 1996).

By their very nature, the transnational supervisory processes form a self-contained regime set around the specific terms of individual treaties. As products of conventional negotiations between states, treaties tend to reflect agreeable compromises rather than the groundbreaking ideals advocated by non-state actors (classed as norm entrepreneurs and their sponsors in Koh's studies). The low expectations that come to be associated with such compromises have, in fact, been exceeded by the overall achievements of the various processes of transnational supervision. Today, the requirements for states to submit periodic reports for the review of progress in domestic human rights practice is taken for granted, as is the fact that the supervisory bodies issue guidelines for the preparation of these reports (Partsch, 1992, p. 350; Opsahl, 1992, p. 400) and the 'constructive dialogue' that directs the review of these reports and the adoption of concluding observations, General Comments and follow-up plans. Within the regional supervision regimes of the Council of Europe, the Organization of American States and the African Union there is an increasingly successful scheme of adversarial contestation of human rights claims. This is surely progress!

However, not everyone is impressed by the achievements of transnational supervision and indeed some seem convinced in their opinion, that with a few notable exceptions such as selected Council of Europe and the Organization of American States procedures, the majority of the transnational supervisory processes are weak and inefficient in practice (Mutua, 1998; Steiner, 2000; Higgins, 1996; Opsahl, 1992, p 369). The political context in which the terms of the supervisory remit was defined is considered a lasting handicap. National self-interest, played out through the Cold War years, and states' deliberate unwillingness to empower the supervisory bodies with effective and coercive powers, are admitted shortcomings of these processes (Mutua, 1998; Opsahl, 1992, pp. 371–72). The deliberate decision on the part of states to establish weak supervisory institutions may seem predictable and, to that extent, forgiveable, but a continuing effort to ensure the ineffectiveness and inefficiency of the work of these institutions is indefensible. Most of the supervisory bodies work on a part-time basis, meeting a couple of times a year over a few weeks each time. During these short designated meetings, they are expected to deal with the various heads of supervision, including state reports and individual petitions. This is an impossible task even for a full-time organization. The predictable consequence of this pressure of work is an unnecessary cutting of corners that leads to overall inefficiency and poor supervision. This problem is compounded by the overburdened office of the High Commissioner for Human Rights, mandated to provide support to the members of these institutions (Opsahl, 1992, pp. 380–81). Other shortcomings of the transnational processes of supervision include the insecurity of members' appointments and the adoption of the United Nations standards of deference to national authorities (Mutua, 1998).

Reform

Despite their differences, both the impressed and the unimpressed agree that progress, if any, has been slow and, in many senses, dated. There is therefore a definite need for reform to take this system of implementation to its next level. This raises the fundamental question of whether the reform should take the form of revision of the supervisory mechanism or a total and radical overhaul of the system of implementation. In their essay, 'Towards a Theory of Effective Supranational Adjudication' (Chapter 8), Laurence Helfer and Anne-Marie Slaughter focus on the work of the United Nations Human Rights Committee. They do not believe in a root-and-branch overhaul but, rather, declare their confidence in the potential evolution of the present system into an effective supranational adjudicatory body. Helfer and Slaughter identify a checklist of three categories of essential factors that underlie their theory of effective supranational adjudication. The first set of factors tend to lie under the control of national authorities, the second are at the discretion and under the control of the supervisory authorities and the third, being opportunistic, are beyond the control of both states and supervisory bodies. Situating the Human Rights Committee at the political end of the legal implementation continuum, Helfer and Slaughter recommend that the most valuable strategy for enhancing its supranational standing is for the Committee to seek to establish itself in a community of law. This, they admit, may seem:

> ... [a] modest proposal ... one that takes into account the Committee's existing and somewhat limited powers, ... the relatively poor record of compliance with the Committee's decisions, and the increasing importance of communication among judicial and quasi-judicial arbiters of individual rights disputes. (p. 357)

The aim of this community of law is:

> ... [to] build a sense of transnational judicial solidarity [where] the resulting decisions can contribute to the development of a genuinely transnational or supranational body of law: a set of principles informed by and building on one another, textually and culturally differentiated as necessary but acknowledging the promise of universality. (p. 363)

This proposal for reform anticipates the establishment of a web of relations between the Committee and national and supranational legal actors, providing incentives for all actors to participate in the Committee's work with a view to securing the integrity of the legal process. Specifically, Helfer and Slaughter conclude that 'the Committee can enhance its effectiveness as a quasi-judicial tribunal by engaging in a dialogue with the ECHR and the European Commission of Human Rights as an important first step toward a broader effort to increase communication with other supranational tribunals and national courts over the interpretation of shared human rights standards' (pp. 363–64). This dialogue should involve an effort to harmonize the decisions of the two supranational institutions, with the Committee drawing on the strengths and lessons of the European experience.

This is, beyond doubt, an extremely attractive, realistic and convincing proposal for reform. Its central quality is its holistic and integrated character as a general theory that is applicable to the full domain of supranational adjudication rather than focusing on an individual procedure. The future of international human rights can be progressive and successful under this theory. In addition, the proposal acknowledges the dynamism and diversity in the implementation of international human rights norms and rightly concedes that it represents a modest start in a narrow dimension of the wider picture. The proposal acknowledges the significance of radical overhaul but only as a long-term strategy because:

> [o]ne of the most important lessons of the European experience is that supranational courts and tribunals must move cautiously in their early years, striking a delicate balance between independence and deference, permitting states to adjust and respond to the mechanisms of supranational adjudication. Only after states develop a level of comfort with these mechanisms – and with complying with unfavorable outcomes in specific disputes – will it be feasible to enhance and extend the architecture of the system itself. (p. 357)

This proposal has been criticized for placing the Human Rights Committee under the tutelage of European institutions with a view to transplanting 'universally generalizable European experiences . . . to institutions outside Europe' (Mutua, 1998, p. 239). In a similar vein, the proposal casts the Human Rights Committee 'in the role of toddling works in progress, projects which must be reared by the more mature intellectual, spiritual and institutional European parents' (ibid., p. 241). Both criticisms represent an unfortunate oversimplification. Although this is the least effectively articulated point in an otherwise excellent and inspiring piece of academic scholarship on this issue,[13] the important point of the relevance of generally applicable principles and strategies of international human rights supervision cannot have been lost on the reader. It is less a matter of the European experience *per se*. The principles have proved relevant and valuable in other institutional contexts, albeit not as effectively as in the European context.

There are some lessons to be learned from the many calls to reform the processes for transnational supervision of national human rights practices. The dynamic character of the subject makes change inevitable. The ground-breaking goodwill of these processes that existed half a century ago has been exhausted and the time has come to move forward. In thinking about the next steps in this field, it may be important to recall that change to the place of human rights in international law has always been slow, gradual and purposive. In the short term, a refinement of existing procedure may meet with less resistance, although this should not preclude thoughts of long-term proposals. As the events leading to the establishment of the ad hoc and permanent international criminal tribunals continue to demonstrate, the idea of governments as guarantors of human rights is a flawed one. Yet, the dynamics of modern political power makes governmental involvement in human rights matters an inevitable fact. Nevertheless, it may be possible to manipulate the short-term reform strategy of refining the procedures of existing institutions but this is not so easy for a long-term ambition of establishing a coercive judicial body. That strategy can only evolve in the light of further failures on the part of states in this responsibility for the protection of human rights. This is how the present gains were made, and change is unlikely to happen as a consequence of the willingness of states. This is a far more realistic expectation and, odd as it sounds, it is the proven process by which power has been wrested out of the hands of states and their national elites, whose interests and privileges are threatened by reform.

Exceptions

Objective and Subjective Regimes

On the surface, exceptions are an abnormality in the law that enable or permit an actor to depart from the defined objectives of a legal undertaking. However, so far as exceptions are not an alternative to the general rule their character can often be exaggerated. In reality, exceptions have no independent existence in the law; they are an inextricable part of the general rule and the conventional norm, tasked to complement the general rule (Pauwelyn, 2003, pp. 162–63) and to expand its relevance and accord actors essential flexibility with which to adjust to its demands (Shaw, 2003, pp. 821–22; Higgins, 1977; MacDonald, 1997; Mahalic and Mahalic, 1987). Exceptions are therefore in a secondary relationship with the general norm, and their meaning and purposes may only be revealed through the prism of the general rule. To be effective, exceptions have to be malleable and adaptable but, as a matter of principle, must necessarily be interpreted restrictively unless a broader interpretation is permitted by the objectives of the general rule. A restrictive interpretation of exceptions is not meant to belittle their importance but, instead, capture their true character in complementing the objectives set out in the general rule.

It is true that this objective and purposeful character of exceptions is an idealistic representation that may not always be followed in practice where exceptions have been known to be misused and abused. In theory, the misuse of exceptions is a departure from their objective and purposeful character but, be that as it may, such a departure may often not be so easily distinguishable from the legitimate differences in the practical perspectives of the diverse legal actors. In the absence of a prescribed application of the objective principle of exceptions, the differences between actors are sufficiently commonplace to acknowledge the place of a subjective regime of exceptions alongside an objective regime of exceptions. In effect, it is the inherent and unavoidable relativity in the practice of exceptions rather than an innate attribute of the principle as such that underlies its conventional characterization as a two-sided legal tool that enables a departure from the primary objectives of the general rule and, at the same time, can be employed to facilitate the objectives of a general rule of law. These seemingly conflicting attributes of exceptions (the subjective and the objective) are employed interchangeably so frequently that both conceptions become equally compelling in practice, making it unwise to speak of an unequivocal purpose of exceptions in law. The true character of the practice of exceptions therefore lies in the balance between its objective potential and the manner in which it is employed in practice by legal actors to determine which of its double edges becomes dominant.

International law is no different in its employment of exceptions for reasons of diversity and flexibility, but its horizontal structure presents an entirely different context in which the subjective employment of exceptions is dominant. The attraction of the subjective attributes of exceptions in international law is a reflection of the freedom and autonomy claimed and exercised by states as part of the Westphalian pedigree of that system of law. Exceptions may be employed to affirm predetermined interests that are affected by legal obligations. Similarly, the decision to participate in, and therefore be bound by, law (custom or treaty) – and the extent of such participation on, or engagement with, the law – is a matter of state discretion that may be expressed through exceptions. The persistent objection to a rule of customary law (Charney, 1985; Stein, 1985; Charney, 1993, pp. 538–42),[14] for example, or the decision not to ratify or accede to a treaty are legitimate exceptions by which state choices and preferences may be expressed. The Vienna Convention on the Law of Treaties (VCLT) expressly acknowledges diverse ways, including reservations (VCLT, 1969, Articles 2, 19–23) and denounciations (VCLT, Articles 54–56, 59, 60), by which states may legitimately depart or exempt themselves from legal obligations. These express exemption opportunities are in addition to choices made available through states' legitimate self-interpretation (Brownlie, 2003, p. 602) of these treaties.

However, the Westphalian model of legal engagement that underwrites an unconstrained employment of exceptions in international law, has come under critical scrutiny during its evolution, resulting in a direct challenge to the freedom that has traditionally been claimed by States to affirm choices through exceptions. The emergence of new social priorities as a result of the increasing fragmentation of international law into specialist regimes (Koskenniemi, 2002; Simma, 1985; Kuiper, 1994), such as human rights, environmental law, international economic law, international humanitarian law and international criminal law, have necessitated a reassessment of some of the foundational principles of international law that support the dominance of the subjective perspective of exceptions (Simma, 1985; Kuiper, 1994). Similarly, the expanding role of non-state actors, such as international organizations (Alvarez, 2005; Sarooshi, 2005), non-governmental organizations (Steiner, 1991) and also individuals, as well as the growing consensus on the emergence of premptory norms (VCLT, Article 53) of international law have informed the challenge to the Westphalian model of legal engagement. The challenges posed by these changing trends in the evolution of international law have validated the significance of a balance of factors in favour of the objective standards relating to exceptions, although the exact interaction of factors depends on the individual circumstances under consideration. In these transitional times, the new and changing priorities in favour of an objective standard of exceptions must coexist with conflicting standards of the old Westphalian priorities. The schizophrenic consequences of this relationship can be extremely confusing at the best of times.

Exceptions and the International Law of Human Rights

Two broad and interrelated factors, one of retrospective and the other of contemporary significance, are prominent in the consideration of exceptions as part of the international law of human rights. The first of these factors relates to the unique nature of the subject of human rights, including its entirely unusual pedigree in international law. The second factor, made much more relevant by contemporary practice, relates to the predominant representation of human rights as positive law through treaties, declarations and resolutions. Both factors have nurtured an objective basis for the application of exceptions in this field of international law, in complete contrast to the subjective practice in the general body of international law. This section assesses some of the issues raised by this thorny subject and the two essays selected for Part IV focus in microcosm on the isolated, but topical, subject of reservations to international human rights treaties.

Of the many distinguishing characteristics of the international law of human rights, its evolution through cooperation between states has had the greatest impact on the management of exceptions in this field of international law. By nature, cooperation requires the employment of standards beyond individual subjective preferences. In the horizontal legal environment of international law, such standards cannot be imposed, but must instead be negotiated or distilled from the diverse interests of its many actors. To the extent that such negotiated or distilled standards are not necessarily the subjective preferences of individual states, they may be perceived as objective standards. Objectivity in this context may not necessarily convey its conventional connotation of an external regime that is independent of its actors but it does serve the crucial purpose of regulating and restraining the freedom of actors. The requirement to cooperate in fields such as the protection of aliens, the protection of victims of war or the protection of minorities challenged national authorities to temper their sweeping claims to unlimited sovereignty with the needs of other states and their citizens (Borchard, 1928). These limitations on states' sovereignty constrained, rather than facilitated, the freedom to employ exceptions for narrow subjective preferences. Viewed in isolation, the individual incidents of human rights in the field of international law during the formative years after the Westphalian treaties could not have altered the general practice of the subjective application of exceptions. While the alteration of state practice was less of an ambition during the formative years of international law, it was nevertheless significant that there were areas of international law where the conventional freedom to employ subjectively exceptions was constrained. In addition, these early challenges facilitated subsequent developments in the field to which we have become accustomed.

The processes of change in international law are slow and gradual, often entailing longer periods of transition during which legal actors are expected to employ a balance between various competing standards, including the subjective standards of Westphalia and the objectivity demands of interstate cooperation. In the early stages of this transition, when standards of cooperation are sporadic and insignificant, the reference to the subjective standards is more likely. By contrast, the expansion in the areas of cooperation further into the transitional regime increases the dominance of objective standards. The law on exceptions in the international law of human rights is currently staged somewhere along this transitional continuum, where both the benefits of an ideal objective standard and the reality of subjectivity are acknowledged. Since 1945 and the Charter of the United Nations, the field of international law relating to human rights has been sufficiently expansive and integrated as to qualify as a specialist regime, with its unique priorities requiring the employment of standards that often depart from the conventional practice in international law (Simma, 1985). Unlike most aspects of international law, the human rights regime defines and prescribes acceptable behaviour for states and seeks to supervise their compliance with these standards, thus considerably limiting the opportunity to employ exceptions for subjective purposes. This is not, however, to suggest that the application of exceptions is an entirely objective enterprise. Rather, the standards relating to exceptions in the international law of human rights are part of a continuing effort to refine a balance between the subjective preferences of national authorities, on the one hand, and the objective demands of the subject itself on the other.

The recent increase in the use of treaties as the leading medium for the conduct of international affairs is due to the evolution of international law in response to the increasing diversity of states and their interests, the uncertainty of customary international law and also the gradual loss of state autonomy to international regimes. Of these factors, it is the loss of autonomy to international regimes that poses the greater challenge to the conventional subjective employment of exceptions in international law, with the other factors exacerbating this handicap. Treaties offer states an opportunity to reassert some control or at least stem the flow of increasing internationalization without abandoning the commitment to international law. The control exercised by states over the terms of treaties and their realization through participation, combined with the greater tangibility and certainty of outcomes, makes them particularly attractive to states. However, as negotiated outcomes, treaties take the loss of primary autonomy for granted, thereby acknowledging that the days of unlimited free action are long gone (or, arguably, that such freedom never existed). Stripped of its formality, the modern treaty is therefore no more than an instrument of reaction to the failings of the Westphalian promise. From that perspective it is a compromised source of law in which individual preferences are melted together into, or replaced by, common agreeable purposes.

The significance of exceptions in such a collaborative engagement is bound to be different from the traditional freedom enjoyed by states to employ exceptions for narrow subjective preferences. In essence, treaty regimes, by their very consensual nature, cannot so easily be reconciled with a subjective standard of exceptions. Instead, it would seem, the applicable standard is an objective one in which exceptions are considered an inseparable part of the specific ambitions of the treaty. The value of exceptions, therefore, is judged by their contribution to the agreed norms and objectives set out in the treaty. The process is by no means precise and may normally tolerate minor departures based on differences in circumstances or changes necessitated by time but not radical departures from the central purposes of the treaty.

The employment of objective standards in the determination of the significance of exceptions in the law of treaties must, however, not be exaggerated on account of the simple fact of negotiation or collaboration alone. The limitations imposed on states by treaty collaboration may not always and necessarily be so severe as to prevent totally the pursuit of narrow subjective interests with exceptions. The precise legal significance of exceptions depends on the nature of the treaty, its origins and objectives. In this regard, the distinction adopted by the International

Court of Justice (ICJ) in its Advisory Opinion in the *Reservations to the Convention for the Prevention and Punishment of the Crime of Genocide*[15] between the modern humanitarian treaty and the traditional contractually-inspired treaty freely negotiated by states to secure their subjective interests, and the integrity of which the unanimity rule of reservations is designed to uphold, is illuminating. Ultimately, it is the object and purpose of humanitarian treaties (an objective standard), rather than the subjective preferences of contracting states, that determine the legal significance of reservations. According to the Court:

> The objects and purpose of the Convention thus limit both the freedom of making reservations and that of objecting to them. It follows that it is the compatibility of a reservation with the object and purpose of the Convention that must furnish the criterion for the attitude of a State in making the reservation on accession as well as for the appraisal by a State in objecting to the reservation.[16]

The Court rejected the argument that a state may enter any reservation it chooses as an attribute of its sovereignty, because 'so extreme an application of the idea of sovereignty could lead to the complete disregard of the object and purpose of the Convention'.[17] The Court's conclusion that reservations are permissible so long as they are compatible with the objects and purposes of the treaty was an unequivocal endorsement of the objective paradigm of reservations. This is the standard reiterated in the VCLT (Article 19(c)) and endorsed in practice before international tribunals dealing with human rights.[18]

This apparent consensus, however, conceals some fundamental differences in the practice relating to reservations law with regard to human rights. In reality, the consensus goes as far as the establishment of the principle of object and purpose but does not stretch as far as the consequences of applying the principle. In this regard, the full import of the ICJ's conclusion that the special characteristics of normative treaties, especially of humanitarian treaties, was an important factor in the permissibility of reservations within the 'object and purpose' standard could not have been appreciated at the time the Court rendered its opinion.

Concerning the consequences of the object and purpose standard, the ICJ in this Advisory Opinion and the International Law Commission through the VCLT, especially in Articles 19, 20(4) and 21(3), both envision wide discretion for states in the determination of the validity of, and any consequences relating to acceptance or objection to, reservations. In addition, the ICJ prescribes guidelines upon which states may exercise their discretion in this matter. The Court advised that the traditional contractual characterization of treaties should not determine the legal significance of reservations 'if having regard to the character of the Convention, its purposes and its mode of adoption, it cannot be established that the parties intended to derogate from that rule admitting the faculty to make reservations thereto'.[19] In the case of the Genocide Convention, the universal auspices of its adoption and the expectation of widespread participation, for which the exclusion of some states would undermine its objective and purposes, were among factors that revealed the intentions of its sponsors and contracting parties to permit reservations. This conclusion did not merely justify the adoption of the object and purpose standard but also injected an invaluable element of flexibility into the reservations regime that enabled the Court to conclude further that, in humanitarian treaties such as the Genocide Convention:

> . . . the contracting States do not have any interests of their own; they merely have, one and all, a common interest, namely, the accomplishment of those higher purposes which are the *raison d'être* of the Convention.[20]

Using the Genocide Convention as illustrative, the Court had acknowledged, at least in principle, that the character and terms of certain treaties may call for engagement of different obligations and consequences with regard to reservations. This view confirms the futility of a prescribed standard, objective or subjective, in this field of the law.

The full significance of this freedom to draw on the distinguishing characteristics of individual treaties in determining the scope and consequences of reservations was not appreciated until it was vigorously applied by international human rights tribunals. These tribunals argued strongly that, having regard to the special character and purposes of human rights treaties, they are distinguishable from other agreements in so far as the consequences of reservations are concerned. They argued that human rights are, in effect, a specialist regime driven by entirely different priorities that tend to engage differently with the standards set out in the VCLT. The sentiments of the Inter-American Court on Human Rights that 'modern human rights treaties in general, and the American Convention in particular, are not multilateral treaties of the traditional type concluded to accomplish the reciprocal exchange of rights for the mutual benefit of the Contracting States',[21] have been echoed by the European Court of Human Rights[22] and the United Nations Human Rights Committee.[23] The Committee took the view that the principle of interstate reciprocity does not apply to obligations under the Covenant to the extent that it does not represent a web of interstate exchanges of mutual obligations.[24]

In the human rights field, the freedom to think 'out of the box' in the determination of reservations policy not only enabled the supervisory tribunals to adopt the objective standard as the most appropriate criterion in this context, but also proved to be a convenient tool of empowerment with which to challenge the subjective claims of national authorities. This power dynamic has become possible not because human rights treaties are untypical in their provenance and structure when compared with most other treaties but as a direct consequence of the establishment of supervisory institutions to ensure that states comply with their obligations. It is this factor that defined a sufficiently unique relationship between states parties as well as with the supervisory tribunals that it affected the treatment of reservations. The scope of this power must, however, not be exaggerated as these bodies are, after all, inherently disadvantaged because of their subsidiary relationship with national authorities and the specifically weakened terms of engagement. Consequently, as is common knowledge, they undertake their tasks and responsibilities at less than full speed (Steiner, 2000; Higgins, 1996; Mutua, 1998; Opsahl, 1992).

The supervisory institutions established under the auspices of the United Nations human rights treaties, including the Human Rights Committee, stand out as the weakest of the implementation schemes, and this makes the legitimacy of their power to depart from traditional subjective standards in matters concerning reservations the most contentious. In 1994 the Committee was confronted with an increasing number of challenging reservations that threatened the integrity of the Covenant (Higgins, 1989; Redgwell, 1997) and, finding no assistance under the standard norms set out in the VCLT, it drew strength from the characterization of human rights treaties as special in order to respond to the threats posed by these reservations. In principle, General Comment No. 24 is a non-binding interpretation of the law relating to reservations under the Covenant but in reality, its impact is far-reaching. With this General Comment, the Committee justified its progressive actions in its routine review of national reports and the consideration of individual communications. In certain aspects of juridical detail, there are differences between the various supervisory bodies but the position in which the Committee found itself, reacting to the subjective claims of national authorities when confronted with reservations, is not an isolated one. The policies of the ECHR and the I-ACHR have been a consequence of having to react to states' claims rather than a proactive engagement. Concerning reservations and human rights, the air of confrontation between sovereign claims of states and the supervisory responsibility of international human rights tribunal is stiff.

Naturally, the reservations policy, as applied to human rights treaties, has not met with universal approval. The US, the UK, France and Trinidad and Tobago have openly challenged and protested the legitimacy of the policy (Tomuschat, 2003, pp. 161–62).[25] These countries are backed by no less an institution than the International Law Commission in insisting on a consistent application of the VCLT standards (ILC, 1996).

Reservations and Non-reciprocal Obligations

Today, the scholarship on reservations policy in the field of human rights treaties is largely contentious, complex and extremely baffling. One of the key concerns of the academic scholarship relates to the claim to uniqueness of human rights treaties upon which the entire policy is developed. The core problem with the claim that human rights treaties are special is its complacent representation as autonomous and self-sufficient. The originality of Matthew Craven's essay on 'Legal Differentiation and the Concept of the Human Rights Treaty in International Law' (Chapter 9) lies in its critical engagement with this particular claim. Craven shows how the claim of autonomy and self-sufficiency of human rights treaties is thin on clarity and precision and heavy on exaggeration for, after all, the roots of human rights law lie in, and indeed the body of human rights knowledge continues to share substantial aspects of its detail with, mainstream international law. At the same time, he notes that it may not be so clever to dismiss lightly the unusual considerations of human rights law as being no more than conventional international law while its objectives, processes and outcomes are often so evidently different from those of conventional international law. Human rights law has less of a state-centred focus, and it engages in an entirely different way with international law doctrine and practice. The law of treaties is a classic case in point. Human rights treaties are the product of an interstate contractual bargain that leaves individuals as the fortuitous beneficiaries of a regime that is otherwise designed to uphold the interests of states, but the philosophy and practice of the regime in requiring states to respect and secure individual rights under the watchful supervision of independent tribunals supposes that the treaties are quasi-constitutional in character in terms, *inter alia*, of underwriting the legitimacy of international law and states' actions. Similarly, the state-centred deference of the VCLT generally, and the fragmentation and bilateralism of obligations that underlie its reservations standard especially, seem woefully inadequate in the human rights field where 'the content and extent of obligations does not vary according to which States are, or are not, party to the treaty, or indeed as to how many States are party' (p. 392). Craven concludes that, to say that the international law of human rights is *lex specialis* may be far less contestable, if for no reason other than because of the decentralized nature of international law. Alas, the diversity principle alone is too broad to justify the claims for specialist treatment of reservations to human rights treaties, the credibility of which has been put on the line by the strong objections from states and the International Law Commission (ILC, 1996).

That the stand-off between the advocates and objectors to a special reservations regime for human rights has yielded little progress makes Craven's proposal for a critical assessment to unpack the *lex specialis* claims for human rights an attractive, if not the only available, option for breaking the impasse. Precision and clarity will no doubt strengthen the terms of the claim for special treatment. The current justifications for uniqueness, including the humanitarian ideals of human rights treaties, are rather general and are therefore not particularly distinctive or conclusive. As Craven rightly points out, there are other treaties with equally compelling humanitarian ideals, such as the Conventions of the International Labour Organization, the Geneva Conventions, the Hague Regulations and the Conventions on Diplomatic and Consular Relations, for which no claims for a special reservations regime have been made. Similarly, the establishment of international supervision or the right to individual petition falters on the same score, taking account of other treaties with similar institutions. There is, further, the focus on the irrelevance of reciprocity in human rights treaties – a factor that has been endorsed by human rights tribunals and so seems to hold the key to unlocking the puzzle.[26] However, this factor, too, is not entirely secure because human rights treaties, including the European Social Charter and the Migrant Workers' Convention, automatically make reciprocity relevant by making nationality a condition for the enjoyment of the rights in the treaty. Clearly, the issue cannot be easily dismissed and requires further investigation. Lacking such an investigation, however, Craven rightly concludes that:

> It would seem then, in speaking of non-reciprocal human rights regimes, we are speaking about a limited category of treaties whose purpose is to recognize and protect individual human rights in a way that is independent of the question of nationality, or of the acceptance of similar obligations by any other particular state party. (p. 395)

This limited category includes the United Nations Covenants, the Convention on the Rights of the Child, the Racial Discrimination Convention, the Women's Convention, the Torture Convention, the European Convention on Human Rights and the Inter-American Convention on Human Rights. This raises at least two interesting questions. Are these treaties sufficiently coherent to constitute a discrete category of special treaties? What exactly is the significance of that key principle of reciprocity? Answers to either or both would enlighten the debate relating to the special regime of reservations.

An awkward point of adjustment at this stage in the debate is the difficulty of conceptualizing a treaty as anything other than a reciprocal exchange of promises, benefits or obligations. At least, in its form if for no other reason, the credibility of human rights treaties does depend on the significance of the principle of reciprocity in treaty law generally. The evidence, according to Craven's essay, does suggest a sense of its indispensability (p. 400), although it need not necessarily be premised on the exchange of material considerations – that is, 'material reciprocity'. Other metaphysical or intangible representations of the principle may well expand the scope and consequences of its application. In this regard, the notion of 'legal reciprocity' entails an expansive versatility that may accommodate the unique characteristics of human rights treaties. How, then, has the principle been employed in relation to human rights treaties? One may have to look back at the 1951 landmark Advisory Opinion on the Genocide Convention to find the basis of a credible answer. Arguably, the clear statement of the object and purpose principle in that Opinion made the further categorization of humanitarian treaties as 'special' superfluous, and yet this is the characterization upon which human rights tribunals have crafted the image of extreme sensitivity of human rights treaties to reservations. Accordingly, they conclude that the strict application of the principles of opposability set out in the VCLT will defeat the objects and purpose of human rights treaties and that it is therefore inappropriate.

In effect, there is nothing particularly new or captivating in this claim by the international human rights tribunals apart from the interpretation of their own powers. In other words, it is their understanding of the object and purpose of human rights treaties that carries these treaties outside of the traditional treaty framework. This interpretation is as compelling as the alternative, proposed by the International Law Commission, of being faithful to the mainstream discourse, and only time and opportunistic circumstances will determine upon which interpretation international consensus eventually settles. Craven concludes, rightly, that '[u]ltimately, therefore, it would seem that the critical point around which the discussion of reciprocity turns is that of "enforcement" and the characteristics of the "supervisory" regimes instituted within human rights treaties' (p. 406).

In the meantime, the scholarship is free to adopt a variety of reconciliatory paradigms including the three discussed in the essay – the 'formalist', the 'purposive' and the 'cognitivist', each with interesting explanations. In the end, none of these is overwhelmingly distinguished as a perfect explanation. In practice, these attempts at reconciliation meld the competing conceptualizations together, leaving confusion and contradiction, of which the impasse relating to reservations is typical. The law of treaties may well be in a transitional phase where, although the replacing norms are not well established, the old norms are under challenge, if not discredited. Ultimately, the critical handicap to unlocking this deadlock may be the supposition that international law is a cohesive and unitary phenomenon. Craven's contribution, in this essay, was to open up the discussion and lay bare the insecurity of the so-called non-reciprocity of human rights obligations.

The Consequences of Invalid Reservations

In Chapter 10 Ryan Goodman, in 'Human Rights Treaties, Invalid Reservations and State Consent', opens up an equally revealing assessment of doctrinal differences relating to the consequences of an invalid reservation to human rights treaties. Inspired by the International Court of Justice in the Genocide Convention Advisory Opinion, the authors of the VCLT affirm the discretion of states freely to decide and determine for themselves the consequences of reservations to treaties to which they are party, including invalid reservations. Concerning invalid reservations, an objecting state may decide either: (a) not to prescribe any consequences; or (b) resolve not to apply the provision that is the subject of the reservation; or (c) oppose the entry into force of the treaty between itself and the reserving state; or (d) choose to sever the reservation (Article 21). States' discretion in this regard is not unlimited since the terms of the treaty may specifically propose limits or other limitations arising from established norms of international law.

By and large, international human rights tribunals recognize the VCLT as a valid statement of international law relating to the consequences of invalid treaties but only as a preliminary and limited determination of the issue. The human rights standard reserves final determination of the consequences of all reservations, including invalid reservation, to the supervisory tribunals.[27] This standard is also founded on the characterization of human rights treaties as special and so outside the realm of standard treaty law practice. The empowerment of supervisory tribunals to determine states' compliance with treaty obligation, coupled with the expectation of wide, if not universal, participation in human rights treaties and the absence of reciprocal undertakings in human rights treaties, have been presented as founding a different policy on the consequences of reservations, especially invalid reservations. In practice, international human rights tribunals have taken the position that an invalid reservation (that is, contrary to Article 19 VCLT) is impermissible, for which the special characteristics of human rights treaties call for one credible consequence, namely, the severance of the reservations.

This policy on the severability of reservations has met with strong policy and normative objections.[28] The anti-severability school argues that international law provides for two possible consequences of an invalid reservation, not including the severability option. In the event of an invalid reservation, it argues, states may disapply the offending reservation or oppose the entry into force of the treaty between itself and the reserving state.[29] From the normative perspective, the severability option is rejected as unjustified because it compels a state to abandon the conditions under which it undertook to enter the treaty in the first place. This is considered an unacceptable attack on state consent. It is the veracity of this normative objection by the anti-severability school that forms the focus of Ryan Goodman's analysis. In considering such a categorical rejection of the severance standard as rather simplistic, he argues, with the aid of a quasi-empirical assessment, that the harms to sovereignty claimed by the anti-severability school are exaggerated. In any case, a severability policy based on an assessment of the true intentions of the reserving state can often complement, rather than undermine, the objectives of the reserving state. Above all else, the alternative proposal to oppose the participation of the reserving state can be counterproductive and can generate worse implications for that state and those within its jurisdiction.

In a general review of states' expectations he concludes that most newly established democracies ratify human rights treaties in the hope of locking their political system into a democratic regime as an insurance against future roll-back of liberal gains. Such a government would rather sever its impermissible reservations than be excluded from the process altogether. For some established democracies, on the other hand, membership of the human rights treaty provides a good framework for exerting pressure on other states to comply as well as the opportunity to keep an eye on the powers exercised by supervisory institutions. Other established democracies are far less opportunistic and ambivalent. Goodman identifies the Netherlands and the Scandinavian states as ones that adopt the severance policy as standard practice for reasons not entirely dissimilar to the 'lock-in' policy advanced by the newly established democracies. For these and other reasons, severance of invalid reservation seems preferable to exclusion. Goodman notes that the perspective of non-democratic states can be complex and may depend on their level of democratic advancement. In general, reservations are a tactical tool either to avoid scrutiny or to secure democratic gains; this suggests a need for further and better investigation of their true intentions before adopting a policy on reservations.

In effect, Goodman's argument that, given the chance, there are times when a state would prefer to sever its reservations to human rights treaties than be excluded compels a critical rethink of both anti-severance policy and the conventional severance policy adopted by international human rights tribunals. Neither the United Nations Human Rights Committee nor the European Court of Human Rights are as rigorous in their investigation of the wishes of states parties in the consideration of reservations. Indeed, their practice is so categorical as to ignore the possibility, even if a minimal one, that some states may stand and die for their reservations,[30] and this reveals a handicap in their processes. The overall contribution of Goodman's essay is to alert us to the dangers of simplistic and categorical answers to complex regimes such as reservations generally, but especially in the field of human rights. Focusing on the need to search for appropriate contexts for different consequences to different reservations, thereby injecting more rigour into the investigation and conclusions about reservations, leads to a better claim to legitimacy in practice.

Despite its strengths, Goodman's essay raises more problems and uncertainties than it resolves. In its stoic defence of the severance policy, the essay is blind to the serious handicaps of the practice of this standard. That it defers to state sovereignty in effect poses an impossible challenge for a strategy that would prioritize human rights. The proposal for a presumption in favour of severance on account of error costs – that is to say that the costs of an error for severance are less than total exclusion – will encounter some serious problems. It would, for instance, cultivate a practice of express comment upon entering a ratification that the reservation is essential to the state's consent, making it unreasonable to sever it. It will also disempower the supervisory bodies in revisiting the significance of such reservations. Above all, it puts reserving states and objecting states in an unnecessary stand-off that compels the objecting state to disregard the express wishes of a reserving state and insist on severing the reservation bilaterally or to accept it as a mark of respect of its sovereignty.

Challenges

The analogy of the international law of human rights as a road well travelled but with so much of it yet unexplored is correct in terms of how much has been achieved and the high expectations that still remain of it. Meaningful progress can only be made if the discipline adapts and responds to the new and complex challenges that emerge from time to time. In effect, one of the key pillars of the law of human rights (domestic or international) is its dynamism, a fact acknowledged by the European Court of Human Rights when it delivered its decision that the Convention is a living instrument and so must be interpreted in the light of contemporary circumstances.[31] If challenges are the test of strength for the international law of human rights, then there is vivid evidence to suggest that the road ahead is not an entirely easy one. Poverty, disease and conflict in our time have raised the stakes so high as to challenge the integrity of human rights to the level of the law's obsession with abstract models such as sovereignty, the state and nationality. In recent times, severe conflicts, which have led to the disintegration of national regimes, have threatened the fibre of international rule of law of which human rights are a key. Former Yugoslavia (Bassiouni and Manikas, 1996), Rwanda (Reyntjens, 1996; Orth, 2001), the Congo (Smis and Oyatambwe, 2002; Boya, 2001), Sierra-Leone (O'Flaherty, 2004; Orogun, 2003) and Chechnya (Bovay, 1995; Blank, 1996) are markers of burning flames, death, inhumanity, poverty, disease, the collapse of law and order and many more failings that continue to test the dependability of the modern strategy to uphold human rights ideals. The necessity of grounding the legal basis of the international response to these atrocities in the wider Security Council mandate to contain threats to international peace and security[32] is one clear indication of how dissipated and unintegrated the international legal regime really is and highlights, in particular, the isolation of the law of human rights from the core areas of disagreement. In practice, the credibility of this effort to secure peace and security has been held together by setting the terms of engagement for these tribunals in terms of redress for human rights violations. The definition of offences, the conduct of the processes and the outcomes reflect the priority of human rights norms. Today, it is no exaggeration to claim that the Yugoslavian and Rwandan tribunals processes are an integral part of an increasingly complex chain of the international law of human rights.

The relationship between international criminal law and the international law of human rights remains unrefined, although the significance of the critical grounds broken with the adoption of the Rome Statute for the permanent International Criminal Court (Cassese, Gaeta and Jones, 2002) is now taken for granted. In this regard, the shift of focus in the international law of human rights from states to individuals, and the addition of individual responsibilities to the traditional perspective of individual rights, is no mean transformation in a legal system premised on Westphalian ideals. In addition, international criminal law marks a gear shift to the next stage in the realization of human rights ideals by seeking to adopt an independent and autonomous regime, that has slipped the clasp traditionally held by states in such supranational adjudicatory regimes. While not totally separate, international criminal law marks the early stages of a true regime of international protection of human rights that is to be distinguished from the (albeit related) established system of international supervision in which states retain a greater degree of control. That the future of the international law of human rights may continue to slip out of states' control is an exciting prospect, although the obstacles that prevent or frustrate this ambition must not be underestimated. International criminal law has not achieved the unanimous endorsement that its standing deserves, and there have been some notable non-ratifications of the Rome Statute, including the United States. The integrity of this enterprise depends largely on the quality of the Court itself, including the standing and expertise of its judges, the imagination with which they approach their tasks and the seriousness with which their judgments are received by states. Although it is too early to draw any definite conclusions, it is a matter of lingering concern that the establishment of the Court, coupled with the lessons from other processes in Yugoslavia, Rwanda and Sierra Leone, have had little deterrent effect on events in the Sudan (Sapienza, 2003; Kobrin, 2004) and in the conduct of the war in Iraq (Weisselberg, 2005; Moeckli, 2005).

How much, if any, of the progress and adjustment in the international law of human rights is attributable to changes in global economic, political, cultural or other structures is unclear. Once the Cold War ceased to be a driving force in international decision-making, the development of international law, including the law of human rights, shifted ever so slightly and yet significantly. There has been an increased expectation of consensus among states that has enabled the adoption of important strategic plans, such as the ad hoc criminal tribunals, the permanent International Criminal Court and the World Trade Organization. For a system based on the rule of law, this consensus has enabled the injection of a reasonable degree of certainty and objectivity into its character. That the end of the Cold War would change the dynamics of global relations is predictable enough, but the precise nature of the change has always been uncertain. From the perspective of the law and practice of human rights, the liberation of Cold War satellite states in Europe and Africa was consistent with the ideals of the right to self-determination (McCorquodale, 2000), the impact of which was almost immediately registered in membership of the Council of Europe and participation in its drive for democracy and human rights.[33] Not all the consequences of this transformation in inter- and intrastate dynamics have been worthwhile and successful in respect of the law of human rights. The disintegration of political and military hegemony was unimaginably violent and incompatible with human rights ideals, as exemplified by the well-documented case of Yugoslavia (Human Rights Watch, 2004b; Alcock, Milivojevic,and Horton, 1998).

Modern technological advancements have also posed significant challenges to the international law of human rights. The core of these challenges is not so much the direct human rights implications of advancements in space technology – especially satellites, computers and telecommunications – as the largely unpredictable consequences of technology on standard relations in the economic, social, cultural and political fields. 'Globalization' is the term that has come to describe this transformation in which nationality and national boundaries have become increasingly less significant. In the economic sphere the emergence of a new economic efficiency model that postulates the shortcomings of public authorities in the conduct of economic affairs has increased the role and influence of non-state actors such as transnational corporations (Blumberg, 1993; Muchlinski, 2001; Ratner, 2001), whose investment decisions are facilitated as much by modern technology as they are by the policies and strategies of international economic institutions such as the International Monetary Fund (IMF) and the World Bank Group (Addo, 1999; Kiely, 2004). Although globalization is a continuing process, the full impact of which is yet to be revealed, there is sufficient evidence to demonstrate that its consequences for international law and human rights are sufficiently radical and overwhelming to represent the modern equivalent of the Peace of Westphalia.

The transformative potential of globalization is captured in the essay on 'Globalization and the Convergence of Values' by Alex Seita (Chapter 11). In characterizing globalization as much as a cause as a consequence of the convergence of basic economic and political systems among nations, leading to the convergence of fundamental values such as democracy, human rights, the rule of law and free enterprise, Seita hints at the complexity and enormity of the challenges presented to the evolving law of human rights. The essay isolates and simplifies difficult concepts and processes in an effort to explain the potential benefits and shortcomings of globalization. As an unsettled and contentious, and yet highly influential, body of knowledge, globalization is of immense sensitivity to the law of human rights, and it is therefore important not to represent it in such a way that it unravels the gains made in the field of human rights in recent decades. In this context, it is important to appreciate the conservative perspective of globalization adopted by Seita with some caution.

Seita's essay represents globalization less as a cooperative engagement and more as a contrived process of political and economic transformation of less developed and non-Western cultures, the origins of which apparently lie in the vision of the United States and its Western allies of establishing the United Nations and companion institutions such as the IMF and the World Bank Group as a means of fostering liberal democratic values. This is a polemical representation of globalization in which the ownership of the key values are Western. Moreover, globalization is primarily a process; as such, it is not an end in itself but is coded as a facilitator to the dissemination and transposition of Western values. This is an enterprise in control and manipulation – the imposition of a particular truth and reality born out of a specific culture and history that may lead to an enlightened world government of new attitudes among peoples. The contribution of the subsidiary cultures in this exercise is largely passive, and the emerging commonality that evolves from this adjustment and transformation forms the stem of the concept of convergence around which the arguments of the essay are woven. This perspective of globalization generates a chilling sense of *déjà vu*, in so much as the impact on the international law of human rights is unlikely to be progressive. Globalization, as a contrived political strategy, is unstable and exhibits an astonishing failure to learn from the lessons of past neo-imperialistic ambitions.

Fortunately, the evidence of recent scholarship contradicts this narrow and conservative perspective by recognizing the universal acknowledgement of ideals not dissimilar to those identified as Western. Time and circumstances, such as technological advancements, wars and colonialism, may have directed emphasis on to a Western representation and vision whose reception into non-Western cultures is more a consequence of the self-evident merit of the ideals than a contrived political strategy to transform civilizations. In this regard, the contribution of globalization is to facilitate the increasing appreciation of the values and ambitions that unite the human family rather than what divides it. In our time, values such as human rights, peace, democracy and environmental sustainability resonate more strongly than factors such as nationality and geographical boundaries which separate and divide us.

In addition, opportunistic factors such as technological advancements, the establishment of international intergovernmental organizations and a well-informed and integrated civil society, as well as the lessons from economic efficiency models that empower private institutions, have all contributed to the quality of interaction between separated and isolated communities. This is the true character of globalization: it is as much a process as a phenomenon whose effect, while undoubtedly transformative, is less that of an imposition and more that of a radical evolution. In this light, the impact of globalization on the international law of human rights can be unimaginably complicated. On the one hand, human rights law, with its focus on the individual and the enhancement of human welfare, has been premised on the insignificance of nationality and national boundaries. Thus, the law and practice of human rights would seem to be related to the objectives of globalization. On the other hand, the law of human rights finds itself separated and isolated from other indicators or agents of globalization, such as the highly empowered transnational corporations and international organizations whose activities tend to marginalize individual actors. In effect, globalization is a double-edged sword – progressive on one side and dangerously reactive on another. The challenge therefore remains how to define an effective balance between these competing characteristics. In attempting this, it is important not to forget that globalization is just a tool in the hands of humans who exercise the discretion to focus on its progressive objectives. For this goal, human rights standards provide a splendid point of reference.

The intellectual separation between the law of human rights and other indicators of globalization forms a thematic foundation in 'Globalization and Human Rights' by Robert McCorquodale with Richard Fairbrother (Chapter 12). This is reflected in the status differentiation between economic globalization as the foremost dimension and the other dimensions that draw inspiration and direction from economic policy. An assessment of the potential impact of economic globalization on human rights policy reveals the two-sided character of globalization, in which economic growth retains the potential to enhance human rights – especially economic rights to adequate standard of living, food, shelter and development – while, at the same time, impacting adversely on other rights. McCorquodale notes that the analysis of the human rights handicaps of foreign direct investment, a notable instrument of economic growth, and the failings of structural adjustment, an equally central pillar of international economic policy, remain unaddressed precisely because none of these carries a human rights point of reference. In effect, the balance in the potential employment of globalization has, in the field of economic affairs, been poorly struck, leaving globalization leaning unhappily towards adverse human rights implications.

The broad conclusions drawn here on the relationship between economic globalization and economic rights are also reflected in its impact on other political and cultural rights. Yet the acknowledgement of the importance of democratic ideals, the rule of law and standards of democratic governance for an effective economic policy vividly implies their secondary and subsidiary relationship with economic globalization. In other words, human rights are neither the ends of economic globalization nor do they inform on its objectives. Rather, human rights are facilitative only of ostensibly different and separate economic aims. The irony in the label of this tenuous relationship as the progressive dimension of economic globalization on political rights is clear enough but, in addition, the label indicates where the balance is struck between the notional double edges of globalization. In the circumstances, rather little value can be expected from the negative implications of globalization that, paradoxically, tend to coincide with priorities of economic policy-making.

The challenges posed by the processes, institutions, agents and objectives of globalization for the law of human rights are critical. The flexible and adaptable character of globalization makes it as much a virtue as a potential curse. Fortunately, its character and impact depends on how it is employed by individuals, groups and the community as a whole. The terrain on which to conduct human rights affairs has been altered as a direct consequence of globalization. The state is a weakened entity and non-state actors have assumed central importance. The empowerment of the individual actor, as well as standards for his or her accountability, need to be structured in a complementary manner for an effective and credible human rights strategy. In addition, the expectations of the law of human rights have been complicated further by the advancements in technology that have made the world a smaller place in which intermingled fates and converging values are recognized. This requires an entirely different approach – one that is integrated at all levels and in all contexts – to the challenges posed by a rapidly changing society. A failure to appreciate the law of human rights as an appropriate point of reference for our changing society may well prove to be an irredeemable error.

Conclusions

From its unplanned and unstructured origins in the subjective, state-centred framework of the Peace of Westphalia, the international law of human rights has evolved into a clearly identifiable regime that is, in many ways, distinguishable from its parent. However, the inappropriateness of the legacy of sovereignty, territorialism and the subjectivity of narrow self-interest, bequeathed by international law to the law of human rights, has defined an unstable and normatively disfunctional discourse. Its ambition to achieve objective standards in a structurally subjective environment reveals contradictions and incoherence. In effect the real brief of the international law of human rights, in the short term at least, is to seek to reconcile these seemingly opposing structures. Even the harshest critics may have to concede that this project has been successful.

The international law of human rights is therefore still caught at a stage of transition in its evolution, with clearly articulated ambitions to secure or protect individual rights. The achievement of this ambition using the medium of the rule of law generates problems of its own. In requiring the suppression, if not the elimination, of non-legal concerns and the subjugation of all actors to the legal standard, the international law of human rights may seem wildly pretentious and exaggerated. For, after all, nowhere are the structurally subjective foundations of international law more evident than in the interface between politics and human rights. Here the landscape is polemical, confrontational and largely insincere. Yet, as the impact of the Cold War confirms, such polarization can spawn credible progress. However, this is a complex phenomenon that refuses to conform or disappear.

It is reassuring that the prognosis for the international law of human rights and its 'wild' ambitions is bright, on account of its adaptability, versatility and goodwill. The Westphalian point of reference has been radically transformed over the years and, in recent times, the power and role of the state has transferred to other sites including international organizations and non-state actors. It is impossible to imagine even the limited gains made in the international law of human rights without the central, and often proactive, intervention of international organizations and the non-governmental organizations that work closely with them. The evidence on this aspect of the process of evolution suggests a continuing consolidation rather than a disintegration. In addition, the increasing enlightenment that is a spin-off from the globalization of modern communications makes it impossible for national authorities to undermine the gradual human rights ideals and processes. An equally important factor in the progressive human rights prognosis lies in the expanding scholarship. In particular, the critical scholarship in the field of human rights has opened the subject to scrutiny that is constructive enough to repair harms of misrepresentation and misunderstanding.

Notes

1 The United Nations Organization is the largest and most well known of the international organizations that have devoted considerable effort to the promotion of its human rights purposes. Other organizations such as the Council of Europe, the Organization of American States and the African Union have given equally significant attention to the subject.

2 Academic scholarship has drawn inspiration from all sources including formal and informal actors at both national and international levels.

3 The Charter sought to address the issue of the marginalization of people by encoding the promotion and respect of fundamental rights among the ambitions of the international community. The human rights aspirations of the emerging international legal order were supported by an integrated institutional framework that made it possible, at all levels and contexts of international practice, to confront the rhetoric of rights with a realistic need for action.

4 At the hub of the human rights strategy stood the ECOSOC and subsequently the Commission on Human Rights that it established in 1946.

5 The Commission's denial of its power to redress human rights petitions in its first 20 years was typical and, no doubt, a source of frustration to human rights activists and disaffected victims.

6 ESCOR, Supp. No. 1 (E/4393) at pp, 17–18 and ESCOR, Supp. No. 1A (E/4832.Add.1), pp. 8–9.

7 See, for example, Committee on Economic, Social and Cultural Rights (CESCR), General Comment No. 4 (1991) on The Right to Adequate Housing, esp. para. 8. Also General Comment No. 12 (1999) on the Right to Adequate Food, para. 8. See also Human Rights Committee (HRC) General Comment No. 17 (1989) on the Rights of Children; General Comment No. 23 on Minorities' Rights. See, further, Committee on the Elimination of Racial Discrimination (CERD), General Recommendation Nos XXI (1996) on Self Determination; XXIII (1997) on the Rights of Indigenous Peoples; XXVII (2000) on Discrimination Against Roma and XXIX (2002) on Descent. See also Committee on the Elimination of Discrimination Against Women (CEDAW) General Recommendation Nos 14 (1990) on Female Circumcision; 19 (1992) on Violence Against

Women; and 21 (1994) on Equality in Marriage and Family Relations, especially paras 11–14 and 41–47.

8 He employs terms such as pluralist, multiculturalist, cultural agnostic and cultural relativist.

9 See note 7 above.

10 Article 9 CERD (1966); Article 16 ICESCR (1966); Article 40 ICCPR (1966); Article 18 CEDAW (1979); Article 19 CAT (1984); Article 44 CRC (1989).

11 Article 11 CERD; Article 41 ICCPR; Article 21 CAT.

12 Article 14 CERD; Article 1 of Optional Protocol No. 1 to ICCPR (1996); Article 2 of Optional Protocol to CEDAW (1999), Article 22 CAT.

13 See, Chapter 8, especially p. 363 *et seq* where, for example, the essay interchangeably calls on the Human Rights Committee to 'harmonize' its decisions with the European case law (p. 364) or to 'consult' with, or not to ignore the relevant body of 'precedent' (p. 364), or to 'follow' or 'seek guidance' (p. 371) or to dialogue with or 'draw inspiration' (p. 371) from the European case law. Some of these usages imply subordination while others capture a true collegial relationship. Such confusion lends room to misunderstanding and misinterpretation.

14 See the Fisheries case (*UK* v. *Norway*) 1951, ICJ Reports, p. 31; Asylum case (*Colombia* v. *Peru*) 1950, ICJ Reports, pp. 277–78 and Continental Shelf cases (*Germany* v. *Denmark and Netherlands*) 1969, ICJ Reports, pp. 26–27.

15 (1952) ICJ Reports, 1951, p. 15.

16 Ibid., p. 24.

17 Ibid.

18 Human Rights Committee, General Comment No. 24 (52) 1994. Text reprinted in United Nations, *Compilation of General Comments and General Recommendations Adopted by Human Rights Treaty Bodies*, UN Doc. HRI/GEN/1/Rev.6 (2003), paras 6 and 17.

19 *Genocide Convention* case, *loc. cit.*, p. 24.

20 Ibid., p. 23.

21 Advisory Opinion on *Entry into Force of the American Convention on Human Rights (Articles 74 & 75)* (1982), para. 29 where the Court took the view that:

> Their [human rights treaties] object and purpose is the protection of the basic rights of individual human beings, irrespective of their nationality and all other contracting States. In concluding these human rights treaties, the States can be deemed to submit themselves to a legal order within which they, for the common good, assume various obligations, not in relation to other States, but towards all individuals within their jurisdiction.

22 See *Loizidou* v. *Turkey*, Application No. 9116/80; *Tameltasch* v. *Switzerland* (1983), paras 62–65; *Belilos* v. *Switzerland*, para. 47. See also Opinions of the European Commission on Human Rights in Application No. 788/60, *Austria* v. *Italy*, 4 *European Yearbook of Human Rights* (1961), p. 116 at 140; *Cyprus* v. *Turkey*, 21 *Yearbook of ECHR* (1979), p. 226 and *France* v. *Turkey*, *Yearbook of ECHR* (1983) (Part II) p. 31 at 42.

23 Human Rights Committee's General Comment No. 24 (52), *op. cit.*, note 18 *supra*, para. 17.

24 Ibid.

25 See GAOR, Suppl. No. 40, Doc. A/50/40, vol. 1 (1995), p. 131; also GAOR, Suppl. No. 40, Doc. A/57/40 (2002), p. 146.

26 See *Austria* v. *Italy*, 4 *European Yearbook of Human Rights* (1961), p. 116 at 140; *Advisory Opinion on Effect of Ratification (Arts. 74 and 75)* (1982) para. 29; and General Comment No. 24 (52), *op. cit.*, note 18 *supra*, para. 29.

27 See *Belilos* v. *Switzerland* (1988) Series A/132; HRC General Comment No. 24.

28 See the objections registered by US; UK; France, *loc. cit*; and the Dissenting Opinion in the *Kennedy* v. *Trinidad and Tobago* case – UN. Doc. A/55/40 p. 258; and the Second Report of the ILC on Reservations, *loc. cit.*

29 This view draws its inspiration from conclusions of the ICJ in the Genocide Convention Advisory Opinion as well as on the narrow reading of the Vienna Convention on the Law of Treaties – Article 21(3).

30 One of the Swiss reactions to the *Belilos* decision before the European Court of Human Rights was to seek to denounce the treaty. Fortunately the government failed to secure the necessary endorsement of the national legislature. Similarly, Trinidad and Tobago denounced the Optional Protocol No. 1 to the ICCPR after the Human Rights Committee's decision in the *Kennedy* v. *Trinidad and Tobago* case: see *Report of the Human Rights Committee*, vol. I (2002) UN Doc. A/57/40, p. 146.

31 See *Tyrer* v. *United Kingdom*, Series A/26 (1978), para. 31; *Loizidou* v. *Turkey*, Series A/310 (1995), para. 71; *Soering* v. *United Kingdom*, Series A/161 (1989), para. 102; *Selmouni* v. *France*, 29 EHRR 403 (1999), para. 101; and *Mamatkulov and Abdurasulovic* v. *Turkey* (2003), para. 94.

32 For ICTY see UN Doc. S/RES/808 (1993) and UN Doc. S/RES/827 (1993). For ICTR see UN Doc. S/RES/955 (1994).

33 See Statute of the Council of Europe at www.coe.fr.

References

Addo, Michael K. (1999), 'The Role of International Financial Institutions in Privatisation and the Need for Constitutional Reform', in John F. McEldowney (ed.), *National and International Perspectives on Law and Privatisation*, London: British Institute of Comparative Law, pp. 145–67.

Alcock, John, Milivojevic, Marko and Horton, John (eds) (1998), *Conflict in Former Yugoslavia: An Encyclopedia*, Denver: ABC-CLIO.

Alston, Philip (1992a), 'Critical Appraisal of the UN Human Rights Regime', in Philip Alston (ed.), *The United Nations and Human Rights: A Critical Appraisal*, Oxford: Clarendon Press, pp. 1–22.

Alston, Philip (1992b), 'The Commission on Human Rights', in Philip Alston (ed.), *The United Nations and Human Rights: A Critical Appraisal*, Oxford: Clarendon Press, pp. 126–210.

Alston, Philip (1996), 'Introduction', in Philip Alston (ed.), *Human Rights Law*, Aldershot: Dartmouth, pp. i–xxvi.

Alvarez, José (2005), *International Organisations as Law-makers*, Oxford: Oxford University Press.

Amerasinghe, C.F. (1967), *State Responsibility for Injuries to Aliens*, Oxford: Oxford University Press.

An-Na'im, Abdullahi (1987), 'Religious Minorities under Islamic Law and the Limits of Cultural Relativism', *Human Rights Quarterly*, **9**, pp. 1–18.

An-Na'im, Abdullahi (1992), 'Towards a Cross-Cultural Approach to Defining International Standards of Human Rights. The Meaning of Cruel, Inhuman and Degrading Treatment or Punishment', in A. An-na'im (ed.), *Human Rights in Cross-Cultural Perspectives*, Philadelphia, PA: University of Pennsylvania Press, pp. 19–43.

Bailey, Sydney D. (1992), 'The Security Council', in Philip Alston (ed.), *The United Nations and Human Rights. A Critical Appraisal*, Oxford: Clarendon Press, pp. 304–36.

Bassiouni, Cherif, M. and Manikas, P. (1996), *The Law of the International Criminal Tribunal for the Former Yugoslavia*, Irvington, NY: Transnational Publishers.

Bayefsky, Ann (1996), 'Cultural Sovereignty, Relativism, and International Human Rights: New Excuses for Old Strategies', *Ratio Juris*, **9**, pp. 42–59.

Blank, Stephen (1996), 'Russian Democracy and the West after Chechnya', *Comparative Strategy*, **15**, pp. 11–30.

Blumberg, Phillip (1993), *The Multinational Challenge to Corporate Law*, Oxford: Oxford University Press.

Borchard, E.M. (1928), *The Diplomatic Protection of Citizens Abroad*, New York: Banks.

Bovay, Nicholas (1995), 'The Russian Armed Conflict in Chechnya and its Human Rights Implications', *ICJ Review*, **54**, pp. 29–48.

Boya, Odette (2001), 'Contentious Politics and Social Change in Congo', *Security and Dialogue*, **32**, pp. 71–86.

Brett, Rachel (1999), 'Non-Governmental Actors in the Field of Human Rights', in Raija Hanski and Markku Suksi (eds), *An Introduction to the International Protection of Human Rights – A Textbook*, Turku: Åbo Akademi, pp. 399–413.

Broomhall, Bruce (2003), *International Justice and the ICC. Between Sovereignty and the Rule of Law*, Oxford: Oxford University Press.

Brownlie, Ian (2003), *Principles of Public International Law*, Oxford: Oxford University Press.
Brownlie, Ian and Goodwin-Gill, Guy S. (2002), *Basic Documents on Human Rights*, Oxford: Oxford University Press.
Buergenthal, Thomas (1977), *Human Rights, International Law and the Helsinki Accord*, Montclair: Allanheld.
Buergenthal, Thomas (1978), 'A Challenge for the Universities', *UNESCO Courier*, **31**, pp. 25–28.
Buergenthal, Thomas (1988), 'The OAS and the Protection of Rights', *Emory Journal of International Dispute Resolution*, **3**, pp. 1–24.
Cassese, Antonio (1992), 'The General Assembly: Historical Perspective 1945–1989', in Philip Alston (ed.), *The United Nations and Human Rights. A Critical Appraisal*, Oxford: Clarendon Press, pp. 25–54.
Cassese, Antonio, Gaeta, Paola and Jones, John R.W.D. (2002), *The Rome Statute of the International Criminal Court: A Commentary*, Oxford: Oxford University Press.
Cerna, Christina M. (1992), 'The Structure and Functioning of the Inter-American Court of Human Rights', *British Yearbook of International Law*, **LXIII**, pp. 135–229.
Charney, Jonathan (1985), 'The Persistent Objector Rule and the Development of Customary International Law', *British Yearbook of International Law*, **LVI**, pp. 1–24.
Charney, Jonathan (1993), 'Universal International Law', *American Journal of International Law*, **87**, pp. 529–51.
Clapham, Andrew (2000), 'UN Human Rights Reporting Procedures: An NGO Perspective', in Philip Alston and James Crawford (eds), *The Future of UN Human Rights Treaty Monitoring*, Cambridge: Cambridge University Press, pp. 175–98.
Coppel, Jason and O'Neil, Aidan (1992), 'The European Court of Justice: Taking Rights Seriously', *Common Market Law Review*, **29**, pp. 669–92.
Corazza, Paolo G. (2003), 'Subsidiarity as a Structural Principle of International Human Rights Law', *American Journal of International Law*, **97**, pp. 38–79.
Davidson, Scott (1992), *The Inter-American Court of Human Rights*, Aldershot: Dartmouth
Donnelly, Jack (1982), 'Human Rights and Human Dignity: An Analytical Critique of Non-Western Conceptions of Human Rights', *American Political Science Review*, **76**, pp. 303–16.
Donoho, Douglas (1991), 'Relativism versus Universalism in Human Rights: The Search for Meaningful Standards', *Stanford Journal of International Law*, **27**, pp. 345–91.
Estébanez, Maria Amor Martin (1999), 'The OECE and Human Rights', in Raija Hanski and Markku Suksi (eds), *An Introduction to the International Protection of Human Rights – A Textbook*, Turku: Åbo Akademi, pp. 329–50.
Evans, Malcolm and Murray, Rachel (2002), *The African Charter on Human and Peoples' Rights*, Cambridge: Cambridge University Press.
Farer, T.J. and Gaer, F. (1993), 'The UN and Human Rights: At the End of the Beginning', in Adam Roberts and Benedict Kingsbury (eds), *United Nations, Divided World*, Oxford: Clarendon Press, pp. 240–96.
Flinterman, Cees (1999), 'Extra-Conventional Standard-Setting and Implementation in the Field of Human Rights', in Raija Hanski and Markku Suksi (eds), *An Introduction to the International Protection of Human Rights – A Textbook*, Turku: Åbo Akademi, pp. 143–50.
Garcia Amador, F.V. (1958-II), 'State Responsibility: Some New Problems', *Recueil des Cours de l'Académie de Droit International de la Haye*, **94**, p. 365.
Gittleman, Richard (1982), 'The African Charter on Human and Peoples' Rights: A Legal Analysis', *Virginia Journal of International Law*, **22**, pp. 667–714.
Hannum, Hurst (ed.) (2004), *Guide to International Human Rights Practice*, New York: Transnational.
Harris, David and Livingstone, Stephen (1998), *The Inter-American System of Human Rights*, Oxford: Clarendon Press.
Higgins, Rosalyn (1977), 'Derogations under Human Rights Treaties', *British Yearbook of International Law*, pp. 281–320.
Higgins, Rosalyn (1989), 'Human Rights: Some Questions of Integrity', *Modern Law Review*, **52**, pp. 1–21.
Higgins, Rosalyn (1996), 'Ten Years on the UN Human Rights Committee: Some Thoughts Upon Parting', *European Human Rights Law Review*, **6**, pp. 570–82.

Howard, Rhoda (1992), 'Dignity, Community and Human Rights', in Abdullahi An-Na'im (ed.), *Human Rights in Cross-Cultural Perspectives*, Philadelphia, PA: Pennsylvania University Press, pp. 81–102.
Human Rights Watch (2004a), *Justice at Risk*, New York: HRW.
Human Rights Watch (2004b), *Genocide, War Crimes and Crimes Against Humanity*, New York: HRW.
International Law Commission (1996), *Second Report on Reservations to Treaties by the Special Rapporteur*. UN Doc. A/CN.4/477/Add.1.
Jackson, John, H. (2003), 'Sovereignty-Modern: A New Approach to an Outdated Concept', *American Journal of International Law*, **97**, pp. 782–802.
Jernow, Allison L. (1996), 'Ad-Hoc and Extra-Conventional Means of Human Rights Monitoring', *New York University Journal of International Law and Politics*, **28**, pp. 785–836.
Kiely, Ray (2004), 'The World Bank and "Global Poverty Reduction": Good Policies or Bad Data?', *Journal of Contemporary Asia*, **34**, pp. 3–20.
Kittichaisaree, Kriangsak (2001), *International Criminal Law*, Oxford: Oxford University Press.
Kobrin, Stephen (2004), 'Oil and Politics: Talisman Energy and Sudan', *New York University Journal of International Law and Politics*, **36**, pp. 425–56.
Koh, Harold H. (1997), 'Why do Nations Obey International Law?', *Yale Law Journal*, **106**, pp. 2599–659.
Koh, Harold, H. (1998), 'Bringing International Law Home', *Houston Law Review*, **35**, pp. 623–81.
Koh, Harold, H. (1999), 'How is International Human Rights Enforced?', *Indiana Law Journal*, **74**, pp. 1379–417.
Koskenniemi, Martti (1990), 'The Pull of the Mainstream', *Michigan Law Review*, **88**, pp. 1946–62.
Koskenniemi, Martti (2002), 'Fragmentation of International Law? Postmodern Anxieties', *Leiden Journal of International Law*, **15**, pp. 553–79.
Kuiper, Pieter Jan (1994), 'The Law of GATT as a Special Field of International Law', *Netherlands Yearbook of International Law*, **25**, pp. 227–57.
McCorquodale, Robert (2000), *Self Determination in International Law*, Aldershot: Ashgate.
MacDonald, Ronald St John (1993), 'The Margin of Appreciation', in R. St J. Macdonald *et al.* (eds), *The European System for the Protection of Human Rights*, Dordrecht: Martinus Nijhoff, pp. 83–124.
MacDonald, R. St J. (1998), 'Derogations under Article 15 of the European Convention on Human Rights', *Columbia Journal of Transnational Law*, **36**, pp. 225–67.
Mahalic, Drew and Mahalic, Joan G. (1987), 'The Limitation Provisions of the International Convention on the Elimination of All Forms of Racial Discrimination', *Human Rights Quarterly*, **9**, pp. 74–104.
Mahoney, Paul (1997), 'Universality Versus Subsidiarity in the Strasbourg Case Law on Free Speech: Explaining some Recent Judgments', *European Human Rights Law Review*, pp. 364–79.
Mahoney, Paul (1998), 'Marvelous Richness of Diversity or Invidious Cultural Relativism', *Human Rights Law Journal*, **19**, pp. 1–6.
Moekli, Daniel (2005), 'The US Supreme Court's "Enemy Combatant" Decisions: A Major Victory for the Rule of Law', *Journal of Conflict and Security*, **10**, pp. 75–99.
Muchlinski, Peter (2001), 'Human Rights and Multinational: Is There a Problem?', *International Affairs*, **77**, pp. 31–47.
Murray, Rachel (2000), *The African Commission on Human and Peoples' Rights*, Oxford: Hart.
Mutua, Makau wa (1998), 'Looking Past the Human Rights Committee: An Argument for De-Marginalizing Enforcement', *Buffalo Human Rights Law Review*, **4**, pp. 211–60.
O'Flaherty, Michael (2004), 'Sierra-Leone's Peace Process: The Role of the Human Rights Community', *Human Rights Quarterly*, **26**, pp. 29–63.
Opsahl, Torkel (1992), 'The Human Rights Committee', in P. Alston (ed.), *The United Nations and Human Rights: A Critical Appraisal*, Oxford: Oxford University Press, pp. 369–443.
Orogun, Paul (2003), 'Blood Diamonds and Africa's Armed Conflicts in the Post Cold War Era', *World Affairs*, **166**, pp. 151–62.
Orth, Rick (2001), 'Rwanda's Hutu Extremist Genocide Insurgency: An Eyewitness Perspective', *Small Wars and Insurgencies*, **12**, pp. 76–109.
Partsch, Karl J. (1992), 'The Committee on the Elimination of Racial Discrimination', in P. Alston (ed.), *The United Nations and Human Rights: A Critical Appraisal*, Oxford: Clarendon Press, pp. 339–68.
Pasqualucci, Jo M. (2003), *The Practice and Procedure of the Inter-American Court of Human Rights*, Cambridge: Cambridge University Press.

Pauwelyn, Joost (2003), *Conflict of Norms in Public International Law*, Cambridge, Cambridge University Press.

Petzold, Herbert (1993), 'The Convention and the Principle of Subsidiarity', in Ronald St J. Macdonald *et al.* (eds), *The European System for the Protection of Human Rights*, Dordrecht: Martinus Nijhoff, pp. 41–62.

Pollis, Admantia and Schwab, Peter (1979), 'A Western Construct with Limited Applicability', in A. Pollis and P. Schwab (eds), *Human Rights: Cultural and Ideological Perspectives*, New York: Praeger, p. 1.

Preis, Ann-Belinda (1996), 'Human Rights as Cultural Practice: An Anthropological Critique', *Human Rights Quarterly*, **18**, pp. 286–315.

Prouvez, Nathalie (2003/4), 'Minorities and Indigenous Peoples' Protection: Practice of UN Treaty Bodies', *European Yearbook of Minority Issues*, **3**, pp. 481–508.

Quinn, John (1992), 'The General Assembly into the 1990s', in Philip Alston (ed.), *The United Nations and Human Rights. A Critical Appraisal*, Oxford: Clarendon Press, pp. 55–106.

Ratner, Steven (2001), 'Corporations and Human Rights: A Theory of Legal Responsibility', *Yale Law Journal*, **111**, pp. 443–545.

Redgwell, Catherine (1997), 'Reservations to Treaties and Human Rights Committee General Comment No. 24 (52)', *International and Comparative Law Quarterly*, **46**, pp. 390–412.

Reyntjens, Flip (1996), 'Rwanda: Genocide and Beyond', *Journal of Refugee Studies*, **9**, pp. 240–51.

Rodley, Nigel and Wiessbrodt (2004), 'United Nations Nontreaty Procedures for Dealing with Human Rights Violations', in Hurst Hannum (ed.), *Guide to International Human Rights Practice*, New York: Transnational.

Sapienza, Lina (2003), 'Classifying the Killings in Sudan as Genocide', *New York Law School Journal of Human Rights*, **19**, pp. 889–94.

Sarooshi, Dan (2005), *International Organisations and their Exercise of Sovereign Powers*, Oxford: Oxford University Press.

Shaw, Malcolm, N. (2003), *International Law*, Cambridge: Cambridge University Press.

Shelton, Dinah (1993), 'Subsidiarity, Democracy and Human Rights', in Donna Gomien (ed.), *Broadening the Frontiers of Human Rights: Essays in Honour of Asbjørn Eide*, Oslo: Scandinavian University Press, pp. 43–54.

Simma, Bruno (1985), 'Self-Contained Regimes', *Netherlands Yearbook of International Law*, **16**, pp. 111–36.

Smis, Stefan and Oyatambwe, Wamu (2002), 'Complex Political Emergencies: The International Community and the Congo Conflict', *Review of African Political Economy*, **29**, pp. 411–30.

Sohn, Louis, B. (1982), 'The New International Law: Protection of the Rights of Individuals Rather Than States', *American University Law Review*, **32**, pp. 1–64.

Sohn, Louis. B. and Buergenthal, Thomas (1973), *International Protection of Human Rights*, New York: Bobbs-Merrill.

Stein, Ted L. (1985), 'The Approach of the Different Drummer: The Principle of the Persistent Objector in International Law', *Harvard International Law Journal*, **26**, pp. 457–82.

Steiner, Henry J. (1991), *Diverse Partners: Non-Governmental Organisations in the Human Rights Movement*, Cambridge, MA: Harvard University Press.

Steiner, Henry J. (2000), 'Individual Claims in a World of Massive Violations: What Role for the Human Rights Committee?', in Philip Alston and James Crawford (eds), *The Future of UN Human Rights Treaty Monitoring*, Cambridge: Cambridge University Press, pp. 15–53.

Tomuschat, Christian (2003), *Human Rights. Between Idealism and Realism*, Oxford: Oxford University Press.

Weiss, T.G. and Gordenker, L. (eds) (1996), *NGOs, the UN and Global Governance*, Boulder, CO: Lynn Rienner.

Weisselberg, Charles (2005), 'The Detention and Treatment of Aliens Three Years After September 11: A New New World', *UC Davis Law Review*, **38**, pp. 815–60.

Willets, Peter (ed.) (1997), *The Conscience of the World: The Influence of NGOs in the United Nations System*, Washington, DC: Brookings Institution.

Woods, Lorna (1999), 'The European Union and Human Rights', in Raija Hanski and Markku Suksi (eds), *An Introduction to the International Protection of Human Rights – A Textbook*, Turku: Åbo Akademi, pp. 35–68.

Part I
Nature

[1]

HUMAN RIGHTS GENEALOGY

*Ruti Teitel**

Introduction

AS the century draws to an end, this Article explores the status and future directions of contemporary human rights theory. It begins with the puzzle that, despite its conceded normative force, contemporary human rights theory is said to be fundamentally flawed, lacking a center, organizing structure, or unifying value. The puzzle is varyingly attributed to incoherence in international human rights theory and to irreconcilable dualisms pervading the theory.[1] This Article critiques the prevailing understanding by elaborating on the implications of theorizing in these oppositional terms, proposing a genealogical perspective to human rights theory. Such a perspective explores international human rights theory's historical and political legacies, its founding structures and rhetoric, with an eye toward a better understanding of the contemporary international human rights movement, its place in history, and its future potential. International human rights theory is reconsidered in light of its historical and political engendering circumstances. This Article will use "genealogy"[2] in a number of senses: first, as the exploration of the organizing structures, logic, and language that comprehend the domain of contemporary human rights theory; second, as the historical and political circumstances of the international human rights movement; and third, as the connection between the relationship of international human rights theory and other philosophical, political, and legal rights theorizing.

The Article attempts to illuminate the status of prevailing international human rights theory by contributing a genealogical perspective to the contemporary theorizing. Part I examines the origins of the reigning theoretical framework by considering the historical and political circumstances that attended the development of the theory. Part

---

* Professor of Law, New York Law School; J.D., 1980, Cornell Law School. My gratitude to Camille Broussard, Brenda Davis-Lebron, and Sabrina Bagdasarian for their research and other assistance.

1. Thus, introductions to texts on human rights law often begin with caveats about the subject area's incoherence. *See* Louis Henkin, International Law: Politics and Values 184-85 (1995); Human Rights Law xiii (Philip Alston ed., 1996); *see also* Martti Koskenniemi, *The Pull of the Mainstream*, 88 Mich. L. Rev. 1946, 1961-62 (1990) (reviewing Theodor Meron, Human Rights and Humanitarian Norms as Customary Law (1989)) (observing that international lawyers have not succeeded in developing any compelling theory on the place of human rights within any grand design of international law and that "the justifying rhetoric" of mainstream international lawyers is in "disarray").

2. On the genealogical perspective, see Michel Foucault, Power/Knowledge: Selected Interviews and Other Writings, 1972-1977 (Colin Gordon ed. & Colin Gordon et al. trans., 1980).

II explains how a genealogical approach clarifies problems in the reigning paradigm. Part III explores further the dichotomies in the prevailing theory, thereby clarifying the puzzling status of contemporary human rights theory. Part IV examines the international human rights movement today, incorporating a genealogical perspective and clarifying the contemporary movement's intimate and uneasy relation to its original historical and political circumstances. This part also proposes a more coherent view of the existing international human rights normative apparatus.

I. Rights Genesis

Consider international human rights theory and its engendering circumstances. The founding is said to go like this: Genesis of the human rights movement, by its own description, begins in postwar Europe. This point of departure for contemporary human rights theory is definitional—the international human rights movement is birthed in the war and the postwar experience. Told this way, international human rights creation, like the war itself, gave rise to a new, paradigmatic view of rights as extraordinary and discontinuous from prior expectations.

As a paradigm supported and engendered by the immediate circumstances of the postwar period, international human rights implies an utterly transformed model regarding individual/state responsibility and relations. International human rights, as both a postwar and post-totalitarian movement, was a radical departure from the prevailing rights theorizing assumptions about the state. A creature of postwar circumstances, the new paradigm was said to mean new rights and a departure from the contractarian tradition associated with pre-existing rights theorizing. International human rights drew their normative force, at the time, not necessarily from social consensus, but rather from the exercise of judicial power. This alternative normative vision is instantiated by the Nuremberg Tribunal, the extraordinary Allied justice brought to bear against human rights abusers.

Later, these norms were ratified in various international charters and conventions as merely the institutionalization of preexisting universal norms. The human rights movement, which blossomed in the war's aftermath, was a phenomenon that largely developed within a newly created international legal system.[3] The postwar construction of international human rights appeared in transnational form: initially, in the Nuremberg Charter, then in the United Nations Charter and other United Nations instruments, and in multilateral treaties and conventions.[4] These alternative conceptions of human rights ulti-

3. For an excellent account, see Henkin, *supra* note 1.

4. On transnationalism, see Harold Hongju Koh, *Why Do Nations Obey International Law?*, 106 Yale L.J. 2599 (1997) (book review); *see also* Lawrence G. Helfer &

mately meant a new system of rights protection—inhering outside of social contract—vindicating a view of human rights within an adjudicatory model and an emerging international legal system. At Nuremberg, after the war, international human rights appeared to have ultimate normative power. Human rights seemingly were protectable, with or without the state, as the massive postwar codification projects made rights with normative force positive.

The postwar paradigm implied a reconceptualization of core rights concepts. First, rights were understood to be protected within a conception of rule of law which was largely conceived as legal accountability, indeed as criminal accountability. While this view of rule of law suffers from being *ex post*, it is best understood in its historical postwar context. After the grave atrocities of the war, the human rights project was largely the ascribing of individual responsibility. Next, and relatedly, the understanding of individual responsibility for rights protection under international law changed, particularly the balance between the individual and the state. These changed understandings implied changes in the content of human rights values. The postwar normative scheme that defined human rights in terms of political persecution was a response to the war and to totalitarianism. As such, postwar justice reflected its engendering circumstances.

The new arrangements forced a rethinking of the meaning of rights. This reconsideration included the extent to which these rights appertained to a corresponding system of duties. The change in the prior expectations, which were the legacy of social contract theory,[5] transformed the human rights paradigm entirely. Whereas in earlier rights theory, individuals were entitled to the contractual rights that the state agreed to protect, these assumptions fell away in the postwar paradigm. Individual rights bore no particular relation to the state's assumption of duties. Indeed, the previous formulation of rights appeared unavailable and the state instead a potential source of evil. Accordingly, rights protection moved to alternative sites and systems, to international human rights conventions, mechanics, and processes.

The human rights movement was nurtured by the concomitant development of a new international legal system, as well as by the parallel explosion of constitutionalism.[6] The notion of rights as judicial in nature is supported by the postwar explosion of constitutionalism and judicial review. As time passed, the postwar paradigm and its ad hoc blend of laws of war and the laws of peace become normalized, despite the absence of political circumstances similar to those that at-

Anne-Marie Slaughter, *Toward a Theory of Effective Supranational Adjudication*, 107 Yale L.J. 273 (1997).

5. *See generally* Ian Shapiro, The Evolution of Rights in Liberal Theory (1986).

6. *See generally* Louis Henkin, The Age of Rights (1990) (discussing the relation of constitutionalism and the international human rights movement).

tended its founding.[7] Born at a time of unparalleled international cooperation, the human rights movement's normative projects would later appear to have fostered unrealistic expectations about the human rights system's potential.

These historical and political developments and contingencies engendered the postwar understanding of human rights. Genesis at Nuremberg and at Auschwitz expresses the paradigm shift's sad paradoxical story of catastrophe and failure in the international order, which somehow nevertheless ends on a hopeful note. Through the international human rights movement and its lead in responding to wartime atrocities, justice becames a liberal means to a redemptive resolution.

II. Rights Generation

The passage of time increased the distance from the engendering historical and political circumstances of the human rights movement. The distance led to questions about the continued viability of international human rights theory. Nevertheless, the international human rights movement is said to be in vital development and rights genesis considered an event capable of repetition. Consider rights "generation" in at least three senses. First, the language represents rights creation as a natural process. The rhetoric of "genesis" at once evokes the language of science and of nature. Scientific rhetoric imbues international human rights theory with legitimacy by implying that the theory follows the natural laws of the universe—as if human rights are just out there, existing as an autonomous and objective reality. Second, generation also conveys rights in a genetic sense.[8] Put this way, rights generation casts the human rights story in terms of the broader human condition—of scientific, historical, and political generations. Third, the rhetoric of genesis and generation propounds the international human rights movement's distinctive account of natural rights made positive.

The passage of time and the accompanying changes in circumstances put pressure on the prevailing rights narrative and the attempt to theorize in terms of a unitary international human rights apparatus. Every aspect of the Nuremberg legacy appeared vulnerable to normative incoherence.

The dominant paradigm, drawing largely from American constitutionalism, suggested that the proper response to human rights viola-

7. *See generally* Immanuel Kant, Perpetual Peace (Lewis White Beck ed., Liberal Arts Press 1957) (1795) (proposing interstate stability as minimal standard); John Rawls, Political Liberalism (1993) (affirming stability standard); *see also* Theodor Meron, Human Rights and Humanitarian Norms as Customary Law (1989) (discussing the changes in the law of war and humanitarian law).

8. *See* Louis Henkin, *A New Birth of Constitutionalism: Genetic Influences and Genetic Defects*, 14 Cardozo L. Rev. 533, 538-45 (1993).

tions was individual accountability. The postwar paradigm instantiated at Nuremberg represented a radical shift in the understanding of prevailing international legal norms. Absolute sovereignty had been violated, seemingly challenging the border between the international and the national, as well as the individual and the collective. While there have been occasional national trials, such as Argentina's military junta or those of unified Germany,[9] there has never been the same sort of adjudication of rights violations as at Nuremberg. The historical and political circumstances surrounding Nuremburg, including the predicates for international sovereignty, and the force of occupation law, were missing from the later trials.

Considering rights theory in concert with localized historical and political knowledge clarifies the postwar precedent and doctrine. The very understanding of human rights and justice is entwined in the postwar paradigm's engendering circumstances. International human rights' historical and political contexts elucidate the theory's putative incoherence. Acknowledging the extraordinary political circumstances of international human rights recognizes their parameters and their limits. As the postwar predicates of the international human rights model have not yet repeated themselves,[10] the question has become: What, if any, is the ongoing vitality of the reigning theory's generating structures and related norms?

This part has explored the human rights narrative that has long dominated our understanding. In addition, it contended that examining the reigning theory, in the light of its historical and political predicates, clarifies existing structures and perceived problems. The Article continues by explaining how a genealogically enriched perspective illuminates the problems said to pervade contemporary human rights theory.

III. Rights-Theoretical Divides

Consider the putative gap between human rights theory and practice: Prevailing human rights theory is generally conceded to lack full normative force because of a perceived gap between the theory and judicialized rights. These are commonly considered to signal incoherence in human rights theory. The absence of remedies is often considered fatal.[11] The juxtaposition of rights theory to rights enforcement

9. For a discussion of contemporary human rights trials relating to periods of political transition, see Ruti Teitel, *Transitional Jurisprudence: The Role of Law in Political Transformation*, 106 Yale L.J. 2009, 2035-51 (1997).

10. Even the ad hoc International Criminal Tribunal for the former Yugoslavia does not reflect the same judicialized human rights model. For a comparative discussion of the Yugoslavia Tribunal in the light of Nuremburg, see Ruti Teitel, *Judgment at The Hague*, E. Eur. Const. Rev., Fall 1996, at 80.

11. *See* Jack Donnelly, *International Human Rights: A Regime Analysis*, 40 Int'l Org. 599, 633-36 (1986) (characterizing the weakness of the human rights system in terms of enforcement).

or rights practices also comprehends other theoretical dichotomies: international and national, universalism and particularism, positivism and natural law.[12]

The postwar story of Nuremberg justice inspires the reigning paradigmatic conception of international human rights as judicial. The post-war model of justice is the all powerful Military Tribunal and judicial rights. This historical legacy generates a view of human rights norms backed by legal sanctions and judicial enforcement. This conception of rights also derived from a largely unspoken analogue of international human rights to constitutional rights on the domestic plane and to rights protection in an age of constitutional democracy. The view construed international human rights as traditional rights at law where meaningful rights were norms backed by sanctions. Indeed, one might think of these as "American" rights,[13] a conception nurtured by the Allied initiative in the postwar judicialized rights response.[14] The prevailing notion that there is a "gap" in rights enforcement is intimately connected to the insistence that as a normative matter human rights ought be protected within a judicial system.[15] In this account, the problem does not derive from the theoretical framework itself, but rather from its lack of actualization.

Despite the animating force of international human rights theory, the twentieth century has been characterized by genocidal massacres and impunity.[16] How can we explain this course of events within the international human rights narrative? Perhaps the most glaring example is the apparent disjunction between the enormous political support for the Genocide Convention and the failure of judicial enforcement.[17] Despite the existence of the World Court, the international community has not enacted an international criminal code or created a permanent international criminal court.[18] Indeed, the first tribunals

12. The attempt here to contribute a genealogical perspective to the prevailing human rights analysis should not be taken as an instance of further juxtaposition of theory and practice.

13. *See* Marbury v. Madison, 5 U.S. (1 Cranch) 137, 162-66 (1803); Martin Shapiro, Courts: A Comparative and Political Analysis (1981).

14. *See* Telford Taylor, The Anatomy of the Nuremberg Trials: A Personal Memoir (1992).

15. The view appears Hohfeldian in its understanding of rights as closely connected to duties. *See* Arthur J. Jacobson, *Hegel's Legal Plenum*, 10 Cardozo L. Rev. 877 (1989).

16. *See, e.g.*, *Final Report of the United Nations Commission of Experts Established Pursuant to Security Council Resolution 780*, at 12-13, U.N. Doc. S/1994/674/ Annex VI (1992).

17. *See* Convention on the Prevention and Punishment of the Crime of Genocide, Dec. 9, 1948, 78 U.N.T.S. 277, 282 (1951); *see generally* Beth Van Schaack, Note, *The Crime of Political Genocide: Repairing the Genocide Convention's Blind Spot*, 106 Yale L.J. 2259 (1997).

18. *See generally* James Crawford, *The ILC Adopts a Statute for an International Criminal Court*, 89 Am. J. Int'l L. 404 (1995) (discussing the International Law Commission's draft statute to create an international criminal court).

in the half century since Nuremberg are the ad hoc international tribunals convened to prosecute violations arising out of the Balkans conflict, and expanded to include the Rwandan genocide.[19]

The perceived gap between human rights theory and its normative enforcement is often explained in terms of political realism. The theoretical apparatus is commonly characterized as unresponsive to political circumstances. A disjunction arises between international human rights theory and its realization. International human rights norms are viewed as somehow existing as autonomous realities spiraling away from other political structures. The characterization is one of internal incoherence, of a theory at war with itself.

Politics is deemed to explain the absence of the reigning normative model's actualization. The lack of enforcement is said to relate to the absence of consent. Without political consent, there is a "race to the bottom." Here is a rare and limited concession to the role of politics within the international legal system. Understanding the role of politics implies commencment of the analysis of the human rights system before the extraordinary story of occupation justice. It entails returning to the Treaty of Westphalia and the view that the subjects of international law were sovereign states,[20] where external sovereignty was bound by international law and its related legal principle of nonintervention. In this regard, the postwar human rights paradigm challenged pre-existing principles of sovereignty,[21] nonintervention, and respect for borders. The conflict is evinced in slippage of the concepts of: international and national, war and peace, private and public, rights and remedies.

Reification of the postwar proceedings has utterly distorted our understanding and derailed contemporary human rights theory. From the postwar perspective of human rights as judicial rights, the normative response to rights abuses is deemed to be adjudicatory and drawing upon the historical legacy with associated punishment. Accordingly, for some time now, the emphasis has been upon expansion of enforcement. The critical human rights question is characterized as one of execution, the problem largely of political will.

Yet, the postwar narrative is itself a substantially idealized version of the historical experience. The precedent is overstated because the statement of the norm exceeded its instantiation—even at the time. Thus, the postwar paradigm is deemed inherently paradoxical, pro-

19. *See* Statute of the International Tribunal for the Former Yugoslavia, *Report of the Secretary-General Pursuant to Paragraph 2 of S.C. Res. 808*, U.N. SCOR, 48th Sess., Annex, U.N. Doc. S/2504 (1993), *reprinted in* 32 I.L.M. 1159 (1993) [hereinafter International Tribunal]; *see also* Statute of the International Tribunal for Rwanda, S.C. Res. 995, U.N. SCOR, 49th Sess., 3453d mtg., Annex, U.N. Doc. S/RES/955 (1994), *reprinted in* 33 I.L.M. 1598 (1994).

20. *See* Stanley Hoffman, *Sovereignty and the Ethics of Intervention*, *in* The Ethics and Politics of Humanitarian Intervention (Stanley Hoffman ed., 1996).

21. *See* Charles R. Beitz, Political Theory and International Relations (1979).

ducing an antinomian tension in its structuring categories. Indeed, a very different story could be told about Nuremberg.

Reconsider the dominant theory incorporating its historical and political circumstances. This reconsideration means another understanding of the core rights paradigm categories: of the relation of individual and collective, of positivism and natural law, of the universal and the particular, and of the law of peace and the law of war. Thus, for example, postwar international human rights are commonly represented as an instance of natural law norms made positive. Nevertheless, reconsideration of the postwar paradigm in a historical light implies something for the debate about authority for the sources of international human rights law,[22] and a move away from strict positivism to a recognition of customary international law.[23] Relatedly, despite postwar claims to the forging of new normative ground in humanitarian law, adjudication of the crime against humanity—a violation at the norm's apex—was, even as applied at Nuremberg restricted to its abiding nexus with war.[24]

The same is true of other normative claims where the postwar precedent is similarly antinomial. Thus, a closer look at the postwar circumstances offers a more nuanced understanding of the categories of sovereignty and jurisdiction.[25] Although the postwar rights paradigm is commonly characterized in terms of universal norms and the norms ratified in the postwar codifying instruments,[26] the postwar proceedings also related to offenses occurring, at least in part, in particular locations, instantiating an alternative positivist normative point. Ultimately, the postwar paradigm incorporates within it the antinomial tension between those opposing normative concepts. While this tension is somewhat mitigated in the extraordinary postwar circumstances, in subsequent periods, it has only grown. Thus, a broader inquiry into the historical and political context of international human rights clarifies, and even reconciles, the purported gap between theory and practice in the contemporary movement.

---

22. *See* Gerald L. Neuman, *Sense and Nonsense About Customary International Law: A Response to Professors Bradley and Goldsmith*, 66 Fordham L. Rev. 319 (1997).

23. *See* Quincy Wright, *Legal Positivism and the Nuremberg Judgment*, 42 Am. J. Int'l L. 405 (1948).

24. Justifying crimes against humanity in terms of this nexus is still true to date. *See* International Tribunal, *supra* note 19, art. 5, at 1193 (granting the International Tribunal the power to prosecute crimes against humanity that were committed in armed conflict, whether international or national); International Criminal Tribunal for the Former Yugoslavia, Excerpts from Prosecutor v. Dusko Tadic, 36 I.L.M. 908, ¶¶ 79-85 (1997) (App. Chamber decision) [hereinafter *Tadic Decision*]. However, in the most recent developments toward a permanent international criminal court, the emerging consensus is a predicate of international armed conflict.

25. *See* W. Michael Reisman, *Sovereignty and Human Rights in Contemporary International Law*, 84 Am. J. Int'l L. 866 (1990).

26. *See* Charter of the International Military Tribunal, Aug. 8, 1945, 59 Stat. 1544, 82 U.N.T.S. 279 (1945).

The international human rights founding story is one that is said to be *sua sponte*, a radical birthing, a discontinuous affair with only an ambivalent relation to preexisting rights theory. Nevertheless, consider the meaning of the idea of rights as being "born" in the mid-twentieth century, seemingly without preexisting rights forbears?[27] This representation as an immaculate conception preserves the natural law claims. Telling the story this way, as an extraordinary narrative that begins in the war's aftermath, represents international human rights in atomistic fashion, as somehow insulated from preexisting rights theory. The account also plays a role in distorting international human rights theory, generating tension and incoherence.

To some degree, the theoretical framework of international human rights rests awkwardly on preexisting theory. Historically, theories of consensus and the social contractarian tradition, predicated on assumptions about the relationship of the individual to the state, justified rights theory. Specifically, the political predicate of the state's role as protector and guarantor of individual rights provided justification for the theory. Indeed, this view drew from the social contract theory underlying the liberal state.[28]

Postwar revelations tragically challenged these theoretic bedrock assumptions, rendering them inappropriate for responding to the central Auschwitz problem of the twentieth century. The contractarian foundations of previous rights theory appeared inapt for comprehending the strange shift in recognition of the position of the modern state—from rights protector to rights violator. The shift could not help but have normative implications for understanding the political regime, as well as for related constitutional and other rights principles. With the move away from social contract as the source of rights authority, new questions arose regarding alternative sources of authority for international human rights and their constraints.

On these questions, the prevailing rights paradigm resolution is paradoxical. In the postwar "genesis" story, international human rights are represented in universal terms deemed of general applicability. Rights, however, are also cast as manifestly positivist creatures of convention. The paradigm is widely understood as having, at some level, moved from natural law ideas to those that are more positivist, for example, in the Nuremberg Charter and the many postwar conventions.[29] This shift raises a central tension that continues to be present

27. On this question, see Maurice Cranston, What are Human Rights? (1973); Louis Henkin, *International Human Rights as "Rights," in* Human Rights 257 (J. Roland Pennock & John W. Chapman eds., 1981); Rights (David Lyons ed., 1979).

28. *See* John Locke, *The Second Treatise of Government, in* Two Treatises of Government 283 (Peter Laslett ed., Cambridge Univ. Press 2d ed. 1967) (1714); Jean Jacques Rousseau, The Social Contract (Charles Frankel trans., Hafner Pub. Co. 1947) (1762).

29. *See, e.g.*, Convention on the Prevention and Punishment of the Crime of Genocide, *supra* note 17.

in contemporary rights debates.[30] Indeed, the question of what should "count" as a right raises a broader methodological question.[31]

The move out of classical rights theory leads to a rethinking of the nature of the sources of and authority for human rights. The postwar paradigm leads away from views of authority as inhering in democratic consensus to other sources. A broader array of sources are available for the construction of human rights, such as customary law.[32] This is nowhere more true than in the gravest abuses of customary law, the so-called "jus cogens" norms, which include conduct considered to be universally condemned.[33] The sources undergirding grave rights abuses mediate both international and national conventions and jurisdictions.[34] Human rights norms mediate international and national law. Indeed, one norm often guides the other and becomes incorporated within governing documents.[35]

Although, historically, international human rights theory generally eschews hierarchizing rights, such hierarchies are implied by the extent of the theory's nexus with its postwar circumstances. Thus, the dominant view of rights adheres closely to those impinged upon during the war—political rights relating to persecution. It is also undeniable that this view of human rights, represented largely as "civil" and "political" rights, bore a close semblance to rights conceptions in preexisting political theory. Human rights, as civil and political, related closely to the core associated with the modern state in working democracies: norms associated with principles of the rule of law and equal protection.

Further, there was a constructive effect on the postwar rights model of political circumstances relating to the conflict with the Soviet Union and later Cold War developments. This historical and political contingency illuminates putative theoretical rights differentiation: for

30. *See* Neuman, *supra* note 22; *see generally*, Human Rights on the Eve of the Next Century Symposium, Panel entitled U.N. Human Rights Standards and U.S. Law (Feb. 28, 1997) (transcript on file with the *Fordham Law Review*).

31. On human rights generally, see Henkin, *supra* note 27. Exploring some differences between rights in the international and domestic contexts, see Henkin, *supra* note 1.

32. Regarding *jus cogens*, see Restatement (Third) of the Foreign Relations Law of the United States § 702 (1986) (listing, for example, slavery and genocide). *See also* Change and Stability in International Law-Making (Antonio Cassese & Joseph H.H. Weiler eds., 1988).

33. *See* Oscar Schachter, International Law in Theory and in Practice 333-42 (1991); *see also* Meron, *supra* note 7.

34. Indeed, the so-called "Alien-Tort" litigation is illustrative. The leading case is *Filartiga v. Pena-Irala*, 630 F.2d 876 (2d Cir. 1980). For a clarifying article, see Anne-Marie Burley, *The Alien Tort Statute and the Judiciary Act of 1789: A Badge of Honor*, 83 Am. J. Int'l L. 461 (1989).

35. One place this is seen is in the comparison of the language of international agreements with that characterizing domestic constitutional rights. *See* Constitutionalism and Rights: The Influence of the United States Constitution Abroad (Louis Henkin & Albert J. Rosenthal eds., 1990).

example, the distinction between "political" and "economic" rights. Another manifestation was the so-called "big compromise," the bifurcation of the post World War II, Cold War era codification of international human rights into the Covenant on Civil and Political Rights and the Covenant on Economic, Social and Cultural Rights. This rights differentiation can only be understood as resulting from the construction of human rights that was set in the context of the postwar conflict with the communist bloc.

Given the massive political changes since the war and those that have taken place since the Soviet collapse, the constitutive distinction between civil/political and economic rights of international human rights theory has fallen under attack. Indeed, the subsequent wave of political and economic transitions in the region invite rethinking of the received wisdom. To what extent should economic rights be recognized as positive rights—whether under constitutional schemes, or within the international human rights system? This question has emerged as a central point of debate in the post communist transitions.[36] The contemporary debate reconsidering the purported distinctions of these rights—just as the political circumstances change—underscores the historical and political contingencies embedded in the prevailing human rights apparatus. Similarly, other differences have appeared over time, signaling the growing chasm that has emerged between the postwar rights model and its generating circumstances. This widening divide is best seen in the tension in the normative scheme that was thought to define human rights. Indeed, the relevant question is whether that old framework would be apt for normative development.

Still, other features of postwar human rights theory have been criticized for their inability to comprehend prevailing phenomena. Consider, for example, the elusive distinction between the public and private spheres in international human rights theory, as well as the theory's related emphasis on state action. The public/private state action distinction is, once again, best explained within its historical and political circumstances, namely, the postwar focus on states persecution. The public/private distinction also inhered in the constitutionalism of the time, emphasizing the view of state action derived from traditional liberal political theory. Nevertheless, massive historical, political, and social change have outstripped the postwar normative apparatus. This reconception implies reconsidering contemporary

36. On the debate over whether economic rights should be constitutionalized, see Cass R. Sunstein, *Against Positive Rights*, *in* Western Rights? Post-Communist Application 225 (András Sajó ed., 1996) [hereinafter Western Rights?]; Ruti Teitel, *Constitutional Costs to Free Market Transitions*, *in* Western Rights?, *supra*, at 361; Ruti Teitel, *Post-Communist Constitutionalism: A Transitional Perspective*, 26 Colum. Hum. Rts. L. Rev. 167 (1994); Richard Falk, *Comparative Protection of Human Rights in Capitalist and Socialist Third World Countries*, Universal Hum. Rts., Apr.-June 1979, at 3.

human rights violations beyond the public domain.[37] Here, the feminist critique is particularly compelling in its reconceptualization and proposed reconstruction of the private and public spheres.[38]

The so-called "third" generation of rights comprehends the rights of groups, collectivity rights, ethnicity rights, rights of "peoples," and rights to self-determination. This generation of rights incorporates the critique of prevailing human rights theory from the communitarian perspective,[39] as well as the critique from cultural relativism.[40] Although reigning normative human rights concepts emphasize the universal, recent rights developments suggest there is little that is essential in these normative distinctions.

Finally, there is the critique of the prevailing rights model—from the vantagepoint of its arch ontological dichotomy—of the claim that human rights inhere in sources in terms of objectivity and reason. Here, the challenge to human rights theorizing reflects broader concurrent epistemological challenges in theorizing of knowledge.[41]

Movement away from the prevailing conception can be seen in contemporary philosophical theorizing.[42] This theorizing offers fresh directions and new paths to human rights—not necessarily in the terms of the prevailing paradigm's rational, objective, and universalizing approach—but instead, through the pathways of friendship and solidarity. Indeed, these approaches indicate the prevailing arch antinomial differences paradigm, offering both normative rights principle and rights practice—a way to relate to the "other." The exhortation is a call for a return to the "human" in human rights and the repair of pervasive dehumanization.

After half a century, the foundational concepts of the reigning postwar model reveal growing slippage. The passage of time and change, both in the relevant political circumstances and in theories of knowledge generally, have put increasing pressure on the paradigmatic rights model. The mounting claim of incoherence in the received international human rights account has had profound consequences for the theory's positive and normative force. Nevertheless, the claim to

37. *See* Andrew Clapham, Human Rights in the Private Sphere (1993).

38. *See, e.g.*, Catherine MacKinnon, *On Torture: A Feminist Perspective on Human Rights*, *in* Human Rights in the Twenty-First Century 21 (Kathleen Mahoney & P. Mahoney eds., 1993), *reprinted in* International Human Rights in Context: Law, Politics, Morals 951 (Henry J. Steiner & Philip Alston eds., 1996).

39. *See* The Rights of Minority Cultures (Will Kymlicka ed., 1995).

40. *See* Michael J. Perry, *Are Human Rights Universal? The Relativist Challenge and Related Matters*, 19 Hum. Rts. Q. 461 (1997).

41. For a critique on the basis of multiplicity and indeterminacy, see Steven Connor, Postmodernist Culture: An Introduction to Theories of the Contemporary (2d ed. 1997); David Harvey, The Condition of Postmodernity: An Enquiry into the Origins of Cultural Change (1989).

42. *See* Annette C. Baier, Moral Prejudices: Essays on Ethics (1994); Richard Rorty, *Human Rights, Rationality, and Sentimentality*, *in* On Human Rights: The Oxford Amnesty Lectures 111 (Stephen Shute & Susan Hurley eds., 1993).

incoherence is best explained in terms of a growing chasm between a unitary human rights theory abstracted from its engendering circumstances, reified with perverse consequences.

IV. Constituting Contemporary Human Rights

What gives contemporary human rights law its force? I want to return to the question with which this Article began. Moving beyond the prevailing narrative enables the analysis of contemporary practices as the ongoing construction of human rights culture. Exploration of the practices, conventions, and discourses illuminates the contemporary meaning of human rights. These manifestations also invite a rethinking of the status and directions of contemporary human rights. Contemporary practices shed light on dynamic human rights norms, illuminating change in the postwar paradigm. Emergent practices lead us to recognize new human rights paradigms.

What is the significance of the contemporary human rights movement's discourse?[43] Practices here are an indication, not of theory gone awry, but rather as what comprises international human rights norms—as all there is.

The enormous expansion of the human rights domain is manifest. The attempt at normalization is seen in the generalizing and ambiguating of the postwar norms far beyond their animating circumstances. Whereas international human rights were previously characterized as largely discontinuous with other law practices, the notion of a bright line separation has disappeared. This melding can easily be seen in a number of areas where human rights law has merged with other established bodies of law, for example, human rights law and the humanitarian law of war, and human rights law and asylum law. Convergence of international human rights law and international humanitarian law can be seen in the normative slippage, whereby the laws of armed conflict have been extended to internal conflict and peacetime.[44] Such convergence in humanitarian and human rights law demarcates a broader domain for human rights. Further areas of convergence can be seen in the incorporation and protection of international and national rights protection in the various regional systems, for example, the European Court and the Inter-American systems.

The convergence in established areas of law relating to human rights challenges the theory's reigning conceptual oppositions. So it is, that in the slippage of the old dichotomies of war and peace, of inter-

43. On the human rights movement, see Jack Donnelly, Universal Human Rights in Theory and Practice (1989); Henkin, *supra* note 1, at 184-226; Henkin, *supra* note 6, at 16-41.

44. *See, e.g.*, Hague Convention IV Respecting the Laws and Customs of War on Land, Oct. 18, 1907, 36 Stat. 2277 (1907); Geneva Conventions for the Amelioration of the Condition of the Wounded and Sick in Armed Forces in the Field, August 12, 1949, 75 U.N.T.S. 31 (1950); *see also supra* note 24.

national and national, that the law of war leads back to the law of peace. Slippage exists in other directions, as international law and its rights protections help to define the rights of citizens under domestic constitutional law. The rights of the foreigner, of the alien, give us those of the citizen.

Human rights practices emphasize the relationship between the international legal system and other legal domains. Despite the postwar momentum within the new international legal system—reflected in instantiated Nuremberg-style justice, as well as the attendant wave of constitutionalism that emphasized individual rights—the international legal system alone could not protect deracinated individual rights. Transitional periods of political crisis revealed the extent to which meaningful rights protection presumes a working state. Responses to rights abuses in periods of national political transformation characterized as "transitional," while affirming individual rights norms are also limited, and as such illuminate the political predicates to a viable human rights system.[45] Thus, half a century later, the postwar primacy of individual rights ultimately leads back to the recognition of the state's role in protecting human rights in a rule of law system. Vindication of individual rights under international law presumes a strong and functioning state with liberal rule of law institutions that are responsive to individual rights.

In the face of ongoing political horror, what is the point of the new direction in human rights law? Of the value to human rights normalization? The focus is on practices, particularly the contemporary responses to the extreme human rights violations of the atrocities in the Balkans, which produce grave charges of crimes against humanity and genocide. In the radical political climate following the collapse of the Soviet Union and the transitions away from military rule, the practices of successor regimes throughout Eastern and Central Europe, Latin America, and Africa appear to instantiate liberalizing political change.

According to the prevailing human rights paradigm, the normative response is to subsume treatment of grave violations within the judicial system. Although there may appear to be some movement in that direction, with the contemporary Ad Hoc International Tribunal convened regarding Yugoslavia and Rwanda, the Tribunal at the Hague responds to a conflict that itself defies facile characterization.[46] Further, Tribunal practices underscore historical and political differences from the postwar Tribunal's prevailing circumstances, such as an absence of custody over the defendants and the evidence. These distinctions ultimately indicate that the leading form of international criminal justice in the contemporary moment is procedural. The role of the law here is largely procedural and hence, seemingly preserva-

45. *See* Teitel, *supra* note 9.
46. *See, e.g.*, *Tadic Decision*, *supra* note 24.

tive of other rights.[47] Procedural human rights emphasize the preparation and distillation of a record of rights abuses, whether through indictment or other processes, such as "truth commissions."[48]

This human rights function is part of a broader phenomenon: Human rights practices suggest that the most effective development of customary law could be characterized as procedural. Thus, for example, consider another area of emergent human rights practices: the response to the paradigmatic human rights violation of the late twentieth century—the disappearance. The responses to disappearances offer a way to understand contemporary human rights violations, their remedies, and ultimately the related conception of a human right. Rather than the reigning paradigmatic focus on criminal legal accountability rights violators, here emerges the move toward victim-centered remedies, for survivors, and the society at large. Hence, the newest human rights construction: the right "to truth" and the rights to an investigation, a record, and a hearing. The turn is toward an alternative understanding of human rights as threshold procedural rights. These understandings of human rights ultimately redefine the understanding of individual rights as well as the relationship of the individual and the state.

Responses to the worst human rights violations of this last half century—political executions and disappearances, totalitarian rule, apartheid, the national security state in Latin America, violations throughout Africa, and ethnic cleansing in the Balkans—reflect a broad phenomenology of international human rights responses that is a shift away from the paradigmatic judicial rights to more informal administrative sanctions and procedural rights.[49] To be sure, the law is highly normative and hortatory in nature.

There is a broader domain for human rights, one encompassing a culture that increasingly frames state behavior and decisionmaking in human rights terms. There is a movement away from an emphasis on the punishment of norm transgression to a broader representation of rights claims. Human rights practices of monitoring and reporting can tell us a lot about the changes in the conception of rights as well as the relation of states to their citizens regarding the protection of human rights. These new practices comprehend complex ideas of rights and ongoing obligations beyond the initial equal protection rights such as the duty to investigate. These ongoing rights obligations fall upon successor regimes temporizing the understanding of the relevant state action and inspiring rethinking of human rights and related obligations.

47. For a rights analogy, drawing from the domestic sphere, see John Hart Ely, Democracy and Distrust: A Theory of Judicial Review (1980) (proposing the view of constititutional rights as procedural).

48. For a catalog of such Truth Commissions, see Priscilla B. Hayner, *Fifteen Truth Commissions—1974 to 1994: A Comparative Study*, 16 Hum. Rts. Q. 597 (1994).

49. *See* Teitel, *supra* note 9.

Contemporary human rights come into the picture much earlier in the process. Whereas the prevailing paradigm conceives of human rights as ex post—of rights as "trumps"[50] or of rights that follow politics—contemporary practices suggest that human rights come into the picture much earlier. Human rights discourse occurs on an ongoing basis in the public sphere and the practices of documentation and reporting are normalized. Thus, reporting on the adherence to human rights takes place on two time lines—on an ordinary yearly basis, as well as on an extraordinary basis reactive to particular crises.[51]

What is also undeniable is that human rights practices are increasingly discursive. The significance given to deliberation in the international setting evidences this change. Such discursive practices are illustrated by the appeals to rights set forth in the Universal Declaration. The United Nations General Assembly is itself the site of regular and ongoing human rights deliberations. "Rights talk" is increasingly offered as performative, as remedy.[52] Rights themselves appear to be constructive in structuring political developments, in part because of the moral and social political force of the language of rights.

What is the point of these rights? Consider the purposes of human rights procedural discourse. These discursive practices are not mere signs of rights, not merely customary law. Adopting that view would be to persist in the received wisdom, in the prevailing insistence of measuring normative rights rhetoric against a putative autonomous rights reality. If the purpose is largely procedural—with an eye toward preserving other rights—one way to think about the value of these rights is as establishing a foundation for a prospective, more complete, international human rights justice. What kind of vision is this? Are these millennial rights? Is the point to ward off a repetition of the wartime events? Yet, a repetition of the Nuremberg circumstances is unlikely. Can we even imagine a similar international tribunal, divorced from its abiding historical and political circumstances?

Interestingly though, there is presently an attempt to reenact the Nuremberg trials with similar international tribunals. These transitional responses to contemporary human rights violations, however, fail to generate a comparable sense of the rule of law or security because they lack the background political conditions associated with the postwar judicialized rights model.[53] These transitional remedies exemplify the limits and ultimate temporizing of rights remedies in the

50. *See* Ronald Dworkin, *Rights as Trumps*, *in* Theories of Rights 153 (Jeremy Waldron ed., 1984).

51. Thus, for example, the U.S. State Department issues worldwide yearly reports and human rights organizations have emulated this. *See, e.g.*, Human Rights Watch, World Report 1997 (1996).

52. On increasing linguistification, see generally Judith Butler, Excitable Speech: A Politics of the Performative (1997).

53. For a broader elaboration of this point, see Teitel, *supra* note 9.

less than ideal circumstances presumed in the prevailing model. Although procedural rights may well comprise a virtue of justice, these ought not be mistaken for full justice. Record making in and of itself is not justice, although it enables preserving an idea of justice not presently realizable.

The above hints at clarifying the puzzle with which the Article commenced, regarding the elusive nature of international human rights' normative force. International human rights offer a widely shared language by which to represent abuses and violations of human dignity.[54] Demands cast in rights language become claims that cannot otherwise be rationalized away in the domestic scheme, such as in terms of war or national security. Indeed, just this role for rights discourse is evinced in the recent wave of liberalizing transformation. The language of international human rights not only captured the prior repression, but also offered a means to inspire and galvanize a liberal opposition as well as an image of hope. Here the language of rights shapes that of political discourse. The claim of right convergent with that of politic's demand promises mediating differences of culture,[55] and building such discourse promises solidarity among diverse peoples.[56] Ultimately, deliberations are thought to enable gradual consensus.[57] At the very least, the rights practices instantiate those of democracy.

Conclusion

This Article's goal has been to illuminate the genealogy, status, and directions of contemporary human rights theory. This alternative critical approach analyzes international human rights theory in terms of its relation to its abiding politics and from the perspective of its organizing language and structures. The approach advanced here seeks to contribute to a moving out of the problematic in present theorizing. Incorporating the genealogical should illuminate the received understanding of contemporary human rights theory. Incorporation of international human rights' engendering context illuminates a renewed coherence in contemporary human rights theory and appreciation of the sources of its normative force.

---

54. *See* Judith N. Shklar, The Faces of Injustice (1990) (describing the significance of representation in terms of injustice and rights violations as opposed to misfortune). For an example of the central role of rights construction in representations of "ethnic" as opposed to political conflict, see Human Rights Watch, Playing the "Communal Card:" Communal Violence and Human Rights (1995).

55. *See* Abdullahi Ahmed An-Na'im, *Human Rights in the Muslim World: Socio-Political Conditions and Scriptural Imperatives* A Preliminary Inquiry, 3 Harv. Hum. Rts. J. 13 (1990).

56. *See* Rorty, *supra* note 42.

57. *See* Rawls, *supra* note 7.

[2]

The Concept of Human Rights in International Law*

Anthony D'Amato**

In the past ten years, the concept of human rights has become a permanent part of the way we think about relations between nations. International human rights are now a legislative condition of foreign aid,[1] have been institutionalized in bureaucratic structures,[2] and, perhaps most importantly, have been stamped indelibly in the minds of the public as one of the most important standards by which we measure other countries.

Human rights is not just a political and moral concept; it is a legal one as well. Not surprisingly, human rights has been the subject of a burgeoning jurisprudential literature. Since the signing of the United Nations Charter the virtual equivalent of a new academic discipline has emerged to champion the idea that international law gives individuals rights against the state.[3] To prove their claim, these scholars can point to a plethora of international treaties, conventions, and United Nations resolutions guaranteeing individuals all sorts of different "rights."

It was inevitable that these advances would be challenged. In the political sphere, the human rights policies of Jimmy Carter have given way to the *realpolitik* of the Reagan administration. In the legal sphere, the proponents of international human rights jurisprudence have come under the vigorous attack of such younger scholars as Professors J.S. Watson and Mark Lane. In various journals and symposia,[4] Watson and Lane have accused their older

---

** Professor of Law, Northwestern University School of Law. A.B. 1958, Cornell University; J.D. 1961, Harvard Law School; Ph.D. 1968, Columbia University. The author would like to thank Professor Oscar Schachter and Professor Roger Fisher for their invaluable critiques of a draft of this Article. In particular, Professor Fisher's writings and teachings deal with the most difficult and realistic aspect of international law: how to get nations to comply with norms. Although the present Article disagrees in some important points with Professor Fisher, it could not have been written without his pioneering work in this field.

1. E.g., 22 U.S.C. § 2151n(a) (1976), which bars United States economic assistance "to the government of any country which engages in a consistent pattern of gross violations of internationally recognized human rights . . . unless such assistance will directly benefit the needy people in such country." See also id. § 2304(a)(2), which bars security assistance to such countries.

2. E.g., id. § 2384(f), which establishes the position of "Assistant Secretary of State for Human Rights and Humanitarian Affairs." The Assistant Secretary's functions include the "gathering [of] detailed information regarding humanitarian affairs and the observance of and respect for internationally recognized human rights."

3. See, e.g., W. Miller, Human Rights: A Bibliography, 1970-1976 (1977); R. Rich & R. Shimane, International Human Rights: A Selected Bibliography (1979); A. Rusis, Human Rights: A Selective Bibliography (1969).

4. See Lane, Demanding Human Rights: A Change in the World Legal Order, 6 Hofstra L. Rev. 269 (1978) [hereinafter cited as Lane, Demanding Human Rights]; Lane, Mass Killing by Governments: Lawful in the World Legal Order?, 12 N.Y.U. J. Int'l L. & Pol. 239 (1979) [hereinafter cited as Lane, Mass Killing by Governments]; Watson, Autointerpretation, Competence and the Continuing Validity of Article 2(7) of the U.N. Charter, 71 Am. J. Int'l L. 60 (1977) [hereinafter cited as Watson, Autointerpretation]; Watson, Legal Theory, Efficacy and Validity in the Development of Human Rights Norms in International Law, 1979 U. Ill. L.F. 609 [hereinafter cited as Watson, Legal Theory]. See also Watson, A Realistic Jurisprudence of International Law, 1980 Y.B. World Affairs 265.

colleagues of seriously overstating the international legal status of human rights. The "old school," they charge, has confused a vision of what international law ought to be with an examination of what it actually is.[5] In concentrating on multilateral treaties and United Nations Resolutions the old school has neglected actual state practice; in laboring to codify the varieties of human rights they have ignored the fact that the current international order contains no means of punishing state violators of such rights.[6] Watson and Lane relentlessly recount the mass atrocities of recent years in Uganda, Burundi, Nigeria, and Cambodia. They marshal Amnesty International reports on shock treatment in Brazil and beatings in Iran.[7] In light of such depradations, they ask, how can anyone realistically claim that there is an international law of human rights?

Watson and Lane's contentions have set off a lively debate.[8] Many of their specific points have been countered.[9] Yet these thrusts and counter-thrusts have been vaguely unsatisfying. The discomfiture of the "younger scholars" (and of the Reagan administration) with the notion that international law extends to the rights of citizens against their own governments cannot easily be brushed aside—especially by academicians' reiterations of previously stated positions. Watson and Lane's attacks are sophisticated symptoms of the unease that the layman must feel when he hears of various governmental practices assailed as violations of international law. Can a realistic system of international law—one that takes full account of the dominance of the "Westphaelian . . . legal order"[10]—effectively comprehend such practices? More importantly, can international law provide an effective remedy for these practices when they turn out to be, in fact, violations of internationally recognized human rights? Professor Watson's forthright response to these questions is a negative one: "What human rights advocates are seeking," he writes, "is a supranational legal order of the hierarchical, coercive type prevalent in domestic systems to act as a check on governmental malfeasance. But international law is not such a system and it cannot be turned into one no matter how desirable that may be from a humanistic standpoint."[11]

This Article will attempt to defend the opposite conclusion: that the concept of human rights can, and does, play a role in international law. To

5. Lane, Mass Killing by Governments, supra note 4, at 279-80; Watson, Legal Theory, supra note 4, at 611-12.

6. Watson, Legal Theory, supra note 4, at 634-35.

7. Id. at 634.

8. See Symposium on the Future of Human Rights in the World Legal Order, 9 Hofstra L. Rev. 337 (1981); Perspectives on Enforcement of Human Rights, 1980 Proc. Am. Soc. Int'l L. 1-30 (panel discussion of Watson's ideas). See also Henkin, International Human Rights as "Rights," *in* J.R. Pennock & J.W. Chapman (eds.), Human Rights (Nomos XXIII) 257 (1981); R. Falk, Human Rights and State Sovereignty (1981).

9. See, e.g., Schachter, The Views of "Charterists" and "Skeptics" on Human Rights in the World Legal Order: Two Wrongs Don't Make a Right, 9 Hofstra L. Rev. 357 (1981); Sohn, The International Law of Human Rights: A Reply to Recent Criticisms, 9 Hofstra L. Rev. 347 (1981).

10. See Falk, A New Paradigm for International Legal Studies: Prospectives & Proposals, 84 Yale L.J. 975 (1975).

11. Watson, Legal Theory, supra note 4, at 609.

meet Watson and Lane's theoretical objections head-on—that is, to answer their call for a theory which heeds the realistic necessity of "implementation and compliance"[12]—I will have to go back to some fundamental notions about international law. In the first part of this Article, I will discuss the all-important "compliance" issue, and will attempt to demonstrate that a substantive human rights law is capable of fitting comfortably into the existing system of international legal enforcement. This argument does not need to posit the existence of these rights; it merely serves to demonstrate that the "current legal order" can accommodate the idea that nations have a legal stake in human rights violations by other nations, and that a flexible system exists for enforcing that stake. The second part of the Article will attempt to fill this vessel: I will argue that an international law of human rights actually exists, and that it is derived from such ostensibly particularistic sources as the Genocide[13] and Slavery[14] Conventions. To do this, however, involves an extended discussion of the theory of customary international law, confronting in particular the ideas of several distinguished scholars who have argued that treaties are incapable of evolving on their own into rules of customary international law. My argument will be that such treaties can and do generate new legal rules. Of course, without a system of "implementation and compliance" these rules are meaningless. So it is to the question of the place of human rights in the existing structure of international law that I turn first.

I. The Place of Human Rights in International Law: Seven Propositions

In this first section, I will try to show how the concept of a human rights law relates to the existing structure of international legal relations. Specifically, I will describe that structure in a way that should illuminate its capacity for correcting illegal deviations from its systemic stability. My model of the international legal order is not idealized or forward-looking. My aim is simply to describe what already exists from a fresh perspective that should portray the international legal enforcement of human rights norms.[15]

My argument reduces to several distinct propositions about international law: that a nation is defined by its interests and its entitlements; that all nations have the same set of entitlements; that each entitlement has equal legal standing vis-a-vis other entitlements; that international law strives to preserve the equilibrium that equal entitlements create by permitting retaliation by nations whose entitlements have been violated; and that if human rights norms are part of international law, they take the form of universally-held entitlements.

---

12. Lane, Demanding Human Rights, supra note 4, at 615.

13. Convention on the Prevention and Punishment of the Crime of Genocide, Dec. 7, 1948, 78 U.N.T.S. 277.

14. Convention to Suppress the Slave Trade and Slavery, Sept. 25, 1926, 46 Stat. 2183, T.S. No. 778, 60 L.N.T.S. 253.

15. In particular, see sections E–G, infra notes 39–65 and accompanying text.

A. *A "Nation" Is a Collection of Interests and Entitlements*

The term "international law" suggests a law of, by, and for nations; they are the "creator-subjects" of international law.[16] Although nations as a whole have the power to shape international law any way they collectively desire,[17] that law itself nevertheless defines what a "nation" is. From the point of view of a given individual nation, whether or not it is a "nation" internationally depends not on what it desires but on whether the "constitutive" rules of international law define it as a "nation." An individual nation in this manner is no different from the "sovereign" described by Professor H.L.A. Hart.[18] A sovereign may be able to make or annul the laws in his own territory, but he cannot regulate the laws that define who the sovereign is or who will succeed to the sovereignty upon his demise.[19] For these "constitutive" laws are the conditions of his own sovereign power. He may influence them, for example, by appeals to the citizenry or by displays of force, but somehow the constitutive laws are larger than the sovereign. The international situation is an a fortiori case. An individual aggregation of people in a territory may try to influence outside groups to label it as a "nation,"[20] but this labeling will or will not occur depending upon the international rules of recognition of nations and whether it comes within those rules.

Thus, at its moment of creation, a "nation" is faced with external rules that have defined it as a "nation." It is already plugged into an international system of rules—by definition. And it finds, upon investigation, that there are many other rules that define nationhood and the nation's standing vis-a-vis other nations—rules that it cannot unilaterally change although it has an equal influence in working with other nations to bring about systemic change acceptable to all.

Our hypothetical new nation might not want to accept any of these rules as obligatory upon itself. For this reason, I will avoid the usual phraseology of "rights" and "obligations" under international law, and instead employ the more objective term of "legal entitlements," or simply entitlements.[21] Thus, although our new nation may want to deny that it has any "obligations" under international law—even if the other nations have chosen to recognize it as a "nation"—it cannot deny that other nations claim for *themselves* certain entitlements. Indeed, our new nation will want to discover what these entitlements are so that it may be more fully aware of its international environment,

16. A. D'Amato, The Concept of Custom in International Law 33 (1971). This argument proceeds on the assumption of a "Westphalian legal order," see supra note 10. For a different conception, see infra note 65.

17. There is no international law external to the international collectivity; but any individual nation may only influence the collective consensus as to what the law is. If a single nation could determine what the law is, there would be no possibility of a violation of international law.

18. H. Hart, The Concept of Law 51-60 (1961).

19. Id. at 74-76.

20. The Palestinian Arabs on the West Bank are a good example.

21. See generally Calabresi & Melamed, Property Rules, Liability Rules, and Inalienability: One View of the Cathedral, 85 Harv. L. Rev. 1089 (1972).

for the expectations of its neighbors will be of great practical importance to it in its relations with them.

Upon investigation, it will find a rather awesome and fully developed set of entitlements. We are familiar with these as the usual rules of customary international law. For example, it will find that other nations claim exclusive sovereignty over their airspaces, that they do not claim exclusive sovereignty over the high seas, that they claim that their boundaries are fixed and not subject to forcible change by the military aggression of others, and that treaty entitlements survive changes of government. They also claim, among many other things, that their own nationals traveling in foreign countries must be accorded a minimal standard of international protection against the governmental or police action of those countries.[22] Our new nation, looking at this list, will probably conclude that these entitlements are not on the whole a bad lot. Although they serve to restrict the activities of our new nation (for instance, it will not be able to have free use of the world's airspace for its new commercial airline but will rather have to engage in negotiations and reciprocal contracts for international flight), they also present it with an important set of entitlements. If our new nation wants to assert these entitlements, it will derive international legal protection for its own boundaries, its own airspace, its own citizens traveling abroad, and so forth. But the crucial point is that even if it does not want to assert these entitlements, it nevertheless will be looking outward at all the other nations that have been asserting and continue to assert these entitlements against it. Our new nation is faced with the fact that other nations have claimed and are claiming these entitlements as a matter of right and expect to continue to claim them, even against our new nation, even if it does not like any or all of them.

In addition to, and conceptually distinct from, entitlements, our new nation and every nation has its own particular "interests."[23] These are the things that the nation wants, and can include wants that are quite illegal—for instance, rapid territorial expansion at the expense of its neighbors. The set of interests may overlap with the set of entitlements. For example, our new nation's interest in the sanctity of its borders overlaps with an entitlement to the same effect. It may have an interest, as it certainly has an entitlement, to the safety of its diplomatic personnel abroad. On the other hand, our new nation may have a very deep interest in something that has not attained the status of an entitlement (and might never attain that status). For instance, the United States might have a deep interest in breaking up international oil cartels. In domestic law, the United States has such an antitrust power. But internationally an oil cartel is not as of the present writing a violation of any American international entitlement.[24] The American legal interest in breaking up an

22. See Root, The Basis of Protection of Citizens Residing Abroad, 4 Am. J. Int'l L. 517, 521–22 (1910).

23. See, e.g., M. Kaplan & N. Katzenbach, The Political Foundations of International Law 240–43 (1961).

24. Cf. International Association of Machinists and Aerospace Workers v. Organization of Petroleum Exporting Countries, 477 F. Supp. 553 (C.D. Cal. 1979) (discussing legality of international resource cartels), aff'd on other grounds, 649 F.2d 1354 (9th Cir. 1981), cert. denied, 102 S.Ct. 1036 (1982).

international oil cartel might be many orders of magnitude greater than the American interest in some of its international entitlements, but to confuse the magnitude of a nation's interests with international entitlements, as these examples suggest, makes no sense.[25] The reverse is also true: a nation may have an entitlement but absolutely no interest in it. Switzerland has an entitlement to jurisdiction over its territorial sea. Lacking a territorial sea and any near-term prospects of obtaining one, Switzerland may be assumed to have a near-zero interest in this particular entitlement. Nevertheless, as a nation, it still "has" the entitlement. A nation may unilaterally control its own interests; it has no unilateral control over its (and every other nation's) entitlements.

Thus, when Professor Watson, at a crucial point in his argument, asserts that "it is an inescapable fact that one state's treatment of its citizens is of little interest to other states,"[26] it is clear that he is not making a legal argument, for he is speaking only of interests, not entitlements. And he may be quite wrong even as to interests: consider Israel's interest in the treatment of Soviet Jews, or the interest of African nations in the treatment of South African blacks. Nevertheless, the degree of interest that a nation has in the affairs of another nation has no direct connection to its legal entitlements.[27] Of course, if every state had no interest whatsoever in what other states do to their own citizens, then it would be *unlikely* that there would have arisen an entitlement to protect oppressed citizens in other states. I say "unlikely" because international law, after all, reflects the aggregate interests of states over time. But there is no theoretical, or necessary, linkage between no-interest and no-entitlement. And certainly, as my previous examples have suggested, if Watson is roughly correct that one state's treatment of its citizens is of "little" interest to other states, that fact certainly would neither prevent an entitlement from arising nor defeat one that had already arisen.

B. *All Nations Have the Same Set of Entitlements*

In sharp contrast to interests that, as we have seen, can vary greatly, each nation's set of entitlements is the same as every other nation's. Occasionally, some writers such as DeVisscher, Kaplan, Katzenbach, and McDougal have made highly curious assertions to the contrary.[28] But those arguments have

---

25. For a critique of the "interests approach" of Kaplan and Katzenbach, see D'Amato, supra note 16, at 145-47.

26. Watson, Legal Theory, supra note 4, at 619.

27. States' interests in such questions, after all, may change over time. Different states may have different degrees of interest (consider, for example, a majority in one state having ethnic or religious ties to a persecuted minority in another state). Indeed, there are signs that people are becoming more empathetic to the plight of other human beings even absent the "old" sorts of ties of religious or ethnic similarity. Evidence for this increasing "interest" is the greater acceptance of nondiscrimination within nations and Professor Schachter's observation that there is a greater world awareness of human-rights violations. See Schachter, supra note 9, at 264-65. Surely this media awareness reflects people's increasing "interest" in this topic, an interest that has been reflected in the actions of government in the human rights area.

28. See C. DeVisscher, Theory and Reality in Public International Law 149 (Corbett trans. 1957); M. Kaplan & N. Katzenbach, supra note 23; M. McDougal et al., Studies in World Public Order 773-843 (1960). I have previously commented upon these assertions that some states are

not been taken seriously. Law, in fact, has an internal dynamism that promotes, if not requires, equality; its prescriptions, in nearly every legal system including the international, apply to all its addressees equally.[29] It is indeed hard to imagine rules and norms of general application that do not apply equally to their addressees. To be sure, within organizations entitlements sometimes are different. In the United Nations, for example, the permanent members of the Security Council have more entitlements regarding the practices of the United Nations than have the other members of the Council, and the Council members as a whole have more entitlements than do the members of the United Nations who are not seated on the Security Council. In any treaty regime, the contracting parties may have differentiable entitlements vis-a-vis each other or as against noncontracting parties (e.g. exclusive trade arrangements). But general customary international law, including the entitlements regarding the entering into and validity of treaties, knows no such differentiations.

C. *Each Entitlement Has Equal Standing*

Each separate entitlement in a national set of entitlements is legally the equivalent of every other entitlement. None has more legal weight or standing than any other. An entitlement either exists or does not exist, but once it exists, it is the equivalent of any other entitlement. This point is by no means obvious, since normally we think of some entitlements as more important than others—for example, the inviolability of national boundaries seems much more important than equal access to the mineral wealth of the ocean floor. But this "importance" is upon analysis simply a matter of what I have defined as national "interests." To an expansionist nation, for example, the inviolability of national boundaries might be an impediment; such a nation would have a very low interest in maintaining that entitlement. Stripped of its "interest" dimension, the system of entitlements appears as an unidimensional set of legal norms legally indistinguishable from each other. Entitlements are like Ronald Dworkin's rules—you have one or you don't, one applies or it doesn't.[30] Even international rules of *jus cogens*, or peremptory norms,[31] are no more important than other rules, for these are simply rules

---

more important than others in terms of rights under international law. See D'Amato, supra note 16, at 64-65 (DeVisscher), 144-47 (Kaplan and Katzenbach), 218-22 (McDougal). See also The Antelope, 23 U.S. (10 Wheat.) 66, 122 (1825) ("perfect equality of nations"). It should be noted that when DeVisscher and other writers talk about special custom, regional custom, or local customs it is clear that the rights appertaining thereto are not shared by the community of nations—any more than all nations share the bilateral treaty rights of two contracting states. The statement in the text that all entitlements are the same refers only, of course, to general rules of international law.

29. See L. Fuller, The Morality of Law 46-49 (rev. ed. 1969); see also A. Gewirth, Reason and Morality 129-89 (1978) (incoherent to assert rights yet deny similar assertions by others).

30. See R. Dworkin, Taking Rights Seriously 26 (1977). Dworkin contrasts "rules" with "principles," the latter having weight that helps impel a decision a certain way without requiring such a decision.

31. See D'Amato, supra note 16, at 132 n.73 (claim oriented perspective on peremptory norms).

that deny the validity of certain substantive provisions that might be included in treaties.[32] As such they are not on a higher plane than, for example, the customary rule of *pacta sunt servanda*; in fact, they may be thought of as conditional specifications of the rule of *pacta sunt servanda*.

That entitlements are mutually equivalent in terms of importance or weight is not a necessary feature of international law. Rather, it reflects the current international legal system. Nations might have evolved a different kind of system. But at least so far they have not. Indeed, it is the present deep divergence in interests among nations that accounts for the equal standing of entitlements. For while nations have been able to agree to a common set of entitlements, their differential interests with respect to any particular entitlement almost ensures the lack of any communal consensus as to relative importance among entitlements. (Of course, some entitlements are trivial—for example, the finer points of diplomatic protocol—and these surely are not equivalent to general norms of customary international law. But among the latter material norms, there is no consensus as to relative importance.)

D. *The Legal System Will Strive to Preserve Entitlement Equilibrium*

Given a common set of entitlements of equal weight, which as a whole defines the international legal system,[33] the legal system itself will act to preserve the equilibrium engendered by that set. This equilibrium or stable balance of legal entitlements is, after all, the result of centuries of international interaction and expresses principles by which nations on the whole have consented[34] to accommodate each other. A disruption in the set may be viewed as a tendency toward imbalance, toward disequilibrium. The legal system may be expected to respond homeostatically—to restore the balance by exacting a legal penalty upon the entitlement violator. The entitlements as a set, worked out by nations over the centuries, represent a coherent system such that the violation of any one of them gives rise on the international level to what Festinger has called "cognitive dissonance" on the level of personal psychology.[35] Other nations will react to remove this dissonance by taking legal action against the violator (which, as we shall see, involves retaliatory entitlement-violation). Additionally, the violating nation itself, having introduced disso-

32. See Vienna Convention on the Law of Treaties, opened for signature May 23, 1969, art. 53, 8 I.L.M. 679, 698-99 [hereinafter cited without cross references as Vienna Convention on the Law of Treaties].

33. The entitlements as a whole contain primary rules regarding the conduct of states, and secondary rules that "specify the ways in which the primary rules may be conclusively ascertained, introduced, eliminated, varied, and the fact of their violation conclusively determined." H. Hart, supra note 18, at 92. See D'Amato, supra note 16, at 41-44; D'Amato, The Neo-Positivist Concept of International Law, 59 Am. J. Int'l L. 321 (1965).

34. See L. Jaffe, Judicial Aspects of Foreign Relations 90 (1933).

35. See L. Festinger, A Theory of Cognitive Dissonance (1957); cf. D'Amato, Psychological Constructs in Foreign Policy Prediction, 11 J. Confl. Res. 294, 306-09 (1967) (proposing that an individual reacts to the foreign policy environment according to certain behavioral structures and that these "constructs" can be used to predict an individual policy-maker's decision in a given foreign policy situation).

nance into the system, will expect retaliation, but will not know what kind of entitlement will be involved in the retaliation. Its inability to predict the retaliation serves to dissuade it from committing the initial entitlement violation (the delict); thus the system as a whole tends toward self-preservation of its set of entitlements. This systemic homeostatic mechanism is enhanced by the nature of rule-formation in the international legal system. General rules of international law now are changeable only by the process of custom or consensus. The latter by definition raises no disruptive problem; nations simply agree as a whole to a new rule.[36] But customary law formation, except when accomplished by the effect of treaties upon nonparties,[37] can be disruptive indeed. Like the Hegelian-Marxist struggle of thesis and antithesis, an entitlement (thesis) is met with a violation (antithesis), which violation, if it "catches hold," may give rise to a new rule (synthesis). The violation of the entitlement may thus contain the seeds of a new rule,[38] but the critical question is what the other nations will do about it. If they accept the violation, a new customary rule is on its way toward being formed. But if they isolate the violation, label it a violation, and punish the transgressor, then instead of the seed of a new rule taking hold, the seed is trampled upon and the original customary rule is reinforced. What might have been an impediment to the formation of a customary rule instead becomes another instance of its confirmation.

Unless the international legal system is psychologically ready for a new rule (in which case there is already an implicit consensus), it will react to the violation of a customary rule with all the means at its dispoal to ensure that the violation does not replace the old rule with its opposite. These means, as we shall see in the discussion of the next principle, are all that the legal system qua legal system can do—namely, to treat the violator as an "outlaw" for the purpose of its transgression, and to respond by a retaliatory deprivation of one or more of the violator's entitlements.

E. *A Nation that Violates Another Nation's Entitlement May Expect Retaliation that Preserves Entitlement Equilibrium*

The entitlements that define any legal system require a mechanism for self-protection. This is simply a consequence of the nature of systems that have survived and become stable.[39] Domestic legal systems have such mechanisms in legislatures, in courts of comprehensive jurisdiction, and in police enforcement. If *A* steals *B*'s car, the state recognizes that *B* retains ownership of the car even though it is now in *A*'s possession, and furthermore will prosecute *A* criminally, repossess the car, and deliver it over to *B*. Thus *B*'s property entitlement in the car is preserved and vindicated. There is no

36. See D'Amato, On Consensus, 8 Can. Y.B. Int'l L. 104 (1970).

37. See D'Amato, supra note 16, at 103–66.

38. Of course, this puts the matter broadly. For a specification, see D'Amato, supra note 16, at 91–98.

39. See L. von Bertalanffy, General System Theory 78, 161–63 (1968); E. Laszlo, Introduction to Systems Philosophy 38–41 (1972); N. Wiener, Cybernetics (1948).

suggestion that the entitlement itself is in jeopardy of being changed by *A*'s action. In other words, there is no process of customary law formation in this example or in domestic examples similar to it. In contrast, if customary international law were involved in such an example, *A*'s theft from *B* would contain the seeds of a new customary rule (for example, that anyone who forcibly takes possession of another person's property becomes the legitimate owner of such property).[40] Depending on how many previous cases there were of the old rule (protecting ownership in private property against forcible takeover), on subsequent reaction to the *A-B* case, and possibly on cases subsequent to the *A-B* case, a new rule of custom may have been presumptively formed, initiated, or defeated.[41] To be sure, in the earliest days of the domestic legal system, before courts knew very much of what was expected of them and before legislatures or monarchs realized that they could create new laws out of thin air, there was a process of customary-law formation akin to that of the international legal system today.[42] But in any modern municipal-law system, the existence of legislatures, which can change any rule the public wants changed, and courts, which preserve existing rules, is sufficient to give the system of entitlements stability through time.

Of course, the international legal system is not devoid of courts, although the courts as a whole certainly do not enjoy comprehensive jurisdiction over all international legal transactions. The present International Court of Justice at the Hague has very limited, consensual jurisdiction, and it has not acted resolutely in recent cases even where jurisdiction was arguably established.[43] The Security Council of the United Nations in principle has central enforcement power to protect against threats to or breaches of the peace, but due to dissension on the Council, it has not yet mobilized an army. There are many regional organizations, arbitral tribunals, bilateral commissions, and so forth in the international legal panoply, but Professor Watson is correct in arguing that there is a "lack of enforcement mechanisms of the hierarchical type."[44] What Watson fails to see, however, is that the international legal system protects its entitlements by processes different from the domestic model.

---

40. In years past, the forcible conquest of another nation's terrritory conferred title upon the conqueror. See J. Brierly, The Law of Nations 171-72 (6th ed. Waldock 1963).

41. See D'Amato, supra note 16, at 91-102.

42. See generally H.S. Maine, Ancient Law: Its Connection with the Early History of Society and Its Relation to Modern Ideas (1861). See also L. Fuller, Anatomy of the Law 76-91 (1968).

To take a speculative example parallel to that given in the text, suppose that in the early days of a legal system *A* stole *B*'s money, purchased some goods from *C*, and then left the country. *B* applies to a court to get his stolen money back from *C*. The notion of theft and of stolen property might very well have given *B* a prima facie claim to his money. However, the usefulness of money as a mechanism for exchange would be compromised by allowing persons to trace stolen money. By not allowing *B*'s claim, the early court would be developing the law in a fashion analogous to custom in international law. (A later court would then hold, as we know, that if *B* could prove that *C* was not a holder in due course *B* could get the money back.)

43. See Dugard, The Nuclear Tests Cases and the South West Africa Cases: Some Realism About the International Judicial Decision, 16 Va. J. Int'l L. 463, 465-68 (1976).

44. Watson, A Realistic Jurisprudence of International Law, 1980 Y.B. World Affairs 265, 267. Even so, there are many kinds of "sanctions" other than force, and the more attenuated the

The way the international legal system protects its entitlements is in effect to declare the nation that violates an entitlement a temporary outlaw and to allow the nation or nations whose entitlements were violated, or even third parties, to retaliate against the outlaw by in turn disregarding one or more of the outlaw nation's entitlements. The criteria as to which entitlements may be violated in retaliation are, in the present stage of international law, quite controversial. There is a strong consensus that the *same* entitlement may be violated, at the very least. For instance, when the Iranian militants held American embassy personnel hostage, there was some talk in the United States of retaliating by arresting Iranian diplomats, consular officials, and students in this country.[45] However, this was widely perceived to be ineffective; the new Iranian revolutionary government might not care about Iranians in the United States who might very well be sympathizers with the old regime of the Shah. Indeed, it is often the case that when state *A* violates state *B*'s entitlement, state *A* has already calculated that retaliation in kind would not be too costly to it. Of course, when it is perceived that retaliation in kind *would* be too costly, the initial violation is probably deterred—and this may be true of the vast majority of cases that never move beyond the planning stage.

As to retaliation by violating a different entitlement, there is a sense in which the retaliation chosen must not be out of proportion to the initial violation.[46] It would not do to punish the Iranians for taking the American hostages by dropping a nuclear bomb on an Iranian city. However, less drastic, but still forceful, military measures were indeed contemplated by the United States during the period the hostages were held captive.[47] A further restriction on the choice of a different entitlement for retaliatory purposes might be some sense that the method of retaliation should be related to the initial delict in time, place, or subject matter. However, all of the foregoing are extremely vague restrictions under present international law. Indeed, it is difficult to imagine how rules could be formulated that deal specifically and usefully with questions of proportionality and relatedness when there is such an enormous variety of possible thrusts and counterthrusts in international relations.

The difficulty, or indeed near-impossibility, of formulating rules constricting the choice of retaliations is itself a deterrent to the initial delict. If nation *A* decides to violate an entitlement of nation *B*, it risks retaliation along a fairly wide and rather undefined front. The risk is, in most cases, not

concept becomes, the harder it is for positivists, such as Lane and Watson, to accommodate it within their theory of law. See D'Amato, What "Counts" as Law?, *in* Law-making in the Global Community 831-88 (N. Onuf ed. 1982).

45. See Appendix, infra notes 138-84 and accompanying text.

46. See R. Fisher, International Conflict for Beginners 148-49 (1969). Professor Fisher does not purport to be discussing international law in this book, but rather is addressing the broader issue of international conflict resolution. To the extent that he is not talking about "law" itself, he may be correct that it is better strategically to retaliate in proportion, time, place, and manner, to the original delict. But cf. J. Gaddis, Strategies of Containment (1982) (discussion of usefulness of "asymmetric containment" in United States foreign policy); discussion in Appendix, infra notes 145-49 and accompanying text. See also R. Fisher, Improving Compliance with International Law 72 (1981) (credibility of sanction a function of relation to the offense) [hereinafter cited as R. Risher, Improving Compliance].

47. See Appendix, infra notes 150-53 and accompanying text.

worth taking. The result is a general condition of systemic stability in which, to use a phrase of Professor Henkin, "almost all nations observe almost all principles of international law and almost all of their obligations almost all of the time."[48]

In the Appendix, I try to present some examples of the contemplation or use of retaliation against entitlements as illustrative of the "enforcement and compliance" mechanism in international law. The mechanism may appear less mysterious if we note here that international law explicitly provides for the kind of entitlement retaliation I have described in the area of breach of treaty. If nations *X* and *Y* have entered into a treaty, then no matter how long the treaty is and how many articles it contains, if *X* commits a material breach of the treaty then *Y* may legally retaliate by disregarding any or all of its treaty obligations to *X*.[49] Another way of putting this is that a treaty sets up contractual entitlements between the parties. If *X* violates one of *Y*'s treaty entitlements, *Y* may legally retaliate by disregarding any or all of its obligations to *X* in the particular treaty that was violated by *X*. As in international customary law, there is no differentiation among entitlements in a treaty as to their relative importance or weight. The only restriction upon *Y*'s power of retaliation is that *X* must have committed a breach of a material entitlement. In the analogous customary-law situation, the violating nation must have committed a breach of a nontrivial customary-law entitlement.

International law is replete with examples of reprisals, retortions, and other forms of self-help, and the (sometimes) accompanying rules of relatedness and proportionality.[50] Only some of these situations have involved entitlement retaliation (which is not circumscribed by rules of relatedness and proportionality). There have been two recent events, however, that provide an outstanding example of the entitlement-retaliation system: the Iranian hostage crisis and Iraqi war, and the Namibian independence movement. The relevance of both of these is explored in depth in the Appendix to this Article.[51]

Retaliation for entitlement violation is a constant possibility in the international legal system, and this fact helps ensure the stability of the entire set of

---

48. L. Henkin, How Nations Behave 47 (2d ed. 1979).

49. See Vienna Convention on the Law of Treaties, supra note 32, art. 60(3). The retaliatory mechanism I have discussed in the text applies to the international legal system as a system in any given time period. I have attempted to describe the structure of entitlement retaliation as a mechanism for preserving entitlements. Of course, at any given historical time there may be rules that disallow certain kinds of retaliation. At present, article 2(4) of the United Nations Charter seems to preclude the use of military force in retaliation for anything except armed attack (article 51). But in the systemic terms I have attempted to describe, article 2(4) is simply a very important entitlement that nations invoke to protect themselves. Conceivably that entitlement might be violated, however, if a nation commits an egregious act that falls short of armed attack upon another nation. For example, if a white minority government began systematically to kill its black nationals, I think that such a blatant example of genocide would trigger military invasion by other nations upon the genocidal state's territory, and article 2(4) would be viewed as simply having been overridden. In sum, I suggest that the entitlement-retaliatory mechanism I have described, while primitive, is the ultimate sanction in international law, more basic even than article 2(4).

50. See, e.g., I. Brownlie, International Law and the Use of Force by States (1963); J. Starke, An Introduction to International Law 548–51 (8th ed. 1977); Bowett, Reprisals Involving Recourse to Armed Force, 66 Am. J. Int'l L. 1 (1972); Paust, The Seizure and Recovery of the Mayaguez, 85 Yale L.J. 774 (1976).

51. See infra notes 138–84 and accompanying text.

entitlements. However, like the old notion of a "just war" in retaliation for what in those days were considered grave entitlement violations,[52] the entitlement-retaliation system I have described could erupt in runaway escalation, given the vagueness of the previously mentioned "restrictions" of relatedness and proportionality. Its escalatory potential constitutes an ever-present threat to world peace. Clearly entitlement retaliation is not the most desirable form of "compliance and implementation," and fortunately it is not the only one. The international legal system contains many of the sanctions that are more typically used in domestic legal systems to secure compliance with norms.[53] For example, when the International Court of Justice has compulsory jurisdiction, its judgments may be implemented by the United Nations under article 94. In addition, the machinery of the United Nations itself, especially the peace-keeping provisions of the Security Council, which have yet to be implemented, allows for international sanctions against lawbreakers. Many treaties set up treaty mechanisms for enforcement. Also there are regional courts, such as the European Court of Human Rights, which have certain powers of enforcement. Finally, international legal questions arise very often in municipal courts, and depending on the kind of case, enforcement can at times be extremely effective.[54] All of these procedures offer traditional "sanctions"—namely, direct punishment of the lawbreaker that is designed to deter similar instances of such conduct. This traditional type of "sanction" is conceptually distinct from the system of retaliation by entitlement violation that I have described in this Article.

However, although the traditional sanctions systems works for many cases, at the present stage of international legal development it falls significantly short of universality. The international system has no pervasive judicial jurisdiction over all cases that may arise, and the United Nations is hobbled by its discretionary veto system.[55]

As a result, the system of retaliatory entitlement violation that I have described is the only truly universal mechanism allowed by the international legal system to secure implementation and compliance in the real sense required by Professors Lane and Watson. Realistically, we have to acknowledge it as such, even as we recognize its potential for runaway destructive escalation and even as we work to expand the traditional sanctions system.

---

52. See D'Amato, Book Review, 72 Am. Pol. Sci. Rev. 804 (1978) (reviewing E.B.F. Midgley, The Natural Law Tradition and the Theory of International Relations (1975)); M. Walzer, Just and Unjust Wars (1977).

53. See generally R. Fisher, Improving Compliance, supra note 46, at 39–72.

54. See Filartiga v. Pena-Irala, 630 F.2d 876 (2d Cir. 1980); Gordon, Current Legal Developments, 15 Int'l Law. 265, 280–85 (1981); Comment, Torture as a Tort in Violation of International Law: Filartiga v. Pena-Irala, 33 Stan. L. Rev. 353 (1981) (loose discussion of international "consensus").

55. If the permanent members of the Security Council were only able to cast vetoes in certain legally prescribed instances, we might have a universal system of law enforcement; however, the totally discretionary veto has ensured so far in United Nations history that no principled system of universal sanctions could come into existence.

F. *If Human-Rights Norms Are Part of International Law, They Are Entitlements*

The preceding analysis of entitlement suggests that the international legal system does allow for sanctions for noncompliance with its norms, the sanctions being the threat or actuality of reciprocal entitlement violation that is generally understood and accepted as restorative of entitlement equilibrium. But now the questions arise: when a nation violates an individual's human rights, has that nation violated an entitlement? If so, is that entitlement a part of the international-law set of entitlements? I want to reserve this last question for the second part of this Article, and deal here only with the structural contention that a nation that violates a human-rights norm can violate what we have defined as an entitlement. While reserving the question of whether or not human rights entitlements actually *do* exist, this section will deal with the more fundamental question of whether or not they *can* exist—that is, whether or not they can fit into the international system of legal entitlements.

Imagine that a soapbox orator begins to make a political speech in state *X*. Among the small group of people listening to him are *A*, a national of *X*, and *B*, who was born in *X* but became a naturalized citizen of *Y* and is now on a vacation in *X*. The *X* police suddenly descend upon the scene, and arrest the orator and the twenty or so persons who had gathered around to listen. *A* and *B* are jailed without any formal arraignment processes; they are subjected to inhuman and degrading treatment and finally are tortured for supporting (by virtue of their listening to) the subversive orator. Let us further stipulate that both *A* and *B* were simply passers-by, and neither was connected in any way with any anti-government political activities in *X*.

On these facts, Lane and Watson would have no difficulty in concluding that nation *X* has incurred international responsibility to nation *Y* for its maltreatment of *B*.[56] That maltreatment fell below the international minimal standard for a state's reponsibility to aliens, and thus clearly violated *Y*'s entitlement that its nationals traveling abroad should not be subjected to such maltreatment by the officials of *X*.[57] There is no difficulty with this conclusion in present-day international law or even in the international law of the nineteenth century. A classicist might say that state *Y* is itself "harmed" by virtue of the harm to one of its nationals, and is thus entitled to redress from state *X*.[58] Since state *Y* is injured, *Y* might want to engage in a reciprocal violation of one of *X*'s entitlements in the event that *X* does not compensate *Y* for the injury.

But what is it, if anything, that sets *B* apart from *A*? Is it the fact that *B* is holding a passport from state *Y*? *B* may not have the passport (he may have lost it), or it may be outdated or invalid for some other reason. Without the passport or some other set of papers, *B* is, in appearance, the same as *A*. Both are, say, men in their forties, apolitical, perhaps of the same religious and

56. See, e.g., Watson, Legal Theory, supra note 4, at 620.

57. See L. Sohn & T. Buergenthal, International Protection of Human Rights 23–136 (1973).

58. See McDougal & Bebr, Human Rights in the United Nations, 58 Am. J. Int'l L. 603, 609–10 (1964).

ethnic group, and were even born in the same town in *X*. Why should Watson and Lane have no difficulty with *B*'s case, which they acknowledge is part of international law in the realistic sense of compliance and sanctions,[59] and yet have enormous difficulty with *A*'s case, which they say is outside the realm of international law? Why do they feel that what state *X* does to its own citizen, *A*, within its own borders, is purely a matter of *X*'s "domestic jurisdiction" protected as such by article 2(7) of the United Nations Charter?[60] A possible answer is that *B* is a "national" of *Y*, and that fact "internationalizes" his situation, whereas *A* is a national of *X*, and thus the *A-X* relation is one of domestic law only. Yet, this begs the question. "Nationality" is only an artificial relationship pertaining to international law. It is merely another way of stating that state *Y* has an entitlement in *B*'s protection from *X*. For if *Y* were the only state in the world, there would not have arisen a concept of nationality. (There might have arisen a concept of citizenship, which has to do with voting or other kinds of political eligibility, but not "nationality.") It is the existence of other states in the world that has given rise to a special relationship between *Y* and certain of "its" people, including those who become its people through naturalization, namely, the relationship of nationality. This special relationship would not have arisen had not other states recognized it (and they recognized it, perhaps, because they saw in it reciprocal advantages to themselves in claims of their own "nationality").[61] Once recognized and accepted, it became an entitlement.

Thus, Watson and Lane's theses come down to this: they agree that what *X* does to *B* is a matter of international law in the fullest sense of the word—namely, that *X*'s duties toward *B* are subject to implementation and compliance to the extent that international law can and does ensure such compliance with its norms. And they also agree that what *X* does to *A* is a matter of domestic jurisdiction wholly outside the realm of international law. Thus Lane and Watson (and their followers in the Reagan administration) are *not* saying that individuals cannot be the subject of international law, or that international law does not exist, or that international law is ineffective, or any of the other discredited positions that from time to time have been asserted by self-styled "realists." Rather, they are saying *only* that international law obtains in the case of *B*, because *B* is a national of *Y*, and does not obtain in the case of *A*, because *A* is not an alien within *X* but rather a national of *X* who is stuck with whatever maltreatment his own country metes out to him within its boundaries. Finally, as we have seen, the only thing that differentiates *A* and *B* is the intangible and indeed question-begging concept of "nationality."

---

59. Watson indeed criticizes Lauterpacht and McDougal for their "lack of understanding as to why there is such a difference in the legal status of aliens and citizens." Watson, Legal Theory, supra note 4, at 620.

60. Watson is more strident on this point than Lane. See Watson, Autointerpretation, supra note 4. Lane, Mass Killing by Governments, supra note 4, focuses more upon the failure to enforce human rights.

61. International law might have developed quite differently—perhaps that anyone physically within a state is totally subject to that state's laws and that there is no concept of an alien, a non-national, or a stateless person.

G. *If Human Rights Norms Are Entitlements, Then They Are Universal Entitlements*

Our next step is therefore apparent. We must try to discover whether *Y* has an entitlement to protect *A* along with its acknowledged entitlement to protect *B*. We have to decide, in other words, whether there is a "human rights" entitlement in *Y* that enables *Y* legally to violate one or more of *X*'s international-law entitlements if *X* maltreats *A*, its own national, in the same sense that *Y* has a "nationality" entitlement that enables *Y* legally to violate one or more of *X*'s international-law entitlements if *X* maltreats *B*, *Y*'s national. Or, to coin a phrase, we must find *A* to be an "international" of state *Y* just as *B* is a "national" of state *Y*.

To writers such as Lane and Watson, what state *X* does to its own national, *A*, within its own borders seems quintessentially a matter of *X*'s domestic jurisdiction. Yet, as Professor Henkin has demonstrated, a matter is exclusively within *X*'s domestic jurisdiction only when it is not a matter of international law.[62] Domestic jurisdiction is a residual concept; it is simply another way of saying that international law does not apply. To be sure, how state *X* treats individuals within its borders seems to be something within state *X*'s exclusive province. Yet we only have to recall our previous hypothetical example to dispel this illusion. State *X* maltreats *A* and *B*, who are individuals within its borders. *B*, we assume, carries no papers or other identification, and appears to be no different from *A*. Yet *B* is a national of state *Y*. Every international lawyer believes that what state *X* does to *B* is not within *X*'s domestic jurisdiction. The reason given for singling out *B* is that there is some international law link between *B* and another state, a link defined and approved by international law and labeled "nationality." Appearances do not tell us about this; rather, the link is entirely a juridical construct. In short, Henkin and before him Kelsen must be correct in arguing that characterizing a matter as one within *X*'s domestic jurisdiction is simply another way of saying that the matter is not cognizable under international law, and no more than that.[63]

---

62. See Henkin, Human Rights and "Domestic Jurisdiction," *in* Human Rights, International Law and the Helsinki Accord 21–40 (T. Buergenthal ed. 1977).

63. See H. Kelsen, Principles of International Law 290–91 (rev. ed. R. Tucker 1966); Henkin, supra note 62.

There are, however, two alternative views of "domestic jurisdiction," both suggested by Professor Oscar Schachter, that should be noted. See Schachter, Book Review, 17 Colum. J. Transnat'l L. 531 (1978) (reviewing Human Rights, International Law and the Helsinki Accord (T. Buergenthal ed. 1977)). The first might view the concept as something of a shield or barrier to international cognizance of minor international law violations that occur within a state's territory. For example, the issue of preferential admissions to blacks in American professional schools, if argued to be racial discrimination against whites, may be too minor an issue to rise to the level of international human-rights concern. Perhaps international law should concern itself only with "consistent patterns or gross abuses," id. at 534. Schachter makes the interesting suggestion that over time the concept of "domestic jurisdiction" might aid the development of standards for determining the nature or frequency of violations that do rise to the international level, which may be preferable to "leaving the drawing of a line entirely to the political judgment of interested States." Id. (Of course, it might be pointed out, the existence of a domestic-jurisdiction line does not mean that its violation will automatically be sanctioned; the political judgment of interested states will still have an impact.) A second possibility is that the concept of domestic jurisdiction

So let us now focus upon *X*'s maltreatment of its own national *A*. Is *X*'s action cognizable under international law? A more precise way of asking this question is to ask if one or more other states can have an entitlement that *A* not be tortured by *X*? If so, which other states? I would suggest that the other states that may claim such an entitlement are *all* the other states, a notion which after all is suggested by the very term "human rights."

The human rights violator is, like the pirate, *hostis humani generis*, an enemy of all mankind, and jurisdiction to punish his violations is universal.[64] In years past, although pirates were theoretically subject to the criminal jurisdiction of any state that captured them, many nations "winked" at the practice so long as the pirates were known to carry out their depredations against other states. For instance, pirate vessels known to focus their attentions upon Spanish galleons might have been allowed a certain freedom of action by England, even though England theoretically had jurisdiction. The state immediately affected, Spain, certainly had every incentive to combat piracy, but other nations often did nothing about it even though they were entitled to act. Similarly, with human rights most nations might not care whether state *X* tortures its own national. Perhaps a particular nation might feel specially affected—for instance, if *A*'s religious or ethnic background is the same as that of a majority of the citizens of *Y*, *Y* might feel some special calling to complain about *X*'s treatment of *A*. Certainly many nations in Africa having black majorities feel a special interest in the plight of blacks in South Africa. But like piracy, human rights may allow for a "universal" entitlement without necessarily guaranteeing that any one nation or group of nations will feel motivated, or have the interest, to do something about it.

For Lane and Watson to contend that the often appalling statistics of human-rights violations by governments vis-a-vis their own nationals are evidence that what those governments are doing is legal under international law would be very much like a seventeenth-century legal scholar stating that piracy must be legal because it is flourishing. Rather, the critical legal question for the seventeenth-century scholar was not whether nations in fact combatted piracy but whether they were legally entitled to do so if they chose. Similarly, if *X*'s maltreatment of *A* is a violation of *Y*'s entitlement, what is important is *Y*'s *potential* enforceability (through reciprocal entitlement-violation) of its entitlement.[65]

---

can act as a sort of "exhaustion of local remedies" requirement, so that if a state recognizes a domestic human-rights violation and takes steps to remedy it, the international community would not have jurisdiction unless there is a failure to remedy that amounts to a denial of justice.

64. Cf. Filartiga v. Pena-Irala, 630 F.2d 876 (2d Cir. 1980) (discussion of the torturer as *hostis humani generis*).

65. Before proceeding to an argument that other nations do have an international law entitlement against certain forms of maltreatment by any one nation of its own nationals, I might mention a much more "radical" view of the human rights issue that I have chosen not to deal with in the present essay. This more radical theory is that individual human beings are in a sense more important than, or legally higher than, nations; therefore it is relatively unimportant whether other nations feel that they have an entitlement to protect individuals against the depredations of their own governments. Indeed, under this theory, to look at the matter from the viewpoint of nations' entitlements is somehow to cheapen the issue, for *A*'s rights do not exist because nations *Y* and *Z* have an entitlement with respect to *A* but simply because *A*'s rights are primary to those

This first section has described the international legal system from a perspective that allows for a substantive international law of human rights. Nations may have an interest in protecting human rights in other countries; what counts, however, is that they have a realistic *entitlement* to do so. None of the foregoing arguments, of course, establishes the existence of these rights. It is now necessary to explore the means by which legally binding human rights may be derived to fit our framework.

II. Treaties Into Custom: Deriving an International Law of Human Rights

The second half of this Article is concerned with the actual process by which various human rights become law. As will be seen below,[66] treaties play a crucial role in the creation of these laws—but not just through the usual method of creating strictly defined obligations that restrict the ratifying parties. More importantly, treaties containing generalizable principles of international law generate rules of customary international law that bind even nonsignatories.

A. *Some Human Rights Are Protected By Treaties*

The most obvious way for nations to secure human-rights norms among themselves is to conclude a treaty to that effect. The earliest forms of treaties—treaties providing for the safety of emissaries and messengers—had individuals as their subject matter.[67] The treaties involved in the Iranian example discussed in the Appendix[68] focused upon the safety of diplomatic and embassy personnel abroad. Of course, these and countless other "classic" treaties were concerned with the rights of nationals in foreign countries. Persons lacking a nationality, refugees, and "stateless" persons were accorded rights by states adhering to the 1951 Convention Relating to the Status of Refugees.[69] Lane and Watson, however, are concerned with a government's treatment of its own nationals within its own territory. As to this class of persons, states adhering to the Genocide Convention that came into force in 1961 have agreed inter se that certain enumerated acts by a government

---

of all governments including *X*, *Y*, and *Z*. Whether this theory can be given operational substance, or whether it is merely rhetoric, is not an issue that needs to be addressed here. Compare Henkin, supra note 8, at 257-80, with M. McDougal, H. Lasswell, and L. Chen, Human Rights and World Public Order 161-85 (1980).

My purpose is simply to take Lane and Watson (and their sympathizers in government) at face value. To them, the question is whether international law applies to *A* in the same way that they concede that it applies to *B*. Given that concession on their part, I see no need to change the theory so that some entirely different view of human rights can be propounded. Indeed, part of their legitimate frustration, expressed in their articles, is that writers have not come to grips with the precise question that they raise. Since their question is, I believe, answerable on its own terms, I eschew any circuitous paths, however tempting they may be.

66. See infra notes 78-96 and accompanying text.

67. See G. Schwarzenberger, The Frontiers of International Law 49 (1962).

68. See infra notes 139-78 and accompanying text.

69. Convention Relating to the Status of Refugees, July 28, 1951, 189 U.N.T.S. 150. See P. Weis, Nationality and Statelessness in International Law 168-69 (2d ed. 1979).

against a group of its own citizens are crimes under international law that all the signatories "undertake to prevent and to punish."[70] The broadest treaty on human rights, the International Covenant on Civil and Political Rights,[71] is explicitly aimed at all individuals within the territory and jurisdiction of the signatory state.

The United Nations Charter, as a treaty, contains a pledge in article 56 that members will take action to achieve the purposes set forth in article 55, including "universal respect for, and observance of, human rights." The many resolutions of the General Assembly adopted over the years may be claimed to constitute an implementation of these treaty provisions and hence are binding upon the member states. Of course, many would argue that the resolutions are merely recommendations without legal force.[72]

B. *Some Human Rights Have Become Part of Customary International Law*

1. *Which Rights.* Apart from treaty entitlements among parties to treaties, we must inquire whether there are any "human rights" that are generally binding upon all states by virtue of such rights having become entitlements of customary international law. Such an inquiry must be highly particular about which human rights, if any, are at issue. Many "rights" have been asserted in print, ranging from the fundamental to the vague, from the consistent to the incoherent. Three examples of fundamental, consistent assertions of human rights that come readily to mind are the entitlement of any one nation that no other nation may commit an act of genocide against a group of persons, including its nationals, within its territory;[73] the entitlement of any one nation that no other nation may torture any human being;[74] and the entitlement of

70. Convention on the Prevention and Punishment of the Crime of Genocide, Dec. 9, 1948, art. I, 78 U.N.T.S. 277 [hereinafter cited without cross references as Genocide Convention].

71. International Covenant on Civil and Political Rights, opened for signature Dec. 19, 1966, art. 2, 6 I.L.M. 368, 369, [hereinafter cited without cross references as International Covenant on Civil and Political Rights]. The fact that the United States, as of this writing, has ratified neither this Convention nor the Genocide Convention may cause some policy makers in the Reagan administration to think that the human rights of foreigners in their own countries are of no legal concern to the United States, but if so this attitude is rarely made explicit—perhaps because of a sense of shame that the treaties are still unratified. In any event, the attitude has little to recommend it from a legal standpoint, since the failure of the United States to ratify these treaties can hardly make a difference to the many states who are parties. As to the latter, they have achieved by their own adherence to those treaties a legal entitlement in the human rights of persons who are nationals of the other contracting parties.

72. See, e.g., Panel Discussion, Contemporary Views on the Sources of International Law: The Effect of U.N. Resolutions on Emerging Legal Norms, 73 Am. Soc'y Int'l Proc. 300 (1979). Professor Sohn has forcefully stated the case for treating General Assembly resolutions as important components of international law. See Sohn, The Universal Declaration of Human Rights, 8 J. Int'l Comm. Jurists 17 (1967); L. Sohn & T. Buergenthal, supra note 57, at 518–22, 551–56.

73. Genocide Convention, supra note 70.

74. International Covenant on Civil and Political Rights, supra note 71, art. 7. In Filartiga v. Pena-Irala, 630 F.2d 876 (2d Cir. 1980), the court held that torture committed against a citizen of Paraguay by a Paraguayan official within Paraguay violated international law and thus jurisdiction was conferred upon United States district courts under 28 U.S.C. § 1350 (1976) (allowing original jurisdiction where an alien sues for a tort "committed in violation of the law of nations").

any one nation that no other nation may enslave human beings or traffic in human slavery.[75]

"Vague" rights tend to be those that are asserted against an entire social system such as apartheid or communism. The ambiguity arises when one considers the results of immediate dismantling of those systems: would other human rights be jeopardized? To make the blanket assertion, for example, that apartheid is a violation of human rights fails to take account of the foreseeable consequences to whites in South Africa if the social system were suddenly dismantled. Finally, there are "incoherent" assertions of human rights. The so-called rights to the necessities of life—minimal food, shelter, and clothing—may reflect what Lon Fuller would call an "aspirational morality."[76] But they are inconsistent if viewed as legally enforceable rights since they may involve redistribution of privately held resources.[77] Much more specification is needed before we can ascribe a clear meaning, much less make out an international entitlement, to such "rights."

In this section I will focus upon the three relatively uncontroversial prohibitions previously given: genocide, torture, and slavery. My purpose is simply to challenge the theses of Watson and Lane that there are *no* universal or general rights. Although I acknowledge the necessity of particularizing any discussion of human rights, these three, or any one of them, are sufficient to my present purpose. I suggest that these three prohibitions are entitlements of general customary international law and thus binding upon all states. Other rights as well may come under my analysis, but they may be left to further research and particularization.

2. *The Effect of Treaties Upon Custom*. My argument is simply that the multilateral conventions containing prohibitions against genocide, torture, and slavery[78] constitute evidence of customary law binding upon all states and not just the parties thereto. I do not claim that this evidence can be found subsequent to, or apart from, the conventions, but rather that the conventions themselves constitute or generate customary rules of law. To prove this argument it will be necessary to depart from our concentration on human rights—since the argument relates to all generalizable treaty provisions, including human rights provisions—and discuss in detail the theory of customary law formation. The present section will describe my argument. The next section

75. International Covenant on Civil and Political Rights, supra note 71, art. 8; Convention to Suppress the Slave Trade and Slavery, Sept. 25, 1926, 46 Stat. 2183, T.S. No. 778, 60 L.N.T.S. 253.

76. L. Fuller, supra note 29, at 5-32.

77. While the argument I have given in the text criticizes economic and social rights from the perspective of requiring others (including the government) to provide them, the rights may be viewed coherently from the standpoint of prohibiting certain kinds of acts. As Professor Schachter has called to my attention, former Secretary of State Cyrus Vance argued that economic rights can be violated by a government "through corrupt official processes which divert resources to an elite at the expense of the needy." Vance, Human Rights and Foreign Policy, 76 Dep't St. Bull. 505-06 (1977), quoted in Schachter, International Law Implications of U.S. Human Rights Policies, 24 N.Y.L. Sch. L. Rev. 63, 77 (1978).

78. See supra notes 70, 71 & 75.

will deal with specific criticisms of my theory that have been made by Dr. Michael Akehurst.[79]

Customary international law is a set of entitlements that have developed through centuries of the "practice" of states. By "practice" I mean not what states do in isolation, but how states interact with each other on any issue: absent *all* interactions, a state is simply acting domestically.[80] Some customary entitlements owe their origin to the following model: state *X* acts, state *Y* reacts, and either *X*'s action or *Y*'s reaction or some other resolution of the issue is accepted or becomes operative between *X* and *Y*. For example, a courier of state *X* delivers an unwelcome message to the king of state *Y*. The king imprisons the messenger. State *X* responds by sending another courier (obviously a reluctant one) who delivers the message that unless *Y* returns the first courier safe and sound *X* will sack and destroy the towns of *Y*. If *Y* releases the first courier with an apology and perhaps a payment of gold, a resolution of the issue in this manner will lead to a rule that offical couriers are entitled to immunity against imprisonment. However, if *Y* were to imprison the second messenger as well, and *X* was unable for any reason to do anything about it or get *Y* to change its mind, a different rule would arise to the effect that offical couriers have no immunity. We cannot say a priori which of these two results must occur; all we have is the history of state behavior to tell us which rules of international law have become manifest in their customary interactions. In fact, we know that, due either to the perceived need to communicate, or the injustice of ill-treatment of couriers, an early rule of diplomatic immunity became well established as an entitlement of any nation against all other nations. This is the classic kind of example of a practice ripening into a rule of law. But many rules of international law—the vast majority of them, in fact—did not originate along the lines of this model. Rather, most rules began as provisions in treaties. State *X* and *Y* agreed in writing to honor the personal safety of their respective diplomats, either because of an earlier incident between them involving the ill-treatment of a messenger, or because they perceived the need to coexist peacefully and avoid problems arising out of the exchange of message-bearing personnel. Early treaties and agreements of friendship, commerce, and/or navigation typically provided for the immunity of diplomatic personnel, a rule that became part of customary law. The treaty in effect replaced the model I suggested in the

79. Akehurst, Custom as a Source of International Law, 47 Brit. Y.B. Int'l L. 1 (1974–75).

80. In IIT v. Vencap, Ltd., 519 F.2d 1001, 1015 (2d Cir. 1975), Judge Friendly noted that the fact that every nation's municipal law might prohibit theft does not incorporate into international law the Eighth Commandment's prohibition against stealing. As Judge Kaufman wrote in Filartiga v. Pena-Irala, 630 F.2d 876, 880 (2d Cir. 1980), "It is only where the nations of the world have demonstrated that the wrong is of mutual, and not merely several, concern, by means of express international accords, that a wrong generally recognized becomes an international law violation within the meaning of the [Alien Tort Statute, 28 U.S.C. 1350 (1976)]." In other words, if two or more nations commit themselves in a treaty not to allow certain domestic acts—for example, torture, or even in Judge Friendly's hypothetical, theft—that treaty provision internationalizes the issue and takes it out of the pure domestic realm of a state's acts. See D'Amato, supra note 16, at 79–80 (1971) (Genocide Convention moves domestic genocide into the domain of international relations).

previous paragraph. Instead of imprisoning a courier and then letting him go to establish a customary rule, the two affected nations committed themselves to that rule in advance by virtue of a binding instrument. (The binding nature of a "treaty" had itself already been established by virtue of customary law.)[81]

Some years ago when I read the classic works of the "positivist" writers of international law, such as Zouche, Wolff, Moser, Vattel, and especially Bynkershoek, I was struck by the fact that nearly everything they claimed to be a rule of international law was in fact a provision of a treaty. The earlier "naturalist" writers, such as Grotius, Suarez, and Gentili, had unabashedly included treaty provisions as sources of customary law. The "positivists" were more of a surprise; though they claimed that international law was based upon consent, they were able to find such consent generally in the system on the basis of treaty provisions concluded by only a subset of the nations in the system. In my book, *The Concept of Custom in International Law*,[82] I tried to give a detailed account of the rules we now accept as part of customary law that orignated in treaties. My impression is that if we were to remove all the rules of international law that originated as provisions in treaties, we would be left with very few rules indeed—the rare rules that were actually the result of clashing acts and claims and the resolutions of these controversies.

To say this is not to assert that all provisions in treaties become part of the general customary international law. Many treaty provisions are simply not generalizable into rules of law without destroying their content—they are not "norm-creating" treaties. For instance, a "most-favored-nation" clause loses its meaning if it is generalized to give most-favored-nation treatment to everyone without exception.[83] The classic writers on international law, including those previously mentioned, were well aware of these limitations, and regarded the sorting out and identification of generalizable provisions in treaties as their scholarly mission.[84]

---

81. Interestingly, the rule that treaties are binding might itself have resulted from provisions in early treaties containing solemn vows that the treaties were binding.

82. A. D'Amato, supra note 16.

83. Additionally, there are many treaties that effect a barter or exchange (e.g., the "destroyers-for-bases" deal between England and the United States prior to World War II), and these too cannot be generalized. Moreover, many treaties and treaty provisions refer to particular places or organizations and thus cannot state a general rule: for example, treaties affecting the title or rights of passage of particular lands or waterways, demilitarization treaties for particular territories, mandates and trusteeships, boundaries, treaties setting up international organizations, and so forth. See generally the list of categories provided by Waldock in 2 Y.B. Int'l L. Comm'n 27, U.N. Doc. A/ CN.4/SER. A/1964/Add. 1. Finally, if some treaties state one rule and other treaties state the opposite rule, the clash between the two, just like a clash of customary practice, cannot give rise to any one customary rule.

84. The classic writers' approach to international law was no different from Lord Mansfield's approach to developing the "law merchant" rules of the common law in England at roughly the same time. Lord Mansfield found many provisions in contracts which were generalizable, and he applied them to other unrelated contracts when the latter lacked specificity. He had no difficulty accepting as the "practices" of the mercantile class the written agreements concluded among merchants. See generally B. Shientag, Moulders of Legal Thought 108-11, 123-50 (1943).

At about the turn of the twentieth century, however, several English publicists, including Oppenheim and Hall,[85] put forth the view that treaties simply laid down contractual obligations for the parties and could have no legal effect outside the parties. This view was repeated as dicta by Lord Alverstone in the much-cited case of *West Rand Central Gold Mining Co. v. The King*,[86] a case now, however, generally acknowledged to have been wrongly decided.[87] I have not been able to find any support for the Oppenheim position apart from the assertion by Oppenheim and Hall that provisions in treaties can either be declaratory or in derogation of the underlying customary law, but do not affect the underlying law.[88] This is more a statement of a conclusion than a reason, a conclusion that follows from equating treaties with contracts and then taking a restrictive view of contracts. Yet, a long line of British and American authors, from Oppenheim to my former teacher, the late Professor (and Judge) Richard R. Baxter, have reiterated this "restrictive-contract" view of treaties.[89]

Several arguments can be made against the restrictive-contract view. First, as Lord McNair and Professor Sohn, among others, have persuasively demonstrated, treaties differ in many fundamental respects from domestic contracts.[90] Second, and much more significantly, the writers who have asserted, with Oppenheim, that provisions in treaties do not affect the underlying customary law have uniformly failed to adduce a single instance of a generalizable treaty provision that has *not* been transmuted into customary law. Third, even these writers accept that provisions in treaties may eventually "pass" into customary international law or "harden" into law. But they have never indicated how or when this "passage" or "hardening" takes place, and they have failed to indicate what evidence we might look for to ascertain that a treaty provision has undergone the rites of passage into customary law. Their inability to give theoretical or practical support to the notions they have invented of "passing" or "hardening," after all these years, suggests that perhaps something is wrong with their initial premise.

---

85. W. Hall, International Law 7–8 (A.P. Higgins 8th ed. 1924); 1 L. Oppenheim, International Law 28 (H. Lauterpacht 8th ed. 1955).

86. [1905] 2 K.B. 391, 398.

87. See, e.g., E. Feilchenfeld, Public Debts and State Succession 380–96 (1931) (eventual diplomatic settlement by England more liberal than the theories advanced in the case would indicate); 1 D. O'Connell, State Succession in Municipal Law and International Law 244, 321, 378 (1967).

88. W. Hall, supra note 87, at 7–8; 1 L. Oppenheim, supra note 87, at 27.

89. See C. Parry, The Sources and Evidences of International Law 29–32 (1965); Baxter, Multilateral Treaties as Evidence of Customary International Law, 41 Brit. Y.B. Int'l L. 275, 285 (1965–66); Baxter, Treaties and Custom, 129 Recueil des Cours 31 (1970) [hereinafter cited as Baxter, Treaties and Custom]; Waldock, General Course on Public International Law, 106 Recueil des Cours 3, 84 (1962).

In contrast, many continental authors have retained the classical view that generalizable provisions in treaties constitute evidence of customary international law. See references in D'Amato, supra note 16, at 138–40.

90. See McNair, The Functions and Differing Legal Character of Treaties, 11 Brit. Y.B. Int'l L. 100 (1930); Sohn, The Many Faces of International Law, 57 Am. J. Int'l L. 868 (1963).

An example from Oppenheim's own text indicates the level of unreality to which insistence upon a theory of "hardening" can lead. As late as the final edition of Lauterpacht's Oppenheim, published in 1955, the author still found it "difficult to say" whether a customary international law contains a prohibition against the international traffic in slaves.[91] The author cited numerous international treaties condemning slave traffic, but because of the commitment to the theory that treaty provisions can either be in derogation of or declaratory of customary law, no conclusion as to the latter could be reached. But not long thereafter, the International Law Commission, commenting upon the *jus cogens* provision of the new Vienna Convention on Treaties, found not only that customary international law prohibited international slave trade but that this prohibition was "one of the most obvious and best settled rules of *jus cogens*" in that even new treaties could not derogate from it.[92] Unlike Lauterpacht's Oppenheim, the I.L.C. did not miss the forest for the trees.

If we press this example a bit further, we might inquire what evidence Oppenheim or Lauterpacht would desire in order to substantiate a customary international law rule prohibiting traffic in slaves. Certainly one more or a dozen more treaties would not do the trick, because Lauterpacht already cited numerous international treaties prohibiting slave traffic. Thus his prescription in practical terms might be inferred to be as follows: let one nation that is not a party to any conventions on slavery actually encourage the taking of a group of humans as slaves, allow or require one of its vessels to transport these slaves to another nation, hope that other nations will intercede forcibly to halt the transportation, and then have the first nation "back down" and agree to free the slaves and punish the ship's captain. This procedure, or something like it, would then substantiate the prior treaty provisions outlawing the international slave traffic, and presumably would allow Lauterpacht in the next edition to write that, finally, the treaty law has indeed "hardened" into customary law. Similarly, if a writer were to contend that "it is difficult to say" whether the Genocide Convention has passed into customary international law, presumably a nation would actually have to engage in genocide and then desist after a few hundred or a few thousand people have been massacred in order to substantiate the antigenocide rule. If Oppenheim's "theory" is accepted, it would appear that nations would have to engage in such post-treaty "practice" in the slavery and genocide cases—as well as in all other human-rights cases—in order to test whether the treaty rule has hardened into customary law. My position, on the other hand, is that nations have not painted themselves into any such theoretical corner, but rather have manifested by virtue of their behavior over the centuries that generalizable provisions in treaties become part of customary law directly without need for such subsequent "practice."

---

91. 1 L. Oppenheim, supra note 87, at 733–34.

92. Report of the International Law Commission to the General Assembly, 18 U.N. GAOR Supp. (No. 9) at 1, U.N. Doc. A/CN.4/SER. A/1963/Add. 1, U.N. Doc. A/5509 (1963), reprinted in [1963] 2 Y.B. Int'l L. Comm'n 187, U.N. Doc. A/CN.4/SER. A/1963/Add. 1.

Finally, the incoherence of the "hardening" theory can be demonstrated theoretically even if we accept the previously described gruesome example of deliberately enslaving human beings as necessary to test whether the treaty rule has become a customary rule. Suppose nation *X* (not a party to any antislavery treaty) enslaves some people and transports them on one of its ships, and nations *Y* and *Z* notify *X* that *X* should cease and desist immediately. By what *law* do nations *Y* and *Z* object to *X*'s acts? The only prior law on the subject, by definition, is the law in the treaties. Yet, if it is by *this* law that *Y* and *Z* object to *X*'s acts, then the law, for international law purposes, is already established prior to *X*'s compliance. In this event, the Oppenheim thesis is redundant. Or to put the point differently, there is no coherent means to establish "hardening" of the sort envisaged by Oppenheim, since its very proof involves invocation of the theory that Oppenheim attacks, namely the theory that provisions in treaties generate customary law immediately and without any such process of "hardening."

To be sure, the subsequent evidence needed to substantiate the "passage" of a treaty provision into customary law might be something other than the action-reaction-resolution model I suggested at the outset. But what might this something else be? The late Professor Baxter in a carefully reasoned lecture argued that this subsequent element must be acquiescence in the rule by the nonparty states.[93] Baxter gave no suggestion, however, as to how this acquiescence might be manifested or proved. And he himself recognized a logical paradox implicit in the idea of acquiescence: the more states that sign a multilateral convention, the fewer nonparties remain and hence the more difficult it becomes to find a consistent attitude of these nonparties to the rule in the treaty.[94] Indeed, suppose all the states in the world that are at all interested in the subject matter of the treaty sign it; we might wait in vain for the nonsignatories to express any attitude toward the rules of the treaty.

Nevertheless, a critic may attempt to support the Oppenheim approach by the argument that since the parties to a treaty intend that the treaty shall be binding only upon themselves—which is, after all, why they enter into the treaty—the provisions cannot therefore have any third-party effect. This argument in a sense restates the restrictive-contract notion of treaties. But it is also answerable on its own terms. In the first place, we cannot be sure that the parties to a treaty intend exclusivity of its provisions. Of course, a treaty involving commercial trade or one delimiting boundaries would seem to be of particular and even exclusive interest to the parties, but I have previously ruled

93. Baxter, Treaties and Custom, supra note 89, at 71–73.

94. Id. at 64. Professor Baxter based much of his reasoning upon the decision of the International Court of Justice in the North Sea Continental Shelf Cases (W. Ger. v. Den., W. Ger. v. Neth.), 1969 I.C.J. 3 (Judgment of Feb. 20). For reasons that I give in the next section of the present essay, see infra notes 97–113 and accompanying text, the *Continental Shelf Cases* are better construed as delineating the requirements of "special custom" and not "general custom." Under this approach, reliance on that decision is misplaced. But even if the reader does not want to accept my analysis of the *Continental Shelf Cases* as turning on the requirements of special custom, one looks in vain at the opinion of the court to find what the court itself would accept as evidence of "acquiescence" under Baxter's theory.

out such treaties as norm-creating because they are not generalizable.[95] But taking those provisions that are generalizable, it is not clear that the parties intend them to be exclusive to themselves. Indeed, a generalizable provision would almost by its very nature be one to which the parties would welcome adherence on the part of other states. Moreover, multilateral conventions, which these days are becoming especially numerous and prominent, nearly always contain provisions to which the parties would want other states to subscribe. Multilateral conventions open to all nations seem to manifest an intent to universal inclusivity.[96] At the very least, we might conclude that parties to treaties do not necessarily intend generalizable treaty provisions to be limited to the signatories.

Second, and more importantly, I would argue that whether the parties' intent is resolved on the side of exclusivity or inclusivity, intent is ultimately irrelevant. What the *parties* to a treaty intend its effect to be has nothing to do with the use to which the international community of states may desire to put the treaty. Take as an analogy a case in domestic law. The judicial system will give the case precedential effect irrespective of the intent of the parties. Indeed, if both plaintiff and defendant were to stipulate that the decision in their case be confined to themselves, I believe that any court would disregard their wishes and reply simply that the use to which the judicial system wants to put the decision in this particular case has nothing to do with the desire or intent of the parties but rather is a question of the jurisprudence of the legal system. In international law, nations have through history incorporated the provisions of treaties into customary law without regard to the intent of the parties—even if such an intent could be determined, and even if it were determined to express a desire for exclusivity.

3. *Dr. Akehurst's Critique*. In a leading article devoted largely to a criticism of my book on the concept of customary international law,[97] Dr. Michael Akehurst contends that I was wrong in asserting that treaties may generate customary law.[98] It will be instructive to see how he goes about attempting to prove this proposition.

95. See supra text accompanying note 82.

96. See D'Amato, Manifest Intent and the Generation by Treaty of Customary Rules of International Law, 64 Am. J. Int'l L. 892 (1970). In a paper that I wrote for a seminar given by Professor Baxter in 1961, published the following year, I argued that parties to a treaty usually hope that "the general rules they adopt in treaties" are "extended to all nations; a rule is essentially a reciprocal accommodation." D'Amato, Treaties as a Source of General Rules of International Law, Harv. Int'l L. Club Bull., Apr. 1962, at 1, 29.

97. Akehurst, supra note 79.

98. Akehurst's criticism is ironic, since he also disputes my position that claims are less important than treaties in generating custom. In the book, I asserted that a claim is only the first step toward a unit of "custom." To complete the unit, what is needed is a reaction by one or more other states and a resolution of the issue. On the other hand, if custom can be generated by a claim only, as Akehurst argues, then all kinds of unilateral desires by nations would become law. For instance, a claim made by one nation that the Soviet Union violates international law by not having more than one political party to give the voters a meaningful choice at election time would, according to Akehurst's reasoning, be evidence of a rule of international customary law of which the Soviet Union's one-party system is in violation. Or, a claim by one or more nations that apartheid violates international law would be evidence of a customary rule to that effect binding upon South Africa. A claim by Switzerland that it owns Antarctica, or by Sweden that it owns the

Since Akehurst recognizes that so many rules of customary law owe their origin to provisions in treaties, and since (with some misgivings) he accepts the cases I cited to prove this proposition,[99] he must find various mechanisms to

moon, or by Saudi Arabia that it owns the mineral wealth under all the oceans would also be constitutive of custom (for Akehurst indeed cites cases involving claims to specific real estate in support of what I would have thought would be the rather different proposition that claims generate general customary law). Akehurst, supra note 79, at 2. In domestic law, if one were to argue that any claim made by any private person or by any lawyer constitutes evidence of what the law is, the argument would be thrown out of court. For clearly there is no conceivable restraint upon what any person—or any nation—might claim. And just as clearly, for every claim there is a potential counterclaim. For these reasons, I find Akehurst's position that a mere claim is enough to constitute evidence of *customary law* to be quite unconvincing.

In turn, Akehurst calls my position on claims "very restrictive." Id. at 1. He makes one argument that on its face has merit: that claims of states regarding the width of the territorial sea or of exclusive fishery zones are regarded as in themselves capable of creating customary law. Id. at 2. While Akehurst does not specify this argument any further, let us suppose that all the nations in the world are requested by the Secretary-General of the United Nations to state their claim for the width of the territorial sea (or, interchangeably, their claim for the width of exclusive fishery zones) in a letter to the Secretary. Suppose all nations respond, and the claims range from 25 miles to 500 miles. On these supposed facts, I would have no difficulty finding a rule of international law to the effect that a 25-mile territorial sea has been established, and that anything beyond 25 miles is still subject to dispute and resolution. But as I made clear in my book, D'Amato, supra note 16, at 33–34, and in a simultaneously published article on consensus, D'Amato, On Consensus, 8 Can. Y.B. Int'l L. 104 (1970), cited in Akehurst, supra note 79, at 7, a minimal consensus reached by all states (for instance, 25 miles) becomes part of general international law *not* by the process of "custom" but simply because international law itself is no more and no less than what the nations of the world think it is. If all the nations in the world think that, at the very least, the territorial sea is 25 miles wide, then that ipso facto is what international law holds. If a label had to be given to this process of law creation, I would call it "consensus." But in any event it is not *custom*. For if it were custom, then logically *any* claim is capable of generating custom. If one or two states in the letter to the Secretary-General claimed a 500-mile territorial sea, Akehurst would have to give that claim weight as part of "customary" law as much as he gives weight to all the other claims. He would then be caught in a welter of conflicting claims (after all, a nation that claims a 25-mile territorial sea is implicitly stating that it will not recognize a claim that exceeds 25 miles). Thus, my conclusion on this particular issue of claims to the width of territorial seas coincides with Akehurst's conclusion only to the limited extent that I would accept a consensus position as to the minimal claim. But I would not accept it as custom, as he does, for all the reasons previously given.

But if all the reasons I have given fail to convince the reader, and if instead Akehurst's position that claims generate customary law is preferred, then it would appear to be quite easy to reach the conclusion that treaties generate customary law as well as claims, for treaties incorporate the claims made by all the parties thereto and go a step farther and resolve those claims. Surely if a bare claim is enough to generate custom, then the frozen evidence of resolved claims in a treaty is an a fortiori case. Yet strangely enough, Akehurst does not take this step that his own logic would seem to impel him to take. Instead, he puts the matter in reverse. He asks: "What logical justification is there for regarding treaties as State practice, while denying that status to other statements (such as claims) made by States?" Akehurst, supra note 79, at 3. My position, which he is criticizing by his rhetorical question, is precisely that treaties are a record of state agreements that legally bind them to act in a certain way, whereas a statement (such as a claim) is merely a negotiating position to which we should not attach much credibility or conviction. But surely if Akehurst wants to attach that much credibility to a mere statement by a state, then what logical justification is there for questioning the position that treaties generate custom?

99. Akehurst, supra note 79, at 42–43. One of his "contrary" cases is *West Rand Central Gold Mining Co. v. The King*, see supra text accompanying note 86. Akehurst takes issue with me on the matter of treaties articulating a rule of custom (the articulation being what I have claimed as the objective evidence of *opinio juris* in D'Amato, supra note 16, at 160–62). Akehurst writes in a footnote that the "fatal flaw" in my reasoning "is that treaties do not, in most cases, articulate the norm as one of *customary* law (unless one assumes that laying down a rule in a treaty automatically means articulating the rule as a norm of customary law—but that is to assume

account for this international practice. One important mechanism builds upon the early Oppenheim view, as significantly modified by Baxter. Oppenheim, it will be recalled, said that treaties are either declaratory or in derogation of the underlying common law, and hence are irrelevant to it.[100] Many years later Baxter argued that those treaties that are declaratory of customary law, but not those in derogation of it, can be cited as evidence of that customary law.[101] I entered the argument at this point and objected that if we are able to determine whether or not a treaty is declaratory of the underlying customary law, as Baxter suggests, then if our answer is positive we would have no need to cite the treaty as evidence at all, for we will have determined independently of the treaty what the customary law on the point in fact is.[102] Before my book was published, I had communicated my objection on this point to Professor Baxter, and he modified his view in his Hague Lectures in 1970, agreeing that the proof of customary law is not "facilitated" by the method of determining what the customary law is dehors the treaty.[103] However, Baxter retained his previous position that treaties that are declaratory of customary international law may be cited as evidence of that custom. After abandoning the idea that proof of whether the treaty is declaratory requires separate research into the custom, Baxter argued that there are two other methods of determining whether a treaty is declaratory of customary law. The first would be "appropriate language in the preamble or elsewhere" that the treaty "incorporates nothing but customary international law."[104] And the second is research into the *travaux préparatoires* to see whether the treaty was intended to be declaratory of international law.[105]

My reply to these latter two methods must now be summarized to set the stage for Akehurst's rejoinder. I argued that the first method—looking for language in the treaty that incorporates customary law—simply would put a high premium upon treaty draftsmanship.[106] And with respect to the *travaux préparatoires*, I argued that any good negotiator on either side would invariably contend that the language that he or she champions is a mere restatement of the customary rule in the absence of a treaty. The reason for so contending would be to convince the other side that the language in question adds nothing

---

without argument the very thing which D'Amato sets out to prove)." Akehurst, supra note 79, at 43 n.7. Quite to the contrary, I have never contended that a treaty must articulate a norm as a norm of *customary* law; there are hardly any treaties which would bother to do so, any more than nations *X* and *Y* in settling a conflict would refer to their resolution of that conflict as articulating a norm of customary law. Rather, I would contend that the articulation of the norm in the treaty *constitutes* an articulation of the rule for the purposes of customary law determination. Perhaps Akehurst did not see the initial discussion in my book of custom as a *secondary rule* of law-determination in the precise sense offered by Professor H.L.A. Hart in his discussion of secondary rules. See D'Amato, supra note 16, at 41-44.

100. See supra note 88 and accompanying text.

101. Baxter, Multilateral Treaties as Evidence of Customary International Law, 41 Brit. Y.B. Int'l L. 275 (1965-66).

102. D'Amato, supra note 16, at 115, 153.

103. Baxter, Treaties and Custom, supra note 89, at 42, 75 n.1.

104. Id. at 42.

105. Id. at 42-46; Baxter, supra note 101, at 291-93.

106. D'Amato, supra note 16, at 157-58.

to existing law and therefore no "bargaining chips" must be paid in order for the other side to accept the language. One may dip at random into the *travaux préparatoires* of any multilateral draft convention and find any number of instances of experienced negotiators resting their case for the adoption of their own drafts on no argument other than the fact that their own draft accurately reflects existing law on the subject in question.

Upon this dialogue, Akehurst builds his exception to his criticism of my theory that treaties generate custom. He takes Baxter's position one step further by arguing that, irrespective of the real intent of the drafters of the treaty, it is possible for us to conclude that a treaty is declaratory of the underlying customary law if we merely find statements to that effect in the treaty or in the *travaux*.[107] Nor is this method defeated, Akehurst adds, if we were to find that the states making those statements (that the treaty is declaratory of customary law) knew them to be untrue.[108] Thus, Akehurst has objectified Baxter's method of proving subjective intent.

Yet it seems to me that the exception that Akehurst thus carves out of his proposition that treaties do not generate custom is large enough to swallow the entire thesis. There will not be many instances, including human-rights conferences, of *travaux* that manifest any intent other than to declare existing customary law. Nor will there be many instances of preambles in treaties stating any intention other than to codify existing law, even if those treaties are the result of conferences originally called into being to engage in the "progressive development" of international law. The more important the treaty, the more likely we are to have language expressly declaring the treaty to be a codification of existing law. An example is the Genocide Convention of 1948 which, in its first article (an article given added significance by virtue of the omission of any preamble), states that "[t]he Contracting Parties confirm that genocide, whether committed in time of peace or in time of war, is a crime under international law which they undertake to prevent and to punish."[109] While I have given my reasons for disagreeing with the entire investigation into whether a treaty is declaratory of customary law, if Akehurst's objective approach leads him to admitting that, say, ninety percent of all multilateral conventions and many bilateral treaties (those containing generalizable provisions) will constitute customary law by virtue of statements that we are sure to find in the *travaux* or in the treaties themselves, I would not object to the practical result that he reaches.

A second important mechanism suggested by Akehurst to show that the provisions in a treaty have become part of customary international law is a subsequent statement made by a state that the provision or the rule it describes has become part of customary law.[110] We might label this mechanism an

107. Akehurst, supra note 79, at 45-48. I had previously suggested the importance of objectifying all the constituent elements of custom; see D'Amato, supra note 16, at 33-41, 74-87.

108. Akehurst, supra note 79, at 47.

109. Convention on the Prevention and Punishment of the Crime of Genocide, supra note 70, art.1. By "confirming" the crime of genocide, rather than recognizing its novelty, the parties obviously used draftsmanship to help ensure the status of genocide as a universal prohibition.

110. Akehurst, supra note 79, at 49.

objective restatement of the old "hardening into law" position. I have previously indicated that no writer has come forth with any mechanism for a treaty provision's "hardening" or "passing" into customary law.[111] But now Akehurst appears to have provided such a mechanism. It occurs, according to Akehurst, when states subsequently make a statement or claim that the legal norm in question has become part of customary law.

Yet if we look more closely at Akehurst's article, we find that he has given no example of this mechanism. Thus we might dismiss this effort by Akehurst with the observation that he is only trying to salvage the old "hardening" test by indicating what would be an objective example of "hardening" even though the real world has apparently failed to provide a single illustration of that objective example. And we might conclude that with Akehurst's prior concession regarding the ease with which we may find that a treaty is intended to be declaratory of customary law, all or nearly all treaties are subsumed within that exception, thus making Akehurst de facto a supporter of the theory that treaties generate custom, despite his insistence that, but for these exceptions, they do not.

Yet we cannot dismiss this latter theory too quickly because of the support Akehurst claims for it from the Vienna Convention on the Law of Treaties[112] and the *North Sea Continental Shelf Cases*.[113] Neither of these eminent sources provides an illustration of a "subsequent statement" of the sort envisaged by Akehurst, although on their surface they seem to support his theoretical position.

Article 38 of the Vienna Convention provides that "nothing in Articles 34 to 37 [relating to the effect of treaties on third states] precludes a rule set forth in a treaty from becoming binding upon a third State as a customary rule of law, recognized as such." Akehurst contends that the phrase "recognized as such" indicates an intention on the part of the framers that something must happen subsequent to a treaty in order to warrant the conclusion that a rule in the treaty has become binding as a customary rule of law.[114] An examination of the *travaux préparatoires*, however, indicates no such singleminded intent and no common understanding of what the phrase "recognized as such" means.[115] To the Soviet delegation and its ideological adherents, "recognized as such" apparently did indicate the need for subsequent *consent* to the rule, but we must bear in mind that the Soviet position (at least as it was at the time of the *travaux*) was that customary law itself is only binding upon states that have consented to it.[116] Given that restrictive, antihistorical, and theoretically unsound[117] view of general customary law, it is no surprise that the adherents

111. D'Amato, supra note 16, at 139–40.

112. Vienna Convention on the Law of Treaties, supra note 32.

113. (W. Ger. v. Den., W. Ger. v. Neth.) 1969 I.C.J. 3 (Judgment of Feb. 20).

114. Akehurst, supra note 79, at 49.

115. U.N. Conference on the Law of Treaties, Official Records (1st sess.) at 197–201, U.N. Doc. A/CONF.39/11 (1969); id. (2d sess.) at 63–72, U.N. Doc. A/CONF.39/11/Add. 1 (1970).

116. See, e.g., Tunkin, Remarks on the Juridical Nature of Customary Norms of International Law, 49 Calif. L. Rev. 419 (1961).

117. See D'Amato, supra note 16, at 187–99.

to the Soviet position would not want to recognize in treaties any mechanism for general generation of customary law; they would not even recognize in custom itself any such mechanism. It is improbable that Akehurst would want to endorse the Soviet position if that were the cost of substantiating his argument, for that would leave him with a restrictive view of custom that would render otiose his entire preceding argument that treaties found through their *travaux* to be declaratory of customary law have that effect upon non-parties.

But there are at least two other meanings that can be attributed to the phrase "recognized as such" that either were expressed during the treaty negotiations or might conceivably have been considered as a meaning by the states that ultimately ratified the convention. For instance, the phrase might mean "understood as such"; it would thus imply that the process of treaty formation of customary rules of law must be understood to create *custom* and not a *treaty obligation* upon third states. Along this line, the delegate from El Salvador acutely observed that it was not the rules of a treaty that could have the effect of becoming binding via custom on third states, but the content of the treaty provisions.[118] Or, "recognized as such" might refer to recognition within the treaty or in its *travaux* (Akehurst's first objective mechanism, but *not* the mechanism of subsequent statements for which he cited article 38). Clearly, article 38 contains great ambiguity in the phrase "recognized as such," which should not obscure the central fact that the article expressly recognizes the process of customary law creation by treaty that I have been describing in the present section of this essay.

More significant than the Vienna Convention for Akehurst's purposes is his invocation of the judgment of the International Court of Justice in the *North Sea Continental Shelf Cases* of 1969. He contends that the need for *opinio juris*—that is, in his view, the need for statements in the treaty, in the *travaux*, or in subsequent remarks by states accepting the treaty provisions that those provisions are declaratory of international law—"is clearly stated in the *North Sea Continental Shelf Cases*."[119] The court, commenting upon the contention of Denmark and the Netherlands that a customary rule corresponding to article 6 of the Geneva Convention on the Continental Shelf[120] had "come into being since the Convention, partly because of its [the conven-

118. U.N. Conference on the Law of Treaties, Official Records (2d sess.) at 64, U.N. Doc. A/CONF.39/11/Add. 1 (1970).

119. Akehurst, supra note 79, at 44.

120. Convention on the Continental Shelf, opened for signature April 29, 1958, art. 6, 15 U.S.T. 471, T.I.A.S. No. 5578, 499 U.N.T.S. 311. Article 6 reads:

> 1. Where the same continental shelf is adjacent to the territories of two or more States whose coasts are opposite each other, the boundary of the continental shelf appertaining to such States shall be determined by agreement between them. In the absence of agreement, and unless another boundary line is justified by special circumstances, the boundary is the median line, every point of which is equidistant from the nearest points of the baselines from which the breadth of the territorial sea of each State is measured.
>
> 2. Where the same continental shelf is adjacent to the territories of two adjacent States, the boundary of the continental shelf shall be determined by agreement between them. In the absence of agreement, and unless another boundary line is justified by special circumstances, the boundary shall be determined by application of the principle

tion's] own impact, partly on the basis of subsequent State practice," said that there must be some showing of *opinio juris* to demonstrate this subsequent behavior that made the Convention's article 6 into a norm of customary law.[121] The court's precise language on this point, which explicitly recognizes the norm-creating process that I have been describing in the present essay, is as follows:

> In so far as this contention is based on the view that Article 6 of the Convention has had the influence, and has produced the effect, described, it clearly involves treating that Article as a norm-creating provision which has constituted the foundation of, or has generated a rule which, while only conventional or contractual in its origin, has since passed into the general *corpus* of international law, and is now accepted as such by the *opinio juris*, so as to have become binding even for countries which have never, and do not, become parties to the Convention. There is no doubt that this process is a perfectly possible one and does from time to time occur: it constitutes indeed one of the recognized methods by which new rules of customary international law may be formed. At the same time this result is not lightly to be regarded as having been attained.[122]

The court then found that as far as article 6 itself was concerned, there was a need to show subsequent acceptance of its rule by other states (for example, by demonstrating *opinio juris*—although the court fails to indicate how *opinio juris* could be shown), and that the contending parties failed to offer such proof of subsequent acceptance.

The court is saying two things. First, there is no doubt that treaty provisions may generate customary rules. Second, article 6 of the Geneva Convention did not do so. At this point in the court's opinion we are left unsure whether the reason given by the court for why this particular provision did not generate the customary rule desired by Denmark and the Netherlands—that there was no subsequent *opinio juris* indicating acceptance of the treaty rule—applies generally to all treaty provisions that generate customary rules, or only to article 6. If it is the former, then the thesis I have been contending for in this Article becomes unnecessary, since any subsequent showing of *opinio juris* should be enough to demonstrate a rule of customary law quite apart from the prior treaty. Thus we are left with the question whether the court is positing the first of these propositions or the second.

Fortunately, we are not remitted to metaphysical speculation for our decision. The court's opinion as a whole makes it abundantly clear that the rule of article 6 was itself inapplicable to the facts of the case and could not

---

of equidistance from the nearest points of the baselines from which the breadth of the territorial sea of each State is measured.

3. In delimiting the boundaries of the continental shelf, any lines which are drawn in accordance with the principles set out in paragraphs 1 and 2 of this article should be defined with reference to charts and geographical features as they exist at a particular date, and reference should be made to fixed permanent identifiable points on the land.

121. North Sea Continental Shelf (W. Ger. v. Den., W. Ger. v. Neth.), 1969 I.C.J. 3, 41 (Judgment of Feb. 20).

122. Id.

have generated a rule binding upon the Federal Republic of Germany with regard to its continental shelf. By omitting the facts of the case, the contentions of the parties, and the court's decisive reasoning in that regard, Akehurst creates the impression that the court was speaking ex cathedra about custom formation. Unfortunately, Akehurst is not alone in dealing with the *Continental Shelf* opinion as if it were cut loose from the moorings of its own pleadings, facts, and judicial holding.[123] Hence we must examine the case itself with some care.

Denmark and the Netherlands contended that the North Sea continental shelf delimitation line between themselves and the Federal Republic of Germany should be decided upon the basis of the equidistance method as specified in article 6 of the Geneva Convention. Germany countered that the continental shelf should be delimited according to the principle that each coastal state is entitled to a just and equitable share. The court, however, held that neither contention was correct under international law. Instead, it found that a nation's continental shelf is as much its territory as is its land above sea level, and that fairness, equity, or equidistance has nothing to do with the matter. To summarize the court's reasoning in this regard, let us imagine two nations, *X* and *Y*, facing each other across a 500-mile wide sea. Suppose that nation *X* has a continental shelf appertaining to its land territory, and that the shelf extends across the sea for a distance of 450 miles. At that point, the shelf drops down to the ocean floor depth, and then rises precipitously to form the land mass of nation *Y*. In other words, *X* "has" a continental shelf and *Y* does not "have" one. In this situation, the equidistance principle might draw the line of delimitation at 250 miles from *X*'s coast, giving the remaining 200 miles of continental shelf over to *Y*. A fair or equitable principle might draw the line in roughly the same place. But according to the court, what is involved in the matter of the continental shelf is not fairness or equidistance, but *title* to territory. "What confers the *ipso jure* title which international law attributes to the coastal State in respect of its continental shelf," the court held, "is the fact that the submarine areas concerned may be deemed to be actually part of the territory over which the coastal State already has dominion—in the sense that, although covered with water, they are a prolongation or continuation of that territory, an extension of it under the sea."[124] Thus, under the court's reasoning, *X* is entitled to the entire continental shelf of 450 miles.

This, then, is the bedrock upon which the court constructed its judgment in the case. But there are two remaining contentions that Denmark and the

123. A leading casebook on international law suggests that excerpts from the *North Sea Continental Shelf Cases* will "provide the answers to, or at least throw further light on," numerous questions posed by the authors regarding the impact of treaties upon custom. L. Henkin, R. Pugh, O. Schachter, & H. Smit, International Law Cases and Materials 38 (1980). The lengthy excerpts from the *North Sea Continental Shelf Cases* that follow, id. at 59–65, 84–85, 366–67, do not indicate the territorial basis upon which the court based its result in the cases or the consequence that the territorial basis entails stricter proof of special custom. These qualifications are also not mentioned in the references to the *North Sea Continental Shelf Cases* in Restatement (Revised) of the Law: Foreign Relations Law of the United States 31–34 (Tent. Draft No. 1, 1980).

124. 1969 I.C.J. at 32.

Netherlands offered. First, they argued that the equidistance principle of article 6 of the Geneva Convention changed matters, so that, whatever title to the continental shelf Germany might have had prior to that Convention, it now only had so much of the North Sea continental shelf as the equidistance principle would allow (a principle that, as we might expect, sharply reduced the total area of the continental shelf that would be allocated to Germany).

The answer to this first contention might best be illustrated by a hypothetical example. Suppose most of the nations in the world conclude a multilateral treaty on the subjects of international law, and that one of the provisions of this supposed treaty contains the following language:

> A "nation" consists of reasonably contiguous territory. No nation may claim as any of its territory land that is separated from the bulk of its territory by more than 1000 miles of ocean.

Suppose further that the United States signs this treaty, but fails to ratify it because it realizes that ratification would mean that its fiftieth state would be forfeited. Is there any process known to international law whereby other states, by entering into a treaty, may deprive the United States of Hawaii? To be sure, the treaty provision I have invented looks generalizable—as does article 6 of the Geneva Convention regarding the equidistance principle.[125] But the fact that the provision appears to be generalizable into a norm of customary law does not make it in fact so generalizable, because the effect of this particular provision would be to change the title to specific territory. To be sure, the situation would be different if Hawaii were *res nullius* or the continental shelf were *res nullius*. But as I pointed out above, the court explicitly held that the continental shelf was as much part of the territory of a nation as its land above sea level. Thus, no matter how many nations ratified the hypothetical treaty I have suggested, the United States could not be bound thereby unless the United States itself ratified the treaty. A nation cannot be deprived of a portion of its territory (such as its continental shelf) except by its own consent.[126] No matter how innocuous a treaty provision might seem to be, if its effect is to change title to specific territory, it cannot have that effect without the consent of the owner.

Second, Denmark and the Netherlands argued that, although Germany did not ratify the Geneva Convention, international conduct subsequent to the Convention had nevertheless elevated the equidistance principle to a rule of customary law. But now we can see that, given the court's primary holding that title to specific territory is involved in this case, the only way that such title may be transferred other than through the process of explicit consent (and there was no showing at all that Germany consented) would be through the

125. Convention on the Continental Shelf, supra note 120, art. 6 (continental shelf between adjacent or opposite states to use the equidistant median line from baselines, in absence of agreement or special circumstances).

126. Present customary international law requires this result. Of course, international law could change. A new norm could come into being, through multilateral conventions that allowed for loss of national territory without the consent of the national owner.

process of special custom, which is indeed a form of implied consent. The concept of a special custom may apply to settle specific questions regarding territory, such as whether "an alleged regional or local custom" settled a question of territorial asylum in the *Asylum Case*,[127] whether specific territorial capitulatory rights existed in Morocco in the *Nationals in Morocco Case*,[128] or whether Portugal had a right of passage or easement over specific Indian territory in the *Right of Passage Case*.[129] In all these cases, specific *opinio juris* on the part of the defendant against whom the rights were asserted had to be proved as part of the plaintiff's (complainant's) case. A proof of such specific *opinio juris* would satisfy Blackstone's original distinction between general and special custom in giving the latter the required element of consent.[130] Hence, the idea of subsequent *opinio juris* in the *North Sea Continental Shelf Cases* was required by the court before it would divest Germany of title to any portion of its continental shelf territory. In a previous article, I attempted to spell out the requirements of special custom at some length, with more detailed references to the preceding cases as well as to the *Anglo-Norwegian Fisheries Case*.[131] The main point of that article bears summarization here: that general custom is entirely distinct from special custom, and that the stringent requirements of proof of the latter (such as a showing of *opinio juris*) should in no way be confused with proof of the former.

Therefore, given its judgment (which I believe was entirely correct) that the continental shelf question was one of title to territory and not fairness of apportionment, the court turned to article 6 as a possible contention—not stated in so many words—that proof of special custom was needed before any change of title could be assumed. (We would expect and insist on the same result in the hypothetical case I gave of Hawaii.) Inasmuch as the court explicitly acknowledged the process of custom generation by treaty, it held only that article 6 was not an example of the generation of general custom. Given the facts of the case and the court's disposition of the matter of title to the continental shelf, the court's remarks on the need for *opinio juris* subsequent to the adoption of the Geneva Convention apply only to this or similar cases of special custom. The use to which Akehurst puts the court's remarks on article 6 is wholly unwarranted.[132]

127. Asylum (Colom. v. Peru), 1950 I.C.J. 265 (Judgment of Nov. 20).

128. Rights of Nationals of the United States of America in Morocco (Fr. v. U.S.), 1952 I.C.J. 176 (Judgment of Aug. 27).

129. Right of Passage over Indian Territory (Port. v. India), 1960 I.C.J. 4 (Judgment of Apr. 12).

130. See 1 W. Blackstone, Commentaries *74–75, *78.

131. Fisheries Case (U.K. v. Nor.), 1951 I.C.J. 114 (Judgment of Dec. 18th). See D'Amato, The Concept of Special Custom in International Law, 63 Am. J. Int'l L. 211 (1969).

132. To be sure, Akehurst prefaced his remarks about the *Continental Shelf Cases* with the qualification, "Despite some ambiguities, the judgment in the *North Sea Continental Shelf* cases supports this [Akehurst's own] view." Akehurst, supra note 79, at 50. But since he leaves the term "ambiguities" undefined, there is only the slightest hint that he may have misconstrued the cases. More significant is Akehurst's own shifting throughout his article between a view of *opinio juris* as an element in the establishment of custom quite apart from any use the customary rule is put to against a third state, and *opinio juris* as a showing by the specific third state against which a rule is being asserted; the latter is what I have argued is only an element of special custom. If it were the

4. *Treaties Into Custom?* It seems to me that the theory that treaties generate customary law stands, at the present writing, upon the following considerations. First, any student of international law reading the literature of the subject, particularly historical texts or the successive editions of a textbook, should conclude that a great many of the rules we now call customary law had their origin as provisions in treaties. Second, as to human rights in particular, treaty law today is clearly the major repository of the rules that we regard as the rules of customary international law of human rights.[133] The most prominent example is perhaps the prohibition against human slavery, as I have already tried to show in this Article; the more recent prohibitions against genocide and torture are also generally regarded as part of customary law. Of course, Lane and Watson seem to regard these latter two, at least, as outside the realm of customary international law binding upon all nations generally. But their position, it would appear, would logically require them to discard all the rules of customary law that have had their origin in treaties, and that would mean nearly all the rules.

Yet, doubts remain that treaties do not of themselves generate custom. Akehurst's position, which I have criticized in the preceding section, probably represents what many, if not most, American and English scholars believe to be the case. The persons sharing Akehurst's stance feel that generalizable provisions in treaties do not give rise instantly, or ipso facto, to customary law binding upon nonparties. I think they feel this way largely because of the "contract" view of treaties that I have previously described, and perhaps in lesser part because they may feel it is unfair in some sense to visit new rules upon states who have not joined (for whatever reason) in the treaty that supposedly creates those new rules. Thus, they might feel that one must view "with caution" the proposition that treaties generate custom, even though they might acknowledge that the process undoubtedly takes place "from time to time."

As much as I acknowledge the reality of these psychological perceptions, the arguments that I have made in the last two decades and continue to make

former, then we would probably have little or no general custom in international law, and we would be reduced to the Soviet conception of consent to each and every rule that is asserted against a state.

133. In any litigated case, counsel will of course cite any and all other possible "sources" of international law in addition to treaties. In Filartiga v. Pena-Irala, 630 F.2d 876 (2d Cir. 1980), for example, the court stated that torture was a violation of international law and cited as support the writings of legal scholars, resolutions of the United Nations General Assembly, the prohibitions against torture contained in the constitutions of various countries, and also, of course, international treaties. But not all of these "sources" are equally persuasive. In particular, resolutions of the General Assembly might on occasion represent political desiderata of a majority of nations but not amount to a statement of "law." See, e.g., Discussion, Contemporary Views on the Sources of International Law: The Effect of U.N. Resolutions on Emerging Legal Norms, 73 Proc. Am. Soc'y Int'l L. 327 (1979). Some writers feel that international law can be shown by an international "consensus." See, e.g., Farer, International Law and Political Behavior: Toward a Conceptual Liaison, 25 World Pol. 430,446 (1973). The problem consists, however, in establishing that the "consensus" exists. Professors Lane and Watson are properly cynical in saying that a consensus on human rights can easily be formed by authors citing each other until something that looks like a consensus emerges. For a restrictive, and perhaps similarly cynical, view of consensus, see D'Amato, supra note 36.

in the present Article stem solely from a conviction that the cautious view in this case is a chimera. No process of treaties "hardening" or "passing" into custom has even been described, much less recorded. Akehurst's attempt to objectify the hardening process (requiring states subsequently to make a statement that they believe a treaty rule has passed into custom—whether or not, Akehurst adds, they actually believe it) again has no real-world exemplar.

Where, then, do we stand? If I am correct in arguing that nothing subsequent to the treaty can be found, or needs to be found, to prove that its generalizable provisions have passed into custom, and if the reader concurs that treaties have furnished us with many if not nearly all the rules of customary law that we now recognize as such, then we are left with two possibilities. The first is that generalizable treaty provisions ipso facto and instantly give us evidence of custom in the same sense that the classic act-conflict-resolution pattern gives us evidence of custom. The second is that such treaty provisions have this effect, but not immediately; some passage of time is required. But how much time? A day, a month, a century? Are there different time requirements for different rules, and if so, how can we discover what they are? These difficulties seem to me to be insuperable, for absent any material thing or process that we can point to subsequent to a treaty that indicates when the treaty rule becomes customary, the time question becomes arbitrary. A "reasonable" time period, however, should perhaps be required so that if two or more states do not like a rule in a treaty signed by other states they may have a reasonable time to enter into a contrary treaty among themselves. Thus, for example, five nations enter into a human-rights treaty that contains a generalizable, yet controversial, provision. Nations *V*, *W*, and *X* do not like this provision and enter into a treaty among themselves that contains the opposite of that provision (i.e., its contradiction). Perhaps we should give *V*, *W*, and *X* time to do this—a reasonable amount of time. If they do not act, then we might say that the first treaty gives rise to customary law.

It should be noted that if *V*, *W* and *X* enter into such a treaty, not only will they carve out a rule for themselves, but their treaty too will generate customary law—a custom that is directly contrary to the custom generated by the first treaty. This is the same process that would occur if some state practices resolved a dispute one way and others, another way; it is like conflicting precedents in domestic law. What an international court might do if faced with conflicting treaties that are argued to generate customary law for a state that is not a party to any of them is a complex question, one that I have previously tried to answer, though the lack of case law on this particular subject makes such enterprises extremely speculative.[134]

Should this "reasonable time" provision be read into the treaty-into-custom process? Perhaps some such provision is all that many scholars would need to secure their concurrence to the proposition that human-rights treaties (among others) by now have generated customary international law binding

134. See D'Amato, supra note 16, at 92–98. See also Onuf, Global Law-Making and Legal Thought, *in* N. Onuf, supra note 44, at 21, 28–29 (critique of D'Amato's theory); D'Amato, What "Counts" as Law?, *in* id. at 79–100 (reply to Onuf).

on all the states. If that is so, my thesis is for the purpose of the present Article complete. There is no doubt that by now nations have had ample opportunity to enter into treaties providing that slavery, genocide, or torture are legal (and perhaps, although one would have to argue each case separately, treaties contradicting other human rights as well). Since no nations have entered into any such treaties, we might conclude that the prohibitions against slavery, genocide, and torture have "passed" into customary international law.

This conclusion of course follows a fortiori if no time is needed for such "passage." Because of the indeterminateness of what would constitute a "reasonable time," and because traditional customary law has no such requirement (the act-conflict-resolution scenario generates custom right away, though of course subsequent contrary practice would modify or change that custom), my own preference would be to acknowledge that generalizable provisions in treaties (especially multilateral treaties) ipso facto generate customary rules. But happily for the purpose of the present essay, this "stronger" version of the thesis is not required.

III. Conclusion

I have tried to show that, through the time-honored process of the generation of customary law by generalizable treaty provisions, international entitlements have arisen that prohibit any nation from engaging in acts of genocide against its own population, or torturing or enslaving any human being. These "human rights," as well as others, may be found in multilateral conventions, but their effect spreads to nonparty states through the customary process of treaty generation of international law. In the second part of this Article, I attempted to defend the thesis of treaty generation of customary law against various contrary contentions that have recently been advanced.

Thus, in the example I gave in the first part of this Article, if *A*, a national of state *X*, is tortured by state *X*, state *Y* has an international-law entitlement against *X* that *X* cease and desist the torture and pay damages to *A* (the damages may be paid to *Y*, which in turn pays them to *A*, following the procedure in the *Lotus Case*[135]). *A*, as it turns out, is an "international" of state *Y* just as he is a "national" of state *X*. If international law provides for "implementation and compliance" for *A* as *X*'s national, it provides, *the same* sanctions for *A* as *Y*'s "international" in those areas secured by the customary law of human rights. As a national of *X*, *A* has certain rights when he is visiting in states other than *X*. As an "international" of *Y*, he has a different set of rights against all states including state *X* when he is back home. These latter rights are precisely those that have been articulated and

---

135. S.S. "Lotus" (Fr. v. Turk.), 1927 P.C.I.J., ser. A, No. 9, at 4 (Judgment of Sept. 7). Although France was the complaining state, and although under traditional theory France was itself complaining of an injury (which might or might not be measured in terms of the damage to its injured citizen), the question posed to the court by the parties indicated that if the court found against Turkey, the citizen, a Lieutenant Demons, would be paid (either directly by Turkey or through the good offices of France); the question was "what pecuniary reparation is due to M. Demons?" Thus, as early as 1927, the real party in interest was the injured person, M. Demons.

protected in the generalizable provisions of treaties, particularly multilateral conventions, dealing with various aspects of human rights. To be sure, these international human rights are defeasible if other conventions are entered into that deny such rights. As of the present writing, I know of no international conventions that contradict the various "human rights" conventions, but we must recognize the possibility that, as far as international entitlements are concerned, those entitlements may be destroyed by conventions just as they have been created. As in all other arguments in this article, I think we must above all recognize that as far as the states of the world are concerned, what they do—and not what we want them to do—constitutes international law. On this point I agree with Lane and Watson, whose theses I have otherwise devoted this article to refuting.

We must also recognize that many powerful sources—particularly the present administration—oppose the concept of a human rights law.[136] The United States lives under a regime of dedication to law and the Constitution.[137] If what nation *X* is doing to its own citizens in *X* is contrary to international law, American policy makers (or some of them) will feel a pressure to denounce *X* or to cut off military or economic aid to *X*. The President, however, generally likes to have wide discretion to decide politically whether or not to give aid to any foreign nation such as *X* and thus is likely to be predisposed against any *legal* argument that such aid must be curtailed. Naturally, any President will tend to oppose a policy that weakens his personal power and discretion, and thus we may expect resistance from the executive branch to the universality of human rights entitlements. On the other hand, this may be an area where, in the United States at least, international law is ahead of national interests. If the President has an international legal right to complain about what nation *X* does to its citizens, a new area for the legitimate exercise of presidential power has opened up and perhaps it will be filled someday. If and when that happens, commentators will undoubtedly say that we are expressing our national interest in how nation *X* treats its own citizens.[138]

But if it is any small comfort to the admirers of executive discretion, I would also reiterate that entitlements and interests are not the same thing. Although we may be entitled to complain about what nation *X* does to its own citizens in *X*, we may, for other overriding political reasons, not want to show our "interest" in the matter. From a purely personal point of view, with the luxury of not being saddled with foreign-policy-making responsibility, I would consider it a matter of morality that we should protest vigorously against any denial of human rights in any foreign country and take all steps necessary to

---

136. See Garment, Lefever's Fight: Who Owns Issue of Human Rights?, Wall St. J., Mar. 6, 1981, at 18, col. 3.

137. The implications, positive and negative, for human rights are carefully delineated in L. Henkin, The Rights of Man Today 115-22 (1978). See also Bilder, Rethinking International Human Rights: Some Basic Questions, 1969 Wis. L. Rev. 170, 185, 192.

138. See D'Amato, Are Human Rights Good for International Business? 1 N.W. J. Int'l L. and Bus. 22 (1979).

influence that country to abandon its illegal practices. But my concern in the present essay is, I hope, a more objective one: to indicate that even if, for political reasons, we do *not* protest against some violations of human rights in some foreign countries, that does not give any favorable coloring of legality to those foreign practices. Rather, the entitlement remains the same even if the interest is not manifested.

At the present level of academic dialogue on the matter of human rights, it is essential to make sure that despair over the wretched state of human rights around the world does not lead to abandonment of the concept of human rights law. I have tried to demonstrate that the concept remains vital, and that no special change in the relationship of states to one another is needed to implement it. It is true that we cannot legally require the executive to combat human-rights violations in foreign countries. Yet that is only a legal concession—and a relatively small one at that. The most difficult issues in the enforcement of human rights are not issues of law, but of politics—and ultimately, of morality.

Appendix: The Entitlement-Retaliation System at Work

A. *The Iranian Example*

The events surrounding the taking of hostages at the United States Embassy in Teheran in 1979 offer several illustrations of different aspects of the workings of entitlement-retaliation in international law. Although multilateral and bilateral treaties signed by Iran and the United States required Iran to protect American diplomatic and consular personnel against such an attack, and although a similar requirement could be made out under general international law, the Iranian government did nothing by way of protection or intervention.[139] Thus an American entitlement against Iran, requiring the latter to protect American Embassy personnel in Iran, was violated. A second American entitlement was violated when Iran officially endorsed the action of the militants, enabling them to hold the hostages for more than a year.[140]

Were Iran's actions a retaliation for a previous entitlement violation by the United States? Iran took such a position in communications to the International Court of Justice. In a letter of March 16, 1980, the Iranian Minister for Foreign Affairs referred to "more than 25 years of continual interference by the United States in the internal affairs of Iran, the shameless exploitation of our country, and numerous crimes perpetrated against the Iranian people, contrary to and in conflict with all international and humanitarian norms."[141] As far as the court itself was concerned, these vague charges were not specified because Iran refused to participate in the proceedings.[142] The court, as one might have expected, viewed Iran's allegations as part of the "political

139. See United States Diplomatic and Consular Staff in Tehran (U.S. v. Iran), 1980 I.C.J. 3, 6-7, 13-14 (Judgment of May 24) [hereinafter cited as Tehran Hostages Case].

140. See id. at 33-34.

141. Id. at 8.

142. Id. at 20.

context" in which the specific dispute (namely, the taking of American hostages) arose.[143] For our own analytical purposes, the labeling of something as "political" is another way of saying that it has not attained the status of a legal entitlement.

This conclusion would follow, under present international law, even if we were to assume that the Iranian charges could be fully specified and proved. The fact is that the customary international law of human rights has not yet reached the level of implicating foreign governments in such situations. Every government's foreign affairs business consists of encouraging or discouraging the actions of other governments, and it is far too soon in the evolution of international law to expect legal responsibility to attach to any such actions of encouragement or discouragement. However, we should not too readily dismiss the Iranian claim. Perhaps Iran has articulated[144] a norm that now needs, for customary corroboration, supporting instances of international behavior that would generate a new customary rule of international law, to the effect that if a government aids and abets another government that is engaged in human-rights violations, the first government has violated an international norm. However, it is clear that although Iran may have articulated such a norm, the articulation has fallen upon deaf ears. The argument made no impression upon the court or the dissenting Soviet judge.[145] At the present time, the proposed Iranian entitlement is clearly rejected by the world community; hence the international legal system, acting to preserve its present set of entitlements, has responded almost uniformly with outrage at the Iranian endorsement of the militants' seizure of American embassy personnel. This seizure was therefore seen to be not in retaliation for a previous entitlement violation, but rather itself an illegal violation of an American entitlement.

Given Iran's violation of the American entitlement of the safety and protection of its diplomatic personnel abroad, let us now consider the posture of the American responses to the Iranian action. Perhaps the most obvious reciprocal entitlement-violation would have been for the United States to seize and hold hostage the approximately 220 Iranian embassy personnel within the United States. Such a move would have satisfied Professor Fisher's criterion of relatedness—the seizure would have been similar in time, place, and manner to the original delict.[146] However, the United States rejected this possibility, reportedly on the ground that it did not want to be accused of following

143. Id.

144. See Fisher, Constructing Rules that Affect Governments, reprinted in Preventing World War III: Some Proposals 342, 348 (Q. Wright, W. Evans & M. Deutsch eds. 1962) (quoted in A. D'Amato, supra note 16, at 74–75).

145. Tehran Hostages Case, supra note 139, at 30 (Judgment of May 24). Compare the discussion by Hermann Kahn about "retortions" and "legal harassment", quoted in B. Weston, R. Falk, & A. D'Amato, International Law and World Order 137–38 (1980).

146. See R. Fisher, supra note 46, at 148–50.

Iran's lead.[147] Instead, the State Department gave Iran five days to reduce the diplomatic staff from about sixty to fifteen and the consulate staffs from a total of 160 to twenty.[148] In light of other alternatives for the United States, to be discussed below, it is interesting to speculate further on why the United States did not do the "obvious" thing and hold Iranian embassy personnel hostage in retaliation for the actions in Teheran. Such an action, I submit, might not be as effective in upholding the entire set of international entitlements as would selecting a different entitlement violation. Instead, what it might do is simply help erode the particular entitlement at issue. The international legal system might lose one of its entitlements instead of protecting it. Crucially, the entitlement would not have been lost through the process of custom, since a change in custom requires both an initial deviating act and an acceptance of that deviation by the affected state.[149] But a "spreading" entitlement violation of the sort I have just described, though it would lead to a loss of the general rule of diplomatic immunity, would not have been effected by acquiescence on the part of the affected states but rather by their attempt—futile in the premises—to secure the original norm. Hence, there is some theoretical support for taking a position contrary to the strategic suggestion of Professor Fisher—namely, for the international system to secure its entitlements by allowing the affected nation to retaliate against a *different* entitlement.[150]

Accordingly, the United States considered several other violations of Iran's entitlements when it became clear that the government of Iran was not immediately going to return the hostages.[151] The options considered ranged from a naval blockade of the Kharg Islands[152] to precision strikes against other oil installations.[153] Although the threats certainly served a purpose, helping to ensure the safety of the hostages, the United States made it clear on numerous occasions that military action would be taken if the hostages were harmed.[154] Anyone reading the media accounts cannot fail to be impressed with the fact that practically no objection was raised to the legality of such possible actions. The discussion instead focused upon possible Iranian retaliation against the hostages and the possible adverse reaction of public opinion in

147. "From the start of the crisis, American officials had considered various ways of retaliating against Iranian diplomats. The possibility of holding them hostage was rejected. The United States did not want to be accused of following Iran's lead." N.Y. Times, Dec. 13, 1979, at A1, col. 5.

148. Id.

149. See A. D'Amato, supra note 16, at 87–98.

150. The slow refinement of customary laws through the centuries indicates that the international system protects its customary entitlements, allowing them to change by custom (since that is the process by which they were created) but is careful lest they change by the destructive process of spreading entitlement violations. For a discussion of the factors supporting and reinforcing custom, see id. at 169–229.

151. See Halloran, A Five-Foot Shelf of Iran "Contingencies," N.Y. Times, Nov. 18, 1979, at E4, cols. 3-5.

152. See N.Y. Times, Nov. 22, 1979, at A10, col. 4.

153. Id. at A10, col. 5.

154. See N.Y. Times, Nov. 24, 1979, at 8, col. 1; N.Y. Times, Nov. 25, 1979, at 14, col. 6; N.Y. Times, Nov. 28, 1979, at A10, col. 3.

other Middle Eastern nations.[155] Although not strong evidence, it is at least some evidence of an underlying acceptance of the international systemic mechanism I have described that would allow an entitlement violation (i.e., attacking the territory of Iran) in retaliation for an initial entitlement violation (the taking of the hostages).

Better evidence in support of that mechanism can be found in the reaction to the American military initiative that was taken—the aborted rescue mission of April 24-25, 1980. Iran appears not to have asked for an American apology for the violation of its airspace and territory, and certainly the United States tendered no apology. International reaction in general focused upon criticism of strategy and tactics and seemed to say little if anything about legality.[156] The International Court of Justice stated in its judgment that it "cannot fail to express its concern in regard to the United States' incursion into Iran."[157] However, the court then made it clear that its concern was that the incursion could "undermine respect for the judicial process," since it took place while the court was deliberating and writing its judgment in the case.[158] Other than that, the court pointed out that the question of the legality of the incursion was not before it, and that in any event the operation of April 24th could have "no bearing on the evaluation of the conduct of the Iranian Government over six months earlier."[159]

Here, as is often true of legal analysis, it is more important to consider what the court did rather than what it said. For the court held not only that Iran violated the American diplomatic and consular entitlements, but also that Iran must make reparation to the United States (the form and amount of such reparation to be settled by the court in a future proceeding).[160] Surely the American incursion was relevant to the question of reparation. And the court had direct notice of its relevance, because the Soviet judge, in dissent, made the precise point. Judge Morozov, referring to economic actions by the United States against Iran that "culminated in a military attack on the territory" of Iran,[161] argued that the United States "has forfeited the legal right as well as the moral right to expect the Court to uphold any claim for reparation."[162] Under article 53 of the Statute of the International Court of Justice, the court is required to satisfy itself that an uncontested claim "is well founded in fact and law."[163] Hence there is no doubt that the military incursion was part of the case.

---

155. There was, of course, loose discussion in the media about article 51 of the United Nations Charter, but it is farfetched to say that an armed attack occurred against the United States within the meaning of that article.

156. Keesing's Contemporary Archives, Oct. 24, 1980, 30,534, cols. 1-2.

157. Tehran Hostages Case, supra note 139, at 43.

158. Id.

159. Id. at 43-44.

160. The vote on reparations was 12 to 3, and the vote deciding that the form and amount of reparation shall be settled in the future by the court was 14 to 1. Id. at 45.

161. Id. at 54 (Morozov J., dissenting).

162. Id. at 53.

163. Statute of the International Court of Justice, June 26, 1945, art. 53, 59 Stat. 1055, 1062, T.S. No. 993 at 32, 1976 U.N.Y.B. 1052, 1066. In a recent article, Professor Stein contends that

Thus we have an apparent contradiction. The court in its judgment said that the question of the legality of the incursion was not before it. Yet, as we have seen, the incursion's legality was implicated in the court's holding. We can only conclude, given the court's holding that reparations were owing, that the court necessarily had to find as a logical condition to its holding that the American incursion was legal. In other words, the American incursion was a retaliatory entitlement violation permitted by the international legal system in the face of Iran's initial clear violation of the American diplomatic and consular entitlements.

A further indication that this is what the court actually had in mind is its disposition of the issue whether the United States could rely on its Treaty of Amity, Economic Relations, and Consular Rights of 1955 with Iran.[164] Judge Morozov, dissenting, said that the United States could not rely on this treaty because it had engaged in "military invasion of the territory of Iran, a series of economic sanctions and other coercive measures which are, to say the least, incompatible with notions such as amity."[165] But in the court's opinion:

> However, all the measures in question were taken by the United States after the seizure of its Embassy by an armed group and subsequent detention of its diplomatic and consular staff as hostages. They were measures taken in response to what the United States believed to be grave and manifest violations of international law by Iran, including violations of the 1955 Treaty itself.[166]

Thus the court explicitly acknowledged what I have called retaliatory entitlement violation. Its use of the word "including" in the last sentence above quoted indicates that apart from the 1955 treaty the actions by the United States were justifiable. And, interestingly, even with respect to the treaty itself the United States was not limited to the remedy of being able in turn to disobey its provisions (referred to loosely by Judge Morozov as "amity"), but could continue to invoke the treaty against Iran even in the face of such departures from the treaty. Thus the measures taken by the United States must be interpreted as supporting the treaty and enforcing Iran's obligations under the treaty, rather than simply rendering the treaty void. In effect the court has treated the Treaty of Amity as an entitlement of the United States, which the

---

the only analytical issue in the case regarding the incursion was not whether it was lawful but whether it amounted to a type of contempt of court. Stein, Contempt, Crisis, and the Court: The World Court and the Hostage Rescue Attempt, 76 Am. J. Int'l L. 499 (1982). However, he seems to conclude both that there was and was not contempt of court. The court, he writes, gave a "sharp rebuke" to the United States but did not penalize it, which according to Stein "seems a proper exercise of discretion." Id. at 530. In any event, contrary to Stein's argument, the damage inflicted by the United States was not only upon the court and the integrity of its proceedings, but also upon the territory of Iran. The court, in awarding reparations to the United States, could easily have provided for a set-off in favor of Iran for the actual dollar amount of the damages sustained by Iran as a result of the unlawful incursion. That the court did not do so indicates that it implicitly held the rescue attempt to be lawful.

164. August 15, 1955, United States-Iran, 8 U.S.T. 899, 284 U.N.T.S. 93.

165. Tehran Hostages Case, supra note 139, at 52 (Morozov, J., dissenting).

166. Id. at 28.

latter may uphold by retaliatory entitlement violations against Iran's entitlements under the same treaty.

Most prominent of all the American responses to the hostage crisis was, of course, the freezing of approximately $13 billion of Iranian assets in American banks, American corporations, and American-controlled bank deposits abroad.[167] Whether the freeze was in violation of Iran's international entitlement to use of its own property abroad, and hence an entitlement violation by retaliation in the sense I have been describing, or whether the freeze was legal, remains a difficult question. I will argue that the freeze's legality is a mixed question, and hence to the extent that it was illegal, it was a partial entitlement retaliation.

The legal position of the United States in regard to the freeze was stated by Roberts B. Owen, Legal Adviser to the Department of State, in oral argument to the International Court of Justice on March 20, 1980, in direct response to a question posed by Judge Morozov requesting explanation of the freeze.[168] First, Mr. Owen argued that the freeze was a direct response to the Iranian threat suddenly to withdraw all Iranian funds from United States banks. The threat "constituted nothing less than an attack on the stability of the world economy and the international monetary system."[169] Legally, this is perhaps an explanation, but hardly a justification. It constitutes a political statement designed to elicit sympathy for the United States in international banking circles, but clearly if Iran had a right to withdraw its money the consequences to the stability of the international monetary system would simply be a price that system would have to pay for allowing Iran to build up such significant reserve assets. Second, Mr. Owen referred to the Iranian threat to repudiate obligations owed to the United States and its nationals:

> In response to Iran's efforts to harm the U.S. economy and the dollar, and having in mind Iran's unlawful detention of American hostages, the President of the United States simply froze all Iranian assets in U.S. control for the time being, in part simply to make it possible for U.S. claimants to be made whole if the Government of Iran carried through with its threats to repudiate all of its obligations to such claimants.[170]

The freezing of assets to guard against repudiation of obligations by Iran is akin to an attachment proceeding in a judicial action, and thus if we regard the entire Iranian situtation as a "case," perhaps the United States acted legally to secure its legitimate expectations. Even if one were to object that the totality of claims that could be asserted against Iran would fall short of $13 billion—and thus the United States blocked more than was necessary—a

---

167. Although the exact figure has been disputed, the $13 billion amount is generally used as a rough measure. See Nickel, Battling for Iran's Frozen Billions, Fortune, Dec. 15, 1980, at 117.

168. Dep't St. Bull., May, 1980, at 56.

169. Id.

170. Id.

rejoinder to that contention could be made to the effect that the hostages themselves might have significant claims for false imprisonment and even maltreatment if that were later revealed. But even with Mr. Owen's argument, as augmented, we still find his phrase "having in mind Iran's unlawful detention of American hostages," which indicates a retaliatory motivation for the freeze. Additionally, nothing was mentioned about interest on the $13 billion that was frozen. Since the money was blocked for more than a year and prevailing interest rates were approximately fifteen percent, there is perhaps as much as $2 billion of interest unaccounted for in the legal arguments before the court. Was the United States threatening to confiscate the "interest" on the frozen assets? If so, that would amount to a violation of an Iranian entitlement. (What happened in the end was that, with the return of the hostages, the United States remitted to Iran, as part of the agreed settlement, an initial interest payment of $800 million.[171] But this was clearly ex post the legal question.)

As matters turned out, the United States "unfroze" the assets in return for the safe delivery of the hostages. The judicial question of whether the freezing of the assets was in whole or in part a violation of an Iranian entitlement thus became moot. Nevertheless, to the extent that my claim that the freeze was a partial violation of an Iranian entitlement is convincing, the fact that it occasioned such little comment from the rest of the world or the International Court of Justice tends to support the legitimacy of the concept of entitlement retaliation.

A much more dramatic, but equally more controversial, entitlement violation that may have been causally connected with the initial Iranian delict was Iraq's military invasion of Iran in early September 1980. In the first place, and relevant though not critical for my present analysis, the Iraqi invasion in fact helped wind up the hostage problem. According to Lloyd N. Cutler, who was a participant at the highest level in the ultimate negotiations for the release of the hostages, "[i]t took the Iraqi invasion to sharpen Iran's need for arms, spare parts, and money."[172] This linkage between the invasion and Iran's need for the return of its $13 billion in banks controlled by the United States may be taken as a response by two members of the international community (the United States and Iraq, acting of course separately) which had the effect of upholding the international norm of diplomatic and consular inviolability. For the effect of their separate efforts was to secure the release of the hostages, quite apart from any motivation on the part of Iraq to help the United States in this particular way. Indeed, any such motive was probably farthest from the minds of the Iraqi leaders, as far as we can know such things. But the international legal system is not explainable on the basis of crude psychological guesses about the motivation of national leaders; objective reality is the only criterion for law-determination.[173] Putting speculations

171. N.Y. Times, Jan. 21, 1981, at A9, col. 1.

172. Cutler, Negotiating the Iranian Settlement, 67 A.B.A. J. 996, 996 (1981).

173. See D'Amato, The Content of International Law as Psychological Data, 10 Colum. J. Transn'l L. 66, 72–77 (1971).

about motive aside, the fact remains that the Iraqi invasion contributed to the relief that the United States sought from Iran for Iran's initial delict.

My second point will be far more controversial. I contend that if we can step back and take a broad historical perspective, we might well conclude that the Iraqi invasion of Iran was legally related to the Iranian violation of the American diplomatic and consular entitlement. Indeed, we might conclude that it was an example of retaliatory entitlement violation. If we can sort out large international movements from the small zigs and zags that preoccupy most present observers, I believe we can recognize that the international legal system itself (acting of course through the states) has attempted to preserve entitlement equilibrium and has done so by allowing the Iraqi invasion as an example of retaliatory entitlement violation.

In support of this proposition, I contend that the initial delict by Iran was universally regarded as an outrageous attack upon a key international entitlement.[174] More importantly, Iraq's invasion of Iran for purposes of territorial aggrandizement, flying in the face of every international prohibition from the Kellogg-Briand Pact[175] to article 2(4) of the United Nations Charter, actually seemed acceptable to the world community. In Professor Falk's words:

> In September 1980, we witnessed for the first time since World War I an example of one country attacking another—Iraq attacking Iran—while the world looked on with indifference. Both superpowers have suggested that this is a context where noninvolvement is the appropriate response. Nor has a dissident voice of any significance been raised in the United Nations or elsewhere in international society. To me, this represents a monumental, unacknowledged retreat from the post-World War I notion that aggression is the most severe form of disruption of international life . . . .[176]

Falk goes on to give some "opportunistic reasons" for the indifference of the world community, but he hardly finds these persuasive.[177] Thus, under Falk's theory, we might have in the Iraq invasion something that is unexplained, unexplainable, totally illegal, and hence a "gap" in the theory of international relations and international law. On the other hand, the theory I have been suggesting in this essay constitutes, I contend, a full explanation. The "wound" inflicted by Iran upon a critical international entitlement was so deep, so much in need of redress, and so shocking—no nation had ever before ratified the imprisonment of foreign diplomats—that the international community mentally branded Iran an "outlaw" and was willing to tolerate a

174. See Dep't St. Bull., May, 1980, at 46. Iran's official endorsement of the seizure of the diplomats, supra note 139, seems to be the first such official endorsement in modern history, an historical factor contributing to the outrage of the international community.

175. Pact of Paris, Aug. 27, 1928, 46 Stat. 2343, T.S. No. 796, 94 L.N.T.S. 57. Though eclipsed by the United Nations Charter, the Kellogg-Briand Pact retains its validity.

176. Falk, Some Thoughts on the Decline of International Law and Future Prospects, 9 Hofstra L. Rev. 399, 399 (1981).

177. Id. at 400–03.

severe violation of one of Iran's basic entitlements in retaliation therefor, no matter who inflicted it. Iran, in the international systemic sense, got what it deserved.

Admittedly, any political realist might object to my theory on the ground that "international law" is not as important as I make it out to be and that certainly Iraq of all countries was not interested in making Iran respect international law. My reply, briefly, is that no one knows exactly how important international law is, but we do know that it has persisted through the centuries and further, that while Iraq may not have had anything in mind about international law and may have attacked Iran simply for territorial expansionist purposes, the important point is the reaction of the world community to that attack. If my theory is correct, Iraq's attack would have been condemned by the world community in no uncertain terms but for Iran's seizure of the hostages. But given that seizure, Iraq's attack was viewed as permissible under international law (just as the possible American military retaliations upon Iranian territory, which I discussed previously, might have been viewed with equal indifference by the world community although they were not carried out by the United States because of its fear for the lives and safety of the hostages).

Even though the reader might find it difficult to accept naked aggression by Iraq as permissible under international law, I would suggest that my theory actually upholds article 2(4) and the general prohibition against aggression, whereas Professor Falk's view would undermine that same prohibiton. For those who share Falk's view, Iraq's invasion is a direct violation of an international norm, and the fact that the world community has greeted it with indifference means that the international norm against aggression is on its way to being replaced, via the processes of customary-law formation resulting from state practice accepted by the international community, with a contrary norm—that such aggression is no longer illegal. Indeed, Professor Falk seems to draw such a conclusion and goes on to view the future with great apprehension—and has dire forebodings as well for the role of international law itself.[178] Quite to the contrary, I argue that the Iraqi invasion occasions no such violation of the international norm against aggression, but rather is a function of the "implementation and compliance" problem we have been

178. See Falk, The American Society of International Law: 75 Years and Beyond, 1981 Proc. Am. Soc. Int'l L.; D'Amato, Comment on Professor Falk's Remarks, id. at (forthcoming). The argument I give in the text may be supported by the following additional consideration by way of analogy. In the event of a violation of article 2(4), the United Nations, acting through the Security Council, has the right to send in an international army to maintain and restore international peace and security (article 42). Such an action by the United Nations army, of course, would not violate 2(4). I suggest that, in the absence of such Security Council procedure, the world community considered Iraq's military action against Iran as privileged in the same sense that the Security Council's action might be. Naturally, the reader is free to reject this analysis, in which case I rest my argument concerning reciprocal entitlement violation on the other examples given in the present section of the Article.

addressing that the international legal system, in looking out for its own preservation, allows in the name of restoring entitlement equilibrium. Hence, although my theory "justifies" the Iraqi invasion in legal terms (personally I deplore the aggression), the consequence of my theory is to preserve intact the international entitlement of every nation against external military invasion of its territory. If this consequence did not follow, I suggest that the world community would not have been indifferent to the Iraqi invasion.

B. *The Namibian Example*

Our investigation of the Iranian situtation in entitlement terms has revealed several aspects of the entitlement-retaliation system, and there is no need to multiply examples for their own sake. However, the gradual emergence of Namibia toward independent statehood deserves brief comment because, absent the international entitlements system, it would be inexplicable.[179]

When South West Africa was given over as a class C mandate to South Africa in 1920, South Africa proceeded to administer the territory as a fifth province and practically to ignore the admittedly vague provisions of the mandate.[180] The mandate provided only the loosest "internationalization" of South West Africa, a frail juridical link to the international legal system. Nations other than South Africa had an entitlement, through the mandate, only to the effect that South Africa itself was required to act for the best interests of the inhabitants of the territory. After the Second World War, South Africa refused to turn the mandate over to the new trusteeship system of the United Nations, and when the League of Nations was formally dissolved in 1946 the juridical link between South West Africa and the world community became even more attenuated. South Africa, through the Odendaal Report, began to plan for *Bantustans*, or homelands, in South West Africa, though the plan upon analysis was sufficiently discriminatory as arguably to violate South Africa's mandatory obligations to the native inhabitants of the territory.[181] Other nations, fearful that South Africa would formally annex the territory, kept up the pressure by a series of United Nations General Assembly resolutions, requests to the International Court of Justice for advisory opinions, and in 1966, a compulsory-jurisdiction proceeding in that court (which proceeding, however, ended in a procedural victory for

179. As of the present writing, Namibia is certainly not independent. But neither is it a mere "fifth province" of South Africa. Apartheid has been legally removed, a multiracial coalition controls the National Assembly, and a one-person/one-vote election process has at least been authorized even though there is no short-term hope of democratic elections (at present the stumbling block is supervision and control over such elections).

180. See The South West Africa/Namibia Dispute 75–88 (J. Dugard ed. 1973); Rovine & D'Amato, Written Statement of the International League for the Rights of Man Filed with the International Court of Justice in the Namibia Question, 4 N.Y.U. J. Int'l. L. & Pol.335, 343–49 (1971).

181. See D'Amato, The Bantustan Proposals for South-West Africa, 4 J. Mod. African Stud. 177 (1966); D'Amato, Apartheid in South West Africa: Five Claims of Equality, 1 Portia L.J. 59 (1966).

South Africa).[182] Disappointing as these initiatives were individually, their total effect was to keep underlining the tenuous link between the world community and South West Africa. Perhaps a few hundred years ago such a link would have been ignored by a nation like South Africa for the juridical construct it undoubtedly was, yet such a course of action was not realistically possible for South Africa in recent decades. It was not possible, I contend, because formal incorporation or annexation of the territory by South Africa would have opened up South Africa to retaliatory entitlement violation by other nations.

The entitlement retaliation I have in mind is not the application of "sanctions" against South Africa. For the latter, in the form of economic boycotts, have been in recent years a constant. They would have been applied against South Africa for its apartheid policies whether or not South West Africa was a mandate, or an independent nation, or an integral part of the South African Republic. Despite the occasional talk that the sanctions policy has been the factor in keeping South West Africa independent,[183] clearly when it is analyzed as a constant, no such power can be attributed to it.[184]

Rather, the gradual emergence of Namibia as an independent state must be attributed to South Africa's self-perceived stake in the entire set of international entitlements. Without those entitlements that enable it to proclaim sovereignty within its own boundaries, that proclaim it as an equal member among nations with equal claims to territorial integrity and political independence, South Africa would be jeopardizing its very existence. It would be vulnerable to the same sort of international indifference that greeted Iraq's invasion of Iran. Hence, South Africa has maintained a careful regard for international entitlements, argued its cases thoroughly and well before the International Court of Justice, objected to all U.N. resolutions directed against it (the objections, as I earlier argued, were of crucial importance in defeating a consensus claim[185]), and refrained from incorporating South West Africa. Instead, it has let the weak mandate entitlement gradually sever the territory administratively from the Union—an underlying corroboration, I maintain, for the efficacy of international law's "implementation and compliance" of its set of entitlements.

---

182. See D'Amato, Legal and Political Strategies of the South West Africa Litigation, 4 L. Trans. Q. 8, 20-22 (1967), reprinted in segments in *The South West Africa/Namibia Dispute*, supra note 180, at 220-21, 279-80, 281-90.

183. See, e.g., Burns, South-West Africa, an Orphan Pretoria Can No Longer Keep, N.Y. Times, Aug. 15, 1976, § 4, at 3, cols. 1-3.

184. See R. Fisher, supra note 46, at 67.

185. See D'Amato, supra note 36, at 117-21.

Part II
Politics

[3]

International Human Rights and Cultural Relativism

FERNANDO R. TESÓN*

Notre conception des droits de l'homme ne varie pas selon les latitudes ni selon les circonstances.[1]

I. INTRODUCTION

We are witnessing an unequivocal process of universalization of the concern for human dignity.[2] As international law becomes more responsive to the demands for individual freedom, however, it necessarily challenges the validity of certain state practices reflecting geographical and cultural particularities. The tension between national sovereignty and the enforcement of international

---

* Associate Professor of Law, Arizona State University. J.D. 1975, Universidad de Buenos Aires; Licencié en Droit International 1982, Université Libre de Bruxelles; currently S.J.D. candidate, Northwestern University. This article grew out of a presentation delivered to the Conference on Third World Legal Studies at Harvard Law School in December 1983. I am grateful to my colleagues David Kaye and David Kader for their valuable suggestions. The remaining mistakes are only mine.

1. President Francois Mitterand on the eve of his trip to the Soviet Union, Le Monde, May 17, 1984, at 1, col. 5. ("Our conception of human rights does not vary with latitudes or with circumstances.") [trans. by eds.].

2. For a survey of the literature dealing with what has been, in the words of Professor Sohn, a true "human rights revolution," Sohn, The New International Law: Protection of the Rights of Individuals Rather than States, 32 Am. U.L. Rev. 1 (1982), see Vincent-Daviss, Human Rights Law: A Research Guide to the Literature-Part I: International Law and the United Nations, 14 N.Y.U. J. Int'l L. & Pol. 209 (1981); Vincent-Daviss, Human Rights Law: A Research Guide to the Literature-Part II: International Protection of Refugees, and Humanitarian Law, 14 N.Y.U. J. Int'l L. & Pol. 487 (1982); Vincent-Daviss, Human Rights Law: A Research Guide to the Literature-Part III: The International Labor Organization and Human Rights, 15 N.Y.U. J. Int'l L. & Pol. 211 (1982) [hereinafter collectively cited as Vincent-Daviss, Human Rights Law Research Guides].

human rights standards is highlighted when governments point to national cultural traditions to justify failures to comply with international law.[3] States espousing such positions have found invaluable allies not only in Third World writers,[4] but also among certain Western legal scholars,[5] anthropologists, and philosophers.[6]

"Cultural relativism" is not a term of art, nor even a legal term. It has been borrowed from anthropology and moral philosophy, a fact that has several consequences. First, because an intimate link exists between the moral and legal dimensions of relativism,[7] both the philosophical aspects of relativism and the status of that doctrine in positive international law will be discussed. Second, the theory of cultural relativism has several different possible meanings.[8] While the core idea of cultural relativism will be discussed and critiqued,[9] arguments that relativists could or should advance will also occasionally be anticipated, even though such arguments may not yet have been articulated by relativist scholars or governments.

In the context of the debate about the viability of international human rights, cultural relativism may be defined as the position according to which local cultural traditions (including religious, political, and legal practices) properly determine the existence and scope of civil and political rights enjoyed by individuals in a given society.[10] A central tenet of relativism is that no transboundary le-

---

3. See, e.g., the statement made by the Saudi Arabian representative to the United Nations, 32 U.N. GAOR C.3 (43rd mtg.) at 11-13, U.N. Doc. A/C.3/32/SR.43 (1977) (different social, cultural, and political traditions justify different interpretations of human rights).

4. See, e.g., Wai, Human Rights in Sub-Sahara Africa, in Human Rights: Cultural and Ideological Perspectives 1 (A. Pollis & P. Schwab eds. 1979) (claiming that Western-oriented human rights notions embodied in the U.N. Charter and the Universal Declaration on Human Rights may not be applicable in non-Western areas); Mani, Regional Approaches to the Implementation of Human Rights, 21 Indian J. Int'l L. 96, 97 (1981).

5. A recent work by E. McWhinney, United Nations Law Making (1984), bears the following subtitle: Cultural and Ideological Relativism and International Law Making for an Era of Transition.

6. See, e.g., M. Herskovits, Man and His Works 61-78 (1949); E. Westermarck, Ethical Relativity 183-219 (1932).

7. See infra notes 79-84 and accompanying text.

8. See infra notes 85-94 and accompanying text.

9. See infra text accompanying notes 10-13.

10. Many contemporary situations exemplify the tension between domestic cultural imperatives and international norms: mutilation and flogging as criminal punishment (see U.S. Dep't of State, Country Reports on Human Rights Practices 1084 (1981); Marett, Some Medical Problems Met in Saudi Arabia, 4 U.S.A.F. Med. J. 31, 36 (1953)); the circumcision of women (see Dullea, Female Circumcision a Topic at U.N. Parley, N.Y. Times, July 18, 1980, at B4, col. 3.); the subjugation of women (see White, Legal Reform as an Indicator of

gal or moral standards exist against which human rights practices may be judged acceptable or unacceptable.[11] Thus, relativists claim that substantive human rights standards vary among different cultures and necessarily reflect national idiosyncracies. What may be regarded as a human rights violation in one society may properly be considered lawful in another, and Western ideas of human rights should not be imposed upon Third World societies.[12] Tolerance and respect for self-determination preclude crosscultural normative judgments. Alternatively, the relativist thesis holds that even if, as a matter of customary or conventional international law, a body of substantive human rights norms exists, its meaning varies substantially from culture to culture.[13]

The critique advanced here of cultural relativism shall be limited in several important ways. First, the paper will only deal with violations of civil and political rights—the so-called "first generation" rights. Cultural relativism will not be analyzed in relation to other human rights that may be part of international law, such as the socioeconomic or "second generation" rights.[14] Second, cultural

---

Women's Status in Muslim Nations, in Women in the Muslim World 52 (L. Beck & N. Keddie eds. 1978); Marshall, Tradition and the Veil: Female Status in Tunisia and Algeria, 19 J. Mod. African Stud. 635, 632-37 (1981)); and various authoritarian methods of government (see Note, Human Rights Practices in the Arab States: The Modern Impact of Shari'a Values, 12 Ga. J. Int'l & Comp. L. 55, 92 (1981) (Shari'a values established a philosophical foundation for human rights abuses)). All of these examples of contemporary practices, while clearly unlawful by international standards, are defended by some as being required or permitted by cultural traditions. See also the discussion of the Iranian position on human rights in E. McWhinney, supra note 5, at 210.

11. Since the main concern of international human rights is the position of the individual vis-á-vis the government, the expression "human rights practices" encompasses, in addition to governmental acts, actions by groups or individuals that governments tolerate or condone (e.g., religious practices carried out by the clergy and tolerated by the state).

12. See supra note 4.

13. See Pollis, Liberal, Socialist and Third World Perspectives on Human Rights, in Toward a Human Rights Framework 1, 23 (A. Pollis & P. Schwab eds. 1982) (arguing that human rights judgments ought to be determined "by the criteria set by the philosophic/cultural/ideological roots of particular states"); Said & Nasser, The Use and Abuse of Democracy in Islam, in International Human Rights: Contemporary Issues 61 (J. Nelson & V. Green eds. 1980) ("freedom exists in Islam as long as it serves the interest of the community").

14. For a complete though somewhat uncritical account of the evolution and meaning of the different "generations" of rights in the United Nations, see Sohn, supra note 2, and references cited therein. The so-called "third generation" of human rights are the "solidarity" rights. The advocacy of this new set of rights may represent an attempt to use the favorable emotive connections of human rights language to expand the "rights" of the state at the expense of individual rights. Cf. Alston, A Third Generation of Solidarity Rights: Progressive Development or Obfuscation of International Human Rights Law?, 29 Neth.

relativism must be distinguished from the thesis that governments, especially those of the Third World, may suppress, delay or suspend civil and political rights in an effort to achieve a just economic order. While the issue of whether socioeconomic rights should in certain situations have priority over civil and political rights has received a great deal of attention in human rights literature,[15] it differs from the problems raised by cultural relativism *stricto sensu*.[16]

The discussion here will be further circumscribed by two assumptions which have solid foundations in international law. The first assumption is that human rights are a substantive part of international law, not only as a matter of treaty, but also as part of customary law.[17] It follows that arguments premised upon the ex-

---

Int'l L. Rev. 307, 321 (1982) (proponents of such rights have a strong burden of proof to show that they are compatible with and do not devalue existing rights).

15. See Forsythe, Socioeconomic Human Rights: The United Nations, the United States and Beyond, 4 Hum. Rts. Q. 433, 434-45 (1982); Zalaquett, An Interdisciplinary Approach to Development and Human Rights, 4 B.C. Third World L.J. 1, 28-31 (1983). Unlike "solidarity" rights, socioeconomic rights represent a positive force in the fight to enhance human dignity. However, the emergence of socioeconomic rights need not entail the demise or contraction of civil and political rights. It should be noted that authoritarian regimes, whether Marxist or not, invariably defend the priority of socioeconomic rights. See Forsythe, supra, at 434. The U.N. majority appears to take the position that socioeconomic rights deserve as much attention as civil and political rights. See G.A. Res. 34/46, 34 U.N. GAOR Supp. (70th mtg.) at para 4, U.N. Doc. A/Res. 34/46 (1979). The philosophical literature has devoted considerable attention to the priority issue since the publication of John Rawls' A Theory of Justice (1971). Rawls suggests a "lexical" order between civil and political freedoms on the one hand and economic principles of justice on the other. Id. at 243-50. Some of the numerous responses to Rawls' solution of the priority problem include B. Barry, The Liberal Theory of Justice ch. 8 (1973), and Hart, Liberty and Its Priority, in Reading Rawls 230 (N. Daniels ed. 1975).

16. The position that socioeconomic rights should have priority over civil and political rights need not embrace cultural relativism. The relativist thesis states that *cultural* standards—and not economic development or the need to implement distributive justice—determine the extent and nature of human rights. A government that justifies human rights deprivations by appealing to economic priorities may well reject cultural relativism. Some of the arguments marshalled in this article, however, are also directed to the thesis of the priority of socioeconomic rights. See infra notes 121-26 and accompanying text.

17. See H. Lauterpacht, International Law and Human Rights 147-52 (1950) (human rights provisions of the U.N. Charter are binding). Accord Haile, Human Rights, Stability and Development in Africa: Some Observations on Concept and Reality, 24 Va. J. Int'l L. 575, 581 (1984). See also M. McDougal, H. Lasswell & C. Chen, Human Rights and World Public Order 7-27 (1980) (human rights are binding as a result of the *combined* effect of treaties, U.N. resolutions, diplomatic intercourse, and the impressive rise of awareness of the problem in world opinion); D'Amato, The Concept of Human Rights in International Law, 82 Colum. L. Rev. 1110, 1128-49 (1982) (human rights have become part of customary international law through the process of generalization of treaty provisions). On the other hand, some commentators deny that human rights are part of international law. See, e.g.,

clusively municipal nature of human rights law are inconsistent with present international law.[18] The cultural relativist may, but need not, disagree with this assumption. He need only hold that the various freedoms have different meanings when applied to different societies.[19] Some relativists would even agree that a few basic human rights, such as the right to life and the freedom from torture, are absolute in the sense that even cultural traditions may not override them. But relativists do not regard other rights, such as the right to physical integrity, the right to participate in the election of one's government, the right to a fair trial, freedom of expression, freedom of association, freedom of movement, or the prohibition of discrimination, as required by international law.[20] While I assume that the core meaning of international human rights law encompasses rights beyond the right to life and to freedom from torture, I do not attempt to prove this assumption. Rather, my main thesis can be condensed into the following two propositions:

a) If there is an international human rights standard—the exact scope of which is admittedly difficult to ascertain—then its meaning remains uniform across borders.

b) Analogously, if there is a possibility of meaningful moral discourse about rights, then it is universal in nature and applies to all human beings despite cultural differences.

The second assumption made in this paper is that an obligation in international law indeed exists to respect the cultural identities of peoples, their local traditions, and customs.[21] For example, the

---

Lane, Demanding Human Rights: A Change in the World Legal Order?, 6 Hofstra L. Rev. 269 (1978); Watson, Normativity and Reality in International Human Rights Law, 123 Stetson L. Rev. 221 (1984); Watson, The Limited Utility of International Law in the Protection of Human Rights, 1980 Am. Soc'y Int'l L. Proc. 1.

18. See L. Goodrich, E. Hambro & A. Simmons, Charter of the United Nations 370-78 (1949); M. Rajan, The Expanding Jurisdiction of the United Nations 98-123 (1982).

19. See, e.g., Pollis, supra note 13, at 22-23.

20. See Murphy, Objections to Western Conceptions of Human Rights, 9 Hofstra L. Rev. 433 (1981).

21. See Declaration on Principles of International Law Concerning Friendly Relations and Co-operation among States in Accordance with the Charter of the United Nations, G.A. Res. 2625, 25 U.N. GAOR Supp. (No. 28) at 123, U.N. Doc. A/8028 (1970) ("Every State has an inalienable right to choose its political, economic, social, and cultural systems without interference in any form by another State.") [hereinafter cited as Declaration on Principles].

classical international law on the treatment of aliens has long recognized that Westerners cannot expect to enjoy Western judicial procedures in non-Western states. Arbitral tribunals have consistently refused to accept the claim that partially nonadversary criminal procedures violate the international minimum standard concerning the right to a fair trial.[22]

However, to say that cultural identities should be respected does not mean that international human rights law lacks a substantive core.[23] Such a core can be gleaned from international human rights treaties, both regional and universal,[24] and diplomatic practice, including the relevant practices of international organizations. Indeed, human rights treaties offer a surprisingly uniform articulation of human rights law. They may safely be used as a reference, regardless of how many or which states are parties.[25] The rights, *inter alia*, to life, to physical integrity, to a fair trial, freedom of expression, freedom of thought and religion, freedom of association, and the prohibition against discrimination are all rights upon which international instruments agree. Unless one wishes to give up the very notion of an international law of human rights altogether, these rights should have essentially the same meaning regardless of local traditions.[26]

---

22. Salem Case (Egypt v. U.S.), 2 R. Int'l Arb. Awards 1161, 1197 (1932); McCurdy Case (U.S. v. Mexico), 4 R. Int'l Arb. Awards 418 (1929).

23. Schachter, The Charter and the Constitution: The Human Rights Provisions in American Law, 4 Vand. L. Rev. 643, 652 (1951). Cf. M. McDougal, H. Lasswell & C. Chen, supra note 17, at 5-6 (while different peoples may assert human rights demands in different modalities, a universal insistence on certain basic values exists among all cultures); Kader, Book Review, 1980 Ariz. St. L.J. 815, 825 (1980) ("The challenge confronting the human rights movement . . . is to recognize and take into account the sociopolitical differences in the world and yet to resist the relativism which is incompatible with the promotion of universal standards of human rights.").

24. See, e.g., African Charter on Human Rights and Peoples' Rights, Organization of African Unity, O.A.U. Doc. CAB/LEG/67/3 Rev. 5 (Jan. 1981), reprinted in 21 I.L.M. 58 (1982) [hereinafter cited as African Charter]; American Convention on Human Rights, O.A.S. Off. Records OEA/Ser. K/XVI/1.1, Doc. 65 (1969), reprinted in 9 I.L.M. 101 (1970) [hereinafter cited as American Convention]; International Covenant on Civil and Political Rights, G.A. Res. 2200, 21 U.N. GAOR Supp. (No. 16) at 49, U.N. Doc. A/6316 (1966) [hereinafter cited as U.N. Covenant]; European Convention on Human Rights and Fundamental Freedoms, 213 U.N.T.S. 221, 1950 Gr. Brit. T.S. No. 71 (Cmd. 8969) (1950) [hereinafter cited as European Convention].

25. As of December 31, 1983, 78 states are parties to the U.N. Covenant, 21 to the European Convention, and 14 to the American Convention. The African Charter is not yet in force. For the view that the treaties themselves have created human rights obligations to third parties, see D'Amato, supra note 17, at 1127-49 nn.70-74.

26. A growing number of Third World scholars reject the relativist approach. See, e.g.,

I will argue that cultural relativism cannot be reconciled with the recognition in international law of fundamental rights of the individual. Part II will demonstrate that positive international law does not recognize cultural diversity as a justification for the failure to observe human rights. In Part III, I will argue further that ethical relativism is a philosophically untenable position. Part IV includes a brief exposition on and critique of two by-products of relativism: the elitist and conspiracy theories of human rights. Finally, Part V sets forth some general conclusions.

II. CULTURAL RELATIVISM AND INTERNATIONAL LAW

A. *Cultural Relativism and the Structure of International Law*

Some commentators have argued that in the absence of centralized international organs, one cannot give a manageable core of meaning to international human rights norms.[27] It may be suggested along these lines that, because the uniform meaning of human rights advanced by the universalist thesis can be achieved only in conjunction with international bodies having jurisdiction to decide conflicting claims regarding the observance of human rights, relativism best accounts for the realities of contemporary international society.[28] This is not a negligible argument. While some encouraging steps are being taken, mainly in regional settings,[29] there

---

Eisemokhai, Towards Adequate Defense of Human Rights in Africa, 21 Indian J. Int'l L. 141 (1981) (criticizing the failure of African governments to comply with human rights law); Haile, supra note 17, at 584 (African traditions are not inconsistent with international human rights law). Some African leaders have also taken a less relativistic position, at least with regard to basic human rights. See, e.g., the speech of President Julius Nyerere of Tanzania criticizing African nations that refrained from condemning President Idi Amin of Uganda on the grounds that Amin was black, 1979 Keesing's Contemporary Archives 29670A (1979) ("blackness has become a certificate to kill with impunity").

27. See Watson, Legal Theory, Efficacy and Validity in the Development of Human Rights Norms in International Law, 1979 U. Ill. L.F. 609, 626 (1979).

28. Indeed, centralized systems for the protection of human rights aim to give uniform meaning to basic rights and freedoms in countries with disparate cultural and legal traditions. The system established by the European Convention provides a striking illustration. In the *Sunday Times Case*, the European Court of Human Rights held that the ancient British institution of contempt of court as applied by British courts was inconsistent with the freedom of speech guaranteed by the European Convention. Sunday Times Case, 23 Y.B. Eur. Conv. Human Rights 480 (1980) (Eur. Comm'n on Human Rights).

29. The creation of the Inter-American Court of Human Rights represents a major development in the human rights enforcement area, particularly because countries like Argentina have accepted the jurisdiction of the court. See generally Buerghenthal, The Inter-American Court of Human Rights, 76 Am. J. Int'l L. 231 (1982). The Inter-American Human Rights Commission, although not endowed with judicial power, has considerable political weight.

is no doubt that the lack of centralized, compulsive judicial machinery represents a major weakness of current international human rights law.

This argument, however, is open to two fatal objections. First, it proves too much. The lack of courts and enforcement agencies characterizes international law generally, not just the law of human rights. Therefore, the relativist who leaves human rights out of the scope of international law solely because of the absence of adjudicatory and enforcement mechanisms ultimately must deny the legal character of international law altogether.[30]

Second, this view overlooks the way that international law works. Unlike domestic societies where legislatures, courts, and government agencies create law, law in the international arena results from the subtle interplay of claims, counterclaims, actions and omissions of many international actors.[31] Thus, what nations do and say, even if they sometimes do not believe it, becomes part of the raw material from which international law ultimately springs. This observation rings particularly true in the field of human rights, precisely because of the absence of enforcement and judicial bodies. Soviet-bloc countries, for example, cannot join the critics of the Chilean regime without at the same time opening the door to criticisms of their own human rights abuses.[32] The process thus underscores the role of reason in international law. Contrary to what some realists contend,[33] national interest alone cannot support valid international claims. Instead, as is true in all legal discourse, such claims must be supported by principles that are neu-

---

The same can be said of the U.N. Human Rights Commission, although the primary importance of both commissions stems from their position as forums for the open discussion of human rights situations. Governments attach great importance to the debates before the U.N. Human Rights Commission.

30. Although those who deny the "legal" character of international law can point to such venerable authority as John Austin's The Province of Jurisprudence Determined 201 (ed. 1954), this position has been fully discredited by modern scholars. See, e.g., H.L.A. Hart, The Concept of Law 222-25 (1961).

31. McDougal, Lasswell & Reisman, The World Constitutive Process of Authoritative Decision, in The Future of the International Legal Order 73 (R. Falk and C. Black eds. 1969). The "New Haven" approach can be supplemented with the contributions of modern political philosophy. See generally infra notes 79-120 and accompanying text.

32. All of the Soviet-bloc countries voted in favor of the U.N. Resolution on the Protection of Human Rights in Chile, G.A. Res. 3219, 29 U.N. GAOR Supp. (No. 31) at 83, U.N. Doc. A/9631 (1974).

33. See, e.g., H. Morgenthau, Politics Among Nations 5-12 (5th rev. ed. 1978).

tral to individual interests.[34] No authoritative judicial bodies are needed for this process, though it would be preferable to have them. The decentralized nature of international law does not, therefore, preclude the existence of a universal human rights standard.

B. *Cultural Relativism and the Human Rights Conventions*

Supporters of cultural relativism argue that the theory creates a legal defense to the general duty incumbent upon governments to observe international human rights. One should therefore expect to find a provision to that effect in the international legal materials. Yet, virtually nothing in the human rights conventions suggests that the respect for human rights depends upon, or can be modified by, local cultural conditions. The U.N. Covenant, the American Convention, and the recent African Charter[35] do not acknowledge any right of governments to avoid compliance by alleging the priority of local traditions.

The only apparent exception is article 63(3) of the European Convention, which states that "[t]he provisions of this Convention shall be applied in [colonial territories] with due regard, however, to local requirements."[36] If one reads this provision as supporting cultural relativism, the parties would be exempted from enforcing the human rights guaranteed by the Convention in those colonial territories where "local requirements" conflict with the Convention.

The European Court of Human Rights rejected this interpretation in the *Tyrer Case*, which involved corporal punishment, a local tradition, on the Isle of Man.[37] The court found that the word "requirement" embodied the idea of necessity, and that corporal punishment, no matter how accepted by public opinion and practice or enshrined in the traditions of the Isle, was not necessary to maintain law and order and consequently ran afoul of the Conven-

34. The "neutral principles" advocated by Herbert Wechsler in a different context are narrower in scope, since they refer to constitutional review. Wechsler, Towards Neutral Principles of Constitutional Law, 73 Harv. L. Rev. 1 (1959). The concern here, more generally, is with *claims*. The "neutrality" requirement holds even where the principles argued from are incorrect or nonexistent. Cf. D'Amato, supra note 17, at 1125-27 (human rights are entitlements of nations which are universal in nature).

35. See supra note 24.

36. European Convention, supra note 24, art. 63(3).

37. Eur. Ct. Hum. Rts., Tyrer Case, Judgment of 25 April 1978, Series A No. 26.

tion.[38] Further, the court wrote that no local requirement could enable a party to the Convention to make use of a criminal sanction in violation of article 3, which prohibits degrading punishment.[39]

The *Tyrer* opinion thus forcefully supports the idea that human rights are non-negotiable in the sense that not even the force of overwhelming public opinion or state practice may impair them. It also stands for the proposition that international human rights possess a transboundary meaning that cannot be modified or ignored on relativist grounds. The *Tyrer* court noted that article 63(3) of the European Convention,[40] drafted in 1950, had been conceived to meet the European perception about the insufficient degree of civilization of colonial peoples.[41] Although the court did not elaborate on this point, it is doubtful that the relativist interpretation of article 63(3) of the Convention, whereby entire populations are less eligible for protection in the enjoyment of human rights, conforms to the anti-colonialist values embodied in present international law.[42]

In assessing the validity of the relativist doctrine, it is noteworthy that each of the major human rights conventions contains a nondiscrimination clause.[43] The classical interpretation of such clauses holds that a government may not discriminate within its own borders on the basis of race, sex, religion or other impermissible criteria in the enforcement of human rights.[44] The clause is commonly regarded as operating purely within national borders, but a broader interpretation is also possible. The nondiscrimination clause arguably forbids governments to treat individuals in ways that substantially depart from the core of meaning of international human rights law, because such treatment would amount to discrimination vis-à-vis the treatment enjoyed by individuals in other states. In other words, one could argue that an individual's

---

38. Id. at 18.

39. Id.

40. See supra note 24.

41. "The Court notes, in this connection, that the system established by article 63 was primarily designed to meet the fact that, when the Convention was drafted, there were still certain colonial territories whose state of civilisation did not, it was thought, permit the full application of the Convention." *Tyrer Case*, Judgment at 19.

42. Such a construction would amount to an elitist version of relativism. See infra notes 121-26 and accompanying text.

43. See, e.g., African Charter, supra note 24, art. 2; American Convention, supra note 24, art. 24; U.N. Covenant, supra note 24, art. 26; European Convention, supra note 24, art. 14.

44. See, e.g., Belgian Linguistics Case, 11 Y.B. Eur. Conv. Human Rights 832, 862-69 (1968) (Eur. Comm'n on Human Rights).

entitlement to human rights does not depend on the particular traditions of the state in which the individual is located, that national boundaries do not affect the imperative of nondiscrimination.

The thrust of article 1(3) of the U.N. Charter is no different. It states that a major purpose of the organization is to achieve international cooperation in encouraging and promoting "respect for human rights and for fundamental freedoms *for all without distinction as to race, sex, language and religion.*"[45] To interpret the clause "for all" to mean for all individuals on earth, and not just for all individuals within a given state, surely violates neither the letter nor the spirit of the Charter. Suppose, for example, states A and B conclude a human rights treaty that contains a nondiscrimination clause. It is insufficient to say that *within* state A there should be no discrimination based on sex, race, and the like. The nondiscrimination clause must also be read to have a transboundary dimension. Accordingly, the rights enjoyed by individuals in state A cannot differ substantially in content and scope from those enjoyed by individuals in state B. Otherwise the human rights treaty would be redundant, at least insofar as the principle of nondiscrimination already existed in those states as a matter of municipal or constitutional law.[46]

C. *Cultural Relativism and Self-Determination*

One may object to the foregoing analysis on the grounds that human rights treaties only bind the parties,[47] and that the status of cultural relativism in international law cannot be ascertained from treaty analysis alone. It is therefore necessary to determine whether customary international law supports the claims of the cultural relativists. The principles of self-determination and nonintervention offer, at first glance, possible legal support for the rela-

45. U.N. Charter art. 1, para. 3 (emphasis added).

46. Admittedly, the interpretation of the nondiscrimination clause suggested in the text is a novel one. But if we accept that the international legal system primarily entrusts the application of human rights law to states, and if we further accept that individuals are the beneficiaries of such law, then it becomes clear that violations premised upon cultural traditions represent transboundary discriminatory treatment. To put it differently, the relativist contention that freedom of religion, for example, means one thing in the West and a different thing in the Third World, requires a discriminatory application of human rights law.

47. See, e.g., the statement of the Chilean representative to the U.N. General Assembly Third Committee, 31 U.N. GAOR C.3 (46th mtg.) paras. 1-25, U.N. Doc. A/C.3/31/SR.46 (1976) (rejecting case law under the European Convention, supra note 24, regarding the Emergency Clause as irrelevant to the Chilean situation).

tivist doctrine.[48] A closer consideration of these principles reveals, however, that this support is only illusory.

Ascertainment of the precise contours of the self-determination principle is not easy.[49] In addition to the important anti-colonialist aspect of self-determination,[50] an internal dimension appears to exist as well.[51] Article 2 of the Declaration on the Granting of Independence to Colonial Countries and Peoples[52] ("Declaration of Colonial Independence"), widely regarded as embodying customary law concerning self-determination, provides that "[a]ll peoples have the right to self-determination; by virtue of that right they freely determine their political status and freely pursue their economic, social and cultural development."[53]

Commentators espouse two conflicting interpretations of this clause. The democratic, anti-authoritarian view holds that internal self-determination requires internal democracy and respect for the human rights of all peoples.[54] This thesis finds support in the intent of the framers of the U.N. Charter,[55] and arguably reflects a correct reading of the self-determination principle as agreed upon

48. For a brief and lucid account of the role played by self-determination concerns in the development of the Third World's distrust toward the human rights movement, see Nickel, Cultural Diversity and Human Rights, in International Human Rights: Contemporary Issues 43, 43-46 (J. Nelson & V. Green eds. 1980).

49. See generally M. Pomerance, Self-Determination in Law and Practice 1-28 (1982).

50. External self-determination means the right of peoples to decide their international status. It represents an expression of modern anti-colonialist values in the international community. The literature on external self-determination is voluminous. See references in id. at 130-38.

51. See id. at 37 nn.209-11.

52. Declaration on the Granting of Independence to Colonial Countries and Peoples, G.A. Res. 1514, 15 U.N. GAOR Supp. (No. 16) at 66, U.N. Doc. A/4684 (1960) [hereinafter cited as Declaration of Colonial Independence].

53. Id. This provision is echoed by the Declaration on Principles, supra note 21, art. 1 ("all peoples have the right freely to determine, without external interference, their political status and to pursue their economic, social and cultural development"), and by the U.N. Covenant, supra note 24, art. 1 ("All peoples have the right of self-determination. By virtue of that right they freely determine their political status and freely pursue their economic, social and cultural development.").

54. See Moore, Grenada and the International Double Standard, 78 Am. J. Int'l L. 145, 154-56, 165 (1984) (Grenada mission was designed to restore self-determination, in the form of democratic rights, to the Grenadian people); Reisman, Coercion and Self-Determination: Construing Charter Article 2(4), 78 Am. J. Int'l L. 642, 643-44 (1984) ("Ongoing self-determination [works] to increase the probability of the free choice of peoples about their government and political structure."); Rosenstock, The Declaration of Principles of International Law Concerning Friendly Relations: A Survey, 65 Am. J. Int'l L. 713, 732 (1971).

55. See Cassese, The Helsinki Declaration and Self-Determination, in Human Rights, International Law and the Helsinki Accord 83, 84 (T. Buergenthal ed. 1977).

by the European states in the Helsinki Accord.[56] Under this interpretation, the word "freely" means "free from *internal*, as well as from external, interference." The right of self-determination in international law would thus represent an expression of the entitlement of all individuals to democratic representative government and to basic human rights.[57]

The relativist version of the rule embodied in article 2 of the Declaration of Colonial Independence differs radically from the one expressed above. According to this view, internal self-determination represents the flip side of the nonintervention principle: it forbids any state from interfering with the cultural and political choices of autonomous peoples.[58] Self-determination in this sense represents the rights-language version of the duty of nonintervention in internal affairs. People have the right to create whatever form of government they want, no matter how repressive, and human rights claims put forward by other states may not interfere with the fulfillment of this right. Under this view, a people exhausts its right to self-determination when it achieves the status of a sovereign state.[59] Once the people choose a political and cultural system, nothing in international law confers a right to change the system.[60] Under this construction, internal self-determination

56. Id. at 99-105.

57. Some Western states defended this position in the negotiations that led to the 1970 Declaration on Principles, supra note 21. The proposals presented by the United Kingdom and the United States suggested that representative government was essential for the realization of the right to self-determination. See U.N. Doc. A/AC.125/L.44, July 19, 1967 (United Kingdom draft); U.N. Doc. A/AC.125/L.32, Apr. 12, 1966 (U.S. draft). In fact, some support for this position may be found in the final wording of the Declaration on Principles, supra note 21, at 123: "[A]ll peoples have the right *freely* to determine, without external interference, their political status and to pursue their economic, social and cultural development." (emphasis added). Arguably, the word "freely" means "without *internal* interference," or else it would be superfluous. Contra Cassese, supra note 55, at 89-90 (Declaration only requires internal self-determination in cases involving racist regimes or foreign domination, in contrast with the Helsinki declaration).

58. See Mojekwu, International Human Rights: The African Perspective, in International Human Rights, supra note 48, at 89 ("Self-determination . . . would involve the right of a people to take into their hands the full responsibility of determining, without coercion, their own political, economic and cultural destiny."). Obviously, "coercion" here means external coercion. Mojekwu's definition clearly tolerates internal coercion, i.e., human rights violations without foreign interference.

59. This is the official position of Soviet-bloc countries. See Poeggel, 1 Volkerrecht (Manual of International Law of the German Democratic Republic) 270 (1973), cited in Cassese, supra note 55, at 85 n.7.

60. The Soviet Union and its allies defended this view during the 1975 Helsinki negotiations. See Cassese, supra note 55, at 99. This position does not simply reflect tactical "power

means that no state may impose a cultural or political system on people living beyond its borders.[61]

However, this version of internal self-determination is at best a misconception, and at worst it can be a rationalization for oppression. First, a contextual interpretation of the Declaration of Colonial Independence yields a very different result. The preamble of the Declaration recalls the commitment of the peoples of the world to "fundamental human rights" and to "the dignity and worth of the human person."[62] The same argument applies *a fortiori* to the self-determination principle embodied in article 1 of the U.N. Covenant,[63] which exactly reproduces article 2 of the Declaration.[64] The relativist interpretation of article 1 grants people "the right to freely . . . pursue their economic, social and cultural development"[65] even where that pursuit would reduce to meaninglessness the remaining fifty-one articles of the Covenant. A more reasonable approach, consistent with sound treaty interpretation, would dictate that the principle of independent cultural development as a part of self-determination be harmonized with human rights law.[66]

Further, the relativist version of internal self-determination often defines the interests of a people in mystical or aggregative terms that ignore or belittle individual preferences. Such mystical definitions may be articulated in the form of axiomatic "true" interests of peoples, as opposed to real or expressed interests.[67] They

---

politics" devices. It is strongly linked to the Leninist conception that the "true" interest of the people can only be expressed by, and result in, the dictatorship of the proletariat. See M. Pomerance, supra note 49, at 40.

61. The proviso "beyond its borders" is crucial, because according to a widespread view, self-determination does not grant rights (of secession or otherwise) to minorities within a sovereign state. See generally Nanda, Self-Determination under International Law: Validity of Claims to Secede, 13 Case W. Res. J. Int'l L. 257 (1981). Thus, many governments (not only those of the Soviet-bloc) hold the inconsistent view that cultural standards determine the scope of human rights, and that minorities within a sovereign state are not entitled to choose their own political institutions and pursue their independent cultural development.

62. Declaration of Colonial Independence, supra note 52, preamble.

63. U.N. Covenant, supra note 24.

64. See supra text accompanying note 53.

65. U.N. Covenant, supra note 24, art. 1.

66. See, e.g., the draft proposed by the Dutch delegation to the Helsinki conference:

> The participating States recognize the inalienable right of the people of every State freely to choose, to develop, to adapt or to change its political, economic, social and cultural systems without interference in any form by any other State or group of States and *with due respect to human rights and fundamental freedoms*.

Doc. CSCE/II/A/8, cited by Cassese, supra note 55, at 96 (emphasis added).

67. See supra note 60.

may also be expressed as a plain rule of political power, whereby those in power automatically are deemed to represent the people, regardless of whether they have been democratically elected and regardless of their human rights record. Consequently, a relativist would maintain that in Pinochet's takeover in Chile or Ho Chi Minh's takeover in Vietnam, the peoples of Chile and Vietnam exercised their right of self-determination, and that the governments so formed are immune from foreign interference even when they deprive people of human rights. It may well be that self-determination, external or internal, exists only as a collective right that can be exercised jointly by individuals.[68] It is equally true, however, that self-determination is a *human* right, not a right of governments, whether they are headed by charismatic revolutionary leaders or military dictators.[69] Therefore, the right to self-determination must ultimately be ascertained by reference to the wishes and rights of individuals.[70] As Professor Schachter has convincingly argued, the concept of human dignity implies that high priority should be given to individual choices in ways of life, beliefs and the conduct of public affairs.[71] This concept, however, simple as it is, clearly contradicts many existing ideologies and political arrangements.[72]

Finally, a consideration of the concerns which prompted the development of the self-determination principle also leads to a rejection of the relativist thesis. The self-determination principle has traditionally been directed against colonialism and various tangible

68. See Dinstein, Collective Human Rights of Peoples and Minorities, 25 Int'l & Comp. L. Q. 102, 103 (1976).

69. Professor Dinstein aptly cautions that "collective human rights retain their character as direct human rights. The group which enjoys them communally is not a corporate entity and does not possess a legal personality." Id.

70. "The state must protect the individual citizen, its units or atoms; *but the international organization also must ultimately protect human individuals, and not its units or atoms, i.e., states or nations.*" 1 K. Popper, The Open Society and its Enemies 288 n.7 (1966) (emphasis added). See also Luban, The Romance of the Nation-State, 9 Phil. & Pub. Aff. 392 (1980) (arguing against the "rights" emphasized by nationalism). Under the relativist version of internal self-determination, the term "state will" does not mean the sum of the individual wills, because then governments would never act against the popular will—which is obviously not the case. "State will," instead, means what the government decides. Relativism asks us to believe that the government necessarily represents the people, and that the government always acts as a surrogate for the "people." The authoritarianism embodied in this notion of "state will" is clearly incompatible with respect for human rights, and must therefore be rejected.

71. Schachter, Human Dignity as a Normative Concept, 77 Am. J. Int'l L. 848, 849 (1983).

72. Id. at 850.

forms of *foreign* domination.[73] It primarily guarantees to people the right to establish their own government and pursue their cultural development without external interference.[74] Yet external pressure for human rights compliance has nothing to do with colonial domination, imperialism and the other evils against which self-determination was conceived. An analysis of the purposive dimension of self-determination, therefore, provides no support for the relativist doctrine.

As to the nonintervention principle, there is broad support today for the proposition that discussing human rights does not amount to "intervention" within the meaning of article 2(7) of the U.N. Charter,[75] unless one takes the position—discarded at the beginning of this study—that human rights are not part of international law.[76] For the relativist, the nonintervention principle and internal self-determination have identical content. Saying that people may choose whatever government they want is the same as saying that other states may not intervene to criticize human rights violations.[77] Thus, *mutatis mutandi*, the same arguments marshalled in the previous paragraphs apply.[78]

In sum, under international law, all individuals, regardless of their state of origin, residence, and cultural environment, are entitled to fundamental human rights. International law does not relieve governments of the obligation to respect these rights simply because a particular right is inconsistent with local traditions.

---

73. See supra note 50.

74. See generally M. Pomerance, supra note 49, at 9-28. The Declaration of Colonial Independence, supra note 52, emphasizes decolonization and independence, which suggests an "externalist" approach to self-determination.

75. See generally R. Higgins, The Development of International Law Through the Political Organs of the United Nations 118 (1963); Gilmour, The Meaning of "Intervene" Within Article 2(7) of the United Nations Charter—An Historical Perspective, 16 Int'l & Comp. L. Q. 330 (1967).

76. Contra Watson, Autointerpretation, Competence and the Continuing Validity of Article 2(7) of the U.N. Charter, 71 Am. J. Int'l L. 60 (1977). Whether international law supports military intervention to protect human rights under certain circumstances is a far more difficult problem. It is the subject of extensive discussion in my forthcoming S.J.D. dissertation, "Humanitarian Intervention in International Law."

77. See Cassese, supra note 55, at 85-86.

78. See supra notes 47-74 and accompanying text. The Argentine military junta used the principle of nonintervention as its main defense against human rights criticisms. The U.S.S.R. also frequently invokes it. Schreman, Gorbachev Meets the Press: A Bantering Style and an Echo of Krushchev, N.Y. Times, Oct. 5, 1985, at 4, col. 2.

III. Cultural Relativism and Moral Philosophy

This part of the paper addresses the philosophical status of cultural relativism. After outlining the link between human rights law and moral philosophy, I draw a distinction between several types of relativism. Ultimately, I reject relativism on the grounds that it violates formal and substantive constraints of moral discourse.

A. *Moral Philosophy and Human Rights Law*

The law of human rights borrows its language from moral philosophy. From its inception at the end of World War II, the modern international law of human rights has been indissolubly linked with the moral concerns prompted by the Nazi horrors. The statesmen who drafted the U.N. Charter were motivated in part by the moral imperative to restore human dignity and give it legal status, and indeed that moral concern permeates the subsequent development of human rights law.[79]

At the same time, the framers of the Charter also worried about problems of conflict avoidance, peace, security, and maintaining the balance of power. Paradoxically, while national sovereignty continues to be strongly asserted both inside and outside the confines of the United Nations, human rights law has developed impressively.[80] Indeed, reconciling national sovereignty and the international law of human rights remains one of the central challenges of our times.[81] Despite serious problems of enforcement, the dynamism of human rights groups throughout the world and the pressure exerted on delinquent governments by democratic nations has achieved remarkable results, demonstrating that the belief in human rights is not a mere illusion created by scholars, but an effective and living tool for political reform.[82]

---

79. See Sohn, supra note 2, at 9-14.

80. See Vincent-Daviss, Human Rights Law Research Guides, supra note 2.

81. Cf. Delbrueck, International Protection of Human Rights and State Sovereignty, 57 Ind. L. J. 567 (1982) ("[T]he sovereign states not only are creating the international norms for the protection of human rights, but also are determining the process of their implementation—or nonimplementation—according to their sovereign will. Seen from this perspective, state sovereignty and the international protection of human rights appear to be incompatible.").

82. Sometimes the importance of the pressure exerted by democratic governments is erroneously downplayed. I can personally attest that President Carter's human rights policy saved thousands of lives in Argentina. Human rights organizations also play a significant role, despite justified criticisms of occasional one-sidedness. See generally Weissbrodt, Strategies for the Selection and Pursuit of International Human Rights Objectives, 8 Yale J.

Another reason for focusing on moral philosophy is that the concern for human rights did not grow from a desire to force governments to comply with the law "as it is." The world regards human rights violations as a moral wrong of the most serious nature, and presumably continues to condemn such practices even though technically the accused government has not violated any unambiguous positive international obligation. Given the intimate historical and conceptual connection between international human rights law and morality and the current emphasis of some writers on relativism as a supposed basis of the contemporary world order,[83] it is important to examine the conclusions about cultural relativism that can be gleaned from moral philosophy.[84]

B. *Descriptive, Metaethical, and Normative Relativism*

To analyze the moral status of relativism, several types of relativism must be carefully distinguished.[85] First, different societies have different perceptions of right and wrong. This assertion—which may be called "descriptive" relativism—finds support among anthropologists who consider themselves relativists.[86] Although descriptive relativism has been challenged,[87] its validity may be conceded for the purposes of the present analysis.

The second type of relativism, "metaethical" relativism, asserts that it is impossible to discover moral truth. Metaethical relativism may take the form of a thesis about the meaning of moral terms.[88] The relativist can adopt either some version of emotivism[89] or a

---

World Pub. Ord. 62 (1981).

83. See generally E. McWhinney, supra note 5. While McWhinney's conception of relativism is broader, it encompasses the one treated here.

84. The relevance of moral inquiry to international law depends, of course, upon one's particular theory of the relation between law and morality. However, if the relativist concedes that his theory is not supported by independent moral reasoning, he must conclude that cultural relativism, although technically legal, is immoral, and he is therefore logically committed to the reform of international law in the sense of eliminating the relativist defense.

85. See Brandt, Ethical Relativism, in 3 Encyclopedia of Philosophy 75 (P. Edwards ed. 1967).

86. See, e.g., M. Herskovits, supra note 6, at 61-78.

87. The debate centers on whether *fundamental* diversities of ethical views exist in different societies. See Brandt, supra note 85, at 75.

88. Id. at 75.

89. Emotivism holds that moral propositions are no more than interjections or emotive utterances. See generally, A. Ayer, Language, Truth and Logic (1946); C.L. Stevenson, Ethics and Language (1944).

straight nihilist position.[90] A milder version of metaethical relativism contends that there is no valid *method* for moral reasoning—that is, no method that would have, on moral matters, the same persuasive force as scientific method.[91]

Finally, "normative" relativism asserts that persons, depending on their cultural attachments, ought to do different things and have different rights.[92] This is the version of relativism equivalent to the one discussed in Part II of this study.[93] It should be clear that descriptive and metaethical relativism do not logically entail normative relativism. Descriptive relativism operates at a different logical level than its normative counterpart. The anthropologist or descriptive relativist says that different cultures in fact have different conceptions of morality. The normative relativist asserts that individuals of different cultures have different rights, and that they *ought* to do or to abstain from doing different things. It is therefore perfectly possible for the descriptive relativist to concede that different societies have different social practices and conflicting views about morality and yet consider some practices or views morally preferable to others.[94]

The relationship between metaethical and normative relativism is more complex, but the two theories are still logically distinguishable. The metaethical relativist doubts the possibility of demonstrating the correctness of any particular moral principle. As a matter of moral decision, he may reject normative relativism while denying that any moral principle or system is demonstrably correct. To create a framework within which to make moral judgments, the metaethical relativist nevertheless has an option: he may subscribe to the "reflective equilibrium" method suggested by John Rawls.[95] Rawls devised a framework within which to make

90. Nihilism, in this context, holds that moral terms lack any meaning whatsoever.

91. Brandt, supra note 85, at 76.

92. See E. Westermarck, supra note 6, ch. 5; Benedict, Anthropology and the Abnormal, 10 J. Gen. Psych. 59 (1934). Even "relativism" is too charitable a name for this theory, which may properly be called "moral positivism." See the brilliant critique in 2 K. Popper, supra note 70, ch. 12, 392-96.

93. See supra text accompanying notes 10-13.

94. See Douglas, Morality and Culture, 93 Ethics 786 (1983) ("Two conversations are running parallel, one the philosophers', about the rational formulation of ethics, one the anthropologists', about the interaction between moral ideas and social institutions. The conversations, as they are set at the present time, will never converge.").

95. J. Rawls, supra note 15, at 48-51. Of course, the acceptance of reflective equilibrium as a plausible description of moral methodology is completely independent from (a) the acceptance of Rawls' contractarian justification for principles of social justice; (b) the ac-

meaningful moral judgments without encountering the problem of demonstration. He suggests that moral conclusions may be reached by checking one's moral intuitions against one's moral principles with the crucial proviso that both be subject to modification.[96] At the very least, Rawls demonstrates that it is unnecessary to have an infallible method of discovering moral truth in order to speak about the rights all people should enjoy.

C. *Critique of Normative Relativism*

As a moral theory, normative relativism cannot withstand scrutiny.[97] First, its straightforward formulation reflects a fundamental incoherence. It affirms at the same time that (a) there are no universal moral principles; (b) one ought to act in accordance with the principles of one's own group; and (c), (b) is a universal moral principle.[98] David Lyons demonstrated that the typical anthropologists' version of relativism ("an act is right if, and only if, it accords with the norms of the agent's group") does not validate conflicting moral judgments, because each group is regarded as a separate moral realm.[99] Consequently, the incoherence attached to normative relativism springs from the fact that the very assertion of universal relativism is self-contradictory, not from the fact that it validates conflicting substantive moral judgments. If it is true that no universal moral principles exist, then the relativist engages in self-contradiction by stating the universality of the relativist principle.[100] As Bernard Williams observed, this is a "logically un-

---

ceptance of the principles themselves; or (c) the acceptance of his solution to the priority problem. For Rawls' view that "undeveloped" societies may fail to observe human rights in certain situations, see infra note 109.

96. J. Rawls, supra note 15, at 48.

97. Bernard Williams calls relativism "the anthropologists' heresy, possibly the most absurd view to have been advanced even in moral philosophy." B. Williams, Morality: An Introduction to Ethics 20 (1972).

98. Id. at 20-21; Lyons, Ethical Relativism and the Problem of Incoherence, 86 Ethics 107, 109 (1975-76).

99. Lyons, supra note 98, at 109.

100. This problem resembles the one exhibited by ideologism, the theory that everything is ideology, which for some mysterious reason does not apply to itself. This paper will not deal with Gilbert Harman's narrower version of moral relativism because Harman intended for his version to apply only to "inner" judgments, i.e., judgments that someone who had already settled upon a moral code ought or ought not to have acted in a certain way. His theory does not apply to the judgment that a given institution is unjust, which is most relevant for the purposes of this paper. Harman, Moral Relativism Defended, 84 Phil. Rev. 3, 4 (1975). See the critique of Harman's theory by Copp, Harman on Internalism, Relativism and Logical Form, 92 Ethics 227 (1981-82).

happy attachment of a nonrelative morality of toleration or noninterference to a view of morality as relative."[101]

However, this objection over the incoherence of normative relativism is not decisive. Normative relativism can be reformulated to avoid the threat of incoherence as follows: (a) there are no universal moral principles, save one; (b) one ought to act in accordance with the principles of one's own group; and (c) the only universal moral principle is (b).[102] Yet, if the normative relativist is also a metaethical relativist, he cannot justify why (b) is a universal moral principle. If the relativist has a method of discovering universal moral principles—for example, Rawls' "reflective equilibrium" or the utilitarian principle—then it is difficult to see why the only principle yielded by such method would be (b) above. Thus, this new version of relativism avoids inconsistency, but it is epistemologically weak.

A second problem with normative relativism is that it overlooks an important feature of moral discourse, its *universalizability*.[103] Independently of substantive morals, when we talk about right and wrong or rights and duties, and act accordingly, we are logically committed to "act in accordance with the generic rights of [our] recipients as well as of [our]selves," on pain of self-contradiction.[104] This not only means that we cannot make exceptions in our own favor, but also that individuals must be treated as equally entitled to basic rights regardless of contingent factors such as their cultural surroundings. The requirement of universalizability may be thought of as having a logical nature,[105] or alternatively, as be-

---

101. B. Williams, supra note 97, at 21. See also a profound criticism of relativism in B. Williams, Ethics and the Limits of Philosophy, ch. 9 (1985).

102. I am grateful to David Kaye for demonstrating this point to me.

103. The requirement of universalizability is usually traced to IV I. Kant, Critique of Practical Reason § 436 (L. Beck trans. 1949). It has been revived in recent philosopical literature, mainly by A. Gewirth, Reason and Morality (1978) and M. Singer, Generalization in Ethics (1961).

104. A. Gewirth, Human Rights: Essays on Justification and Application 52, 128-41 (1982).

105. See id. at 89; IV I. Kant, supra note 103, § 436 ("All maxims have . . . a form, which consists in universality; and in this respect the formula of the moral imperative requires that the maxims be chosen as though they should hold as universal laws of nature."); M. Singer, supra note 103, at 34 ("The generalization principle . . . is involved in or presupposed by every genuine moral judgment, for it is an essential part of . . . distinctively moral terms."); Frankena, The Concept of Morality, 63 J. Phil. 688, 695-96 (1966). Professor D'Amato makes a convincing linguistic case against relativism, showing that when we ordinarily refer to some conduct as "moral," we usually mean that it is universally valid. Conversely, when we are prepared to be tolerant about some conduct (for example, sexual hab-

ing a requirement of moral plausibility.[106] If the first approach is correct, the relativist simply refuses to engage in meaningful moral discourse. Under the second approach, the relativist endorses the highly implausible position that in moral matters we can pass judgments containing proper names, and that consequently we may make exceptions in our own favor.[107]

The relativist has two responses to the universalizability argument. First, the relativist may argue that belonging to different communities is a morally relevant circumstance.[108] Universalizability, he would argue, is not violated when individuals are situated in different factual conditions. To say that if A ought to do X in circumstances C, then B also ought to do X in circumstances C, presupposes a similarity of circumstances. If such circumstances vary substantially, that is, if cultural traditions, creeds, and practices differ, then we would not violate the universalizability requirement by holding that individuals who belong to different cultures ought to have different basic rights.[109] Sometimes relativists articulate this position in the form of an attack on the assertion of the existence of abstract rights, as opposed to the assertion of concrete rights and duties in materially defined social conditions.[110]

---

its), we regard such conduct as "mores" or "custom," and not as "morality in the stronger sense." D'Amato, Lon Fuller and Substantive Natural Law, 26 Am. J. Juris. 202, 204 (1981).

106. See, e.g., J. Rawls, supra note 15, at 132 (principles apply to everyone by virtue of their being moral persons).

107. See J. Hospers, Human Conduct 276-77, 285 (1972).

108. See the elementary but excellent discussion in id. at 283-90.

109. John Rawls asserts that in societies which have not attained certain minimal material conditions, individuals may be denied human rights. J. Rawls, supra note 15, at 151-52. This seems a surprising statement in the context of Rawls' impressive defense of the "rights" conception of justice. As Brian Barry put it:

> Why this should be so is not at all clear to me. Is there anything in the material condition of, say, a group of nomadic Bedouin eking a bare subsistence from the desert or a population of poor peasant cultivators which prevents them from being able to use personal liberty?

B. Barry, supra note 15, at 77.

In his most recent article, Rawls expressly refused to deal with the issue of whether his theory "can be extended to a general political conception for different kinds of societies existing under different historical and social conditions." Rawls, Justice as Fairness: Political not Metaphysical, 14 Phil. & Pub. Aff. 223, 225 (1985). It would be unfair, however, to charge Rawls with yielding to relativism, since he expressly avoids "prejudging one way or the other." Id.

110. See Tushnet, An Essay on Rights, 62 Tex. L. Rev. 1363, 1364-65 (1984) ("It does not advance understanding to speak of rights in the abstract. It matters only that some specific right is or is not recognized in some specific social setting. . . . In this way rights become identified with particular cultures and are relativized."). Tushnet's article astonishes in several regards. For example, he states that "[t]he use of rights in contemporary discourse

Such arguments are flawed, however, because the fact that one belongs to a particular social group or community is not a *morally* relevant circumstance. The place of birth and cultural environment of an individual are not related to his moral worth or to his entitlement to human rights. An individual cannot be held responsible for being born in one society rather than in another, for one "deserves" neither one's cultural environment nor one's place of birth. There is nothing, for example, in the nature of a Third World woman that makes her less eligible for the enjoyment of human rights (though she may, of course, consensually waive her rights) than a woman in a Western democracy.[111] If the initial conditions are not morally distinguishable, the requirement of universalizability fully applies to statements about individual rights, even where the agents are immersed in different cultural environments.

The relativist's first objection to universalizability also confuses the circumstances in which one learns moral concepts with the *meaning* of those concepts.[112] A person who learns a moral concept (such as that of "wrong") by applying it in fact situations peculiar to his culture, is perfectly able to apply that concept to a set of facts he has never encountered before. As Bernard Williams said in his most recent work:

> The fact that people can and must react when they are confronted with another culture, and do so by applying their existing notions—also by reflecting on them—seems to show that the ethical thought of a given culture can always stretch beyond its boundaries. Even if there is no way in which divergent ethical beliefs can be brought to converge by independent inquiry or rational argument,

---

impedes advances by progressive social forces." Id. at 1364. Such criticism, of course, assumes that it is morally desirable for the "progressive social forces" (whatever that means) to dictate conducts and impose ends and conceptions of moral excellence on other individuals (i.e., on those who presumably would be accused of militating in the ranks of the "regressive social forces"). John Rawls artfully responded to this assertion in an oft-quoted sentence: "Each person possesses an inviolability founded on justice that even the welfare of society as a whole cannot override." J. Rawls, supra note 15, at 3. This is what I mean by "rights" in the "abstract." See also infra text accompanying notes 116-17.

111. One must be careful not to overstate this exception. Dictators typically assert that they represent the people or that they have their support. Even if a particular dictator enjoys popular support, however, such support does not entitle him to oppress dissenters who have not consented to his rule. The majoritarian principle is thus useless when assessing human rights violations. See the discussion in J. Rawls, supra note 15, at 356-62.

112. See R. Trigg, Reason and Commitment 20 (1973).

> this fact will not imply relativism. Each outlook may still be making claims it intends to apply to the whole world, not just to that part of it which is its 'own world.'[113]

By claiming that moral judgments only have meaning within particular cultures, the relativist underestimates the ability of the human intellect to confront, in a moral sense, new situations.

The relativist's second objection to universalizability has a logical nature. As noted above, the relativist may contend that (a) his only principle is that culture determines human rights; and (b), (a) is universal.[114] The relativist thus universalizes a principle. But the requirement of universalizability applies to *substantive* moral statements, which (a) is not. The principle that culture determines human rights is a principle of *renvoi*; that is, it refers us to different normative systems in order to determine the rights of individuals. The principle does not establish rules governing the rights of any particular individual. Universalizability requires that *if* we make a statement about the right of X to freedom of thought, we are committed to grant that right to Y under similar, morally relevant circumstances. Because the relativist principle does not address issues of substantive morality in this respect, it is not susceptible to being universalized in the same way. The violation of universalizability becomes apparent when one translates the relativist principle into substantive moral statements (i.e., X, who lives in culture C1, has the right R; while Y, who lives in culture C2, does not have the right R). In other words, the relativist principle may be regarded as *metamoral*, even where it is asserted as the basis of normative morality.[115]

Third, normative relativism runs counter to the principle that persons have moral worth *qua* persons and must be treated as ends in themselves, not as functions of the ends of others—a non-trivial version of the Kantian principle of autonomy.[116] This principle of moral worth forbids the imposition upon individuals of cultural

113. B. Williams, supra note 101, at 159.

114. See supra text accompanying note 102.

115. The characterization of relativism as metamoral differs from the assertion of metaethical relativism. This part of the paper deals with normative relativism, which does not need support from metaethical skepticism. See supra notes 88-97 and accompanying text. But normative relativism is still not strictly a substantive moral theory. It only tells us where to look for the norms that determine individual rights.

116. See Ping-Cheung Lo, A Critical Reevaluation of the Alleged "Empty Formalism" of Kantian Ethics, 91 Ethics 181, 182 (1980-81). See also Schachter, supra note 71, at 849.

standards that impair human rights. Even if relativists could show that authoritarian practices are somehow required by a community—a claim which in many cases remains to be proven—they would still fail to explain why individuals should surrender their basic rights to the ends of the community. If women in Moslem countries are discriminated against, it is not enough to say that a tradition, no matter how old and venerable, requires such discrimination.[117] The only defense consistent with the principle of autonomy would be a showing that each subjugated woman consented to waive her rights. However, because of the mystical and holistic assumptions underlying relativism, presumably the relativist would not regard such a test as relevant or necessary.

Quite apart from the moral implausibility of normative relativism, it is worth noting the extreme conservatism of the doctrine.[118] Normative relativism tells us that if a particular society has always had authoritarian practices, it is morally defensible that it continue to have them. It works as a typical argument of authority: it has always been like this, this is our culture, so we need not undertake any changes.[119] In the final analysis, normative relativism thus conceived amounts to the worst form of moral and legal positivism:

---

117. For examples see supra note 10.

118. A similar point is made by Amy Gutman in her response to modern critics of liberalism. Gutman, Communitarian Critics of Liberalism, 14 Phil. & Pub. Aff. 308, 309 (1985). As the text demonstrates, anti-liberal theories that emphasize the priority of communal values are necessarily relativist.

119. Tushnet asserts that his radical critique of rights "is a Schumpeterian act of creative destruction that may help us to build societies that transcend the failures of capitalism." Tushnet, supra note 110, at 1363. Tushnet later expressed this idea in relativistic terms: "The critique of rights takes a strong relativist position: it insists that rights-talk is meaningful only when placed within a full social and legal context." Id. at 1394. Thus, relativism to Tushnet is a basic assumption of radical politics, an essential underpinning of left-wing scholarship and politics. Yet nothing is farther from the truth. Relativism is tantamount to moral positivism and to "legalism," two of the most reactionary doctrines in the history of ideas. Tushnet himself seems to realize this. He tells us that "to say that some specific right is (or ought to be) recognized in a specific culture is to say that the culture is what it is, ought to recognize what its deepest commitments are, or ought to be transformed into some other culture." Id. at 1365. Thus, for Tushnet the only way to talk about rights is to *describe* rights as they are recognized by this or that culture. Those are the only *existing* rights. True, he accepts that we can say that this culture "ought to be transformed into some other culture." He thus avoids the charge of moral positivism. But because he has been precluded from even talking about rights in the abstract, he loses the best and most effective philosophical tool for criticizing positive law: the idea that individuals have rights independent of contingent cultural standards. Thus, when criticizing a particular culture, a Tushnet-type relativist may not rely on the proposition that individuals are entitled to some other social arrangement or that their rights have been violated.

it asserts that the rules enacted by the group are necessarily correct as a matter of critical morality.[120] If there is a particularly unfit domain for arguments of authority, it is surely that of human rights.

Admittedly, the force of the moral critique of relativism articulated here depends on the intuitive acceptance of certain moral premises. The relativist can successfully resist the attack by rejecting metaethical relativism so as to avoid logical incoherence, denying that universalizability is an ingredient of moral judgments, and rejecting the principle of autonomy. But this is a high price to pay. Normative relativism would then be a poor and implausible moral doctrine, and it is doubtful that many relativists, upon careful reflection, would accept the harsh implications. Furthermore, cultural relativism as defined in the first part of this article expressly or impliedly assumes the validity of normative relativism. Not only does positive international law fail to provide any basis for the relativist doctrine, but the underlying philosophical structure of relativism also reveals profound flaws.

IV. Two By-Products of Relativism: Elitism and Conspiracy

In this Part I will briefly consider two doctrines closely associated with relativism. The first theory asserts that one can appropriately honor human rights in certain societies, usually the most sophisticated ones, but not in others, on account, for example, of the latter's insufficient economic development. This doctrine, which can be called "elitism," necessarily follows from relativism. The second theory states that the law of human rights results from a conspiracy of the West to perpetuate imperialism. The "conspiracy theory," by contrast, does not follow inevitably from, and is not required by, cultural relativism.

A. *The Elitist Theory of Human Rights*

During the dark years of the military dictatorship in Argentina, one commonly heard many well-intentioned commentators exclaiming: "It is really a shame! Argentina, a country that springs

120. See supra note 92. This indictment only attacks what Professor Carlos Nino has called "ideological positivism," the theory that the norms of a group are necessarily correct as a matter of critical morality. C. Nino, Introduccion al Analisis del Derecho 32-35 (1980). This paper is not concerned with the more fertile concept of "methodological positivism," the theory of the separation between law and morality defended by H.L.A. Hart and others.

from Western tradition, cannot be excused for not respecting human rights." The statement implies that countries that do not spring from a Western tradition may somehow be excused from complying with the international law of human rights. This elitist theory of human rights holds that human rights are good for the West but not for much of the non-Western world.[121] Surprisingly, the elitist theory of human rights is very popular in the democratic West, not only in conservative circles but also, and even more often, among liberal and radical groups.[122] The right-wing version of elitism embodies the position, closely associated with colonialism, that backward peoples cannot govern themselves and that democracy only works for superior cultures.[123] The left-wing version, often articulated by liberals who stand for civil rights in Western countries but support leftist dictatorships abroad, reflects a belief that we should be tolerant of and respect the cultural identity and political self-determination of Third World countries (although, of course, it is seldom the people who choose to have dictators; more often the dictators decide for them).[124]

The position of relativist scholars who are human rights advocates illustrates an eloquent example of concealed elitism.[125] Such persons find themselves in an impossible dilemma. On the one hand they are anxious to articulate an international human rights standard, while on the other they wish to respect the autonomy of individual cultures. The result is a vague warning against "ethnocentrism,"[126] and well-intentioned proposals that are deferential to tyrannical governments and insufficiently concerned with human suffering. Because the consequence of either version of elitism is that certain national or ethnic groups are somehow less entitled than others to the enjoyment of human rights, the theory is fundamentally immoral and replete with racist overtones.

---

121. I am indebted to Professor Guido Pincione from the University of Buenos Aires for our stimulating discussions on this point.

122. See, e.g., Pollis, supra note 13, at 22-23; Tushnet, supra note 110, at 1394.

123. Relativism influenced the British colonial administrators. See B. Williams, supra note 97, at 20.

124. See supra notes 67-72 and accompanying text.

125. See, e.g., Pollis, supra note 13, at 22-23.

126. Id. McWhinney's work is another example of this paradox. See E. McWhinney, supra note 5, at 209 ("eurocentrism").

B. *The Conspiracy Theory of Human Rights*

The final aspect of relativism to be discussed is what Karl Popper might describe as "the conspiracy theory of human rights."[127] This theory asserts that human rights are a Macchiavelian creation of the West calculated to impair the economic development of the Third World. Starting from the Marxist assumption that civil and political rights are "formal" bourgeois freedoms that serve only the interests of the capitalists,[128] the conspiracy theory holds that human rights serve the same purpose in the international arena. It sees them as instruments of domination because they are indissolubly tied to the right to property, and because in the field of international economic relations, the human rights movement fosters free and unrestricted trade which seriously hurts the economies of Third World nations. Furthermore, proponents of the conspiracy theory charge that human rights advocacy amounts to moral imperialism.[129] In short, "the effect, if not the design, of such an exclusive political preoccupation [is] to leave the door open to the most ruthless and predatory economic forces in international society."[130]

The conspiracy theory, however, fails to justify the link between the support for human rights and support for particular property rights or trade policies—a fundamental flaw. The argument made in this paper does not presuppose or imply any position in this regard. Moreover, to claim that civil and political rights must be suppressed as a necessary condition for the improvement of Third World economies grossly distorts the facts. As Louis Henkin put it:

> [H]ow many hungry are fed, how much industry is built, by massacre, torture, and detention, by unfair trials and other unjustices, by abuse of minorities, by denials of freedoms of conscience, by suppression of political association and expression?[131]

The contention that the West imposed human rights on the world and that "poor peoples" do not care about freedom is clearly

127. 2 K. Popper, supra note 70, at 94.

128. See, e.g., Marx, On the Jewish Question, in The Marx-Engels Reader 42 (2d ed. Tucker 1978).

129. For an account of the Marxist critique, see Murphy, supra note 20, at 438-42.

130. E. McWhinney, supra note 5, at 211. Cf. Tushnet, supra note 110, at 1398 (the fact of unnecessary human suffering alone is enough to support the critique of "rights" theory).

131. L. Henkin, The Rights of Man Today 130 (1978).

a myth.[132] First, it contradicts the plain fact that a growing awareness exists in the Third World about the need for reinforcing the respect for human rights.[133] Second, even if, *gratia argumentandi*, some Western plot created human rights philosophy, that fact alone would not necessarily undermine its moral value. Conspiracy theories (such as vulgar Marxism, "ideologism," and Critical Legal Studies) assert that the true explanation of a phenomenon consists of discovering the groups of people or hidden interests which are interested in the occurence of the phenomenon and which have plotted to bring it about.[134] To be sure, conspiracies do occur. As Popper conclusively showed, however, the fact that conspiracies rarely succeed ultimately disproves the conspiracy theory. Social life is too complex and the unforeseen consequences of social action too many to support conspiracy as the explanation of every social phenomenon.[135] Institutions originally designed for a certain purpose often turn against their creators. Thus, even if the law of human rights was originally conceived as an ideological tool against communism, today human rights have achieved a universal scope and inspire the struggle against all types of oppression.[136] In other words, the circumstances surrounding the origins of human rights principles are irrelevant to their intrinsic value and cannot detract from their beneficial features.

V. CONCLUSION

The human rights movement has resisted the relativist attack by emphasizing that social institutions, including international law,

132. Id.

133. Cf. the statement by the All Africa Council of Churches/World Council of Churches (1976), cited by Haile, supra note 17, at 584 (describing the system of checks and balances that prevented gross abuses of human and civil rights in traditional African societies); the statement by the Arab Lawyers' Union at their meeting of December, 1983, reprinted in 9 Hum. Rts. Internet Rep. 564 (1984) ("The basis of the legitimacy of any regime or system of government is related to its effective observance of human rights, particularly those set forth in the Universal Declaration."). See also Nickel, supra note 48, at 45 (human rights appeal to many peoples, not just to Westerners).

134. 2 K. Popper, supra note 70, at 94.

135. Id. at 95.

136. South Africa is a case in point. Maybe in 1948 the framers of the Universal Declaration on Human Rights did not intend for it to apply to the black majority in South Africa. Maybe they thought that democracy "among whites" was enough to comply with the Declaration. The international community has subsequently rejected that interpretation, however, and today the law and philosophy of human rights are the main bases for the claims for freedom by the black majority.

are created by and for the individual. Consequently, as far as rights are concerned, governments serve as but the agents of the people. International norms aim to protect individuals, not governments, by creating concrete limits on how human beings may be treated.[137]

I have suggested that cultural relativism is not, and ought not to be, the answer to human rights concerns. Supported neither by international law nor by independent moral analysis, cultural relativism exhibits strong discriminatory overtones and is to a large extent mistaken in its factual assumptions.

I also demonstrated that regardless of its historical origins, the international law of human rights cannot mean one thing to the West and another to the Third World. International human rights law embodies the imperfect yet inspired response of the international community to a growing awareness of the uniqueness of the human being and the unity of the human race. It also represents an eloquent body of norms condemning the effects of organized societal oppression on individuals. Fortunately, the Third World is now starting to play a role in the process of universalizing human rights. The significance of its new role will increase when governing elites cease to use authoritarian traditions as a shield against legitimate demands for basic human rights.

137. For example, the purpose of the prohibition of the use of force, U.N. Charter, article 2, para. 4, is to spare humanity from the horrors of war—to prevent human suffering. Although the Charter articulates the rule as an inter-governmental prohibition, its humanitarian underpinnings should be kept in mind. Governments are thus made responsible for the maintenance of peace as agents of humanity, not merely for their own benefit.

[4]

The Ideology of Human Rights

Makau wa Mutua*

Introduction

Over the last fifty years the international law of human rights has steadily achieved a moral plateau rarely associated with the law of nations.[1] A diverse and eclectic assortment of individuals and enti-

* Associate Professor of Law, State University of New York at Buffalo Law School; Co-Director, Human Rights Center at SUNY Buffalo; L.L.B. 1983, University of Dar-es-Salaam; L.L.M. 1984, University of Dar-es-Salaam; L.L.M. 1985, Harvard Law School; S.J.D. 1987, Harvard Law School. This Article is the result of my participation in the human rights movement over the last two decades. The Article would not have been possible, however, without the privileged access that I have enjoyed to the major authors and actors in the movement. I am indebted to them all. Many thanks are also due to the faculty at SUNY Buffalo Law School in general, and to Lucinda Finley and Stephanie Phillips in particular, for giving me an opportunity to be heard. I am deeply appreciative for the insightful comments of James Gathii, Athena Mutua, and Peter Rosenblum on earlier drafts of this Article. I am especially grateful to Randall Kennedy and Henry J. Richardson whose many contributions to my academic and professional development have been invaluable and steadfast. This Article is dedicated to the late Haywood Burns whose commitment to the attainment of human dignity will continue to live in us.

1. In the wake of World War II, member states of the United Nations adopted on December 10, 1948, the Universal Declaration of Human Rights, G.A. Res. 217 A(III), U.N. Doc. A/810, at 71 (1948) [hereinafter UDHR]. Although the UDHR was adopted without opposition by a vote of 48 to zero, it was the subject of eight abstentions: Byelorussia, Czechoslovakia, Poland, Soviet Union, Ukraine, Yugoslavia, Saudi Arabia, and South Africa. See Antonio Cassese, The General Assembly: Historical Perspective 1945-1989, in The United Nations and Human Rights: A Critical Appraisal 25, 31 n.22 (Philip Alston ed., 1992) [hereinafter United Nations and Human Rights]. It is significant to note that many of the triumphant Western powers who formulated the UDHR held colonies and other dependent territories at the time. Moreover, these possessions, which were largely located in Africa and Asia, did not participate in the Declaration's creation. The UDHR, though only a declaration without binding authority on member states, was the lowest threshold, the most basic common denominator, on which the states then represented at the United Nations could agree as representative of a general understanding of the relationship between the individual and the state and the freedoms and rights of individuals in organized political society. See id. at 31. Now widely viewed as the "gospel" of the human rights movement, the UDHR has been the predominant road map in the development and elaboration of a "universal" jurisprudence of human rights.

ties now invoke human rights norms and the attendant phraseology with the intent of cloaking themselves and their causes in the paradigm's perceived power and righteousness.[2] What is interesting is the failure of this universal reliance on the language of human rights to create agreement on the scope, content, and philosophical bases of the human rights corpus. Intellectual and policy battles have focused on its cultural relevance, ideological and political orientation, and thematic incompleteness.[3] Notwithstanding these

The parental basis and condensed "philosophy" of the U.N. human rights corpus, the UDHR is now regarded by some leading authorities as a normative instrument, a part of customary international law in spite of its peculiarly "Western" orientation and content. See Thomas Buergenthal & Harold G. Maier, Public International Law In a Nutshell 119-20 (1990). More general and less controversial, however, is the view that some UDHR rights, particularly those that implicate state action against personal security, such as freedom from torture, slavery, illegal detention, and disappearances, have achieved the status of customary international law. See Thomas Buergenthal, International Human Rights In a Nutshell 32 (1988) [hereinafter Buergenthal Nutshell]; see also Filartiga v. Pena-Irala, 630 F.2d 876 (2d Cir. 1980) (holding deliberate torture perpetrated under color of official authority violates universally accepted norms of human rights); Restatement (Third) of Foreign Relations § 702 (1986) (enumerating seven types of conduct considered to be violations of the customary international law of human rights).

2. See, e.g., Statement to the World Conference on Human Rights on Behalf of the Committee On Economic, Social and Cultural Rights, U.N. ESCOR, 7th Sess., Supp. No. 2, Annex III, at 82, U.N. Doc. E/1993/22 (1993) (making the point that economic, social, and cultural rights should not be treated as inferior to civil and political rights); Stephen Cohen, Conditioning U.S. Security Assistance On Human Rights Practices, 76 Am. J. Int'l L. 246 (1982) (arguing that international human rights law imposes corresponding obligations on one government not to support another that violates human rights); Karl E. Klare, Legal Theory and Democratic Reconstruction, 25 U. Brit. Colum. L. Rev. 69, 95 (1991) (concluding, despite his critique of rights, that the post-communist regimes of Eastern Europe should be founded on human rights guarantees); Michael Reisman, Sovereignty and Human Rights in Contemporary International Law, 84 Am. J. Int'l L. 866, 869-71 (1990) (arguing that a new human rights-based conception of "popular sovereignty" permits the world community to intervene militarily in a country to remove coup-makers who abrogate that sovereignty, particularly if the popular will has been expressed through internationally supervised free and fair elections). For additional causes that claim the mantle of human rights, see Farooq Hassan, The Right to be Different: An Exploratory Proposal for the Creation of a New Human Right, 5 Loy. L.A. Int'l & Comp. L.J. 67 (1982); Eric Heinze, Sexual Orientation: A Human Right (1995); Ours By Right: Women's Rights as Human Rights (Joanna Kerr ed., 1993); Henry J. Richardson, The Right to Food: The International Human Rights Response, 30 How. L.J. 233 (1987); Eugene W. Rostow, Peace as a Human Right, 4 N.Y.L. Sch. J. Int'l & Comp. L. 215, 217 (1983); Melissa Thorme, Establishing Environment as a Human Right, 19 Denv. J. Int'l L. & Pol'y 301 (1991).

3. For discussions of different and conflicting cultural, historical, and intellectual bases and traditions in human rights, see Josiah A.M. Cobbah, African Values and the Human Rights Debate: An African Perspective, 9 Hum. Rts. Q. 309 (1987); Jack Donnelly, Cultural Relativism and Universal Human Rights, 6 Hum. Rts. Q. 400 (1984); Bilahari Kausikan, Asia's Different Standard, 92 Foreign Pol'y 24 (1993) (advancing the view that Asia has its own distinctive historical and cultural values which may differ or should not be easily analogized with the "universal" human rights norms promoted by the West); Makau

questions, the seduction of human rights discourse has been so great that it has, in fact, delayed the development of a critique of rights.[4]

This Article focuses upon what these polar impulses and positions—the fight over the content of human rights, on the one hand, and their captivating allure, on the other—have obscured: that although it seems implausible to openly deny that the human rights corpus is the construction of a political ideology, the discourse's major authors present it as non-ideological. They use a vocabulary that paints the movement as both impartial and the quintessence of human goodness. They portray it as divorced from base materialism, self-interest, and "ideology." Perhaps they do so because "ideology" has a negative connotation: it is the instrument that the "other," the adversary, the opponent, uses to challenge and seek the marginalization of the forces of "good." In reality, however, the human rights corpus is not a creed or a set of normative principles suspended in outer space; the matters that it affects are earthly and concern immediate routine politics.[5] The larger political agenda of the human rights regime has, however, been blurred by its veneration and by attempts to clean it of the taint of partisanship.

---

wa Mutua, The Banjul Charter and the African Cultural Fingerprint: An Evaluation of the Language of Duties, 35 Va. J. Int'l L. 339 (1995) [hereinafter Mutua, African Cultural Fingerprint]; Raimundo Pannikar, Is the Notion of Human Rights A Western Concept?, 120 Diogenes 75 (1982). For discussions on the hierarchy and "importance" of some rights over others, see Philip Alston & Gerard Quinn, The Nature and Scope of States Parties' Obligations under the International Covenant on Economic, Social and Cultural Rights, 9 Hum. Rts. Q. 156 (1987) (arguing against a prejudiced hierarchy of rights which subordinates economic, social, and cultural rights to civil and political rights); Theodor Meron, On a Hierarchy of International Human Rights, 80 Am. J. Int'l L. 1 (1986). For discussions on the inclusion or exclusion and enforcement of women's rights as human rights, see Sandra Coliver, United Nations Machineries on Women's Rights: How Might They Better Help Women Whose Rights Are Being Violated?, in New Directions in Human Rights 25 (Ellen L. Lutz et al. eds., 1989); Margaret E. Galey, International Enforcement of Women's Rights, 6 Hum. Rts. Q. 463 (1984).

4. Cf. Karen Engle, International Human Rights and Feminism: When Discourses Meet, 13 Mich. J. Int'l L. 517, 518-19 (1992) (exploring the different "affirmative" human rights approaches taken by advocates of international women's rights even as they have critiqued extant rights frameworks to better the lives of women); Klare, supra note 2, at 95 (arguing that the "critique of rights" debate raises issues that should play a role in the democratic legal reconstruction of Eastern Europe).

5. Cf. Southern Pac. Co. v. Jensen, 244 U.S. 205, 222 (1917) (Holmes, J., dissenting) ("The common law is not a brooding omnipresence in the sky but the articulate voice of some sovereign or quasi-sovereign that can be identified . . . .").

This Article examines the theoretical and practical work of the major authors[6] of human rights discourse and develops the proposition that human rights and Western liberal democracy are virtually tautological. Although the two concepts seem different from a distance, one is in fact the universalized version of the other; human rights represent the attempted diffusion and further development at the international level of the liberal political tradition. These processes have contributed to the reexamination and reconstruction of liberalism, and have in some respects refined and added to the liberal tradition. It seems to be true historically that for political movements and ideologies, from nationalism to free enterprise and beyond, totems or myths are necessary to remove them from their earthly moorings.[7] For liberal democracy that totem appears today to be the human rights corpus, the moralized expression of a political ideology. Although the concept of human rights is not unique to European societies, I argue here that the specific philosophy on which the current "universal" and "official"[8]

---

6. I use the term "authors" more broadly here to describe all those individuals and entities that have exerted discernible influence in the normative development and practical enforcement of human rights law. These include the United Nations and its factions, leading non-governmental human rights organizations, based almost exclusively in Western Europe and North America, and academic and other conceptual writers. In the past several decades, thousands of organizations, activists, and scholars in Africa, Asia, Latin America, and everywhere in between, have adopted and adapted the message of the authors and added to its "globality" and "universality." Regional human rights systems in Africa, the Americas, and Europe have also contributed to the "worldization" of human rights. These are anchored by the following instruments: (i) the African Charter on Human and Peoples' Rights, June 27, 1981, OAU Doc. CAB/LEG/67/3/Rev.5 (1981), reprinted in 21 I.L.M. 59 (1982) [hereinafter African Charter]; (ii) the American Convention on Human Rights, Nov. 22, 1969, 36 O.A.S.T.S. No. 36, at 1, O.A.S. Off. Rec. OEA/Ser. L/V/II.23 Rev.2, reprinted in 9 I.L.M. 673 (1970); (iii) the [European] Convention for the Protection of Human Rights and Fundamental Freedoms, Nov. 4, 1950, 213 U.N.T.S. 221 (1955); and (iv) the European Social Charter, Oct. 18, 1961, 529 U.N.T.S. 89 (1965).

7. Myths of racial superiority and other "justifications" for the repression of one group by another have often served as a pretext for the control of political power and resources. The White American "rationale" for the enslavement of Africans or the White South African construction of the concept and practice of apartheid—both steeped in religion and pseudo-science—enhanced White nationalism and the control by Whites of state power. Similarly, philosophical justifications for free enterprise rest on nebulous conceptions of the "nature" of individual human beings, their relationships, and their motivations to acquire property.

8. I use the term "official" to describe the "mainstream" and popular conceptions of the human rights movement, that is, as norms and codes of conduct developed and promoted by Westerners after the 1939-45 war for the purposes of limiting the abuse of individuals by their governments. This version of human rights has been largely authenticated and mediated through the United Nations. See, e.g., UDHR, supra note 1; the International Covenant on Economic, Social and Cultural Rights, G.A. Res. 2200 (XXI), U.N. GAOR,

human rights corpus is based is essentially European.[9] This exclusivity and cultural specificity necessarily deny the concept universality. The fact that human rights are violated in liberal democracies is of little consequence to my argument and does not distinguish the human rights corpus from the ideology of Western liberalism; rather, it emphasizes the contradictions and imperfections of liberalism. In other words, the elusive state of perfection in which human rights are *fully* respected and realized tells us, among other things, that both human rights and democracy are works in progress. They are projects that are essentially infinite, open-ended, and highly experimental in nature.

Since World War II, the United Nations, non-governmental organizations, and scholarly writers have created a thicket of norms, processes, and institutions that purport to promote and protect human rights. Working with the so-called International Bill of Rights as their basis,[10] the key but diverse collection of organizations and scholars has tended to agree on an irreducible human rights core.[11] This core, although stated in human rights terms, is now being formulated into the emergent norm of democratic gov-

---

21st Sess., Supp. No. 16, at 49, U.N. Doc. A/6316 (1966) (entered into force Jan. 3, 1976) [hereinafter ICESCR]; the International Covenant on Civil and Political Rights, G.A. Res. 2200 (XXI), U.N. GAOR, 21st Sess., Supp. No. 16, at 52, U.N. Doc. A/6316 (1966) (entered into force Jan. 3, 1976) [hereinafter ICCPR]; the Optional Protocol to the International Covenant on Civil and Political Rights, G.A. Res. 2200 (XXI), U.N. GAOR, 21st Sess., Supp. No. 16, at 59, U.N. Doc. A/6316 (1966) (entered into force Mar. 23, 1976) [hereinafter Optional Protocol].

9. See Jack Donnelly, Human Rights and Western Liberalism, in Human Rights in Africa: Cross-Cultural Perspectives 31 (Abdullahi Ahmed An-Na'im & Francis M. Deng eds., 1990) [hereinafter Cross-Cultural Perspectives]; Virginia Leary, The Effect of Western Perspectives on International Human Rights, in Cross-Cultural Perspectives, supra, at 15. A system of human rights is comprised of the norms, processes, and institutions that protect human dignity, an ideal that is prevalent in all cultures of the world. Different cultures, however, have evolved different systems for protecting human dignity. As has been argued elsewhere, the duty/rights dialectic was essential in the protection of human rights in pre-colonial Africa. See generally Mutua, African Cultural Fingerprint, supra note 3. Societies evolve particular systems of human rights protection based on their histories and philosophical and religious traditions. Within their own cultural spaces, various traditions evolve norms and processes that safeguard individuals, communities, and political societies. See id.

10. The International Bill of Rights consists of: (i) the UDHR, supra note 1; (ii) the ICCPR, supra note 8; (iii) the ICESCR, supra note 8; and (iv) the Optional Protocol, supra note 8.

11. This core includes personal security rights, rights that implicate state power. In conventional jargon, they are negative, "hands off" rights that individuals enjoy in relation to the state.

ernance in international law.[12] The routes different authors of human rights have taken to arrive at these conclusions are, of course, varied. Nevertheless, I have identified the four defining approaches or schools of thought into which I believe all the paramount voices writing and acting in the human rights discourse fall.[13] I believe that these voices express the synonymity and close fit of the human rights corpus with its parent, Western liberalism.

The proponents of and adherents to the four dominant schools of thought may be classified as (i) conventional doctrinalists, (ii) constitutionalists or conceptualizers, (iii) cultural agnostics or multiculturalists, and (iv) political strategists or instrumentalists. Although most of these voices differ—in some instances radically—on the content of the human rights corpus and whether or how the contents should be ranked, they are nevertheless united by the belief that *there are* basic human rights. They also believe that these human rights should be promoted and where possible protected by the state, the basic obligor[14] of human rights law. These

12. For discussion of the norm of democratic governance in international law, see Gregory H. Fox, The Right to Political Participation in International Law, 17 Yale J. Int'l L. 539 (1992); Thomas M. Franck, The Emerging Right to Democratic Governance, 86 Am. J. Int'l L. 46 (1992) [hereinafter Franck, The Emerging Right]. The democratic project, which can be stated in explicitly human rights terms, builds on the conception that "core" rights can only be realized and protected in a political society organized through the liberal democratic framework.

13. There are, of course, other major voices, such as Martti Koskenniemi, whose work has focused on the deconstruction of human rights discourse and the unveiling of the interests, struggles, and politics that are hidden behind the rhetoric of international law and human rights. But when I speak of the paramount voices in the movement, I do not mean Koskenniemi or those with similar approaches; I speak primarily of the originators, the conceptualizers of the movement, those who are responsible for its construction. See, e.g., Martti Koskenniemi, The Politics of International Law, 1 Eur. J. Int'l L. 4 (1990).

14. Human rights law, like all other law, is a statist or structural construct in that it is the formulation of the package of obligatory relationships—rights as well as duties—from the state to the individual and vice versa. The dominant tradition of the human rights movement derives from that brand of Western liberalism which atomizes and alienates the singular individual from both the state and the society. See Donnelly, Human Rights and Western Liberalism, supra note 9, at 31. John Locke is the most prominent early Western thinker to condense this compact into a philosophy. See John Locke, Two Treatises of Government (Peter Laslett ed., 1988). In effect, human rights law is only possible because of the existence of the state, whose basic duty, at least in the dominant Western tradition, has been to protect the individual and property. More progressive interpretations of human rights have now forced the implication of state action even under circumstances where causation is not directly attributable to the state, as in cases of domestic violence against women or other discriminatory practices by private entities. See, e.g., Karen Engle, After the Collapse of the Public/Private Distinction: Strategizing Women's Rights, in Reconceiving Reality: Women and International Law 143 (Dorinda G. Dallmeyer ed., 1993) (critiquing the understanding of the public/private distinction in international law); Elizabeth Schneider, The Violence of Privacy, 23 Conn. L. Rev. 973, 974 (1991) (discussing

different schools disagree, however, on the political orientation of human rights, the weight accorded to certain rights, and strategies and tactics for the enforcement of the human rights movement's norms. These disagreements reflect the different visions and trajectories of liberalism, the types of societies intended by advocates of human rights, and the purposes to which they feel the human rights discourse should be directed.

This Article argues that the human rights corpus, taken as a whole, as a document of ideals and values, particularly the positive law of human rights, requires the reconstruction of states to reflect the structures and values of governance that derive from Western liberalism, especially the contemporary variations of liberal democracy practiced in Western democracies. While these democracies differ in the content of the rights they guarantee and the organizational structures they take, they are nevertheless based on the idea of constitutionalism.

Viewed from this perspective, the human rights regime has serious and dramatic implications for questions of cultural diversity, the sovereignty of states, and ultimately the "universality" of human rights. The purpose here, however, is not to mediate these conflicts, but rather to expose them and to allow diverse stakeholders to reflect on their meaning and the policy issues they raise. The four schools of thought serve as a starting point to explore the divergent pathways that each school's proponents take to converge on the concept of human rights in international law.

The first two approaches, which are espoused by conventional doctrinalists and conceptualizers or constitutionalists, are closest in ideological orientation and share an unequivocal belief in the redemptive[15] quality and power of human rights law. Admittedly, there is a wide and contrasting diversity of attitudes towards the human rights corpus within the two schools. While the doctrinalists tend to be statisticians of violence, conceptualizers are at their core systematizers of the human rights corpus. For the latter, human rights norms arise out of the liberal tradition, and their application should achieve a type of a constitutional system broadly referred to as constitutionalism. Such a system generally has the following characteristics, although the weight accorded to

the effect of the public/private dichotomy on societal understandings about the rights of abused or battered women).

15. By "redemptive quality" I mean their faith in the power of the human rights regime, if fully enforced, to substantially eliminate violations of the individual. According to them, the enforcement of human rights norms stands between tyranny and freedom.

each differs from one state to the next: (i) political society is based on the concept of popular sovereignty; (ii) the government of the state is constitutionally required to be accountable to the populace through various processes such as periodic, genuine, multi-party elections; (iii) government is limited in its powers through checks and balances and the separation of powers, a central tenet of the liberal tradition; (iv) the judiciary is independent and safeguards legality and the rule of law; and (v) the formal declaration of individual civil and political rights is an indispensable facet of the state.[16]

While conceptualizers are more critical of the corpus, many of the conventional doctrinalists see it in almost religious dimensions. Nevertheless, many of the voices in the two schools see themselves in a variety of guises: as inheritors of the Western historical tradition pitting individual rights against the state, as guardians of human rights law, or as founders, conceptualizers, and elaborators of the human rights corpus. The two schools constitute what I call the human rights "orchestra" in which their proponents are the composers and conductors of the discourse; they "control" the content and map the margins of the discourse. Conventional doctrinalists are marked by their heavy and virtually exclusive reliance on positive law in treaties, custom, and other sources of international law as the basis for their activist advocacy or scholarly inquiry. The vast majority of doctrinalists "who matter" operate in the context of human rights non-governmental organizations (NGOs) in the West, although a number of academics also write in this mold.[17] In contrast, constitutionalists are usually found in the realm of theory.

---

16. See Henry J. Steiner & Philip Alston, International Human Rights in Context: Law, Politics, Morals 710-725 (1996) [hereinafter Steiner & Alston, International Human Rights in Context].

17. Conventional doctrinalists profess almost blind allegiance to "standards" and fashion their mandates or points of reference strictly on those standards. For example, the New York-based Lawyers Committee for Human Rights, one of the major American NGOs with an international mandate, proclaims in every human rights report that "its work is impartial, holding each government to the standards affirmed in the International Bill of Human Rights." This claim conceals more than it reveals and could even be interpreted as misleading in a number of respects. The Lawyers Committee does not address human rights issues in *all* countries or simply apply the International Bill of Human Rights in its work. Instead, it focuses on a very small number of countries in the lesser-developed nations of the South—usually those with historically strong ties to the United States—and only deploys a highly select list of rights from the ICCPR. See Lawyers Committee for Human Rights, Critique: Review of the Department of State Country Reports on Human Rights Practices for 1990, back leaf (1991); Lawyers

Both schools enjoy a spirited supporting cast in the non-Western world. In the last several decades, the number of national human rights NGOs and human rights academics has mushroomed in the South. In virtually all cases, they reproduce intellectual patterns and strategies of advocacy similar to those in the West. Although there are some significant differences on the emphasis placed on certain rights, there has been little originality as the corpus has conquered new territory outside the West.

Substantively, doctrinalists stress the primacy of civil and political rights[18] over all other classes of rights. Thus, only a small number of "traditional" civil and political rights comprise the heart of the human rights regime. In addition, doctrinalists seek immediate and "blind" application of these rights without regard to historical, cultural, or developmental differences among states and societies. Many constitutionalists, on the other hand, recognize the supremacy of these "core" rights but point out that the list could or should be expanded. They see the difficulties of "immediate" implementation and prefer a more nuanced approach, staggered to take into account variables of culture, history, and other cleavages. Although many who adopt this approach are positivist, some are critical thinkers who subject the human rights regime to a probing critique. I call them constitutionalists because they believe that, as a whole, human rights law is or should be a constitutional regime and a philosophy that is constitutive of a liberal democratic society, along a spectrum that stretches from a bare republican state to the social democratic state. In the republican "minimum" state, the archetypal nineteenth century liberal state, the government protects the privileges of the few against the poor masses, as well as ethnic, racial, religious, and sexual minorities. In the twentieth century, however, the liberal tradition is developed and constructs

---

Committee for Human Rights, Impunity: Prosecutions of Human Rights Violations in the Philippines, back leaf (1991). Some academics, such as Louis Henkin, the distinguished Columbia Law School professor, should be perceived as both doctrinalist and constitutionalist; although he is primarily an academic, he is also a strong advocate of positive human rights law. See, e.g., Louis Henkin, The Age of Rights x (1990) (challenging those who argue for broad, vague declarations of rights and extolling the virtues of the UDHR).

18. Although the term "negative" rights is for all intents and purposes meaningless when talking about categories of rights and the role of the state in their realization, it is the image that conventionally describes a very small collection of civil and political rights which are seen as the "core" of human rights. Such rights usually involve personal security and freedom from the state. See also supra note 11 and accompanying text.

the social welfare state in which the government progressively and affirmatively seeks to give substance to formal equality.

Cultural agnostics are generally outsiders who see the universality or convergence of some human rights norms with certain non-Western norms and as a result partially embrace the human rights corpus. Many are scholars and policymakers of multicultural heritage or orientation who, though familiar and sometimes even comfortable with the West, see cross-cultural referencing as the most critical variable in the creation of a universal corpus of human rights.[19] They critique the existing human rights corpus as culturally exclusive in some respects and therefore view parts of it as illegitimate or, at the very least, irrelevant in non-Western societies. Some, including this author, have called for a multicultural approach to reform the human rights regime so as to make it more universal.[20] Many proponents of the first two schools who regard themselves as universalists have labelled many cultural agnostics "cultural relativists," a form of type-casting or human rights name-calling that has generally had the effect of stigmatizing those who resist the Eurocentric formulation of human rights.[21] Were this Article confined to this dichotomous view, it would be fair to label the universalists cultural relativists, as well, because universalists operate in a specific cultural space and distinct historical tradition. The perspective reflected here is not, however, sympathetic to cynical elites who purposely manipulate cultural images to justify despotic rule.[22] Rather, by cultural agnostics I refer to academics and

19. For views of cultural agnostics, see Mutua, African Cultural Fingerprint, supra note 3 (arguing that the current human rights regime is Eurocentric and that the creation of a truly universal human rights jurisprudence can result only from the multicultural elaboration of norms); Kausikan, supra note 3, at 25 (contending that Asian countries rely on their own traditions, and not just Western pressure, to govern their citizens in a way which respects the human dignity of individuals); see also Human Rights: Cultural and Ideological Perspectives (Adamantia Pollis & Peter Schwab eds., 1979) (examining the relevance of a universal standard of human rights to societies with a non-Western cultural tradition); see generally Cross-Cultural Perspectives, supra note 9; Human Rights in Cross-Cultural Perspectives: A Quest for Consensus (Abdullahi Ahmed An-Na'im ed., 1992) [hereinafter Quest for Consensus].

20. See Mutua, African Cultural Fingerprint, supra note 3, at 345-46.

21. For bold universalist views and a rejection of the multiculturalist approach, see Jack Donnelly, Universal Human Rights in Theory and Practice (1989); Rhoda E. Howard, Group Versus Individual Identity in the African Debate on Human Rights, in Cross-Cultural Perspectives, supra note 9, at 159.

22. Some of the world's notorious dictators have on occasion misappropriated tradition to justify repression. For example, Hastings Kamuzu Banda, formerly the absolute leader of Malawi, instituted "traditional courts" through which his political opponents were dispatched after sham trials. See Makau wa Mutua, Confronting the Past: Accountability

policymakers who see the potential dynamism of the human rights corpus as an opportunity for the creation of a multicultural conception of human rights.

The last school, that of political strategists or instrumentalists, abounds with governments and institutions that selectively and inconsistently deploy human rights discourse for strategic and political ends.[23] While all states—socialist or capitalist, developed or underdeveloped—are generally cynical in their deployment of human rights norms, my focus here is not on all states. If that were the case, I would discuss the hypocrisies of the Zairian state under Mobutu Sese Seko, those of the former Soviet Union, and of many

---

for Human Rights Violations in Malawi (1994). Similarly, some oppressive Asian states have cynically invoked tradition and culture to ward off human rights challenges. Human Rights Watch (HRW), the dominant American human rights NGO with an international mandate, has repeatedly attacked Asian governments for promoting an "Asian concept of human rights." Human Rights Watch, Human Rights Watch World Report 1995: Events of 1994, at xiv (1995)[hereinafter World Report 1995]. HRW has argued that Asian governments falsely maintain that Asians "sought economic development before political liberty, valued communal obligations over individual rights, and supported national rather than universal human rights standards." Id. For a powerful critique of the positions espoused by Asian governments, see Yash Ghai, Human Rights and Governance: The Asia Debate, 15 Austl. Y.B. Int'l L. 1 (1994).

23. A good example of such a government is that of the United States which, using human rights as the pretext, nevertheless applies two distinct policies to two countries with similar political systems. The United States has developed its economic and diplomatic relationships with The People's Republic of China (PRC) but has steadfastly rejected the normalization of relations with Cuba even though both countries are ruled by one-party communist regimes. According to Western human rights groups, human rights abuses in both countries are plentiful. See World Report 1995, supra note 22, at 85-89, 142-49; Diane F. Orentlicher & Timothy A. Gelatt, Public Law, Private Actors: The Impact of Human Rights on Business Investors in China, 14 Nw. J. Int'l L. & Bus. 66 (1993) (discussing the role played by human rights in the decisions of private corporations to invest in China); Douglas Jehl, U.S. is to Maintain Trade Privileges for China's Goods, N.Y. Times, May 27, 1994, at A1 (describing the U.S. decision not to use trade as a lever to force an improvement of China's human rights practices); see also Roger Sullivan, Discarding the China Card, 86 Foreign Pol'y 3 (1992)(examining a revision in U.S. China policy). There seems little doubt that it is China's significant size, population, military capability (nuclear), and potential market which has drawn the United States close to it. See Mary McGrory, The Fog of Morality, Wash. Post, Feb. 10, 1991, at C1 (contrasting the cynical reactions of the Bush administration to the Iraqi abuses in Kuwait and the Chinese crackdown against its dissidents). Human rights concerns, which have historically been used by the United States as a weapon of foreign policy, were trumped by the need for a better relationship with China. On the other hand, Cuba's continued isolation appears to be more closely related to Cold War nostalgia and American domestic politics—political pandering to the Cuban-American lobby—than simply the human rights record of the Castro government. In any event, states that have committed egregious human rights violations such as Egypt, Israel in the Occupied Territories, Turkey, Vietnam, and Russia, have enjoyed U.S. support. Rhetorically, however, the United States continues to promote democracy and human rights abroad.

other states across the political spectrum that professed allegiance to human rights but violated them as official policy. My concern here is not with claims of states about their internal application of human rights norms. Rather, I am only interested in Western democracies and their institutions which alone rhetorically champion the universalization of human rights. Such institutions include the World Bank and the North Atlantic Treaty Organization (NATO), whose primary purposes are related to the preservation or the enhancement of liberalism and free markets. Increasingly, they have invoked human rights when dangers to these two goals have been deemed unacceptably high. Examples of such unacceptable dangers include civil war or regional conflicts that threaten "vital" Western interests, such as access to strategic resources. In the view of international financial institutions, donor agencies, and donor countries, such a risk could involve autocratic forms of governance that encourage intolerable levels of corruption and economic mismanagement and negatively affect the growth or functioning of markets and international trade.[24] Responses to such risks, including military ones, have in the past often been couched in human rights terminology.[25]

Obviously, human rights issues cannot be, nor should they be, the only factors that determine foreign policy choices. Other "vital" interests such as trade could trump human rights because in the calculus of geopolitics states have "many fish to fry." Yet it is precisely this "necessity" to balance competing objectives that

24. In general, popular demands for open political competition gained near universal recognition in the West after the collapse of the Soviet bloc in the late 1980s. Donor countries and agencies began to press one-party states in Africa to allow multi-partyism, liberalize their economies, and show more respect for human rights. In November 1991, for example, a World Bank-led group of donors interested in Kenya suspended aid to that country pending political and economic reforms. The donors stressed that "good governance is a prerequisite for equitable economic development" and urged Kenya to move towards "greater pluralism." They "underlined the importance of the rule of law and respect for human rights, notably the basic freedoms of expression and assembly, and called for firm action to deal with issues of corruption." Press Release of the World Bank 3 (Paris Nov. 26, 1991) [hereinafter Meeting of the Consultative Group for Kenya] (summing up the proceedings at the meeting of the Consultative Group for Kenya) (on file with the Virginia Journal of International Law). See also Lawyers Committee for Human Rights, The World Bank: Governance and Human Rights 43-60 (1993) [hereinafter Governance and Human Rights].

25. See, e.g., Diane Bartz, Amnesty International Scores Washington for Hypocrisy in Human Rights, UPI, July 9, 1991, available in LEXIS, News Library, ARCNWS File (reporting that Amnesty International accused the United States of "selectively using human rights abuses as a foreign policy tool").

makes states unreliable, unprincipled, and manipulative proponents of the human rights corpus.

By grouping the authors of human rights discourse into these four schools, I do not mean to suggest that the typologies or categories delineated are finite, completely separate and irreconcilable, or that one could not understand the "creators" of the discourse differently. I also do not mean to imply that the proponents of various typologies are one-dimensional; one author could fall into several categories depending upon the circumstances. Any number of critiques—from the feminist to the post-modern—would yield interesting results. This Article, however, is concerned with correlating the recent and "lofty" mantra of human rights to liberalism, arguably the most dominant political ideology of our time.

Part I of this Article briefly discusses the basic notions and requirements of liberal democracy and relates them to the central tenets of the human rights corpus. Part II focuses on the first school, that of the abolitionists or doctrinal conventionalists. Part III explores the assumptions and views of constitutionalists, while Part IV examines the dilemmas of the cultural agnostic. Lastly, Part V looks at political strategists.

This Article analyzes each of the four schools of thought and action to determine how they may be traced back to liberal democracy. It attempts to respond to the challenges and questions raised for the human rights corpus by these typologies. In particular, it revisits questions of the universality and legitimacy of the human rights corpus, and raises the possibility of a new internationality in human rights including its potential implications for the post-liberal society.

I. LIBERALISM, DEMOCRACY, AND HUMAN RIGHTS: A HOLY TRINITY?

Liberalism is distinguished from other traditions by its commitment to formal autonomy and abstract equality. It is a tradition that in its contemporary expression requires a constitutional state with limited powers, a state that is moreover accountable to the broad public. These aspirations are the basis for the development and elaboration of liberal democracy and, as this Article contends, the construction and universalization of the jurisprudence of human rights. In the historical continuum, therefore, liberalism gave birth to democracy, which, in turn, now seeks to present itself internationally as the ideology of human rights. This Part briefly explores the relationships among liberalism, political democracy, and human rights norms.

While many definitions of Western liberal democracy abound, the most dominant cast it in other than substantive terms. Samuel Huntington, for example, emphasizes the Schumpeterian[26] tradition, defining democracy in purely procedural language.[27] For Huntington, the democratic method involves two basic dimensions: contestation and participation, where the "most powerful collective decision makers are selected through fair, honest, and periodic elections in which candidates freely compete for votes and in which virtually all the adult population is eligible to vote."[28] Participation and contestation, according to Huntington, also imply certain civil and political freedoms which are necessary to free and fair elections, namely, the right to speak, publish, assemble, and organize.[29]

Significantly, Huntington does not believe that a system is democratic to the extent that it denies "voting participation" to segments of its population on the basis, for instance, of race or gender.[30] Thus the United States was not a democracy until it allowed its population of African ancestry the right to vote.[31] Likewise, South Africa was undemocratic until it granted its black African majority

26. Joseph Schumpeter, Capitalism, Socialism, and Democracy (3d ed. 1950). Schumpeter rejected the means and ends paradigm—which he called the "classical theory of democracy"—in which the "common good" was achieved through recourse to the "will of the people." Id. at 250-52. Schumpeter posited that the "democratic method is the institutional arrangement for arriving at political decisions in which individuals acquire the power to decide by means of a competitive struggle for the people's vote." Id. at 269.

27. Samuel Huntington, The Third Wave: Democratization in the Late Twentieth Century 6 (1991).

28. Id. at 7. Thus, a system is undemocratic where the following factors obtain: the opposition is not permitted to participate in elections, or is prohibited or curbed; opposition media, especially newspapers, are closed down or censored; or votes are tampered with or miscounted. Competition could be insufficient where an opposition experiences sustained failure over long periods to win elections. Id. at 7-8.

29. Id. at 7. These rights are central features of the human rights corpus. See, e.g., UDHR, supra note 1, arts. 19-21; ICCPR, supra note 8, arts. 19-22.

30. Huntington, supra note 27, at 7.

31. Although the Fifteenth Amendment to the U.S. Constitution prohibited the denial of the right to vote on the basis of race, many Southern states enacted laws designed to obstruct the exercise of that right by African-Americans. For example, some laws imposed the ability to read or write as a precondition for registration, a requirement that excluded many African-Americans. See Gerald Gunther, Individual Rights in Constitutional Law 625-31 (5th ed. 1992); see also Voting Rights Act of 1965, 42 U.S.C. §§ 1973-1973aa-3 (1988) (prohibiting various methods of obstructing citizens from exercising their right to vote).

the right to vote in 1994.[32] Many European countries, such as Switzerland, were undemocratic until they granted women the right to vote, likewise the United States until 1920.[33] The norm of non-discrimination is here extended to political participation. The formal right to vote is clearly in itself an insufficient measure of democracy because quite often it has masked other hindrances to political participation such as institutional biases and barriers based on race, gender, religion, social status, and wealth. Nevertheless, the political scientist Robert Dahl has argued that elections are the critical element in the definition of democracy and the central device for ordinary citizens to exert a high degree of control over their leaders.[34]

The minimalist definition of democracy does not betray traditional or conventional conceptions of liberalism; rather, it responds to liberalism's basic commitment to guarantee citizens their formal autonomy and political and legal equality. Thus, as Henry Steiner puts it, the traditional liberal understanding of the state requires that it "protect citizens in their political organizations and activities,"[35] guaranteeing autonomy and legal equality, but does not require that it remove impediments to actual equality which may result from lack of resources and status. Steiner says it clearly:

> Choices about types and degrees of [political] participation may depend on citizens' economic resources and social status. But it is not the government's responsibility to alleviate that dependence, to open paths to political

32. For a description of the formal transformation of South Africa from a racist state to a democracy, see Adrien K. Wing, Towards Democracy in a New South Africa, 16 Mich. J. Int'l L. 689 (1995) (reviewing Ziyad Motala, Constitutional Options for a Democratic South Africa: A Comparative Perspective (1994)).

33. Based on the gender criteria alone, most states long regarded as democratic were in fact undemocratic until recently. Women were not allowed to vote on an equal footing with men in the following states until the early twentieth century: Austria (1920); Belgium (1948); France (1944); Germany (1919); the United States (1920); and the United Kingdom (1928). See Fox, supra note 12, at 546. See also Thomas F. Mackie & Richard Rose, The International Almanac of Electoral History (3d rev. ed. 1991). Until 1948, university graduates and businessmen in the United Kingdom were allowed two votes each. Id. at 438-39.

34. See Robert R. Dahl, A Preface to Democratic Theory 125 (1956).

35. Henry J. Steiner, Political Participation as a Human Right, 1 Harv. Hum. Rts. Y.B. 77, 109 (1988) [hereinafter Steiner, Political Participation]. Steiner identifies some of these activities as "forming political parties, mobilizing interest groups, soliciting campaign funds, petitioning and demonstrating, campaigning for votes, establishing associations to monitor local government, lobbying." Id.

> participation which lack of funds or education or status would otherwise block.[36]

In reality, of course, participation in the political process requires more than the state's permission and protection. Increasingly, states not only provide these two services but also expend enormous resources constructing the electoral machinery for participation; legislative reforms in many democracies now attempt to address historical, socioeconomic, and ethnic, racial, and gender-related barriers to participation.[37] Such interpretations of political democracy have attempted to build into their frameworks notions of social or economic democracy. In human rights law, the International Covenant on Economic, Social and Cultural Rights (ICESCR) most closely resembles this aspiration.[38]

The main focus of human rights law, however, has been on those rights and programs that seek to strengthen, legitimize, and export political or liberal democracy.[39] Inversely, most of the human rights regime is derived from bodies of domestic jurisprudence developed over several centuries in the West.[40] The emphasis, by academics and practitioners, in the development of human rights law has been on civil and political rights.[41] In fact the currency of civil and political rights has been so strong that they have become

36. Id. at 109-10.

37. See id. at 110-11.

38. See ICESCR, supra note 8. As noted by Alston, however, the rights enumerated in the ICESCR, unlike those in the ICCPR, were "not based upon any significant bodies of domestic jurisprudence." Philip Alston, The Committee on Economic, Social and Cultural Rights, in United Nations and Human Rights, supra note 1, at 473, 490 [hereinafter Alston, ECOSOC]. Thus, with the exception of some labor-related rights, there is still little understanding of the normative content of the rights to food, education, health care, clothing, and shelter, to mention a few. See id.

39. In terms of emphasis and political importance, the two most significant human rights documents are the UDHR and the ICCPR. Although the UDHR lists a number of economic, social, and cultural rights, its first 21 articles, which include the right to own property individually, read like a manifesto for a political democracy. See UDHR, supra note 1, arts. 1-21. The ICCPR is itself mainly a repetition and elaboration of the rights and processes that liberal democracies have evolved. See ICCPR, supra note 8.

40. See Alston, ECOSOC, supra note 38, at 490. For an example, Alston notes that "phrases like 'cruel, inhuman or degrading treatment or punishment' had been the subject of in-depth judicial and academic analysis" prior to its inclusion in the ICCPR. Id.

41. Although the formal body of human rights law includes economic, social, and cultural rights, the rhetoric and practice of the human rights movement, and especially its most vocal wing, the international non-governmental organizations (INGOs), have centered on civil and political rights. The three human rights organizations most closely associated with the human rights movement, Amnesty International, the International Commission of Jurists, and Human Rights Watch, focus on state action against the individual. There is no major INGO in the West that addresses economic and social rights.

synonymous with the human rights movement, even as the so-called second and third generation rights have attempted to make inroads into the mainstream of the discourse.[42]

There is virtual agreement that the early formulation and codification of human rights standards was dominated by Western cultural and political norms.[43] This was particularly true with the formulation and adoption of the Universal Declaration on Human Rights (UDHR), the "spiritual parent of and inspiration for many human rights treaties."[44] As one author has remarked, the West was able to "impose" its philosophy of human rights on the rest of the world because in 1948 it dominated the United Nations.[45] The minority socialist bloc abstained after it put up ineffectual resistance on grounds that economic, social, and cultural rights were downgraded.[46] More important, non-Western views were largely unrepresented because the so-called Third World at the United Nations was mainly composed of Latin American countries whose dominant worldview was European.[47] In 1948, most African and Asian states were absent from the United Nations because they were European colonies.[48] On account of this exclusivity of major cultural blocs, it was presumptuous and shamelessly ethnocentric for the UDHR to refer to itself as the "common standard of achievement for all peoples and all nations."[49]

---

42. Sometimes writers and actors in human rights refer to "generations" of rights, a euphemism that variously describes ranking, acceptability, or even the order in which rights "ought" to be implemented or realized. Thus, civil and political rights are regarded as "first generation" rights while economic, social, and cultural rights are termed "second generation" rights. Group rights, such as the right to self-determination, and peoples' rights, such as the right to development, which are listed in the African Charter on Human and Peoples' Rights, are referred to as "third generation" rights. African Charter, supra note 6. Given the inadequate attention given to rights in the second and third "tiers," it seems fair to conclude that "generations" are the human rights movement's proxy for the importance it attaches to the particular category of rights. For more on these distinctions, see Buergenthal Nutshell, supra note 1, at 234-35; Jean-Bernard Marie, Relations Between Peoples' Rights and Human Rights: Semantic and Methodological Distinctions, 7 Hum. Rts. L.J. 195 (1986).

43. See Leary, supra note 9, at 15.

44. Steiner, Political Participation, supra note 35, at 79.

45. See Cassese, supra note 1, at 31-32.

46. Id. at 31.

47. Id. at 32.

48. As Leary puts it, the drafting of the Universal Declaration of Human Rights was entrusted to the Human Rights Commission, which in turn gave the responsibility to people who were from "Western Europe or the Americas or were non-Europeans educated in the West." Leary, supra note 9, at 20.

49. UDHR, supra note 1, pmbl. Leary provides a very good summary of the origin and cultural orientation of the drafters of the UDHR. She lists the following persons as the

A closer examination of the rights listed in both the UDHR and the International Covenant on Civil and Political Rights (ICCPR) leaves no doubt that both documents—which are regarded as the two most important human rights instruments[50]—are attempts to universalize civil and political rights accepted or aspired to in Western liberal democracies. Many articles in the Universal Declaration echo or reproduce provisions of the U.S. Constitution and the jurisprudence of Western European states such as France and the United Kingdom. The UDHR prohibits "cruel, inhuman or degrading treatment or punishment;"[51] the U.S. Constitution prohibits the infliction of "cruel and unusual punishments."[52] Other parallels include due process protections,[53] speech rights,[54] and privacy.[55] During the drafting of the ICCPR and the ICESCR, both of which were opened for signature in 1966, there was some discernable influence from the newly independent states of Africa and Asia, though the ICCPR retained its distinctly Western character.[56] Although non-Western perspectives on human rights, such as the African conceptions of peoples' rights and duties and the more celebrated right to development,[57] have acquired some notoriety in

key drafters: Rene Cassin of France, John P. Humphrey of Canada, Eleanor Roosevelt of the United States, Hernan Santa Cruz of Chile, Charles Malik of Lebanon, P. C. Chang of China, and Fernand Dehousse of Belgium. She notes that although this group appears culturally diverse—three from the Americas, two Europeans, and two Asians—it was in reality Eurocentric. All the drafters had received their education largely from Western institutions; Chang and Malik, the only non-Westerners, were educated at Clark College and Harvard University respectively. Malik, who had taught at Harvard, even urged the inclusion of the phrase that each person is "endowed by the Creator with unalienable rights." The phrase, which was lifted from the United States Declaration of Independence, was rejected. See Leary, supra note 9, at 20. Chang referred "with approval, to eighteenth-century Western philosophical theories as the source of the declaration." Id.

50. Although the ICESCR is included in the trilogy referred to as the International Bill of Rights, it is the least prominent of the three. It has been relegated to the backwater of human rights discourse. See supra note 42.

51. UDHR, supra note 1, art. 5.

52. U.S. Const. amend. VIII.

53. U.S. Const. amends. V, VI; UDHR, supra note 1, arts. 7-11.

54. U.S. Const. amend. I; UDHR, supra note 1, art. 19.

55. U.S. Const. amend. IV; UDHR, supra note 1, art. 12.

56. The ICCPR repeated, almost verbatim, with the exception of the right to property, many of the civil and political rights enumerated in the UDHR. The most visible demonstration of the presence of emergent states of Africa, Latin America, and Asia was the inclusion of article 1, common to both the ICCPR and the ICESCR, on the group right to self-determination. See ICCPR, supra note 8, art. 1; ICESCR, supra note 8, art. 1; Leary, supra note 9, at 28.

57. In 1986, the United Nations General Assembly adopted the Declaration on the Right to Development. G.A. Res. 128, U.N. GAOR, 41st Sess., Supp. No. 53, at 186-87, U.N. Doc. A/41/53 (1986). Leading Western states, including the United States, Germany,

human rights debates, they remain marginal to the mainstream practice of human rights.[58] The same has been true of economic, social, and cultural rights since their relegation to the "other" human rights treaty.[59]

The purpose of this segment was to track some of the historical roots of the human rights corpus and to establish its evolution from liberal thought and political democracy. This connection leads to the conclusion that the post-1945 elaboration and codification of human rights norms has been the process of the universalization of liberalism and its outgrowth, Western political democracy. Seen in this light, the human rights movement is a proxy for a political ideology, a fact that would shear it of the pretense of non-partisanship. Although the movement's authors present it as non-ideological, and as universal and non-contentious, the human rights regime does not transcend or stand removed from politics. The human rights movement is not post-ideological, although its mantra of universal morality and timeless righteousness attempts to mask its deeply political character.

II. CONVENTIONAL DOCTRINALISM: CONTENT AND CONTEXT

Perhaps no other school in the human rights movement has been more influential in the promotion of the "universalization" of human rights norms than that of the conventional doctrinalists, even though the formal creation of human rights law is carried out by collections of states—the so-called international community—

---

the United Kingdom, the Nordic countries (except Norway), and Japan, either voted against the declaration or abstained. See John Quinn, The General Assembly into the 1990s, in United Nations and Human Rights, supra note 1, at 55, 65.

58. Even Leary, who is more optimistic about the normative universalization of human rights, is careful not to overstate the influence of non-Western thinking on human rights. She notes that such thinking has "*begun* to influence Western thinking on the subject." Leary, supra note 9, at 29.

59. Opposition from the West to one human rights covenant covering all human rights—civil and political as well as economic, social, and cultural—led to the two instruments, the ICCPR and the ICESCR. Traditional Western thinking on rights, which used the Soviet bloc emphasis on economic, social and cultural rights as a pretext for opposing a single covenant, makes a distinction between "negative" and "positive" rights. Although this distinction has for the most part been demystified, civil and political rights have retained their prominence in the West because their implementation does not necessarily involve the redistribution of wealth or inception of programs that drastically curtail an individual's right to accumulate unlimited property. Cf. Donnelly, supra note 9, at 31, 49 (demonstrating that the positive-negative distinction fails to provide accurate labels for negative rights like the protection from torture, which requires positive governmental action, and the right to political participation, which seems to be "more a positive than a negative right").

acting in concert and separately within and outside the ambit of the United Nations. It is generally accepted that the full-court press for the universalization of human rights ideals was not applied until after the Hitler atrocities half a century ago, although the development of human rights norms and ideals preceded the Holocaust. Prior to 1945, the antecedents to the human rights corpus included the 1926 Slavery Convention,[60] the work of the International Labor Organization,[61] and some opinions of the Permanent Court of International Justice.[62] After Hitler, the United Nations set out on a crusade to codify "universal" human rights norms.

The most active element in the internationalization of the human rights movement has been the so-called international non-governmental organization (INGO),[63] the movement's prime engine of growth. The most prominent INGOs in this regard are based in the West and seek to enforce the application of human rights norms internationally, particularly towards repressive states in the South. They are ideological analogues, both in theory and in method, of the traditional civil rights organizations which preceded them in the West. The American Civil Liberties Union (ACLU), one of the most influential civil rights organizations in the United States, is the classic example of the Western civil rights organization.[64] Two other equally important domestic civil rights organizations in the United States are the National Association for the Advancement

---

60. Slavery Convention, Sept. 25, 1926, 46 Stat. 2183, 60 L.N.T.S. 253.

61. Established by the League of Nations on April 11, 1919, the ILO has focused on the creation of common labor standards. For a general description of the origin and purposes of the ILO, see Human Rights Directory: Western Europe 235-36 (Laurie S. Wiseberg & Hazel Sirett eds., 1982) [hereinafter Western Europe Directory].

62. See, e.g., Advisory Opinion No. 64, Minority Schools in Albania, 1935 P.C.I.J. (ser. A/B) No. 64 (examining whether Albania violated the 1919 Minorities Treaty Between the Principal Allied and Associated Powers and Poland by prohibiting private schools for the Albanian Greek-speaking minority).

63. INGOs may be contrasted with non-governmental organizations (NGOs) which, though also referring to private, non-governmental groups, is often used to describe "domestic" or national organizations. So-called NGOs address human rights issues only in the country in which they are based.

64. Initially founded in 1920 to advocate the rights of conscientious objectors, the ACLU sees itself as the "guardian of the Bill of Rights which guarantees fundamental civil liberties to all of us." These rights include the freedoms of speech, press, and religion (First Amendment); freedom from abuses by the police, domestic spying, and other illegal intelligence activities (Fourth Amendment); equal treatment and fair play (Fifth Amendment); fair trial (Sixth Amendment); prohibition against cruel and unusual punishment (Eighth Amendment); and privacy and personal autonomy (Fourth, Fifth, and Ninth Amendments). See North American Human Rights Directory 19 (Laurie S. Wiseberg and Hazel Sirett eds., 1984) [hereinafter North American Directory].

of Colored People (NAACP)[65] and the NAACP Legal Defense and Educational Fund (LDF).[66] Although these organizations are called civil rights groups by Americans, they are in reality human rights organizations. The historical origin of the distinction between a "civil rights" group and a "human rights" group in the United States remains unclear. The primary difference is that Western human rights groups focus on abusive practices and traditions in what they see as relatively repressive, "backward" foreign countries and cultures, while the agenda of civil rights groups concentrates on domestic issues. Thus, although groups such as Human Rights Watch publish reports on human rights abuses in the U.S., the focus of their activity is the human rights "problems" or "abuses" of other countries.[67]

In American popular culture, several assumptions are implicit in this thinking: "human rights problems" do not apply to "people like us," but rather to "backward" peoples or those who are "exotic;" these "problems" arise where the political and legal systems do not work or cannot correct themselves; and "we are lucky" and should "help those less fortunate" overcome their history of despotism. Unfortunately, this dichotomy has calcified in academic institutions where civil rights questions are taught and explored under the rubric of "American" courses while human rights offerings and activities are treated under the rubric "foreign" or "international" disciplines and classifications.[68] For example, American law school graduates who have taken courses on race, gender, employment law, sexuality, housing, or the criminal justice system probably associate those fields with civil rights, not human

65. The NAACP, the United States' oldest civil rights organization, was founded in 1909 to seek equal treatment—the removal of racial discrimination in areas such as voting, employment, housing, business, courts, and transportation—for African-Americans through peaceful reform. See id. at 161.

66. Although today the LDF and the NAACP are separate legal entities, the LDF was founded in 1939 as the legal arm of the NAACP. It has initiated legal action in courts to challenge discrimination and promote equality in schools, jobs, the electoral system, land use, and other services and areas. Id. at 159.

67. See, e.g., Human Rights Watch, Questions and Answers 3 (undated pamphlet, on file with the *Virginia Journal of International Law*) ("We examine both how the U.S. government promoted human rights abroad and how it respects human rights at home.").

68. Human rights programs at American University (Washington College of Law), Columbia, Harvard, Virginia, and Yale, among others, have adopted this bifurcated approach: civil rights belong to courses and pursuits that explore "American" issues and dilemmas while human rights offerings concern the "foreign," the "international," the "other." Perhaps there is a fear that exploring human rights under this umbrella may blunt the importance of the civil rights courses and activities at American universities and relegate them to the margins.

rights. This organizational format could lead to a sense of cultural superiority and may exacerbate problems of nationalism. In turn, this development could adversely affect attempts at an international consensus on human rights, as non-Western cultures see crusading human rights activists from the West as the "civilizers" that many of the activists cast themselves as.

At any rate, the half-dozen leading human rights organizations, the prototypical conventional doctrinalists, have arisen in the West over the last half-century with the express intent of promoting certain basic Western liberal values—now dubbed human rights—throughout the world, especially the non-Western world. These INGOs were the brainchildren of prominent Western civil rights advocates, lawyers, and private citizens. The International League for the Rights of Man, now the International League for Human Rights (ILHR), is the oldest such organization, founded in New York in 1942.[69] At various times it has focused on victims of torture, religious intolerance, the rights of human rights monitors at its affiliates abroad, the reunification of Eastern Europeans with relatives in the West during the cold war, and the human rights treaty state reporting system within the United Nations.[70] Roger Baldwin, the founder of the ACLU, also founded the ILHR.[71]

The ILHR itself was responsible for establishing in New York in 1975 the Lawyers Committee for International Human Rights, now known as the Lawyers Committee for Human Rights (LCHR), another of the more important Western INGOs. The LCHR claims to promote the human rights standards contained in the International Bill of Rights.[72] The New York-based Human Rights Watch (HRW)[73] was founded in 1978[74] and has developed into the most dominant American INGO working to expose violations of

69. See North American Directory, supra note 64, at 135.

70. Id.

71. See Rita McWilliams, Who Watched Americas Watch?, 19 Nat'l Interest 45, 53 (1990). Jerome Shestack, a prominent American lawyer who long served as the President of the ILHR and is the organization's current honorary chair, was replaced in May 1996 by Scott Horton, a partner in a New York law firm. Telephone Interview with the ILHR (Sept. 13, 1996).

72. On the mandate of the LCHR, see supra note 17.

73. Human Rights Watch is divided into five geographic units covering Africa, the Americas, Asia, the Middle East, and the signatories of the Helsinki Accords. It also has five thematic projects on arms transfers, children's rights, free expression, prison conditions, and women's rights. See World Report 1995, supra note 22, at vii.

74. Id. Human Rights Watch began in 1978 with the founding of the Helsinki Watch.

basic liberal freedoms.[75] The founder of HRW is Aryeh Neier, a former national executive director of the ACLU.[76]

The last major American INGO is the Washington DC-based International Human Rights Law Group, which was established by the Procedural Aspects of International Law Institute (PAIL), a private American organization that explores issues in international law.[77] Some American domestic civil rights NGOs are acutely aware of their pioneering role in the creation of similar organizations abroad.[78] Until recently, and to a large extent even today, none of these American INGOs focused on human rights issues in the United States, except to seek the reform of U.S. foreign policy and American compliance with aspects of refugee law.[79]

75. HRW asserts that it "defends freedom of thought and expression, due process and equal protection of the law; it documents and denounces murders, disappearances, torture, arbitrary imprisonment, exile, censorship, and other abuses of internationally recognized human rights." Id.

76. See Aryeh Neier, Political Consequences of the United States Ratification of the International Covenant on Civil and Political Rights, 42 DePaul L. Rev. 1233, n.* (1993).

77. See North American Directory, supra note 64, at 133. PAIL itself was established in 1965 and has devoted considerable resources to the promotion of the idea of human rights. Richard Lillich, its former president, is a professor of law at the University of Virginia School of Law, and one of the leading writers on human rights. See, e.g., Richard B. Lillich, International Human Rights: Problems of Law, Policy, and Practice (2d ed., 1991); Richard B. Lillich, Preface, in Hurst Hannum et al., Materials on International Human Rights and U.S. Criminal Law and Procedure (1989); Richard B. Lillich, The Constitution and International Human Rights, 83 Am. J. Int'l L. 851 (1989); Richard B. Lillich, Invoking International Human Rights Law in Domestic Courts, 54 U. Cin. L. Rev. 367 (1985); Richard B. Lillich, The Role of the U.N. Security Council in Protecting Human Rights in Crisis Situations: U.N. Humanitarian Intervention in the Post-Cold War World, 3 Tul. J. Int'l & Comp. L. 1 (1995).

78. At a 1992 LDF symposium of public interest law NGOs from around the world, Julius Chambers, then director-counsel of the LDF, recalled how Thurgood Marshall, his most celebrated predecessor, had in 1959 helped write the Kenya Constitution, and had helped to endow it with doctrines of due process, equality, and justice. Mr. Chambers also remembered how Jack Greenberg, another predecessor, had laid the groundwork for the Legal Resource Centre of South Africa, one of that country's leading public interest law firms under apartheid. Instructively, he noted that he did not view the symposium "primarily as an occasion for the LDF to *teach* others." See NAACP Legal Defense & Education Fund, Public Interest Law Around the World 1 (1992) [emphasis added]. See also Lawyers Committee for Human Rights, The Establishment of the Right of Non-Governmental Groups to Operate, (1993) (noting the progress made in establishing human rights NGOs around the world and arguing for the removal of restrictions on NGOs to allow them to operate more freely).

79. American INGOs argue, with some justification, that there is a glut of civil rights organizations addressing civil (human) rights problems in the United States. They therefore see little purpose in duplicating the excellent work of local NGOs. This posture is self-defeating in several respects. First, charges of "imperialism" undercut the effectiveness of American INGOs, even with some of their kindred spirits in the South and the former Soviet bloc. Secondly, domestic American NGOs remain unaware of the uses

The two other leading INGOs are located in Europe, in the United Kingdom and Switzerland. The Geneva-based International Commission of Jurists (ICJ) was "founded in 1952 to promote the 'rule of law'[80] throughout the world."[81] The ICJ has been accused of being a tool of the West in the Cold War, spending considerable resources exposing the failures of Soviet bloc and one-party states.[82] Today, however, it is regarded as a bona fide INGO, concerned with rule of law questions in the South.[83]

Lastly, the London-based Amnesty International (AI), the most powerful human rights INGO, is today synonymous with the human rights movement and has inspired the creation of many similar human rights groups around the world. It was launched by Peter Benenson, a British lawyer, writing in the May 28, 1961, issues of the London Observer and Le Monde.[84] Benenson's article, "Forgotten Prisoners," urged moral outrage and appeals for amnesty for individuals who were imprisoned, tortured, or exe-

of the international rights regime and the solidarity of advocates elsewhere, facts which conspired to delay the ratification by the United States of major international human rights treaties. The absence of domestic U.S. NGOs from the international human rights movement served, among other things, to delegitimatize the movement in the eyes of other cultures. Nevertheless, in a rare effort, Human Rights Watch and the ACLU in 1993 produced a report on human rights abuses in the United States. See Human Rights Watch & American Civil Liberties Union, Human Rights Violations in the United States (1993). Two things were unusual about the effort: first, that an American INGO produced a human rights report on the United States, and second, that it did so in collaboration with a domestic American NGO. In a rare call, Dorothy Thomas, the director of Human Rights Watch Women's Project, has urged the use of international human rights norms in protecting human rights in the United States. Dorothy Q. Thomas, Advancing Rights Protection in the United States: An Internationalized Advocacy Strategy, 9 Harv. Hum. Rts. J. 15 (1996).

80. This term is commonly understood to describe a state that is accountable to the governed through the application of fair and just laws enforced by an independent and impartial judiciary. See, e.g., Andrea J. Hanneman, Note, Independence and Group Rights in the Baltics: A Double Minority Problem, 35 Va. J. Int'l L. 485, 523 ("The extent to which a society protects human rights in general and minority rights in particular has been called the 'litmus test of liberty and the rule of law.'") (citing Ralf Dahrendorf, Minority Rights and Minority Rule, in Minorities: A Question of Human Rights 79, 79 (Ben Whitaker ed., 1984)).

81. Western Europe Directory, supra note 61, at 216.

82. See Issa G. Shivji, The Concept of Human Rights in Africa 34 (1989). At its inception, the ICJ was funded in part by covert CIA funds. "It followed an essentially American set of priorities in its early years, then expanded and became less politically partial." Claude E. Welch, Jr., Protecting Human Rights in Africa: Roles and Strategies of Non-Governmental Organizations 163 (1995).

83. As of September 1996, the ICJ's secretary general was Adama Dieng, the Senegalese jurist who had risen from the legal officer responsible for Africa to become the organization's first non-Western head.

84. See Western Europe Directory, supra note 61, at 265.

cuted because of their political opinions or religion.[85] The recipient of the 1977 Nobel Peace Prize, AI claims that its object is "to contribute to the observance throughout the world of human rights as set out in the Universal Declaration of Human Rights"[86] through campaigns to free prisoners of conscience;[87] to ensure fair trials within a reasonable time[88] for political prisoners; to abolish the death penalty, torture, and other cruel treatment of prisoners;[89] and to end extrajudicial executions and disappearances.[90]

Some structural factors provide further evidence of the ideological orientation of INGOs. They concern the sources of their moral, financial, and social support. The founding fathers of major INGOs—they have all been White males—were Westerners who either worked on or had an interest in domestic civil and political rights issues; they sought the reform of governmental laws, policies, and processes to bring about compliance with American and European conceptions of liberal democracy and equal protection. Although the founders of the INGOs did not explicitly state their "mission" as a crusade for the globalization of these values, they nevertheless crafted organizational mandates that promoted liberal ideals and norms. In any case, the key international human rights

---

85. See Ian Martin, Lecture by the Edward A. Smith Visiting Fellow presented by the Harvard Law School Human Rights Program, (Apr. 14, 1993), in The New World Order: Opportunity or Threat for Human Rights? at 4-5 [hereinafter New World Order]. From 1986-1992, Martin was the secretary general of Amnesty International. Benenson's article accompanied photos of six political prisoners: three were imprisoned in Romania, Hungary, and Czechoslovakia; the other three were a Greek communist and unionist imprisoned in Greece, an Angolan doctor and poet incarcerated by the Portuguese colonial rulers in Angola, and the Rev. Ashton Jones, an American who had repeatedly been beaten and jailed in Louisiana and Texas for advocating the civil rights of Black Americans. Id. Although AI now focuses most of its attention on Africa, Central America, and South America, the trigger for its creation was, ironically, the official conduct of Soviet-bloc and Western governments, including the United States.

86. Statute of Amnesty International arts. 1 and 2, reprinted in Amnesty International, Amnesty International Report, app. II at 332 (1994) [hereinafter AI Report].

87. Prisoners of conscience are individuals detained anywhere for their beliefs or because of their ethnic origin, sex, color or language who have not used or advocated violence. Id. at 333. It is interesting to note that Nelson Mandela and many in the African National Congress were not regarded as prisoners of conscience by this standard. See Peter Worthington, Dancing to Castro's Tune, Toronto Sun, Aug. 16, 1994, at 11, available in LEXIS, News Library, ARCNWS File; Sousa Jamba, An Ex-Convict Runs out of Convictions, The Times, Dec. 9, 1993, available in LEXIS, News Library, ARCNWS File. For a more comprehensive discussion of the reasons and motivations behind the narrow mandate of Amnesty International, see Peter R. Baehr, Amnesty International and Its Self-Imposed Limited Mandate, 12 Neth. Hum. Rts. Q. 5 (1994).

88. AI Report, supra note 86, at 332.

89. Id. at 332-33.

90. Id. at 333.

instruments such as the UDHR and the ICCPR pierced the sovereign veil for the purposes of protecting and promoting human rights. The mandates of INGOs are lifted, almost verbatim, from such instruments. AI also deploys jurisprudential arguments developed in the context of Western liberal democracy to cast the death penalty as the "ultimate form of cruel, inhuman and degrading punishment."[91]

The pool for the social support of INGOs has therefore come from the private, non-governmental, and civil society segments of the industrial democracies: prominent lawyers, academics at leading universities, the business and entertainment elite, and other professionals. In the United States, these circles are drawn from the liberal establishment; the overwhelming majority vote for and support the Democratic Party and its politics and are opposed to the Republican Party. The board of directors of Human Rights Watch, for example, counts among its members such luminaries as Robert Bernstein, formerly the top executive at Random House; Jack Greenberg, the former director-counsel at LDF and provost at Columbia University; and Alice Henkin, spouse of the acclaimed professor of international law, Louis Henkin, and an important human rights personality in her own right.[92] The board of directors of the Lawyers Committee for Human Rights includes its chair, Norman Dorsen, the prominent New York University law professor, former ACLU president, and First Amendment expert; Louis Henkin; Sigourney Weaver, the actress; Kerry Kennedy Cuomo, the daughter of the late Robert F. Kennedy and the founder of the Robert F. Kennedy Memorial Center for Human Rights; Deborah Greenberg, the spouse of Jack Greenberg and a professor at Columbia Law School; Marvin Frankel, formerly the Chairman of the Board and a named partner in a major New York City law firm; and Tom Bernstein, the Committee's president, a senior business executive and scion of Robert Bernstein.[93] The board of directors of the International Human Rights Law Group is composed of sim-

91. AI Report, supra note 86, at 21. In addition, AI attacks the "arbitrary and irrevocable nature of the death penalty," its use as a "tool of political repression," and its disproportionate imposition on "the poor and the powerless." It disagrees with the argument that the death penalty has a deterrent effect on crime. Id.

92. See World Report 1995, supra note 22, at 387.

93. Lawyers Committee for Human Rights, Critique: Review of the U.S. Department of State's Country Reports on Human Rights Practices 1994, at 305 (1995). Telephone Interview with Lawyers Committee for Human Rights (Sept. 13, 1996).

ilar personalities.[94] These boards are predominantly White and male and almost completely American; some, such as those of the Lawyers Committee or HRW, typically have one or several African-Americans or a member of another non-White minority.

The boards of the European-based INGOs, the ICJ and AI, tend to differ, somewhat, from American INGOs, although they too are dominated by Westerners, Western-trained academics, professionals, and policymakers, or non-Westerners whose worldview is predominantly Western. Thus, even these Asians and Africans—who, though non-White, nevertheless "think White" or "European"—champion, usually uncritically, the universalization of the human rights corpus and liberal democracy. In 1994, for example, the seven members of the executive committee of the ICJ included a German, an Australian, a Brazilian (a Westerner), and four establishment figures from India, Ghana, Sri Lanka, and Jordan. The non-Westerners in the group were prominent legal professionals steeped in either the common law or the civil law traditions.[95] AI's International Executive Committee, its principal policymaking organ, is arguably "more global looking"—it includes a number of members from the South—although it too has historically been dominated by Westerners.[96] The staffs of all the major INGOs, including AI's headquarters in London, are similarly dominated by Westerners, although both AI and ICJ now have African heads.[97]

94. See International Human Rights Law Group, Ethiopia in Transition: A Report on the Judiciary and the Legal Profession, front leaf (1994) [hereinafter Ethiopia in Transition]. To "broaden" its international credibility, the Law Group has constituted an International Advisory Council which includes noted activists, scholars, and pro-establishment figures from Asia, Africa, and Latin America. Id.

95. For a list of the members of the ICJ, see International Commission of Jurists, The Civilian Judicial System in the West Bank and Gaza: Present and Future 134-35 (1994). The president of the ICJ was Joaquim Ruiz-Gimenez, a Spanish professor of law and a former Ombudsman of Spain. Id. at 134.

96. See Henry J. Steiner, Diverse Partners: Non-Governmental Organizations in the Human Rights Movement 61-64 (1991) [hereinafter Steiner, Diverse Partners].

97. Id. Pierre Sané, a Senegalese, became AI's first non-European secretary-general in October 1992. Amnesty International, Press Release, Amnesty International Announces Appointment of New Secretary General, Oct. 1, 1992. Adama Dieng, also a Senegalese, became the secretary-general of the ICJ in 1991. Although both AI and the ICJ accepted non-Western heads, the choices were more "safe" and less radical than they initially appeared. Sané came from the International Development Research Centre, a Canadian development aid organization, for which he had worked since 1978. Dieng was working for the ICJ before his appointment. Both were nationals of Senegal, with a reputation in the West as a stable formal democracy, and one of the most Francophillic countries in Africa. Leopold Sedar Senghor, Senegal's first president, whose wife was French, was educated in France and later appointed as the first black African to the *Academie Francaise*, the pinnacle of French culture. The forty "immortals," as the members of the *Academie* are

The selection of the boards and staffs of INGOs seems designed to guard against individuals, even if they are Westerners, who may question the utility or appropriateness of the conventional doctrinalist approach. This vetting perpetuates their narrow mandates and contradicts the implied and stated norms of diversity and equality, the raison d'etre for the existence of these organizations.[98]

The relationship between social, financial, and other material support provides further evidence of the political character of INGOs. Except for AI, which relies heavily on membership dues, most INGOs are funded by a combination of foundation grants, private donations, corporations, businesses, and governments.[99] While most do not accept government funds, some, among them the ICJ and the International Human Rights Law Group, have accepted financial support from governmental sources such as the United States Agency for International Development (USAID) and its Canadian and Nordic counterparts.[100] Those who reject government funds cite concerns for their independence of action and thought. It seems fair to conclude that to be considered for acceptance financial support must come from an industrial democracy with a commitment to promoting human rights abroad; presumably, support from Saudi Arabia or Zaire, clearly authoritarian states, would be unacceptable.

---

known, are chosen for their contribution to the legacy of French culture and statecraft. See generally Janet G. Vaillant, Black, French, and African: A Life of Leopold Sedar Senghor (1990).

98. When INGOs engage Southerners, it is ordinarily for area-specific responsibilities, usually their native region. For example, Africa Watch, the division of Human Rights Watch that addresses sub-Saharan African human rights problems, has been headed by Africans since its founding in 1988. Similarly, Americas Watch has been headed by Latin Americans virtually since its inception in 1981. This author, an African, was in 1989-91 the director of the Africa Project at the Lawyers Committee for Human Rights, having succeeded Rakiya Omaar, another African. This "ghettoization"—conscious or not—seeks to legitimize the organization in the particular region while retaining its commitment to Western liberal values. It also "pigeon-holes" non-Westerners as capable of addressing issues in only their native region and incapable of dealing with questions from other regions. In effect, these hiring patterns leave the impression that only Westerners have the ability to develop a "universal" outlook.

99. AI categorically states that "no money is sought or accepted from governments." AI Report, supra note 86, app. VIII at 352. HRW states that it "accepts no government funds, directly or indirectly." See World Report 1995, supra note 22, at vii.

100. In 1993 this author led a USAID-funded "rule of law" study mission to Ethiopia for the International Human Rights Law Group and wrote a report on the mission's findings. See Ethiopia in Transition, supra note 94.

The value of the board of directors is critical for groups that rely on private funding. Those networks and associations signify an INGO's reputation and acceptability by political and business elites. In the past decade, some INGOs, especially those based in the United States, have devised a fund-raising gimmick. At an annual dinner they present an award to a noted activist from a repressive country in the South or to a Westerner with superstar quality, such as Senator Edward Kennedy or George Soros, the philanthropist, and invite well-to-do, if not wealthy, citizens, corporations, law firms, and foundations to "buy a table"—a euphemism by which it is meant an invitee purchases the right to the dinner by reserving a table for a certain number of guests for a substantial donation. This tapestry of social and business ties, drawn from leading Americans who believe in liberal values and their internationalization through the human rights regime, underlines the agenda of INGOs.[101]

Substantively, conventional doctrinalists stress a narrow range of civil and political rights, as is reflected by the mandates of leading INGOs like Amnesty International and Human Rights Watch. Throughout the Cold War period, INGOs concentrated their attention on the exposure of violations of what they deemed "core" rights in Soviet bloc countries, Africa, Asia, and Latin America. In a reflection of this ideological bias, INGOs mirrored the position of the industrial democracies and generally assumed an unsympathetic, and at times, hostile posture towards calls for the expansion of their mandates to include economic and social rights.[102]

In the last few years since the collapse of the Soviet bloc, however, several INGOs have started to talk about the "indivisibility" of rights; a few now talk about their belief in the equality of the ICESCR and the ICCPR, although their rhetoric has not been matched by action and practice.[103] Many, in particular Human

101. In 1986, for example, the Lawyers Committee for Human Rights honored President Corazon Aquino of the Philippines for "her achievement in leading the people of her nation to peacefully reclaim democracy." See Lawyers Committee for Human Rights, 10th Anniversary Annual Report (1988). In 1987, it honored Robert Bernstein, senior executive at Random House and the founder of Human Rights Watch. NBC news anchor Tom Brokaw was the master of ceremonies at the 600-guest event which attracted prominent businessmen and lawyers. Id.

102. See Aryeh Neier, Human Rights, in The Oxford Companion to Politics of the World 401, 403 (Joel Krieger et al. eds., 1993).

103. Of all American INGOs, the International League for Human Rights (ILHR) has, until recently, taken the most favorable position towards economic and social rights. Testifying before the U.S. Congress in 1988, Jerome Shestack, the ILHR president,

Rights Watch, for a long time remained hostile, however, to the recognition of economic and social rights as "rights." HRW, which considered such rights "equities," instead advanced its own nebulous interpretation of "indivisible human rights" which related civil and political rights to survival, subsistence, and poverty, "assertions" of good that it did not explicitly call rights.[104] It argued that subsistence and survival are dependent on civil and political rights, especially those related to democratic accountability.[105] According

---

attacked American foreign policy as deeply flawed because of its omission of economic and social rights. See Recent Developments in U.S. Human Rights Policy: Hearings Before the Subcomm. on Human Rights and International Organizations of the House Comm. on Foreign Affairs, 100th Cong., 2d Sess. 64-65 (1988) (statement of Jerome Shestack, President, ILHR). Another American INGO, the Lawyers Committee for Human Rights, has (at least since 1988) called for the ratification of the ICESCR, although it has not taken any concrete steps in its monitoring, reporting, and advocacy to underline the importance of economic and social rights. See Lawyers Committee for Human Rights, Human Rights and U.S. Foreign Policy: Report and Recommendations 39 (1988); Lawyers Committee for Human Rights, Human Rights and US Foreign Policy: Report and Recommendations 46 (1992). More recently, the LCHR stated in a position paper arguing for the ratification of the ICESCR, that it believed "strongly that the two sets of rights (economic, social and cultural, and civil and political) are inseparable, and of equal importance. Neither can claim priority over the other." See Lawyers Committee for Human Rights, United States Draft Human Rights Action Plan: A Commentary 5 (June 1993) [hereinafter LCHR, Draft Action Plan Commentary]. The Lawyers Committee has stressed elsewhere that ratification of the ICESCR would recognize as rights what is already American domestic practice through historical evolution. See Lawyers Committee for Human Rights, The International Covenant on Economic, Social and Cultural Rights: The Case for US Ratification (June 1993) [hereinafter Lawyers Committee, ICESCR Ratification].

104. See Human Rights Watch, Indivisible Rights: The Relationship of Political and Civil Rights to Survival, Subsistence and Poverty (1992) [hereinafter HRW, Indivisible Rights]. In 1993, Aryeh Neier, the former executive director of HRW, expressed his opposition to the deployment of rights rhetoric to economic and social concerns:

> When it comes to the question of what are called economic rights, I'm on the side of the spectrum which feels that the attempt to describe economic concerns as rights is misguided. I think that when one expresses this opinion, it is often thought that one is denigrating the significance of economic misery and inequities. I would like not to be accused of that. I regard economic equity and economic misery as matters of enormous significance. I just don't think that it's useful to define them in terms of rights.

Aryeh Neier, Remarks to East Asian Legal Studies & Human Rights Program Symposium (Harvard Law School) (May 8, 1993), in Human Rights and Foreign Policy: A Symposium 16 (1994). For a critique of NGOs and their restrictive mandates, see James Gathii & Celestine Nyamu, Note, Reflections on United States-based Human Rights NGOs' Work on Africa, 9 Harv. Hum. Rts. J. 285, 291 (1996).

105. See HRW, Indivisible Rights, supra note 104, at vi-vii. One of the most coherent rationalizations of the opposition to economic and social rights was expressed in a meeting of American INGOs:

> One participant felt strongly that it would be detrimental for U.S. human rights NGOs to espouse the idea of economic, social and cultural rights. Although they refer to important issues, they concern distributive justice rather than corrective justice, like civil and political rights. But distributive justice is a matter of policy,

to this view, civil and political rights belong to the first rank because the realization of other sets of concerns or rights, however they are termed, depend on them.[106]

In September 1996, however, Human Rights Watch tentatively abandoned its long-standing opposition to the advocacy of economic and social rights.[107] It passed a highly restrictive and qualified one-year policy—effective January 1997—to investigate, document, and promote compliance with the ICESCR. Under the terms of the new policy, HRW's work on the ICESCR will be limited to two situations: where protection of the ICESCR right is "necessary to remedy a substantial violation of an ICCPR right,"[108] and where "the violation of an ICESCR right is the direct and immediate product of a substantial violation of an ICCPR right."[109] Furthermore, HRW will only intervene to protect ICESCR rights where the violation is a "direct product of state action, whether by commission or omission;"[110] where the "principle applied in articulating an ICESCR right is one of general applicability;"[111] and where "there is a clear, reasonable and practical remedy that HRW can advocate to address the ICESCR violation."[112]

While an important step by HRW, this policy statement can be seen as a continuation of the history of skepticism toward economic and social rights HRW has long demonstrated; it sees economic and social rights only as an appendage of civil and political rights. Its construction seems to condition ICESCR rights on ICCPR rights—in other words, economic and social rights do not

---

> rather than principles; and human rights NGOs must deal with principles, not policies. Otherwise, their credibility will be damaged. Supporting economic demands will only undermine the ability of NGOs to promote civil and political rights, which are indispensable.

M. Rodriguez Bustelo & Philip Alston, Report of a Conference held at Arden House (1986) 26 (unpublished), quoted in Philip Alston, U.S. Ratification of the Covenant on Economic, Social and Cultural Rights: The Need for an Entirely New Strategy, 84 Am. J. Int'l L. 365, 390 n.107 (1990).

The credibility of American INGOs to which the speaker referred was unlikely to be credibility among those whose economic and social rights are denied. It seems fair to suppose that the concern here was the reputation of NGOs with the governments of industrial democracies and the elites who support the INGO community.

106. HRW, Indivisible Rights, supra note 104, at vi-vii.

107. Human Rights Watch, Human Rights Watch's Proposed Interim Policy on Economic, Social, and Cultural Rights, Sept. 30, 1996.

108. Id.

109. Id.

110. Id.

111. Id.

112. Id.

exist outside the realm of civil and political rights. Thus, one interpretation of the HRW policy could be that civil and political rights are the fundamental, primary rights without which other rights are less meaningful and unattainable. The policy also continues HRW's stress on state-related violations, an orientation that overlooks other important violators, such as businesses and international corporations. What is important about the policy, however, is the commitment by the largest and most influential American INGO to begin advocacy of economic and social rights. No other major INGO has gone that far in its practical work. Nonetheless, the policy is experimental and may be revised or terminated in a year.[113]

Steiner has put the character of INGOs succinctly:

> [T]he term "First World" NGOs both signifies an organization's geographical base and typifies certain kinds of mandates, functions, and ideological orientations. It describes such related characteristics as a concentration on civil and political rights, a commitment to fair (due) process, an individualistic rather than group or community orientation in rights advocacy, and a belief in a pluralist society functioning within a framework of rules impartially applied to protect individuals against state interference. *In a nutshell, "First World" NGOs means those committed to traditional Western liberal values associated with the origins of the human rights movement.* Many of these NGOs work exclusively within their home countries, but the "First World" category also includes most of the powerful international NGOs that investigate events primarily in the Third World.[114]

Traditionally, the work of INGOs has typically involved investigation,[115] reporting,[116] and advocacy.[117] Investigation usually takes

113. Id. HRW is unlikely to expand this mandate to cover more ICESCR rights for a number of reasons, including the lack of adequate human resources. Telephone Interview with Kenneth Roth, Executive Director, Human Rights Watch (Oct. 8, 1996).

114. Steiner, Diverse Partners, supra note 96, at 19 (emphasis added). The ACLU and the LDF are typical domestic "First World" NGOs. HRW, AI, and other INGOs fit Steiner's categorization.

115. An investigation, known as a human rights fact-finding mission, is conducted by the staffs of INGOs who typically spend anywhere from several days to a number of weeks in a "Third World" country interviewing victims of repression, government officials, local activists, local media, and academics. See generally Diane F. Orentlicher, Bearing Witness: The Art and Science of Human Rights Fact-Finding, 3 Harv. Hum. Rts. J. 83 (1990).

place in a "Third World" country while reporting and advocacy aim at reforming policies of industrial democracies and intergovernmental agencies to trigger bilateral and multilateral action against the repressive state. Some INGOs now go beyond this denunciatory framework and work to foster and strengthen processes and institutions—rule of law, laws and constitutions, judiciaries, legislatures, and electoral machineries—that ensure the protection of civil and political rights.[118] Although the ideological commitment of these INGOs seems clear through their mandates and work, they nevertheless cast themselves as non-ideological. They perceive themselves as politically neutral modern-day abolitionists whose only purpose is to identify "evil" and root it out. Steiner again notes that:

> Although committed to civil-political rights and in this sense taking clear moral and political positions, First World NGOs prefer to characterize themselves as above the play of partisan politics and political parties, and in this sense as apolitical . . . . Their primary self-image is that of monitors, objective investigators applying the consensual norms of the human rights movement to the facts found. They are defenders of legality.[119]

Thus, although INGOs are "political" organizations that work to vindicate political and moral principles that shape the basic characteristics of a state, they consciously present themselves as disinterested in the political character of a state. When HRW asserts that it "addresses the human rights practices of governments of all political stripes, of all geopolitical alignments, and of all ethnic and

---

116. Reporting involves compiling data and information from the fact-finding mission and correlating it to human rights standards to bring out discrepancies and disseminating it through reports or other media. This method is also called "shaming" because it spotlights the offending state to the international community. See, e.g., Lawyer's Committee for Human Rights, Zimbabwe: Wages of War: A Report on Human Rights (1986); World Report 1995, supra note 22.

117. This includes lobbying governments and international institutions to use their leverage to alleviate violations.

118. For example, according to its statute, Amnesty International works to "promote as appears appropriate the adoption of constitutions, conventions, treaties and other measures which guarantee the rights contained in the provisions referred to in Article 1 hereof." AI Report, supra note 86, app. II at 333. The International Human Rights Law Group undertakes rule of law assessments which aim at identifying institutional weaknesses and proposing structural reforms. See generally Ethiopia in Transition, supra note 94.

119. Steiner, Diverse Partners, supra note 96, at 19.

religious persuasions,"[120] it is anticipating charges that it is pro-Western, pro-capitalist, and unsympathetic to Islamic and other non-Western religious and political traditions. The first two charges could have been fatal to a group's credibility at the height of the cold war. In reality, however, INGOs have been highly partial: their work has historically concentrated on those countries that have not attained the stable and functioning democracies of the West, the standard for liberal democracy. Target states have included the Soviet bloc and virtually the entire South, where undemocratic or repressive one-party state and military dictatorships have thrived.

The content of the work of INGOs reveals their partiality as well. The typical INGO report is a catalogue of abuses committed by a government against liberal values. As Steiner notes:

> Given the ideological commitments of these NGOs, their investigative work naturally concentrates on matters such as governmental abuses of rights to personal security, discrimination, and basic political rights. By habit or established practice, NGOs' reports stress the nature and number of violations, rather than explore the socioeconomic and other factors that underlie them.[121]

Reports further document the abridgement of the freedoms of speech and association, violations of due process, and various forms of discrimination.[122] Many INGOs fear that explaining why abuses occur may justify them or give credence to the claims of some governments that civil and political rights violations take place because of underdevelopment. Such an argument, if accepted, would destroy the abolitionists' mission by delaying, perhaps indefinitely, the urgency of complying with human rights standards. Abolitionists fear that this argument would allow governments to continue repressive policies while escaping their obligations under human rights law. INGOs thus demand the immediate protection and respect of civil and political rights

---

120. See World Report 1995, supra note 22, at vii. For a systematic explanation of the mandate, structure, and objectives of Human Rights Watch, see Human Rights Watch, Human Rights Watch: Questions and Answers, supra note 67.

121. Steiner, Diverse Partners, supra note 96, at 19.

122. Virtually all reports by INGOs are catalogues of cruelties and abominations of civil and political rights. See, e.g., Lawyers Committee for Human Rights, Promise Unfulfilled: Human Rights in Tunisia Since 1987 (1993); Alice Jay, Persecution by Proxy: The Civil Patrols in Guatemala (Robert F. Kennedy Memorial Center for Human Rights, Kerry K. Cuomo et al. eds., 1993); Middle East Watch, Human Rights in Syria (1990).

regardless of the level of development of the offending state. By taking cover behind the international human rights instruments, INGOs are able to fight for liberal values without appearing "partisan," "biased," or "ideological."

Conventional doctrinalists also perpetuate the appearance of objectivity by explicitly distinguishing themselves from agencies, communities, and government programs that promote democracy and democratization. The "democracy" and "human rights" communities see themselves in different lights.[123] The first is made up of individuals and institutions[124] devoted to "democracy assistance programs" abroad, while the second is primarily composed of INGOs.[125] The human rights community has created a law-versus-politics dichotomy through which it presents itself as the guardian of international law, in this case human rights law, as opposed to the promoter of the more elusive concept of democracy, which it sees as a political ideology.[126] A complex web of reasons, motivations, and contradictions permeate this distinction.

The seeds of the dichotomy are related to the attempt by the human rights community not to "side" with the two protagonists of the Cold War, and in particular Ronald Reagan's crusade against communism and his efforts to pave the way for democracy and free markets across the globe.[127] The human rights community, whose activists and leaders are mostly Democrats or sympathetic to the

---

123. For a comprehensive journalistic account of the differences between the two communities, see Thomas Carothers, Democracy and Human Rights: Policy Allies or Rivals?, Wash. Q., Summer 1994, at 109 [hereinafter Enlarging Democracy].

124. These include governmental agencies such as USAID or their European and Canadian equivalents, quasi-governmental and non-governmental organizations, programs at major Western universities, policy institutes, foundations, and academic and policy specialists. Id. at 110.

125. Although INGOs constitute the core of this group, the community also draws from government agencies—especially in the state departments or foreign ministries—universities, development institutes, and law firms. Id.

126. Id. at 111.

127. During Reagan's terms in office, the United States was criticized quite heavily for its strong-arm tactics, such as those employed in support of the Nicaraguan Contras or the invasion of Grenada, that Reagan frequently used to defend U.S. strategic and "vital" interests, but did not use against U.S. *allies* to enforce compliance with human rights norms. See, e.g., Joanne Omang, Human-Rights Groups Hit 'Narrow' U.S. View, Wash. Post, Dec. 30, 1987, at A7 (reporting on the critical appraisal of the Reagan administration human rights policy by human rights groups); Michael Posner, Reagan Becomes a Force for Rights, N.Y. Times, Mar. 16, 1986, § 4 at 27 (criticizing the Reagan administration's lack of enthusiasm for promotion of human rights); Kenneth Roth, Inconsistency is Mark of Reagan Latin Policy, N.Y. Times, Aug. 17, 1988, at A22 (letter to the editor criticizing administration's unwillingness to censure human rights violations among its "democratic" allies).

Democratic Party, in the case of the United States, or Social Democrats and Labor Party sympathizers in Europe—liberals or those to the left-of-center in Western political jargon—viewed with alarm Reagan's and Margaret Thatcher's push for free markets and support for any pro-Western government, notwithstanding its human rights record. This hostility was exacerbated by the Reagan administration's attempts to reverse the rhetorical prominence that the Carter administration had given to human rights in American foreign policy.[128] Although INGOs delighted in Reagan's opposition to communist rule within the Soviet bloc—their own human rights reports on Soviet bloc countries were scathing—they sought "impartiality" and a "principled" use by the administration of human rights as a tool of foreign policy.[129] INGOs also feared that "democracy programs" would focus only on elections without entrenching basic civil and political rights.[130] In addition, INGOs believed that the focus on democracy blurred the focus on violators and dulled the clarity of physical violations of rights.

The differentiation between democratic and free market crusades and human rights had another advantage: Western governments and human rights groups could play "good cop, bad cop" roles in the spread of Western liberal values. While the West in bilateral agreements and projects opened up previously closed or repressive, one-party societies to markets and "encouraged" democratization, human rights groups would be unrelenting in their assault of the same government for violating civil and political rights. Ordinarily, staffs of INGOs consulted extensively with the State Department or relevant foreign ministry, Western diplomats[131] in the "repressive" state, and elements of the United Nations charged with human rights oversight, such as the Commission on Human Rights, the Committee Against Torture, and the Human Rights Committee.

128. INGOs charged the Reagan administration with the perversion of Carter's human rights policy by applying it almost exclusively to communist states. By the end of his second term, however, INGOs started to admit that Reagan's policy had evolved to institutionalize human rights as a fixed concern of U.S. policy. See Human Rights Watch & Lawyers Committee for Human Rights, The Reagan Administration's Record on Human Rights in 1988, at 1 (1989).

129. See id. at 11-12.

130. See LCHR, Draft Action Plan Commentary, supra note 103, at 4.

131. Meetings at the request of INGOs with State Department officials responsible for policies in particular countries are indispensable to INGOs, whose clout often comes from their association with rich and powerful Western states. Ordinarily, INGO fact-finding missions also meet with Western diplomats to raise "concerns" and seek "inside information" about political issues in the country.

Other factors indicate the commitment of INGOs to liberal democracy as a political project. At least one American NGO, the Lawyers Committee for Civil Rights Under Law, a domestic NGO with an INGO dimension, expressly linked the survival of its international operations to the "attainment" of democracy by, for example, shutting down its Southern Africa Project after the 1994 South African elections. Some INGO reports explicitly lament the failure of democratic reform.[132] They defend and seek to immortalize pro-democracy activists in repressive states.[133] At least one former leader of an INGO recognizes that the distinction made between democracy and human rights is a facade:

> This determination to establish impartiality in the face of human rights violations under different political systems led Amnesty International to shun the rhetorical identification of human rights with democracy. But in fact the struggle against violations, committed mostly by undemocratic authoritarian governments, was closely bound up with the struggle for democracy. Thousands of prisoners of conscience for whom Amnesty International worked in its first three decades were political activists challenging the denial of their rights to freedom of expression and association.[134]

Recently, some INGOs have started seeking the deployment of the resources of other institutions, in addition to those of the United Nations, in their advocacy for liberal values. The Lawyers Committee for Human Rights, for example, has instituted a project that explores ways of encouraging international financial institutions such as the World Bank to build human rights concerns into their policies.[135] Perhaps INGOs should openly acknowledge the inescapable and intrinsic linkage between human rights and

132. See, e.g., Amnesty International, Zaire: Violence Against Democracy 23 (1993); Africa Watch, Zaire: Two Years Without a Transition 45-46 (1992).

133. The Robert F. Kennedy Memorial Center for Human Rights, for example, has often given its annual award to pro-democracy activists, including Gibson Kamau Kuria of Kenya, a leading figure in the struggle to end repressive one-party rule by introducing multiparty democracy in his country. See Robert F. Kennedy Memorial Center for Human Rights, Justice Enjoined: The State of the Judiciary in Kenya (1992); Makau Mutua, Confronting the Past: Accountability for Human Rights Violations in Malawi (Robert F. Kennedy Memorial Center for Human Rights, 1994).

134. New World Order, supra note 85, at 6.

135. See Governance and Human Rights, supra note 24, at 2-3.

democracy, a fact consciously recognized by quasi-governmental agencies in the North.[136]

III. THE CONCEPTUALIZERS: CONSTITUTIONALIZING HUMAN RIGHTS

Constitutionalists, as the label suggests, see, or would like to see, the human rights corpus as a constitutional framework: a set of norms, ideals, and principles—moral, philosophical, legal, even cultural—that cohere to determine the fundamental character of a state and its society. They do not openly distinguish or distance themselves from doctrinalists whom they see as the human rights movement's critical core, its foot soldiers, those on whom the practical advocacy, proselytization, and universalization of its creed depend. Rather, constitutionalists are the "thinking" corps of the movement; as its ideologues they provide intellectual direction and rigor. They explore and explain issues relating to the movement's origin, its philosophical and historical bases, its normative content, and the connections among social, political, and cultural structures and values, as well as the questions that arise from the norms' enforcement and internationalization. When constitutionalists critique the human rights corpus and its movement, it is in language that is internal and "friendly" to the discourse, that is, conversations which are meant to sharpen the movement's focus, expand its influence, and bare its dilemmas. Such critiques explore moral and political dilemmas, normative conflicts within the corpus, the scope of the movement, and differences in the strategies deployed in the vindication of the movement's values. Constitutionalists were among the founders of INGOs and many serve on their boards.[137]

In this section, I will explore the works of a number of leading constitutionalists in order to extract and underline the basic messages and themes they advance to create and crystallize what I call the "defining" character of the human rights movement. Principal among the constitutionalists has been Louis Henkin.[138] Per-

136. See, e.g., David Gillies, Human Rights, Democracy and "Good Governance": Stretching the World Bank's Policy Frontiers (1993) (report of the Canadian International Centre for Human Rights and Democratic Development).

137. Examples include Professor Louis Henkin, who serves on the board of directors of the Lawyers Committee for Human Rights, and Professor Norman Dorsen, who chairs the Lawyers Committee board of directors.

138. Some of Louis Henkin's human rights works include: Louis Henkin, The Age of Rights (1990) [hereinafter Henkin, Age of Rights]; Louis Henkin, The Rights of Man Today (1978); Human Rights: An Agenda for the Next Century (Louis Henkin & John L. Hargrove eds., 1994).

haps more than any other proponent in this school, Henkin has combined extensive and authoritative scholarship with active association with the "nerve center" of the American human rights community in New York.[139] Among others in this school, I will also briefly explore the work of Philip Alston,[140] Henry Steiner,[141] and Thomas Franck.[142] I contend here that while these thinkers do not completely agree on the content or even the normative importance of different human rights, they nevertheless are generally united in their vision of the political society intended by the human rights corpus.

In the preface to *The Age of Rights*, a collection of essays that crystallizes his ideas on human rights, Henkin underlines his belief in the omnipotence of human rights by elevating them to a near-mythical, almost biblical plateau. To him, the universality of the acceptance of the idea of human rights sets it apart from all other ideas and puts it in a most distinctive place in modern times. He boldly states:

> Ours is the age of rights. Human rights is the idea of our time, the only political-moral idea that has received universal acceptance. The Universal Declaration of Human Rights, adopted by the United Nations General Assembly in 1948, has been approved by virtually all governments representing all societies. Human rights are enshrined in the constitutions of virtually every one of today's 170 states—old states and new; religious, secular, and atheist; Western and Eastern; democratic, authoritarian, and totalitarian; market economy, socialist, and mixed; rich and poor, developed, developing, and less developed. Human rights is the subject of numerous international

139. Except for the International Human Rights Law Group, all the major American INGOs are based in New York. These include the Lawyers Committee for Human Rights and Human Rights Watch. Amnesty International and the International League for Human Rights are also based there. Key American (domestic) human rights NGOs such as the ACLU and LDF are also based in New York. See generally North American Directory, supra note 64.

140. Alston's works include: Alston, ECOSOC, supra note 38; Philip Alston, Conjuring Up New Human Rights: A Proposal for Quality Control, 78 Am. J. Int'l L. 607 (1984).

141. Steiner's writings include: Steiner, Diverse Partners, supra note 96; Steiner, Political Participation, supra note 35; Henry J. Steiner, Ideals and Counter-Ideals in the Struggle Over Autonomy Regimes for Minorities, 66 Notre Dame L. Rev. 1539 (1991) [hereinafter Steiner, Autonomy Regimes]; Henry J. Steiner, The Youth of Rights, 104 Harv. L. Rev. 917 (1991) (reviewing Henkin, Age of Rights, supra note 131) [hereinafter Steiner, Youth of Rights].

142. See Franck, supra note 12.

> agreements, the daily grist of the mills of international politics, and a bone of continuing contention among superpowers.[143]

This celebratory and triumphant passage uses a quantitative approach—the idea's dissemination and diffusion to most corners of the earth—as the standard for determining the superiority of human rights over other ideas.[144] But the quantitative approach, while persuasive, has its own problems. One might plausibly argue, based on this criterion, that ideas about free markets as the engine of economic development, among others, are equally, if not more universally accepted, than human rights. Furthermore, depending on how universal acceptance is calibrated, and who the participants are, might it not have been possible to argue at the close of the last century that colonialism enjoyed a similar status?

In any case, it seems highly doubtful that many of the states which constitute the international community are representative of their societies and cultures. It is certainly questionable whether the homage such states pay to human rights is part of a cynically manipulative strategy to be seen "to belong" among the "civilized" members of the international community. Universality obtained at the expense of genuine understanding and commitment cheapens and devalues the idea of human rights. Ultimately, such universality is of little normative value in the reconstruction of societies.

Like other Western pioneers of the concept of human rights, Henkin rejects claims of "cultural relativism" or a multicultural approach to the construction of human rights.[145] He accuses those who advocate cultural and ideological diversity in the creation of the human rights corpus of desiring a vague, broad, ambiguous, and general text of human rights.[146] He sees such an approach as fatal because it would allow different societies to read into human

---

143. Henkin, Age of Rights, supra note 138, at ix.

144. Henkin acknowledges that although the universal consensus on human rights may be formal, even hypocritical and cynical in some societies, it is important that it is the idea that

> has commanded universal nominal acceptance, not (as in the past) the divine right of kings or the omnipotent state, not the inferiority of races or women, not even socialism. Even if it be hypocrisy, it is significant—since hypocrisy, we know, is the homage that vice pays to virtue—that human rights is today the single, paramount virtue to which vice pays homage, that governments today do not feel free to preach what they may persist in practicing.

Id. at ix-x.

145. Id. at x.

146. Id.

rights texts what they will. Instead, he turns to the Universal Declaration of Human Rights, which he sees as the bedrock, the constitution, of human rights.[147] Although Henkin insists that human rights are universal, he does not offer any non-Western political or moral underpinnings for them. Rather, he emphasizes that human rights are derived from "natural rights theories and systems, harking back through English, American, and French constitutionalism to John Locke."[148] The truth is that human rights instruments did not articulate the Western philosophical basis for the corpus because of the need to present the image of universality; it was not, as Henkin suggests, because the framers were politicians and citizens as opposed to philosophers.[149]

Henkin draws many parallels between human rights and American or Western constitutionalism but concludes, surprisingly, that the human rights corpus does not require a particular political ideology. This conclusion, with which this Article disagrees, has been popular among the pioneers of the human rights movement for a number reasons, including their basic assertion that human rights are distinct from politics—defined here as a particular ideology—and can be achieved in different political traditions such as socialist, religious, or free market systems. A further examination of the views of Henkin and other constitutionalists indicates just the opposite: that taken as a whole, their philosophy of human rights leads to the construction of liberal democratic states.

Henkin outlines and uses the basic precepts of American constitutionalism to argue that they are not required by the human rights corpus. He identifies these as: "original individual autonomy translated into popular sovereignty;" a social contract requiring self-government "through accountable representatives; . . . limited

147. The UDHR, Henkin says, reflects a "general commitment to ideas . . . that have become part of our zeitgeist." Id. The framers of the international human rights texts, Henkin writes, did not seek to build an "umbrella large enough to encompass everyone, but rather to respond to a sensed common moral intuition and to identify a small core of common values." Id.

148. Id. at 6.

149. Id. Henkin writes that the human rights expressions "claim no philosophical foundation, nor do they reflect any clear philosophical assumptions; they articulate no particular moral principles or any single, comprehensive theory of the relation of the individual to society." Id. Henkin has suggested that the diversity of cultures and political traditions has caused the human rights movement to eschew inquiries into the philosophical origins and justifications for the human rights corpus, fearing that such inquiry would prove "disruptive and unhelpful." Steiner, Youth of Rights, supra note 141, at 919.

government for limited purposes;" and basic individual rights.[150] He argues that in contrast, the human rights regime "reflect[s] no comprehensive political theory"[151] about how the individual should relate to the state and vice versa; that a state's failure to respect individual rights does not trigger the right of revolution, although the corpus gives a "nod to popular sovereignty;"[152] and that it requires the state to be more active because of the ideas of socialism and the welfare state.[153] Henkin concedes that human rights instruments point to particular principles, but quickly denies that such principles imply a particular political theory:

> Necessarily, however, the idea of rights reflected in the instruments, the particular rights recognized, and the consequent responsibilities for political societies, imply particular political ideas and moral principles. International human rights does not hint at any theory of social contract, but it is committed to popular sovereignty. "The will of the people shall be the basis of the authority of government" and is to "be expressed in periodic elections which shall be by universal and equal suffrage." It is not required that government based on the will of the people take any particular form.[154]

In addition to the UDHR, the ICCPR gives citizens the right to political participation through elections and the guarantee of the right to assemble, associate, and disseminate their ideas.[155] These and the rights to equality and a fair trial imply a society with the following structure: a regularly elected government, real competition for political office, and the separation and independence of powers among the branches of government. The protection of the

150. Henkin, Age of Rights, supra note 138, at 6.

151. Id. Note, though, Henkin's acknowledgment that at the start the United States saw the human rights movement as an instrument to "improve the condition of human rights in countries other than the United States (and a very few like-minded liberal states)." Id. at 74.

152. Id. at 6.

153. Id.

154. Id. at 7 (footnote omitted) (quoting UDHR, supra note 1, art. 21(3)). Henkin notes that Western-style presidential and parliamentary regimes as well as communist "democratic centralism" could presumably meet this standard, provided that the governed can control how they are governed and by what policies they are governed, and that they can replace their governors at frequent and regular intervals. Id.

155. On assembly, see ICCPR, supra note 8, arts. 21 and 22. The right to political participation is contained in article 25; the right to expression in article 19; the rights of free speech in article 18. Id.

individual, his autonomy, and property are among the key goals of such a society. The human rights regime does not dictate the particular variant of liberal society or the color of democracy it envisions; but the rights it guarantees, the ones that Henkin champions as the cornerstone of the human rights regime, seem to require a Western liberal democracy.

Although Steiner seems to agree with Henkin—that association and participation rights do not impose a particular government or political ideology—he identifies liberal democratic systems such as parliamentary or presidential systems, unicameral or bicameral legislatures, proportional representation, or "first past the post" system, as permissible under human rights standards.[156] Steiner notes, however, that dictatorships, inherited leadership, and many forms of one-party states would likely violate associational rights.[157]

Henkin seeks to distinguish human rights from American constitutionalism on the bases for which government is instituted. He argues that while "American rights" originally required a government for limited purposes, human rights, born after socialism and the welfare state, "imply a government that is activist, intervening, [and] committed to economic-social planning" to meet the needs of the individual.[158] This distinction, which relies on the traditional bifurcation of the responsibilities of government—either as the hands-off, negative instrumentality or the regulating, positive interventionist—is more fictitious than real.[159] The social democratic strand of liberalism, which Jack Donnelly credits with the welfare state,[160] has deep roots in liberalism and has historically challenged the individualist formulations of American constitutionalism. As Henkin himself acknowledges, the United States is not a welfare state by constitutional compulsion; but it is a welfare state nevertheless.[161] The political struggles of working Americans and in particular historically excluded groups, such as African-Ameri-

156. Steiner, Youth of Rights, supra note 141, at 930.

157. Id. at 930-31. Steiner allows that some one-party states may meet "generous interpretations" of pluralist participation if they have "extensive intraparty democracy." Id. at 931. But the human rights corpus requires more than pluralist participation; it imposes the respect and recognition for diversity and difference, judicial independence, and a private sector, conditions which are unlikely to be met in societal typologies found in the one-party state. Id.

158. Henkin, Age of Rights, supra note 138, at 145.

159. For a discussion of this positive-negative distinction and the ends of government, see generally Donnelly, supra note 9.

160. Id. at 54-55.

161. Henkin, Age of Rights, supra note 138, at 153.

cans and women, have transformed "original American rights" and explicitly imposed interventionist commitments on the American state to alleviate economic and social disparities. Thus the distance between "American rights" and human rights that Henkin creates is somewhat exaggerated.[162]

Henry Steiner, another constitutionalist whose writing has concentrated on the content of human rights norms and the structure of the human rights regime, is more inclined to the view that human rights norms are best accomplished, and in most cases only accomplished, within liberal democracy. There is no suggestion that a theocracy or a military regime could accomplish human rights. Although he does not state it explicitly, a number of his writings suggest this conclusion.[163] In his first major article on human rights, for example, Steiner chose to explore the question of political participation, a foundational norm in liberal democracies, from a human rights perspective.[164] The article, which was published in the inaugural issue of the *Harvard Human Rights Journal* (then called the *Harvard Human Rights Yearbook*), explores the different understandings of the right to political participation in various political contexts, from liberal democracies to communist states. Drawing primarily on the UDHR and the ICCPR, which Steiner terms the "two most significant" human rights instru-

162. For a discussion of the use of rights rhetoric to advance economic and social rights (including the right to health) in the United States and internationally, see generally Harvard Law School Human Rights Program & François-Xavier Bagnoud Center for Health and Human Rights, Economic and Social Rights and the Right to Health (1995).

163. See, e.g., Steiner & Alston, International Human Rights in Context, supra note 16. This substantial work presents the inquiry into human rights as the contradiction between authoritarian, oppressive, non-democratic, non-Western societies on the one hand, and Western liberal core values such as the rights of association, speech, due process, and the ideals of equal protection on the other. In the view of this author, the text is the most comprehensive and provocative human rights coursebook to date.

164. Steiner, Political Participation, supra note 35, at 77.

ments,[165] the article sidesteps any discussion about the philosophical and historical origins or justifications for human rights.[166]

Steiner categorizes the rights enumerated in the ICCPR in five sets which slide on a spectrum of universal acceptability and normative clarity. These are: traditional "negative" rights "which lie at the heart of the liberal tradition's commitment to individual autonomy and choice;"[167] rights that assure procedural fairness when a state seeks restrictions on individual liberty;[168] rights that involve anti-discrimination norms;[169] so-called expressive rights, which include free speech, association, and assembly;[170] and finally, the right to political participation.[171] While there is at least formal, near-universal consensus on the normative content of the rights in the first category—the negative rights—there has been no such unanimity on the meaning of the last category, the right to political participation.[172] However, respect for the first four categories of rights is unlikely to materialize in any systemic manner unless the right to political participation is understood and exercised from a particular ideological perspective. Steiner argues that an abusive regime can terminate some of the rights without altering the existing patterns of economic and political power under that regime. However, the "termination" of, say, one-party or military rule and its replacement by a participatory electoral system most

---

165. Id. at 79. Steiner calls the UDHR the "spiritual parent" of many human rights treaties; the ICCPR's importance hinges on its acceptance by most of the world's states in all regions and ideological blocs. These facts give the two instruments "universal scope." Id. Elsewhere, Steiner writes:

> To this day, it [the UDHR] retains its symbolism, rhetorical force and significance in the human rights movement. It is the parent document, the initial burst of idealism and enthusiasm, terser, more general and grander than the treaties, in some sense the constitution of the entire movement. It remains the single most invoked human rights instrument.

Steiner & Alston, International Human Rights In Context, supra note 16, at 120.

166. Continuing the theme of universality, Steiner notes, however, that the "rights may be understood to be rooted in natural law or positive enactment. They may be justified by liberal postulates or by the imperative of socialist construction." Steiner, Political Participation, supra note 35, at 80.

167. Id. at 81. These are physical integrity rights. Id.

168. Id. at 82. These rights involve an individual's fair treatment within the criminal justice system. Id.

169. Id. These rights protect individuals and groups against discrimination on the basis of race, gender, color, religion, and political opinion. "Such norms respond to liberal ideology's stress on individuals' civil and political equality and on the state's neutrality." Id. at 82-83.

170. Id. at 83.

171. Id. at 84.

172. Id.

likely would be "fatal to those in power."[173] This is particularly the case since such participation involves the exercise of expressive and other rights.

Debates during the drafting sessions of the relevant provisions of the UDHR and the ICCPR revealed divisions among different states about the content of the right to political participation. Although there is almost a twenty-year gap between the UDHR and the ICCPR, with non-Western states achieving a numerical majority in the UN in the interim, it is significant to note that the political participation articles—21 of the UDHR[174] and 25 of the ICCPR[175]—are nearly identical. Divisions on the content of these provisions were strictly ideological. The West and its philosophical allies in Latin America sought language to guarantee competitive multi-party elections through the secret ballot while Soviet bloc countries wanted open-textured provisions that would meet their more closed electoral systems.[176] Article 25 is deliberately vague enough to accommodate differing views. Both the "elections" and "take part" clauses do not spell out a liberal pluralist theory, although that seems to have been their original intention.

---

173. Id. at 85.

174. UDHR, supra note 1, art. 21, provides:

> 1. Everyone has the right to *take part* in the government of his country, directly or through freely chosen representatives.
>
> 2. Everyone has the right of equal access to public service in his country.
>
> 3. The will of the people shall be the basis of the authority of government; this will shall be expressed in periodic and genuine elections which shall be by universal and equal suffrage and shall be held by secret vote or by equivalent free voting procedures.

(Emphasis added).

175. ICCPR, supra note 8, art. 25 provides:

> Every citizen shall have the right and the opportunity, without any of the distinctions mentioned in article 2 and without unreasonable restrictions:
>
> *(a)* To *take part* in the conduct of public affairs, directly or through freely chosen representatives;
>
> *(b)* To vote and to be elected at genuine periodic elections which shall be by universal and equal suffrage and shall be held by secret ballot, guaranteeing the free expression of the will of the electors;
>
> *(c)* To have access, on general terms of equality, to public service in his country.

(Emphasis added).

176. During the drafting of the UDHR, for example, the Belgian delegate to the Third Committee argued that the "very essence of the democratic system was the electoral competition between different political parties," otherwise the "whole democratic character of free, equal, periodical and secret elections might be distorted." U.N. GAOR 3d Comm., 3d Sess., 133d mtg. at 464, U.N. Doc. A/C.3/SR.133 (1948). But the Soviet delegate countered that such language would be "absolutely irreconcilable with the social structure of certain Member States." Id. at 471.

> The International Covenant does not, then, offer the explicit guidance for the interpretation of Article 25 that a reference to Western pluralist theory would have provided. Its provision for elections fails to resolve some basic issues. Countries of radically different political systems which included *some* form of electoral process ratified it, without considering themselves to be in instant violation of Article 25 and without expressing their willingness to conform to any one political tradition's prescription of basic political processes.[177]

Steiner realizes the complex character of the norm of political participation and even argues that different political systems could meet it as formulated in article 25. He nevertheless pushes for an understanding of it that comes closer to a liberal pluralist formulation.[178] Such an understanding would reject as inadequate hereditary, non-competitive, one-party, or ritualistic "yes-or-no" electoral systems where the citizenry votes to evaluate only a single candidate. Seen as part of the gamut of the other four categories of rights that Steiner identifies, an interpretation of article 25 brings it closer to liberal political democracy. Steiner seems to echo this view when he concludes that:

> Fresh understandings and different institutionalizations of the right in different cultural and political contexts may reveal what an increasing number of states believe to be a necessary minimum of political participation for all states. That minimum should never require less of a government than provision for meaningful exercise of choice by citizens in some form of electoral process permitting active debate on a broad if not unlimited range of issues. But it could require much more.[179]

Elsewhere, Steiner is more explicit about the association of human rights norms with liberalism and the political structures of liberal democracy. In an article on autonomy regimes for minorities, Steiner imagines the application of norms and ideals which are essential to liberalism.[180] He argues for a political regime that recognizes the rights of ethnic, racial, or religious minorities to cul-

177. Steiner, Political Participation, supra note 35, at 93.
178. See id.
179. Id. at 134.
180. See Steiner, Autonomy Regimes, supra note 141, at 1539.

tural survival and freedom from violence and repression by the majority. He notes that repressive and authoritarian governments preclude an effective voice for minorities, as would majoritarian democracies where the political structures give the "minority no effective electoral power or political leverage."[181] He further notes that minorities can use the ICCPR to argue for the "kind of fair or equitable political participation that [ICCPR] article 25 should be interpreted to require."[182] He finds the basis for the protection of the rights of minorities in the human rights regime's insistence and promotion of difference and diversity:

> The Universal Declaration and the Civil-Political Rights Covenant accept and, indeed, encourage many forms of diversity. They insist on respect for difference . . . . The value placed on the survival (and creation) of diversity in cultural, religious, political, and other terms permeates human rights law, which evidences throughout its hostility to imposed uniformity.[183]

Steiner emphasizes that the norm of equal protection—"perhaps the preeminent human rights norm"[184]—plays a key role in the protection and encouragement of diversity. He cites the freedoms of association, assembly, and expression as the vital complement to the project of equal protection.[185] In my view, the following passage sums up Steiner's "philosophy" of human rights and reveals his biases, although in most of his writings he seems to studiously avoid identifying human rights law with any one ideological orientation. He states that

> the aspirations of the human rights movement reach beyond the goal of preventing disasters. The movement also has a "utopian" dimension that envisions a vibrant and broadly based political community. Such a vision underscores the potential of the human rights movement for conflict with regimes all over the world. *A society honoring the full range of contemporary human rights would be hospitable to many types of pluralism and skeptical about any one final truth, at least to the point of allowing and protecting difference. It would not stop at the*

181. Id. at 1546.
182. Id.
183. Id. at 1547-48.
184. Id. at 1548.
185. Id.

> ***protection of negative rights but would encourage citizens to exercise their right to political participation, one path toward enabling peoples to realize the right to self-determination. It would ensure room for dissent and alternative visions of social and political life by keeping open and protecting access to the roads toward change.***[186]

Steiner differs from the conceptualizers explored here in that he views the right to political participation as a work in progress while the others tend to see it as a completed norm. For him, political participation is a programmatic right. It is not enough to carry out periodic elections; the "take part" clause is fertile ground for the development of the norm.

Among the constitutionalists, few have had the rare combination of high-level practical and scholarly experience that has characterized the work of Philip Alston.[187] A leading advocate of a broader conception of human rights, one that treats economic, social, and cultural rights as an integral part of the corpus, Alston has stated with approval that "the characterization of a specific goal as a human right elevates it above the rank and file of competing societal goals, gives it a degree of immunity from challenge and generally endows it with an aura of timelessness, absoluteness and universal validity."[188] Hence, Alston's efforts to promote the legitimacy of rights such as the right to development,[189] and other eco-

---

186. Steiner, Youth of Rights, supra note 141, at 931 (emphasis added).

187. Alston, an Australian, has served as the chair of the pivotal Committee on Economic, Social and Cultural Rights, the body that has overseen the implementation of the ICESCR since 1991. Between 1978 and 1984, he was an official of the United Nations Centre for Human Rights in Geneva. He has taught at Harvard Law School and the Fletcher School of Law and Diplomacy at Tufts University, and has been professor of law and director of the Australian National University's Centre for International and Public Law. Currently, he is a professor of international law at the European Law Institute in Florence, Italy. He has undertaken numerous high level activities for the United Nations and its specialized agencies.

188. Philip Alston, Making Space for New Human Rights: The Case of the Right to Development, 1 Harv. Hum. Rts. Y.B. 3, 3 (1988) [hereinafter Alston, Right to Development].

189. Alston rejects the arguments of opponents of the right to development, that either development is "incompatible with the philosophy underlying the existing body of international rights law" or that it is "non-justiciable." Id. at 7. In response to the first contention, he argues that the United Nations' conception of human rights does not rest exclusively on natural rights theory; he finds incoherence within the UDHR itself, which lists some rights he considers outside the natural rights theory such as economic and social rights. Id. at 29-30. With respect to the second objection to a right to development, he argues that human rights law privileges notions of "implementation" and "supervision" as opposed to "justiciability" or "enforceability." Thus, the existence of "judicial remedies"

nomic, social and cultural rights whose status as "rights" remains contested.

In a statement to the 1993 World Conference on Human Rights, Alston's Committee on Economic, Social and Cultural Rights lamented that the massive violations of economic and social rights would have provoked "horror and outrage" if they had occurred to civil and political rights.[190] The Committee noted that it was "inhumane, distorted and incompatible with international standards" to exclude the one-fifth of the global population which suffered from poverty, hunger, disease, illiteracy, and insecurity from human rights concerns.[191] It noted that although "political freedom, free markets and pluralism" had been chosen by a large percentage of the global population in recent years because they were seen as the best routes for attaining economic, social and cultural rights, democracy will inevitably fail and societies will revert to authoritarianism unless those rights are respected.[192] The Statement, which underlines Alston's central goal, seeks the globalization of more humane economic and social structures—a social democracy—to complement the open political society of liberal democracy.

Thomas Franck is the first prominent constitutionalist to argue that democratic governance[193] has evolved from moral prescription to an international legal obligation.[194] Franck sees three recent occurrences as the unmistakable signs of the emergent right to governance: first, the failure of the August 1991 coup in the Soviet Union; second, the unanimous October 1991 resolution by the UN General Assembly to restore to power Jean-Bertrand Aristide, the then-ousted Haitian president; and third, the proliferation of states

may not be required depending on the nature of the rights and the terms of the instrument in question. Id. at 35-36.

190. See Statement to the World Conference on Human Rights on Behalf of the Committee on Economic, Social and Cultural Rights, supra note 2, at 83.

191. Id.

192. Id.

193. Franck uses the term to describe a legal and practical commitment to "open, multiparty, secret-ballot elections with a universal franchise." Franck, The Emerging Right, supra note 12, at 47. I use only this one article by Franck because among all his numerous writings, it best expresses the views relevant to my argument.

194. Id. Franck traces the notion of "democratic entitlement" to the U.S. Declaration of Independence, with its assertion that governments are instituted to secure the "'unalienable rights' of their citizens . . . [and] derive their just powers from the consent of the governed." Id. at 46. He also traces the international legitimacy of governments to their demonstration of "a decent respect to the opinions of mankind," hence, through their recognition and legitimization by other nations. Id.

committed to competitive elections.[195] In celebratory fashion, Franck highlights the rejection of the "dictatorship of the proletariat,"[196] "people's democracy,"[197] and the dictatorships of Africa and Asia by "people almost everywhere"[198] who "now demand that government be validated by western-style parliamentary, multiparty democratic process."[199] He emphasizes that "[o]nly a few, usually military or theocratic, regimes still resist the trend."[200] With great optimism he concludes that:

> This almost-complete triumph of the democratic notions of Hume, Locke, Jefferson and Madison—in Latin America, Africa, Eastern Europe and, to a lesser extent, Asia—may well prove to be the most profound event of the twentieth century and, in all likelihood, the fulcrum on which the future development of global society will turn. It is the unanswerable response to those who have said that free, open, multiparty, electoral parliamentary democracy is neither desired nor desirable outside a small enclave of western industrial states.[201]

After exploring the involvement of regional and international organizations and governments in activities that enhance the right to democratic governance—such as sanctions systems and election monitoring—Franck lists the human rights instruments that constitute "the large normative canon"[202] which promotes democratic entitlement. These instruments recognize individual rights and

---

195. Id. at 46-47.

196. Id. at 48.

197. Id. at 47.

198. Id. at 49.

199. Id.

200. Id. He adds that "[v]ery few argue that parliamentary democracy is a western illusion and a neocolonialist trap for unwary Third World peoples." Id.

201. Id.

202. Id. at 79. This includes the U.N. Charter; UDHR, supra note 1; ICCPR, supra note 8; the Declaration on the Elimination of all Forms of Intolerance and of Discrimination Based on Religion or Belief, G.A. Res. 55, U.N. GAOR, 36th Sess., Supp. No. 51, at 171, U.N. Doc. A/36/51 (1981), reprinted in 21 I.L.M. 205 (1982); the Convention on the Elimination of all Forms of Discrimination Against Women, G.A. Res. 180, U.N. GAOR, 34th Sess., Supp. No. 46, at 193, U.N. Doc. A/34/46 (1979), reprinted in 19 I.L.M. 33 (1980) (entered into force Sept. 3, 1981) [hereinafter CEDAW]; the International Covenant on the Suppression and Punishment of the Crime of Apartheid, G.A. Res. 3068, U.N. GAOR, 28th Sess., Supp. No. 30, at 75, U.N. Doc. A/9030 (1973), reprinted in 13 I.L.M. 56 (1974) (entered into force July 18, 1976); and the International Convention on the Elimination of All Forms of Racial Discrimination, opened for signature Mar. 7, 1966, 660 U.N.T.S. 195, reprinted in 5 I.L.M. 352 (1966) (entered into force Jan. 4, 1969) [hereinafter CERD].

require equal protection. Franck here deploys human rights law to underpin the right to democratic governance.

While the majority of constitutionalists are reluctant to make explicit connections between the human rights corpus and political democracy, they generally use typically Western conceptions of rights to explain the content and implications of human rights law. Although many make references to the influence of the different types of socialism on the fashion of human rights, such references are spotty and carry minor significance in these analyses. In virtually no instances do constitutionalists explore in an inclusive manner non-Western ideals and notions of rights or duties. There is no paucity of references, however, to non-Western ideas, practices, and political and social structures that contradict human rights norms.

IV. THE DILEMMAS OF THE AGNOSTIC

One of the most probing critiques of the human rights corpus has come from non-Western thinkers who, though educated in the West or in Western-oriented educational systems, have philosophical, moral, and cultural questions about the distinctly Eurocentric formulation of human rights discourse. They have difficulties accepting the specific cultural and historical experiences of the West as the standard for all humanity. As outsider-insiders,[203] cultural agnostics understand and accept certain contributions of Western (largely European) civilization to the human rights movement but reject the wholesale adoption or imposition of Western ideas and concepts of human rights. Instead, they present external critiques to human rights discourse, while generally applying language internal to that discourse. By agnostics, I do not refer to external critiquers who think that as a Western project the human rights system is irredeemable and cannot rearrange its priorities or be transformed by other cultural milieus to reflect a genuinely uni-

203. I use the term "outsider-insiders" to bunch together Africans, Asians, Latin Americans, non-mainstream Western scholars, and certain members of racial and cultural minorities in the West, such as African-Americans and Asian-Americans. The latter have historically been part of the struggle to vindicate non-European cultural viewpoints in the West. In feminist jurisprudence, for example, Black scholars have advocated the recognition of views other than those of mainline White feminists. See, e.g., Hope Lewis, Between Irua and "Female Genital Mutilation": Feminist Human Rights Discourse and the Cultural Divide, 8 Harv. Hum. Rts. J. 1 (1995) (distinguishing black feminist human rights approaches from mainstream perspectives and calling for a cross-cultural discussion to improve the quality of debate).

versal character and consensus.[204] Rather, I mean those who advocate a multicultural approach in the reconstruction of the entire edifice of human rights. They could also be termed human rights pluralists.

There is no dispute about the European origins of the philosophy of the human rights movement; even Westerners who advocate its universality accept this basic fact. Refuge from this disturbing reality is taken in the large number of states, from all cultural blocs, which have indicated their acceptance of the regime by becoming parties to the principal human rights instruments.[205] Others argue that as more non-Western states have become significant members of the international community, their influence on international lawmaking has corrected the initial lopsidedness of the enterprise and allowed other historical heritages to exert themselves.

This positivistic approach has some value, but it does not answer the agnostic challenge or endow the human rights corpus with multicultural universality. There are fundamental defects in presenting the state as the reservoir of cultural heritage. Many states have been alien to their populations and it is questionable whether they represent those populations or whether they are little more than internationally recognized cartels organized for the sake of keeping power and access to resources.[206] It is difficult to identify the motivations, for example, that led the abusive Zairian state of Mobutu Sese Seko to ratify the major human rights instruments;[207] respect for international standards could not have been high among them. Many states seem to ratify human rights instruments to blunt criticism, and because as a general rule the cost to their sovereignty is nominal.

---

204. For a view that advocates the incompatibility of human rights norms with non-Western needs and views, see Pannikar, supra note 3.

205. As of July 1994, 127 states had ratified, acceded or succeeded to the ICCPR, arguably the principle human rights treaty. See Report of the Human Rights Committee, U.N. GAOR, 49th Sess., Supp. No. 40, at 1, U.N. Doc. A/49/40 (1994).

206. I have argued elsewhere that the state in Africa was organized for the purposes of colonial exploitation, it was decolonized as a tool of the international state system and the Cold War, and it has survived without internal legitimacy or coherence because of external support. See Makau wa Mutua, Why Redraw the Map of Africa: A Moral and Legal Inquiry, 16 Mich. J. Int'l L. 1113 (1995); Makau wa Mutua, Putting Humpty Dumpty Back Together Again: The Dilemmas of the Post-Colonial African State, 21 Brook. J. Int'l L. 505 (1995) (book review).

207. See Makau wa Mutua & Peter Rosenblum, Zaire: Repression As Policy (Lawyers Committee for Human Rights, 1990) (documenting the abuses of the Zairian state against its own citizens).

Agnostics look beyond the positive law and explore the historical and cultural imperatives that are essential for the creation of a legitimate corpus. Some point, for instance, to the celebration of the individual egoist in human rights law as a demonstration of its limited application. As this author has noted elsewhere:

> The argument by current reformers that Africa merely needs a liberal democratic, rule-of-law state to be freed from despotism is mistaken. The transplantation of the narrow formulation of Western liberalism cannot adequately respond to the historical reality and the political and social needs of Africa. The sacralization of the individual and the supremacy of the jurisprudence of individual rights in organized political and social society is not a natural, "transhistorical," or universal phenomenon, applicable to all societies, without regard to time and place.[208]

Some African scholars have been particularly uncomfortable with this emphasis, resisting the unremitting emphasis on the individual. Okere notes, for instance, that "[t]he African conception of man is not that of an isolated and abstract individual, but an integral member of a group animated by a spirit of solidarity."[209] Individuals are not atomistic units "locked in a constant struggle against society for the redemption of their rights."[210] The concept of the group-centered individual in Africa delicately entwines rights and duties, and harmonizes the individual with the society. Such a conception does not necessarily see society—organized either as the community or the state—as the individual's primary antagonist.[211] Nor does it permit the over-indulgence of the indi-

---

208. Mutua, African Cultural Fingerprint, supra note 3, at 341. This author further noted that, "[t]he ascendancy of the language of individual rights has a specific historical context in the Western world. The rise of the modern state in Europe and its monopoly of violence and instruments of coercion gave birth to a culture of rights to counterbalance the invasive and abusive state." Id. at 341-42.

209. B. Obinna Okere, The Protection of Human Rights in Africa and the African Charter on Human and Peoples' Rights: A Comparative Analysis with the European and American Systems, 6 Hum. Rts. Q. 141, 148 (1984). John Mbiti has argued that in Africa the individual's rights, needs, sorrows, and duties are woven in a tapestry that denies runaway individualism. "I am because we are; and since we are, therefore I am." John Mbiti, African Religions and Philosophy 141 (1990).

210. Richard N. Kiwanuka, The Meaning of "People" in the African Charter on Human and Peoples' Rights, 82 Am. J. Int'l L. 80, 82 (1988).

211. See Mutua, African Cultural Fingerprint, supra note 3, at 363.

vidual at the expense of the society.[212] This conception resists casting the individual as the center of the moral universe; instead, both the community and the individual occupy an equally hallowed plane.

In the context of Asia, a number of writers have also cast doubt on the individualist conception of rights and its emphasis on negative rights.[213] Although many of these commentators are connected to governments in the region, and therefore have an interest in defending certain policy and development approaches, it would be sloppy to dismiss them out of hand. Such dismissals, which the INGO community issues with haste and without much thought about the cultural character of the human rights corpus, have aggravated differences between the West and certain Asian countries over the interpretation of human rights.[214] The University of Hong Kong's Professor Ghai powerfully critiques the cynical distortion of Asian conceptions of community, culture and religion, as well as the use of state apparatuses to crush dissent. He argues that the political elites manipulate cultural imagery to further eco-

---

212. Dunstan Wai argues that African conceptions of human rights guaranteed a "modicum of social justice and values concerned with individual and collective rights." Dunstan Wai, Human Rights in Sub-Saharan Africa, in Human Rights: Cultural and Ideological Perspectives 115, 116 (Adamantia Pollis & Peter Schwab eds., 1979).

Asmarom Legesse notes the importance of this balance between the individual and the society so that "individuals do not deviate so far from the norm that they can overwhelm the society." Asmarom Legesse, Human Rights in African Political Culture, in The Moral Imperatives of Human Rights: A World Survey 123, 125 (Kenneth W. Thompson ed., 1980).

213. A vocal advocate of the Asian conception of human rights has argued, for instance, that

> many East and Southeast Asians tend to look askance at the starkly individualistic ethos of the West in which authority tends to be seen as oppressive and rights are an individual's "trump" over the state. Most people of the region prefer a situation in which distinctions between the individual, society, and state are less clear-cut, or at least less adversarial. It will be far more difficult to deepen and expand the international consensus on human rights if East and Southeast Asian countries believe that the Western promotion of human rights is aimed at what they regard as the foundation of their economic success.

Kausikan, supra note 3, at 36.

Kausikan has served as the director of the East Asian and Pacific bureau of the Ministry of Foreign Affairs of Singapore. Id at 24. For an elaboration of Kausikan's views on the universality of human rights, see Bilahari Kausikan, An Asian Approach to Human Rights, 89 Am. Soc'y Int'l L. Proc. 146 (1995); Bilahari Kausikan, An East Asian Approach to Human Rights, 2 Buff. J. Int'l L. 263 (1996). For a forceful repudiation of Kausikan, see Aryeh Neier, Asia's Unacceptable Standard, 92 Foreign Pol'y 42 (1993).

214. Human Rights Watch in particular has been very vocal in its rejection of the so-called Asian concept of human rights, which emphasizes economic development over respect for civil and political rights. See World Report 1995, supra note 22, at xiv.

nomic development and retain power.[215] That critique does not elaborate, however, on the cultural and philosophical differences between different Asian traditions and Western ones and on how those differences might manifest themselves in the construction of human rights norms.

Cultural agnostics do not reject the Western conception of human rights in toto; nor do they even deny that a universal corpus may ultimately yield societal typologies and structures similar to those imagined by the present human rights regime. At stake for them is the availability of the opportunity for all major cultural blocs of the world to negotiate the normative content of human rights law and the purposes for which the discourse should be legitimately deployed. Many African agnostics and some Africanists, for example, have demonstrated the similarity of human rights norms in Western states to pre-colonial African states and societies. These included due (fair) process protections;[216] the right to political participation;[217] and the rights to welfare, limited government, free speech, conscience, and association.[218] These rights, however, were not enjoyed as an end in themselves or with the sole

215. See Ghai, supra note 22, at 20. Ghai attacks the notion of a unique or singular Asian perspective on human rights because of the religious, political, and economic diversities prevalent in the region. Id. at 5. See also Susan Sim, Human Rights: The East Asian Challenge, The Straits Times (Singapore), Feb. 18, 1996, at SR1, SR4, available in LEXIS, News Library, CURNWS File.

216. Kwasi Wiredu, for example, contends that the principle of innocent until proven guilty was an essential part of Akan (West African peoples') consciousness. "[I]t was an absolute principle of Akan justice that no human being could be punished without a trial." Kwasi Wiredu, An Akan Perspective on Human Rights, in Cross-Cultural Perspectives, supra note 9, at 243, 252. Timothy Fernyhough notes that Africa's preoccupation with the right to life was manifested in the power to hand down the death penalty, which was reserved for a few elders "only after elaborate judicial procedure, with appeals from one court to another, and often only in cases of murder or manslaughter." Timothy Fernyhough, Human Rights and Precolonial Africa, in Human Rights and Governance in Africa 39, 56 (Ronald Cohen, et al. eds., 1993). He notes, further, that "in the Tio kingdom north of modern Brazzaville, . . . as elsewhere in Africa, a strong tradition of jurisprudence existed, with specific rulings for penalties cited as precedents, such as levels of fines for adultery." Id. at 62.

217. See Wiredu, supra note 216, at 248-49.

218. For example, Wiredu writes:

> Akan thought recognized the right of a newborn to be nursed and educated, the right of an adult to a plot of land from the ancestral holdings, the right of any well-defined unit of political organization to self-government, the right of all to have a say in the enstoolment or destoolment of their chiefs or their elders and to participate in the shaping of governmental policies, the right of all to freedom of thought and expression in all matters, political, religious, and metaphysical, the right of everybody to trial before punishment, the right of a person to remain at any locality or to leave, and so on.

intent of fulfilling just the individual. Among the major human rights instruments, only the African Charter on Human and Peoples' Rights attempts the comprehensive unification of these conflicting notions of community, individual rights, and duties to the family, the community, and the state.[219]

Agnostics agree that many of the human rights in the current corpus are valid as human rights, their Western origin notwithstanding. The difficulty lies in the emphasis placed on certain rights, their ranking within that universe, and ultimately the political character of the state required or implied by that conception of rights. Although African agnostics, for example, bitterly oppose the violations of civil and political rights by the post-colonial state, they see little redemption in a campaign or worldview that seeks merely to transplant Western notions of political democracy and "negative" rights to African states. The contrived nature of the African state and its inability to claim the loyalties of its citizenry have been compounded by the delegitimization of cultural and philosophical identities by European values and practices. Africa appears to have lost its pre-colonial moral compass and fallen prey to the machinations of bands of elites who exist in cultural suspension, neither African nor foreign.

Some agnostics call for reconnection with certain human rights ideals from Africa's pre-colonial past to address social problems and to attempt to arrest political disintegration. The reconstruction of the ancient duty-rights dialectic, which was essential to the vitality of Africa's social and political fabric, has been advanced as a critical starting point in the redefinition of the relationship between individual and community, and individual and state. As this author has stated elsewhere:

> The duty/rights conception of the African Charter could provide a new basis for individual identification with compatriots, the community, and the state. It could forge and instill a national consciousness and act as the glue to reunite individuals and different nations within the modern state, and at the same time set the proper limits

---

Id. at 257. See also Mutua, African Cultural Fingerprint, supra note 3, at 346-47 (discussing human rights in various pre-colonial African cultures).

219. African Charter, supra note 6. The African Charter codifies all three "generations" of rights: civil and political rights; economic, social and cultural rights; and peoples' rights, such as the right to development, self-determination or political sovereignty over natural resources. Id.

> of conduct by state officials. The motivation and purpose behind the concept of duty in pre-colonial societies was to strengthen community ties and social cohesiveness, creating a shared fate and common destiny. This is the consciousness that the impersonal modern state has been unable to foster. It has failed to shift loyalties from the lineage and the community to the modern state, with its mixture of different nations.[220]

The human rights corpus' over-emphasis on the individual runs counter to this African worldview; it would most likely delay or arrest Africa's reconstruction if applied without the restraint of balance, the tempering of the ego with the fuller understanding of rights that sees them in all their political, economic, and social dimensions. Agnostics feel that while ultimately the state that emerges from this conception may resemble a Western-style democracy in certain respects, such an outcome need not be predetermined or required by the human rights corpus. Asian agnostics accept that changes in the political character of the state are inevitable as their societies become more prosperous economically, but they are reluctant to conclude that this evolutionary process will automatically lead to a Western-type democracy.[221]

The dilemma of the agnostic, therefore, is not that he sees an "evil" in the Eurocentric formulation of the human rights corpus; although he sees much good in it, he does not agree with its zealous Western construction and its close identification with liberal democracy. Ultimately, of course, the major bone of contention is the cultural legitimacy of the corpus in non-Western settings.

V. Political Strategists: Instrumentalism in Human Rights

The school of political strategists, of all the four typologies explored here, is the least principled and the most open-textured in the manner and the purposes for which it deploys human rights

---

220. Mutua, African Cultural Fingerprint, supra note 3, at 368 (footnote omitted).

221. Kausikan, supra note 3, at 38. Kausikan suggests that the collapse of communism, which many in the West saw as the triumph of its liberal democratic values and systems, has been used as a "lens through which [Western media, NGOs, and human rights activists] view developments in other regions." Id. at 33. Kausikan warns that an approach which gauges states by the progress of democracy is ideological because democracy is "a value-laden term, itself susceptible to multiple interpretations, but usually understood by Western human rights activists and the media as the establishment of political institutions and practices akin to those existing in the United States and Europe." Id.

discourse. Apart from the United Nations, whose Center for Human Rights is responsible for human rights matters, Western governments, and particularly the United States, have been the principal advocates for the use of human rights as a tool of policy against other states. In this respect, human rights standards have been viewed as norms with which non-Western, non-democratic states must comply. The United States, from the birth of the movement half a century ago, viewed human rights "as designed to improve the condition of human rights in countries other than the United States (and a very few like-minded liberal states)."[222] Henkin believes that because individual rights "dominate [America's] constitutional jurisprudence, and are the pride of its people, their banner to the world,"[223] such a view is natural. Western European industrial democracies hold similar viewpoints, as evidenced by their trade and aid policies towards each other, as well as towards non-Western states.[224] Western international financial institutions such as the World Bank and the IMF have followed the lead of these major powers and have started to link some of their activities to human rights concerns.[225]

The United States was a principal player in the drafting of the major international human rights instruments, although it has been reluctant to become a party to most of them.[226] It was not until the 1970s that the United States started institutionalizing human rights

222. Henkin, Age of Rights, supra note 138, at 74. This view, according to Henkin, results from the fact that the United States is "a principal ancestor of the contemporary idea of rights." Id. at 65.

223. Id.

224. For an eloquent exploration of Western European (European Union, formerly European Community) policies linking human rights and democracy to aid and trade in their relationship with non-Western countries, see Demetrios James Marantis, Human Rights, Democracy, and Development: The European Community Model, 7 Harv. Hum. Rts. J. 1 (1994).

225. See F.L. Osunsade, IMF Support for African Adjustment Programs: Questions and Answers 8 (IMF, 1993); cf. Balakrishnan Rajagopal, Crossing the Rubicon: Synthesizing the Soft International Law of the IMF and Human Rights, 11 B.U. Int'l L.J. 81, 100 (1993) (noting that the charter of the IMF allows linkage between human rights and IMF activities).

226. The United States has only recently ratified two important human rights instruments: the Convention on the Prevention and Punishment of Genocide of December 9, 1948, ratified by the United States in 1988; and the ICCPR, ratified by the United States in 1992. Among others, the United States has still not ratified the ICESCR, the Convention on the Elimination of All Forms of Racial Discrimination, the Convention for the Elimination of All Forms of Discrimination Against Women, and the American Convention on Human Rights. See Henkin, Age of Rights, supra note 138, at 74-75; see also Lawyers Committee, ICESCR Ratification, supra note 103.

within its foreign policy bureaucracy.[227] Policy upheavals triggered by the conflict in Vietnam, American support for repressive regimes in Latin America, and the crises of the Nixon presidency precipitated a more systematic evaluation of human rights concerns in American foreign policy.[228] As a result, laws were amended to restrict assistance to countries with particular levels of human rights abuses.[229] In 1977, President Jimmy Carter elevated the head of the Human Rights Bureau[230] within the Department of State to the rank of Assistant Secretary of State for Human Rights and Humanitarian Affairs.[231] Perhaps Carter's lasting achievement will be the rhetorical prominence that his administration gave human rights in American foreign policy.

The Carter legacy has not resulted in continued support for consistency in the application of human rights to foreign policy. There have always been glaring gaps between declared U.S. policy and actual practice toward foreign countries. Under Carter, inconsistent attempts were made to link support for particular countries to their human rights records, a task made all the more difficult by the logic of the cold war. As a general rule, pro-Western but despotic states such as the Shah's Iran, Zaire, South Korea, and Indonesia continued to receive U.S. military assistance.[232] This fact was understated by the Carter administration official responsible for human rights in the National Security Council in 1979-80:

---

227. See American Association for the International Commission of Jurists, Human Rights and US Foreign Policy: The First Decade 1973-1983, at 6 (1984) [hereinafter US Foreign Policy].

228. Id. at 9. As a result of these upheavals, in 1973 the U.S. Congress launched hearings to determine the type and level of recognition that human rights should receive in foreign policy considerations. Id. See also Makau wa Mutua, The African Human Rights System in a Comparative Perspective, 3 Rev. of Afr. Comm'n Hum. & Peoples' Rts. 5, 6 (1993).

229. See Foreign Assistance Act, Pub. L. No. 93-559, § 46, 88 Stat. 1795, 1815 (1974) (creating § 502B) (codified at 22 U.S.C. § 2304 (1994)); International Development and Food Assistance Act, Pub. L. No. 94-161, title III, § 310, 89 Stat. 849, 860 (1975) (creating Foreign Assistance Act § 116) (codified at 22 U.S.C. § 2151n (1994)). The amendments made human rights a "principal goal" of U.S. foreign policy.

230. Congress mandated the establishment of this office and instructed it to report annually on the human rights conditions in every country in the world. International Security Assistance and Arms Export Control Act, Pub. L. No. 94-329, § 301(b), 90 Stat. 729, 750 (1976) (amending Foreign Assistance Act of 1961 § 624(f)) (codified as amended at 22 U.S.C. §§ 2151n, 2304, 2384) (1994).

231. US Foreign Policy, supra note 227, at 17.

232. Id. at 21 (quoting Secretary of State Cyrus Vance: "'In each case,' the Secretary explained, 'we must balance a political concern for human rights against economic and security goals.'").

> When it came to specifics, whether the aid was military or nonmilitary, complex interests had to be balanced in reaching decisions on individual cases. Inescapably, there were numerous cases in which the administration was exposed to the charge of inconsistency. Human rights performance became a dominant factor in conventional arms transfers to Latin America; but such considerations were clearly subordinate in weighing military aid to Egypt, Israel, North Yemen and Saudi Arabia.[233]

While Carter was inconsistent and continued American support for abusive client states, the Reagan administration found the "perfect" use for human rights in American foreign policy. Rather than push for the unlikely repeal of human rights concerns from American policy, which many human rights advocates feared, the administration quickly enlisted human rights as a key ally in the greater struggle against Communism, which many officials saw as the prime evil of the day. Thus, as Henkin noted:

> For the Reagan administration, the struggle between good and evil was itself a struggle for the values commonly associated with human rights. The overriding concern for the United States was to resist, contain, and defeat Communist expansion. That was not only seen as in the United States [sic] interest generally, but it furthered human rights since Communism was the epitome of disrespect for human rights, and where Communism was, or came, human rights were lost irretrievably. Opposition to Communism, including criticism of any new and particular human rights violations by Communist states (as when military rule came to Poland, or Sakharov was confined and mistreated), should be strong and loud and clear.[234]

This reasoning eventually led the administration to solidify its human rights policy around the promotion of democracy. This policy was outlined as the promotion of "democratic processes in order to help build a world environment more favorable to respect

233. Id. (quoting Lincoln P. Bloomfield, From Ideology to Program to Policy: Tracking the Carter Human Rights Policy, 2 J. Pol'y Analysis Mgmt. 1, 8 (1982)).
234. Henkin, Age of Rights, supra note 138, at 71.

for human rights."[235] It was billed as a dual policy that opposed human rights violations while strengthening democracy. The policy aimed singularly at the promotion of democracy "as *the* human right, rejecting in principle not only military 'juntas' but the many one-party states of Africa and Asia."[236] In reality, of course, the administration coddled right-wing dictatorships and oppressive pro-Western regimes, including apartheid South Africa.[237] With the end of the Cold War, however, political conditionality has frequently been used to push one-party states towards the creation of more open, democratic political structures.[238]

The Bush administration did not dramatically depart from the substance of the Reagan policy, although it countenanced the withdrawal of knee-jerk U.S. support for some pro-Western regimes primarily because of the collapse of Communism.[239] Despite its rhetorical defense of human rights, the Clinton administration has been more concerned with the promotion of democratic initiatives and trade opportunities than with the principled application of human rights norms.[240] The United States has frequently used human rights as a weapon of its foreign policy, but that use has rarely been principled. The invocation of human rights has variously been used to justify access to markets or resources vital to the United States, as was the case with the U.S.-led military defeat of Iraq in 1991. The support and the promotion of popularly elected regimes has, however, been privileged by the Clinton administration as the more effective method for advancing what it

---

235. Department of State, Country Reports for Human Rights Practices for 1985, at 3 (1986) (Report submitted to House Comm. on Foreign Affairs and Senate Comm. on Foreign Relations, 99th Cong., 2d Sess.).

236. Henkin, Age of Rights, supra note 138, at 72.

237. See, e.g., Mutua & Rosenblum, supra note 207. For a more comprehensive review of the repressive regimes supported by the Reagan administration, see The Watch Committees & Lawyers Committee for Human Rights, The Reagan Administration's Record on Human Rights in 1986 (1987).

238. See Meeting of the Consultative Group for Kenya, supra note 24; see also Jane Perlez, On Eve of Talks with Aid Donors, Kenya is under Pressure to Democratize, New York Times, Nov. 25, 1991, at A9. In May 1992, the World Bank-led groups of Malawi donors also suspended aid pending moves towards political pluralism by the Banda regime. See Lawyers Committee for Human Rights, Malawi: Ignoring Calls for Change 10 (1992).

239. See generally Human Rights Watch, Human Rights Watch World Report 1992: Events of 1991, at 1-2 (1991) (lamenting the Bush administration's "downgrading the significance of human rights in the formulation of US foreign policy").

240. In October 1994, for example, the Clinton administration forced the restoration to power of the democratically elected Haitian government of President Aristide. See World Report 1995, supra note 22, at 99. But in May of the same year, it also ended the linkage of China's Most Favored Nation status to human rights conditions. Id. at 146-47.

sees as the three inseparable goals of democracy, human rights, and, most important, free markets.[241]

International financial institutions and donor agencies also constitute an increasingly important component of the political strategy approach. World Bank-led groups of donors that keep many states in the South from total economic collapse have used human rights conditionalities to force economic liberalization, a measure of public accountability, and political pluralism. But the World Bank's concern with "good governance" has not been altruistic. That attitudinal change came after the Bank's utter failure to reverse economic decline in Africa. Overlooking its own role in exacerbating Africa's underdevelopment, the Bank concluded in 1989 that "underlying the litany of Africa's development problems is a crisis of governance."[242] In what amounted to a prescription for liberal democracy, it defined governance in the following familiar language:

> By governance is meant the exercise of political power to manage a nation's affairs. Because countervailing power has been lacking, state officials in many countries have served their own interests without fear of being called to account. . . . The leadership assumes broad discretionary authority and loses its legitimacy. Information is controlled, and many voluntary organizations are co-opted or disbanded. This environment cannot readily support a dynamic economy. At worst the state becomes coercive and arbitrary. These trends, however, can be resisted. . . . It requires a systematic effort to build a pluralistic institutional structure, a determination to respect the rule of law, and vigorous protection of the freedom of the press and human rights.[243]

The Bank has used its forbidding political and economic muscle to stare a few states down and push for political reform. Through its consultative groups (CGs)—the collection of donors—it pressed for political change in Kenya and Malawi in the early 1990s,

241. As a demonstration of the view that human rights, democracy, and free markets are intrinsically linked, the Assistant Secretary of State for Human Rights and Humanitarian Affairs has been renamed the "Assistant Secretary of State for Democracy, Human Rights, and Labor." See 22 U.S.C. § 2151n(c) (1994).

242. World Bank, Sub-Saharan Africa: From Crisis to Sustainable Growth, a Long-Term Prospective Study 60 (1989).

243. Id. at 60-61.

although it did not heed its own message in continuing support for China, Zaire, Morocco, and Indonesia, to name just a few undemocratic states with serious human rights problems.[244] INGOs have seized this opening to seek a more systematic application of human rights norms by multilateral donors.[245] The significance of the Bank's general attitude lies in its conclusions: economic liberalization and free markets are less likely in undemocratic regimes that abuse basic liberal freedoms.[246] Authoritarian but economically prosperous Asian states, such as Singapore, China (PRC), Indonesia, and South Korea, have attacked the linkage of human rights to aid and trade as an abuse of human rights and a new form of imperialism by the West.[247] The trademark of political strategists is their unabashed deployment of human rights and democracy interchangeably for the advancement of a variety of interests: strategic, tactical, geopolitical, security, "vital," economic, and political. None of the preceding three schools of thought equals their cynicism.

244. See Governance and Human Rights, supra note 24, at 37-42.

245. Id. The report of the Lawyers Committee for Human Rights is a prime example of the enlistment of donors by INGOs in the human rights crusade. INGOs now work with donors to exploit this willingness to include human rights concerns in their relations with recipient countries.

246. The Bank's 1991 World Development Report read, in part:

> Few authoritarian regimes, in fact, have been economically enlightened. Some of the East Asian [newly industrialized economies] are the exceptions, not the rule. Dictatorships have proven disastrous for development in many countries—in Eastern Europe, Argentina, Central African Republic, Haiti, Myanmar, Nicaragua, Peru, Uganda, and Zaire, to name only a few. Democracies, conversely, could make reform more feasible in several ways. Political checks and balances, a free press, and open debate on the costs and benefits of government policy could give a wider public a stake in reform.

World Bank, The Challenge for Development, in World Development Report 1991, at 133 (1991), cited in Governance and Human Rights, supra note 24, at 41-42.

247. See Report of the Regional Meeting for Asia of the World Conference on Human Rights, UN Doc. A/CONF.157/ASRM/8-A/CONF.157//PC/59 (1993) [hereinafter Bangkok Declaration]; Kausikan, supra note 3, at 33-34; Ali Alatas, Minister for Foreign Affairs and Head of the Delegation of the Republic of Indonesia, Statement before the Second World Conference on Human Rights at Vienna, 9 U.N. Doc. A/48/214 (June 14, 1993). See also Information Office of the State Council of the People's Republic of China, Human Rights in China, Nov. 1, 1991, available in LEXIS, News Library, ARCNWS File. For more on China's positions on human rights, see Information Office of the State Council of the People's Republic of China, The Progress of Human Rights in China (1996), Jan. 31, 1996, available in LEXIS, News Library, CURNWS File.

VI. CONCLUSIONS

This Article has attempted to make a more explicit link between human rights norms and the fundamental characteristics of liberal democracy as practiced in the West, and to question the mythical elevation of the human rights corpus beyond politics and political ideology. In the past, the main authors of the human rights discourse have been reluctant to make this connection either, as I suspect, because they sincerely did not believe that an honest inquiry could pin the human rights movement down to a specific political structure, or because it would have been an admission against interest in the context of the Cold War, amidst states only too eager to exploit cultural and political excuses to justify or continue repressive policies and practices. Now that the end of the Cold War has lifted at least part of that injunction, it seems imperative that probing inquiries about the philosophical and political raison d'etre of the human rights regime be encouraged and welcomed.

While I do not think that the human rights movement is a Western conspiracy to deepen its cultural stranglehold over the globe, I do believe that its abstraction and apoliticization obscure the political character of the norms that it seeks to universalize. As I see it, that universe is at its core and in many of its details, liberal and European. The continued reluctance to identify liberal democracy with human rights delays the reformation, reconstruction, and the multiculturization of human rights. Defining those who seek to reopen or continue the debate about the cultural nature and the raw political purposes of the human rights regime as "outsiders" or even as "enemies" of the movement is the greatest obstacle to the movement to bring about true universalization.

A half century after the Universal Declaration of Human Rights laid the foundation for the human rights movement, those ideas have been embraced by diverse peoples across the earth. That fact is undeniable. But it is only part of the story. Those same people who have embraced that corpus also seek to contribute to it, at times by radically reformulating it, at others by tinkering at the margins. The human rights movement must not be closed to the idea of change or believe that it is the "final" answer. It is not. This belief, which is religious in the evangelical sense, invites "end of history"-type conclusions and leaves humanity stuck at the doors of liberalism, unable to go forward or imagine a post-liberal society. It is an assertion of a final truth. It must be rejected.

From the perspective of this Article, the human rights corpus—as a philosophy that seeks the diffusion of liberalism and its primacy around the globe—can ironically be seen as favorable to political and cultural homogenization and hostile to difference and diversity, the two variables that are at the heart of the vitality of the world today. Yet, strangely, many human rights instruments explicitly encourage diversity through the norm of equal protection, which Steiner sees as the cardinal human rights norm.[248] As he correctly notes:

> Other rights declared in basic human rights instruments complement the ideal of equal respect and confirm the value placed on diversity. Everyone has a right to adopt "a religion or belief of his choice" and has freedom "either individually or in community with others and in public or private" to manifest belief or religion in practice and teaching. Rights to "peaceful assembly" and "freedom of association with others," in each case qualified by typical grounds for limitation like public order or national security, further commit the human rights movement to the protection of people's ongoing capacity to form, develop, and preserve different types of groups.[249]

The paradox of the corpus is that it seeks to foster diversity and difference but does so only under the rubric of Western political democracy. In other words, it says that diversity is good so long as it is exercised within the liberal paradigm, a construct that for the purposes of the corpus is not negotiable. The doors of difference appear open while in reality they are shut. This inelasticity and cultural parochialism of the human rights corpus needs urgent revision so that the ideals of difference and diversity can realize their true meaning. Since we now live in the Age of Skepticism,[250] the long-term interests of the human rights movement are not likely to be served by the pious and righteous advocacy of human rights

248. See Steiner, Autonomy Regimes, supra note 141, at 1548. For example, some human rights conventions are fully fashioned on the principle of equal protection. See, e.g., CEDAW and CERD, the gender and race conventions, respectively, supra note 202.

249. Steiner, Autonomy Regimes, supra note 141, at 1548 (footnotes omitted).

250. By the "Age of Skepticism" I mean the era of post-industrialism during which the technological revolution and the failure of political democracy to end injustice have dashed the popular expectation that the improvement of the lot of humanity will always be a constant. It is an age during which naiveté has given way to skepticism and paved the way for the realization that the organizational norms and structures that have evolved so far are merely experimental. The Age of Skepticism has the potential to free humanity from tradition and allow it to think more creatively and imaginatively about the future.

norms as frozen and fixed principles whose content and cultural relevance is unquestionable.

Based on this premise, the human rights movement needs to alter its orientation, which has been an orientation of moral, political, and legal certitude. There needs to be a realization that the movement is young and that its youth gives it an experimental status, not a final truth. The major authors of human rights discourse seem to believe that all the most important human rights standards and norms have been set and that what remains of the project is elaboration and implementation. This attitude is at the heart of the push to prematurely cut off debate about the political and philosophical roots, nature, and relevance of the human rights corpus.

Debates about the universality of the corpus between Westerners[251] and Southerners[252] should not be viewed with alarm or as necessarily symptomatic of a lack of commitment to the human rights project by Southerners. Attempts to question the normative framework of human rights, their cultural relevance, and the need for a cross-cultural re-creation of norms will not be silenced or wished away by universalists who are unwilling to engage in the debate. As Deng and An-Na'im argued in a volume exploring these issues, the debate is just beginning:

> Whatever the reason for the controversy surrounding cross-cultural perspectives on human rights, the essays in this volume clearly demonstrate that the debate has just begun and that its parameters are still to be defined and its course is still to be charted. The central issue in this debate is whether looking at human rights from the various cultural perspectives that now coexist and interact in the world community promotes or undermines international standards.[253]

There is little doubt that certain states and governments will hide behind the veil of cultural sovereignty to perpetuate practices that are harmful to their populations. That cynicism, however, must not be confused with genuine attempts to bequeath cross-cultural legit-

251. I use the term "Westerners" loosely here to denote advocates of universality, the most prominent of whom are drawn largely from the West and their soul mates in the South.

252. "Southerners" is a term I use here as a shorthand for "dissidents" within the human rights movement, that is, those who question the Eurocentric formulation of the corpus and call for a multicultural approach for its recreation. Many Southerners are non-Western and hail from Asia and Africa.

253. See Cross-Cultural Perspectives, supra note 9, at 9.

imacy to a universal human rights corpus. Deng and An-Nai'm ask a series of biting questions that leave little doubt about the indispensability of cross-culturalism.[254] Richard Schwartz affirms this point of view: he sees the necessity of a cross-fertilization of cultures if a universal human rights corpus is to emerge. According to him:

> Every culture will have its distinctive ways of formulating and supporting human rights. Every society can learn from other societies more effective ways to implement human rights. While honoring the diversity of cultures, we can also build toward common principles that all can support. As agreement is reached on the substance, we may begin to trust international law to provide a salutary and acceptable safeguard to ensure that all people can count on a minimum standard of human rights.[255]

The failure of most universalists, particularly the conventional doctrinalists, to positively engage in this debate unnecessarily antagonizes cultural agnostics and may lend itself to legitimate charges of cultural imperialism. This is particularly the case if the human rights corpus is seen purely as a liberal project whose overriding goal, though not explicitly stated, is the imposition of a Western-style liberal democracy. The forceful rejection of dialogue also leads to the inevitable conclusion that there is a hierarchy of cultures, an assumption that is not only detrimental to the human rights project but is also inconsistent with the human rights corpus' commitment to equality, diversity, and difference.[256] Ultimately,

---

254. An-Na'im and Deng ask:

> Is this [cross-cultural approach to creating a universal corpus] a fanciful ideal or an achievable objective? Are we being romantic and are we unnecessarily complicating the process of universalizing the cause of human rights, or are we presenting a cultural challenge for all members of the human family and their respective cultures that can help shape the lofty ideals of universal human rights? And could such worldwide involvement in itself lead to a realization of the universality of human dignity, which is the cornerstone of international human rights? *Or would it be more practical to assume that some cultures are just not blessed with these human ideals, and that the sooner they recognize this and try to adjust and live up to the challenge presented by the pioneering leadership of those more endowed with these lofty values, the better for their own good and for the good of humanity?*

Id. at 10-11 (emphasis added).

255. Richard D. Schwartz, Human Rights in an Evolving World Culture, in Cross-Cultural Perspectives, supra note 9, at 382.

256. Belief in cultural superiority violates more than the norms of the human rights movement. As this author has written elsewhere:

the unrelenting universalist push seeks to destroy difference by creating the rationale for various forms of intervention and penetration of other cultures with the intent of transforming them into the liberal model. This view legitimizes intervention and leaves open only the mode of that intervention, that is, whether it is military, through sanction systems, bilateral or multilateral, as a cultural package bound in one or another form of exchange, or through trade and aid.

What should not be at stake when conversations about human rights are held is a singular obsession with the universalization of one or another cultural model. Rather, the imagination of norms and political models whose experimental purpose is the reduction—if not the elimination—of conditions that foster human indignity, violence, poverty, and powerlessness ought to be the overriding objective of actors in this discourse. For that to be possible, and to resonate in different corners of the earth, societies at their grassroots have to participate in the construction of principles and structures that enhance the human dignity of all, big and small, male and female, believer and unbeliever, this race and that community. But those norms and structures must be grown at home, and must utilize the cultural tools familiar to the people at the grassroots. Even if they turn out to resemble the ideas and institutions of political democracy, or to borrow from it, they will belong to the people. What the human rights movement must not do is to close all doors, turn away other cultures, and impose itself in its current form and structure on the world. A post-liberal society, however that will look, cannot be constructed by freezing liberalism in time.

> No one culture or religion is sovereign in relationship to any other culture or religion. From the perspective of the human rights movement, all cultures are equal. This view rejects the notion that there is a hierarchy of cultures or religions; that some cultures are superior to others even though technologically they may be more advanced. Belief in the contrary has led to military invasions to "civilize," colonize, and enslave, as was the case with Christianity in Africa.

Makau wa Mutua, Limitations on Religious Rights: Problematizing Religious Freedom in the African Context, in 2 Religious Human Rights in Global Perspective: Legal Perspectives 417 (Johan D. van der Vyver & John Witte, Jr. eds., 1996).

[5]

Cultural Relativism and Universal Human Rights

Jack Donnelly *

Cultural relativity is an undeniable fact; moral rules and social institutions evidence an astonishing cultural and historical variability. Cultural relativism is a doctrine that holds that (at least some) such variations are exempt from legitimate criticism by outsiders, a doctrine that is strongly supported by notions of communal autonomy and self-determination. Moral judgments, however, would seem to be essentially universal, as suggested not only by Kant's categorical imperative but also by the common sense distinction between principled and self-interested action. And if human rights are, literally, the rights (every)one has simply because one is a human being, they would seem to be universal by definition.

How can the competing claims of cultural relativism and universal human rights be reconciled? In this article I shall try to specify the nature of their relationship, and argue for an approach that preserves the tension between, and the insights of, both relativism and universalism.

DEFINING "CULTURAL RELATIVISM"

The two extreme positions on cultural relativism can be called radical cultural relativism and radical universalism. Radical cultural relativism would hold that culture is the sole source of the validity of a moral right or rule. Radical universalism would hold that culture is irrelevant to the validity of moral rights and rules, which are universally valid.

* Rhoda Howard's criticisms of earlier drafts forced me to greater clarity and precision, and saved me from several errors – although I have stubbornly insisted on leaving a few in here. John Vincent started me thinking along these lines and provided helpful comments on an earlier draft. Ted Lewellen offered useful observations from an anthropologist's point of view. I am grateful to them for their help.

These radical views are ideal types that mark the end points of a continuum. The body of that continuum, those positions involving varying mixes of relativism and universalism, can be roughly divided into what we can call strong and weak cultural relativism.

Strong cultural relativism holds that culture is the *principal* source of the validity of a moral right or rule. In other words, the presumption is that rights (and other social practices, values, and moral rules) are culturally determined, but the universality of human nature and rights serves as a check on the potential excesses of relativism. At its furthest extreme, just short of radical relativism, strong cultural relativism would accept a few basic rights with virtually universal application, but allow such a wide range of variation for most rights that two entirely justifiable sets might overlap only slightly.

Weak cultural relativism holds that culture may be an *important* source of the validity of a moral right or rule. In other words, there is a weak presumption of universality, but the relativity of human nature, communities, and rights serves as a check on potential excesses of universalism. At its furthest extreme, just short of radical universalism, weak cultural relativism would recognize a comprehensive set of *prima facie* universal human rights and allow only relatively rare and strictly limited local variations and exceptions.

Strong and weak are relative terms referring to the extent of cultural variation permitted. We must be careful, however, not to use merely quantitative measures of relativism; qualitative judgments of the significance of different cultural variations must also be incorporated.

Across the continuum of strong and weak relativisms there are several levels or types of relativity. In a rough way, three hierarchical levels of variation can be distinguished, involving cultural relativity in the *substance* of lists of human rights, in the *interpretation* of individual rights, and in the *form* in which particular rights are implemented. The range of permissible variation at a given level is set by the next higher level. For example, "interpretations" of a right are, logically, limited by the specification of the substance of a right. The range of variation in substance is set by the notions of human nature and dignity, from which any list of human rights derives. In other words, as we move "down" the hierarchy we are in effect further specifying and interpreting, in a broad sense of that term, the higher level.

I shall ultimately try to defend a weak cultural relativist position that permits limited deviations from "universal" human rights standards[1] primarily at the levels of form and interpretation. On the way to this conclusion, I argue, in the following section, that radical relativism and radical universalism are

1. Cultural relativism, of course, applies *prima facie* to practices and moral standards other than human rights, but henceforth I shall be concerned here almost exclusively with cultural relativist arguments applied to human rights, and in particular lists of human rights in widely accepted international documents such as the Universal Declaration of Human Rights.

misguided. I then explore, in greater detail, the levels and types of cultural relativism, and address the problem of the cultural basis of relativism. Finally, in the last two sections, I try to show that the international consensus represented by the Universal Declaration of Human Rights and the International Human Rights Covenants, in the conditions of the modern world, support a weak cultural relativist approach to human rights; that is, an approach that views human rights as *prima facie* universal, but recognizes culture as a limited source of exceptions and principles of interpretation.

RELATIVITY AND UNIVERSALITY: A NECESSARY TENSION

The dangers of the moral imperialism implied by radical universalism hardly need be emphasized. Radical universalism, however, is subjected to other moral objections as well.

Moral rules, including human rights, function within a moral community. Radical universalism requires a rigid hierarchical ordering of the multiple moral communities to which individuals and groups belong. In order to preserve complete universality for basic rights, the radical universalist must give absolute priority to the demands of the cosmopolitan moral community over all other ("lower") moral communities. This complete denial of national and subnational ethical autonomy and self-determination is dubious at best.

Even if the nation is a doomed, transitory stage in the development of human moral community, there is no logical or inescapable moral reason why peoples cannot accept or choose it as their principal form of social organization and the primary locus of their extrafamilial moral and political commitments. Once we allow the moral validity of such commitments, we are bound to accept at least certain types of substantive moral variability, including variability in human rights practices.

Such moral "nationalism" may be based on reasons such as an inability to agree on the structure of a supranational organization or a fear of creating an instrument of universal tyranny. More directly moral reasons might also be advanced, such as the advantages of international diversity provided by a strong commitment to national or local customs. Most importantly, it rests on the notion of self-determination. But however it is justified – and the various arguments are likely to be mutually reinforcing – at least certain choices of such moral communities demand respect from outsiders; not necessarily uncritical acceptance, let alone emulation, but in some cases at least, tolerance. Therefore, radical universalism cannot be justifiably maintained.

This is perhaps too strong a conclusion. There may be some formal principle, such as the universalizability of moral judgments, that might plausibly be argued to be universally valid. There may even be a very short list of universal rights. Advocates and theorists of human rights, however, rarely if ever restrict themselves to either of these extremely limited claims. For any robust substantive list of basic human rights—for example, the lists in the Universal Declaration of Human Rights and the International Human Rights Covenants—at least some allowance must be made by outsiders for the special practices of national and other noncosmopolitan moral communities.

A cultural relativist account of human rights, however, seems to be guilty of logical contradiction. If human rights are based in human nature, on the simple fact that one is a human being, and if human nature is universal, then how can human rights be relative in any fundamental way?

The simple answer is that human nature is itself in some measure culturally relative. There is a sense in which this is true even at the biological level; for example, if marriage partners are chosen on the basis of largely cultural preferences concerning height, weight, skin tone, or other physical attributes, the gene pool in a community would be altered in ways equivalent to "natural" mechanisms of selection. More importantly, culture can significantly influence the presence and expression of many less easily quantified aspects of human nature, for example, by encouraging or discouraging the development or perpetuation of certain personality types.

The impact of culture on the shaping of individuals is systematic and may lead to the predominance of distinctive social types in different cultures. There can be little doubt that there are important, structurally determined differences, for example, between the modal "natures" of men and especially women in modern western and traditional Islamic societies. In any particular case, "human nature," the realized nature of real human beings, is a social as well as a "natural" product.

Whether we conceive of this process as involving cultural variation around an inalterable "natural" core or largely cultural variation within a physiologically fixed range, there is an undeniable social side to human nature, at least insofar as that nature is expressed. Human nature, at the levels of the individual, the group, and the species alike, is a range of possibilities, varying, in part in response to culture, within apparently fixed psychobiological limits; it is as much a project, and an individual and social discovery, as a given. Even if all behavior should prove to be ultimately genetic, the expression of that genetic endowment—which also merits being called "human nature"—is in considerable measure culturally determined.

Elsewhere I have sketched a theory of human rights consistent with such an account of human nature.[2] Here I simply want to stress that the cultural variability of human nature not only permits but requires significant allowance for crosscultural variations in human rights.[3]

---

2. Jack Donnelly, *The Concept of Human Rights,* forthcoming, Chapter 3.
3. Note that I am *not* arguing that all such cultural variations are morally justifiable; below, I will argue explicitly that they are not. My point is that *some* such variations are justifiable, on a variety of moral and practical grounds. Particular arguments concerning the justifiability of individual practices, however, are largely beyond my scope here.

But if all rights rested solely on culturally determined social rules, as radical cultural relativism holds, then there could be no human rights, no rights one has simply as a human being. This denial of human rights is perfectly coherent. Furthermore, as I have argued elsewhere, "traditional" societies generally do not recognize rights held simply because one is a human being.[4] Nonetheless, I shall argue that radical cultural relativism is morally indefensible today.

The strongest form of radical cultural relativism would hold that the concept "human being" is of no moral significance; the mere fact that one is a human being is irrelevant to one's moral status. It is true that premodern societies typically have not recognized "human being" even as a descriptive category, but instead define persons by social status or group membership. For example, the very names of many cultures mean simply "the people" (e.g., Hopi, Arapahoe), and their origin myths define them as separate from outsiders, who are somehow "not-human." Similarly, in ancient Greece there were Hellenes and barbarians. This view, however, is almost universally rejected in the contemporary world.

For example, chattel slavery and caste systems, which implicitly deny the existence of a (morally significant) common humanity, are almost universally condemned, even in the most rigid class societies. Likewise, the basic moral distinction between insiders and outsiders has been seriously eroded by greatly increased individual mobility and by an at least aspirational commitment to the idea of a universal human moral community.

Today there is near universal international agreement, at least in theory, although often not in practice, that certain things simply cannot legitimately be done to human beings – regardless of the difficulties in specifying those things.[5] Failure to act or even speak out against the grossest affronts to human dignity overseas on the grounds of cultural relativism would be widely – and I believe correctly – perceived as moral cowardice.[6]

Even more striking is the apparent crosscultural consensus on a few particular practices that cannot be justified by even the hoariest of traditions, and certainly not by any new custom. For example, the prohibition of torture and the requirement of procedural due process in imposing and exe-

4. Jack Donnelly, "Human Rights and Human Dignity: An Analytic Critique of Non-Western Conceptions of Human Rights," *American Political Science Review* 76 (June 1982), 303–316.
5. Such international agreement, of course, tends to reflect primarily the views of those who are politically active in the modern sector. Exceptions, therefore, continue to exist, particularly in relatively isolated areas where status-based societies still persist with some vigor. Nonetheless, I would argue that even such exceptions are subject to defensible (although perhaps not necessarily decisive) criticism, on grounds discussed below.
6. Compare R. J. Vincent, "Human Rights and Cultural Relativism" Paper presented at the 25th Annual Convention of the International Studies Association, Atlanta, Georgia, March 1984. This article is largely the result of my efforts to come to grips with the issues raised in Vincent's paper.

cuting legal punishments seem to be accepted as binding by virtually all cultures, despite profound differences in specifying the practical and substantive meanings of these notions.

The radical relativist might respond that such consensus is irrelevant. Logically, this is correct; crosscultural consensus does not necessarily entail any additional force for a moral rule. Nonetheless, I would submit that virtually all people do view such consensus as adding substantial force to the rule, and thus in an important sense this sort of radical relativism, while logically impeccable, is morally defective.

In effect, a moral analog to customary international law seems to operate. If a practice is nearly universal and generally perceived as obligatory, international community standards require that practice of all members of the community, and preclude the legitimate development of alternative practices. There is – or at least one might plausibly argue that there is – a weak cosmopolitan moral community, which imposes minimal substantive limitations on the range of permissible cultural moral variation.

Notice, however, that I have argued only that there are at least a few crossculturally valid moral *values*. This still leaves open the possibility of a radical cultural relativist denial of human *rights*. Such an argument would hold that while there may be universal moral rules or values, human rights – inalienable entitlements held equally by all, grounding particularly strong claims that may be made against the state and society – are but one of several defensible mechanisms to protect human dignity (which in any case is largely a culturally determined notion).[7]

Plausible arguments can be advanced to justify alternative mechanisms to guarantee human dignity; for example, natural *law*, which imposes transcultural moral obligations that are not correlative to rights.[8] Few if any states, however, actually advance such arguments. In the First, Second, and Third Worlds alike, a strong commitment to human *rights* is almost universally proclaimed, even where practice throws that commitment into question.

It is too easy to dismiss such proclamations as mere rhetorical fashion; such a widespread international moral "fashion" must have some substantive basis. That basis, I would suggest, is the moral hazard presented by the modern state.

Traditional rulers usually faced substantial moral limits on their political power, customary limits entirely independent of human rights. Furthermore, the relative technological and administrative weakness of traditional states

7. The argument here rests on the conceptual distinction between *rights*, in the strong sense of titles grounding claims of a special type, and righteous; that is, between rights, in the sense in which one *has* rights, and (mere) righteousness, in the sense in which something *is* right. For a further discussion of this distinction, see Donnelly, note 3 above, Chapter 1 and Vincent, note 6 above, 303–306.

8. Compare Jack Donnelly, "Natural Law and Right in Aquinas' Political Thought," *Western Political Quarterly* 33 (December 1980), 520–535.

and nonstate political institutions provided considerable practical restraints on arbitrary abuses of power. In such a world, at least some human rights—inalienable entitlements of individuals held against state and society—might plausibly be held to be superfluous (in the sense that basic dignity was being guaranteed by alternative mechanisms) if not positively dangerous to well-established practices that realized a cultural conception of human dignity.

Such a world, however, exists today only in a relatively small number of isolated areas. And the modern state, particularly in the Third World, not only operates relatively free of the moral constraints of custom but has far greater administrative and technological reach. It thus represents a serious threat to basic human dignity, whether that dignity is defined in "traditional" or "modern" terms.

To the extent that modernization or Westernization has reached into, and transformed, traditional communities, traditional approaches to guaranteeing human dignity seem objectively inappropriate; traditional limits on political power are unlikely to function effectively in modern conditions. In such circumstances—to which we will return in more detail below—at least certain basic human rights seem necessary rather than optional. In most instances, then, radical or unrestricted relativism is as inappropriate as unrestricted universalism; some sort of intermediate position is required.[9] This requires us to consider in greater detail the various levels and types of cultural relativism.

LEVELS AND TYPES OF RELATIVISM

In discussing foreign practices, we can distinguish between what can be called "internal" and "external" evaluations. An internal judgment asks whether the practice is defensible within the basic value framework of that society; the issue here is whether a plausible and coherent defense of the practice can be made in response to universalistic criticism. Practices that do not even stand up to such evaluations can in no sense be defended on cultural terms. An external judgment applies the standards of the evaluator (modified, as appropriate, by relativistic arguments) in order to determine whether the practice can or should be accepted or defended, all things considered. Clearly the most important controversies are likely to arise over practices that are defensible according to internal standards but unacceptable by external standards; these are the practices we are most concerned with in the discussion of cultural relativism and universal human rights.

To a considerable degree this distinction between internal and external

9. Note that this argument is largely empirical and functional. While others may wish to construct a more ambitious, "universal" argument for human rights, I shall restrict myself here to this historically "limited" horizon.

evaluations matches up with, and further elaborates, the distinction between strong and weak cultural relativism; the stronger one's relativism, the greater one's reliance on internal evaluations. It also helps to elucidate the dilemma we face in judging culturally specific practices, torn between the demands of relativism and universalism, demands that require us to renounce radical relativism and radical universalism in favor of some combination of internal and external judgments.

As I have already emphasized, relativism rests on the notions of moral autonomy and communal self-determination. Respect for autonomous moral communities would seem to demand internal evaluations. But to rely entirely on internal judgments would seem to abrogate one's moral responsibilities as a member of the cosmopolitan moral community; such membership would seem to demand the application of universal standards in external judgments. Membership in one's own national or local moral community also might demand (a different type of) external judgments. Furthermore, moral judgments by their nature are universal, or at least universalizable, even though we know that moral values and particular judgments are, at least in part and in their genesis, historically specific and contingent.

The choice between internal and external evaluations thus is itself a moral choice. However, the choice is not entirely free or simply a matter of personal moral judgment. Within each system – the "universal" standards of the cosmopolitan moral community, the standards of one's home community, and those of the foreign community whose practice is being evaluated – we can rank practices in terms of their moral worth. As a general rule, we can suggest that the more "important" a practice within a particular system, the greater the force of internal standards, which can be overridden only by particularly strong external judgments.

Such a general rule hardly solves all our problems. Besides the obvious difficulties of providing even a very crude system for weighing competing internal and external standards, in some instances at least "important" values, judged by external standards, will compete with internally "important" values or practices, presenting a dilemma of immense proportions. However, such a rule can greatly simplify the process of evaluation – assuming we are able to make at least rough internal judgments of "importance."

As I noted above, strong and weak relativism cannot be distinguished solely by the number of deviations they allow from "universal" standards; some qualitative measure also is required. The distinction between variations in substance, interpretation, and form is a useful place to begin discussing this issue.

Even very weak cultural relativists – that is, relatively strong universalists – are likely to allow considerable variation in the form in which most rights are implemented. For example, whether free legal assistance is required by the right to equal protection of the laws is best viewed as a technical issue of the form in which the right is implemented, and thus largely beyond the legitimate reach of universal standards. Important differences between strong and weak relativists are likely to arise, however, when we move to the levels of interpretation and substance.

While the distinction between variations in form and in interpretation is difficult to draw with precision, it is fairly clear and quite important, as we can see by looking at a particular right, such as the right to political participation. In specifying the right to political participation, we can begin by distinguishing electoral from nonelectoral forms of participation. We can also distinguish direct democracy from representative government, and both of these from participation through occasional plebiscites. Representative elections can be further divided into relatively open and closed multiple-party and one-party elections. We can also distinguish elections where voting is a basic right from those where it is a privilege or even a duty, elections intended to determine the will of the people from elections that serve principally to mobilize popular support for government policy, and so forth. All of these variations in "interpretation" clearly are qualitatively different from questions of form such as how often elections, town meetings, or plebiscites will be held.

But while all these mechanisms represent plausible interpretations of the right to political participation, we need not – and should not – hold that all "interpretations" are equally plausible or defensible. They are *interpretations*, not free associations or arbitrary stipulations; the meaning of "the right to political participation" is controversial, but the range of controversy is limited by the concept. For example, an election in which a people were allowed to choose an absolute dictator for life – "one man, one vote, once," as a West African quip puts it – in no way represents a defensible interpretation of the right.

Particular human rights are like "essentially contested concepts," in which there is a substantial but rather general consensus of meaning, coupled with a no less important, and apparently unresolvable, conflict of interpretations.[10] In such circumstances, culture provides one plausible and defensible mechanism for selecting interpretations (and forms). Nonetheless, there are strong conceptual limits on the acceptable range of variation.

In addition to essential contestability, scarcity also implies permitting variations in form and interpretation. The effective political implementation of virtually all human rights consumes resources. While frequently noted for economic and social rights, this is equally true of many civil and political rights. For example, there are significant direct costs, as well as indirect costs such as the diversion of resources, in running an election, operating a legal system in accord with principles of due process, and protecting citizens

10. See W. B. Gallie, "Essentially Contested Concepts," *Philosophy and the Historical Understanding* (New York: Shocken Books, 1964), 157.

against arbitrary or inhumane and degrading treatment by officials of the state.[11]

Fiscal constraints may also require difficult decisions concerning priorities, decisions that are in part tied to culture. In setting such priorities, however, an especially extreme emphasis or deemphasis of a right (or set of rights) brings us to the edge of the third type of relativity, namely, variations in substance, differences in lists of human rights.

Rights that vary in form and interpretation still are clearly "universal" in an important sense, particularly if the substantive list of rights is relatively universal. But while variations in substance involve much more extreme relativity, even here talk of universality can be meaningful.

If we look at complete lists rather than particular rights, there may be an essential universality even in the midst of considerable substantive diversity. Such universality may take the form of a large common core with relatively few differences "around the edges." It may involve strong statistical regularities, in which outliers are few and are clearly overshadowed by the central tendency. There may be clusterings, or lesser but still significant overlaps, that allow us to speak of "universality" in a very extended sense. And if we distinguish between "major" and "minor" rights, we might have still another sort of universality amidst substantive diversity: the definition of such categories is of course extremely controversial, but to the extent that variations in substance are concentrated among "minor" rights, a fundamental universality would be retained.

The extent to which the listed rights are aggregated is another important consideration. At the level of broad categories such as civil, political, economic, and social rights, there is widespread agreement – except for a very small minority that still rejects economic and social rights – that "universality" is required; any defensible list must include rights from all these categories. As we disaggregate, however, the permissible range of relativity expands, in part because each listed right is more minor," and in part because disaggregation is largely a process of interpretation, in a broad sense of that term.

Consider, for example, the right to work, which is almost universally recognized in disaggregations of economic rights. This right might be interpreted as a right to seek employment, to be compensated for unemployment, to be employed, or even a right to employment appropriate to one's interests and talents. Certain rights specified at this level, however, will be missing from some defensible lists of human rights, including many lists that recognize a right to work. Further disaggregation – for example, specifying

11. Compare Henry Shue, "Rights in the Light of Duties," in *Human Rights and U.S. Foreign Policy*, ed. Peter G. Brown and Douglas MacLean (Lexington, Mass.: Lexington Books, 1979), 65–81 and Henry Shue, *Basic Rights: Subsistence, Affluence and U.S. Foreign Policy* (Princeton: Princeton University Press, 1980), 35–53.

the length and amount of unemployment benefits, or the extent of vocational training or retraining made available – is likely to bring us into the realm of formal variation, where universality usually is an inappropriate demand.

Thus in considering the various levels and types of relativism, we see once more, and now more deeply and in greater detail, that the problem of cultural relativism and universal human rights cannot be reduced to an either-or choice. Claims of cultural relativism show a great diversity in meaning, substance, and importance. Therefore, any evaluation of such claims must be sensitive to this diversity, which is all too often overlooked when the issue of cultural relativism is raised in the discussion of human rights.

CULTURE AND RELATIVISM

So far we have focused on relativism, in general. The cultural basis of cultural relativism also must be considered, especially in light of the fact that numerous contemporary arguments against universal human rights standards strive for the cachet of cultural relativism but in fact are entirely without cultural basis.

Standard arguments for cultural relativism rely on examples such as the precolonial African village, Native American tribes, and traditional Islamic social systems. Elsewhere I have argued that human rights – rights/titles held against society equally by all persons simply because they are human beings – are foreign to such communities, which instead employed other, often quite sophisticated, mechanisms for protecting and realizing defensible conceptions of human dignity.[12] The claims of communal self-determination are particularly strong here, especially if we allow a certain moral autonomy to such communities and recognize the cultural variability of the social side of human nature. It is important, however, to recognize the limits of such arguments.

Where there is a thriving indigenous cultural tradition and community, arguments of cultural relativism based on the principle of the self-determination of peoples offer a strong defense against outside interference – including disruptions that might be caused by the introduction of "universal" human rights. But while autonomous communities that freely decide their destiny largely according to traditional values and practices still do exist throughout the Third World,[13] they are increasingly the exception

12. Donnelly, note 4 above.

13. In what follows, I largely restrict myself to relativist arguments made on behalf of indigenous cultural practices in the Third World. This is not because of any greater inherent universality of western or northern practices or values. Rather, it reflects the "western" genesis of international standards and the fact that arguments of cultural relativism today are made largely on behalf of practices in Third World countries.

rather than the rule. They are not, for example, the communities of the teeming slums that hold an ever-growing proportion of the population of most states. Even most rural areas have been substantially penetrated, and the local culture "corrupted," by foreign practices and institutions ranging from the modern state, to the money economy, to "western" values, products, and practices.

In the Third World today, more often than not we see dual societies and patchwork practices that seek to accommodate seemingly irreconcilable old and new ways. Rather than the persistence of traditional culture in the face of modern intrusions, or even the development of syncretic cultures and values, we usually see instead a disruptive and incomplete westernization, cultural confusion, or the enthusiastic embrace of "modern" practices and values.[14] In other words, the traditional culture advanced to justify cultural relativism far too often no longer exists.

Therefore, while recognizing the legitimate claims of self-determination and cultural relativism, we must be alert to cynical manipulations of a dying, lost, or even mythical cultural past. We must not be misled by complaints of the inappropriateness of "western" human rights made by repressive regimes whose practices have at best only the most tenuous connection to the indigenous culture; communitarian rhetoric too often cloaks the depredations of corrupt and often westernized or deracinated elites. In particular, we must be wary of self-interested denunciations of the excessive individualism of "western" human rights.

Human rights are inherently "individualistic"; they are rights held by individuals in relation to, even against, the state and society.[15] But while traditional cultures, both western or nonwestern, usually view persons primarily as parts of a family or community, rather than as autonomous individuals, not all forms of nonindividualistic or antiindividualistic politics are based in traditional culture – even where that culture remains vital. In particular, communitarian defenses of traditional practices usually cannot be extended to modern nation states and contemporary nationalist regimes.

Arguments of cultural relativism are far too often made by economic and political elites that have long since left traditional culture behind. While this may represent a fundamentally admirable effort to retain or recapture cherished traditional values, even in such cases it is at least ironic to see

14. Compare Rhoda Howard, "Is There an African Concept of Human Rights?" in *Human Rights in Foreign Policy: Issues and Responses*, ed. R. J. Vincent, forthcoming. (Currently available as Working Paper No. A:8, Development Studies Programme, University of Toronto.) I have also benefited greatly from reading preliminary versions of Howard's ongoing research on human rights in contemporary Commonwealth Africa.

15. For a further elaboration and defense of this understanding of human rights see Donnelly, note 2 above, and "Human Rights as Natural Rights," *Human Rights Quarterly* 4 (August 1982), 391–405, where, in addition to the argument based on the nature of modern society developed here, I present arguments relying on conceptual analysis and the international consensus represented by the Universal Declaration of Human Rights.

largely westernized elites warning against the values and practice they have adopted. At their best, such arguments tend to be dangerously paternalistic—for example, villagization, which was supposed to reflect traditional African conceptions, was accomplished in Tanzania only by force, against the vocal and occasionally even violent opposition of much of the population—and even such a troubling sincerity is unfortunately rare.

Arguments of cultural relativism regularly involve urban elites eloquently praising the glories of village life—a life that they or their parents or grandparents struggled hard to escape, and a life to which they have not the slightest intention of returning. Government officials denounce the corrosive individualism of western values—while they line their pockets with the proceeds of massive corruption, drive imported luxury automobiles, and plan European or American vacations. Leaders sing the praises of traditional communities, which they claim as the source of their political practices—while they wield arbitrary power antithetical to traditional values, pursue development policies that systematically undermine traditional communities, and replace traditional leaders with corrupt cronies and party hacks.

In other words, appeals to traditional practices and values all too often are a mere cloak for self-interest or arbitrary rule. For example, the All Africa Council of Churches has condemned the fact that "some leaders have even resorted to picking out certain elements of traditional African culture to anesthetize the masses. Despite what is said, this frequently has little to do with a return to the positive, authentic dimensions of African tradition."[16] While this cynical manipulation of tradition occurs everywhere, let me mention just a few African illustrations.

In Malawi, President Hastings Kamuzu Banda utilizes "traditional courts" in order to deal with political opponents outside of the regular legal system. For example, Orton and Vera Chirwa, after being kidnapped from Zambia, were brought before a "traditional court" made up of five judges and three tribal chiefs, all appointed directly by Banda. While there was a prosecutor, no defense attorney was allowed, and the only possible appeal was to Banda personally.[17] Such procedures have not the slightest connection with authentic traditional practices.

In Zaire, President Mobutu has created the practice of *salongo*, a form of communal labor with a supposedly traditional basis. In fact, it has little or no connection with indigenous traditional practices; rather, it is a revival of the colonial practice of *corvee* labor.[18] In Niger, *samarias*, traditional youth

16. All Africa Council of Churches/World Council of Churches Human Rights Consultation, Khartoum, Sudan, 16–22 February 1975, "Factors Responsible for the Violation of Human Rights in Africa," *Issue* 6 (Winter 1976), 45.
17. *Africa Report* 27 (September/October 1982), 35; *Africa Report* 27 (November/December 1982), 35.
18. Thomas M. Callaghy, "State-Subject Communication in Zaire: Domination and the Concept of Domain Consensus," *Journal of Modern African Studies* 18 (September 1980), 490.

organizations, have been "revived" – but not so much out of a respect for traditional culture as "to replace party organizations so as to channel youthful energies away from politics."[19] And Macias Nguema of Equatorial Guinea, probably the most vicious ruler independent black Africa has seen, called himself "Grand Master of Popular Education, Science and Traditional Culture,"[20] a title that would be comical if it weren't so tragic.

The cynicism of many claims of cultural relativism can also be seen in the fact that far too often they are for external consumption only. The same elites that raise culture as a defense against external criticisms based on universal human rights are often ruthless in their suppression of inconvenient local customs, whether of the majority or a minority. National unification certainly will require substantial sacrifices of local customs, but the lack of local cultural sensitivity shown by many national elites that strongly advocate an international cultural relativism suggests a very high degree of self-interest.

Furthermore, numerous and regretably common practices, such as disappearances, arbitrary arrest and detention, or torture, are entirely without cultural basis. Idi Amin, Pol Pot, and the death squads of El Salvador cannot be attributed to local culture; while these names have become justly synonymous with modern barbarism, such practices are not an expression of established cultural traditions. Rigged elections, military dictatorships, and malnutrition caused by government incentives to produce cash crops rather than food are just a few of the widespread abuses of generally recognized human rights that are in no sense a positive expression of indigenous cultures. Such practices can be condemned on the basis of both internal and external evaluations and thus are in no sense capable of plausible defense.

In traditional cultures – at least the sorts of traditional cultures that would readily justify cultural deviations from international human rights standards – people are not victims of the arbitrary decisions of rulers whose principal claim to power is their control of modern instruments of force and administration. In traditional cultures, communal customs and practices usually provide each person with a place in society and a certain amount of dignity and protection. Furthermore, there usually are well-established reciprocal bonds between rulers and ruled, and between rich and poor.

The human rights violations of most Third World regimes are as antithetical to such cultural traditions as they are to "western" human rights conceptions. In fact, authentic traditional cultural practices and values can be an important check on abuses of arbitrary power. Traditional African cultures, for example, usually were strongly constitutional, with major customary

19. *Africa Contemporary Record*, 14 (1981–1982), B490–491.
20. Rene Pelissier, "Equatorial Guinea: Autopsy of a Miracle," *Africa Report* 25 (May/June 1980), 11.

limits on rulers; as a Basotho maxim says, "A chief is a chief by the people."[21] Not only are these traditional checks a resource that human rights advocates may be able to tap, but it has even been argued that transgressions of traditional limits have figured in the collapse of some recent regimes.[22]

Finally, as I argued above, there are substantive human rights limits on even well-established cultural practices, however difficult it may be to specify and defend a particular account of what those practices are. For example, while slavery has been customary in numerous societies, today it is a practice that no custom can justify. Likewise, sexual, racial, ethnic, and religious discrimination have been widely practiced, but are indefensible today; the depth of the tradition of anti-Semitism in the West, for example, simply is no defense for the maintenance of the practice.

This is not to say that certain cultural differences cannot justify even fundamental deviations from "universal" human rights standards; I have already argued that they may. However, if cultural relativism is to function as a guarantee of local self-determination, rather than a cloak for despotism, we must insist on a strong, authentic cultural basis, as well as the presence of alternative mechanisms guaranteeing basic human dignity, before we justify cultural derogations from "universal" human rights.

RESOLVING THE CLAIMS OF RELATIVISM AND UNIVERSALISM

Despite striking and profound international differences in ideology, levels and styles of economic development, and patterns of political evolution, virtually all states today have embraced – in speech if not in deed – the human rights standards enunciated in the Universal Declaration of Human Rights and the International Human Rights Covenants. This consensus presents a strong *prima facie* case for a relatively strong universalism; that is, for weak cultural relativism. Even if this "consensus" is largely the complement of vice to virtue, it reveals widely shared notions of "virtue," an underlying "universal" moral position compelling at least the appearance of assent from even the cynical and corrupt.

While human rights – inalienable entitlements of individuals held in relation to state and society – have not been a part of most cultural traditions, or even the western tradition until rather recently, there is a striking similarity in many of the basic values that today we seek to protect through human rights. This is particularly true when these values are expressed in relatively general terms. Life, social order, protection from arbitrary rule,

21. See Richard F. Weisfelder, "The Decline of Human Rights in Lesotho: An Evaluation of Domestic and External Determinants," *Issue* 6 (Winter 1976), 23.
22. See, e.g., Victor T. LeVine, "African Patrimonial Regimes in Comparative Perspective," *Journal of Modern African Studies* 18 (December 1980), 672.

prohibition of inhuman and degrading treatment, the guarantee of a place in the life of the community, and access to an equitable share of the means of subsistence are central moral aspirations in nearly all cultures.

This fundamental unity in the midst of otherwise bewildering diversity suggests a certain core of "human nature" – for all its undeniable variability, and despite our inability to express that core in the language of science. And if human nature is relatively universal, then basic human rights must at least initially be assumed to be similarly universal.

In the conditions of modern society, rights, especially human rights, are a particularly appropriate mechanism for protecting this basic, relatively universal core of human nature and dignity. The modern state, the modern economy, and associated "modern" values tend to create communities of relatively autonomous individuals, who lack the place and protections provided by traditional society. Furthermore, regardless of the relative degree of individual autonomy, people today face the particularly threatening modern state, and the especially fierce buffeting of the ever-changing modern economy. Rights held equally by all against the state, both limiting its legitimate range of actions and requiring positive protections against certain predictable economic, social, and political contingencies, are a seemingly natural and necessary response to typically modern threats to human dignity, to basic human values, traditional and modern alike.

Such an analysis seems to be confirmed by an examination of, for example, the Universal Declaration of Human Rights. In the Universal Declaration we can see a set of rights formulated to protect basic human – not merely cultural – values against the special threats posed by modern institutions.

The stress on equality and nondiscrimination, particularly in Articles 1, 2, and 7, reflects an essentially individualistic modern view of man, state, and society. Autonomous individuals are easily viewed as essentially equal. Basic equality, however, is likely to be an incoherent or incomprehensible notion where people are defined, as they usually are in traditional society, by ascriptive characteristics such as birth, age, or sex. Much the same is true of the guarantees in Articles 4 and 6 of an individual's fundamental status as a person and full member of the community by outlawing slavery and assuring to all equal recognition as a person before the law.

Articles 3 and 5 guarantee life, liberty, and security of the person, and prohibit torture and cruel, inhuman, or degrading treatment or punishment. These rights reflect basic, very widely shared values, expressed in the modern form of rights held against the state; they represent a minimal modern consensus on certain virtually universal guarantees against the state.

Articles 8 through 11 list fundamental legal guarantees such as access to legal remedies and impartial judges, protection against arbitrary arrest and detention, and the presumption of innocence. These rights can be seen as specifications of seemingly universal ideas of fairness, again formulated with a special eye to the threat to individual dignity posed by the modern state, especially in the absence of the constraining web of customary practices characteristic of traditional society.

Article 12, which recognizes a limited right to privacy, is peculiarly modern. Privacy is of great value to the relatively autonomous individual; it helps to protect his individuality. It is, however, fundamentally foreign to traditional, communitarian societies, as we can see even in English in the etymological connection between privacy and privation. Articles 13, 14, and 15, which recognize rights to freedom of movement, asylum, and nationality, are likewise basic in the relatively fluid, individualistic modern world, but probably would seem odd, at least as basic rights, in most traditional societies.

Article 16, which deals with the right to marry and found a family, is in part of universal applicability, but the requirement of "free and full consent of the intending spouses" reflects a peculiarly modern view of marriage as a union of individuals rather than a linking of lineages. The right to private property, articulated in Article 17, also is of some universal validity – virtually all societies permit individual ownership of at least some goods – although in the modern sense of a right to individual ownership of the means of production it is clearly appropriate only in economies with a large capitalist sector.

The rights to freedom of thought, conscience and religion, opinion and expression, assembly and association, and participation in government, laid out in Articles 18 through 21, are clearly based on modern individualistic conceptions of man and society. For example, traditional societies often do not distinguish clearly between the religious and the political, require conformity of thought and belief, enforce deference, restrict association, and deny popular political participation, all of which are incompatible with such rights. Within the modern framework, however, these rights represent minimum guarantees of basic personal dignity; they are essential guarantees of individual autonomy.

Finally, the economic and social rights recognized in Articles 22 through 27 guarantee, as individual rights, basic protections that in traditional society usually are provided by the family or the community as a whole: social security, work, rest and leisure, subsistence, education, and participation in the cultural life of the community. But not only are these rights directed against the modern state, they are held by individuals simply as human beings, and thus correspond to the individualization of the person in modern society. And Article 28, which guarantees a social and international order in which the previously listed rights can be realized, clearly reflects a peculiarly modern notion of international responsibility for the protection and provision of basic rights.

This review of the rights in the Universal Declaration is perhaps simultaneously superficial and overly long. However, if my argument is correct and the Universal Declaration does represent a minimal response to the convergence of basic crosscultural human values and the special threats to human dignity posed by modern institutions, then this set of rights has a very strong claim to relative universality. Therefore, the presumption must be that these rights apply universally, although that presumption can be overcome by particular cultural arguments. This, of course, is the position I have called weak cultural relativism.

ASSESSING CLAIMS OF CULTURAL RELATIVISM

Rights are formulated with certain basic violations, or threats to human dignity, in mind.[23] Therefore, the easiest way to overcome the presumption of universality for a widely recognized human right is to demonstrate either that the anticipated violation is not standard in that society, that the value is (justifiably) not considered basic in that society, or that it is protected by an alternative mechanism. In other words, one would have to show that the underlying cultural vision of human nature or society is both morally defensible and incompatible with the implementation of the "universal" human right in question. I would argue that such a test can be met only rarely today, and that permissible exceptions usually are relatively minor and generally consistent with the basic thrust of the Universal Declaration.

For example, it is hard to imagine cultural arguments against recognition of the basic personal rights of Articles 3 through 11. Rights to life, liberty, and security of the person; the guarantee of legal personality; and protections against slavery, arbitrary arrest, detention, or exile, and inhuman or degrading treatment are so clearly connected to basic requirements of human dignity, and are stated in sufficiently general terms, that any morally defensible contemporary form of social organization must recognize them (although perhaps not necessarily as inalienable rights). In fact, I am tempted to say that conceptions of human nature or society incompatible with such rights would be almost by definition indefensible; at the very least, such rights come very close to being fully universal.

Civil rights such as freedom of conscience, speech, and association would be a bit more relative; as they assume the existence and a positive evaluation of relatively autonomous individuals, they are of questionable applicability in strong traditional communities. In such communities, however, they would rarely be at issue. If traditional practices truly are based on and protect culturally accepted conceptions of human dignity, then members of such a community simply will not have the desire or need to claim such civil rights. But in the more typical contemporary case, in which the relatively autonomous individual faces the modern state, they would

23. See Donnelly, note 2 above, Chapter 2. Compare Henry Shue, *Basic Rights*, note 11 above, 29–34.

seem to be close to universal rights; it is hard to imagine a defensible modern conception of human dignity that did not include at least most of these rights. A similar argument can easily be made for the basic economic and social rights of the Declaration.

The Declaration does list some rights that are best viewed as "interpretations," subject to much greater cultural relativity. For example, the already mentioned right of free and full consent of intending spouses not only reflects a specific cultural interpretation of marriage, but an interpretation that is of relatively recent origin and by no means universal today even in the West. Notice, however, that the right, as Section 2 of Article 16, is subordinate to the basic right to marry and found a family. Furthermore, some traditional customs, such as brideprice, provide alternative protections for women, and a sort of indirect conditionality to marriage that addresses at least some of the underlying concerns of Article 16(2). Such factors make it much easier to accept cultural relativity with regard to this right.

When we consider the much more detailed International Human Rights Covenants, a number of listed rights approach specifications at the level of form. For example, Article 10(2)(b) of the International Covenant on Civil and Political Rights requires the segregation of juvenile defendants. In many cultures, the very notion of a juvenile criminal defendant does not exist. Similarly, penitentiary systems, mentioned in Article 10(3), are culturally specific institutions.

Finally, we should note that even the strongest cultural relativist faces a particularly serious problem where cultures clash or are undergoing substantial transformation – as is the case in much of the Third World. In evaluating customary practices that involve otherwise justifiable deviations from or interpretations of *prima facie* universal human rights, we often face the problem of "modern" individuals or groups who reject traditional practices. Should we give priority to the idea of community self-determination, and permit the enforcement of customary practices against modern "deviants," even if this involves violations of "universal" human rights? Or should individual self-determination prevail, thus sanctioning claims of universal human rights against traditional society?

In a recent discussion of women's rights in Africa, Rhoda Howard suggests an attractive, and widely applicable, compromise strategy. Howard argues, on a combination of practical and moral grounds, against an outright ban on practices such as child betrothal and widow inheritance. However, she also argues strongly for national legislation that permits women (and the families of female children) to "opt out" of traditional practices.[24] Where

24. Rhoda Howard, "Women's Rights in English-Speaking Sub-Saharan Africa," in *Human Rights and Development in Africa*, ed. Claude E. Welch, Jr. and Ronald I. Meltzer (Albany: State University of New York Press, 1984), 66–68. On the particularly volatile issue of "female circumcision," Howard also argues for educational programs aimed at reducing

practical, guaranteeing a right to "opt out" of traditional practices in favor of "universal" human rights or alternative human rights interpretations seems ideal, for it permits an individual in effect to choose his or her culture, or the terms on which he or she will participate in the traditional culture.

Sometimes, however, allowing such choice is impossible, because the conflicting practices are irreconcilable. For example, a right to private ownership of the means of production is incompatible with the maintenance of a village society in which families hold only rights of use to communally owned land; allowing individuals to opt out and fully own their land would destroy the traditional system. Similarly, although less dramatically, full freedom of religion, including a right to apostasy, is incompatible with certain well-established traditional Islamic views.

Sometimes such conflicts can be resolved, or at least minimized, by the physical separation of adherents of old and new values. Even a separation of old and new values may be difficult and traumatic, given, for example, the interpenetration of rural and urban sectors, but such a course frequently may be possible, particularly with practices that are not material to the maintenance or essential integrity of either culture.

Nevertheless, a choice must sometimes be made, at least by default, between competing practices or conceptions of human rights. Such cases, I would suggest, take us out of the realm in which useful general guidelines are possible.

Such cases, however, are the exception rather than the rule. And if my arguments above are correct, we can justifiably insist on some form of weak cultural relativism; that is, on a fundamental universality of basic human rights, tempered by a recognition of the possible need for limited cultural variations. Basic human rights are, to use an appropriately paradoxical phrase, relatively universal.

---

the popularity of such practices, particularly in their more extreme, and health threatening, forms. This seems to me generally defensible, and particularly appropriate in this instance, but it does raise the controversial issue of the modern or majority culture exerting pressure against minority cultural practices.

[6]

RETHINKING THE "UNIVERSALITY" OF HUMAN RIGHTS LAW

by Dianne Otto*

INTRODUCTION

The conclusion of the Cold War brought with it reinvigorated assertions of modern European[1] knowledges as universal.[2] In 1991, U.S. President George Bush heralded, with echoes of President Roosevelt's 1941 Four Freedoms vision,[3] the birth of a new world order based on an international consensus embracing the great U.S. ideal of freedom for all.[4] There has been a revival of Kantian liberalism in international legal circles[5] and an expansion of the criteria for the recognition of new states to include, at least in Europe, liberal democratic governmental

---

* Senior Lecturer in Law, The University of Melbourne, Australia; B.A., Adelaide University (1973); LL.B Melbourne University (1992); LL.M Melbourne University (1997); J.S.D. Candidate, Columbia University School of Law. I would like to thank Rosemary Hunter, Wayne Morgan, and Sarah Pritchard for their thoughtful support for this project. This Article is the third in a series of interrelated articles. The other two articles are forthcoming as follows: *Everything Is Dangerous: Some Poststructural Tools for Rethinking the Universal Knowledge Claims of Human Rights Law,* Austl. J. Hum. Rts. (1998); *Rethinking Universals: Opening Transformative Possibilities in International Human Rights Law*, Austl. Y.B. Int'l L. (1997).

1. In using the term "Europe," I do not mean the geographical entity. The term refers to the West in the broad sense of those interests or regimes of power which benefit from the reproduction of European knowledges and, in so doing, affirm European or Western dominance. This term includes postcolonial elites who have embraced European knowledges and institutions, albeit with indigenous variations, as well as the elites of the West.

2. Francis Fukuyama, The End of History and the Last Man 48-50 (1991) [hereinafter Fukuyama, End of History]; *see also* Francis Fukuyama, Trust: The Social Virtues and the Creation of Prosperity (1995) [hereinafter Fukuyama, Trust]. Fukuyama extends this argument to include European forms of sociality and economics.

3. Address of the President of the United States, (Jan. 6, 1941), *in* 87 Cong. Rec., pt. 1, at 46-47 (1941), *quoted in* Virginia A. Leary, *The Effect of Western Perspectives on International Human Rights, in* Human Rights in Africa: Cross-Cultural Perspectives 15, 19 (Abdullahi Ahmed An-Na'im & Francis M. Deng eds., 1990).

4. George Bush, *The Possibility of a New World Order: Unlocking the Promise of Freedom*, 57 Vital Speeches of the Day 450, 452 (1991).

5. Ferdinand Teson, *The Kantian Theory of International Law,* 92 Colum. L. Rev. 53, 53-55 (1992).

institutions and constitutional protections of human rights.[6] Human rights abuses have been used to justify, for the first time, armed intervention in the internal affairs of states,[7] as in the U.S.-led coalition to reinstate democracy in Haiti.

Despite the rhetoric of unmitigated "good" associated with these developments, the ideal of a world without domination is as far as it ever was from the main agenda of nation-states. In the post-Cold War environment the knowledges of modernity,[8] including the liberal discourse of universal human rights, have the potential to serve a new set of powerful political agendas which have little to do with fundamental human dignity. As international lawyer Martti Koskenniemi observes in his questioning of the Security Council's authorization of the Haiti invasion, we need to be cautious about the applicability of liberal ideals to non-European traditions. He says, "we simply do not know what 'democracy' would mean for a Russian, Somali, Chinese, Algerian, or other non-Western, non-liberal society. . . . Our Kantian ethics invites us to assume that everyone wishes to be treated like we would like. This is rubbish."[9] Human rights violations have also been used as an excuse to vilify certain non-European traditions, particularly Islam.[10]

The realignments of global power have brought to the fore a different configuration of priorities with respect to the universality of human rights. The assertion of global free market policies by the new

---

6. Roland Rich, *Recognition of States: The Collapse of Yugoslavia and the Soviet Union*, 4 Eur. J. Int'l L. 36, 42–43 (1993).

7. *See* U.N. SCOR, 47th Sess., 3046th mtg. at 2–3, U.N. Doc S/23500 (1992). The Security Council agreed that "[t]he non-military sources of instability in the economic, social, humanitarian and ecological fields have become threats to international peace and security" and thus are capable of triggering enforcement measures by the Council to maintain or restore peace and security. *Id.* at 3.

8. "Modernity" is the dominant philosophical production of present day Europe. Modernity has its origins in eighteenth-century Enlightenment thinking and is aptly described by feminist jurist Margaret Davies as "the attempt to find absolute grounds for knowledge, to discover abstract, transcendent principles which would be the foundation for all philosophical questioning." *See* Margaret Davies, Asking The Law Question 221 (1994).

9. Martti Koskenniemi, *The Police in the Temple, Order, Justice and the UN: A Dialectical View*, 6 Eur. J. Int'l L. 325, 343 (1995).

10. Ferdinand Teson, *International Human Rights and Cultural Relativity*, 25 Va. J. Int'l L. 869, 893 (1985); *see also* Anne F. Bayefsky, *Cultural Sovereignty, Relativism, and International Human Rights: New Excuses for Old Strategies*, 9 Ratio Juris 42, 51 (1996).

coalition of the former East and West has allowed, even endorsed, the worldwide promotion of reduced state obligations with respect to basic social and economic rights. The result is a narrowing of human rights discourse and a deepening of the North-South divide.[11] Further, as I will argue, the emergence of the deeply polarized debate over the "universality" of human rights, ostensibly about whether universality can be qualified by cultural differences, is directly related to the current struggle for global economic dominance.

One consequence of the polarization of the mainstream universality debate is that "transformative"[12] critiques of human rights orthodoxy, which seek to alter dominating global economies and practices of power, are silenced by the imperative to express absolute, uncompromising positions on both sides. Transformative critiques are those which have emerged from non-elite scholars and activists on the "margins"[13] of modernity, such as feminists, postcolonial and subaltern[14] groups, lesbians and gay men, critical race theorists, and indigenous peoples, as well as many other local expressions of dissent that are erased by the dominant debate. There is a fundamental tension in these transformative projects between a respect for the classic egalitarian ideals of modernity and an acute awareness of their limitations in their allegiance to European and masculinist regimes of power and their

---

11. Brenda Cossman, *Reform, Revolution, or Retrenchment? International Human Rights in the Post-Cold War Era*, 32 Harv. Int'l L.J. 339, 345, 348 (1991).

12. Drucilla Cornell, Transformations: Recollective Imagination and Sexual Difference 1 (1993). The author attributes a double meaning to "transformative":

> [The first meaning], change radical enough to so dramatically restructure any system—political, legal or social—that the "identity" of the system is itself altered. The second meaning, defined as broadly as possible, turns us to the question of what kind of individuals we would have to become in order to open ourselves to new worlds.

Id.

13. As the metaphor of the "margin" indicates, I understand such critiques are made possible by modern knowledges despite their resistance to modernity's hegemony.

14. Edward W. Said, *Foreword, in* Selected Subaltern Studies i–x (Ranajit Guha & Gayatri Chakravorty Spivak eds., 1988). The author traces the origins of the term "subaltern" to Antonio Gramsci, Prison Notebooks (1971). Subaltern Studies scholars, whom I will refer to later in this article, use the term broadly to include all those subordinated in South Asian society whether because of class, gender, caste, religion, age, office, or any other system of hierarchizing difference into relations of domination and subordination. *See infra* notes 76–77 and accompanying text.

silencing and erasing of "difference." I will argue that the egalitarianism of modernity may yet assist the struggle toward a world without domination if it is rethought from the margins of modernity using "poststructural"[15] tools of analysis. Modernity is not "the end of history," as Francis Fukuyama has claimed,[16] and European knowledges are not universal in the modern sense of articulating absolute, transcendent Standards.

I locate my discussion in the context of the current debates between nation-states about universality and cultural relativity, which I analyze critically in Part I. I argue that the debate reflects the contest over universal Truth[17] between the liberal capitalism of the "North" (Europe, the West) and the new economic systems emerging from the non-liberal context of some "Asian" (Southern)[18] states. Consequently, neither side of the debate represents a transformative commitment to global multiplicity and antidiscipline. Instead, the debate is serving a variety of elite macroeconomic interests, and will continue to do so while articulated ın modernity's dualistic terms.

In Part II, I examine the difference between modernity's egalitarian strategies for change and the transformative strategies from the margins of modernity. Despite opposing analyses of power and Truth, I suggest that both types of knowledge are critical to devising a new understanding of universality and I explore how they might cooperate in producing transformative human rights strategies.

---

15. The terms "poststructural" and "postmodern" are often used interchangeably and there is considerable overlap between the two projects in their challenges to the certainties of modern knowledges. I prefer the term "poststructural" because it indicates a concern with the local, embodied, situated construction of knowledge, whereas "postmodernism" is oriented towards a critique of the epistemological foundations of modernity. *See* Carol Smart, Law, Crime and Sexuality: Essays in Feminism 7-9 (1995).

16. Fukuyama, End of History, *supra* note 2, at 2.

17. *See* Michel Foucault, *Two Lectures, in* Power/Knowledge 78, 93 (Colin Gordon ed., 1980) [hereinafter Foucault, *Two Lectures*]. Foucault understands knowledge or Truth as the product of a complex of power relations whereby Truth is produced through power and power is exercised by the production of Truth. It follows that modern knowledges are the product of power and not of objective, universal reason operating independently of power. *See also* Michel Foucault, *Truth and Power, in* Power/Knowledge 109, 131-32 (Colin Gordon ed., 1980) [hereinafter Foucault, *Truth and Power*].

18. I use the terms "Northern," "Western," and "European" interchangeably, and similarly the terms "Asian" and "Southern," because of their utility in this particular discussion. However, in doing so I need to emphasize that all these terms are discursive constructions that group together diverse identities and histories in a monolithic idea that erases contingencies and disguises relations of power within the category.

Drawing on the work of critical race feminists in particular, I suggest that there is still a place for universality in a transformative paradigm, but that it is universality understood as dialogue, in the sense of struggle, rather than as a disciplinary civilizing mission of Europe. Transformative universality depends on an ethical dialogue located in the intersections of modernism and poststructuralism, local and global knowledges, and the individual and her or his community.

In Part III, I outline five strategies for transformative intervention in the current human rights debates that emerge from rethinking universality as dialogue and struggle: (1) rejecting the universalizing knowledge claims of modernity, (2) refusing the hierarchy of the generational development of human rights and insisting on their indivisibility, (3) replacing the myopic silencing of the language of dualistic alternatives with the consciousness of multiplicities and incommensurabilities, (4) decentering the nation-state in the global community, and (5) recognizing the limits of law as a means of transformative change.

I. THE "UNIVERSALITY" VERSUS "CULTURAL RELATIVITY" DEBATES

While human rights debates have assumed increased prominence in post-Cold War contests of political and legal power, they continue to raise the old issues of European and masculinist hegemony and state sovereignty—this time, however, in the changed context of the high stakes of global capitalism rather than global *detente*. During the Cold War, challenges to human rights law came from the Communist bloc, which emphasized the lack of substantive commitment to material equality, and from the Non-Aligned Movement (NAM),[19] which highlighted the privileging of European interests in human rights law. These challenges led to a *generational* expansion of the categories of human rights. The human rights enumerated in the Universal Declaration of Human Rights (UDHR)[20] were segmented into two Covenants containing the "first" generation of civil and political rights[21]

---

19. The Non-Aligned Movement (NAM), also known as the Group of 77 (G77), formed in the early 1970s as a lobby group of developing states united in their goal to challenge global European economic domination.

20. G.A. Res. 217, U.N. GAOR, 3d Sess., U.N. Doc. A/819, Dec. 10, 1948.

21. International Covenant on Civil and Political Rights, Mar. 23, 1976, 999 U.N.T.S. 171 [hereinafter ICCPR]; *see also* G.A. Res. 2200, U.N. GAOR, 21st Sess., Supp. No. 16, at 52, U.N. Doc. A/6316 (1966) (U.N. resolution adopting the ICCPR).

and the "second" generation of social, economic and cultural rights[22] reflecting the contrasting interests of the Cold War division between West and East. The rights advanced during the 1960s and 1970s by the postcolonial states of the NAM, in an effort to achieve more equitable social and economic development, became known as the "third" generation of solidarity rights.[23] Subsequently, in the final years of the Cold War, the emerging rights claims of indigenous peoples were characterized as constituting a "fourth" generation of human rights.[24] While the expansion of the human rights corpus is to be applauded, the hierarchization of categories of rights imputes an increasingly questionable universality to the later generational categories. The result is to affirm the unquestionable universality, and thereby the dominance, of the rights in the first generation and legitimate lower standards of accountability and enforcement with respect to succeeding generations.

In this Part, I argue that, unlike the Cold War challenges, the post-Cold War questioning of the universality of human rights is unlikely to be satisfied by a further expansion of the generational hierarchy. First, I outline the current, so-called universality versus cultural relativity debates, often characterized as a struggle between "Western" and "Asian" values. In order to do this, I examine the particular expression of the conflict in the preparations and outcomes of two intergovernmental world conferences: the 1993 Vienna World Conference on Human Rights (WCHR) and the 1995 Beijing Fourth World Conference on Women (FWCW). I will then show that the two sides of the debate are in agreement over certain fundamental points, despite the appearance of polarization and intense disagreement. Second, I suggest that the debate is fueled by competing versions of capitalism rather than by a desire to address issues of cultural diversity in human rights discourse. I contend that deployment of the

---

22. International Covenant on Economic, Social and Cultural Rights, Jan. 3, 1976, 993 U.N.T.S. 3 [hereinafter ICESCR]; *see also* G.A. Res. 2200, U.N. GAOR, 21st Sess., Supp. No. 16, at 49, U.N. Doc. A/6316 (1966) (U.N. resolution adopting the ICESCR).

23. Declaration on the Right to Development, G.A. Res. 41/28, U.N. GAOR 41st Sess., 97th mtg., U.N. Doc. A/RES/41/128 (1987) was adopted by 146 votes to one, with eight abstainers. The United States of America cast the only vote against adoption. Abstainers were Denmark, Finland, Germany, Iceland, Israel, Japan, Sweden, and the United Kingdom.

24. The fourth generational terminology was first used in an affirmative sense by George Manuel and Michael Poslins. *See* George Manuel & Michael Poslins, The Fourth World: An Indian Reality 7, 11-12 (1974).

sameness/difference dualities of modernity by both sides of the debate furthers the interests of the elites of both camps rather than those of the non-elite majority. Third, I maintain that this argument will remain polarized and constitutive of a North/South antithesis, reflecting the post-Cold War realignments of power, while it remains shaped by dualized technologies of difference.

A. Cultural Relativism and Universality: The Bangkok Declaration and its Aftermath

That a universal law of human rights has the potential to erase cultural diversity is hardly disputable. In 1947, the American Anthropological Society cautioned the U.N. Commission on Human Rights about this danger during the drafting of the UDHR. The Society pointed to the West's history of "ascribing cultural inferiority" to non-European peoples, which has led to the "demoralization of human personality and the disintegration of human rights."[25] They outlined the challenge confronting the drafters as follows:

> The problem is thus to formulate a statement of human rights that will do more than just phrase respect for the individual as an individual. It must also take into full account the individual as a member of the social group of which he [or she] is a part. . . . It must embrace and recognize the validity of many different ways of life.[26]

Despite the best intentions of the drafters to produce an "innocent"[27] UDHR that was without political and cultural allegiances, poststructural critiques of modern knowledges indicate why this was impossible. The achievement of universality in a transcendent sense relies on the modern assumption that objective, True knowledge is possible, and that the historical, situated contingencies of the

25. American Anthropological Association, *Statement on Human Rights*, 49 Am. Anthropologist 539 (1947), *reprinted in* Henry J. Steiner & Philip Alston, International Human Rights in Context: Law, Politics, Morals 198 (1996).

26. *Id.* at 198, 200.

27. *See* Jane Flax, *The End of Innocence, in* Feminists Theorize the Political 445, 447 (Judith Butler & Joan W. Scott eds., 1992). The author describes the knowledge of Western philosophy as "innocent" in its assumption that it is possible to discover "some sort of truth which can tell us how to act in the world in ways that benefit or are for the (at least ultimate) good of all." *Id.*

production and interpretation of knowledge can be transcended by modern scientific or dialectical methods.[28] In contrast, a poststructural perspective understands all knowledge/Truth as the contingent product of particular, situated ways of comprehending the world and the outcome of a complex of power relations.[29]

In contemporary debates, the "universalists," who are primarily Northern states, predict that even the slightest "dilution" of universalism will give the green light to tyrannical governments, torturers, and mutilators of women.[30] The universalist position completely denies that the existing universal standards may themselves be culturally specific and allied to dominant regimes of power. As political philosopher Daniel Bell observes, "[e]ven some of the most thoughtful proponents of human rights in the West do not admit the possibility that every society need not settle on exactly the same conception of vital human interests."[31] At the same time, "cultural relativist" counterarguments from Southern states entrench an intense polarization of views. The relativist position advances alternative claims to universal Truth that have their foundations in non-European cultural traditions and rejects the current human rights paradigm as oppressive for developing states with different cultures.

A useful starting point for a critical analysis of the contemporary debate is the 1993 Bangkok Declaration, which was devised by proponents of the cultural relativist position at the Regional Meeting for Asian-Pacific states in preparation for the WCHR.[32] Surprisingly, given the polarized rhetoric of the debate, the Bangkok Declaration welcomes the "increased attention" to human rights,[33] reaffirms commitment to the UDHR,[34] encourages the ratification of the International Covenant on Civil and Political Rights (ICCPR) and the

---

28. Margaret Davies, *supra* note 8, at 96–97.

29. Foucault, *Truth and Power*, *supra* note 17, at 109, 131–32.

30. Teson, *supra* note 10, at 870–71.

31. Daniel A. Bell, *The East Asian Challenge to Human Rights: Reflections on an East West Dialogue,* 18 Hum. Rts. Q. 641, 667 (1996).

32. The Bangkok Declaration, Mar. 29–Apr. 3, 1993, *reprinted in* Human Rights and Chinese Values 205–09 (Michael C. Davis ed., 1995).

33. *Id.* at pmbl., ¶ 4.

34. *Id.* at pmbl., ¶ 3, art. 1. It should be noted that this position may be changing. Dr. Mahathir, the Prime Minister of Malaysia, has recently suggested that a review of the UDHR is necessary because it was "formulated by the super-powers which did not understand the needs of poor countries." Mark Baker, *Row as Malaysia Seeks to Rewrite the Book on Human* Rights, The Age (Melbourne), July 30, 1997, at 1.

International Covenant on Economic, Social and Cultural Rights (ICESCR),[35] and stresses the "universality, objectivity and non-selectivity of all human rights."[36] Even accounting for the geopolitical posturing that inspired the Bangkok Declaration, this language does not in fact depart from the underlying normative framework and principles of the U.N. Charter and the UDHR, although the strongly-critical reactions to it from Northern states and many nongovernmental organizations (NGOs)[37] suggest otherwise. The Bangkok Declaration does not take issue with the foundational philosophical assumptions of human rights orthodoxy about human "dignity" or "reason." Nor does it question the generational categorizations or the overarching commitment to equality in human rights law.

However, the Bangkok Declaration does endorse various positions and priorities that are consistent with those which the NAM has been espousing for many years.[38] In confirming the interdependence and indivisibility of human rights, it stresses the "inherent interrelationship between development, democracy, universal enjoyment of all human rights, and social justice"[39] and urges giving "equal emphasis to all categories of human rights."[40] In listing types of human rights violations, the Bangkok Declaration includes "foreign aggression and occupation, and the establishment of illegal settlements in occupied territories."[41] Such inclusions reflect the ongoing concern about imperialism and neocolonialism in the South. The Bangkok Declaration also emphasizes that adherence to human rights standards ought to be encouraged by consensus and "not through confrontation and the imposition of incompatible values."[42] All of these positions are cogently supported by reference to U.N. Charter principles of self-

35. The Bangkok Declaration, *supra* note 32, at pmbl., ¶ 7.

36. *Id.* at pmbl., ¶ 9, art. 7.

37. Asian Cultural Forum on Development, *Our Voice: Bangkok NGO Declaration on Human Rights*, Reports of the Asia Pacific NGO Conference on Human Rights and NGOs' Statements to the Asia Regional Meeting 106 (1993).

38. Virginia A. Leary, *The Asian Region and the International Human Rights Movement, in* Asian Persp. on Hum. Rts. 13, 16–18 (Claude E. Welch & Virginia A. Leary eds., 1990).

39. The Bangkok Declaration, *supra* note 32, at pmbl., ¶ 11.

40. *Id.* at art. 10.

41. *Id.* at art. 14.

42. *Id.* at pmbl., ¶ 10, arts. 4, 5. Article 4 expressly rejects making development assistance conditional on human rights and Article 5 abhors any use of human rights as an instrument of political pressure.

determination, sovereignty, territorial integrity, and international cooperation.

It is the Bangkok Declaration's emphasis on state sovereignty and nonintervention that reads as rejecting or qualifying the universality of human rights standards, particularly in its statement about the significance of cultural difference:

> [W]hile human rights are universal in nature, they must be considered in the context of a dynamic and evolving process of international norm-setting, bearing in mind the significance of national and regional particularities and various historical, cultural and religious backgrounds.[43]

Yet, as Bilahari Kausikan from Singapore's Ministry of Foreign Affairs argues in his unofficial capacity, surely this statement only describes what is obvious—that all human rights are in a constant process of evolution which relies on debate and contending claims.[44] Speaking at the American Society of International Law Annual Meeting two years after the WCHR, he stated that the "Western overreaction to this simple description of reality—that moreover explicitly recognized the ideal of universality . . . still poisons the atmosphere and fuels misunderstanding."[45]

The "poisonous" atmosphere reached its zenith at the WCHR. The United States and others accused the Southern states, who argued for some consideration of cultural specificities,[46] of promoting a "screen behind which authoritarian governments could perpetrate human rights abuses."[47] The defensive response from Indonesia's Foreign Minister Ali Alatas, as spokesperson for the NAM at the WCHR, was that Asian states "have not come to Vienna to engage in confrontation, nor to advocate an alternative conception of human rights, based on some

---

43. *Id.* at art. 8.

44. Bilahari Kausikan, *An Asian Approach to Human Rights*, 89 Am. Soc'y Int'l L. Proc. 146, 148 (1995).

45. *Id.*

46. These states included China, Columbia, Cuba, Indonesia, Iran, Iraq, Libya, Malaysia, Mexico, Myanmar, Pakistan, Singapore, Syria, Vietnam, and Yemen.

47. Christina M. Cerna, *Universality of Human Rights and Cultural Diversity: Implementation of Human Rights in Different Socio-Cultural Contexts,* 16 Hum. Rts. Q. 740, 741 (1994) [hereinafter Cerna, *Universality*].

nebulous notion of 'cultural relativism' as spuriously alleged by some quarters."[48]

The official outcome of this confrontation, adopted by consensus by the 172 states in attendance, was the reaffirmation of the universality of human rights, repeated throughout the Vienna Declaration and Programme of Action[49] almost to the point of redundancy, as human rights theorist Christina Cerna notes.[50] However, the commitment to universality was also qualified in paragraph 5 in language reminiscent of the Bangkok Declaration:

> All human rights are universal, indivisible and interdependent and interrelated. The international community must treat human rights globally in a fair and equal manner, on the same footing, and with the same emphasis. While the significance of national and regional particularities and various historical, cultural and religious backgrounds must be borne in mind, it is the duty of States, regardless of their political, economic and cultural systems, to promote and protect all human rights and fundamental freedoms.[51]

That the overall outcome can be read as supporting either the universalist or relativist position reflects the paralysis of the debate and leaves the issue firmly on the international human rights agenda for another day.

An opportunity to reopen the debate came two years later, in the shape of the FWCW. The preparatory processes saw a solid confirmation of the polarized positions that had been marked out in Vienna between the universalists and relativists. The antipathy between the two sides was compounded by the capriciousness of some states from the cultural relativity camp who inserted "universality" into the draft conference documents in such a way that it operated as a modifier and thereby served the relativist rather than the universalist agenda. For example, phrases like "universally recognized" and

48. Christina M. Cerna, *East Asian Approaches to Human Rights*, 89 Am. Soc'y Int'l L. Proc. 152, 155 (1995) [hereinafter Cerna, *East Asian*].

49. *Report of the World Conference on Human Rights, Vienna Declaration and Programme of Action*, Vienna, June 1993, at ¶¶ 1, 5, 18, 32, 37, U.N. Doc. A/CONF.157/24 (1993) [hereinafter WCHR Report].

50. Cerna, *Universality*, *supra* note 47, 742.

51. *WCHR Report*, *supra* note 49, at ¶ 5.

"universally accepted" human rights limited the scope of human rights to those that had been formally accepted by *all* states—arguably very few. This action undermined the credibility of the positions taken by more conciliatory Southern spokespeople like Alatas and also strengthened the hand of Northern conservatives who were eager to vilify the non-Western cultural relativists.

The result was the bracketing of universality every time it appeared in the draft conference documents, indicating that the use of the word was contentious.[52] Also, a footnote in the section on women's health which addressed the important issues of sexuality and reproduction sought to ensure that all the health actions outlined were not universally applicable but subject to domestic regulation consistent with "the various religious and ethical values and cultural backgrounds of [a state's] people."[53] The debate seethed for the entire FWCW and the participants did not finish negotiations until its closing hours.[54] In the end, the footnote was deleted, the egregious use of "universality" was expunged, and the Vienna language that affirmed universality while repeating that "cultural and religious backgrounds must be borne in mind"[55] was retained. Deepening the ambiguity of this clause, the same paragraph goes on to say that "full respect for various religious and ethical values . . . should contribute to the full enjoyment by women of their human rights . . . ."[56]

The debate about universality highlights the centrality of concepts of gender, particularly the control of women's reproductive and sexual identities, to the universal knowledges of global regimes of power. It also raises many important questions about the modern egalitarian ideals reflected in human rights discourse and their potential to promote a world without domination. However, it is not these issues that are at the "real" center of the debate, as I will argue in the following Part.

---

52. The use of square brackets indicates that states have not agreed on the wording in the brackets.

53. *Draft Platform for Action*, Fourth World Conference on Women, at 43, U.N. Doc. A/CONF.177/L.1 (1995).

54. Dianne Otto, *Holding Up Half the Sky, but for Whose Benefit? A Critical Analysis of the Fourth World Conference on Women*, 6 Austl. Feminist L.J. 7, 19 (1996).

55. *Report of the Fourth World Conference on Women*, Fourth World Conference on Women, ¶ 9, U.N. Doc. A/CONF.177/20 (1995).

56. *Id.*

B. Regimes of Power Served by the Debate

The characterization of the debate between Northern and Southern states as a dispute about universality and cultural relativity obfuscates many issues of fundamental importance. As I have argued, the dualized characterization of the debate conceals many commonalities between the two sides, particularly in their acceptance that at least a core of human rights is universal. As human rights advocate Michael Davis observes, even the sovereign-centric Peoples Republic of China conceded more about universal human rights in the Bangkok Declaration and its statements in Vienna than it attacked,[57] and postcolonial theorist Admantia Pollis notes that the West made "major concessions" about the primacy of state sovereignty.[58]

Also hidden is the ongoing unanimity within and between both camps that no *new* human rights will be recognized, an accord which has held strong throughout the WCHR and FWCW. This agreement protects the interests of the elites of *all* nation-states from, for example, the erosion of sovereign power by the recognition of universal indigenous rights, and the reduction of male, heterosexual privilege by the inclusion of women's, children's and sexuality rights in the category of fundamental human rights. In short, arguments of cultural difference and of universality, while important in themselves, are being used to serve a variety of macroeconomic, social, and political interests.[59]

Feminist Arati Rao usefully develops the view that the debate is serving other agendas within the context of women's rights. She observes that "[n]o social group has suffered greater violation of its human rights in the name of culture than women."[60] She goes on to argue that cultural arguments disguise the "special agenda that [all] states have developed to control . . . women's reproductive capacities, to torture women, and to curtail women's freedom through specific social policies."[61] In this project, states share a masculinist interest in

57. *See* Michael C. Davis, *Chinese Perspectives on the Bangkok Declaration and the Development of Human Rights in Asia,* Am. Soc'y Int'l L. Proc. 157, 164 (1995).

58. Admantia Pollis, *Cultural Relativism Revisited: Through A State Prism*, 18 Hum. Rts. Q. 316, 331-32 (1996).

59. *Id.*

60. Arati Rao, *The Politics of Gender and Culture in International Human Rights Discourse, in* Women's Rights, Human Rights 167, 169 (Julie Peters & Andrea Wolper eds., 1995).

61. *Id.*

defending the *status quo* of gender, albeit with manifold local variations. Thus, both sides of the debate–between the universalists and the cultural relativists–reproduce a masculinist narrative of legitimation. The underlying agenda in the current historical conjuncture is to shore up the economic interests of dominant states in the global economy. To this end, the debate about women's rights creates a space for shifts in the production of genders, ethnicities, and sexualities that will enhance the globalization of capital by encouraging more extensive, flexible, and exploitable workforce participation by women.[62] It is not a debate that is seriously motivated to challenge masculinist regimes of power.

In the view of Kausikan, the "disproportionate" response from Northern states to the cultural relativist arguments of many Southern states is the outcome of fears and insecurities stirred by the economic success of Asian states in the post-Cold War environment.[63] He remarks that "the problems are particularly acute for those Western societies that define themselves in relation to a universal mission."[64] Thus, the anxiety of the universalist North, in response to post-Cold War contestations and rearrangements of global power, manifests itself in human rights arguments about cultural relativity and universality.

At the same time, the Southern states, who most vehemently promote cultural relativity, seem largely motivated by a desire to limit international scrutiny of their authoritarian regimes. Their assertion that autocratic governance is consistent with Asian values disguises the reality that it is essential to Asian-style capitalism. The emphasis of the relativists on "bearing in mind the significance of national and regional particularities, and various historical, cultural and religious backgrounds"[65] is not a commitment to challenging dualized technologies of sameness and difference, and the patterns of domination that such binaries normalize. The relativist argument simply promotes a reversal of the dualisms. As philosopher Pheng Cheah notes, the difference championed by the Bangkok Declaration is not the same as the diversity of Asian peoples.[66] Thus, the cultural relativist challenge to universality bears no resemblance to a transformative commitment

---

62. *See* Cynthia Enloe, *Silicon Tricks and the Two Dollar Woman*, 1/12 New Internationalist 12 (1992).

63. *See* Kausikan, *supra* note 44, at 151.

64. *Id.*

65. *See* Bangkok Declaration, *supra* note 32, at art. 8.

66. *See* Pheng Cheah, *Posit(ion)ing Human Rights in the Current Global Conjuncture*, 9 Pub. Culture 233, 236 (1997).

to multiplicity and antidiscipline, or to local and transnational solidarities.

In this way, the human rights debate is inextricably linked to a global struggle over Truth that has been precipitated by post-Cold War shifts in power. In the transition from one constellation of dominating global power to another, the human rights discourse shaped by the Cold War is an important site of struggle. The opposition constructed between universality and cultural relativity is politically coded to advance the interests of competing claims to "genuine" universal knowledge. The debate diverts attention from pressing issues, like those of challenging masculinist domination, of realizing the interdependence and indivisibility of the Cold War-inspired generations of human rights, of implementing the right to development as something more than opening state borders to transnational capital, and of achieving global economic and social justice. The debate functions as a means of obscuring the issues of power and depoliticizing the struggle for economic dominance that is taking place. Understood in this way, the universalists are defending Europe's dominance and the relativists are seeking to reverse the duality that presently constitutes the South as Europe's Other.

C. The "Impossible Choice" of Modernity's Dualisms

Those who would wish to see more fundamental change than a reversal of the North/South dualism in the struggle over what constitutes universal knowledge face the conundrum of how to intervene in a modern regime of power without accepting its terms and thereby merely reconstituting its dualities in another guise which, ultimately, leaves dominating relations of power intact. The options from *within* modernity for seeking liberation from the dualisms of domination (Standard) and subordination (Other), or at least for curbing the intensity of their effects, are analogous to those that feminists face in debates about gender equality and whether standards should be based on sameness or difference with respect to the male Standard. The "impossible choice" that feminist Joan Scott identifies in competing strategies to achieve gender equality is also produced by the dualized universality debate: Either what is *different* to the masculinist Standard is reimagined as *the same* thereby losing its autonomy, or the difference is confirmed and different (nonuniversal) treatment and outcomes are legitimated.[67] Either way, the masculinist Standard is validated and difference remains secondary. This insight does not discredit the goals and motivations of modern strategists who seek justice in the equality paradigm of modernity. Rather, it reveals the limits of modern egalitarianism and the need for a reimagining of difference.

Extrapolating to the universality debates, there are several "sameness" arguments that are made, including the following three: that universality is restricted to a core of gross violations (sameness) and everything else (difference) remains within the domestic jurisdiction of states;[68] that human rights really do exist in non-European traditions but require a process of reinterpretation or reunderstanding that will bring them into commensurability (sameness) with the Standard;[69] and that the European bias of human rights discourse can be corrected by empirical research which will confirm the rationality, dignity, and "civilization" (sameness) of non-European traditions and, as a result, their human rights credentials.[70] But because all of these strategies remain uncritical of modernity and assume that universal, *innocent* knowledge is possible, they do not fundamentally challenge Europe's dominance.

There are also several "difference" arguments that are made: (1) difference surpasses sameness such that universal human rights are not possible without subsuming traditions outside Europe, thereby leaving human rights issues solely to the domestic jurisdiction of states;[71] (2) difference is the result of colonialism and exploitation and requires special measures, such as prioritizing the right to development over other human rights, until such time as the disadvantage has been

---

67. Joan W. Scott, *Deconstructing Equality-Versus-Difference: or, the Uses of Poststructuralist Theory for Feminism*, 14 Feminist Stud. 33, 43 (1988).

68. This is one way to read the approach of the *Bangkok Declaration*. *See* Kausikan, *supra* note 44.

69. Abdullahi Ahmed An-Na'im, *Human Rights in the Muslim World: Socio-Political Conditions and Scriptural Imperatives*, 3 Harv. Hum. Rts. J. 13, 22 (1990); Du Gangjian & Song Gang, *Relating Human Rights to Chinese Culture: The Four Paths of the Confucian Analects and the Four Principles of a New Theory of Benevolence*, *in* Davis, *supra* note 57, at 35.

70. Jack Donnelly, *Post-Cold War Reflections on the Study of Human Rights*, 8 Ethics & Int'l Aff. 97, 112, 116 (1994).

71. This view is sometimes heavily implied by the leaders of some Asian states like Singapore, Malaysia, Indonesia, and the Peoples Republic of China.

ameliorated;[72] and (3) difference needs to be *tolerated* as part of a *pluralist* world order, which allows for the inclusion of difference on terms that do not threaten the dominant paradigm,[73] as illustrated by the generational development of human rights. These arguments also leave the dominant Standard of Europe unchallenged. The difference acknowledged, even as a positive attribute, remains defined in relation to the Standard and thereby subordinated. Even the strategy of rejecting universality altogether amounts more to a withdrawal than a challenge. This strategy suggests that it is possible to take a position of strength *outside* Europe which, given Europe's hegemony, amounts to choosing (to the extent that choice is involved) incommensurability with Europe, and thus isolation and erasure.[74]

In the assertion of their respective claims to universal Truth, both sides of the universality debate are employing dualized and hierarchized concepts of difference. This means that the *form* of the debate is itself problematic because it structures the discussion in terms of polar claims which suit the competition between dominating global regimes of power by silencing transformative alternatives. As a result, the important issues of global diversity are clouded and silenced, and the dichotomy between universality and cultural relativity is confirmed as a True antithesis. As Rao says, "geopolitical borders are erased and a multitude of cultures are collapsed into two falsely unified packages, one bearing the stamp of human rights and the other lacking it."[75] Each side depends on the other for the generation of its own identity and meaning, and thus, paradoxically, both are reliant on the shared assumptions of modernity.

The dualized form of debate illustrates the extent of the hegemonic hold of Europe in the world today wherein difference is recognizable only if it is coextensive with the European imagination. As

72. *Bangkok Declaration*, *supra* note 32, arts. 18, 19.

73. *See* Dianne Otto et al., *Rejecting (In)tolerance: Critical Perspectives on the United Nations Year for Tolerance*, 20 Melbourne U. L. Rev. 190 (1995); *see also* Jonathan Chaplin, *How Much Cultural and Religious Pluralism Can Liberalism Tolerate?*, *in* Liberalism, Multiculturalism and Toleration 48 (John Horton ed., 1993).

74. Dipesh Chakrabarty, *Marx After Marxism*, 52 Meanjin 421, 426 (1993). Chakrabarty notes that the presence of subaltern knowledges is marked by moments of disruption and discontinuity in the knowledges of modernity, which he likens to a Derridean "trace" of something that cannot be completely erased by modernity's assertions of universality.

75. Rao, *supra* note 60, at 168.

Indian Subaltern Studies[76] scholar Ranajit Guha argues, all other difference is relegated to a shadow world of superstition, randomness, or criminality because it is incommensurable with the European frame.[77] Therefore, as long as the debate remains uncritical of modernity, the dualistic Standard of Europe will prevail. We need to move on from the choice of arguing sameness or difference to a deeper understanding of modern mechanisms of power in order to extricate ourselves from the grip of dominant knowledges and formulate transformative strategies.

II. Difference and Resistance at the Margins

Would the General Assembly adopt the UDHR in 1998? There are strong indications that it would, not least of which is the unanimity with which states have guarded the present human rights heartland against expansion outside the generational developments of the Cold War era. If any change in content were to occur, the most likely would be the inclusion of a reference to third generation rights, particularly the right to development. Also, the identity of those abstaining from the vote would almost certainly see some change.[78] But a 1998 adoption would not end the disputes about the universality of the UDHR. It would merely reconfirm the dominance of European, masculinist

---

76. The Subaltern Studies Collective is a group of Indian historiographers who are informed by critical Marxist and poststructural perspectives. The initial focus of their work in the early 1980s was to understand how, in the formation of the independent nation-state of India, the nationalists came to represent an Indian elite that was closely allied to the British colonialists, rather than the mass of the Indian people. Their work quickly became multidimensional, producing critiques of modernity and nationalism, and addressing complex epistemological questions. *See* Selected Subaltern Studies (Ranajit Guha & Gayatri Chakravorty Spivak eds., 1988). I do not want to suggest that there is a single, unified Subaltern Studies perspective. My representation of Subaltern Studies analyses is of course shaped by my own experience and interpretations, and developed with the assistance of one member of the Collective, Dipesh Chakrabarty.

77. Ranajit Guha, *The Prose of Counter-Insurgency, in* Selected Subaltern Studies, *supra* note 76, at 45.

78. There were 48 states who voted to adopt the UDHR in 1948. Eight states abstained from voting including, Saudi Arabia, South Africa, the Soviet Union, and five other members of the Eastern European bloc. Today, it is probable that the former communist states would support its adoption and, depending on the status of third generation rights, the United States and some East Asian states might also abstain. Saudi Arabia would undoubtedly continue to hold its dissenting views and might be joined by some other Islamic states.

Standards and the interests of the modern nation-state in the post-Cold War era. The contradiction of "claiming universal and concrete applicability in a world fraught with social, economic, and political inequality," pointed out by the USSR in 1948, [79] would remain. Also, the questions raised by the American Anthropological Society about recognizing the validity of many different ways of life would remain unaddressed. These issues would continue to produce various resistant voices from the margins of modernity calling for transformative change.

In this Part, I begin with a discussion of the difference between what I have been calling the *egalitarian* strategies of modernity and the *transformative* strategies advanced by those on modernity's margins. I suggest that the two frameworks are not necessarily mutually exclusive, despite their differing understandings of power and Truth, and that strategies for change in the post-Cold War environment can draw something useful from both bodies of knowledge. Secondly, I canvas some new approaches to making power transparent in the discourse of human rights and outline some related embryonic thinking about how we might understand difference in nondominating, antidisciplinary ways. Finally, I turn to the question of the implications of marginal perspectives for the idea of universality, and suggest some ways in which universality might be rethought in a transformative paradigm.

A. Working in the Tensions between Modernity and its Margins

There are two discrete locations at which dualized notions of difference construct exclusionary boundaries between the Standards of modernity and its Others. Understanding this difference in location enables a distinction to be drawn between egalitarian human rights strategies from within modernity which will tend to reinforce the *status quo* and transformative strategies from the margins which may disrupt it. But first, I must explain an important aspect of poststructural critiques of modernity which relates to the constitutive power of language.

In modernity, language is understood as a way of giving nomenclature to preexisting meaning. The work of structuralist linguist

79. Marnia Lazreg, *Human Rights, State and Ideology: An Historical Perspective*, *in* Human Rights: Cultural and Ideological Perspectives 32, 37 (Admantia Pollis & Peter Schwab eds., 1979).

Ferdinand de Saussure fundamentally challenged this view in the 1950s and revealed how language creates meaning through patterns of dualistic relationships between "signs."[80] The meaning of a sign emerges from the contrasting meaning of other signs which it is not. For example, the meaning of the universal North is dependent on the contrasting concept of the different (nonuniversal) South.

Poststructural linguist Jacques Derrida takes this analysis a step further by showing how the binaries which create meaning/knowledge are invested with the power hierarchy of domination (the Standard) and subordination (its Other).[81] Derrida also emphasizes that both sides of the dualisms created by language exist in a *codependent* relationship.[82] Therefore, the concept of dominant Man depends on its contrast with the subjugated idea of Woman, and vice versa; and the notion of the "civilized" Occident relies on the "undeveloped" status of the Orient, and vice versa. Derrida highlights the violence that is involved in the exclusionary force used to marginalize, debase, or disqualify the subordinated term.[83] Yet, while the secondary sign is subordinated and to some extent excluded by the positive value attributed to the primary term, it is not erased or completely silenced because it plays a necessary role as an antithesis in the construction of meaning in the dominant discourse.

The dualisms that constitute meaning, with which Derrida is concerned and to which Scott also refers, provide one location for modernity's construction of exclusionary boundaries. This boundary lies between the dominant sign and its subordinated Other. The duality of universality and cultural relativity creates one such boundary. It is at this boundary that the egalitarian equality strategies of modernity arise. Such strategies seek to expand what is included in the universal by broadening what is considered the same as the Standards of Europe.

---

80. *See* Ferdinand de Saussure, Cours de Linguistique Générale (Tullio de Mauro ed., 2d ed. 1985). Saussure's concept of the "sign" ("le signe") consists of both the "concept" which he calls the "signified" ("le signifié") and the "sound-image" which he calls the "signifier"("le signifiant"). *Id.* at 99. The relationship between any particular sign and signifier is not determined by a consistent or prior system but is the result of convention. *See* Davies, *supra* note 8, at 231–32.

81. Jacques Derrida, Positions 41 (Alan Bass trans. 1981) [hereinafter Derrida, Positions].

82. *Id.* at 26.

83. Jacques Derrida, *Force Of Law: The "Mystical" Foundation of Authority*, 11 Cardozo L. Rev. 920, 1042–43 (1990) [hereinafter Derrida, *Force of Law*].

As I have argued in the previous Part, in assuming that universal knowledge is possible, such strategies leave the dominant Standard of Europe unchallenged. But the Derridean insight, that the dualities are interdependent, adds a further dimension to our understanding of this problem. The codependence of the dualism, for example, that of universality and difference (nonuniversality), is actually reproduced by strategies that merely shift the boundaries of the universal. This is so despite the amelioration, material or symbolic, of the disadvantage of at least some in the subjugated category who become included in the dominant idea (the universal) as a result of the movement of the boundary. While the duality remains intact, the strategy ultimately reinforces the dominance of European masculinist norms, even though it might alter their content. Recognizing the interdependence of egalitarian strategies and the hierarchies of modernity is one way to understand the limits of such change and illustrate the need for reimagining difference in nondualistic paradigms.

I became aware of the second boundary through the work of the Subaltern Studies Collective.[84] This boundary lies between the Inside of the *aggregate* of Europe's dualistic Standard and its Other, and the Outside of knowledges that are incommensurable with Europe. In other words, the Inside is constituted by the totality of knowledges which rely on Europe's terms and the Outside consists of knowledges which are not interpretable in the terms of Europe. The erasure of incommensurable knowledges creates an "outside" to modernity in a sense different from the outsider status of the Other created by modernity's dualisms.

In the current universality debates, this second boundary lies between the Inside of the monolithic notions of universality and cultural difference, and the Outside of the manifold incommensurable cultural identities of local people and non-elite groups that are erased by the dualisms of the dominant framework. Erasure does not mean that such knowledges do not exist, but rather that they cannot be articulated on their own terms within modernity. These spaces, outside modernity, are reduced to silence or to the disempowered categories of superstition and randomness because of their incommensurability. They can more accurately be considered erased than the subjugated figure of Europe's Other because they have no relationships of duality with a dominant sign that can bring them into being. This second boundary, between modernity and incommensurability, marks the margins of modernity,

84. *See generally* Guha & Spivak, *supra* note 76.

and these margins, in turn, produce transformative human rights strategies that challenge the form of the dominant paradigm as well as its content.

The strategies for change produced at the two boundaries rely on different analyses of power. The resistant knowledges associated with the first boundary, between Europe's Standard and its Other, produce egalitarian strategies based on modern conceptions of power as centralized, monolithic, and dualistic.[85] These egalitarian strategies emphasize the way macropolitical global categories shape and subjugate the sign of the Other. Also, the struggle for change focuses on the goal of either replacing the centralized Standard with another or increasing its inclusionary scope. For example, strategies aimed at achieving the equal participation of women or ensuring equitable geographical representation in decisionmaking forums remain uncritical of the form of the decisionmaking structures in which they aim to participate. In so doing, such strategies legitimate the very structures that reproduce dominating forms of power.

Yet, it is important not to overstate my critique of egalitarian politics. Modern egalitarianism promotes many worthwhile projects and provides an important defense against fundamentalist agendas. As Subaltern Studies scholar Dipesh Chakrabarty observes, despite his searing rejection of the modern liberatory project:

> [T]o help erect the subaltern as the subject of modern democracies . . . to expand the history of the modern in such a way as to make it more representative of society as a whole . . . is a laudable objective in its own terms, and has undoubted global relevance.[86]

The point is that the responses of democratic politics and liberal pluralism fall a long way short of confronting the realities of Europe's hegemony and the world's diversities.

Unlike modern analyses of power, poststructural analyses confront the issues of hegemony and multiplicity directly. Transformative theories of power are produced by resistant knowledges associated with the second boundary that exists at the margins of modernity, between modernity and what is incommensurable with it. In contrast to modern theories of centralized power, a poststructural

85. Foucault, *Truth and Power*, *supra* note 17, at 115–16.
86. Chakrabarty, *supra* note 74, at 427.

framework like Foucault's theorizes power as dispersed and circulating unevenly in discursive networks throughout the entire social fabric.[87] Exploring the transformative potential of incommensurable knowledges relies on what Foucault has called an "ascending" analysis of power.[88] Such an analysis credits local antidisciplinary knowledges, which initially lack any relationship with the assumptions of Europe, with the power to resist dominant knowledges.

Foucault did not make it clear how the multiplicity of local knowledges can survive modernity's tactics of erasure, colonization, and discipline and become harnessed and coordinated into networks powerful enough to challenge dominant forms of power. Although this question was not part of Foucault's project, it lies at the center of poststructural inquiry. It is the question posed by postcolonial feminist Gayatri Chakravorty Spivak about whether the subaltern can "speak."[89] The answer, within modernity, is that she cannot because her incommensurability makes her an absence. Thus, only at the margins of modernity does the subaltern have the potential to speak. Third World feminist Chandra Mohanty refers to such transformative knowledge as the "plural consciousness" of the "borderlands,"[90] where the dualistic thinking of modernity might be denaturalized[91] and possibly transcended.

In contrasting modern egalitarianism and transformative strategies from the margins of modernity, I construct to some extent a false duality. Recognizing their different emancipatory potential is an important strategic insight, but it should not be allowed to overshadow the ways in which the two types of resistant knowledges might cooperate to influence strategies for change. For example, critical race theorist and feminist Angela Harris suggests that the task for critical race theory (CRT) is to develop in the tension between modernism and postmodernism, "to continually rebuild modernism in the light of

---

87. *Id.* at 98.

88. Foucault, *Two Lectures*, *supra* note 17, at 99.

89. *See* Gayatri Chakravorty Spivak, *Can the Subaltern Speak?*, *in* Marxism and the Interpretation of Culture 271, 294 (Cary Nelson & Lawrence Grossberg eds., 1988).

90. Chandra Talpade Mohanty, *Introduction: Cartographies of Struggle: Third World Women and the Politics of Feminism*, *in* Third World Women and the Politics of Feminism 1, 36 (Chandra Talpade et al. eds., 1991). Mohanty refers to Gloria Anzaldua's term "mestiza consciousness," the outcome of perceiving and negotiating the multiple and often contradictory knowledges of Anglo and Mexican cultures and frames of reference.

91. Chakrabarty, *supra* note 74, at 430.

postmodernist critique."[92] Echoing the views of many other CRT scholars, she observes that "[f]or people of color, as well as for other oppressed groups, modern concepts of truth, justice, and objectivity have always been both indispensable and inadequate."[93] Thus, while the global category of Race has had many empowering effects in mobilizing race-based solidarities and having an impact upon the modern discourse of rights, it has also failed in the project of realizing the egalitarian promises of the Enlightenment.

Harris suggests that poststructuralism, in confronting the impossibilities of the "dilemma of difference" within modernity, has two things to offer: sophistication and disenchantment.[94] By "sophistication" Harris means new understandings of the subject as multiplicitous and contingent, and of power's productive relationship with knowledge; by "disenchantment" she means the need to distrust the authenticity, unity, and certainty that modern categories such as Race promise. It is in the tensions at the intersection of their respective analyses of power and strategy that modern and poststructural theories can be mutually coproductive in building strategies that link, multiply, and empower local transformative challenges to dominating regimes of Truth.

B. Revealing Power and Pluralizing Difference

I will explore two ways in which modern and poststructural knowledges might cooperate to produce transformative human rights strategies: first, these knowledges can increase the transparency of the power relationships created by modernity's dualisms in order to generate transformative resistance and move the contestation of inequality from a paradigm of difference to one of power; second, using these knowledges we can rethink the modern taxonomy of difference in order to base human rights strategies on multiplicities and contingencies, rather than depend on their erasure.

---

92. Angela P. Harris, *Foreword: The Jurisprudence of Reconstruction,* 82 Cal. L. Rev. 741, 744 (1994). Although Harris uses the term "postmodernism," for present purposes I am taking it to have the same meaning as "poststructuralism."

93. *Id.* Others have also cogently argued this view. *See, e.g.,* Patricia Williams, The Alchemy of Race and Rights (1991); Mari J. Matsuda, *Looking to the Bottom: Critical Legal Studies and Reparations,* 22 Harv. C.R.-C.L. L. Rev. 323 (1987); Richard Delgado, *The Ethereal Scholar: Does Critical Legal Studies Have What Minorities Want?*, 22 Harv. C.R.-C.L. L. Rev. 301 (1987).

94. Harris, *supra* note 92, at 766.

First, it is imperative to bring issues of power to the fore. Foucault's point in critiquing modern theories of monolithic power and in proposing an alternative ascending analysis was not to deny or transcend relations of power, as modern knowledges including human rights law claim to do by asserting the possibility of objectivity and universality. His purpose was to increase our understanding of the mechanisms of power within modernity and thereby multiply resistances. In Foucault's paradigm, resistances or "counter politics"[95] exist everywhere in the networks of power relations and can be strategically recoded and integrated to have global counterhegemonic effects.[96] As human rights theorist Sharon Hom suggests, this strategic recoding involves, among other things, reimagining the Others of modernity as agents rather than victims, as "already possessing the power to transform their/our lives and societies."[97] Her view is consistent with Foucault's ascending analysis in its recognition of the vitality of local knowledges as sites of power and struggle. However, one danger of the poststructural focus on localized agency (and diversity) is that it has the potential to assert new forms of individualism[98] and produce new, local forms of hegemonic paternalism, as exemplified in the efforts of some human rights NGOs to be "sensitive" to local cultural traditions in order to convince non-Europeans of the relevance of universal human rights standards (a *sameness* strategy).[99]

To counter the individualist and neoimperialist potential of poststructuralism, modern representational categories, like Race, can help harness and organize local resistances. Thus, the global category

---

95. Colin Gordon, *Governmental Rationality: An Introduction, in* The Foucault Effect 5 (Graham Burchell et al. eds., 1991).

96. Foucault, *supra* note 17, at 142; 1 Michel Foucault, The History of Sexuality 95-96 (1976).

97. Sharon Hom, *Female Infanticide in China: The Human Rights Specter and Thoughts Towards (An)Other Vision,* 23 Colum. Hum. Rts. L. Rev. 249, 310 (1991); *see also* Penny Andrews, *Violence Against Aboriginal Women in Australia: Possibilities for Redress Within the International Human Rights Framework*, 60 Alb. L. Rev. 917 (1997).

98. Linda J. Nicholson, Feminism/Postmodernism 4, 14 (Linda J. Nicholson ed., 1990).

99. Bell, *supra* note 31, at 657-59. Bell mentions several "positive" reasons for drawing on indigenous cultural traditions to persuade East Asians of the value of human rights including identifying cultural resources most likely to lead to a long term human rights commitment and groups most likely to bring about "desirable" social change. Paradoxically, he is also critical of others for adopting a more "sensitive" approach to local traditions in order to be more persuasive about the relevance of "universal" standards, yet this seems to amount to the same thing. *See id.* at 667.

of Race can work against the construction of racism as an individual problem that can be resolved by the exercise of individual agency by drawing attention to the structural dimensions of racial oppression. Furthermore, the global category fosters transnational links which bring to light evidence of worldwide patterns of racism. In turn, poststructural awareness of the falsely universalizing effects of global categories[100] can assist in the struggle to resist the unquestionability and the status of Truth which are attributed to such categories by modernity.

A small but positive example of recognizing the role that local agency can play in human rights discourse is provided by the 1993 Declaration on the Elimination of Violence Against Women (DEVAW),[101] which draws attention to the ongoing importance of women's movements in identifying and responding to gendered violence.[102] The dangers of the global category of Woman are potentially counteracted, at least to some extent, by the emphasis on local self-determination in the form of dialogue with grass roots women's movements. At the same time, the category of Woman suggests that links can be made between the multitude of dispersed local forms that gendered violence takes.[103]

However, as Mohanty emphasizes, it is important to understand agency as an outcome of opposition to domination[104] rather than as based on the Truths of identity politics sponsored by modern forms of law and governance. Achieving this shift involves fostering a new understanding of inequality as an issue of power rather than difference by bringing transparency to the relations of power that lie behind the familiar equality arguments of sameness and difference. Radical feminists like Catharine MacKinnon have developed the forefronting of power relations as a modern strategy.[105] The DEVAW provides a pioneering example of this work in the human rights field in its attempt

---

100. Smart, *supra* note 15, at 7 .

101. *Declaration on the Elimination of Violence Against Women*, G.A. Res. 48/104 U.N. GAOR., 48th Sess., Supp No. 49, 85th mtg. at 217-19, U.N. Doc. A/RES/48/104 (1993) [hereinafter DEVAW].

102. *Id.* at pmbl., cl. 10, arts 4(o), 4(p).

103. *Id.* at art. 2(a) (providing examples of violence against women "including battering, sexual abuse of female children in the household, dowry-related violence, marital rape, female genital mutilation and other traditional practices harmful to women, nonspousal violence and violence related to exploitation").

104. Mohanty, *supra* note 90, at 38.

105. *See* Catharine MacKinnon, Feminism Unmodified 40 (1987).

to relocate antidiscrimination narratives in a jurisprudence of power rather than difference. The DEVAW recognizes that:

> [V]iolence against women is a manifestation of historically unequal power relations between men and women, which has led to domination over and discrimination against women by men and . . . is one of the crucial social mechanisms by which women are forced into a subordinate position compared to men.[106]

The DEVAW's identification of power as the central issue and its acknowledgment that men are the beneficiaries of discrimination against women also mark a radical departure from the masculinist "neutrality" of the heavily guarded Standards of modernity erected by other human rights instruments. In place of the masculinist prototype, the DEVAW constructs a gender-differentiated Standard in its *female* embodiment of the target of gendered violence. However, in its *dualized global* mapping of gendered power, of male beneficiaries and female subordination, the DEVAW stays firmly within a modern framework.

The DEVAW provides, in other ways, an example of a fledgling cooperative endeavor between modern and poststructural knowledges. If poststructural perspectives had been more consciously attended to, the Declaration would emphasize the importance of giving voice to the diversity of local experience of gendered violence, including its racialized and heterosexualized dimensions. The result would be to acknowledge the contingency and fluidity of the Standards erected by the Declaration. A poststructural sensitivity would necessitate vigilance in contesting the dominating tendencies of global categories in the poststructural sense of continual reconstruction, rather than in the modern sense of reshuffling dualistic conceptions of power distributed between the Standard and its Other.

Second, in addition to forefronting the local and global operations and distributions of power, a key issue in building transformative human rights strategies is that of rethinking modernity's dualistic and hierarchical construction of difference. This issue can also be tackled by drawing on a combination of modern and poststructural knowledges. To start with, we need to acknowledge that categorical thinking enables us to communicate and to act. Without

106. DEVAW, *supra* note 101, at pmbl., cl. 6.

classifications and comparisons, we are left with a world of infinite *sui generis* items and without a basis for making judgments of justice, ethics, or rights.[107] Yet categories also always exclude other possibilities by obscuring the multiple strands that make up the whole and the ways in which the strands interrelate.[108] Therefore the issue is not one of dispensing with abstractions or of refining them until they are "correct." It is, rather, of continually questioning which categories we use in human rights discourse and contesting the power that is attributed to them by modernity's dual constructions of Standard and Other, or commensurability and erasure.

However, poststructural analyses suggest we can go farther than continually questioning dualistic categories and reject dichotomous thinking itself. Scott reasons that because power is constructed on difference, it must be challenged from that premise. As she says,

> [t]he only alternative . . . is to refuse to oppose equality to difference and insist continually on differences—differences as the condition of individual and collective identities, differences as the constant challenge to the fixing of those identities . . . differences as the very meaning of equality itself.[109]

Many CRT feminists have made significant contributions to how we might "insist continually on differences" and begin to reconceive the world in nondominating multiplicities and pluralities. Harris, for example, observes that everyone is constituted by a diversity of *selves* or *voices* that are involved in "a constant contradictory state of becoming, in which both social institutions and individual wills are deeply implicated."[110] This idea of "multiple consciousness"[111] is similar to Mohanty's notion of borderland "plural consciousness."[112]

---

107. *See* Angela P. Harris, *Race and Essentialism in Feminist Legal Theory,* 42 Stan. L. Rev. 581, 586 (1990).

108. *See* Stephanie M. Wildman & Adrienne D. Davis, *Language and Silence: Making Systems of Privilege Visible, in* Critical Race Theory: The Cutting Edge 573, 578 (Richard Delgado ed., 1995).

109. Scott, *supra* note 67, at 46.

110. Harris, *supra* note 107, at 584.

111. Mari Matsuda, *When The First Quail Calls: Multiple Consciousness as Jurisprudential Method,* 11 Women's Rts. L. Rep. 7, 9 (1989) (first coined the term "multiple consciousness"); *see also* Deborah King, *Multiple Jeopardy, Multiple Consciousness: The Context of a Black Feminist Ideology,* 14 Signs 42 (1988).

112. Mohanty, *supra* note 90, at 36-38.

Harris's concept of multiple consciousness suggests that if the diversities that coexist *within* us enable a multiplicitous sense of self, then differences can also structure our relations *between* each other without threatening our ability to communicate and make ethical judgments. This paradigm enables a more *sophisticated* understanding, in Harris's sense, of the complex interplay of differences in constructing our social realities than the unidimensional and absolute dualisms of modernity. Dualistic thinking simply cannot account for the interacting, intersecting,[113] and shifting positions of domination and subordination that the same person occupies—perhaps Inside because of their Sexuality, Other due to their Race, and incommensurable on account of their Indigeneity. Multiple consciousness also suggests that we make constant choices about whether and how we conceive of justice. The idea that "wholeness and commonality are acts of will and creativity, rather than passive discovery,"[114] is also consistent with poststructural thinking.

However, there is the danger that we attribute too much power to multiple consciousness as a means of making the whole world accessible. The danger lies in assuming that coherent ways of knowing the pluralities of global experience can be found and, as feminist international lawyer Isabelle Gunning proposes, that "world travelling" and "multicultural dialogue" are always possible.[115] I prefer the approach of feminist philosopher Rosi Braidotti, who suggests that it is better to imagine the diversities of the world in terms of "multiple literacies" and to "relinquish the dream of a common language in favour of the recognition of the complexity of the semiotic and material context in which we operate."[116] Poststructural Donna Haraway agrees, warning that "all dreams for a perfectly true language, of a perfectly faithful

---

113. *See* Kimberlé Crenshaw, *Demarginalizing the Intersection of Race and Sex: A Black Feminist Critique of Anti-Discrimination Doctrine, Feminist Theory and Anti-Racist Politics*, 1989 U. Chi. Legal F. 139, 150–51 (1989).

114. Harris, *supra* note 107, at 608.

115. Isabelle Gunning, *Arrogant Perception, World-Travelling and Multi-Cultural Feminism: The Case of Female Genital Surgeries*, 23 Colum. Hum. Rts. L. Rev. 189, 227 (1991). The term "'world'-travelling" was devised by Maria Lugones, *Playfulness, "World"-Travelling and Loving Perception*, 2 Hypatia: A Journal of Feminist Philosophy 3 (1987).

116. Rosi Braidotti, *The Exile, The Nomad, and The Migrant: Reflections on International Feminism*, 15 Women's Stud. Int'l F. 7, 10 (1992).

naming of experience, [are] totalizing and imperialist."[117] In sum, we need not only learn how to make differences the basis for our interrelationships, but also how to live with incommensurabilities, which are outside dialogue. We need to remind ourselves constantly of the limits of what is possible in relation to all knowledge.[118]

Similar to Mohanty's proposal that resistance be organized around commonalities based on opposition to domination rather than on the static categories of identity politics, Haraway highlights a model of political identity theorized by women of color called "oppositional consciousness."[119] This approach is "born of the skills for reading webs of power by those refused stable membership in the social categories of race, sex or class,"[120] and recognizes that strategic coalitional affinity, rather than identity, unites resistances. Poststructuralist feminist Judith Butler also endorses a coalitional approach, emphasizing its strategic and contingent nature.[121] That is, we need to learn how to build coalitions of interest across the divisions that identity categories construct. In giving up certainty and prescription, the idea of oppositional consciousness potentially opens the space for solidarities across incommensurabilities.

Despite their limitations, modern categories may still prove useful in providing some starting points for coalitional dialogue. At a minimum, modern knowledges facilitate the process of communication that is necessary for their rejection. However, I think their usefulness is much more extensive. The modern ideals of human rights, democracy, equality, and self-determination, employed with poststructuralist caution about their totalizing and dominating potential, may assist the development of processes of coalitional dialogue across vast disparities in power, experience, and literacy. This proposal is not intended to draw the liberal jurisprudential distinction between substance and process which suggests that the latter can be neutral, but to acknowledge the constitutive power of "procedure" and build this power into transformative politics.

---

117. Donna Haraway, *A Manifesto For Cyborgs*, *in* Feminism/Postmodernism 190, 215 (Linda J. Nicholson ed., 1990).

118. *See* Spivak, *supra* note 89, at 283.

119. Haraway, *supra* note 117, at 197. Haraway attributes the term "oppositional consciousness" to Chela Sandoval, a Chicana critical feminist. *Id.*

120. *Id.*

121. *See* Judith Butler, *Gender Trouble, Feminist Theory, and Psychoanalytic Discourse*, *in* Feminism/Postmodernism 324 (Linda J. Nicholson ed., 1990).

It is still unclear how the ideas of multiple literacies and coalitional affinities might reshape human rights instruments. Returning to the example of the DEVAW, its recognition that some groups of women may be particularly vulnerable to violence goes some way towards acknowledging women's diversities.[122] The DEVAW formulation is an advance on the CEDAW, which makes only one reference to differently-situated women in its acknowledgment of the specific needs of rural women.[123] However, the DEVAW approach is limited insofar as it suggests what Chakrabarty has disparagingly called the erection of the subaltern as the subject of modern democracies, and what Scott decries as the invocation of a "happy pluralism."[124] The marginal critiques of modernity's hierarchies of difference and silencing of incommensurabilities demand much more than a rainbow coalition.

C. Rethinking Universality as Dialogue and Ethical Struggle

The next question to address is whether the notion of universality is fundamentally inconsistent with poststructural analyses of power and marginal critiques of human rights discourse. How does universality sit within a framework that emphasizes local agency, situated knowledges, multiple subjectivities, and contingent politics? Clearly, the dominating universality of modernity has no place in such a framework. But does this mean an acceptance of the *sui generis* approach of individual nation-states and an end to transnational communication about human dignity and worth, as the universalists in the current human rights debates would suggest? I agree with Scott and Butler that the exaggerated "outcry" which responds to poststructuralist critiques by portending chaos and nihilism is little more than a defense of privileged epistemic positions.[125] Universality

---

122. The DEVAW refers to "women belonging to minority groups, indigenous women, refugee women, migrant women, women living in rural or remote communities, destitute women, women in institutions or detention, female children, women with disabilities, elderly women and women in situations of armed conflict." DEVAW, *supra* note 101, at pmbl., ¶ 7.

123. *Convention on the Elimination of All Forms of Discrimination Against Women*, G.A. Res. 180, U.N. GAOR, 34th Sess., Supp. No. 46, at art. 14, U.N. Doc. A/34/46 (1980) (entered into force Sept. 3, 1981) [hereinafter CEDAW].

124. Scott, *supra* note 67, at 48.

125. Judith Butler & Joan W. Scott, Feminists Theorize the Political xv (1992).

still has a role in a transformative paradigm, but it is universality understood as dialogue, in the sense of struggle against domination, rather than as a disciplinary civilizing mission of Europe.

Many human rights theorists and activists advocate the importance of dialogue.[126] Postcolonial theorist Raimundo Pannikar, for example, suggests that while human value exists only in a particular cultural context, "there may be cross-cultural values and a cross-cultural critique is indeed possible."[127] He advocates a "healthy pluralism" whereby people are made aware that human rights is only one of a plurality of windows through which different cultures imagine human dignity.[128] However, this kind of approach, while consistent with the CRT idea of multiple consciousness, can easily slip into the rainbow coalition classification wherein anything becomes acceptable, without some "methodological precautions," to borrow a Foucauldian idea.[129] I prefer to use the term "ethics."

The articulation of ethical struggle is, in my view, at the center of the transformative project of universality. Smart is correct when she says:

> [I]f we abandon the idea of an ultimate Truth or correctness, then we have to allow ethics back into the discussion. Ethics should not be the subtext on which we rely to negate oppositional stances, they should be openly addressed.[130]

Also, Harris, arguing for *disenchantment* with the presumed cohesion of modern identity categories, stresses that solidarity is produced by struggle that includes moral and ethical struggle, not solely political struggle.[131] I suggest three ethical struggles, not an exhaustive list, that are critical to the idea of transformative universality in human rights law. These struggles might perhaps be likened to the principles that

---

126. Gunning, *supra* note 115, at 190; Abdullahi An-Na'im, *Islam, Islamic Law and the Dilemma of Cultural Legitimacy for Universal Human Rights*, *in* Human Rights in Cross-Cultural Perspective: A Quest For Consensus 31 (Abdullahi An-Na'im ed., 1992).

127. Raimundo Pannikar, *Is The Notion of Human Rights a Western Concept?*, 120 Diogenes 76, 87-88 (1982).

128. *Id.* at 79.

129. Foucault, *Two Lectures*, *supra* note 17, at 96.

130. Smart, *supra* note 15, at 215.

131. Harris, *supra* note 92, at 784.

have guided, though admittedly not necessarily progressively, the development of the law of equity in the common law.[132]

First, transformative dialogue can take place only in a context where participants acknowledge and address disparities in power.[133] Human rights lawyer Abdullahi An-Na'im highlights this issue when he says that "ideally participants [in dialogue] should feel on an equal footing but, given existing power relations, those in a position to do so might seek ways of redressing the imbalance."[134] I would go much farther and insist that transparency of the operations of global networks of power, of exploitation and domination, is a vitally important component of transformative dialogue. Human rights tribunals and monitoring mechanisms must be redesigned to take account of inequalities in power, in order to find ways to admit the voices of modernity's Others and incommensurables. This reshaping goes well beyond the modern project of expanding the pluralist democratic polity by including the views of Others. It involves acting ethically by interrogating any privileges we might enjoy as a result of Europe's masculinist hegemony, and taking responsibility for the associated relations of dominating power. In other words, transformative strategies involve transformation of the self[135] as concomitant to rethinking the systems of which we are all a part.

Second, transformative dialogue involves the *unlearning* of privileged epistemologies by those who benefit from them. We have an ethical responsibility to recognize and positively assert the diversity of the world. Spivak raises this issue in the context of the possibility of dialogue between European feminists and subaltern women:

> In seeking to learn to speak to (rather than listen to or speak for) the historically muted subject of the subaltern woman, the postcolonial intellectual *systematically* "unlearns" female privilege. This systematic unlearning involves learning to critique postcolonial discourse with the best tools it can

132. Michael Chesterman, *Equity in the Law, in* A Just Society? Essays in Equity in Australia 51, 63 (P.N. Troy ed., 1981); *see also* Sir Anthony Mason, *Themes and Prospects, in* Essays in Equity 242 (Paul Finn ed., 1985).

133. Anne Orford, *Citizenship, Sovereignty and Globalization: Teaching International Law in the Post-Soviet Era*, 6 Legal Educ. Rev. 251, 251-52 (1995).

134. Abdullahi An-Na'im, *What Do We Mean By Universal?*, 5 Index on Censorship 120, 122 (1994).

135. *See* Tracey E. Higgins, *Anti-Esssentialism, Relativism and Human Rights*, 19 Harv. Women's L.J. 89, at 115 (1996).

> provide and not simply substituting the lost figure of the colonized.[136]

This unlearning means making a radical break from "the ferocious standardizing benevolence"[137] of European knowledges that force the translation of difference into the terms of the dominant discourse. Speaking *to* and *among* Europe's Others and incommensurables requires acknowledging one's own positionality, resisting the hierarchization and erasure of difference, and opening oneself to uncertainty—attributes that are unfamiliar to modernity. It requires too that international lawyers and human rights activists confront, in our work, Chakrabarty's ethical question of whether "genuinely 'non-violative' relations between the Self (the 'West') and its Other" are possible.[138]

Third, transformative dialogue must also be based on an ethical commitment to address the *material* aspects of human dignity, and thus to promote global economic justice and substantive equality. As the Soviet Union pointed out in 1948, gross disparities in social, economic, and political power contradict the idea of universal principles. As these inequalities are deepened by post-Cold War economic restructuring,[139] transformative dialogue between the various interests of the people of the world, without a redistribution of wealth, becomes ever more inconceivable.[140] The dialogue of transformative universality must make the ethical move of embracing, in its practice, the indivisibility of the pursuit of individual and collective liberty, and the achievement of global material justice. At the very least, this move means ensuring that the concept of human rights includes social rights and economic justice.

Thus, universality, in the transformative sense, involves continuous political and ethical struggle between differences and across incommensurabilities. These struggles, as I have argued, are usefully informed by aspects of both modern and poststructural ideals and

136. Spivak, *supra* note 89, at 295.

137. *Id.* at 294.

138. Chakrabarty, *supra* note 74, at 423.

139. *See* Julie Stephens, *Running Interface: An Interview with Gayatri Chakravorty Spivak,* 7 Austl. Women's Book Rev. 19, 20 (1995); *see also* J. Brecher & T. Costello, Global Village or Global Pillage: Economic Restructuring From the Bottom Up (1994).

140. *See* Martti Koskenniemi, *The Future of Statehood,* 32 Harv. Int'l L.J. 397, 403-04 (1991).

practices. Following Harris, universality rethought in this way might be understood as lying in the tensions or intersections between modernism and poststructuralism. There are many other intersections which might inform transformative universality, two of which are particularly relevant to human rights discourse: one, the tension between local and global knowledges; two, the tension between the interests of the individual and the collective interests of their community.

Turning to the first issue, the problem of the relationship between the local and the global has always been present in human rights law. However, to assert the local in a transformative paradigm is not to claim greater authenticity or validity for certain knowledges over others. Nor is the meaning of *local* equivalent to the nation-state as it is often understood in international law. Instead, local knowledges can be found in many locations that are not necessarily territorially defined. For example, the *locality* of women's or sexuality movements or of subaltern peoples may traverse many territorially local constituencies, and may even be transnational in certain instances.

In this way, transformative universality opens spaces for dialogue within and beyond the nation-state, in transnational as well as intranational solidarities. It also readmits the embodied and situated subject to human rights discourse; displacing the preconstituted, universal Subject (Man) of modernity. A transformative notion of local might be likened to international legal theorist James Boyle's image of the unreified expression of politics that would accompany a rejection of the Enlightenment search for essences in international law.[141] Rather than addressing the imponderables of the relationship between local and global knowledges by searching for an absolute statement, the relationship should be recognized as one of the productive intersections which are integral to transformative dialogue. As postcolonial feminist Chantal Mouffe explains this process, "[u]niversalism is not rejected but particularized."[142]

A second tension which can inform transformative dialogue is that between the individual and her or his community. This tension may also be described as lying between independence and interdependence, between state sovereignty and international

141. James Boyle, *Ideals and Things: International Legal Scholarship and the Prison-House of Language,* 26 Harv. Int'l L.J. 327, 330–32 (1985).

142. *See* Chantal Mouffe, *Radical Democracy: Modern or Postmodern?, in* Universal Abandon? The Politics of Postmodernism 31, 36 (Andrew Ross ed., 1988).

community, and between what Foucault refers to as the totalizing and individualizing impulses of liberalism.[143] In Mohanty's figuring of resistant agency in the everyday struggles of Third World women, she suggests that we need to rethink what we mean by community:

> The very practice of remembering against the grain of "public" or hegemonic history, of locating the silences and the struggle to assert knowledge which is outside the parameters of the dominant suggests a rethinking of sociality itself. . . . We need to renegotiate how we conceive of the relation of self–and collective consciousness and agency.[144]

This rethinking involves rejecting notions of solidarity and community that are based narrowly on identity and geography, and exploring more contingent ideas of communality associated with coalition and strategy. As with other tensions that cradle transformative universality, there is no "solution" to the perplexities of the relationship between autonomy and interconnection. Rather, enormous productivity lies in the acknowledgment and contestation of this relationship.

In sum, both modernism and poststructuralism have contributions to make to transformative human rights strategies. Relations of power must be made transparent, agency must be reunderstood as opposition rather than identity, and dichotomous thinking must be replaced by consciousness of multiplicities and incommensurabilities. Consistent with these changes is a rethinking of universality as dialogue and ethical struggle. Transformative universality involves the ethical struggles of taking responsibility for the relations of power in which we are implicated, unlearning epistemological privilege, and achieving global economic and material justice.

III. Transformative Human Rights Strategies

Clearly, transformative strategies in human rights must move beyond the dualistic and hierarchical Standards of modernity that have shaped the identity politics and inclusionary strategies of human rights movements since 1945. Yet modern ideas, while assisting the universalization of European and masculinist norms, have also provided

---

143. Gordon, *supra* note 95, at 8.
144. *See* Mohanty, *supra* note 90, at 38–39.

a starting point for many local and global resistances to such hegemonies and have been important in precipitating critiques from the margins of modernity. We must resist the duality of modernity and poststructuralism and find ways to draw on both reservoirs of knowledge in order to work towards a world without domination.

I conclude with five strategies which help reposition the current universality debates in the ethical struggles and tensions of transformative dialogue: rejecting universalizing knowledge claims; refusing the generational hierarchies of categories of human rights; resisting the posing of dualistic alternatives; decentering the nation-state; and recognizing the limits of law as a means of change.

A. Rejecting Universalizing Knowledge

The strategy of rejecting universalizing knowledge claims is based on the Foucauldian recognition of the productive relationship between knowledge and power. To contest the foundational assumptions of the universality debates is to bring into question the claims to Truth that are being produced and reveal their allegiances to power. As I have argued, the debate is largely a contest between two universalizing forms of capital, one side (the North) reliant on confirmation of the supremacy of the Standards of Europe and the other side (the South, particularly Asian states) intent on reversing the dualism that has constructed its secondary status as the Other of Europe. The debate is shaped by the interests of nation-states and has focused on a rearrangement of the global hierarchies produced by modernity, not on their rejection.

A transformative strategy would seek to disrupt the polarized and absolute configurations of the debates by refusing to participate on those terms. Human rights NGOs are one means of bringing local knowledges to the fore in order to confound the certainties of the dominant positions and destabilize the closure brought about by the binary opposition. This strategy involves exposing the cultural allegiances and imperialist potential of the universalist arguments, bringing to light the narrowness of the diversity promoted by the cultural relativist position and revealing the many commonalities between the two sides. Such a strategy would lend transparency to state-based elite interests being served by the debate and to the multitude of local interests erased by it, and open the possibility of new paradigms for understanding context and diversity.

Transformative dialogue needs to draw on the productive tension between local and global knowledges, a tension which is glaringly absent from the globally dominated present debates. Encouraging local communities to participate in the debate on their own terms, whatever those terms might be, is one way of bringing this tension to the fore. For example, non-elite groups might be empowered to have control of agenda-setting, determine the questions of importance, and run meetings according to procedures that they understand. Integral to the success of dialogue between the local and the global is the ethical struggle in which participants take responsibility for developing mechanisms which enable them to identify voices that have hitherto been marginalized or erased and to address inequalities in power. In these ways, the process toward reunderstanding universality and human dignity in context can be commenced. The emphasis is on the human potential for questioning and change and the continuing productivity of the dialogue, rather than on reaching agreement whereby everyone endorses a grand design.

B. Refusing Hierarchies

The second transformative strategy is the refusal of hierarchical arrangements of human rights. The Cold War generational development of human rights law reflected and confirmed dominant arrangements of global power. This hierarchy, as well as the duality which the universality debates are ostensibly contesting, places Europe at the pinnacle of global development. A reimagining of the categories of human rights from the margins involves developing coalitional and intersectional strategies within each category of human rights, as well as across the terrain of them all, with the goal of achieving their indivisibility. This strategy also necessarily entails refusing the hierarchy of North and South.

Promoting the interdependence and indivisibility of human rights is a tactic that already has a place in mainstream human rights rhetoric. The question is how to realize it in practice. The new commitments to indivisibility that accompanied the end of the Cold War have, in fact, veiled a contraction in states' obligations with respect to second and third generation human rights. In particular, the social justice potential of the right to development has been severely compromised by the way in which both Northern and Southern versions of global capital have used the development agenda to promote free market agendas. While the realization of human dignity can hardly be divorced from achieving economic rights and social justice, the modern language of individual human rights has diverted attention from addressing this fundamental issue.

Transformative dialogue must rebuild most human rights movements from the ground up in order to anchor them in an ethical commitment to global social and economic justice. Human rights struggles have largely been shaped by the categories of the generational developments of human rights. Consequently, these struggles have predominated in the area of civil and political rights. Movements for social and economic rights, as well as solidarity rights, have tended to identify themselves as aid or economic development lobbies instead of using the language of human rights.[145] This focus needs to change and, as with the first strategy, the productive tensions between local and global knowledges are important in this endeavor. We in the West understand so little about how counterhierarchies might function. The building of transformative forms of universality involves disengaging human rights discourse from the dominant regimes of power and coming to grips with the material aspects of justice. The starting point must be the manifold, embodied, non-elite subjects of human rights law who understand dignity in particularized yet multiple ways.

C. Resisting Dualisms

The third strategy is to resist the posing of the debate in dualistic alternatives and to link with the various attempts by feminist, critical race, and queer theorists to create a single politics out of multiple differences. Modern knowledges' claim of Truth in their insulation from the contingencies of human diversity has confirmed the masculinist, racist, heterosexist, and imperialist Standards of Europe as universal. Contesting this Truth requires building a transformative paradigm that recognizes difference as an issue of power and encourages solidarity in difference rather than in the sameness of identity politics.

Disrupting the dualisms of the universality debates might commence with renaming the central issue as one of plural literacies, or at least of cultural *diversity* rather than *relativity*. Doing so would dispense with the dualistic Standard that is implicit in the notion of relativity. Such a renaming would help to make the power struggles of

---

145. Michael Posner & Candy Whittome, *The Status of Human Rights NGOs*, 25 Colum. Hum. Rts. L. Rev. 269, 272–76 (1994).

the present debates transparent and reduce their momentum by the assertion of nondominating forms of power. Multiple conceptions of difference and specificity, as alternatives to the comparative hierarchies of cultural relativity, need to be introduced. This approach links with the strategy of promoting the indivisibility of human rights in that rejecting the generational hierarchy involves replacing dualistic notions of difference with an integrated but fluid network of interconnections.

Transformative dialogue must pay particular attention to the productive tension between the individual and her or his community and the identification of strategic commonalities as alternatives to the dualized notions of difference from which the elites of the global community have benefitted. Mohanty has similarly suggested such a rethinking of sociality as a strategic approach.[146] This approach involves an ethical commitment to assert the world's multiple literacies and address the disparities in power that dyadic difference has naturalized.

D. Decentering the State

The strategy to decenter the nation-state is an inescapable component of a transformative rethinking of universality and difference. The self-evidence of the state as the preeminent subject of international law has proved to be an effective means of instituting Europe's hegemony. The entity of the nation-state has erased diversities of "We, the Peoples of the United Nations"[147] that cannot be represented by the National. It has subjugated diversities against which the Nation is defined and, thus, silenced and thwarted a multiplicity of local resistances and affinities from within states and across them. The centralized institutions of the nation-state have organized, and depend upon, the power relations of differences, including those based on gender, class, race, culture, and sexuality.[148]

States provide an important defense against the potential totalitarianism of the international order, as Koskenniemi has

---

146. Mohanty, *supra* note 90, at 73-74.

147. U.N. Charter pmbl.

148. *See, e.g.*, Gendered States: Feminist (Re)Visions of International Relations Theory (V. Spike Peterson, ed., 1992); M. Jacquie Alexander, *Not Just (Any)Body Can Be A Citizen: The Politics of Law, Sexuality and Postcoloniality in Trinidad and Tobago and the Bahamas,* 48 Feminist Rev. 5 (1994); Tony Anghie, *Francisco de Vitoria and the Colonial Origins of International Law,* 5 Soc. & Legal Stud. 321 (1996).

argued.[149] At the same time, a transformative dialogue would work towards new conceptions of the state. As Robert Malley and his colleagues suggest, this reconceptualization would involve divesting states of their fixed territory and constant population. It would require

> envisaging a state . . . as constructed, boundless, and open, a constellation of authoritative behaviours, or authoritative exercises of jurisdiction. . . . It has no permanent inside and outside, no identifiable interests. . . . [It] elicits a different mapping of the world . . . [in which the state becomes] a forum for the competition of particular claims brought by persons whose own movements and contacts may crisscross the globe.[150]

Foucault too suggests that the state is not a unity but a "composite reality," made possible by the tactics of modern governance, and much more tenuous than we think.[151] Feminist international lawyer Karen Knop takes this idea a step further by outlining ways in which recognizing the limited or overlapping nature of state sovereignties could enhance the participation of non-state groups in international law.[152]

Transformative dialogue seeks to ensure that the voices of non-National affinities and oppositions assume a central role in the current debates. Despite the present power of states, transnational and intranational human rights movements have assumed increasing importance and influence in the U.N. system as NGOs, but they are in continual danger of having their local accountabilities and ethical principles compromised by the financial and discursive capacity of states to shape their agendas.[153] In human rights discourse, this danger is particularly acute because, as states are the greatest violators of

---

149. *See* Koskenniemi, *supra* note 140, at 397.

150. Robert Malley et al., Note, *Constructing the State Extraterritorially: Jurisdictional Discourse, the National Interest, and Transnational Norms*, 103 Harv. L. Rev. 1273, 1295-96 (1990).

151. Foucault, *Two Lectures*, *supra* note 17, at 103.

152. Karen Knop, *Re/Statements: Feminism and State Sovereignty in International Law*, 3 Transnat'l L. & Contemp. Probs. 293, 342-43 (1993).

153. *See* Antonio Donini, *The Bureaucracy and the Free Spirits: Stagnation and Innovation in the Relationship Between the UN and NGOs*, *in* NGOs, the U.N., and Global Governance 83 (Thomas G. Weiss & Leon Gordenker eds., 1996).

human rights, states' power to determine what constitutes a right and a violation is strongly defended.

Coalitional strategies are obviously crucial in increasing the power of local knowledges in the context of the present state-centric global. Without coalitional interventions, the current universality debates will remain in the hands of nation-states. Indigenous peoples have led the way in developing coalitional strategies with their efforts to influence the drafting of a Declaration concerning indigenous rights.[154]

Most other NGOs in the U.N. system have yet to realize the importance of strategic unity and cooperation. Transnational coalitions and interventions have become even more imperative in the post-Cold War economic environment as new forms of supranational capital emerge in the context of an embryonic polity that is ill-equipped to demand accountability and mobilize resistance.

E. Resisting "Legal Imperialism"

The final transformative strategy is to recognize the limitations of law as a means of change. The snowballing of international human rights instruments and claims since 1945 has corresponded with a general increase in the legalization of life in the West.[155] In Foucault's view, turning to law in search of protection from modern disciplinary forms of power is a blind alley because law is less powerful than discipline.[156] Smart, however, argues that the two forms of power are complementary.[157] Both Foucault and Smart believe that legal discourse offers, at best, limited and precarious tools for transformative challenge. Furthermore, human rights activist Rajni Kothari warns that the strategy of human rights tends to depoliticize the understanding of an issue by deflecting attention from the structural sources and patterns

---

154. The U.N. Draft Declaration on the Rights of Indigenous Peoples, U.N. Doc. E/CN.4/1995/2, Aug. 26, 1994, *reprinted in* 34 I.L.M. 541, 541–43 (1995).

155. *See* Wendy Brown, States Of Injury: Power and Freedom in Late Modernity 27-28 (1995); Carol Smart, Feminism and the Power of Law 17 (1989).

156. Foucault, *Two Lectures*, *supra* note 17, at 108.

157. Smart, *supra* note 15, at 17.

of violations and focusing narrowly on particular instances of atrocities committed by the state.[158]

A transformative strategy seeks to introduce marginal and incommensurable knowledges to the universality debates and refuse the singular definition of the issue as a question of law. Political, social and economic counterknowledges must be brought into the debates to assist in the contestation of legal Truths and the deconstruction of legal unity. Moreover, we must be careful that the discourse of rights does not silence other languages—of needs, obligations, community, empowerment, ethics, economic justice, and material equity.[159] These extralegal, local languages may have been what Foucault meant when he suggested we turn to the possibility of a new form of "antidisciplinary" right.[160]

At the same time, the power of law cannot be ignored. It must be utilized as well as challenged. As Cheah has pointed out, "an outright realist dismissal of human rights denies their very real enabling force in the current conjuncture."[161] Yet the seduction of law's claim to power is moderated when we remember that law has legitimated particular hierarchies of knowledge and silenced or erased others. Law has also extended legal (global) power by replacing nonlegal (local) mechanisms that also protect and promote human dignity. Thus, law is an important site of struggle which must be simultaneously engaged and critiqued in the project of rethinking and resisting dominating notions of universality.

In the context of transformative dialogue, we must develop a more contextually-responsive, open-ended and ethically-accountable legal order. The current debates provide an opportunity to explore and advance this goal. Formal legal knowledge characterizes justice as an outcome of the abstractions of reason and order, in contrast to more substantive and situated notions of human dignity. Yet, as Koskenniemi notes, the resort to more contextually-determined legal standards is increasingly apparent in mainstream international legal practice where

---

158. Rajni Kothari, *Human Rights—A Movement in Search of a Theory, in* Rethinking Human Rights: Challenges for Theory and Action 19 (Smitu Kothari & H. Sethni eds., 1989), *quoted in* Steiner & Alston, *supra* note 25, at 460–62.

159. *See* Williams, *supra* note 93; *see also* Nancy Fraser, *Women, Welfare and the Politics of Need Interpretation, in* Unruly Practices: Power, Discourse and Gender in Contemporary Social Theory 144 (1989).

160. Foucault, *supra* note 17, 108.

161. Cheah, *supra* note 66, at 266.

the standards of equity, justice, and general principles of law are assuming a more prominent role.[162] Liberal international lawyer Thomas Franck also emphasizes the importance of the *soft* standards of fairness and justice in international law.[163] One challenge for human rights theorists and activists is to make critical links with such developments in order to build a transformative paradigm that responds to human multiplicity, rejects the privileging of elite human experience, resists the creation and subjugation of its converse in an Other, and guards against the erasure of its incommensurabilities.

CONCLUSION

Rethinking, from the margins of modern human rights orthodoxy, the way in which universality and difference are conceived is an important transformative project. This project is especially urgent in the post-Cold War environment in which European knowledges have reasserted their universal applicability and promoted the egalitarian ideals of modernity as the foundation of a new world order based on freedom. Yet, the egalitarianism of modernity has supported the globalization of capital, which has sponsored reduced state obligations with respect to economic and social rights and deepened the economic disparities between North and South. Poststructural thinking articulates in a new way a crisis of confidence in modernity's claim to universal Truth, building on the longstanding critiques of many groups on the margins of modernity.

My discussion of the tension in transformative human rights projects between a respect for classic egalitarian ideals and an acute awareness of their limitations focuses on the current human rights debate over universality and cultural relativity. I argue that the debate is not concerned with the important issues of global diversity, gender oppression, and economic and social justice. Rather, it is inextricably linked to a global struggle over universal Truth, between the Northern and "Asian" states, a struggle that is vital to the fight for post-Cold War economic dominance.

162. Koskenniemi, *supra* note 9, at 31.

163. *See generally* Thomas Franck, Fairness in International Law and Institutions (1995). *See also* Gerry Simpson, *Is International Law Really Fair?*, 17 Mich. J. Int'l L. 615, 618 (1996).

I suggest that the egalitarianism of modernity may yet assist the struggle for a world without domination if it is rethought by drawing on critiques of feminist, race, subaltern, postcolonial, and queer scholars from modernity's margins and by using poststructural tools of analysis. As a way of understanding the differences between the two types of knowledge, I suggest that they are located at two different boundaries produced by modern knowledges: one at the borderline between modernity's Standards and their antithetical Others; the second at the boundary between modernity and its incommensurabilities. Strategies for change from the first boundary tend to reinforce modernity's hegemony, even while they expand the inclusionary scope of the Standard. In contrast, strategies for change arising from the second boundary are critical of modernity and contest issues of power and diversity more directly.

I explore two ways in which modern and poststructural knowledges might cooperate in the development of transformative human rights strategies. The first approach is to increase our understanding of the mechanisms of power within modernity in order to move the contestation of inequality from a paradigm of difference to one of power, and thereby generate transformative resistance. The second method is to rethink the modern taxonomy of difference that relies on dualistic and hierarchical orderings of diversity. In its place, the concepts of "multiple consciousness" and "multiple literacies" suggest that we relinquish the modern desire for a common language and for universal knowledge, and look instead to diversities, incommensurabilities, and contingencies to structure our interrelationships.

It is the cooperative endeavor between modern and post-structural knowledges that suggests the potential for rethinking universality, rather than dispensing with it. I argue that universality still has a place in a transformative paradigm, provided we re-understand universality as continuing dialogue and struggle rather than as a civilizing mission of Europe. Such transformative dialogue involves creating a politics out of multiple differences and incommensurabilities in place of the modern dualities of sameness and difference. At the center of a transformative project of universality is the articulation of ethical principles which address disparities in power, insist on the unlearning of privileged epistemologies, and promote the indivisibility of the material aspects of human dignity. Furthermore, universality in a transformative sense is informed by the productive tensions and intersection between local and global knowledges, and the interests of the individual and her or his community.

Finally, I suggest five strategies of transformative universality which respond to the current universality versus cultural relativity debates: rejecting its universal claims to knowledge by bringing other knowledges to the fore; promoting the indivisibility and interdependence of all categories of human rights thereby rejecting their hierarchization; disrupting the dualized terms of the debate by linking with efforts to create a politics out of multiple difference; decentering the nation-state by giving voice to non-national identities and claims; and recognizing the limits as well as the power of law as a means of change.

In keeping with feminist legal theorist Drucilla Cornell's view, transformative change challenges not only the discursive structures and institutions of domination, but also requires that individuals take responsibility for their participation in relations of power.[164] Seeking to embrace multiplicity and difference in the framework of modern knowledge will always be a "dangerous"[165] endeavor because there is the potential that the dualisms and hierarchies that confirm the dominance of European masculinist knowledges are merely reproduced. However, there is also always the chance that transformative strategies might replace the closed, dualistic, and disciplinary paradigms of modernity with approaches that emphasize human potential for exploring margins and for seeking equity and justice.

164. Cornell, *supra* note 12, 1-2.

165. *See* Gordon, *supra* note 95, at 46. Gordon refers to Foucault's use of the term "dangerous" when explaining that nothing is "evil" in itself but that knowledges contain the possibilities of both domination and emancipation.

Part III
Implementation

[7]

How Is International Human Rights Law Enforced?†

Addison C. Harris Lecture
January 21, 1998

HAROLD HONGJU KOH*

I am greatly honored to deliver this distinguished Lecture, particularly given the illustrious list of lecturers who have preceded me to this podium.[1] My own path to this podium began in Washington, D.C., where as a private lawyer I specialized in issues of international business and trade law: what most American law schools now think of as "international business transactions."[2] But even while working on these matters, I became increasingly diverted toward the novel, growing field of international human rights. While in private practice in the early 1980s, I became involved in the representation of the American hostages who had been held for 444 days in the U.S. embassy in Tehran.[3] Once starting an academic career, I took occasional forays into international human rights advocacy,[4] but my main focus remained on the law of international business transactions and United States foreign policy, two examples of what Henry Steiner and Detlev Vagts have felicitously dubbed "Transnational Legal Problems."[5]

---

* Gerard C. and Bernice Latrobe Smith Professor of International Law and Director, Orville H. Schell, Jr. Center for International Human Rights, Yale Law School (on leave), Assistant United States Secretary of State, Democracy, Human Rights and Labor. These remarks were originally delivered as the January 1998 Addison Harris Lecture at the University of Indiana School of Law-Bloomington. They grow out of a chapter in a forthcoming book entitled *Why Nations Obey: A Theory of Compliance With International Law*, which I am writing under the auspices of the Century Foundation and the Guggenheim Foundation. This Lecture also shares thoughts with my 1998 Frankel Lecture at the University of Houston Law Center, Houston, Texas, and the 1997 Waynflete Lectures at Magdalen College, Oxford University. I am deeply grateful to Dean Alfred Aman, Acting Dean Lauren Robel, Dean Kelly Townes, Professor David Williams, the Harris Lecture Speaker's Committee, and the Editors of the *Indiana Law Journal* for their enormous hospitality while I was in Hoosier country.

Not long after delivering this Lecture, I was nominated and confirmed as Assistant Secretary for Democracy, Human Rights and Labor in the Clinton Administration. These lightly edited remarks, which have been footnoted for publication, obviously represent only my own views, and not necessarily those of the United States Department of State.

1. Past Harris lecturers include my former Harvard professors Paul Bator and Charles Fried, as well as my current Yale colleagues Guido Calabresi, Owen Fiss, Jules Coleman, and Robert Gordon.

2. *See generally* Harold Hongju Koh, *International Business Transactions in United States Courts*, 261 RECUEIL DES COURS 13 (1996).

3. *See* Persinger v. Islamic Republic of Iran, 729 F.2d 835 (D.C. Cir. 1984).

4. *See, e.g.*, David Cole et al., *Interpreting the Alien Tort Statute: Amicus Curiae Memorandum of International Law Scholars and Practitioners in* Trajano v. Marcos, 12 HASTINGS INT'L & COMP. L. REV. 1 (1988).

5. *See generally* HENRY J. STEINER ET AL., TRANSNATIONAL LEGAL PROBLEMS (4th ed. 1994).

As this decade began, international human rights law became the primary focus of both my theoretical and academic work, when I became involved with my students in a number of lawsuits in U.S. courts against human rights violators. In 1992, my students and I brought suits on behalf of the Haitian and Cuban refugees against the U.S. government[6] and a number of lawsuits against foreign human rights violators who had come to the United States—the former Guatemalan Minister of Defense, the former dictator of Haiti, an Indonesian general responsible for the 1991 Dili massacre in East Timor, and most recently a suit that is still ongoing in the Southern District of New York against Radovan Karadzic, the leader of the Bosnian Serbs.[7]

In each of these legal lives, as a scholar and a lawyer, I have asked the question that titles this Lecture, namely, "How is International Human Rights Law Enforced?" I wouldn't be surprised if many of you hearing that question were to give a pessimistic answer: international human rights law is *not* enforced, you might say. Just take a look at the massive human rights violations in Bosnia, violations that have gone unredressed in Cambodia and Iraq; the continuing crises in the Congo, Sierra Leone, Algeria, and Burundi. Look at indicted war criminals, like Radovan Karadzic in Republica Srpska, who continue to flout the jurisdictions of the Bosnian war crimes tribunal. Look, you might say, at the world's willingness to overlook human rights violations committed by more powerful nations, such as Russia's activities in Chechnya, or China's continuing repression after Tienanmen Square. International human rights law is not enforced, you might say, because human rights norms are vague and aspirational, because enforcement mechanisms are toothless, because treaty regimes are notoriously weak, and because national governments lack the economic self-interest or the political will to restrain their own human rights violations. So if the question is "how is international human rights law enforced?", many of you might answer: "not at all, or hardly at all." If you hold to this common, skeptical view of human rights enforcement, you would say that international human rights law is not enforced, like "real" domestic law; instead, it is only occasionally "complied with," by nation-states acting out of transparent convenience or self-interest.

In this Lecture, let me take a somewhat different tack, asking first, "What do we mean when we say that *any* laws are enforced?" Are any laws perfectly enforced? Even here in Bloomington, Indiana, the height of civilization, are the parking laws or burglary laws perfectly enforced? Of course, you would concede, parking violations occur here in Bloomington, and burglaries occur, perhaps even daily;

---

6. *See* Cuban-American Bar Ass'n v. Christopher, 43 F.3d 1413 (11th Cir. 1995); Haitian Ctrs. Council, Inc. v. McNary, 969 F.2d 1326 (2d Cir. 1992), *vacated as moot sub nom.* Sale v. Haitian Ctrs. Council, Inc., 509 U.S. 155 (1993); Haitian Ctrs. Council, Inc. v. Sale, 823 F. Supp. 1028 (E.D.N.Y. 1993). For an account of these cases, written by three of my students, see Victoria Clawson et al., *Litigating as Law Students: An Inside Look at* Haitian Centers Council, 103 YALE L.J. 2337 (1994).

7. *See* Xuncax v. Gramajo, 886 F. Supp. 162 (D. Mass. 1995); Todd v. Panjaitan, No 92-12255WD (D. Mass. decided Oct. 25, 1994) ($14 million judgment awarded); Doe v. Karadzic, 886 F. Supp. 734 (S.D.N.Y. 1994), *rev'd sub nom.* Kadic v. Karadzic, 70 F.3d 232 (2d Cir. 1995); Paul v. Avril, 812 F. Supp. 207 (S.D. Fla. 1993) ($41 million judgment awarded); Ortiz v. Gramajo, No. 91-11612WD (D. Mass. filed Sept. 17, 1992) ($47.5 million judgment awarded).

sometimes egregiously. But those facts alone hardly mean that there is no enforcement of laws against parking violations or burglary. Here in Indiana, the laws against burglary may be underenforced, they may be imperfectly enforced, but they are enforced, through a well-understood *domestic legal process* of legislation, adjudication, and executive action. That process involves prosecutors, statutes, judges, police officers, and penalties that interact, interpret legal norms, and work to internalize those norms into the value sets of citizens like ourselves.

But if we are willing to give that answer to the question "how is domestic law enforced?", why not similarly answer the question whether *international human rights* law is enforced? In this Lecture, I will argue that in much the same way, these international norms of international human rights law are underenforced, imperfectly enforced; but they *are* enforced through a complex, little-understood legal process that I call *transnational legal process*. As I have elaborated in other writing,[8] for shorthand purposes, transnational legal process can be thought of in three phases: the institutional *interaction* whereby global norms of international human rights law are debated, *interpreted*, and ultimately *internalized* by domestic legal systems. To claim that this complex transnational legal process of enforcing international human rights law via *interaction*, *interpretation*, and *internalization* exists is not to say that it always works or even that it works very well. As I will be the first to concede, this process works sporadically, and that we often most clearly see its spectacular failures, as in Cambodia, Bosnia, and Rwanda. But the process of enforcing international human rights law also sometimes has its successes, which gives us reason not to ignore that process, but to try to develop and nurture it. Just as doctors used early successes in addressing polio to push our understanding of how the prevention and healing process works, lawyers can try to globalize the lessons of human rights enforcement. So if the question is "how is international human rights enforced?", my short answer is through a transnational legal process of institutional *interaction*, *interpretation* of legal norms, and attempts to *internalize* those norms into domestic legal systems.

With that introduction, let me divide the balance of these remarks into two parts: First, how, in theory, does transnational legal process promote national obedience of international human rights law? Second, how does transnational legal process—this process that I call "interaction, interpretation and internalization"—work in real cases?

I. The Theory of Transnational Legal Process

The first question, why do nations obey international human rights law, is really a sub-set of a much broader question: why do nations obey international law of any kind? That timeless question, which has troubled thinkers over historical eras dating back to the Roman Empire, is the subject of a book I am writing, under the title

8. For fuller discussion of transnational legal process, see Harold Hongju Koh, *Transnational Legal Process*, 75 Neb. L. Rev. 181 (1996); Harold Hongju Koh, *The 1998 Frankel Lecture: Bringing International Law Home*, 35 Hous. L. Rev. 623 (1998) [hereinafter Koh, *Frankel Lecture*], and Harold Hongju Koh, *Why Do Nations Obey International Law?*, 106 Yale L.J. 2599 (1997) [hereinafter Koh, *Why Do Nations Obey International Law?*].

"Why Nations Obey?". My forthcoming book examines both the theoretical and the historical answers to that question.[9]

A. From Compliance to Obedience

Let us start by asking what it means to "obey" international law at all. Imagine four kinds of relationships between rules and conduct: coincidence, conformity, compliance, and obedience. For example, I have lived my whole life in the United States; but a few years ago, I took a sabbatical year in England. While there, I noticed that everybody drives on the left side of the road, as a matter of both practice and of law. Yet what is the relationship between the law and the observed practice?

One remote possibility is *coincidence*. It could be coincidence that the law is that everyone must drive on the left and that in practice everybody follows that norm. Yet coincidence might explain why one person follows a rule, but not why millions of people throughout the country do the same. That suggests a second possibility: *conformity*. If people know of the rule that you must drive on the left, they may well choose to conform their conduct to that rule when convenient; but feel no obligation to do so when inconvenient. (Perhaps some Scots, for example, swerve over and drive on the right, in remote unpopulated areas of the Hebrides). But, is there a third possibility, *compliance*? Perhaps people are both aware of the rule and accept the rule for a variety of external reasons, for example, to get specific rewards, to receive insurance benefits, or to avoid certain kinds of bad results, such as traffic tickets, or getting hit by an oncoming car. These are instrumental reasons why someone might decide to comply with a rule even if they felt no moral obligation to obey it. Finally, there is a fourth possibility, *obedience:* the notion that a person or an organization adopts the behavior that is prescribed by the rule because he or it has somehow internalized that rule and made it a part of their internal value system.

Notice that as we move down this scale from coincidence to conformity to compliance to obedience, we see an increase of what I will call "norm-internalization." As you move from grudgingly accepting a rule one time only to habitually obeying it, the rule transforms from being some kind of external sanction to becoming an internal imperative. We see this evolutionary process regularly in our daily lives: when you put on a bicycle helmet; when you snap on your seatbelt; when you recycle a tin can; when you do not smoke in the law school cafeteria. All of these are examples of people moving from conformity with a rule to compliance and gradually obedience, which is driven by a sense of an internalized norm. Over time, we also witness a rise in what one might call "normativity." If you see someone driving 100 mph, and then suddenly they see a police car and slow dramatically to 60 mph, you might say they are complying with; but not really obeying the speed limit. But, if one witnesses people routinely driving at the speed limit (without witnesses around), or routinely disposing of litter, or recycling without being told, we are seeing an *internalized normative form of behavior*—an

9. For the gist of both answers, see Koh, *Why Do Nations Obey International Law?*, *supra* note 8.

increase in normativity, if you will—which derives from the incorporation of external norms or values into a person's or organization's internal value set.

There is a further point as well: namely, that the most effective form of *law-enforcement* is not the imposition of external sanction, but the inculcation of internal obedience. Most traffic laws, litter laws, tax laws and the like are enforced primarily not by enforcement officers, but by the social internalization of norms of obedience! Indeed, enforcement is maximized when a norm is so widely obeyed that external sanctions become virtually unnecessary. As my Yale colleague Bob Ellickson has demonstrated, when everyone in a community follows certain social norms out of felt internal normativity, order can be maintained without rigid systems of external legal enforcement, because self-enforcement is both more effective and more efficient than third-party controls.[10] Social psychologists who study why individuals obey the law have reached the same conclusion.[11]

B. The Relationship Between Enforcement and Obedience

With this background, let us now turn to the question of how *international human rights law* is enforced, which is a subset of the larger question: why do nations obey international law of any kind? In earlier writing, I have suggested that, over time, five distinct explanations have emerged to answer the question "why nations obey?": *power*; *self-interest* or rational choice; *liberal explanations* based on rule-legitimacy or political identity; *communitarian explanations*; and *legal process explanations* at the state-to-state level (what I will call "horizontal" or "international legal process" explanations) and from the international-to-national level (what I will call "vertical" or "transnational legal process explanations").[12]

In their current form, each of these five approaches gives their own short answer to the question "how is international human rights law enforced?" Let me start with the realists, who date back to Thomas Hobbes, but include such modern-day theorists as George Kennan, Hans Morgenthau, and Henry Kissinger. To the question "why do nations obey international law?", their short answer is *power*: nations never truly "obey" international law, they only comply with it, because

---

10. *See* ROBERT C. ELLICKSON, ORDER WITHOUT LAW: HOW NEIGHBORS SETTLE DISPUTES 132 (1991) ("A person who has 'internalized' a social norm is by definition committed to self-enforcement of a rule . . . ."); *id.* at 126 n.8 (1991) ("Whatever the origin of self-enforced moral rules, there is broad agreement that the overall system of social control must depend vitally on achieving cooperation through self-enforcement."); Robert C. Ellickson, *Bringing Culture and Human Frailty to Rational Actors: A Critique of Classical Law and Economics*, 65 CHI.-KENT L. REV. 23, 44 (1989) (arguing that the primary system of social control is a "*first-party* system of social control that would operate without external enforcers") (emphasis in original).

11. *See, e.g.*, TOM R. TYLER, WHY PEOPLE OBEY THE LAW (1990) (concluding, after extensive empirical study, that people comply with law not so much because they fear punishment as because they feel that legal authorities are legitimate); *see also id.* at 4 (urging authorities who seek to promote voluntary compliance with laws to apply "[a] normative perspective [which] leads to a focus on people's internalized norms of justice and obligation," rather than "an instrumental perspective [which] regards compliance as a form of behavior occurring in response to external factors").

12. Both the historical and theoretical analysis are fleshed out in Koh, *Why Do Nations Obey International Law?*, *supra* note 8, from which this portion of the Lecture derives.

someone else makes them. Why, for example, why did Iraq ultimately respect the borders of Kuwait? In the end, because the other nations of the world came in and drove Saddam out! Under this view, nations can be coerced or bribed to follow certain rules, or even induced to bargain in the shadow of such incentives. But in the end, the critical factor is neither altruistic or normative, only the realist values of power and coercion.[13] Thus, the familiar power explanation traces back to Thucydides: the strong states do what they can, the weak states suffer what they must, but in the end there is no real "obedience" of international law, only such coincidence between national conduct and international rules that results from power and coercion.

There is a second, kinder and gentler explanation, based on the self-interest rationales favored by the vibrant school of "rational choice" theory.[14] Under this explanation, nations may choose rationally to follow certain global rules out of a sense of self-interest. After participating in game-theoretic discussions, to avoid multi-party prisoners' dilemma, nations may decide to cooperate around certain rules, which lead them to establish what international relations theorists call "regimes": governing arrangements in which certain governing norms, rules, and decisionmaking procedures come to predominate because the nations in their long-term self-interests have calculated that they should follow a presumption favoring compliance with such rules.

This "self- interest" rationale helps explains why, for example, complex global rules have emerged in a whole variety of international areas in which nations have established regimes structured around legal rules born of self-interested cooperation. In the contemporary era, for example, talented international relations scholars such as Robert Keohane, Duncan Snidal, and Oran Young have applied increasingly sophisticated rational choice techniques to argue for such an instrumental, interest-based view of international law. Recently, a number of legal scholars, most prominently Kenneth Abbott, Alan Sykes, and John Setear have espoused a similar, "rationalistic" legal vision. Under the rationalist account, participants in a given issue area will develop a set of governing arrangements, along with a set of expectations, rules, and decisionmaking procedures—in other words, a regime—both to restrain the participants and to provide means for achieving their common aims. Within these regimes, international law stabilizes expectations and promotes compliance by reducing transaction costs, providing dispute-resolution procedures, performing signaling functions, triggering negative responses, and promoting information disclosure.

---

13. The "power" rationale is captured in a famous joke often told about Henry Kissinger, who after he ceased to be the Secretary of State, reportedly went to work as a zoo keeper. After the first day, zoo patrons noticed an amazing phenomenon: that after all of these centuries, the lion was finally lying down with the lamb. The patrons ran excitedly to Dr. Kissinger, and asked, "How have you achieved this miraculous result?" The famous realist replied, "It's simple. A lamb a day!"

14. *See, e.g.*, Kenneth W. Abbott, *Modern International Relations Theory: A Prospectus for International Lawyers*, 14 YALE J. INT'L L. 335 (1989); Kenneth W. Abbott, *The Trading Nation's Dilemma: The Functions of the Law of International Trade*, 26 HARV. INT'L L.J. 501 (1985); Kenneth W. Abbott, *'Trust But Verify': The Production of Information in Arms Control Treaties and Other International Agreements*, 26 CORNELL INT'L L.J. 1 (1993).

Recently, more sophisticated instrumentalists have begun to disaggregate the state into its component parts, to introduce international institutions and transnational actors, to incorporate long-term self-interest, and to consider the issue within massively iterated multi-party games.[15] Subtler instrumentalists even recognize that global rules form part of the environment faced by a state and thus alter the incentives of domestic interest groups and organizations. But even so, their analysis remains thin.

The rationalists recognize *nonstate actors* as players in the transnational system, but too often ignore them because of the complexity their inclusion adds to their *game-theoretic* analysis. Nor do these analysts tell much of a domestic politics story, because they tend to operate largely at the horizontal level of the international system. Their chosen issue areas thus tend to be areas like trade and arms control, where nation-states remain the primary players and traditional realist assumptions still largely prevail. Such rationalistic, state-centric theories thus work less well, for example, in such areas as human rights, debt restructuring, or international commercial transactions, where nonstate actors abound, pursue multiple goals in complex nonzero-sum games, and interact repeatedly within institutions nested within broader informal regimes. Rationalists see law as regulating behavior by changing incentives, not altering interests or identities. The role of norms, in their view, is to reduce transactions costs in dynamic interactions among exogenously constituted actors. Shared norms, and the interactive processes by which those norms are interpreted, have little effect on state policies. In effect, they see international law as a kind of mechanical device, a switching mechanism, which facilitates the interactions of autonomous states, not as a communal decisionmaking structure that helps generate options, modify preferences, and build a normative interpretive community.

In short, my major complaint about the self-interest explanation is that it does not take account of what I consider to be an important factor—the "vertical" internalization of international norms into domestic legal systems. The rationalists' picture takes too little account of the internalizing, normative, or constitutive impact of participating in the transnational legal process. For the rationalists, the decision to obey the law remains perpetually calculated, never internally felt. Compliance always remains an instrumental computation, never an internalized normative imperative.[16]

This brings me to a third possible explanation for why international human rights laws are enforced, so-called "liberal" theories, which I divide into those scholars who follow principles of "rule legitimacy" and those who focus on national "political identity." Both sets of theorists derive their analysis from Immanuel Kant's pamphlet in 1795, *Perpetual Peace*. Rule-legitimacy theorists, led by Thomas Franck of NYU, argue that nations do feel some sort of internal "compliance pull" toward certain rules that they feel are legitimate; for example,

---

15. Duke's Robert Keohane is the leading exemplar of such a sophisticated approach. *See* Robert O. Keohane, *When Does International Law Come Home?*, 35 HOUS. L. REV. 699 (1998).

16. It would be as if every time you got into a car, you calculated *for the first time* whether or not to put on a seat belt or to stop for a red light, rather than relying upon internalized norms of obedience.

the rules against genocide or the rules favoring diplomatic immunity. When nations perceive that rules are legitimate, either because they meet some procedural standard of legitimacy or some substantive notion of due process or distributive justice, they will obey that rule because they are "normatively pulled" toward that rule by its legitimacy.[17]

In my view, this rule-legitimacy approach is problematic because it claims to draw its power from the legitimacy of rules themselves, rather than from communitarian and legal process pressures. In fact, most of us do not litter when others are watching, but not because the no-littering *rule* itself has such compliance pull, but because of a combination of internal impulse and felt peer pressure. In the same way, Franck's rule-legitimacy ends up being another way of saying that a state obeys a norm because it has been both internalized, and is being enforced by "communitarian peer pressure" (which, I will argue below, is really a form of transnational legal process).[18]

A second view, pressed strongly by other members of this liberal school, argues that whether or not nations comply with international law depends crucially on the extent to which their political identity is based on liberal democracy. This approach derives from a branch of international relations literature known as the "Democratic Peace" literature, pioneered by Michael Doyle of Princeton, my Yale colleague Bruce Russett, and many others who have sought to verify a basic tenet of Kant's writing that liberal democracies do not go to war with each other. The many adherents of this view include President Clinton, who in October of 1995 opined that promoting democracies that participate in the new global marketplace is the right thing to do because we know that these democracies are less likely to go to war.

Transposing this basic maxim to international law, several Harvard theorists, Anne-Marie Slaughter and Andrew Moravcsik, have flipped this maxim, arguing not so much that democracies do not fight each other, but rather, that democracies are more inclined to "do law" with one another. For these analysts, the key variable for whether a nation will or will not obey international law is whether they can be characterized as "liberal" in identity, i.e., having certain democratic attributes such as a form of representative government, civil and political rights, and an independent judicial system dedicated to the rule of law. Not surprisingly, many liberal scholars focus on European Union law, noting that the European system of human rights works because it is largely composed of liberal democracies, who share reasons for collective obedience. This helps explain why, for example, the embryonic African human rights system—a collection of democracies and authoritarian systems—does not work nearly as well.

What is troubling about this view is that it suggests that liberal states interact mainly in a zone of law, while liberal and illiberal states interact in a zone of politics. But in my view, any analysis that treats a state's identity as somehow

---

17. Franck calls this the "compliance pull" of particular international legal rules. *See generally* THOMAS M. FRANCK, THE POWER OF LEGITIMACY AMONG NATIONS (1990).

18. Franck defines rule-legitimacy as "a property of a rule which exerts a pull towards compliance on those addressed normatively, because they believe that the rule has come into being and operates in accordance with generally accepted principles of right process," that is, an internalized view of fair legal process. *Id.* at 24 (emphasis omitted).

exogenously or permanently given, is overly essentialist. National identities, like national interests, are socially constructed products of culture, ideology, learning, and knowledge. As we have witnessed, nations like South Africa, Nigeria, Indonesia, Poland, Argentina, Chile, and the Czech Republic are neither permanently liberal nor illiberal, but transition back and forth from dictatorship to democracy. As Laurence Whitehead has argued, democratization has powerful international dimensions, potentially spreading from one country to another by contagion, control, or consent.[19] Liberal identity analysis does not directly address the impact of compliance on democratization, and thus leaves unanswered a critical, constructivist question: to what extent does compliance with international law itself help *constitute the identity* of a state as law-abiding, and hence, as "liberal" or not? The notion that "only liberal states do law with one another" can be empirically falsified, particularly in such areas as international commercial law, where even rogue states like Libya tend to abide fastidiously by private international law rules on letters of credit without regard to whether they are representative democracies. Finally, like the "cultural relativist" argument in human rights, the claim that nonliberal states somehow do *not* participate in a zone of law denies the universalism of international law and effectively condones dealing with nonliberal states within a realist world of power politics.

In more recent writings, some liberal authors have revised their positions to say that they view liberal states not as actors, but as representative *agents* for various institutions and groups within civil society. These institutions and groups are more likely to engage in transborder cooperation with one another, thus predicting greater levels of transnational legal relations among liberal states. But if this is so, what it suggests is that the density of a state's *interactions* in the transnational legal process—not its label as liberal or illiberal—is the key to explaining its level of compliance with international law.

A fourth possible explanation—"communitarian" reasons—can be found in the English "International Society" school of International Relations, particularly in the work of Martin Wight and Hedley Bull, who traced their international origins back to the Dutch international law scholar Grotius. These theorists argue that nations obey international law because of the values of the international society of which they are a part. So, for example, the Czech Republic, Poland and Hungary now feel peer pressure to obey international law because of their community ties, now as NATO nations. The idea is that one's membership in a community helps to define how one views the obligations of that community. So, for example, when someone becomes a member of a church, they decide they will conduct their lives differently because they now view themselves as Catholic, Jewish, or Muslim. Similarly, under this view, the governments of Russia, Ukraine, and Turkey should all feel communitarian pressure to obey the European Convention on Human Rights—the "rules of their church"—because they have all now become members of the Council of Europe.

19. Laurence Whitehead, *Three International Dimensions of Democratization*, *in* THE INTERNATIONAL DIMENSIONS OF DEMOCRATIZATION 3, 5-22 (Laurence Whitehead ed., 1996) ("In the contemporary world, there is no such thing as democratization in one country, and perhaps there never was.").

Unlike a liberal approach, this communitarian, constructivist approach at least recognizes the *positive transformational effects* of a state's repeated participation in the legal process. At the same time, however, the approach gives too little study to the vertical "transmission belt" whereby the norms created by international society infiltrate into *domestic* society. The *existence* of international community may explain the *horizontal* pressures to compliance generated among nation-states on the global plane, but it does not clarify the *vertical process* whereby transnational actors interact in various fora, generate and interpret international norms, and then seek to internalize those norms domestically, as future determinants of why nations obey.

Fifth and finally, there are so-called "legal process" explanations for why nations obey international law. Let me distinguish here between what I call "international legal process" or horizontal reasons for compliance, which tend to function at a government-to-government level,[20] and the so-called "vertical" explanation, which focuses on the relationship between the international and the domestic legal systems. Suppose, for example, that the government of Canada wishes to urge Japan to join the global land mine treaty. Initially, the two governments will engage in government-to-government discussions at the "horizontal" nation-state level within an intergovernmental process organized by the United Nations. But at the same time, there is also a "vertical," transnational process whereby governments, intergovernmental organizations, nongovernmental organizations, and private citizens argue together about why nations should obey international human rights law. Through this vertical dynamic, international rules that are developed at a government-to-government level gradually work their way down and become internalized into domestic legal structure. Take, for example, recent legal enactments whereby global norms regarding genocide, war crimes, torture, and religious freedom have become internalized into American legal rules.

What I have just recounted is a very compressed version of a small bookshelf of political science and international law and literature. But my broader point, simply speaking, is that all five explanations—power, self-interest, liberal theories, communitarian theories, and legal process explanations—work together to help explain why nations obey international law. These five explanatory strands work together as complementary conceptual lenses to give a richer explanation of why compliance with international law does, or does not, occur in particular cases.

To clarify, let me ask the parallel question, how is domestic law enforced? What is the explanation, for example, for why we now buckle our seatbelts, even though nobody wore seatbelts only a quarter of a century ago? Of course, there are many reasons, but if you thought to explain the change in compliance, you probably would give a variety of explanations. If you organized those explanations in your own mind, they would likely fall under five headings: power or coercion, self-

---

20. The best exemplar of this international process view is ABRAM CHAYES & ANTONIA HANDLER CHAYES, THE NEW SOVEREIGNTY: COMPLIANCE WITH INTERNATIONAL REGULATORY AGREEMENTS (1995), which treats the primary instrument for maintaining compliance with treaties as "an *iterative process of discourse* among the parties, the treaty organization, and the wider public," *id.* at 4 (emphasis added).

interest, liberal theories, communitarian explanations, and legal process explanations.

Why do I now wear a seatbelt, when I never did before? First, because after the seatbelt rule issued, a lot of tickets were given out and I felt coerced to comply: a power explanation. A second factor: self-interest. People calculated that it is more rational to wear your seatbelt to avoid injury, sanction, or to gain insurance benefits. Third, the seatbelt rule acquired "rule-legitimacy" and over time developed a compliance pull. Over time, this became part of one's sense of personal identity. Individuals calculated: "If I am a law abiding person, I ought to obey the seatbelt laws." Partly, the rationale was communitarian. Authorities exhorted people with slogans such as "Seatbelts Save Lives." And fifth and finally, the seatbelt rule was inculcated via legal process. Seatbelts were required by state laws, required by federal highway standards; incorporated into federal automotive standards and became part of the way the automobiles were made. Now you cannot get into a car and drive without buckling your seatbelt without every bell and whistle and electronic voice in the car erupting into a cacophony of noise, making your life miserable until you buckle your seatbelt!

So in short, how are seatbelt laws enforced? Not by any one of these factors acting alone, but by all of them acting in combination. As we move through the five explanations—from power to legal process—we also move from external enforcement of legal rules to internal obedience with legal rules. True compliance is not so much the result of externally imposed sanctions so much as internally felt norms. In other words, as we move from external to internal factors, we also move from coercive to constitutive behavior. My children, who have been wholly socialized to wear seatbelts, have wholly internalized the norm. They view wearing seatbelts as an integral part of what it means to be a law-abiding person. As always, the best way to enforce legal norms is not to coerce action, not to impose sanctions, but to change the way that people think about themselves: whether as teetotalers, safe drivers, or regular taxpayers. In short, our prime way to enforce the law is to encourage people to bring rules home, to internalize rules inside themselves, to transform themselves from lawless into law-abiding individuals.

What does this have to do with international human rights law? I would argue that in the international arena, we are seeing the exact same process at work; a process by which norms and rules are generated and internalized and become internal rules, normative rules, and rules that constitute new nations. The best example we have is South Africa; a country which for many years was an outlaw, was subjected to tremendous external pressure and coercive mechanisms over a long period of time. Through a gradual process, South Africa has converted itself into a country that has undergone a fundamental political transformation. It has now reconstituted itself as a law-abiding country that through its constitutional processes has internalized new norms of international human rights law as domestic law.

In the same way, if the United States is attempting to encourage China to follow norms of international human rights law, the analysis above suggests the need to act at all five levels: at the level of power and coercion, to apply external and political sanctions; at the level of self-interest, to develop carrots that can be offered to China in terms of trade benefits or other kinds of economic incentives; at the level of liberal theory, to encourage Hong Kong's liberal legal identity to bubble up to the Beijing government; at the level of communitarian values, to seek to encourage

China to ratify the International Covenant on Civil and Political Rights and other multilateral communities of international human rights observance; and finally, from a legal process perspective, to seek to engage the Chinese people and groups in civil society in a variety of international interactions that will cause them to internalize norms of international human rights law. As with the seat belt example, our goal is not simply to coerce conduct. More fundamentally, we seek to encourage a change in the nature of the Chinese political identity to reconstitute China as a nation that abides by core norms of international human rights law. In short, a theory of transnational legal process seeks to enforce international norms by motivating nation-states to *obey* international human rights law—out of a sense of internal acceptance of international law—as opposed to merely conforming to or complying with specific international legal rules when the state finds it convenient.

II. How Is International Human Rights Law Enforced?

Against this background, how should we now understand the recent history of international human rights enforcement? Here let me contrast the two "process" stories, the one that everyone usually looks at and the one that I think people should look at. Let me contrast what I will call the horizontal story of enforcement with what I prefer: the vertical, transnational story of human rights enforcement.

A. The "Horizontal" Story

The conventional "horizontal" story about international human rights law enforcement is that international human rights law was born about fifty years ago, the product of the U.N. Charter, the Nuremberg and Tokyo war crimes trials, and the Universal Declaration of Human Rights. Under this view, the principal enforcers of human rights law have always been nation-states, who have always interacted with one another on an interstate, government-to-government level. The U.N. Charter introduced into this picture U.N. organizations and U.N. norms, which soon led to regional human rights systems as well: in Europe, the Strasbourg (Council of Europe) and Helsinki (Organization of Security and Cooperation in Europe) process; in the Americas, the Inter-American Commission and Court of Human Rights; and far less well developed regional human rights systems in Africa, the Middle East, and Asia.

In this post-war order, an international regime developed in which governments and inter-governmental organizations began to put pressure on each other—always at a horizontal, intergovernmental level—to comply with human rights, invoking such universal treaty norms as the international covenants on civil and political and economic, social and cultural rights. U.N. organizations, such as the U.N. Human Rights Commission, and treaty-based organizations, such as the U.N. Human Rights Committee, participated as intergovernmental actors in this horizontal international regime, which addressed all manner of global issues: worker rights, racial discrimination, the rights of children, women, and indigenous peoples. As we soon saw, the difficulties of this horizontal, state-to-state enforcement mechanism were legion: the rules were largely declaratory and precatory, and the few mechanisms created had virtually no enforcement. Occasionally new mechanisms would be created: judicial fora, such as the Yugoslav and Rwandan War Crimes Tribunal, or new executive actors, such as the U.N. High Commissioner on Human Rights, or new quasi-legislative fora, such as the Vienna Conference on Human Rights or the 1995 Beijing Women's Conference. Despite these occasional advances, the overall picture of this standard enforcement story is one of impotence, ineffectiveness, of a horizontal system where the key actors are nation-states and intergovernmental organizations, the key forums are governmental forums, and the key transactions are transactions between states and other states.

B. The "Vertical" Story

If one accepts the horizontal story as the entire picture of human rights enforcement, than the glass is indeed more than half empty. But what is the vertical picture? The "vertical" story of human rights enforcement, I would argue, is a much richer picture: one that focuses on a transnational legal process that includes a different set of actors, fora, and transactions. As I have recently argued in my Frankel Lecture, "Bringing International Law Home," the key agents in this transnational legal process are transnational norm entrepreneurs, governmental norm sponsors, transnational issue networks, interpretive communities and law-declaring fora, bureaucratic compliance procedures, and issue linkages among issue areas.[21]

Many efforts at human rights norm-internalization are begun not by nation-states, but by "transnational norm entrepreneurs," private transnational organizations or individuals who mobilize popular opinion and political support within their host country and abroad for the development of a universal human rights norm. Such norm entrepreneurs first became prominent in the nineteenth century, when activists such as Lord William Wilberforce and the British and Foreign Anti-Slavery Society pressed for treaties prohibiting the slave trade,[22] Jean-Henri Dunant founded the International Committee of the Red Cross,[23] and Christian peace activists, such as America's William Ladd and Elihu Burritt promoted public international arbitration and permanent international criminal courts.[24] Modern-day entrepreneurs have included individuals as diverse as Eleanor Roosevelt, Jesse Jackson, the Dalai Lama, Aung Sang Suu Kyi, and Princess Diana. These nongovernmental actors seek to develop *transnational issue networks*[25] to discuss and generate political solutions

21. *See* Koh, *Frankel Lecture*, *supra* note 8, at 647-70.

22. On the transnational work of Wilberforce and the British anti-slavery movement, see generally BETTY FLADELAND, MEN AND BROTHERS: ANGLO-AMERICAN ANTI-SLAVERY COOPERATION (1972), and Ethan A. Nadelmann, *Global Prohibition Regimes: The Evolution of Norms in International Society*, 44 INT'L ORG. 479, 495 (1990).

23. On the work of Dunant and the International Committee of the Red Cross, which spurred the Geneva Convention of 1864 and the Hague Convention of 1899 and the movement toward codified rules of conduct in warfare, see generally PIERRE BOISSIER, HISTORY OF THE INTERNATIONAL COMMITTEE OF THE RED CROSS: FROM SOLFERINO TO TSUSHIMA (1985), and MARTHA FINNEMORE, NATIONAL INTERESTS IN INTERNATIONAL SOCIETY 69-88 (1996).

24. On the work of Ladd and Burritt, see Mark W. Janis, *Protestants, Progress and Peace in the Influence of Religion*, *in* THE INFLUENCE OF RELIGION ON THE DEVELOPMENT OF INTERNATIONAL LAW 223 (Mark W. Janis ed., 1991).

25. *See* Kathryn Sikkink, *Human Rights, Principled Issue-Networks, and Sovereignty in Latin America*, 47 INT'L ORG. 411 (1993).

among concerned individuals at the domestic, regional and international levels, among government agencies, intergovernmental organizations, international and domestic, academics, and private foundations. Moreover, these norm entrepreneurs seek national government officials and bureaucracies concerned with the same issue areas and seek to enlist them as allies in their transnational cause. These *governmental norm sponsors*—for example, U.N. Human Rights Commissioner Mary Robinson, Presidents Oscar Arias of Costa Rica, Jimmy Carter of the United States, and the Pope, to take just a few prominent ones, use their official positions to promote normative positions. These transnational actors then seek governmental and nongovernmental fora competent to declare both general norms of international law (e.g., treaties) and *specific interpretation* of those norms in particular circumstances (e.g., particular interpretations of treaties and customary international law rules). Such law-declaring fora thus include treaty regimes; domestic, regional, and international courts; ad hoc tribunals; domestic and regional legislatures; executive entities; international publicists; and nongovernmental organizations: law-declaring fora that create an "interpretive community" that is capable of defining, elaborating and testing the definition of particular norms and their violation.[26]

The next vertical step is for national governments to internalize norm-interpretations issued by the global interpretive community into their domestic bureaucratic and political structures. Within national governments and intergovernmental organizations, for example, in-house lawyers and legal advisers acquire institutional mandates to ensure that the government's policies conform to international legal standards that have become imbedded in domestic law. Such institutional mandates to justify noncompliance with international legal norms may be found within the legal advising apparatus of national governments, in the Executive Branch, (e.g., the Legal Adviser's Office at the U.S. State Department), the legislature, as well as in intergovernmental organizations (e.g., the United Nations, the OAS, etc.).[27]

In the same way as corporations develop standard operating procedures to address new domestic mandates regarding corporate sentencing guidelines, occupational health and safety, and sexual harassment, domestic institutions adopt standard operating procedures, and other internal mechanisms to maintain habitual compliance with the internalized international norms. These institutions evolve in path-dependent routes that avoid conflict with the internalized norms.[28] Thus, over time, domestic decisionmaking structures become "enmeshed" with international

---

26. The norm with respect to the recent genocide in Bosnia, for example, has been interpreted before such law-declaring fora as the U.N. General Assembly, the U.N. Security Council, the International Court of Justice, the International Criminal Tribunal for the Former Yugoslavia and Rwanda; the International Court of Justice, numerous scholarly groups, human rights organizations, as well as both the Congress of the United States and a U.S. federal appellate court.

27. *See* Antonio Cassese, *The Role of Legal Advisers in Ensuring that Foreign Policy Conforms to International Legal Standards*, 14 MICH. J. INT'L L. 139 (1992); Robert C. Clark, *Why So Many Lawyers? Are They Good or Bad?*, 61 FORDHAM L. REV. 275, 282 (1992) (calling lawyers "specialists in normative ordering").

28. *See* Mark J. Roe, *Chaos and Evolution in Law and Economics*, 109 HARV. L. REV. 641, 643-44 (1996) (explaining path-dependence).

legal norms, so that institutional arrangements for the making and maintenance of an international commitment become entrenched in domestic legal and political processes.[29] Gradually, legal ideologies come to prevail among domestic decision-makers so that they seek to avoid perceptions that their actions will be perceived as domestically unlawful. Finally, strong process linkages exist across issue areas. Thus, when the United States adopts a twelve-mile limit in the ocean law area, for example, it is bound by it when dealing with refugees sailing toward U.S. shores.[30] Because international legal obligations tend to be closely interconnected, even a single deviation tends to lead noncompliant nations into vicious cycles of treaty violation. These institutional habits soon lead nations into default patterns of compliance. These patterns act like riverbeds, which channel conduct along compliant pathways. When a nation deviates from that pattern of presumptive compliance, frictions are created.

By so saying, I do not mean to suggest that international legal violations never occur. I merely suggest viewing human rights enforcement through vertical, "transnational legal process" lenses can help explain why in Louis Henkin's famous phrase, "almost all nations observe almost all principles of international law almost all of the time."[31] To avoid such frictions in its continuing interactions, a nation's bureaucracies or interest groups may press their leaders to shift over time from a policy of violation into one of compliance. Thus it is through this repeated cycle of interaction, interpretation, and internalization—this transnational legal process—that international law acquires its "stickiness," and that nations come to "obey" international human rights law out of a perceived self-interest that becomes institutional habit.

---

29. *See* Robert O. Keohane, ***Compliance with International Commitments: Politics Within a Framework of Law, International Law and International Relations Theory: Building Bridges***, 86 AM. SOC'Y INT'L L. PROC. 167, 179 (1992) (discussing "institutional enmeshment," which "occurs when domestic decision making with respect to an international commitment is affected by the institutional arrangements established in the course of making or maintaining the commitment").

30. For example, Presidential Proclamation 5928, which extended the U.S. territorial sea from three to twelve miles in breadth, has since been followed throughout the U.S. executive branch as if it were internal law, and has become the basis for binding, internal Coast Guard standard operating procedures. In May 1992, the United States adopted a policy of interdicting fleeing Haitians on the high seas and repatriating them summarily to Haiti, while bringing into the United States for exclusion proceedings those Haitians who entered territorial waters. In November 1992, the U.S. Coast Guard interdicted a boat containing fleeing Haitian refugees ten miles off the coast of Florida, and began making plans to repatriate the occupants. When the 1988 opinion of the Justice Department's Office of Legal Counsel was drawn to the Deputy Associate Attorney General's attention, the Coast Guard consulted with the State and Justice Departments and brought the boat into shore, rather than repatriating the occupants. *See* Harold Hongju Koh, ***Protecting the Office of Legal Counsel from Itself***, 15 CARDOZO L. REV. 513, 517-18 (1993).

31. LOUIS HENKIN, HOW NATIONS BEHAVE 47 (2d ed. 1979).

C. The Pattern Illustrated

By telling the vertical story of transnational legal enforcement, I am not saying that the "horizontal," international legal process picture is wrong. I am just saying it is incomplete. A state-to-state process account simply does not capture the full picture of how international human rights norms are currently generated, brought into domestic systems, and then brought back up to the international level. Take, for example, the recent international drive to limit the use of landmines, which began almost twenty years ago.[32] Despite the development and ratification of a treaty earlier this century banning the use of landmines against civilians, an international norm against the practice had not developed.

Instead, the key step toward a global ban on landmines was taken by non-governmental organizations in conjunction with the efforts of one U.S. senator. At the end of 1991, a group of nongovernmental activists met in Washington, D.C. and decided to create the International Campaign to Ban Landmines, which had the elimination of landmines as its goal.[33] The organization enlisted the support of a governmental norm entrepreneur, Sen. Patrick J. Leahy, who introduced a measure, passed by the Congress and signed by President Bush in 1992, which prohibited the export of landmines by the United States for one year.[34] Soon, the non-governmental organizations received the support of other transnational figures, including Pope John Paul II,[35] Princess Diana,[36] and the International Committee of the Red Cross. Frustrated with what they perceived to be a lack of progress toward a total ban through the U.N.-sponsored efforts, non-governmental organization and other countries created a new law-declaring forum, the so-called "Ottawa process," in the process enlisting another governmental sponsor, Canadian Foreign Minister Lloyd Axworthy. In the end, the Ottawa process reached agreement on the Convention on the Prohibition of the Use, Stockpiling, Production and Transfer of Anti-Personnel Mines and on Their Destruction,[37] which has now been signed by more than 120 countries. Although the United States initially declined to sign the Convention, the new regime prodded the United States to enact a moratorium on the sale of landmines, to develop new technologies to aid in mine detection and demining, and to increase the amount of money that it spends on these programs to at least $100 million per year.[38] The United States further committed itself to stop using all antipersonnel mines except in Korea by 2003, and to sign the

32. For a fuller account of this campaign, see Koh, *Frankel Lecture*, *supra* note 8, at 655-63.

33. *See* Raymond Bonner, *How a Group of Outsiders Moved Nations to Ban Land Mines*, N.Y. TIMES, Sept. 20, 1997, at A5.

34. *See id.*

35. *See id.*

36. *See, e.g.*, Roxanne Roberts, *From London, a Blitz with Glitz; Princess Diana Dazzles a Red Cross Benefit for Land Mine Victims*, WASH. POST, June 18, 1997, at D1. Princess Diana visited landmine victims in Angola and Bosnia in early 1997. *See* Raymond Bonner, *Pentagon Weighs Ending Opposition to a Ban on Mines*, N.Y. TIMES, Mar. 17, 1996, at A1.

37. Sept. 18, 1997, 36 I.L.M. 1507 (1997).

38. *See* Anthony DePalma, *Some See Opportunity in Global Push to Remove Land Mines*, N.Y. TIMES, Dec. 7, 1997, at A14.

treaty itself by the year 2006. Although it remains to be seen whether the Senate will soon ratify the Convention, the United States government may, within the next decade, *obey* the Convention by fully internalizing the Convention's norms into the governing practices of the U.S. government.

Note that under the vertical, transnational enforcement story that I have told, the central actors are not so much governmental entities as nongovernmental organizations and individuals. Today, modern transnational norm entrepreneurs include most of our recent Nobel Peace Prize winners: Burma's Aung San Suu Kyi, East Timor's Bishop Belo and Jose Ramos-Horta, Tibet's Dalai Lama, Britain's Amnesty International, and America's Martin Luther King, Jr. and Jody Williams of the Landmines Coalition. These are people who without governmental portfolio are able to transact a different kind of process, focusing at times on creating new forums to develop new international norms. Their focus is less on the horizontal process among nation states as upon what I call "vertical" or transnational process. Their effort is to try to bring human rights law home, by trying to internalize it into domestic systems through a process of interaction, interpretation, and internalization.

How, precisely, is this internalization accomplished? In earlier work, I have sought to distinguish among social, political and legal internalization:

- *Social internalization*, I argue, occurs when a norm acquires so much public legitimacy that there is widespread general adherence to it.
- *Political internalization* occurs when the political elites accept an international norm, and advocate its adoption as a matter of government policy.
- *Legal internalization* occurs when an international norm is incorporated into the domestic legal system through executive action, legislative action, judicial interpretation, or some combination of the three. Some legal systems establish their receptivity to internalization of international norms through constitutional law rules regarding the extent to which treaties are or are not self-executing and rules of customary international law are or are not automatically incorporated into domestic law.[39] Virtually all legal systems also have explicit mechanisms whereby executive, legislative, and judicial institutions may domesticate international norms. Thus, the landmines case exemplified the incorporation of an emerging norm of international law into U.S. law and policy largely through the *executive action* of the President and his agencies. *Legislative* internalization occurs when international law norms are embedded into constitutional norms or binding domestic legislation that officials of a noncomplying government must obey as part of the domestic legal fabric. *Judicial internalization* occurs when litigation in domestic courts provokes judicial incorporation of international law norms into domestic law, statutes, or constitutional norms.

The precise sequencing among political, legal, and social internalization, and among the different forms of legal internalization, will vary from case to case.

---

39. The national constitutions of Ireland, the Netherlands, and Italy, for example, refer to the recognition of international legal principles as a broad policy goal, thereby requiring policymakers to take account of foreign policy guidelines deriving from international law. *See* IRISH CONST. art. 29, § 3; GRONDWET [Constitution] [GRW. NED.] art. 90 (Netherlands); COSTITUZIONE [Constitution] [COST.] art. 10 (Italy).

Sometimes an international norm is socially internalized long before it is politically or legally internalized. Thus, for example, the United States was the moving force behind the drafting and signature of the Genocide Convention in 1948, but the U.S. Senate did not formally ratify the Convention and implement it as U.S. domestic law until November 1988, long after the norm against genocide had acquired widespread social legitimacy.[40] In other cases, *legal* norm-internalization prompted by a transnational legal process of interaction and internalization helps to trigger the process of political and social internalization of global norms. By domesticating international rules, transnational legal process thereby spurs internal acceptance of international human rights principles.

The process can be viewed as having four phases: interaction, interpretation, internalization, and obedience. One or more transnational actors provokes an *interaction* (or series of interactions) with another in a law-declaring forum, which forces an *interpretation* or enunciation of the global norm applicable to the situation. By so doing, the moving party seeks not simply to coerce the other party, but to *internalize* the new interpretation of the international norm into the other party's internal normative system. Its aim is to "bind" that other party to obey the interpretation as part of its internal value set. That party's perception that it now has an internal obligation to follow the international norm as it has been domestically interpreted leads it to step four: *obedience to* the newly interpreted norm.

Take, for example, the efforts of U.S. courts to define a U.S. law of torture under the Alien Tort Statute since *Filartiga v. Pena-Irala*.[41] The U.S. Senate has been traditionally reluctant to ratify human rights treaties, even though the U.S. Government was one of the primary drafters of these treaties in the postwar era. The Torture Convention, the Genocide Convention, and many others lay unratified by the U.S. government despite this initial input. In 1980, beginning with *Filartiga*, private U.S. human rights lawyers began to bring a series of domestic lawsuits against foreign violators to promote domestic judicial incorporation of the norm against torture under a little-known eighteenth century statute, the Alien Tort Statute. Over fifteen decades, a string of U.S. courts have ruled that torture is a violation not only of international law, but also of U.S. law. In the early 1990s, these legal internalizations of the norm against torture were cited as precedents for Congress to enact a Torture Victim Protection Act,[42] a statute whose drafting and enactment helped persuade skeptical officials of the Bush Administration to acquiesce in U.S. ratification of the U.N. Torture Convention. Once again, an international law norm trickled down, was internalized, and bubbled back up into new international law.

---

40. *See* Genocide Convention Implementation Act of 1987 (The Proxmire Act), Pub. L. No. 100-606, 102 Stat. 3045 (codified in 18 U.S.C. §§ 1091-1093 (1994)).

41. Filartiga v. Pena-Irala, 630 F.2d 876 (2d Cir. 1980) (holding that Paraguayan human rights victims may sue Paraguayan official under Alien Tort Statute, 28 U.S.C. § 1350 (1994), in U.S. court for civil damages arising from official torture). For a theoretical analysis of this line of doctrine, see Harold Hongju Koh, *Transnational Public Law Litigation*, 100 YALE L.J. 2347 (1991).

42. Pub. L. No. 102-256, 106 Stat. 73 (1992) (codified at 28 U.S.C. § 1350 (1994)).

In the United Kingdom, the issue of legislative internalization has similarly been brought to the forefront in recent years by the election of the Labour party, which promised, if elected, to incorporate the European Convention on Human Rights into United Kingdom law. This issue has been a major human rights issue in British politics since the Clement Attlee Government first ratified the Convention in the early 1950's. Since then, the Convention has been internalized in part through judicial construction. When total judicial incorporation efforts failed, a political internalization movement arose, which at this writing will shortly bring about *legal* internalization of the European Convention into U.K. law by an act of Parliament.[43]

Or, take finally the cases of the Haitian and Cuban boat people, in which my students and I were involved for several years. The United States had signed and ratified the Refugee Convention of 1951,[44] a multilateral treaty at the "horizontal" level whereby it agreed not to return refugees to their persecutors. But when the Haitian refugees began fleeing to the United States in 1991, it effectively reneged on that commitment and began to return the refugees, claiming that the Refugee Convention did not bar extraterritorial repatriations. In fact, Congress had passed a statute as part of the Immigration and Nationality Act which required unequivocally that refugees not be returned to their persecutors, thus ostensibly internalizing the treaty into domestic statute. And so on behalf of the Haitian refugees my students and I brought a lawsuit in which we argued that the courts should enforce the extraterritorial nonreturn rule as a matter of U.S. domestic law. We used a "judicialization strategy" to try to reinforce the concept of legal internalization of the international norm against extraterritorial repatriations.

In the end, the Supreme Court rejected our arguments, leaving the United States legally free to continue the extraterritorial return policy.[45] But other international forums, such as the U.N. High Commission on Refugees, the Inter-American Commission on Human Rights, and other bodies began to condemn the U.S. action. Various legislative efforts were made to overturn the Supreme Court's ruling, and

---

43. The debate over incorporation of the European Human Rights Convention is the subject of a voluminous literature. For a political history of the incorporation effort, see generally MICHAEL ZANDER, A BILL OF RIGHTS? (4th ed. 1997). For a comparative study, see ANDREW Z. DRZEMCZEWSKI, EUROPEAN HUMAN RIGHTS CONVENTION IN DOMESTIC LAW: A COMPARATIVE STUDY 177-87 (1983); ASPECTS OF INCORPORATION OF THE EUROPEAN CONVENTION OF HUMAN RIGHTS INTO DOMESTIC LAW (J.P. Gardner ed., 1993); Jorg Polakiewicz & Valerie Jacob-Foltzer, *The European Human Rights Convention in Domestic Law*, 12 HUM. RTS. J. 65, 65-85, 125-42 (1991). For discussion of compliance without incorporation, see DAVID KINLEY, THE EUROPEAN CONVENTION ON HUMAN RIGHTS: COMPLIANCE WITHOUT INCORPORATION (1993). *See also* 8(2) HALSBURY'S LAWS OF ENGLAND (4th ed. 1996) (including human rights law as part of constitutional law). For bills urging incorporation, see Human Rights Bill, *as approved by the House of Lords*, 577 PARL. DEB., H.L. (5th Ser.) 1726 (1997). For arguments as to why the Convention should be incorporated, see generally HUMAN RIGHTS IN THE UNITED KINGDOM (Richard Gordon & Richard Wilmot-Smith eds., 1996); Hon. Sir John Laws, *Is the High Court the Guardian of Fundamental Constitutional Rights?*, 1992 PUB. L. 59; Lord Lester, *The Mouse that Roared: The Human Rights Bill 1995*, 1995 PUB. L. 198; Rt. Hon. Lord Browne-Wilkinson, *The Infiltration of a Bill of Rights*, 1992 PUB. L. 397.

44. Convention Relating to the Status of Refugees, July 28, 1951, 19 U.S.T. 6259, 189 U.N.T.S. 137.

45. For analysis of the opinions, see Clawson et al, *supra* note 6.

the issue later became the subject of domestic political pressure from the African-American community, the Congressional Black Caucus, and Trans-Africa, all of whom began to promote the notion of a safe haven for Haitian refugees. Finally, in the fall of 1994, the U.S. government changed its Haitian policy, and intervened to return the refugees. When the issue arose again the following year, with regard to fleeing Cuban refugees, the Administration first resisted, then ultimately admitted into the United States those Cuban refugees being detained at offshore refugee camps. Although the U.S. stated policy remains problematic, at this writing, the actual practice of the U.S. government has moved into greater compliance with international law.

III. CONCLUSION

Let me close with two thoughts. First, the foregoing analysis teaches something about our duty, as citizens, to participate in transnational legal process. It is sometimes said that someone who, by acquiring medical training, comes to understand the human body acquires as well a moral duty not just to observe disease, but to try to cure it. In the same way, I would argue, a lawyer who acquires knowledge of the body politic acquires a duty not simply to observe transnational legal process, but to try to influence it. Once one comes to understand the process by which international human rights norms can be generated and internalized into domestic legal systems, one acquires a concomitant duty, I believe, to try to influence that process, to try to change the feelings of that body politic to promote greater obedience with international human rights norms.

In that effort, every citizen counts. To this, many Americans might say, "What can one person really do? Isn't such influence beyond the capacity of any one person?" But if you look at these people I have mentioned in this lecture—Aung Sun Suu Kyi, Jody Williams, Nelson Mandela, Martin Luther King Jr.—could they have not said the same thing? In response, many students might say: "But surely, I am not such a world historical figure," to which I would answer, "You don't need to be a Nobel Prize winner to make a difference. Just look at Rosa Parks, or Linda Brown, or Fred Korematsu, ordinary people who simply said that they would not go to the back of the bus, or attend a segregated school, or live in a Japanese internment camp." In short, we need look no further than those individuals who have triggered these legal processes in our own lifetime to promote the enforcement of human rights norms.

The struggle of these individuals reminds us again of the remarkable words of Robert Kennedy, which are etched on his grave in Arlington Cemetery:

> Each time a man stands up for an ideal, or acts to improve the lot of others, or strikes out against injustice, he sends forth a tiny ripple of hope, and crossing each other from a million different centers of energy and daring, those ripples build a current that can sweep down the mightiest walls of oppression and resistance.

What he is talking about, in the end, is the need for individuals to activate transnational legal process. As proof that what he says is indeed possible, one need look only at the country in which he said those words: South Africa, in 1966, a country which only three decades later has now been totally transformed by international human rights law.

So, in closing, if my question is "how is international human rights law enforced?", my answer is simple. International human rights law is enforced, I would say, not just by nation-states, not just by government officials, not just by world historical figures, but by people like us, by people with the courage and commitment to bring international human rights law home through a transnational legal process of interaction, interpretation, and internalization.[46] Thank you very much.

46. Author's note: Since I wrote these words, my life has fundamentally changed. In November 1998, I took an oath as our nation's chief human rights official. At this writing, I have now spent eight months in office, traveling to some twenty-five countries. As I have traveled from Belgrade to Beijing, Colombia to Kosovo, I have become increasingly convinced of the correctness of the basic thesis I have expressed in this Lecture. Although I now spend my time as a "governmental norm sponsor," rather than as a private "transnational norm entrepreneur," I continue to witness, and to attempt to influence, the transnational legal process described herein. I look forward to returning to academic life before too long, not only to finish my book manuscript on "Why Nations Obey," but also to illustrate my basic thesis with reference to my governmental experiences in Kosovo, China, Colombia, Indonesia, and elsewhere.

[8]

Toward a Theory of Effective Supranational Adjudication

Laurence R. Helfer†
Anne-Marie Slaughter††

CONTENTS

---

† Associate Professor of Law, Loyola Law School, Los Angeles.

†† J. Sinclair Armstrong Professor of International, Foreign, and Comparative Law, Harvard Law School. We are grateful to Amanda Frost, Stephen Frug, Stuart Grider, Amir Licht, Sharon Kasok, Miriam Porter, Tamar Shapiro, and Tim Wu for research assistance. Lyonette Louis-Jacques, Foreign and International Law Reference Librarian at the University of Chicago School of Law, and Stephen Wiles of the International Legal Studies Library at Harvard Law School were also indefatigable in tracking down sources. Joseph H.H. Weiler provided inspiration and encouragement at a critical point. We also wish to thank Robert Wintemute for comments on an earlier draft and Martha Minow and Henry Steiner for particularly helpful comments at a Harvard Law School faculty lunch.

Supranational adjudication in Europe is a remarkable and surprising success. Over the past few decades, it has become increasingly clear that the European Court of Justice (ECJ) and the European Court of Human Rights (ECHR) have convinced national governments, individual litigants, and the European public to endorse and participate in frequent and often high-stakes adjudication at a level above the nation-state. Both tribunals began their existence as creatures of classic public international law, established by treaties—the Treaty of Rome[1] and the European Convention for the Protection of Human Rights and Fundamental Freedoms (the Convention)[2]—and perched atop national governments and national law with no direct relationship to either.[3] Somehow, however, through a combination of perspicacity, foresight, and tenacity, both tribunals developed successful strategies to make their judgments as effective, for the most part, as national court rulings.[4]

The central question motivating this Article is whether the success of supranational adjudication in Europe can be translated or transplanted to other regions of the globe. Alleged obstacles are easy to find.[5] The nations of Western Europe that form the core of the European Union and the Council of Europe are established liberal democracies with strong domestic traditions of the rule of law.[6] They also share a common core of social, political, and legal values that European jurists themselves have linked to the effectiveness of the two tribunals.[7] Their hopes for economic integration and their determination

1. TREATY ESTABLISHING THE EUROPEAN ECONOMIC COMMUNITY, Mar. 25, 1957, 298 U.N.T.S. 11 (1958) [hereinafter TREATY OF ROME].

2. Nov. 4, 1950, 213 U.N.T.S. 222 [hereinafter Convention].

3. Both European tribunals were originally established as "international" tribunals in the sense that they were created by intergovernmental agreements and charged with interpreting and applying those agreements as international law. The impact of their decisions on domestic law was intended to be a function of the actions of the states party to those agreements.

4. *See infra* Sections II.A-B (discussing compliance with ECJ and ECHR rulings).

5. For example, Jost Delbrueck argues:

> [T]he regional experience of today is of such a particular nature, made in more or less culturally and politically homogeneous regions, that it hardly could be taken as a model that could be easily transferred elsewhere and that could thereby possibly make a universal approach to the implementation of human rights obsolete.

Jost Delbrueck, *International Protection of Human Rights and State Sovereignty*, 57 IND. L.J. 567, 576 (1982).

6. *See* Michael W. Doyle, *An International Liberal Community*, *in* RETHINKING AMERICA'S SECURITY: BEYOND COLD WAR TO NEW WORLD ORDER 307, 329-31 (Graham T. Allison & Gregory F. Treverton eds., 1992); Michael W. Doyle, *Kant, Liberal Legacies, and Foreign Affairs*, 12 PHIL. & PUB. AFF. 205, 206-09 (1986) [hereinafter Doyle, *Foreign Affairs*]. Doyle defines liberal democracies as having four major characteristics: (1) protection of private property; (2) a market economy; (3) equality under the law and respect for human rights; and (4) a representative government deriving its authority from the consent of individuals. *See* Doyle, *Foreign Affairs*, *supra*, at 206-09.

7. As Judge Rudolf Bernhardt of the ECHR states:

> The main reason for the effectiveness of the European Convention and the Court is the considerable measures of homogeneity among European states. The member states of the Council of Europe and the parties to the Convention have recognized that the interpretation and the application of the European Convention can contribute to uniform European standards. . . . [T]here is a feeling among the member states that there exists a common European standard and that this standard should be further developed.

to safeguard basic human rights were rooted in the searing experience of two world wars. These conditions do not hold for the global community of nations;[8] they may well be absent even for geographically linked nations in other regions.[9]

Yet, what impact, if any, do these factors have on successful supranational adjudication? We suggest that a critical component of the ECJ's and the ECHR's success is the distinctive nature of their jurisdiction. Although both tribunals have the power to adjudicate state-to-state disputes—the province of traditional international adjudication—each has compiled a more successful compliance record in cases involving private parties litigating directly against state governments or against each other. We define adjudication of these cases as supranational adjudication and jurisdiction over these categories of cases as supranational jurisdiction. The provisions for such jurisdiction in the founding documents of both tribunals provide a point of departure for penetrating the surface of the state, allowing the tribunals to interact directly with the principal players in national legal systems.[10] Further, stripping the state of its unitary facade creates the possibility of direct relationships between the tribunals and different governmental institutions such as courts, administrative agencies, and legislative committees. The result, at least in Europe, has been the emergence of a "community of law": a partially insulated sphere in which legal actors interact based on common interests and values, protected from direct political interference.

The simple provision of supranational jurisdiction, however, is not a guarantee of effective adjudication. We contend that the European tribunals have been at least the partial architects of their own success and that their experience can form the basis of a potentially universalizable model. What is needed is an actual theory of effective supranational adjudication, an effort to isolate the various factors that have contributed to the European success story and to identify those that can be replicated beyond Europe. Developing such

---

Rudolf Bernhardt, *Commentary: The European System*, 2 CONN. J. INT'L L. 299, 299-300 (1987); *see also* Henry G. Schermers, *International Human Rights in the European Community and in the Nations of Central and Eastern Europe: An Overview*, 8 CONN. J. INT'L L. 313, 319 (1993) ("In the internal debates in the [ECHR] the legal approach to problems by the different members is very similar. Ideas about issues like a fair trial, a reasonable time, or the protection of private life are very much the same amongst all lawyers in Western Europe.").

8. *Cf.* Rosalyn Higgins, *The United Nations: Still a Force for Peace*, 52 MOD. L. REV. 1, 8 (1989) ("What may be an appropriate and sensitive interpretation for the Western European democracies is not necessarily so for a global system embracing highly diverse political and economic systems.").

9. *See* Andrew Moravcsik, *Explaining International Human Rights Regimes: Liberal Theory and Western Europe*, 1 EUR. J. INT'L REL. 157, 159, 178-80 (1995) (examining conditions under which effective human rights regimes are likely to emerge and concluding that the relative success of the European regime is best explained by factors internal to the countries concerned).

10. The ECJ has a direct link to individual citizens through the Article 177 provision of the Treaty of Rome, allowing national courts to refer cases brought by individuals to the ECJ in cases involving questions of European Community law. *See* TREATY OF ROME art. 177. The ECHR has such a link through the right of individual petition first to the European Commission of Human Rights (the Commission) and then through the Commission to the Court. *See, e.g.*, *infra* Subsection III.B.2.a.

a theory first requires defining "effective" supranational adjudication as precisely as possible. We define effective adjudication in terms of a court's basic ability to compel or cajole compliance with its judgments. In the supranational context, effective adjudication depends on a supranational tribunal's ability to secure such compliance by convincing domestic government institutions, directly and through pressure from private litigants, to use their power on its behalf.

The next step is to distill the factors that observers of and participants in ECJ and ECHR adjudication have identified as common elements in the two tribunals' success.[11] We organize these factors into a "checklist" of effective supranational adjudication, categorizing and ranking them in rough order of their presumed importance. We make no effort to test these factors systematically, a process that would require expanding the range of tribunals examined, ensuring variation in their relative performance, and controlling across factors. We instead offer the checklist primarily as a distillation of current knowledge and as a starting point for further research into these and other tribunals.

Even as a preliminary effort, however, the checklist should prove a useful tool for at least a rough assessment of the effectiveness of other supranational tribunals relative to the ECJ and the ECHR. States around the world have increasingly recognized the right of private parties to bring claims against them before supranational tribunals and adjudicatory bodies.[12] This trend is

11. By focusing on the ECHR, we do not mean to exclude the abundant decisional law of the Commission, a quasi-judicial tribunal that screens claims by individuals before they may be appealed to the court. Under a revision to the European Convention expected to take effect in the next one to two years, however, the Commission will be abolished and will be replaced by a permanent court that, for the first time, individuals can access directly. *See infra* notes 92-98 and accompanying text (discussing the structure of claims under the European Convention and Protocol No. 11).

12. United Nations treaty bodies that are authorized to hear claims against governments by private parties include the Human Rights Committee, the Committee on the Elimination of Race Discrimination, and the Committee Against Torture. *See generally* Andrew Byrnes, *The Committee Against Torture*, *in* THE UNITED NATIONS AND HUMAN RIGHTS 509 (Philip Alston ed., 1992); Karl Joseph Partsch, *The Committee on the Elimination of Racial Discrimination*, *in* THE UNITED NATIONS AND HUMAN RIGHTS, *supra*, at 339; *infra* Part IV (discussing the Human Rights Committee). The Committee on the Elimination of All Forms of Discrimination Against Women cannot as yet receive communications from individuals but has recommended that an optional protocol to the Convention on the Elimination of All Forms of Discrimination Against Women be drafted. *See* Andrew Byrnes & Jane Conners, *The Adoption of a Petition Procedure Under the Convention on the Elimination of All Forms of Discrimination Against Women*, 21 BROOK. J. INT'L L. 679 (1996).

Under Chapters 11 and 19 of the North American Free Trade Agreement (NAFTA), private parties may seek review from supranational panels to resolve investment-related and antidumping disputes with foreign national governments and administrative agencies. *See* David Lopez, *Dispute Resolution Under NAFTA: Lessons from the Early Experience*, 32 TEX. INT'L L.J. 163, 173-84 (1997); Alexandra Maravel, *Constructing Democracy in the North American Free Trade Area*, 16 J. INT'L BUS. 331, 334-45 (1996). Similar, although not identical, review was available under the Canada-United States Free Trade Agreement. *See* Jonathan T. Fried, *Two Paradigms for the Rule of International Trade Law*, 20 CAN.-U.S. L.J. 39, 47-49 (1994); Andreas F. Lowenfeld, *Binational Dispute Under Chapter 19 of the Canada-United States Free Trade Agreement: An Interim Appraisal*, 24 N.Y.U. J. INT'L L. & POL. 269 (1993).

The ad hoc panels and the standing appellate body recently established within the World Trade Organization (WTO) may currently entertain trade and trade-related disputes only between governments,

particularly evident in international human rights law.[13] Human rights law is a particularly suitable area for testing the generalizability of the European experience with supranational adjudication because the global and regional human rights regimes protect common legal norms that, on the whole, are grounded upon identical or substantially similar treaty texts.[14]

We thus proceed in the second half of the Article to apply the checklist to the United Nations Human Rights Committee (the Committee or the UNHRC), an eighteen-member panel of experts that issues nonbinding "views" indicating whether a state has violated the International Covenant on Civil and Political Rights (ICCPR or the Covenant).[15] Under the First Optional Protocol to the Covenant (the Optional Protocol),[16] states parties may authorize individuals alleging human rights violations to file complaints against the states directly with the Committee. Since its first meeting in 1977, the Committee has established, through a slow accretion of case law, a more precise understanding of global human rights norms in a variety of complex factual settings.

Although the Committee is the most active global counterpart to the European human rights tribunals, its work is far less well-known to scholars, litigants, and human rights activists, and its success as a supranational

---

but commentators have already argued in favor of granting standing to private and other nongovernmental parties. *See* G. Richard Shell, *Trade Legalism and International Relations Theory: An Analysis of the World Trade Organization*, 44 DUKE L.J. 829, 911-22 (1995); Glen T. Schleyer, Note, *Power to the People: Allowing Private Parties To Raise Claims Before the WTO Dispute Resolution System*, 65 FORDHAM L. REV. 2275 (1997).

13. For the purposes of this Article, we have limited our focus to the civil and political liberties that comprise the "first generation" of international human rights. It is only for this category of rights that states have developed complaint procedures permitting individuals to seek review of governmental practices before impartial international tribunals and review bodies. Even in Europe, "second" and "third" generation human rights, which include social, economic, cultural, development, and group-based rights, *see* Brenda Cossman, *Reform, Revolution, or Retrenchment? International Human Rights in the Post-Cold War Era*, 32 HARV. INT'L L.J. 339, 344 & n.18 (1991), have not yet become subject to even a limited form of supranational adjudication. *See* Protocol Amending the European Social Charter Providing for a System of Collective Complaints, *opened for signature* Nov. 9, 1995, Europ. T.S. No. 158, 34 I.L.M. 1453. As of June 1997, this protocol had been ratified by only two states and had not yet entered into force. *See* COUNCIL OF EUROPE, CHART OF SIGNATURES AND RATIFICATIONS OF EUROPEAN TREATIES, JUNE 6, 1997 UPDATE [hereinafter CHART OF SIGNATURES 1997].

14. *See infra* Section V.C (comparing rights protected by the International Covenant on Civil and Political Rights to those protected by the European Convention).

15. International Covenant on Civil and Political Rights and Optional Protocol, *adopted* Dec. 16, 1966, G.A. Res. 2200, U.N. GAOR, 21st Sess., Supp. No. 16, at 52, 59, U.N. Doc. A/6316 (1966), 999 U.N.T.S. 171, 301 (1967) (entered into force Mar. 23, 1976) [hereinafter Covenant and Optional Protocol, respectively]. The Covenant is also known as one part of the "International Bill of Rights." *See* THE INTERNATIONAL BILL OF RIGHTS: THE COVENANT ON CIVIL AND POLITICAL RIGHTS (Louis Henkin ed., 1981) [hereinafter THE INTERNATIONAL BILL OF RIGHTS]; *cf.* MANFRED NOWAK, U.N. COVENANT ON CIVIL AND POLITICAL RIGHTS: CCPR COMMENTARY at xvii (1993) (referring to the Universal Declaration of Human Rights, the Covenant on Civil and Political Rights, and the Covenant on Economic, Social and Cultural Rights as the "International Bill of Human Rights"). As of April 1997, 136 states had ratified the Covenant, and 86 states had ratified the Optional Protocol. *See* UNITED NATIONS, ECONOMIC AND SOCIAL COUNCIL, HUMAN RIGHTS COMMITTEE, PRESS RELEASE: HUMAN RIGHTS COMMITTEE CONCLUDES THREE-WEEK HEADQUARTERS SESSION, U.N. Doc. HR/CT/494 (1997) [hereinafter HUMAN RIGHTS COMMITTEE PRESS RELEASE].

16. Optional Protocol, *supra* note 15.

institution (including the record of compliance with its decisions) is far less certain.[17] Recently, however, the Committee's activities have sparked renewed interest.[18] Emboldened by the success of regional regimes, by the end of the Cold War and the rise of fledgling democracies in Eastern Europe, and by several recent high-profile cases, commentators have begun to explore whether a legally binding individual complaint procedure can be replicated at the global level. Some of their proposals have focused on creating new institutions,[19] and others have considered whether the Optional Protocol should be amended to permit the Committee to issue legally binding opinions similar to the judgments of the ECHR.[20]

Measuring the Committee's performance against the various factors enunciated in the checklist reveals an important trend: In numerous and diverse ways, the Committee, even without the power to issue legally binding judgments, is behaving more and more like a court. Although by no means a court in the formal sense and lacking many of the institutional characteristics possessed by the ECJ and the ECHR, the Committee has, within the limits of

17. *See* HENRY J. STEINER & PHILIP ALSTON, INTERNATIONAL HUMAN RIGHTS IN CONTEXT: LAW, POLITICS, MORALS 550 (1996) ("The record of compliance by states with views rendered by the Committee under the Optional Protocol is patchy."); TOM ZWART, THE ADMISSIBILITY OF HUMAN RIGHTS PETITIONS 22 (1994) (noting that prior to 1990 the UNHRC "received a growing number of complaints from victims stating that no appropriate remedy had been provided by the State party concerned" and that as a result the Committee adopted new procedures to monitor compliance with its views); *see also* DOMINIC MCGOLDRICK, THE HUMAN RIGHTS COMMITTEE 504 (1991) ("It is very difficult to provide positive evidence that the existence of the Covenant and the work of the HRC is having any concrete and positive effect on the human rights position in the States parties."); Torkel Opsahl, *The Human Rights Committee*, *in* THE UNITED NATIONS AND HUMAN RIGHTS, *supra* note 12, at 369, 437 (identifying "the absence of direct and effective fact-finding" as a "basic weakness in the system" and linking such absence to the ineffectiveness of the UNHRC). McGoldrick goes on to urge that the Committee document carefully all instances of compliance. *See* MCGOLDRICK, *supra*, at 504.

18. *See* Manfred Nowak, *The Activities of the UN-Human Rights Committee: Developments from 1 August 1989 Through 31 July 1992*, 14 HUM. RTS. L.J. 9, 10 (1993) [hereinafter Nowak, *UNHRC Activities*] ("The growing importance of human rights in general and of the Covenant in particular is . . . reflected by a steady expansion of the legal literature on this subject." (emphasis omitted)); Manfred Nowak, *UN-Human Rights Committee: Survey of Decisions Given up till July 1989*, 11 HUM. RTS. L.J. 139, 152 (1990) ("The comparably high number of communications against Western industrialized countries shows that lawyers are increasingly aware of this individual communication procedure being available in addition to or as an alternative to the one under the European Convention on Human Rights.").

19. In a recent law review article, for example, John Barton and Barry Carter suggest that the United States should "push[] for a global umbrella organization comprised of all those democracies willing to submit themselves to the type of international judicial human rights review now available in Europe." John H. Barton & Barry E. Carter, *International Law and Institutions for a New Age*, 81 GEO. L.J. 535, 557 (1993). The key feature of such an organization, they argue, is that the human rights protections it provides "should be important and strict; countries should only be allowed to join if they are willing to accept formal legal surveillance, and there should be an effective enforcement mechanism that allows individuals to initiate cases and to have at least a role in pursuing their case." *Id.*

20. *See* Markus G. Schmidt, *Individual Human Rights Complaints Procedures Based on United Nations Treaties and the Need for Reform*, 41 INT'L & COMP. L.Q. 645, 650 & n.17 (1992); *see also* Thomas Buergenthal, *International Human Rights Law and Institutions*, 63 WASH. L. REV. 1, 13 (1988) (noting the weak powers of the Committee but stressing the importance of "pushing for impartial international human rights institutions with judicial and quasi-judicial powers"). *But see* Nisuke Ando, *The Future of Monitoring Bodies—Limitations and Possibilities of the Human Rights Committee*, 1991-1992 CAN. HUM. RTS. Y.B. 169, 172 (arguing that it may be premature to expect states parties to authorize the Committee to issue legally binding decisions).

its powers, followed an increasingly judicial method of operation. Its efforts to enhance its effectiveness as a supranational tribunal will remain handicapped by a number of factors on the checklist that are either within the control of the states party to the Covenant or inherent in the universal scope of its jurisdiction; nevertheless, it is moving in the right direction with respect to the factors within its control.

We conclude by proposing a strategy whereby the UNHRC could enhance its effectiveness further by helping to construct a global community of law. We recommend that Committee members engage in an active dialogue with the ECHR and the European Commission of Human Rights (the Commission) as the first step toward a broader effort to increase communication with both national and supranational courts and tribunals over the interpretation and evolution of human rights norms. In particular, we propose that the Committee adopt a policy of thoughtful convergence with European jurisprudence, supplemented by informed divergence from that jurisprudence based on specific and articulated reasons.

Part I discusses effective domestic adjudication, distinguishes between international and supranational adjudication, and defines effective supranational adjudication. Part II recounts the "story of Europe," summarizing the successes achieved by the ECJ and the ECHR over the last forty years and focusing on the methods used by both tribunals to build a constituency among the individuals, lawyers, interest groups, and national courts that refer cases to them. Part III develops the checklist, dividing factors into those within the control of states responsible for establishing a supranational tribunal, those within the control of the tribunal itself, and those that are arguably beyond the control of either. Part IV applies the checklist to the recent practice and procedure of the UNHRC. Finally, Part V elaborates the principal elements of a community of law as it has evolved in Europe. It also describes the recent increase in communication and interaction among national and supranational courts and tribunals that could mark the beginnings of a global community of law. This final part also outlines our proposal for structured interaction between the UNHRC and its European counterparts.

Taken as a whole, this Article seeks to contribute to the existing literature along three different dimensions. First, we hope that the preliminary model of effective supranational adjudication developed here will spur the gathering of additional data from the experience of other supranational tribunals, tribunals concerned with diverse substantive areas of the law and exercising jurisdiction over many different groups of countries. At a time when the right of individual petition is spreading rapidly, both to other human rights tribunals and to various entities charged with resolving trade-related disputes, efforts to develop such a model are both timely and important. Second, we use our model to develop a concrete proposal for improving the effectiveness of the UNHRC and thus to strengthen hopes for proceeding simultaneously along regional and universal tracks to strengthen the global protection of human rights. Third, we develop the concept of a global community of law, constituted not by a world court but rather by overlapping networks of national, regional, and global tribunals. By communicating with one another in a form of collective deliberation about common legal questions, these tribunals can reinforce each other's legitimacy and independence from political interference. They can also promote a global conception of the rule of law, acknowledging its multiple historically and culturally contingent manifestations but affirming a core of common meaning.

I. THE MEASURE OF SUCCESS: DEFINING "EFFECTIVE" SUPRANATIONAL ADJUDICATION

Defining effective supranational adjudication first requires defining effective adjudication and supranationalism. The definitions offered here cannot be definitive; both terms are broad and already subject to multiple meanings. Our purpose is instead to develop an agreed upon terminology that is as precise as possible for the analysis that follows.

A. *Defining Effective Adjudication by Domestic Courts*

When can adjudication be said to be "effective"? The effectiveness of a particular court or of courts in general quickly becomes intertwined with larger jurisprudential questions such as the nature of law and the sources of compliance. Defining effectiveness also inevitably requires asking the question "effective for what purpose?"—an inquiry that will in turn depend on a prior conception of the functions of specific courts within specific legal systems. These functions can include dispute resolution, "social control,"[21] lawmaking,[22] articulating social and political ideals,[23] protecting individual and minority rights, and securing social change.[24] These functions may conflict with one another; they may also each generate a different metric of effectiveness.

21. "Social control" here means the imposition of preexisting rules on disputants. *See* MARTIN SHAPIRO, COURTS: A COMPARATIVE AND POLITICAL ANALYSIS 26 (1981).

22. Courts typically make new rules as an inevitable part of their interpretation of existing law. *See id.* at 28-36.

23. *See* Eugene V. Rostow, *The Democratic Character of Judicial Review*, 66 HARV. L. REV. 193, 208 (1952) ("The Supreme Court is, among other things, an educational body, and the Justices are inevitably teachers in a vital national seminar."); *see also* ALEXANDER M. BICKEL, THE LEAST DANGEROUS BRANCH: THE SUPREME COURT AT THE BAR OF AMERICAN POLITICS 26 (2d ed. 1986) (endorsing and elaborating on Rostow's observation). For further discussion, see Christopher L. Eisgruber, *Is the Supreme Court an Educative Institution?*, 67 N.Y.U. L. REV. 961 (1992).

24. *See* Abram Chayes, *The Role of the Judge in Public Law Litigation*, 89 HARV. L. REV. 1281, 1288-304 (1976) (describing a model of "public law litigation" in which judges must resolve disputes involving multiple parties, prospective rather than retrospective consequences, and a range of remedies enjoining categories of undesirable social and economic behavior).

We offer a much more basic definition of effective adjudication. In the first instance, the effectiveness of a particular court rests on its power to compel a party to a dispute to defend against a plaintiff's complaint and to comply with the resulting judgment. This power is the characteristic that typically distinguishes courts from other dispute resolvers such as go-betweens, mediators, and arbitrators.[25] Thus formulated, this power is one that is exercised during the pendency of a particular dispute and immediately after a dispute is resolved through the issuance of a judgment. The effects of this power are felt ex ante as well as ex post, however, in that parties who are in a similar legal position to actual litigants are likely to comply with the court's judgment "in the shadow" of prospective litigation.[26]

The power of a court to compel parties to appear before it and to comply with its judgments also determines its significance as a political actor. To the extent that it can exercise this power against other government institutions, it can change the dimension and scope of the political bargaining space. Domestic debates in the United States about the power of the Supreme Court, for instance, begin from the premise that it is an important actor on the political landscape, equal to Congress and the President.[27] In this sense, the United States is the "peculiar home of the expansion of judicial power,"[28] a

25. *See* SHAPIRO, *supra* note 21, at 7. Even in domestic adjudication, however, judicial effectiveness is easy to overestimate. Lawyers and legal scholars are often likely to posit a congruence between paper commands and popular practice. The debate between Abram Chayes, on the one hand, and Theodore Eisenberg and Stephen Yeazell, on the other, illustrates the point. Chayes posits a traditional model of "private law litigation" in which the judge issues a retrospective judgment with which parties more or less automatically comply, while Eisenberg and Yeazell point out the frequent need for judges to issue repeated compliance orders against recalcitrant litigants. *Compare* Chayes, *supra* note 24, at 1283, 1285-88, *with* Theodore Eisenberg & Stephen C. Yeazell, *The Ordinary and the Extraordinary in Institutional Litigation*, 93 HARV. L. REV. 465, 481-91 (1980).

26. *See* Robert H. Mnookin & Lewis Kornhauser, *Bargaining in the Shadow of the Law: The Case of Divorce*, 88 YALE L.J. 950, 968-69 (1979) (arguing that in divorce proceedings the parties' bargaining is a direct result of the "shadow of the law" under which they bargain). It is important to distinguish between the above definition of the power of courts and the power of law generally to compel compliance; the latter is a related but larger subject beyond the scope of this Article. Legal rules may be obeyed independent of the power of courts, through what H.L.A. Hart calls "habits of obedience." H.L.A. HART, THE CONCEPT OF LAW 50-60 (1961); *see also* ARCHIBALD COX, THE ROLE OF THE SUPREME COURT IN AMERICAN GOVERNMENT 103-04 (1976) (discussing the operation of law without force or with only a minimum of force against "a few recalcitrants"). Such tranquil visions are hardly the result only of the effectiveness of courts; they rely also on deeply ingrained historical experience, political design, and collective culture. For an empirical study of compliance, see TOM R. TYLER, WHY PEOPLE OBEY THE LAW (1990).

27. *See, e.g.*, COX, *supra* note 26, at 104 (arguing that the Supreme Court "command[s] acceptance and support not only for its decisions but also for its role in government"); *see also* THE GLOBAL EXPANSION OF JUDICIAL POWER (C. Neal Tate & Torbjorn Vallinder eds., 1995) (describing the enhanced policymaking role of courts in different countries around the world, with a particular focus on the rise of judicial power relative to legislative or executive power).

28. Martin Shapiro, *The United States*, *in* THE GLOBAL EXPANSION OF JUDICIAL POWER, *supra* note 27, at 43, 43. Robert McCloskey's classic treatment of the Supreme Court similarly begins with a chapter titled "The Genesis and Nature of Judicial Power." ROBERT G. MCCLOSKEY, THE AMERICAN SUPREME COURT 1 (2d ed. 1994).

phenomenon now being documented around the world.[29]

The power of a court to compel litigants to appear before it and to comply with the resulting judgment stems in part from its ability to harness the coercive power of the state. Supplementing and surrounding this core of potential coercion, however, is the power of legitimacy: a court's ability "to command acceptance and support from the community so as to render force unnecessary."[30]

Legitimacy, in turn, is a concept or attribute that often eludes precise definition, more susceptible to subjective perception than to objective measurement.[31] Various formulations of the sources of judicial legitimacy include the following components, related to both structure and process: impartiality; principled decisionmaking; reasoned decisionmaking; continuity of court composition over time;[32] consistency of judicial decisions over time; respect for the role of political institutions at the federal, state, and local levels;[33] and provision of a meaningful opportunity for litigants to be heard. This list is not intended to be exhaustive; further, many of the factors overlap. Nevertheless, it offers a sense of the judicial attributes that undergird the "compliance pull" of judicial decisions.[34]

B. *Assessing the Effectiveness of International Adjudication*

Assessing the effectiveness of courts, whether domestic or international,

---

29. *See* THE GLOBAL EXPANSION OF JUDICIAL POWER, *supra* note 27, at 27 (arguing that "there is an expansion of judicial power afoot in the world's political systems"). The volume includes chapters discussing the growth of judicial power throughout Western Europe, as well as in Canada, Scandinavia, Malta, Israel, Australia, several post-communist states, the Philippines, and Namibia. Judicial power in this sense, however, often depends on the granted or assumed power of judicial review of legislation, a power quite distinct from the power to compel compliance that we identify as the linchpin of effective adjudication.

30. COX, *supra* note 26, at 103. The question of judicial legitimacy arises in different contexts. Legal scholars in the United States tend to concentrate on the legitimacy of judicial review. *See, e.g.*, BICKEL, *supra* note 23; JESSE H. CHOPER, JUDICIAL REVIEW AND THE NATIONAL POLITICAL PROCESS: A FUNCTIONAL RECONSIDERATION OF THE ROLE OF THE SUPREME COURT (1980); JOHN HART ELY, DEMOCRACY AND DISTRUST: A THEORY OF JUDICIAL REVIEW (1980); William A. Fletcher, *The Discretionary Constitution: Institutional Remedies and Judicial Legitimacy*, 91 YALE L.J. 635 (1982). From this vantage point, judicial legitimacy depends largely on maintaining the proper boundaries between the judiciary and its fellow branches. Equally important, however, is the role of judicial legitimacy in the relationship between the citizen and the state. *See, e.g.*, TYLER, *supra* note 26, *passim*. We attempt to consolidate the two perspectives.

31. A useful overview of the literature on judicial legitimacy is Susan P. Sturm, *A Normative Theory of Public Law Remedies*, 79 GEO. L.J. 1357, 1390-411 (1991). *Cf.* BICKEL, *supra* note 23, at 49 (discussing the importance of procedural justice to legitimacy); TYLER, *supra* note 26, at 6, 163-64 (same). A complementary analysis, identifying several of the factors that we list in Part III with regard to supranational tribunals, is contained in Scott C. Idleman, *A Prudential Theory of Judicial Candor*, 73 TEX. L. REV. 1307, 1388 (1995). Idleman finds three factors affecting judicial legitimacy: (1) unanimity or near unanimity in decisions; (2) professional civility in opinions; and (3) continuity of the law over time. *See id.*

32. *See* BICKEL, *supra* note 23, at 25-31.

33. *See* Sturm, *supra* note 31, at 1380.

34. THOMAS M. FRANCK, THE POWER OF LEGITIMACY AMONG NATIONS 24 (1990).

is not a binary determination. It instead requires locating courts along a continuum of effectiveness. Applying the criteria set forth above, international dispute resolution tribunals are substantially less effective than most domestic courts.[35]

The problem is relatively straightforward. International tribunals lack a direct coercion mechanism to compel either appearance or compliance. They must rely instead on such factors as the immediate perceived interests of states involved in particular disputes in securing judicial settlements, their own legitimacy and the legitimacy of any particular judgment reached, the strength and importance of the international legal rules governing a specific dispute, and the general force of normative obligation. In practice, reliance on these mechanisms has been problematic. Consider the following assessment of the International Court of Justice (ICJ) by the authors of a popular American international law casebook:

> [T]he [ICJ] has not lived up to the hopes of many of its early supporters that the Court, along with the United Nations, would evolve into an international government. To begin with, 90 cases in almost 50 years is not a heavy caseload . . . . Moreover, many of the cases have not been of great international importance. And, in more than 20 contentious cases, the Court's jurisdiction . . . was challenged, with the Court dismissing almost half of these cases. When the Court did reach a judgment on the merits, the affected parties have generally complied with it, but there have been exceptions, especially in recent years.[36]

This assessment reflects the problems of international adjudication on several levels. To begin with, states are reluctant to sue one another. The decision to invoke the jurisdiction of an international tribunal, even where it

35. We use the term "international tribunals" to include not only entities officially designated "courts," such as the International Court of Justice (ICJ), but also less formal or permanent bodies established to resolve specific disputes or clusters of disputes. Examples include panels convened under the 1947 General Agreement on Tariffs and Trade (GATT), dispute settlement procedures available under various environmental treaties, the underutilized Permanent Court of Arbitration, and ad hoc interstate arbitration tribunals. *See generally* David A. Wirth, *Reexamining Decision-Making Processes in International Environmental Law*, 79 IOWA L. REV. 769, 779-90 (1994) (identifying interstate dispute resolution mechanisms).

36. BARRY E. CARTER & PHILLIP R. TRIMBLE, INTERNATIONAL LAW 300 (2d ed. 1995). Similar problems arose with the interstate dispute settlement system of GATT. Under this system, a GATT member country that lost before a dispute settlement panel could effectively block the adoption by the GATT Council of the panel's report, thereby preventing the decision from becoming legally binding. *See* JOHN H. JACKSON, RESTRUCTURING THE GATT SYSTEM 66 (1990). Through use of this veto procedure, delaying tactics, or outright recalcitrance, several states, particularly politically powerful industrialized nations, refused to adhere to certain GATT panel recommendations. *See id.* at 67; Kenneth W. Abbott, *The Uruguay Round and Dispute Resolution: Building a Private-Interests System of Justice*, 1992 COLUM. BUS. L. REV. 111, 140. In the years immediately prior to the completion of the Uruguay Round, the rate of noncompliance increased. *See* Ernst-Ulrich Petersmann, *The Dispute Settlement System of the World Trade Organization and the Evolution of the GATT Dispute Settlement System Since 1948*, 31 COMMON MKT. L. REV. 1157, 1193 (1994).

is available in the context of a specific dispute, inevitably involves a host of political and legal considerations. As David Wirth has observed in his analysis of compulsory third-party dispute resolution as a mechanism for enforcing international environmental law,

> a state whose own performance of international obligations is inadequate may hesitate to proceed against others for fear of calling attention to itself or establishing undesirable precedents. Notwithstanding a meritorious legal claim on an environmental matter, one State may be reluctant to initiate a third-party dispute settlement process against another State for fear of jeopardizing other strategic or economic bilateral relationships.[37]

Further, even once a suit has been filed and the tribunal has determined that it has jurisdiction over both the subject matter and the defending state, the tribunal has no means of compelling the defendant to appear—other than the often hollow threat of a default judgment.

A fresh set of problems arises at the enforcement stage. The mechanisms of coercion available to enforce international judgments are those generally available to states or groups of states to enforce international law against one another. States litigating before the ICJ are formally obligated to comply with its judgments.[38] Failure by a losing party to comply with a judgment provides the winning party with recourse to the Security Council, which may make recommendations or decide upon measures to be taken to give effect to the judgment.[39] The same political calculations involved in the initial decision to bring a suit, however, also affect any unilateral or collective decision to undertake such measures. In addition, the use of collective measures such as sanctions raises the standard panoply of collective action problems.[40]

Perhaps the best measure of the relative ineffectiveness of international tribunals is the degree of effort expended by international lawyers to demonstrate that compulsory third-party adjudication is neither a necessary nor a sufficient condition to ensure compliance with international legal regimes.[41] Louis Henkin dodges the problem with his celebrated assertion: "[A]lmost all nations observe almost all principles of international law and almost all of their

---

37. Wirth, *supra* note 35, at 779; *see also* Petersmann, *supra* note 36, at 1169 ("States are often reluctant to initiate inter-state complaints . . . .").

38. *See* U.N. CHARTER art. 94, para. 1; Statute of the International Court of Justice, Oct. 24, 1945, art. 59, 59 Stat. 1055, 1063.

39. *See* U.N. CHARTER art. 94, para. 2.

40. Indeed, the Security Council has never taken any measures pursuant to these provisions. *See* CARTER & TRIMBLE, *supra* note 36, at 301; *cf.* Petersmann, *supra* note 36, at 1185-86 (noting that GATT contracting parties authorized suspension of trade concessions as a result of a GATT panel ruling "only once over the past 45 years").

41. For a review of decades, if not centuries, of scholarship, see Harold Hongju Koh, *Why Do Nations Obey International Law?*, 106 YALE L.J. 2599 (1997) (review essay).

obligations almost all of the time."[42] Thomas Franck provides a theory of compliance that rests on the independent "compliance-pull" of particular international legal rules and norms based on their degree of legitimacy.[43] Abram Chayes and Antonia Chayes reject the "criminal law model" of forcible enforcement of legal rules by courts as inappropriate for the international legal realm; they develop a "managerial" theory of compliance that emphasizes capacity-building, diplomatic "jawboning," and sustained participation and engagement in international regulatory regimes.[44] Finally, Harold Koh argues that compliance depends on a "transnational legal process."[45] "Once nations begin to interact," he claims, "a complex process occurs, whereby international legal norms seep into, are internalized, and become embedded in domestic legal and political processes."[46]

C. *Defining Effective Supranational Adjudication*

Defining effective *supranational* adjudication first requires a definition of supranational, as opposed to international, law and institutions. The term "supranational" has no canonical definition but is typically used to identify a particular type of international organization that is empowered to exercise directly some of the functions otherwise reserved to states.[47] The distinguishing feature in this regard between supranational and international organizations is the greater transfer of or limitation on state sovereignty involved in the establishment of a supranational organization.[48] The paradigmatic example of a supranational organization is the European Union.[49]

---

42. LOUIS N. HENKIN, HOW NATIONS BEHAVE: LAW AND FOREIGN POLICY 47 (2d ed. 1979) (emphasis omitted).

43. FRANCK, *supra* note 34, at 24; *see also infra* Subsection III.B.2.d (discussing components of legitimacy).

44. *See* ABRAM CHAYES & ANTONIA HANDLER CHAYES, THE NEW SOVEREIGNTY: COMPLIANCE WITH INTERNATIONAL REGULATORY AGREEMENTS 22-28 (1995).

45. Harold Hongju Koh, *Transnational Legal Process*, 75 NEB. L. REV. 181 (1996).

46. *Id.* at 205.

47. *See, e.g.*, FOREST L. GRIEVES, SUPRANATIONALISM AND INTERNATIONAL ADJUDICATION 14 (1969) ("The term 'supranational' signifies that signatory states have transferred to an international institution certain limited decision-making powers normally exercised only by the governmental organs of a sovereign state . . . ." (emphasis omitted)). Henry Schermers and Niels Blokker define six "fundamental characteristics" of a true supranational organization, including the power to make decisions binding on the member states; at least partial independence of the organization from the member states; the ability of the organization to "make rules which directly bind the inhabitants of the member states"; the "power to enforce its decisions"; "some financial autonomy"; and the impossibility of unilateral withdrawal. HENRY G. SCHERMERS & NIELS M. BLOKKER, INTERNATIONAL INSTITUTIONAL LAW § 61, at 41-42 (3d rev. ed. 1995).

48. Grieves argues that the best way to grasp the distinctive nature of supranational organizations is to locate them on a spectrum between "loose international organization[s]" and "strong federal organization[s]." GRIEVES, *supra* note 47, at 13.

49. The original treaty of the European Coal and Steel Community used the term "supranational" apparently for the first time in an international legal document. Article 9(5) provides that the members of the High Authority "shall refrain from any action incompatible with the supra-national character of their functions." TREATY INSTITUTING THE EUROPEAN COAL AND STEEL COMMUNITY, Apr. 15, 1951, 261

More precise definitions of supranational organizations emphasize their ability to penetrate the surface of the state. Giuseppe Schiavone, for example, observes: "Supranational organizations have the ability to make decisions which are directly binding upon member states, public and private enterprises, as well as individuals within these states, whereas traditional international organizations can act or execute decisions only by or through member states."[50] Similarly, in listing six "fundamental characteristics" of an ideal-typical supranational organization, Henry Schermers and Niels Blokker note that "[t]he organization should be empowered to make rules which directly bind the inhabitants of the member states."[51]

This relationship between supranational institutions and the citizens and subjects of domestic governments represents another departure from the bedrock assumption of traditional public international law: that states, functioning as unitary entities, are the only subjects of international rules and institutions and hence the only recognized actors in the international realm.[52] Supranationalism, like contemporary human rights law, acknowledges that states are themselves composed of governments interacting with a panoply of nonstate actors: individuals, groups, corporations, and voluntary organizations.[53] Recognizing rights for these nonstate actors and granting them distinct and independent status before supranational institutions dismantles the fiction of the unitary state.

The move away from the unitary state entails an equally important move away from the fiction of a unitary government. Efforts by supranational institutions to make and enforce rules directly affecting the citizens of domestic governments will overlap and potentially alter the relationship between those citizens and their domestic government institutions: courts, administrative agencies, legislatures, and executives. For instance, private parties are likely to try to enforce rights granted them by a supranational tribunal through

U.N.T.S. 140, 143 (entered into force July 25, 1952). One scholar has suggested that the term was devised to avoid the more controversial term "federal." *See* SCHERMERS & BLOKKER, *supra* note 47, § 61, at 41 (citing H. WAGNER, GRUNDBEGRIFFE DES BESCHLUßRECHTS DER EUROPAISCHEN GEMEINSCHAFTEN 81-82 (1965)). Schermers and Blokker suggest, however, that no true supranational organization exists, at least according to their ideal-typical definition, although they agree that the European Union comes the closest. *See id.* § 62, at 42. Additional authorities defining supranational organization with reference to the European Union are collected in John Head, *Supranational Law: How the Move Toward Multilateral Solutions Is Changing the Character of "International" Law*, 42 KAN. L. REV. 605, 622 n.109 (1994).

50. GIUSEPPE SCHIAVONE, INTERNATIONAL ORGANIZATIONS: A DICTIONARY AND DIRECTORY 3 (3d ed. 1993).

51. SCHERMERS & BLOKKER, *supra* note 47, § 61, at 41.

52. *See* IAN BROWNLIE, PRINCIPLES OF PUBLIC INTERNATIONAL LAW 58-59 (4th ed. 1990) ("It is states and organizations (if appropriate conditions exist) which represent the normal types of legal persons on the international plane.").

53. In domestic politics, we would refer to these "nonstate actors" as citizens, both individual and corporate, or groups and organizations of citizens. From the perspective of the international system, however, it is their nonstate status that is noteworthy.

domestic courts.[54] In response to this intrusion, domestic government institutions may choose to assert their traditional sovereignty or to forge direct relationships with their supranational counterparts. The result is the "disaggregation" of governments into their component parts or branches.[55]

This web of potential relationships between private parties, supranational entities, and domestic government institutions lies at the heart of supranational adjudication. We define supranational adjudication, in its purest form, as adjudication by a tribunal that was established by a group of states or the entire international community and that exercises jurisdiction over cases directly involving private parties—whether between a private party and a foreign government, a private party and her own government, private parties themselves, or, in the criminal context, a private party and a prosecutor's office.[56] Traditional international adjudication, by contrast, involves only state-to-state litigation.[57] Tribunals engaged in supranational adjudication may also exercise jurisdiction over state-to-state cases, but in their supranational capacity they have the potential to be far more effective than their pure international counterparts.

As a result of their ability to penetrate the surface of the state, supranational tribunals have an additional set of potential mechanisms for compelling litigants to appear and to comply with the resulting judgments. In pure international litigation, in which states are treated as unitary actors, the government of a particular state is represented by the head of state or the foreign office. Other domestic government institutions may be involved in determining the position taken by the head of state or the foreign office, but

54. *Cf.* Ernst-Ulrich Petersmann, *Constitutionalism and International Organizations*, 17 NW. J. INT'L L. & BUS. 398, 443 (1996-1997). As Petersmann writes:

> [A] rights-based approach, enabling self-interested individuals to enforce international guarantees of freedom and non-discrimination through [national] courts, has likewise enabled a dynamic evolution of the European Convention on Human Rights . . . . The very small number of complaints among member state governments at the E.C. Court, as well as at the European Court of Human Rights, confirms that individuals . . . may be the best guardians and promoters of rule-oriented international cooperation.

Id.

55. For related discussions of the disaggregation of the state, see Anne-Marie Slaughter, *International Law in a World of Liberal States*, 6 EUR. J. INT'L L. 503, 522-23 (1995) [hereinafter Slaughter, *International Law*]; and Anne-Marie Slaughter, *The Real New World Order*, 76 FOREIGN AFF. 183 (1997).

56. For another definition of "elements which give an international court a supranational character," see GRIEVES, *supra* note 47, at 16-17. Grieves argues that a court can be said to have supranational powers only when it transcends the usual limitations of the prototype international court, that is, that only states are litigants and must consent to litigation. He enumerates several elements that reflect supranationalism in practice: a court's ability to determine its own jurisdiction; the identity of parties before the court; disposition for and against states where individuals have standing; judicial impartiality; and, significantly, enforcement of judgments and compliance. *See id.* He thus assumes that a supranational tribunal by definition is more effective than an international one. We seek to uncover the mechanisms by which such effectiveness is achieved.

57. Between these two pure examples are a range of tribunals before which private parties do not have standing but whose rulings may have a direct bearing upon their pecuniary or political interests in the domestic realm, motivating them to monitor and influence the process of interstate adjudication. We discuss the applicability of our checklist to these tribunals in the conclusion. *See infra* Part VI.

the international tribunal has no way to interact directly with those institutions. In pure supranational adjudication, by contrast, the direct link between supranational tribunals and private parties creates opportunities for those tribunals to establish direct or indirect relationships with the different branches of domestic governments. Through these relationships, a supranational tribunal can harness the power of domestic government to enforce its rulings in the same way that the judgments and orders of a domestic court are enforced.[58]

In sum, we measure the effectiveness of a supranational tribunal in terms of its ability to compel compliance with its judgments by convincing domestic government institutions, directly and through pressure from private litigants, to use their power on its behalf. Part III of this Article spells out the various specific ways in which supranational tribunals and the states that establish them can maximize their effectiveness along these dimensions. The resulting "checklist" is based on the experience of two European supranational tribunals: the ECJ and the ECHR. We turn first, however, to the history of these two tribunals, focusing on the role played by private parties in securing compliance with their rulings and highlighting the empirical judgments of scholars and practitioners that the tribunals are regarded as effective much in the way that domestic courts are viewed as effective.

II. The Story of Europe

The two principal supranational tribunals in Europe, the ECJ and the ECHR, have proved to be remarkably effective. This part traces the history of each in turn and then briefly compares their experiences.

A. *The European Court of Justice*

The European Court of Justice was established by the Treaty of Rome as a court of limited international jurisdiction charged with interpreting and applying the treaty in disputes between member states of the European Community or between the Commission of the Community and one or more member states.[59] At the outset, the ECJ's powers appeared no greater than those of the ICJ; it had jurisdiction over disputes between states, but no direct means of enforcing its decisions. Yet, over a forty-year period, the ECJ succeeded in transforming the Treaty of Rome and secondary Community

58. Schermers and Blokker similarly conclude that "[i]t may well be possible that other organs of the member states are used to aid the [supranational organization]" with regard to enforcing supranational rules. SCHERMERS & BLOKKER, *supra* note 47, § 61, at 41. "Thus, a national parliament and the national judiciary may coerce their government to fulfill its obligations to the organization." *Id.*

59. *See* TREATY OF ROME art. 169 (permitting the Commission of the Community to refer cases of noncompliance with its opinions to the Court of Justice); *id.* art. 170 (permitting member states to bring before the Commission of the Community and the Court of Justice other member states that have allegedly failed to fulfill treaty obligations).

legislation into law directly enforceable in cases brought by private parties in the domestic courts. European Union law is supreme over domestic law and recognized as such by domestic courts—not, in most cases, by action of domestic constitutions or legislative provisions, but by decree of the ECJ itself, a decree ultimately accepted even by the highest national courts.[60]

The task facing the ECJ was the penetration of national legal systems. It accomplished this task by exploiting a relatively obscure provision in the Treaty of Rome, Article 177, which allowed all national courts, and required national courts of last resort, to refer cases involving the application of European law to the ECJ for a preliminary ruling on the European law issues.[61] The ostensible purpose of this provision was to ensure uniformity of interpretation of the treaty by ensuring that six (now fifteen) sets of national judges did not develop divergent interpretations of the treaty and Community secondary legislation. In one of the earliest referrals, however, the ECJ took matters into its own hands and declared the doctrine of "direct effect," holding that certain provisions of the Treaty of Rome are directly applicable to individuals within national legal systems.[62] Individuals could thus invoke these provisions in national court against contrary provisions of national law; the national court was then to refer the issue to the ECJ for resolution.

Over the course of several decades, the number of references from national courts to the ECJ steadily increased, effectively providing the ECJ with domestic enforcement mechanisms for its judgments.[63] The doctrine of direct effect was quickly followed by the doctrine of supremacy of European

---

60. The classic account of the construction of the European Community's legal system is found in J.H.H. Weiler, *The Transformation of Europe*, 100 YALE L.J. 2403 (1991). Weiler follows in the footsteps of Eric Stein, *Lawyers, Judges, and the Making of a Transnational Constitution*, 75 AM. J. INT'L L. 1 (1981), which first alerted international lawyers to the potential significance of the ECJ's achievements. For an influential account by a member of the ECJ, see G. Federico Mancini, *The Making of a Constitution for Europe*, 26 COMMON MKT. L. REV. 595 (1989). Two more general accounts, the first written from a legal realist perspective highlighting the motives of ECJ judges in developing a teleological interpretation of the Treaty of Rome and the second seeking to integrate legal accounts with political science theory, are HJALTE RASMUSSEN, ON LAW AND POLICY IN THE EUROPEAN COURT OF JUSTICE (1986); and Anne-Marie Burley & Walter Mattli, *Europe Before the Court: A Political Theory of Legal Integration*, 47 INT'L ORG. 41 (1993).

61. Article 177 of the Treaty of Rome provides: "The Court of Justice shall be competent to make a preliminary decision concerning . . . the validity and interpretation of acts of the institutions of the Community; and . . . the interpretation of the statutes of any bodies set up by an act of the Council . . . ." TREATY OF ROME art. 177. Any court of a member state may refer a case involving such issues to the ECJ. Further, national courts of last resort, "from whose decisions no appeal lies under municipal law," must refer cases raising questions of European law to the ECJ. *Id.* Article 171 requires member states to "take the measures required for the implementation of the judgment" of the ECJ. *Id.* art. 171.

62. *See* Case 26/62, N.V. Algemene Transp. & Expeditie Onderneming Van Gend & Loos v. Nederlandse administratie der belastingen, 1963 E.C.R. 1, 12; *see also* Weiler, *supra* note 60, at 2413-14 (discussing the doctrine of direct effect).

63. A quantitative illustration of the growing importance of Community law is the number of cases referred to the ECJ by domestic courts. The number jumped from a low of nine in 1969 to a high of 119 in 1978; by 1993, domestic court referrals were "in fact the most common kind of case on the Court's docket (about one-half), numbering over 150 per year." GEORGE A. BERMANN ET AL., EUROPEAN COMMUNITY LAW 245 (1993); *see also* Burley & Mattli, *supra* note 60, at 43 n.8.

Community law over conflicting national law, a much more direct enforcement mechanism than the system of national implementing legislation that the treaty's drafters originally envisioned.[64] Other ECJ innovations included implied powers for Community lawmaking, preemption of conflicting national legislation, and the development of a human rights jurisprudence to check potential excesses of Community law and actors.[65]

Acceptance of these doctrines by national courts has given the judgments of the ECJ in cases referred to it under Article 177 roughly the same effect as judgments issued by domestic courts in the member states of the European Union.[66] Individuals, corporations, and government agencies anticipate the ECJ's position on important economic and political questions; its decisions are carefully reported and analyzed not only in legal reporters, but also in major national newspapers.[67] Indeed, the ECJ's success has been such that it has been widely credited with transforming the Treaty of Rome from an international instrument into the "constitution" of the European Community.[68]

The ECJ's effectiveness has traditionally been measured with regard to its adjudication of Article 177 cases.[69] By contrast, its record in cases brought by states against one another and by the Commission of the Community against member states has been spotty. States have been hesitant to sue one another, preferring to bring their complaints to the Commission.[70] The

64. *See* Weiler, *supra* note 60, at 2413-19 (discussing the doctrines and citing major authorities analyzing them).

65. *See id.*

66. *See, e.g.*, Geoffrey Garrett, *International Cooperation and Institutional Choice: The European Community's Internal Market*, 46 INT'L ORG. 533, 555 (1992) ("The system [implemented by the ECJ] has been quite effective. There is no systematic difference within countries in the extent to which EC laws are followed relative to purely national laws."); Weiler, *supra* note 60, at 2464 (noting that, although noncompliance with ECJ judgments does occur, "[i]n this respect the Community is no different (in principle) than, for example, any state of equivalent size and complexity," and that noncompliance occurs "in a constitutional context with an ethos of domestic rather than international law"); *see also* Petersmann, *supra* note 54, at 465 ("The experience of . . . EC law . . . clearly suggests that cooperation between international and national courts, and the right of individuals to invoke the international obligations of governments before the national judiciary, are of crucial importance for rendering international law more effective within domestic legal systems.").

67. *See, e.g.*, *Deichmann To Go to EU Court over Commission Anti-Dumping Proposals*, FRANKFURTER ALLGEMEINE ZEITUNG, Oct. 15, 1996, at 29; David Rowan, *Gay Rights: Coming Out of the Shadows; A Notable Ruling in Europe in Favour of a Homosexual British Man Heralds the Last Stages in the Long Struggle for Equality*, GUARDIAN (London), Oct. 9, 1997, at 17.

68. *See* Case 294/83, Parti écologiste 'Les Verts' v. Parliament, 1986 E.C.R. 1339, 1365 (describing the Treaty of Rome as "the basic constitutional charter" of the Community); *see also* Weiler, *supra* note 60, at 2413 (referring to the ECJ's efforts as "'[c]onstitutionalization' of the Community legal structure"). For a recent comprehensive discussion of the constitutional character of European Union law, see J.H.H. Weiler & Ulrich R. Haltern, *The Autonomy of the Community Legal Order—Through the Looking Glass*, 37 HARV. INT'L L.J. 411 (1996).

69. *See* J.H.H. Weiler, *The European Court, National Courts and References for Preliminary Rulings—The Paradox of Success: A Revisionist View of Article 177 EEC*, *in* ARTICLE 177 EEC: EXPERIENCES AND PROBLEMS 366, 366-67 (Henry G. Schermers et al. eds., 1987).

70. *See* Alan Dashwood & Robin White, *Enforcement Actions Under Articles 169 and 170 EEC*, 14 EUR. L. REV. 388, 409 (1989) ("In practice the Member States have shown little enthusiasm for their independent right of action under Article 170. . . . The preferred approach . . . seems to be to complain to the Commission and leave it to that body to take action."); *see also* KAREN ALTER, THE EUROPEAN COURT

Commission, in turn, was also initially reluctant to sue member states because of its need to establish its own political legitimacy.[71] Further, even in those cases brought to the ECJ, compliance with resulting judgments has been mixed.[72] Strikingly, the ECJ solved these enforcement problems by turning again to private parties and domestic courts, holding in *Francovich v. Italy*[73] that a state that failed to implement a Community directive could be required to pay compensation to injured private parties.

B. *The European Court of Human Rights*

Beginning from a similarly modest position, the ECHR has succeeded in transforming a relatively empty docket into a relatively teeming one. It has declared its principal text, the European Convention for the Protection of Human Rights and Fundamental Freedoms,[74] a "constitutional instrument of European public order,"[75] just as the ECJ gave the Treaty of Rome constitutional status within the European Community. In addition, the ECHR has successfully established itself as the final interpreter of the Convention's provisions.[76] And it has witnessed its rulings change the shape of domestic law, through both legislative revision and judicial decision.[77]

AND NATIONAL COURTS DOCTRINE AND JURISPRUDENCE: LEGAL CHANGE IN ITS SOCIAL CONTEXT [EXPLAINING NATIONAL COURT ACCEPTANCE OF EUROPEAN COURT JURISPRUDENCE: A CRITICAL EVALUATION OF THEORIES OF LEGAL INTEGRATION] 33 n.17 (European Univ. Inst., Florence, Working Paper RSC No. 95/27, 1995) ("In the history of the Community, Member States have only raised 3 cases against another member state.").

71. *See* ALTER, *supra* note 70, at 34 ("The Commission's reluctance to pursue breaches was most likely based on political concerns."); Stein, *supra* note 60, at 6 ("[U]ntil quite recently, the Commission obviously hesitated to aggravate its fragile relationships with member governments by bringing them into Court—and a decision by a member government to sue another posed political difficulties of a similar nature.").

72. *See* Weiler, *supra* note 60, at 2464-65 & nn.177-78 (noting the increasing lack of compliance by states in cases brought by the Commission of the Community or another member state). *But see* Dashwood & White, *supra* note 70, at 411 (concluding that member states have "almost always taken the steps necessary to comply with [Article 169 judgments], although sometimes after considerable delay").

73. Cases C-6/90 & C-9/90, Francovich v. Italy, 67 C.M.L.R. 66 (1991); *see also* J. Dutheil de la Rochere, *Member State Liability for Infringement of European Community Law*, 11 TUL. EUR. & CIV. L.F. 1, 3-5 (1996) (analyzing *Francovich* and its progeny).

74. Convention, *supra* note 2.

75. Loizidou v. Turkey, 310 Eur. Ct. H.R. (ser. A) at 27 (1995); *see also* RALPH BEDDARD, HUMAN RIGHTS AND EUROPE 5-6 (3d ed. 1993) (characterizing the Convention "as a kind of constitutional document for a united Europe").

76. *See, e.g.*, Barfod v. Denmark, 149 Eur. Ct. H.R. (ser. A) at 12 (1989) (claiming that the ECHR is "empowered to give [a] final ruling" on whether a state's interference with a protected right is compatible with the Convention); Muller v. Switzerland, 133 Eur. Ct. H.R. (ser. A) at 21 (1988) (same); Lingens v. Austria, 103 Eur. Ct. H.R. (ser. A) at 25 (1986) (same).

77. *See* J.G. MERRILLS, THE DEVELOPMENT OF INTERNATIONAL LAW BY THE EUROPEAN COURT OF HUMAN RIGHTS 12 (2d ed. 1993) ("The most dramatic impact of the Court's work is certainly to be found in the changes in domestic law and practice which have been introduced as a result of cases at Strasbourg . . . ."); Richard S. Kay, *The European Convention on Human Rights and the Authority of Law*, 8 CONN. J. INT'L L. 217, 218 (1993) (observing that the European Convention is "accept[ed] as a genuine system of law" and that judgments of the ECHR are "routinely[] honored by the respondent states who both pay the compensation ordered by the Court and also adjust their laws and governmental practices to the Court's interpretations").

The Convention arose out of a broader effort to promote social and economic progress among European states after World War II. It codifies a basic catalog of civil and political liberties and confirms the desire of its signatories to achieve "a common understanding and observance" of those rights.[78] Although originally ratified by few countries outside of Western Europe, as of 1997 forty nations from Iceland to Russia have signed on to the treaty and one or more of its various protocols.[79]

In addition to setting forth substantive guarantees, the Convention creates an intricate enforcement mechanism to permit individuals and groups to file complaints against their national governments alleging violations of European human rights norms. Although the treaty does not compel states parties to recognize this right of petition or the compulsory jurisdiction of the ECHR, in practice all of the treaty's signatories have filed permanent or renewable declarations accepting both obligations.[80] Commentators have stressed the importance of this individual access right as crucial to the success of the Convention in altering the domestic legal landscape.[81]

Individuals who allege that their human rights have been violated first present their claims to the European Commission of Human Rights (the Commission), a quasi-judicial tribunal which screens the claims for possible violations of the Convention.[82] The Commission dismisses the majority of claims for failing to satisfy the Convention's admissibility criteria[83] or for being without merit ("manifestly ill-founded" in the parlance of the Convention[84]). For those cases in which a violation of the Convention is clearly apparent or that present unresolved questions of interpretation, the Commission declares the complaint admissible and receives additional evidence and arguments from the parties. If no amicable resolution can be negotiated, the Commission issues a decision explaining whether the state party has breached its obligations under the Convention.[85]

---

78. Convention, *supra* note 2, pmbl., 213 U.N.T.S. at 222.

79. *See* COUNCIL OF EUR., CHART OF SIGNATURES AND RATIFICATIONS OF EUROPEAN TREATIES, JULY 1, 1996 UPDATE [hereinafter CHART OF SIGNATURES 1996].

80. *See* COUNCIL OF EUR., DECLARATIONS PURSUANT TO ARTICLES 25 AND 46 OF THE CONVENTION FOR THE PROTECTION OF HUMAN RIGHTS AND FUNDAMENTAL FREEDOMS, JULY 1, 1997 UPDATE.

81. *See, e.g.*, BEDDARD, *supra* note 75, at 1; A.H. ROBERTSON & J.G. MERRILLS, HUMAN RIGHTS IN EUROPE 258-59, 284 (3d ed. 1993); P. VAN DIJK & G.J.H. VAN HOOF, THEORY AND PRACTICE OF THE EUROPEAN CONVENTION ON HUMAN RIGHTS 34-35 (1984).

82. The Commission has decided thousands of cases concerning virtually all of the substantive rights guaranteed by the European Convention. Because cases dismissed at a preliminary stage may not be appealed to the ECHR by the aggrieved individual, only a few hundred of these cases have actually reached the court. *See* Henry G. Schermers, *The European Court of Human Rights After the Merger*, 18 EUR. L. REV. 493, 495 (1993).

83. Before filing a petition, an individual must exhaust all available and effective national remedies and must file his or her complaint with the Commission within six months of any "final decision" by a national authority. *See* Convention, *supra* note 2, art. 26, 213 U.N.T.S. at 238.

84. *Id.* art. 27, 213 U.N.T.S. at 238.

85. *See id.* art. 31, 213 U.N.T.S. at 240.

At this point, either the Commission or the defending state (or states) may appeal the decision directly to the ECHR. Under the Convention itself, individuals have no right of appeal.[86] Once seized of an appeal, the court reviews the evidence and legal argument de novo and renders a final judgment.[87] If neither the Commission nor the state appeals the decision, the case is referred to the Committee of Ministers, the executive arm of the Council of Europe, which is composed of the ministers of foreign affairs or their designees from each of the member states of the Council. The Committee, which is also charged with ensuring compliance with the judgments of the court, then renders a final decision on the case.[88]

Although all of the treaty parties "undertake to abide by the decision of the Court in any case to which they are parties,"[89] the legal effect they give to the court's judgments varies considerably. Approximately half of the signatories to the Convention have incorporated the treaty into domestic law, thereby allowing individuals to invoke the treaty and the ECHR's judgments in national judicial proceedings.[90] The remaining states fulfill their Convention obligations by giving effect to specific judgments of the ECHR, in nearly all cases agreeing to introduce legislative amendments, reopen judicial proceedings, grant administrative remedies, and pay monetary damages to individuals whose treaty rights have been violated.[91]

---

86. *See* RALPH BEDDARD, HUMAN RIGHTS AND EUROPE 43 (2d ed. 1980). In 1990, however, several states ratified an optional protocol to the treaty that permits individuals and groups to appeal a decision of the Commission to a three-judge panel of the court. The panel has the authority to dispose of the case if it "does not raise a serious question affecting the interpretation or application of the Convention and does not for any other reason warrant consideration by the Court." Protocol No. 9 to the Convention for the Protection of Human Rights and Fundamental Freedoms, *opened for signature* Nov. 6, 1990, art. 5, para. 2, Europ. T.S. No. 140 (entered into force for 23 states June 10, 1996).

87. *See* DeWilde, Ooms & Versyp Cases (The Vagrancy Cases), 12 Eur. Ct. H.R. (ser. A) at 29 (1971).

88. *See* Convention, *supra* note 2, art. 32, 213 U.N.T.S. at 240-42.

89. *Id.* art. 59, 213 U.N.T.S. at 250.

90. *See* ANDREW DRZEMCZEWSKI, THE EUROPEAN HUMAN RIGHTS CONVENTION IN DOMESTIC LAW 260-303 (1983).

91. The European Convention's influence on domestic legal systems is addressed in a growing literature. For a succinct discussion of the scope of the Strasbourg organ's influence on domestic courts, see Andrew Drzemczewski & Jens Meyer-Ladewig, *Principal Characteristics of the New ECHR Control Mechanism, as Established by Protocol No. 11, Signed on 11 May, 1994*, 15 HUM. RTS. L.J. 81, 82 (1994), which documents changes in Austrian, Belgian, Dutch, and Irish law as a result of ECHR decisions. Other sources provide in depth, country-by-country discussions of the ECHR's far-reaching effects on legislative reform, case law, and revision procedures. *See* Jörg Polakiewicz & Valérie Jacob-Foltzer, *The European Human Rights Convention in Domestic Law: The Impact of the Strasbourg Case-Law in States Where Direct Effect Is Given to the Convention* (pts. 1 & 2), 12 HUM. RTS. L.J. 65, 67-68, 125, 137 (1991) (detailing 30 years of the ECHR's influence on legislative reform and case law in the states party to the Convention, including the reopening and modification of purportedly final judicial decisions). For studies of the effect of the Strasbourg case law on domestic legislation in the countries of Eastern and Central Europe, see Michael O'Boyle, *Right To Speak and Associate Under Strasbourg Case-Law with Reference to Eastern and Central Europe*, 8 CONN. J. INT'L L. 263 (1993); and Jörg G. Polakiewicz, *The Domestic Implementation of the European Convention on Human Rights in Eastern and Western Europe*, 2 ALL-EUR. HUM. RTS. Y.B. 11 (1992).

In response to the widespread success of the individual petition mechanism in Europe, the growth in the number of states party to the Convention, and an increasing backlog of cases,[92] the Council of Europe has sought to improve upon the existing judicial review machinery. In May 1994, after years of study and months of arduous negotiations, a majority of states parties signed Protocol No. 11 to the Convention.[93] The Protocol, once ratified by all of the states,[94] will revolutionize the treaty's enforcement machinery, abolishing the European Commission of Human Rights and creating a permanent European Court of Human Rights.[95] Under the new regime, all states parties must recognize the compulsory jurisdiction of the permanent court and permit individuals direct access to it in all cases.

The rate of compliance by states with the ECHR's rulings is extremely high. Indeed, its judgments have been described as being "as effective as those of any domestic court."[96] As with the ECJ, however, this record of success has occurred principally in cases brought by individuals against their national governments. By contrast, the effectiveness of the handful of interstate complaints[97] filed with the European Commission and the ECHR is doubtful,

92. Cases decided in 1992 took an average of five years and six months to be resolved—four years and four months before the Commission and 13 months before the Court. *See* Andrew Drzemczewski, *Putting the European House in Order*, 144 NEW L.J., 645, 646 (1994).

93. Protocol No. 11 to the Convention for the Protection of Human Rights and Fundamental Freedoms, *opened for signature* May 11, 1994, Europ. T.S. No. 155 [hereinafter Protocol No. 11].

94. As of May 1997, all 40 contracting states had signed Protocol No. 11, but seven had yet to ratify it. *See* COUNCIL OF EUROPE CHART OF SIGNATURES AND RATIFICATIONS: PROTOCOL NO. 11 TO THE CONVENTION FOR THE PROTECTION OF HUMAN RIGHTS AND FUNDAMENTAL FREEDOMS, MAY 23, 1997 UPDATE. The ratification process has been described as "extremely slow" and has been encumbered by foot dragging by states such as Turkey. Patrick Smyth, *European Court Vacancy Arises in Early 1998*, IRISH TIMES, Mar. 14, 1997, at 5. Nevertheless, complete ratification is anticipated in 1998 or 1999. *See id.*

95. The court will screen cases in committees of three judges, with admissible cases being considered by a chamber of seven judges. In exceptional cases, such as "to ensure the quality and consistency of the Court's case law," an appeal may be referred to a grand chamber of 17 judges. Drzemczewski, *supra* note 92, at 644.

96. CARTER & TRIMBLE, *supra* note 36, at 309; *see also* R. Ryssdal, *The Enforcement System Set Up Under the European Convention on Human Rights*, *in* COMPLIANCE WITH JUDGMENTS OF INTERNATIONAL COURTS 49, 67 (M.K. Bulterman & M. Kuijer eds., 1996) (analyzing the effectiveness of ECHR judgments as measured by compliance with judgments and quoting the President of the ECHR as stating that "to date judgments of the [ECHR] have . . . not only generally but always been complied with by the Contracting States concerned," although noting some delays in compliance); Colin Warbrick, *Expansion of Rights Protection by the European Convention on Human Rights*, *in* CONTROL OVER COMPLIANCE WITH INTERNATIONAL LAW 139, 140 (W.E. Butler ed., 1991) [hereinafter CONTROL OVER COMPLIANCE] ("With no exceptions, the judgments of the [ECHR] have been complied with by the States without the need for 'enforcement.'").

One significant exception to this trend, however, occurred when the United Kingdom formally derogated from the ECHR's ruling in *Brogan v. United Kingdom*, 145-B Eur. Ct. H.R. (ser. A) at 30 (1988), in which the court held that prolonged pretrial detention of suspected terrorists in Northern Ireland violated the Convention. *See* Brannigan v. United Kingdom, 258 Eur. Ct. H.R. (ser. A) at 56 (1993) (upholding the government's actions under the Convention's derogation clause). Nevertheless, with this sole exception, the British government has formally taken the position that "Britain complies meticulously with every adverse decision of the Court once it has been made." A.W. Bradley, *The United Kingdom, the European Court of Human Rights, and Constitutional Review*, 17 CARDOZO L. REV. 233, 250 (1995).

97. *See* Scott Leckie, *The Inter-State Complaint Procedure in International Human Rights Law: Hopeful Prospects or Wishful Thinking?*, 10 HUM. RTS. Q. 249, 255 (1988) (noting that there have been

again demonstrating the crucial role played by private parties in securing compliance with supranational court rulings.[98]

C. *The European Courts Compared*

The trajectories of the ECJ and the ECHR reflect important differences. The ECJ interacts with national courts in a kind of partnership based on distinct but complementary spheres of jurisdiction; the ECHR is more likely to be in the position of reviewing the handiwork of national courts in a more traditional hierarchical relationship. Further, the ECJ superintends a treaty that has the stated objective of creating "an ever closer Union" of fifteen European nations;[99] the ECHR oversees compliance with a specific catalog of human rights obligations in forty countries. The ECJ is thus a tribunal of much wider substantive jurisdiction, addressing economic issues with an explicit political dimension. In comparison, the ECHR has a narrower and more traditional judicial role. On the structural side, the ECHR does not have an Article 177 mechanism allowing it to communicate directly with national courts. The ECHR thus faces a different task of convincing national legislatures, at least in the first instance, to conform to its judgments.

Notwithstanding these differences, it is possible to identify many similarities in the structure and practice of the ECJ and the ECHR that transcend the differences between them. They are both supranational courts with no direct means of enforcing their judgments and thus are apparently dependent on the goodwill of national governmental institutions. Within these constraints, they have built a remarkable record, becoming important actors on the domestic as well as the international legal scene. Moreover, their experience confirms the theoretical analysis of effective supranational adjudication set forth in Part I. Each court achieved substantial compliance with its judgments by forging relationships with domestic government

---

only 18 interstate complaints concerning "six distinct human rights violations").

98. As van Dijk and van Hoof point out:

> [I]t is evident that the right of complaint of States has proved not to be very effective. . . . [T]he contracting States have not been willing to expose situations in other States if no interest of their own is involved. Such a step generally runs counter to their own interest in that a charge of violation of the Convention will be considered an unfriendly act by the other party, with all the political consequences that may be involved.

VAN DIJK & VAN HOOF, *supra* note 81, at 33; *see also* BEDDARD, *supra* note 75, at 9 (characterizing interstate petitions as "unsatisfactory" and based on "unfriendliness in the relations between states"); ROBERTSON & MERRILLS, *supra* note 81, at 284 (criticizing the settlement of an interstate complaint against Turkey as a political compromise that failed to protect adequately individual rights and stating that "[i]n a comparable case brought by an individual it is inconceivable that an arrangement so patently unsatisfactory would have been approved"); *id.* at 284-85 (arguing that "political considerations are likely to influence the way the Convention works in inter-state cases to a much greater extent than in cases brought by individuals").

99. TREATY OF ROME pmbl.

institutions, both directly and indirectly through relationships with private parties.

Further, the collective European experience of supranational adjudication is greater than the sum of its parts. The ECJ and the ECHR have become part of a larger European "community of law": a network of legal actors self-consciously interacting with one another on the basis of both self-interest and shared values in a nominally apolitical context. The existence of a community of law as a precondition for a well-functioning legal system within a state is taken for granted; the expansion of such a community beyond the boundaries of any one state, however, is a remarkable phenomenon. A community of law is both a cause and a consequence of effective supranational adjudication. We return to the relationship between these two phenomena, in both the European and the global context, in Part V. First, however, we turn to a more specific analysis of the factors contributing to effective supranational adjudication.

III. A Checklist for Effective Supranational Adjudication

The purpose of generating a "checklist" for effective supranational adjudication is to develop a tool that can be used to assess the effectiveness of other supranational tribunals and to guide the members of those tribunals in seeking to enhance their own effectiveness. We thus divide the checklist into several categories of factors that plausibly affect the effectiveness of supranational tribunals. First are those factors within the power of the states responsible for establishing a supranational tribunal and dictating its relationship to domestic tribunals. Second are those factors within the power of the supranational tribunal itself. Third are more general factors relating to the types of cases presented to a supranational tribunal and to the domestic political configuration and ideology of the states subject to its jurisdiction. Factors in the third category are not fully within the control of states or judges but do not vitiate the importance of factors in the first two categories.

A. *A Methodological Note*

We have developed the following compilation of the attributes of effective supranational adjudication by distilling commentary and analysis by judges, lawyers, and political scientists who have closely observed the workings of the ECJ and the ECHR, supplementing these findings with our own analysis. The checklist is intended as a first step toward the development of a more rigorous model of supranational adjudication, one that will ultimately be informed by data from a wider range of tribunals and dispute resolution bodies, such as panels convened under the North American Free Trade Agreement (NAFTA), the Canadian-United States Free Trade Agreement, the Inter-American Court of Human Rights, United Nations treaty bodies authorized to receive complaints from individuals, and the War Crimes Tribunals for Rwanda and the former Yugoslavia. From a political science perspective, we have "selected on the dependent variable,"[100] focusing only on two relatively effective tribunals rather than correlating explanatory factors with a range of effective and less effective tribunals.

In compiling this list, we have been guided by three principal considerations. First, we have been as detailed as possible. For instance, many accounts of supranational tribunals attribute their success to attributes like "legitimacy" and "authority." We have sought to break down these umbrella terms into more specific components. Second, we have included the widest possible range of factors: legal, political, social, and cultural. It is quite likely that some factors are partially or even wholly derivative of others. At this stage of the analysis, we value comprehensiveness over parsimony, although we recognize that some classes of factors may prove to be more potent explanatory variables than others.

Third, we have tried to compensate for our inclusionary bias by listing the factors in each category in descending order of importance. Our judgments here are based on both our sense of the literature and our own analysis, although these are precisely the types of determinations that are likely to change in light of additional data from other tribunals. In assigning even a preliminary weight to each factor, we have taken into account the degree of consensus among observers regarding the impact of the particular factor on either the ECJ or the ECHR independently, as well as across both tribunals. It follows that factors listed toward the bottom of each category in the checklist are more context-specific and likely to vary across different tribunals.[101] A related problem is the possibility that some factors are, in fact, counterproductive, though this possibility is outweighed by the simultaneous presence of other more powerful factors. It is again difficult to isolate the impact of specific factors with such a limited initial data set; where possible, however, we have sought not only to list the factors identified by judicial observers, but also to trace the mechanisms by which they exercise their purported impact.

---

100. GARY KING ET AL., DESIGNING SOCIAL INQUIRY: SCIENTIFIC INFERENCE IN QUALITATIVE RESEARCH 129-32 (1994).

101. In some cases, for instance, a factor and its opposite may be equally cited as contributing to the effectiveness of the two different courts under consideration. In such cases, we are not inclined to rank the factor highly in terms of relative importance; nevertheless, we seek to analyze the circumstances in which one alternative is likely to work better than the other.

B. *The Checklist*

1. *Factors Within the Control of States Party to an Agreement Establishing a Supranational Tribunal*

a. *Composition of the Tribunal*

If states party to a treaty establishing a supranational tribunal hope to enhance its legitimacy and authority, the experience of the ECJ and ECHR suggests that they should give careful consideration to the background and experience of jurists who serve on it.[102] Seeking to explain the legitimacy of the constitutional interpretations given to the Treaty of Rome by the ECJ, for example, Joseph Weiler observes that the Court is composed of "senior jurists from all member states [of the European Union]."[103] The implicit point is that where a supranational tribunal depends on acceptance of its judgments by national tribunals, it will wield greater authority if its members are known and respected by national judges.[104]

A further implication, however, may be that special expertise in the field of law to be applied by the supranational tribunal is not necessarily the most important qualification for potential tribunal members, at least at the outset of the tribunal's life. For instance, to the extent that international and domestic law are perceived as quite distinct and mutually insulated fields in a particular country, staffing an international tribunal solely with experts in *international* law may have the paradoxical effect of ensuring that the tribunal's members are less well-known to national judges than appointees of equal distinction who have made a career in *domestic* law.[105] The point may carry beyond the need

102. Both the Treaty of Rome and the European Convention on Human Rights provide that their judges must be respected jurists or jurisconsults of high achievement and character. Both specify that judicial appointments are for a fixed term of years and that judges may be reappointed after serving their initial terms. *See* TREATY OF ROME art. 167 (requiring that judges, who serve for a renewable term of six years, be "persons whose independence is beyond doubt and who possess the qualifications required for appointment to the highest judicial offices in their respective countries or who are jurisconsults of recognised competence"); Convention, *supra* note 2, arts. 39(3), 40(1), 213 U.N.T.S. at 244 (requiring that judges, who serve for a renewable term of nine years, be of "high moral character" and "either possess the qualifications required for appointment to high judicial office or be jurisconsults of recognized competence").

103. J.H.H. Weiler, *A Quiet Revolution: The European Court of Justice and Its Interlocutors*, 26 COMP. POL. STUD. 510, 521 (1994).

104. Consider, for example, the increased domestic attention that might be paid to World Trade Organization (WTO) or NAFTA panel rulings if one of the panel members were a widely respected retired Justice of the U.S. Supreme Court.

105. It is perhaps not insignificant in this regard that Robert Lecourt, the enormously influential first President of the European Court of Justice, was a former French Minister of Justice. *See* RASMUSSEN, *supra* note 60, at 230. Rudolf Bernhardt, a judge on the ECHR since 1981 and Vice President since 1992, implicitly confirms the importance of judges' substantive areas of expertise when he notes that the ECHR is staffed by "judges of high national courts, professors of law and holders of various other positions in their home country (advocates, government officials, etc.)" and that only "a limited number of the members of the Court has special experience in the area of international law." Rudolf Bernhardt, *Human Rights and*

to gain acceptance of particular decisions from national judges, extending also to a greater impact on national administrators and even legislators.

On the other hand, special expertise undoubtedly carries its own authority. One English lawyer, commenting on the willingness of English courts to accept ECJ judgments, emphasizes the recognized expertise of the ECJ in European Union law, an area that can often be arcane to even an experienced and highly competent national judge.[106] Moreover, it cannot be questioned that expertise in human rights law enhances the prestige of international human rights tribunals. The development of a particular area of law often coincides with the growth and strength of a tribunal charged with interpreting and applying it. National judges in the European Community for instance, would have been unlikely to perceive the value of special expertise in European Community law if the ECJ and its many helpers had not succeeded in making that law a formidable force. If so, the question remains how best to compose a fledgling supranational tribunal so that it is poised to secure the authority and enhance the scope of the body of law it oversees. The ideal may be a mix of international experts and distinguished national practitioners—who themselves may be drawn from the judiciary, the government, or the private bar.[107]

b. *Caseload or Functional Capacity of the Court*

A second category of factors relevant to the effectiveness of a supranational tribunal that is, at least initially, within the control of member states concerns the caseload and functional capacity of the court. A court that is scarcely used, for whatever reason, cannot hope to make much of a mark.[108] Similarly, a court that is perceived as effective will attract more claimants. The trick is to build a sufficiently high-profile caseload at the outset to attract a steady stream of claimants. The material and financial resources that states devote to the tribunal, together with the degree of complexity they impose regarding its procedures and operations, can assist or hamper this endeavor.

Attracting cases was the prime concern for ECJ judges in the early years of the Court. To build their docket, they had to attract references from national

Judicial Review: The European Court of Human Rights, in HUMAN RIGHTS AND JUDICIAL REVIEW: A COMPARATIVE PERSPECTIVE 297, 301-02 (David M. Beatty ed., 1994). For a general discussion of the professional background of both judges and advocates general, see L. NEVILLE BROWN & TOM KENNEDY, THE COURT OF JUSTICE OF THE EUROPEAN COMMUNITIES 55-59, 67-69 (4th ed. 1994).

106. *See* P.P. CRAIG, THE EUROPEAN COURT AND NATIONAL COURTS DOCTRINE AND JURISPRUDENCE: LEGAL CHANGE IN ITS SOCIAL CONTEXT [REPORT ON THE UNITED KINGDOM] 26 (European Univ. Inst., Florence, Working Paper RSC No. 95/29, 1995) (noting the increased willingness of judges to refer cases to the ECJ as they become more familiar with the European Union's legal system and recognize the expertise of the ECJ in dealing with Union legal problems).

107. The particular mix should also take into consideration the range of subject matters likely to arise on a particular court's docket.

108. *See* MERRILLS, *supra* note 77, at 16.

courts under Article 177. As Judge G. Federico Mancini recounts, the "Court's first preoccupation" was to win the "co-operation and goodwill of the state courts."[109] To this end, the Court engaged in an extensive education campaign aimed at national judges, including seminars, dinners, regular invitations to Luxembourg, and visits around the Community.[110] As will be discussed further below,[111] the formulation of this strategy was within the control of the ECJ itself, but the judges were substantially aided by factors such as a large budget, a permanent and attractive home with a large library and research staff, and substantial educational and public relations resources.[112] The growth of the Court's reputation among litigants over time depended in part on the ready availability of its decisions in multiple languages and the efforts of its research staff in making information available to lawyers, litigants, and scholars on demand.[113]

The ECHR faced a similar task and was similarly aided. The court's docket swelled from a relative trickle of cases in the 1950s and 1960s to a flood in the 1980s.[114] Many factors contributed to this increase, including the rapid growth of the members of the Council of Europe and the resulting increased number of potential plaintiffs.[115] Nevertheless, the ECHR's relatively comfortable working conditions (which make it easier to attract distinguished judges), its physical location in Strasbourg, its relatively ample budget, and its ability to publicize its decisions have all contributed to its visibility and success.[116]

States responsible for establishing international tribunals can thus help ensure that the tribunals will have a sufficient caseload to be effective by

---

109. Mancini, *supra* note 60, at 605.

110. *See* RASMUSSEN, *supra* note 60, at 247.

111. *See infra* Subsection III.B.2.a.

112. *See* BROWN & KENNEDY, *supra* note 105, at 15-42.

113. *See id.* Brown and Kennedy describe in detail the resources made available to the Court, including interpreters, information officers, extensive library and documentation services, as well as an impressive court building.

114. Although the Commission has "continuously tried to increase its productivity," Schermers, *supra* note 82, at 497, it has been unable to keep up with the rise in complaints. In 1985, the number of applications rose to 600, in 1987 to 863, in 1989 to over 1300, and in 1992 to 1862. More than 2500 cases were pending before the Commission as of December 1995. *See id.* at 495. Only a fraction of these cases actually reached the court, of course; nevertheless, the pattern of expansion is evident.

115. *See* Henry G. Schermers, *The Eleventh Protocol to the European Convention on Human Rights*, 19 EUR. L. REV. 367, 368 (1994) (noting an increase in cases due to the court's acceptance by all participating states and the need to render judgment in all important cases); Karel de Vey Mestdagh, *Reform of the European Convention on Human Rights in a Changing Europe*, *in* THE DYNAMICS OF THE PROTECTION OF HUMAN RIGHTS IN EUROPE 337, 339-40 (Rick Lawson & Matthijs de Blois eds., 1994) (discussing the unexpected burden placed on the ECHR by the increase in member states and the unforeseen number of serious individual petitions).

116. *See* Marcus Binney, *Where Justice Can Be Seen To Be Done*, TIMES (London), June 27, 1995, *available in* 1995 WL 7678063; Denis Rousseau, *European Rights Court, Commission Get New Headquarters*, AGENCE FRANCE-PRESSE, June 29, 1995, *available in* 1995 WL 7822707; *cf.* Lynda E. Frost, *The Evolution of the Inter-American Court of Human Rights: Reflections of Present and Former Judges*, 14 HUM. RTS. Q. 171, 177-80 (1992) (arguing that the Inter-American Court of Human Rights's slim docket is linked to an inadequacy of judicial resources).

providing requisite resources. These resources can help to: (1) ensure that judges on the tribunal can educate potential constituencies of litigants concerning both the existence of the tribunal and the law it is charged to apply; (2) dispatch quickly and efficiently the complaints that the tribunal receives; and (3) publicize the results. At the most basic level, this is a matter of money and staffing. But beyond the commitment of material resources, states should give careful attention to the ease and efficiency of the procedures that litigants must follow to bring a case and that judges must follow to hear it. Cumbersome procedures can block the development of a docket in the first instance and prevent its ready dispatch once cases begin to arrive. That the states party to the European Convention on Human Rights were attuned to these concerns is demonstrated by their willingness to streamline the Convention's judicial review machinery to address a growing backlog of cases.[117]

c. *Independent Factfinding Capacity*

States contemplating the establishment of a supranational tribunal also have the authority to control the specific powers of the tribunal in carrying out its adjudicative function. An important dimension of these powers is the ability to elicit credible factual information on which to base the tribunal's decisions. A guaranteed capacity to generate facts that have been independently evaluated, either through a third-party factfinding process or through the public contestation inherent in the adversary system, helps counter the perception of self-serving or "political" judgments.

Several analysts of the ECHR have emphasized the importance of the Commission's, and hence ultimately the court's, ability to test independently the truth of the allegations of the parties.[118] Once the Commission determines that a case is admissible, it is bound by Article 28 of the Convention to examine the application "with a view to ascertaining the facts."[119] Under the established procedure, the state in question is legally bound to cooperate with such an investigation once the Commission has determined, on the basis of an

---

117. *See* Schermers, *supra* note 115, at 368-69.

118. *See, e.g.*, ROBERTSON & MERRILLS, *supra* note 81, at 11. According to Robertson and Merrills, the Commission's investigation is "carried out together with the representatives of the parties, which means in practice a hearing of a judicial nature with the individual applicant and the respondent government represented by counsel on a footing of complete equality." *Id.* For particular examples of the Commission's effective factfinding procedure, see *id.* at 274-81, which discusses with respect to a series of prominent cases the importance of the Commission's ability to establish crucial elements of fact through investigation. *See also* Kersten Rogge, *Fact-Finding*, *in* THE EUROPEAN SYSTEM FOR THE PROTECTION OF HUMAN RIGHTS 677 (R. St. J. Macdonald et al. eds., 1993) (discussing the Commission's competence to verify relevant facts, procedural issues related to on-site investigations, and standards of evidence).

119. Convention, *supra* note 2, art. 28(a), 213 U.N.T.S. at 238 (declaring that the Commission "shall, with a view to ascertaining the facts undertake together with the representatives of the parties an examination of the petition and, if need be, an investigation").

adversary hearing in which both parties are represented, that one is required.[120] On appeal, the ECHR's analysis of the dispute is aided by the Commission's findings of fact, but the court is also empowered to review those findings de novo.[121] Thus the legitimacy of both the ECHR's judgments and the decisions of the Commission depend in large part on their ability to generate an accurate factual record.

When sitting as appellate tribunals charged only with answering specific questions of law, courts like the ECJ do not have such factfinding capacity.[122] The ECJ, however, sits atop a system of courts and tribunals that do have such capacity. Further, the ECJ has the authority to compel the parties to produce documents and "to supply all information which the Court considers desirable," to examine witnesses and the parties themselves, and to seek expert opinions from third parties.[123]

d. *Formal Authority or Status as Law of the Instrument That the Tribunal Is Charged with Interpreting and Applying*

Also relevant to effectiveness is whether the instrument that the tribunal is charged with interpreting and the tribunal's decisions themselves are regarded as binding and hence accorded formal status as law.[124] Both the Treaty of Rome and the European Convention on Human Rights provide that the decisions of the ECJ and the ECHR shall be binding on member states brought before it.[125] These provisions establish the authority of these bodies

120. Article 28 also obligates the state or states concerned to "furnish all necessary facilities, after an exchange of views with the Commission." *Id.*

121. *See* DeWilde, Ooms & Versyp Cases (The Vagrancy Cases), 12 Eur. Ct. H.R. (ser. A) at 29 (1971).

122. Independent factfinding capacity of an inquisitorial nature is one way of assuring accuracy, but such a system arguably works best when complemented by a modicum of adversary process. In the United States, adversary process rests on the assumption "that truth is likely to emerge more from bilateral investigation and presentation, motivated by the strong pull of self-interest, than from judicial investigation motivated only by official duty." FLEMING JAMES, JR. ET AL., CIVIL PROCEDURE 5 (4th ed. 1992). The element of personal representation in adversary process also serves values of individual dignity and autonomy, as discussed below. *See infra* note 212 and accompanying text. Most civil law systems incorporate some element of the adversary process in addition to enhanced "inquisitorial" powers for the judge; while the judge has dominant authority to determine the legal theory to be applied, he or she is highly dependent on the parties for presentation of the evidence. *See* GEOFFREY C. HAZARD, JR. & MICHELE TARUFFO, AMERICAN CIVIL PROCEDURE: AN INTRODUCTION 86 (1993).

123. Protocol on the Statute of the Court of Justice of the European Communities, Apr. 17, 1957, art. 21, 298 U.N.T.S. 147, 152; *id.* art. 22, 298 U.N.T.S at 152; *id.* art. 25, 298 U.N.T.S. at 153; *id.* art. 29, 298 U.N.T.S. at 154.

124. We do not use the term "binding" here in the Anglo-Saxon sense of binding precedent, to be followed by all subsequent courts in subsequent cases, but rather in the more general sense as requiring compliance by virtue of a formal treaty provision.

125. *See* TREATY OF ROME art. 171 ("If the Court of Justice finds that a Member State has failed to fulfil an obligation under this Treaty, the State shall be required to take the necessary measures required to comply with the judgment of the Court of Justice."); *id.* art. 176 (mandating that "the Institution whose act has been declared void or whose failure to act has been declared contrary to this Treaty shall be required to take the necessary measures to comply with the judgment of the Court of Justice"); Convention, *supra* note 2, art. 53, 213 U.N.T.S. at 248 (requiring the parties to "undertake to abide by the decision of

as legal tribunals, a factor to which commentators assessing their effectiveness give considerable weight.[126]

"Legal" status, however, operates on several levels. These treaties establish the status of court decisions as binding pronouncements of *international* law. Conventional wisdom would place equal or greater weight on the status of treaties and supranational court decisions as domestic law. Thus, for instance, states that have "incorporated" a treaty as part of domestic law, via constitutional or statutory provisions, are expected to comply more readily with its requirements. After all, the treaty can then be enforced directly by domestic courts. This belief animates incorporation campaigns such as the drive to convince Britain to implement the ECHR through a domestic statute.[127]

Incorporation offers no guarantee, however, that domestic courts and their fellow branches of government will comply more readily with the judgments of the supranational tribunal charged with interpreting and applying the incorporated treaty. Incorporation, for instance, may trigger a *Kompetenz-Kompetenz* struggle,[128] in which domestic courts decide that they should be the ones to determine the extent to which the treaty provisions override or otherwise effect the interpretation and application of purely domestic law.[129]

---

the Court in any case to which they are parties"). Article 46(2) of Protocol No. 11 contains essentially identical language. *See* Protocol No. 11, *supra* note 93, art. 46(2).

126. *See, e.g.*, P.J.G. KAPTEYN & P. VERLOREN VAN THEMAAT, INTRODUCTION TO THE LAW OF THE EUROPEAN COMMUNITIES 38 (Laurence W. Gormley ed., 2d ed. 1989) ("The extensive powers of the Court of Justice ensure that the law is respected, as regards the functioning of the Community, in a way that is without precedent in the law of international organisations."); Merja Pentikainen & Martin Scheinin, *A Comparative Study of the Monitoring Mechanisms and the Important Institutional Frameworks for Human Rights Protection Within the Council of Europe, the CSCE and the European Community*, *in* MONITORING HUMAN RIGHTS IN EUROPE 93, 104 (Arie Bloed et al. eds., 1993) ("When considering the advantages of the ECHR system, . . . the fact that the complaint procedures end with decisions which are legally binding upon the states parties . . . must be emphasized."); *see also* M.A. Eissen, *L'Interaction des Jurisprudences Constitutionnelles Nationales et de la Jurisprudence de la Cour Europeene des Droits de l'Homme*, *in* CONSEIL CONSTITUTIONNEL ET COUR EUROPEENNE DES DROITS DE L'HOMME 137 (Dominique Rousseau & Frederique Sudre eds., 1990).

127. *See Unconventional Human Rights*, ECONOMIST, Sept. 24, 1994, at 56. In 1991, Lord Ackner noted, in a decision holding that lack of proportionality was not a separate ground of review under English administrative law, that until Parliament incorporated the Convention into domestic law, there was no basis upon which the proportionality doctrine applied by the ECHR could be followed by the courts of the United Kingdom. *See* R. v. Secretary of State for the Home Dep't (*Ex Parte* Brind), [1991] 1 App. Cas. 696 (H.L. 1991).

128. The term "*Kompetenz-Kompetenz*" carries two separate meanings due to its origins in German constitutional law. As used in discussions of the European Union, it refers both to the power of the Union to determine (or enlarge) its own competences and to the power of the ECJ to determine which norms come within the sphere of application of Union law. The latter meaning is also known as judicial *Kompetenz-Kompetenz*. For a discussion and additional sources, see Theodor Schilling, *The Autonomy of the Community Legal Order: An Analysis of Possible Foundations*, 37 HARV. INT'L L.J. 389, 406 (1996); and Weiler & Haltern, *supra* note 68, at 413. *See also* Weiler, *supra* note 60, at 2414.

129. For specific discussion of how this struggle manifests itself within the Union, see the European University Institute 1995 Working Paper Series, *The European Court and National Courts Doctrine and Jurisprudence: Legal Change in Its Social Context*, including JULIANE KOKOTT, THE EUROPEAN COURT AND NATIONAL COURTS DOCTRINE AND JURISPRUDENCE: LEGAL CHANGE IN ITS SOCIAL CONTEXT [REPORT ON GERMANY] 20 (European Univ. Inst., Florence, Working Paper RSC No. 95/25, 1995); and JENS PLOTNER, THE EUROPEAN COURT AND NATIONAL COURTS DOCTRINE AND JURISPRUDENCE: LEGAL CHANGE IN ITS SOCIAL CONTEXT [REPORT ON FRANCE] 11 (European Univ. Inst., Florence, Working Paper

Similarly, national governmental officials may feel that they can interpret the provisions of the treaty *as incorporated into national law* as well as the supranational tribunal can.

In fact, the empirical record concerning the impact of incorporation is mixed. On the one hand, Dutch courts were the first national courts to refer cases to the ECJ and to abide by its decisions even in the face of opposition from other branches of government, a posture that is difficult to separate from Dutch monism, or willingness to accept international law as automatically part of domestic law.[130] Similarly, in his study of the legal authority of ECHR decisions in domestic legal proceedings, Andrew Drzemczewski observes: "[A] basic distinction may have to be made between those states in which the Convention possesses the status of internal law and those in which it does not."[131] Jörg Polakiewicz and Valérie Jacob-Foltzer concur: Most important among the factors "which determine the impact of Strasbourg case-law in domestic law . . . is certainly the status of the Convention in the hierarchy of internal norms."[132]

On the other hand, France, also a monist state, resisted the direct effect and supremacy of European Community law, while both Italy and Belgium, dualist states, were more willing to comply.[133] Observers of the ECHR also reach divergent conclusions. Mirielle Delmas-Marty, for instance, claims that "the correlation that one could have expected to find between the status of the Convention in the national laws and the degree of effectiveness or resistance that may be observed is not clearly established."[134] While international lawyers might be expected to have a professional interest in finding that refusal to incorporate the provisions of an international treaty into domestic law does not decisively determine the impact of those provisions, it is noteworthy that even scholars who are prepared to acknowledge the significance of this factor qualify their conclusions.[135]

RSC No. 95/28, 1995).

130. *See* MONICA CLAES & BRUNO DE WITTE, THE EUROPEAN COURT AND NATIONAL COURTS DOCTRINE AND JURISPRUDENCE: LEGAL CHANGE IN ITS SOCIAL CONTEXT [REPORT ON THE NETHERLANDS] 21 (European Univ. Inst., Florence, Working Paper RSC No. 95/26, 1995).

131. DRZEMCZEWSKI, *supra* note 90, at 268.

132. Polakiewicz & Jacob-Foltzer, *supra* note 91, at 141.

133. *See* ALEC STONE SWEET, CONSTITUTIONAL DIALOGUES IN THE EUROPEAN COMMUNITY 10-13 (European Univ. Inst., Florence, Working Paper RSC No. 95/38, 1995).

134. Mireille Delmas-Marty, *Abuses of the Reason of State*, *in* THE EUROPEAN CONVENTION FOR THE PROTECTION OF HUMAN RIGHTS 101, 103 (Mireille Delmas-Marty & Christine Chodkiewicz eds., 1992); *see also* Rudolf Bernhardt, *The Convention and Domestic Law*, *in* THE EUROPEAN SYSTEM FOR THE PROTECTION OF HUMAN RIGHTS, *supra* note 118, at 25, 40 ("Our conclusion is that irrespective of the formal incorporation of the Convention in the domestic law of States, Convention law and domestic law are so closely interconnected that only together can they be adequately addressed.").

135. Andrew Drzemczewski, for example, writes:

> Even in countries which have not incorporated the Convention, the judiciary may be inclined to take judicial notice of the findings of the Strasbourg organs (especially when the latter elaborate or clarify the meaning of the Convention's provisions), since there exists a general presumption that the courts should interpret domestic law in such a way as to make it consistent with the state's international obligations.

Several factors reinforce the potential impact of international treaties even in the absence of incorporation provisions. First, where an international instrument is not accorded status as domestic law, either through a monist constitutional provision or specific implementation through a domestic statute, it may nevertheless be effective in filling gaps in domestic law. Drzemczewski, for example, attributes the impact of the European Convention on Human Rights on the Austrian legal system to gaps in Austrian domestic law concerning due process safeguards in criminal prosecutions.[136] Several observers of the British judicial scene also comment on the relative willingness of English courts to look to the Convention in light of the absence of a written bill of rights in England.[137] Second, courts can frequently draw on canons of interpretation requiring them to interpret domestic law consistently with international treaties, even where those treaties have not themselves been made self-executing.[138]

On balance, we conclude that the effectiveness of a supranational tribunal is enhanced where states make its decisions legally binding on the parties to the dispute before it. By contrast, our view of the legal status of an international agreement as domestic law is more tempered. Formal incorporation into domestic law appears to have some positive impact on enhancing a tribunal's effectiveness, suggesting that states should take steps to incorporate or otherwise to endow international law with the same force as domestic law. The ultimate impact of such direct or indirect implementation, however, will depend on a host of other factors, such as the relationship between courts and other branches of government and a state's openness to the international legal system. Thus, we include this factor in the checklist, but without the pride of place it might be expected to enjoy. Those who would put their faith in incorporation campaigns should be forewarned that such a step may be only the first step. Conversely, those who fear decisive political resistance to incorporation from the legislature or the executive should not lose hope.

2. *Factors Within the Control of the Judiciary*

Even assuming that the states party to an international agreement establishing a supranational tribunal are fully cooperative and establish all the above conditions to enhance its effectiveness, much remains for the tribunal itself to do. It is the ECJ itself that is popularly credited with the

---

DRZEMCZEWSKI, *supra* note 90, at 261.

136. *See id.* at 93.

137. *See, e.g., Unconventional Human Rights*, *supra* note 127, at 56. *The Economist* further notes that reliance on the European Convention has strengthened the power of lower British courts vis-à-vis Parliament. *See id.*

138. *See* DRZEMCZEWSKI, *supra* note 90, at 261.

transformation of the Treaty of Rome from an international agreement into the constitution of the European Union, by convincing national courts to apply European Union law directly and supremely to national law.[139] The ECJ benefited greatly from the structural relationship with national courts that Article 177 created, providing a ready-made entrée into national legal systems. Nevertheless, the Court still faced the task of wooing the national courts, convincing them to refer cases and to listen and respond to the resulting ECJ judgments.[140]

The ECHR has no structural provision equivalent to Article 177. It has instead faced a situation in which a number of national courts have been inclined to apply the law of the Convention, especially where the Convention has been incorporated into national law, without necessarily following the interpretations developed by the ECHR.[141] It has thus had to rely equally on government officials and on national legislators to heed its judgments, a situation more typical of classic international tribunals.

In both cases, however, the question remains: Why have national actors listened and responded? More precisely, how did these two tribunals manipulate factors within their control to maximize their impact on the relevant national actors? This section of the checklist identifies those factors. They include the tribunals' awareness of their audiences, their demonstrated autonomy from political interests, their incremental style of decisionmaking, the quality of their legal reasoning, their dialogue with other supranational tribunals, and the forms of their opinions. Many of these factors overlap; many may strike readers as the standard elements of "good judging." We present them here as specific components of a sustained effort by two supranational tribunals to enhance their effectiveness.

a. *Awareness of Audience*

The ECJ and the ECHR have both been aware of constituencies for their

---

139. *See supra* note 60 and accompanying text.

140. The story as recounted here focuses primarily on the contributions of the ECJ itself to the establishment and strengthening of its relationship with the national courts. National courts, however, had independent reasons to listen and respond. The most comprehensive account of the motives of national judges is contained in ALTER, *supra* note 70, at 5-23. *See also* WALTER MATTLI & ANNE-MARIE SLAUGHTER, CONSTRUCTING THE EUROPEAN COMMUNITY LEGAL SYSTEM FROM THE GROUND UP: THE ROLE OF THE INDIVIDUAL LITIGANTS AND NATIONAL COURTS 20-27 (European Univ. Inst., Florence, Working Paper RSC No. 95/39, 1995) (using evidence from a country study to discuss three strands of judicial interest: judicial review, judicial competition, and promotion of substantive policies).

141. For general discussions on national courts' acceptance of the Strasbourg court's interpretations, see DRZEMCZEWSKI, *supra* note 90, at 268; and Polakiewicz & Jacob-Foltzer, *supra* note 91, at 66. For discussion of specific countries, see DRZEMCZEWSKI, *supra* note 90, at 270, which discusses Austria; Polakiewicz & Jacob-Foltzer, *supra* note 91, at 72, which discusses Belgium; and *id.* at 129, which discusses the Netherlands. The situation described in the text is similar to the relationship between the ECJ and supreme national courts, many of which have been noticeably more reluctant than lower national courts to refer cases to the ECJ and to follow its rulings. *See* ALTER, *supra* note 70, at 18-19.

decisions other than the monolithic "states" that are their apparent creators and subjects. The ECJ has targeted both national courts and individual litigants. The ECHR has focused more on individual subjects of state governments. In both cases, the tribunals have recognized an audience beyond the parties to the case at hand and have crafted their opinions to encourage additional cases by appealing to both the material interests and professional ideals of prospective litigants or referring courts. They have also used these appeals to penetrate the surface of the state, linking up to different domestic political actors with actually or potentially divergent interests.

The ECJ helped create its own constituency by deliberately aiming many of its landmark opinions at individual litigants who stood particularly to gain from the enforcement of European Community law, from importers and exporters to individual taxpayers. *Van Gend & Loos*[142] is explicit on this score:

> [T]he Community constitutes a new legal order . . . for the benefit of which the states have limited their sovereign rights, albeit within limited fields, *and the subjects of which comprise not only Member States but also their nationals.* Independently of the legislation of the Member States, Community law *therefore imposes obligations on individuals but is also intended to confer on them rights which become part of their legal heritage.*[143]

This passage served as an announcement that the ECJ was prepared to enforce the rights of individuals under the Treaty of Rome against the individuals' own state governments in instances where those governments proved recalcitrant about fulfilling treaty obligations of potential benefit to classes of individuals.

Van Gend & Loos also reveals a keen awareness of the importance of establishing a good relationship with national courts, the sources of potential references under Article 177. The case involved one of the first references from a national court (the Dutch Tariefcommissie). The ECJ was anxious to encourage additional references while simultaneously establishing its own authority within the sphere of Community law. It thus adopted a strategy of manifest deference to those national courts acting within their proper sphere of jurisdiction, combined with an appeal to those courts to use Community law in exercising their primary function of protecting individual rights.[144]

142. Case 26/62, N.V. Algemene Transp. & Expeditie Onderneming Van Gend & Loos v. Nederlandse administratie der belastingen, 1963 E.C.R. 1; *see supra* note 62 and accompanying text.

143. *Van Gend & Loos*, 1963 E.C.R. at 12 (emphasis added).

144. For instance, in response to a contention by the Belgian government that no ruling by the ECJ could have any bearing on further proceedings in the Tariefcommissie, the ECJ emphasized that it was up to the national court to decide whether to seek assistance on questions of Community law, and that the "considerations which may have led a national court or tribunal to its choice of questions as well as the relevance which it attributes to such questions in the context of a case before it are excluded from review by the Court of Justice." *Id.* at 11. After concluding that Article 12 of the Treaty of Rome was directly applicable to the national courts, the ECJ concluded that the actual application of the Article on the specific

The ECJ's next task was to encourage direct references from lower national courts in the face of opposition from their own supreme courts. The Court responded by again emphasizing, court to court, the duties of the national courts to protect individual rights. Where such rights flow from supranational law, the ECJ declared, national courts have an obligation to enforce them in accordance with instructions from the ECJ rather than from higher national courts.[145] Over time, the ECJ depicted itself as a partner of the national courts, collaborating with them to enforce Community law. National courts responded in kind, increasing the number of references under Article 177 from 9 in 1968, to 119 in 1978, to over 150 per year in the 1990s.[146]

This partnership ultimately has evolved into a form of powersharing in which national courts, particularly national supreme courts, communicate their preferences to the ECJ concerning the content and scope of European Community law. The German Constitutional Court has been the ECJ's most active interlocutor in this regard. It announced in the early 1970s that it would not accept the ultimate authority of the ECJ in cases involving the human rights of German citizens because the ECJ had not established a comparable system of human rights protections in European Community law.[147] When

---

facts of the case presented was a matter for the Tariefcommissie to resolve. The court contented itself with a final declaration that "Article 12 . . . produces direct effects and creates individual rights which national courts must protect." *Id.* at 16.

145. In Case 106/77, *Amministrazione delle Finanze dello Stato v. Simmenthal S.p.A.*, 1978 E.C.R. 629, a lower Italian court asked the ECJ to resolve a conflict between a provision of Community law and an apparently conflicting provision of the Italian constitution, notwithstanding a decision by the Italian Constitutional Court that such conflicts should be referred to the Constitutional Court itself. The ECJ held that the provisions of Community law

> are . . . a direct source of rights and duties for all those affected thereby, whether Member States or individuals, who are parties to legal relationships under Community law. This consequence also concerns any national court whose task it is as an organ of a Member State to protect, in a case within its jurisdiction, the rights conferred upon individuals by Community law.

Id. at 643. It followed that any provision of national law that threatened to impede the ability of national courts to enforce Community law was itself a violation of Community law and should thus be disregarded by the national court. *See id.* at 645-46.

146. *See* BERMANN ET AL., *supra* note 63, at 245. This interaction between the ECJ and national courts has been described as a form of "judicial dialogue." Anne-Marie Slaughter, *A Typology of Transjudicial Communication*, 29 U. RICH. L. REV. 99, 100, 135-36 (1994). Commentators on the ECHR have also observed the beginnings of a similar dialogue between the ECHR and national courts. *See* Polakiewicz & Jacob-Foltzer, *supra* note 91, at 66. As Polakiewicz and Jacob-Foltzer write:

> Faced with an ever-increasing case-law from Strasbourg, domestic courts have gradually abandoned their reserved attitude with regard to the Convention. We are witnessing the beginning of a true dialogue between the European Human Rights Court and national jurisdictions whereby principles like the proportionality test that have been developed in certain national legal orders are taken up by the European Court of Human Rights and later accepted in other countries as part of a common European standard.

Id.

147. *See* Internationale Handelsgesellschaft mbH v. Einfuhr- und Vorratsstelle fur Getreide und Futtermittel (Solange I), Entscheidungen des Bundesverfassungsgerichts [BVerfGE] [Federal Constitutional Court] 37, 271 (271-79) (1974) (F.R.G.), *translated in* [1974] 2 C.M.L.R. 540, 540-51 (concluding that Community law, which did not protect fundamental rights to the degree required by the constitution of the Federal Republic of Germany, would not be accorded priority over German law that was designed to

the ECJ responded by establishing such a system, which blended a mixture of national and international human rights guarantees, the German court in turn softened its stance.[148] In such cases, awareness of audience becomes responsiveness to audience, but such necessities are the ultimate fruits of a supranational tribunal's success.

Without the benefits of the structural provisions of Article 177, the ECHR has had to target a broader and more diffuse audience of individual victims of human rights abuses.[149] One device that has served it well in this regard is the "doctrine of effectiveness."[150] According to this doctrine, the Convention's "special character as a treaty for the collective enforcement of human rights"[151] requires that its provisions be interpreted and applied so as to make its safeguards "practical and effective"[152] rather than "theoretical or illusory."[153]

"Practical and effective" in this context means a willingness to find for individual litigants against their national governments, a position the ECHR is quite willing to broadcast.[154] Indeed, in *Cossey v. United Kingdom*,[155] dissenting Judge Martens described the ECHR as the "last resort protector of

---

protect those rights).

148. *See In re* Wünsche Handelsgesellschaft (Solange II), BVerfGE 73, 339 (377) (1986) (F.R.G.), *translated in* [1987] 3 C.M.L.R. 225, 259 (concluding that the 14 years of ECJ practice since *Solange I* had created a climate of effective protection of fundamental rights within Community law). Accordingly, the German court declined to police further the compatibility of European Community law with German fundamental rights. *See* Jochen A. Frowein, Recent Case, 25 COMMON MKT. L. REV. 201, 205 (1988); *see also* Weiler, *supra* note 60, at 2428.

The German Constitutional Court's ambivalence regarding European Union law was repeated in its recent decision in a case challenging the constitutionality of the Masstricht Treaty, which established the European Union. *See* Judgment of Oct. 12, 1993 (Brunner v. European Union Treaty), BVerfGE 89, 155 (F.R.G.), *translated in* [1994] 1 C.M.L.R. 57. The German court found the treaty constitutional, but only so long as the competences of the European Union remained sufficiently limited to assure German citizens of the guarantees of democracy provided them in their constitution. To keep the institutions of the Union within these limits, the German court proposed that it enter into a "relationship of co-operation" with the European Court of Justice, "under which [the ECJ] guarantees protection of basic rights in any particular case for the whole area of the European Communities, and the [German] Constitutional Court can therefore restrict itself to a general guarantee of the constitutional standards that cannot be dispensed with." *Id.* at 79.

149. The ECHR has not, however, ignored the important role that national courts can play in interpreting and applying the Convention. Thus, when a claimant failed to raise arguments based on the Convention in a country whose courts gave its provisions direct effect, the ECHR dismissed the case for failure to exhaust domestic remedies. *See* Van Oosterwijck v. Belgium, 40 Eur. Ct. H.R. (ser. A) at 16-17 (1980).

150. Bernhardt, *supra* note 105, at 306 (noting that the doctrine of effectiveness means that the ECHR sees the Convention's object and purpose as the protection of the individual and that the interpretation of its provisions must guarantee that these protections become effective).

151. Soering v. United Kingdom, 161 Eur. Ct. H.R. (ser. A) at 34 (1989).

152. McCann v. United Kingdom, 324 Eur. Ct. H.R. (ser. A) at 45 (1995); *accord* Loizidou v. Turkey, 310 Eur. Ct. H.R. (ser. A) at 27 (1995).

153. Artico v. Italy, 37 Eur. Ct. H.R. (ser. A) at 16 (1980).

154. *See, e.g.*, Ribitsch v. Austria, 21 Eur. H.R. Rep. 573, 577 (Commission report) (stating that the "proceedings instituted under the European Convention on Human Rights are not aimed at punishing the authors of violations, but at protecting the victims and providing redress for damage caused by the acts of state responsibility"), *aff'd*, 336 Eur. Ct. H.R. (ser. A) at 26-28 (1995).

155. 184 Eur. Ct. H.R. (ser. A) (1990).

oppressed individuals."[156] The ECHR is particularly active in interpreting the Convention "effectively" when reviewing the treatment of especially vulnerable groups. Its receptiveness on these questions signals to disadvantaged individuals throughout member countries the court's willingness to review carefully alleged violations of both procedural and substantive rights by their governments.[157] With Protocol No. 11's entry into force, the court will find it easier to target individual claimants; for the first time, these claimants will be given direct access to the ECHR in every case.[158]

Individuals and their lawyers, voluntary associations, and nongovernmental organizations are ultimately the users and consumers of judicial rulings to redress a particular wrong or advance a particular cause or set of interests. Their power still ultimately depends on their influence with respect to state political institutions—courts, legislatures, administrative agencies, or executives. But an appreciation of the relationship between these social actors and the institutions of state government opens the door to deploying them as forces for expanding the power and influence of supranational tribunals. Just as a supranational tribunal may align its case law with the independent incentives facing some national courts, it can also address itself to the individuals and groups who are likely to be the ultimate beneficiaries of the enforcement of international norms and instruments.

b. *Neutrality and Demonstrated Autonomy from Political Interests*

Commentators have emphasized the link between a supranational tribunal's authority and its neutrality, here defined not only in terms of equidistance between litigants but also with regard to a tribunal's ability to explicate a decision based on generally applicable legal principles. The alternative is

156. *Id.* at 29 (Martens, J., dissenting).

157. *See, e.g.*, Young v. United Kingdom, 44 Eur. Ct. H.R. (ser. A) at 25 (1981) ("Although individual interests must on occasion be subordinated to those of a group, democracy does not simply mean that the views of a majority must always prevail: a balance must be achieved which ensures the fair and proper treatment of minorities and avoids any abuse of a dominant position."); *see also* C.A. Gearty, *The European Court of Human Rights and the Protection of Civil Liberties*, 52 CAMBRIDGE L.J. 89, 108 (1993) ("In the Convention there are no articles dealing specifically with disadvantaged groups, and the Court has had to deploy general provisions in the pursuit of its overall objectives; it is a case of protecting especially vulnerable individuals whose plight happens to be shared by others . . . ."). Examples of the disadvantaged groups aided by the ECHR include prisoners, the mentally ill, and those involved in child custody cases. *See id.*

158. Article 34 of Protocol No. 11 states:

> The Court may receive applications from any person, non-governmental organisation or group of individuals claiming to be the victim of a violation by one of the High Contracting Parties of the rights set forth in the Convention or the Protocols thereto. The High Contracting Parties undertake not to hinder in any way the effective exercise of this right.

Protocol No. 11, *supra* note 93, art. 34; *see* Henry Schermers, *Adaptation of the 11th Protocol to the European Convention on Human Rights*, 20 EUR. L. REV. 559, 569 (1995). Many regard this section of the Protocol as a positive trend towards granting individuals more access to and presence in the ECHR. *See, e.g.*, Schermers, *supra* note 115, at 382 (criticizing the Protocol overall but adding that it does contain improvements, "especially by making the right of the individual petition compulsory").

"political" dispute resolution, in which the dispute resolver seeks above all to satisfy or reconcile the parties' competing interests.[159] The challenge for a court seeking to present itself as a judicial rather than a political body is thus to demonstrate its independence from both political authorities and political modes of dispute resolution. The judicial selection and tenure process (discussed in the first set of factors above)[160] are obviously key factors here. In addition, a tribunal can to some extent manage perceptions of its impartiality by refusing to pander to the governments at whose sufferance it exists. As the history of supranational adjudication in Europe makes plain, both the ECJ and the ECHR have been willing to decide against governments in big cases.[161]

Such willingness does not, however, imply that the tribunals are always aggressive in seeking to find treaty violations. To the contrary, they have often used procedural mechanisms to avoid reaching the merits of a dispute. Thus, both the ECHR and the Commission require claimants to satisfy all of the preconditions for the admissibility of their complaints, and the Commission has regularly dismissed claims where the petitioner failed to proffer evidence in support of his or her case.[162] As a further guarantee of fairness, the ECHR decided in its earliest cases that it had the competence to reconsider a government's objections to admissibility after the Commission had rejected them, a doctrine that has resulted in cases being dismissed on appeal.[163]

159. A classic statement of this position is Lon Fuller's explication of the distinctive features of adjudication. *See* Lon L. Fuller, *The Forms and Limits of Adjudication*, 92 HARV. L. REV. 353, 365-72 (1978). We fully recognize the decades of debate, both before and after Fuller's article, over the validity of the "law/politics" divide. Whatever the proper framing of the interaction between law and politics regarding the activities of a mature judicial tribunal, however, we contend that a young tribunal must be very careful to draw and maintain a very basic version of this distinction with regard to other decisionmaking bodies.

Observers of the ECHR also stress the distinction between legal and political decisionmaking. Drzemczewski, for instance, notes that the decisions of the Committee of Ministers, a "political body," "are likely to carry less weight than the reasoned judgments of the [ECHR]." DRZEMCZEWSKI, *supra* note 90, at 323-24. Paul Sieghart concurs, emphasizing that the Committee of Ministers "is not an impartial tribunal composed of independent individuals, but a political body made up of governmental representatives." PAUL SIEGHART, THE INTERNATIONAL LAW OF HUMAN RIGHTS 27 (1983).

160. *See supra* Subsection III.B.1.a.

161. *See, e.g.*, McCann v. United Kingdom, 324 Eur. Ct. H.R. (ser. A) at 174 (1995) (finding a violation of the Convention in the killing of IRA service unit members); Loizidou v. Turkey, 310 Eur. Ct. H.R. (ser. A) at 18 (1995) (rejecting important aspects of Turkey's reservations on the right of individual petition and the court's jurisdiction); Funke v. France, 256-A Eur. Ct. H.R. (ser. A) at 22 (1993) (finding a violation of the Convention resulting from seizure of documents from the applicant's home and imposing monetary sanctions for failure to produce additional documents); Cases C-6/90 & C-9/90, Francovich v. Italy, 67 C.M.L.R. 66 (1991) (recognizing the right of private parties to sue for damages caused by the state's failure to implement Community law); Case C-221/89, The Queen v. Secretary of State for Transp. (*Ex parte* Factortame Ltd.), 1991 E.C.R. I-3905 (invalidating British laws on the registration of shipping vessels); Case 176/84, Commission v. Hellenic Republic, 1987 E.C.R. 1193 (invalidating a Greek law that effectively prohibited the sale of foreign beer in Greece).

162. *See* ROBERTSON & MERRILLS, *supra* note 81, at 264, 273 (characterizing the Commission's admissibility decisions as strict and noting that under current practice 90% of cases are dismissed at the admissibility stage).

163. *See, e.g.*, Van Oosterwijck v. Belgium, 40 Eur. Ct. H.R. (ser. B) at 26 (1980). This doctrine is not without its critics, however. *See, e.g.*, Brozicek v. Italy, 167 Eur. Ct. H.R. (ser. A) at 22-28 (1989)

Similarly, the ECJ has refused to accept referrals where no genuine controversy concerning an issue of Community law exists, even if the national court or administrative body believed that such issues should be decided.[164] The Court thus has assured member states that it will not decide issues of Community law that are not directly relevant to the disputes before national courts.[165]

For fledgling tribunals, however, counseling autonomy and neutrality presents a dilemma. Members of such tribunals may feel that their authority and legitimacy depends on not antagonizing those governments on which their power ultimately depends, and on proceeding diplomatically. To the extent that a particular tribunal is composed of some individuals from nations without a tradition of an independent judiciary, and to the extent the states under the jurisdiction of the tribunal do not have such a tradition, accommodationist pressures are likely to be particularly strong. In this context, neutrality can come to mean "avoiding political confrontation," a euphemism for choosing not to remind governments of their legal obligations.[166]

The solution to this dilemma turns on a prior conception of identity as a *court*, or at least as a quasi-judicial tribunal. "Court-ness" does not rule out incrementalism or strategic decisionmaking, as discussed further in the next subsection. It does, however, mandate decisionmaking premised (at least formally) on principle rather than power. As studies of "legalization" of international decisionmaking suggest, secrecy and compromise are the hallmarks of diplomacy, not law.[167] Thus, tribunals must be willing to brave political displeasure, searching always for generalizable principles, even as they search for formulations or procedural mechanisms to render the principles more palatable to the states concerned.

c. *Incrementalism*

Bold demonstrations of judicial autonomy by judgments against state interests and appeals to constituencies of individuals must be tempered by incrementalism and awareness of political boundaries. The ECJ originally borrowed a leaf from Chief Justice John Marshall's book, edging principles

---

(separate opinion of Martens, J.).

164. *See, e.g.*, Case 244/80, Pasquale Foglia v. Mariella Novello (Foglia II), 1981 E.C.R. 3045.

165. *See id.* at 3066-77.

166. Robertson and Merrills note that the Commission, in its early years of operation, dismissed at the admissibility stage 98% of all petitions filed, a figure they characterize as unduly high. *See* ROBERTSON & MERRILLS, *supra* note 81, at 264. Beddard concurs that the Commission "trod very carefully and timidly in its early days," but he maintains that this early caution was "essential for the Convention's success." BEDDARD, *supra* note 75, at 227.

167. *See, e.g.*, John H. Jackson, *The Legal Meaning of a GATT Dispute Settlement Report: Some Reflections, in* TOWARDS MORE EFFECTIVE SUPERVISION BY INTERNATIONAL ORGANIZATIONS 149, 151 (Niels Blokker & Sam Muller eds., 1994).

forward while deciding for those most likely to oppose them in practice.[168] Only skilled lawyers could predict the far-reaching outcomes of the early landmark cases, the pregnant potential in a carefully couched phrase. Each case supported the next—from direct effect of selected treaty articles, to the supremacy of Community law over national law, to the direct effect of directives—but the Court took its time and generally responded to strong political signals that it had gone too far.[169]

Overall, the forms and language of law insulated an emerging legal community from the political realm. Again, this is not to suggest a strict divide between law and politics, but rather a mediated interaction. The overall boundaries for the ECJ are set by the political institutions of the Community, above all the member states. If the Court pushes teleological interpretation of the treaty—a mode of interpretation biased toward achieving the ever closer union described in the Treaty's preamble—too far too fast, the member states can act to curtail its jurisdiction or urge their national courts to disregard its judgments.[170] They might also seek to shift the composition of the Court.

The Court has thus used the Commission of the Community, the executive-political branch of the Community, as a political bellwether, watching its position on major cases as a sign of what the political traffic will bear.[171]

---

168. As Weiler explains:

> There was a slow change of climate and ethos [in the early days of the ECJ] whereby strict enumeration was progressively, relentlessly, but never dramatically, eroded. Extension, absorption, incorporation, and powers implied by the Court, all feed on each other in cog-and-wheel fashion so that no dissonances are revealed within the constitutional architecture itself as it is changing.

Weiler, *supra* note 60, at 2447 (analogizing this tactic to U.S. Chief Justice John Marshall's reasoning in *McCulloch v. Maryland*, 17 U.S. (4 Wheat.) 316, 421 (1819)); *see also* ALTER, *supra* note 70, at 282 (noting how the ECJ followed a well-known judicial practice, expanding "its jurisdictional authority by establishing legal principles, but not applying the principles to the cases at hand").

169. The Court retrenched somewhat in the face of strong political opposition to the *ERTA* case, Case 22/70, Commission v. Council, 1971 E.C.R. 263, in which it held that powers granted to the Commission of the Community in internal Community matters implied concomitant powers to represent the Community in external affairs. The ECJ similarly retrenched after opposition to its decision in Case 41/74, *van Duyn v. Home Office*, 1974 E.C.R. 1337, in which the Court granted direct effect to some categories of directives.

170. In 1992, Chancellor Helmut Kohl of Germany voiced distress over what he saw as "unwarranted judicial activism": "[The Court of Justice] does not only exert its competencies in legal matters, but goes far further. We have an example of something that was not wanted in the beginning." *Chancellor Kohl Accuses the Court of Going Beyond Its Competencies: The 'Paletta' and 'Boetel' Cases*, EUROPE, Oct. 14, 1992, at 9. Walter Mattli and Anne-Marie Slaughter argue that, notwithstanding this rhetoric, member states recognize that although "they can limit the court's sphere of operation by curtailing its jurisdiction, they cannot intervene within that sphere by asserting their preferences against the court's creeping extension of community norms." Walter Mattli & Anne-Marie Slaughter, *Law and Politics in the European Union: A Reply to Garrett*, 49 INT'L ORG. 183, 189 (1995).

171. After analyzing 11 landmark cases, one experienced Court watcher concluded that "the Court has been led by the Commission in the inexorable progression toward more legal integration and more Community power. The close alliance between the [two] . . . has probably alleviated some of the concern members of the Court may have felt regarding the legitimacy and acceptance of its rulings." Stein, *supra* note 60, at 24. Judges themselves have referred to the overall climate of the Community as a rationale for more or less activism. Most recently, as accusations of undue activism have been flying from important politicians within the Community, the Court has pulled in its horns a bit. *See* Giuseppe Federico Mancini & David T. Keeling, *Language, Culture and Politics in the Life of the European Court of Justice*, 1 COLUM. J. EUR. L. 397, 406-08 (1995) (noting the recent minimalist posture of the Court due in part to

Over the last decade, in response to political forces and the Maastricht Treaty, the Court has visibly been practicing restraint.[172] It is also discovering the "passive virtues"[173] of rulings that dispose of contentious issues on grounds of jurisdiction (admissibility) and justiciability. In the celebrated Irish abortion case, for instance, the ECJ held that the question of whether Ireland could regulate abortion fell outside its competence, ruling instead only on the much narrower question of whether Ireland could prevent Irish citizens from traveling to England to get abortions.[174] In other decisions, the Court has proven increasingly willing to share power with national courts—perhaps for reasons of docket crowding as much as of political expediency. Much of the pattern of ECJ jurisprudence in the 1990s, however, has demonstrated its renewed awareness of the virtues of incrementalism.

The ECHR has also demonstrated an acute awareness of the tension between the preferences of national decisionmakers and the requirements of the European Convention. To address this tension, the ECHR has developed the concept of a "margin of appreciation," acknowledging an area of discretion for national governments when applying and interpreting the treaty.[175] The court has emphasized that some deference is appropriate because it is not always as well-equipped as national actors to strike an appropriate balance between competing interests in complex areas of law and policy.[176] It has also stressed, however, that any discretion to national decisionmakers is limited by a "European supervision" that "empower[s the ECHR] to give the final ruling" on whether a challenged practice is compatible with the Convention.[177]

In striking the balance between deference and independent judicial review, the ECHR looks to the degree of consensus or harmony among the national

---

the disenchantment of judges who once believed they alone could implement integration).

172. *See id.*

173. BICKEL, *supra* note 23, at 267.

174. *See* Case C-159/90, Society for the Protection of Unborn Children, Ir. v. Grogan, 1991 E.C.R. I-4685.

175. In an early argument before the court, the President of the Commission explained the margin of appreciation doctrine as follows:

> The concept of the margin of appreciation is that a government's discharge of [its] responsibilities is essentially a delicate problem of appreciating complex factors and of balancing conflicting considerations of the public interest; and that, once the Commission or the Court is satisfied that the Government's appreciation is at least on the margin of [its] powers . . . , then the interest which the public itself has in effective government and in the maintenance of order justifies and requires a decision in favour of the legality of the Government's appreciation.

Lawless v. Ireland, 1 Eur. Ct. H.R. (ser. B) at 408 (1960-1961). For a detailed discussion of the margin of appreciation doctrine, see HOWARD CHARLES YOUROW, THE MARGIN OF APPRECIATION DOCTRINE IN THE DYNAMICS OF EUROPEAN HUMAN RIGHTS JURISPRUDENCE (1996). *See also* MERRILLS, *supra* note 77, at 136-59.

176. *See, e.g.*, Handyside v. United Kingdom, 24 Eur. Ct. H.R. (ser. A) at 22 (1976) (noting that the ECHR cannot assume the role of national courts and legislatures when balancing conflicting interests); Belgian Linguistics Case, 6 Eur. Ct. H.R. (ser. A) at 34-35 (1968) (stating that the court cannot assume the role of national authorities).

177. Sunday Times v. United Kingdom, 30 Eur. Ct. H.R. (ser. A) at 36 (1979); *see also* Barfod v. Denmark, 149 Eur. Ct. H.R. (ser. A) at 12 (1989).

laws of signatory states in deciding how wide or narrow a margin to afford the respondent state in the case before it.[178] This approach allows the court to narrow the margin of discretion allotted to national governments in an incremental fashion, finding against state respondents according to the underlying treatment of the right at issue within other European nations.[179] As a result, the ECHR is able to identify potentially problematic practices for the contracting states before they actually become violations, thereby permitting the states to anticipate that their laws may one day be called into question.[180] In the meantime, a state government lagging behind in the protection of a certain right is allowed to maintain its national policy but is forced to bear a heavier burden of proof before the ECHR—whose future opinions will turn in part on its own conception of how far the "trends" in European domestic law have evolved.[181] The conjunction of the margin of appreciation doctrine and the consensus inquiry thus permits the ECHR to link its decisions to the pace of change of domestic law, acknowledging the political sovereignty of respondent states while legitimizing its own decisions against them.[182]

---

178. The ECHR has applied the consensus principle in a few recent cases. *See, e.g.*, X v. United Kingdom, No. 75/1995/581/667, slip op. at 13 (Eur. Ct. H.R. Apr. 22, 1997) ("The Court observes that there is no common European standard with regard to the granting of parental rights to transsexuals. . . . Since the issues in the case, therefore, touch on areas where there is little common ground amongst the member States of the Council of Europe and, generally speaking, the law appears to be in a transitional stage, the respondent State must be afforded a wide margin of appreciation."); Otto-Preminger Inst. v. Austria, 295-A Eur. Ct. H.R. (ser. A) at 19 (1994) (finding that the lack of a uniform European conception of rights to freedom of expression "directed against religious feelings of others" dictates a wider margin of appreciation); *see also* Paul Mahoney, *Universality Versus Subsidiarity in Strasbourg Case Law on Free Speech*, 1997 EUR. HUM. RTS. L. REV. 364, 368-71.

179. *See* YOUROW, *supra* note 175, at 194 (arguing that the existence of progressive European consensus leads to a narrower margin and applicant outcomes favorable to applicants); Nadine Strossen, *Recent U.S. and International Judicial Protection of Individual Rights: A Comparative Legal Process Analysis and Proposed Synthesis*, 41 HASTINGS L.J. 805, 862 (1990) (arguing that consensus is an important factor influencing the scope of deference to state decisionmakers).

180. *See* Laurence R. Helfer, *Consensus, Coherence and the European Convention on Human Rights*, 26 CORNELL INT'L L.J. 133, 141 (1993); *see also* MERRILLS, *supra* note 77, at 81 (interpreting the ECHR's statement in *Rees v. United Kingdom*, 106 Eur. Ct. H.R. (ser. A) at 19 (1986), that "'[t]he need for appropriate legal measures [to protect transsexuals] should therefore be kept under review having regard particularly to scientific and societal developments'" as a "strong hint that while British practice currently satisfied [the Convention], the court's duty to interpret the Convention as a living instrument may lead it to a different conclusion in the future").

181. *See* Strossen, *supra* note 179, at 862; *see also* MERRILLS, *supra* note 77, at 74-75 (discussing Marckx v. Belgium, 31 Eur. Ct. H.R. (ser. A) at 15 (1979)). In *Marckx*, the ECHR decided that Belgian legislation distinguishing between legitimate and illegitimate children contravened the right to respect for family life. In finding a violation, the ECHR stressed that European laws were evolving significantly toward equal treatment. *See Marckx*, 31 Eur. Ct. H.R. (ser. A) at 16. Merrills argues, however, that the court overstated the evolution of state practice. *See* MERRILLS, *supra* note 77, at 74.

182. *See* YOUROW, *supra* note 175, at 196 ("[T]he Court will continue to build its authority incrementally and cautiously, retaining the margin doctrine, pinning it to the security of the consensus principle . . . ."); *see also* Goodwin v. United Kingdom, 22 Eur. H.R. Rep. 123, 143-44 (1996) (Eur. Ct. H.R.) (acknowledging national discretion expressly in the context of finding that the government had violated a journalist's freedom of expression).

d. *Quality of Legal Reasoning*

Judges on supranational tribunals tend to attribute their relative success or failure, according to their own measures, to the quality of their legal reasoning. Judge Mancini, for instance, notes that approximately ninety-five percent of national courts in the European Community accept ECJ rulings.[183] "Why did this happen?" he asks.[184]

> The only reason I can see . . . is the cleverness of my predecessors. If what makes a judge 'good' is his awareness of the constraints on judicial decision-making and the knowledge that rulings must be convincing in order to evoke obedience, the Luxembourg judges of the 1960s and 1970s were obviously *very* good.[185]

The early ECJ judges "developed a style that may be drab and repetitive, but explains as well as declares the law"[186] and they followed a "courteously didactic method."[187] Judge Ulrich Everling concurs, crediting the Court with "creat[ing] its own legitimacy primarily by the internal logic and consistency of the actual results expressed in its judgments and by the significance of those results for the development of the Community legal order."[188]

Joseph Weiler, one of the most sophisticated observers of the ECJ from both a legal and a political perspective, lists formalism as a principal reason for the remarkable record of the ECJ in convincing the national courts to follow its lead in building a Community legal system supreme over national law.[189] He refers to the "per se compliance pull of a dialogue conducted between courts in legalese. Courts are charged with upholding the law."[190] One of the sources of this "compliance pull," in his view, is "the legal language itself: the language of reasoned interpretation, logical deduction, systemic and temporal coherence—the artifacts that national courts would partly rely on to enlist obedience within their own national orders."[191]

183. *See* Mancini, *supra* note 60, at 595.

184. *Id.*

185. *Id.* at 605.

186. *Id.* at 606.

187. *Id.*

188. Ulrich Everling, *The Court of Justice as a Decisionmaking Authority*, 82 MICH. L. REV. 1294, 1309 (1984). He notes further: "The inherent power of persuasion of their judgments entitles courts to expect acceptance by those affected by the decisions." *Id.* at 1308. For the views of yet another member of the ECJ, see Thijmen Koopmans, *The Birth of European Law at the Crossroads of Legal Traditions*, 39 AM. J. COMP. L. 493, 505 (1991), which attributes the attention paid by national courts to the ECJ's reasoning in part to "the intellectual strength of its comparative methods."

189. *See* Weiler, *supra* note 103, at 510-19.

190. *Id.* at 520-21.

191. *Id.* at 521. Weiler borrows the term "compliance pull" from Thomas Franck, who uses it to motivate his important study of the sources of legitimacy of international law. *See* Thomas M. Franck, *Legitimacy in the International System*, 82 AM. J. INT'L L. 705 (1988). Franck reasons that compliance pull flows from legitimacy, and that legitimacy in turn derives from four attributes: determinacy, pedigree, coherence, and adherence. *See id.* Weiler's formulation in the text substantially overlaps Franck's definition

The ECHR has also benefited substantially from the quality of its reasoning, at least according to experienced observers. Polakiewicz and Jacob-Foltzer conclude their study by noting that, with a few rare exceptions, the ECHR has "never been openly defied by national courts."[192] They attribute this "persuasive authority" in large part to "the weight of the Court's arguments."[193] Francois Ost concurs, finding "the judgments of the Court [to be] exceptionally well reasoned. . . . Each of the questions it seeks to answer . . . is scrupulously examined as to the facts, the law and the practice . . . ."[194] And for J.G. Merrills, looking ahead, the factor that "will ultimately determine the importance of the European Court's contribution is the quality of the work. . . . [I]n the last analysis its contribution to the development of the law depends on the technique to be found in its decisions."[195]

Although these scholars would be less likely to agree on precisely what elements or attributes make legal reasoning good, they would probably all acknowledge the value of "systemic and temporal coherence," to borrow Weiler's phrase,[196] or, in Thomas Franck's formulation, "coherence" and "adherence."[197] Merrills, for instance, attributes the "wider significance" of the Court's judgments to its consistent efforts "to justify its decisions in terms which treat its existing case-law as authoritative. In other words, it follows judicial precedent."[198] Adherence to precedent, even when used only as authoritative guidepost and not as binding obligation, ensures a minimum degree of both temporal and systemic consistency.

In a social or legal culture that venerates tradition for its own sake, consistency with earlier decisions provides an autonomous bulwark of legitimacy. It also provides a crucial monitoring device to facilitate judicial

---

of each of these attributes.

192. Polakiewicz & Jacob-Foltzer, *supra* note 91, at 141.

193. *Id.*

194. Francois Ost, *The Original Canons of Interpretation of the European Court of Human Rights*, *in* THE EUROPEAN CONVENTION FOR THE PROTECTION OF HUMAN RIGHTS, *supra* note 134, at 283, 283-84.

195. MERRILLS, *supra* note 77, at 18-19.

196. Weiler, *supra* note 103, at 520-21.

197. FRANCK, *supra* note 34, at 152. Franck defines coherence as the precept that rules must conform to principles of general applicability. *See id.* Coherence endows a rule or rulemaking institution with authority by providing "a reasonable connection between a rule or the application of a rule, to (1) its own principled purpose, (2) principles previously employed to solve similar problems, and (3) a lattice of principles in use to resolve different problems." *Id.* at 147-48 (emphasis omitted). Adherence connects legitimacy to Franck's theory of the international rule system. Adherence is the "vertical nexus between a *primary rule of obligation* . . . and a hierarchy of secondary rules identifying the sources of rules and establishing normative standards that define how rules are to be made, interpreted, and applied." *Id.* at 184.

198. MERRILLS, *supra* note 77, at 12. The ECHR itself has proclaimed a general principle of fidelity to precedent as "being in the interests of legal certainty and the orderly development of the Convention case-law." Cossey v. United Kingdom, 184 Eur. Ct. H.R. (ser. A) at 14 (1990). *See generally* Matthijs de Blois, *The Fundamental Freedom of the European Court of Human Rights*, *in* THE DYNAMICS OF THE PROTECTION OF HUMAN RIGHTS IN EUROPE, *supra* note 115, at 35, 47 (describing precedential decisionmaking as motivated, not only by a desire—often commercially motivated—for predictability, but also by a deeper "quest for rationality" that is a predominant factor in the theory of law).

accountability, allowing concerned constituents to track judges' fidelity to self-imposed rules. It is not, however, a guarantee of analytical quality. Later decisions can only be as good or bad as their predecessors. If *Van Gend & Loos*[199] were widely regarded as a poorly reasoned opinion, consistency with its basic premises and principles would presumably be less desirable. It follows that an additional increment of legitimacy must flow from the quality of the decisions themselves, both past and present.

We search thus for a set of more fundamental attributes of sound legal reasoning, the qualities that Weiler encompasses when he refers to "reasoned interpretation" and "logical deduction."[200] Yet, it is here that assessments of quality diverge, based on the type of legal reasoning and the logical mode a particular author prefers. Merrills stresses clarity of communication, persuasiveness, and completeness.[201] Ost points to "the injection . . . of certain indeterminate elements (. . . elastic criteria, methods of balancing conflicting interests, proportionality)" that forsake binary logic in favor of the flexible evolution of a few general principles.[202] Mary Ann Glendon highlights the ECHR's "searching and tentative style . . . , its open wrestling with the weaknesses as well as the strength of [its] positions."[203] In short, and not surprisingly, scholarly evaluation of the ECJ and ECHR reflects many of the same debates about the distinctive and effective attributes of legal reasoning found in any national or international jurisprudential literature. These debates are likely to be similarly insightful—and similarly inconclusive.

We suggest that the precise nature of the reasoning involved, whether deductive, syllogistic, analogical, or some combination of these styles, is less important than that judicial decisions *be reasoned* in the first place: Reasons should explain why and how a particular conclusion was reached. To reason, in this context, means to give reasons for a particular result, regardless of the logic or mode of reasoning underlying those reasons.[204] The giving-reasons requirement is the prerequisite for the exercise of persuasive rather than

199. Case 26/62, N.V. Algemene Transp. & Expeditie Onderneming Van Gend & Loos v. Nederlandse administratie der belastingen, 1963 E.C.R. 1.

200. Weiler, *supra* note 103, at 521.

201. *See* MERRILLS, *supra* note 77, at 26-28.

202. Ost, *supra* note 194, at 312.

203. MARY ANN GLENDON, RIGHTS TALK 155 (1991). Glendon goes on to note that the ECHR judges "have become proficient at the principled, modest, collegial, flexible, pragmatic techniques of judicial decision-making that were once the pride of the American common law." *Id.* at 157.

204. Martin Shapiro reminds us of Carl Friedrich's proposition that "in the Western tradition, the very concept of political authority . . . implies the capacity to give reasons." Martin Shapiro, *The Giving Reasons Requirement*, 1992 U. CHI. LEGAL F. 179, 181 (citing Carl J. Friedrich, *Authority, Reason, and Discretion*, *in* AUTHORITY 28 (Carl J. Friedrich ed., 1958)); *see also* Fuller, *supra* note 159, at 366 ("Adjudication is . . . a device which gives formal and institutional expression to the influence of reasoned argument in human affairs."). Merrills makes the point equally succinctly as applied to the ECHR: "The Court should support its decisions with adequate reasons because the provision of a reasoned decision is the *raison d'être* of a court of law." MERRILLS, *supra* note 77, at 30.

coercive authority, the assurance that "the authority of a judgment derives from its intrinsic rationality rather than from an 'argument' of authority."[205]

Courts can give reasons in many different ways.[206] What form of reason-giving is most likely to be persuasive? We draw here on the school of thought that equates the explication of a judicial decision with the recognition, albeit not the reconciliation, of competing social, political, and economic values.[207] An opinion that systematically canvasses the arguments for and against a particular position, approving some and answering or rejecting others, is a public acknowledgment that there are a range of different perspectives on a particular issue. These perspectives often are informed either by different fundamental values or at least by different priorities in the difficult task of choosing one set of values over another and assessing the costs and benefits of different choices. For Ost, this mode of explanation is "the 'casuist' method of *pro et contra*," whereby "the Court progresses to its final choice without failing to confront the objections to its position and without minimising what hesitations are to be overcome."[208]

This method has both psychological and political benefits. First, it dignifies the opposing arguments, signaling the proponents of these arguments that they have been heard and recognized as important participants in a debate,

---

205. Ost, *supra* note 194, at 284; *see also* H. Patrick Glenn, *Persuasive Authority*, 32 McGILL L.J. 261, 263 (1987) (defining persuasive authority as "authority which attracts adherence as opposed to obliging it").

206. Anglo-Saxon lawyers are perhaps most forcefully reminded of this point when they contrast common law with civil law decisions. Michael Wells summarizes the difference between American and French decisions as follows: "Rather than a reasoned and candid essay, an opinion in the highest courts [in France] is a terse and opaque summary of the outcome and the reasons for it." Michael Wells, *French and American Judicial Opinions*, 19 YALE J. INT'L L. 81, 92 (1994). Both decisions are "reasoned," but the stylistic and structural differences reflect a divergence of much deeper premises concerning the function of judicial decisions and the role of courts in society:

> For many Americans, the opinion is a vehicle for setting forth the judges' views of the substantive considerations bearing on the outcomes of cases, as well as the interplay between policy concerns and such formal constraints as precedent and rules. French judges begin from a radically different premise. In their view, the role of the opinion is to apply settled law to the facts, or rather, to create the appearance that the court is merely applying law to fact.

Id. But see Mitchel de S.-O.-l'E. Lasser, *Judicial (Self-)Portraits: Judicial Discourse in the French Legal System*, 104 YALE L.J. 1325, 1342-43 (1995) (describing the traditional role of a French judge as a "syllogism machine" and countering this portrayal with the assertion that there exists an alternative conception—the "unofficial portrait" of the French civil judge).

207. Cass Sunstein offers a forceful recent exposition of this position. *See* CASS R. SUNSTEIN, LEGAL REASONING AND POLITICAL CONFLICT at viii (1996) ("When legal reasoning operates at its best, participants in law are attuned to the fact that people legitimately disagree on basic principles. They try to resolve cases without taking sides on large-scale social controversies. They produce *incompletely theorized agreements on particular outcomes*, a central feature of legal reasoning . . . ."); *cf.* EDWARD H. LEVI, AN INTRODUCTION TO LEGAL REASONING 5 (1949) (arguing that reasoning by example, in the sense of presenting "competing analogies" to a court, "bring[s] into the law the common ideas of the society").

208. Ost, *supra* note 194, at 284. Merrills agrees, quoting Hersch Lauterpacht for the proposition that "'governments as a rule reconcile themselves to the fact that their case has not been successful—provided the defeat is accompanied by the conviction that their argument was considered in all its relevant aspects.'" MERRILLS, *supra* note 77, at 28 (quoting HERSCH LAUTERPACHT, THE DEVELOPMENT OF INTERNATIONAL LAW BY THE INTERNATIONAL COURT 39 (1958)).

participants whose arguments must be answered.[209] Second, and relatedly, it suggests that these arguments could still prevail in another case, when the balance of fact and circumstance might tip the other way. Third, it presents the law as a carefully woven tissue of opposites, the fabric of a diverse community.[210] Fourth, this self-presentation of the law fosters a dialogue between judges, lawyers, politicians, and even lay people, as the court's response to each argument can be responded to in turn. If the giving-reasons requirement bolsters a court's legitimacy by justifying its conclusions in terms of a particular polity's legal traditions and underlying social, economic, and political values, a casuist mode of presentation recognizes the inevitability and validity of debate on many if not all of these points while nevertheless insisting that such debate can ultimately produce a determinate and considered outcome. Judicial decisionmaking thus itself becomes a mode of collective deliberation.[211]

These arguments in favor of casuistry can be further grounded both in political philosophy and political science. As a matter of political philosophy, they emphasize the values of individual dignity and democratic participation.[212] A reasoned opinion assures individual litigants that their day in court was meaningful, in that their arguments were actually heard by the judge. The judge's opinion both disseminates their arguments and dignifies them with a response. As a matter of political science, the arguments in favor of the casuist mode are arguments with "microfoundations," in the sense that

---

209. *See* GLENDON, *supra* note 203, at 155-56.

210. We borrow this conception of the law from James Boyd White, who praises "openness" in judicial opinions as a means of exposing to the reader "the grounds upon which [the judge's] judgment actually rests, with as full and fair a statement of her doubts and uncertainties as she can manage." JAMES BOYD WHITE, JUSTICE AS TRANSLATION 224 (1990). Such openness would both reflect and compel "the suspension of judgment, . . . perhaps the central virtue for the lawyer." *Id.* It would also confirm

> that the art of law is not that of linear reasoning to a secure conclusion, but an art, fundamentally literary and rhetorical in kind, of comprehension and integration: the art of creating a text—a mind and a community—which can comprise two things at once, and two things pulling in different directions. In speaking for one side as a lawyer, or for one result as a judge, that is, the legal mind should recognize (implicitly in the lawyer's case, explicitly in the judge's) what can be said for the other, thus by an art of integration creating a world in which differences can coexist.

Id. at 224-25.

211. Sunstein relates this view of judicial decisionmaking to a Madisonian model of deliberative democracy. *See* SUNSTEIN, *supra* note 207, at 195-96.

212. Frank Michelman identifies "dignity values" and "participation values" as two of the four types of values that are implicitly furthered by allowing people to litigate. *See* Frank I. Michelman, *The Supreme Court and Litigation Access Fees: The Right To Protect One's Rights*, 1973 DUKE L.J. 1153, 1172. Michelman argues,

> Dignity values reflect concern for the humiliation or loss of self-respect which a person might suffer if denied an opportunity to litigate. Participation values reflect an appreciation of litigation as one of the modes in which persons exert influence or have their wills 'counted' in societal decisions they care about.

Id. (emphasis omitted). For a discussion of the continuing acknowledgment of the value of individual dignity in the rules regulating litigation in the United States, see Jerry L. Mashaw, *The Supreme Court's Due Process Calculus for Administrative Adjudication in* Mathews v. Eldridge*: Three Factors in Search of a Theory of Value*, 44 U. CHI. L. REV. 28, 49-52 (1976).

they offer an account of how the incentives of key individuals could be shaped in support of judicial authority.[213] Lawyers and litigants who are convinced that their arguments have been heard and carefully considered are more likely to conclude that the judicial system is sufficiently fair to decide in their favor in a subsequent case, and perhaps to feel partially vindicated even on the losing side.

In sum, many commentators seeking to analyze the success of the ECJ and the ECHR emphasize the fact of legal reasoning, in the sense that judicial opinions are reasoned at all, as much as the quality of that reasoning. Both courts provide reasons for their decisions and create a framework within which reasoned debate can be conducted by acknowledging the weight of precedent. The ECJ may seem more lax in this regard than the ECHR, yet the detailed and careful analyses of the Advocate General often compensate for the terseness of the actual text of an ECJ decision.

Once the obligation to give reasons for a particular decision is acknowledged, we suggest further that a casuist mode of reaching or, at least, presenting a particular decision may have particular benefits for bolstering judicial authority and legitimacy. A supranational court, in particular, is essentially in the business of constructing its own polity, defining the boundaries of a legal community constituted by adherence to an international instrument. A mode of judicial decisionmaking that acknowledges competing values while emphasizing dignity and democratic participation has a particular value in this context.

e. *Judicial Cross-Fertilization and Dialogue*

The ECJ and the ECHR enhance each other's authority by referring to one another's decisions. The ECHR (or individual judges writing for it) periodically refers to ECJ decisions both to assert its primary authority in a case of potentially conflicting jurisdiction and to bolster its own power over national courts by referring to a similar power of the ECJ. Cases in the first category are relatively straightforward, essentially involving doctrinal interpretations designed to resolve confusion created by conflicting judicial rulings. In *Funke v. France*,[214] for example, the ECHR held that France had violated the applicant's right to remain silent and to avoid self-incrimination by imposing monetary sanctions on him for failing to produce certain documents. The ECHR's decision was in direct conflict with a ruling of the ECJ four years earlier.[215]

213. *See* JON ELSTER, NUTS AND BOLTS FOR THE SOCIAL SCIENCES 13 (1989) (describing methodological individualism).

214. 256-A Eur. Ct. H.R. (ser. A) at 22 (1993).

215. *See* Case 374/87, Orkem A.S. v. Commission, 1989 E.C.R. 3283; *see also* Walter B.J. van Overbeek, *The Right To Remain Silent in Competition Investigations: The* Funke *Decision of the European*

Cases in the second category are more interesting. In *Fischer v. Austria*,[216] for instance, Judge Martens commented on the influence of ECJ case law in convincing member states of the European Community that state administrative organs should be accountable to the judiciary, a power being exercised by the ECHR in the case before it.[217] Similarly, in *Konig v. Federal Republic of Germany*,[218] Judge Matscher justified the ECHR's interpretation of a provision of the Convention by reference to the principles of treaty interpretation developed by the ECJ in a case decided two years earlier.[219] Both *Fischer* and *Konig* depict the two tribunals as pursuing parallel trajectories, establishing the principle of supranational review and developing a common body of rules or doctrines to guide the exercise of their newfound powers.

Cases in which the ECJ cites ECHR decisions result from the particularities of the ECJ's own human rights jurisprudence, based on constitutional traditions common to the fifteen European Union member states and international human rights treaties to which they are signatories, particularly the European Convention on Human Rights.[220] It thus periodically falls to the ECJ to use both the provisions of the Convention and interpretations of those provisions by the ECHR as a starting point for its own analysis of the nature and extent of specific human rights provisions under Community law.[221] Even when the Court itself does not directly reference ECHR decisions, it often hears argument invoking these decisions either by its Advocate General or by the parties.[222]

In other cases, parties before the ECJ, as well as the Advocate General, have relied on ECHR decisions as evidence of emerging international or

Court of Human Rights Makes Revision of the ECJ's Case Law Necessary, 15 EUR. COMP. L. REV. 127 (1994).

216. 312 Eur. Ct. H.R. (ser. A) (1995).

217. *See id.* at 27 n.5 (separate opinion of Martens, J.).

218. 27 Eur. Ct. H.R. (ser. A) (1978).

219. *See id.* at 46 (separate opinion of Matscher, J.) (citing Case 29/76, Lufttransportunternehmen GMbH v. Eurocontrol, 1976 E.C.R. 1541).

220. *See, e.g.*, Case 4/73, Nold v. Commission, 1974 E.C.R. 491.

221. *See, e.g.*, Cases 46/87 & 227/88, Hoechst AG v. Commission, 1989 E.C.R. 2859, 2924 (explaining that "there is no case law of the [ECHR] on [the] subject" of interpreting Article 8(1) of the Convention); Case 152/84, Marshall v. Southhampton & S.-W. Hampshire Area Health Auth., 1986 E.C.R. 723, 743-44 (citing the ECHR for the proposition that fundamental human rights, incorporated as part of the general principles of Community law, "must be given a wide interpretation").

This intertwining of case law becomes even more complex when parties argue that a particular action of a European Community organ is itself a violation of the Convention. *See* Cases 209 to 215 & 218/78, Heintz van Landewyck S.a.r.l. v. Commission, 1980 E.C.R. 3125 (ruling on a claim that an action of the Commission of the Community violated Article 6(1) of the Convention and referencing an ECHR decision interpreting the Article).

222. *See, e.g.*, Case 326/88, Anklagemyndigheden v. Hansen & Son I/S, 1990 E.C.R. 2911 (opinion of the Advocate General) (referencing the ECHR's interpretation of Article 6(2) of the Convention as supporting a presumption of innocence until proven guilty); Cases 175/86 & 209/86, M v. Council, 1988 E.C.R. 1891, 1896 (referencing the ECHR's interpretation of Article 6 of the Convention in the pleadings).

regional consensus[223] and as a general source of ideas and analysis.[224] The ECJ has only infrequently cited the referenced decisions directly in its own opinions, but has presumably taken such pleadings and argumentation into account in reaching its decisions. It should be noted as well that not all of these pleadings ask the Court to "follow" the ECHR; they sometimes invoke an ECHR position only to distinguish it or to justify a different line of reasoning or outcome.[225]

Each tribunal's willingness to refer to the other's rulings has interesting implications for enhancing their influence and effectiveness generally. Judge Thijmen Koopmans of the ECJ speculates that the Court "has become one of the major sources of legal innovation in Europe not only because of its position as the Community's judicial institution, but also because of the intellectual strength of its comparative methods."[226] It is the Court's ability to canvass different national and supranational approaches to a particular legal problem, he argues, that convinces national courts to pay attention to its rulings.[227] The underlying premise here assumes the intrinsic value of widespread and diverse input in a deliberative process: Two minds are better than one, and fifteen minds, particularly minds from different perspectives and cultures, are better than two.

Koopmans's justification of the ECJ's comparative method focuses on the enhanced quality of decisions resulting from the likelihood that cross-national research will either turn up potential errors in and problems with a particular legal solution or open the door to innovation based on a wider range of potential models.[228] Of course, comparative canvassing of precedents from national courts serves these same ends.[229] But the citation of a coequal

223. *See, e.g.*, Case 155/79, AM & S Eur. Ltd. v. Commission, 1982 E.C.R. 1575, 1600 (arguing that the decisions of the ECHR support the view that legal privilege is a practical guarantee of fundamental individual rights).

224. *See, e.g.*, Case 34/79, Regina v. Henn, 1979 E.C.R. 3795, 3821 (opinion of the Advocate General) (relying on the ECHR judgment in *Handyside v. United Kingdom*, 24 Eur. Ct. H.R. (ser. A) (1979), to interpret Article 36 of the Treaty of Rome).

225. *See, e.g.*, Case 112/83, Societe des Produits de Mais SA v. Adminisration Des Douanes et Droits Indirects, 1985 E.C.R. 719 (considering the plaintiff's rejection of an analogy to an ECHR decision); Case 61/77, Commission v. Ireland, 1978 E.C.R. 417, 464 (opinion of the Advocate General) (objecting to the Irish government's effort to invoke ECHR case law due to "the different wording used" in the Convention and the Treaty of Rome).

226. Koopmans, *supra* note 188, at 505.

227. *See id.*

228. Some criticize Protocol No. 11 to the Convention—which abolishes the two-stage procedure providing for review of cases first by the Commission and only then by the ECHR—for destroying "the possibility of mutual criticism which now exists between the Commission and the Court." Schermers, *supra* note 158, at 560. Judge Schermers fears that "the loss of this mutual education will create the risk that the new Court will accentuate its own mistakes." *Id.*

229. In this respect, both the ECHR and the ECJ can also be seen as engaging in what might be termed an "intermediated dialogue," in which the supranational tribunal acts as a broker for communication among national courts of Europe. As noted by Polakiewicz and Jacob-Foltzer, "principles like the proportionality test that have been developed in certain national legal orders are taken up by the [ECHR] and later accepted in other countries as part of a common European standard." Polakiewicz & Jacob-Foltzer, *supra* note 91, at 66. The authors characterize this process as "the beginning of a dialogue between

supranational court fulfills a distinct and equally important function, that of mutual legitimation of the very act of adjudication above the level of the nation-state. By citing to other supranational decisions as authoritative and worthy of consideration, the citing court acknowledges its engagement in a common enterprise with the cited court, an acknowledgment that implies the possibility of an objectively "better" legal solution to a common legal problem and of some degree of cultural cross-communication.

Such recognition does not deny the necessity of tailoring solutions to the specific cultural and political requirements of a particular legal system; on the contrary, a number of the examples cited above refer to a case from a parallel tribunal only to distinguish it. Nevertheless, acknowledged engagement in a common enterprise at least partially independent of particular jurisdictional and substantive instruments, cultures, and countries is the essence of the idea (and ideal) of a global "community of law," which we discuss in Part V. For the moment, however, it is striking and significant that two of the world's most effective supranational tribunals appear to benefit more from solidarity than insularity.

f. *Form of Opinions*

A final point raised by observers of both the ECJ and the ECHR in assessing the tribunals' effectiveness is the forms of their opinions. The principal issue with respect to form is whether the opinion should be written as if the judgment were unanimous or if dissents and concurring opinions should be allowed. Opinions differ substantially on this question as do the two courts themselves: The ECJ disallows individual concurring and dissenting opinions, whereas the ECHR permits them.[230]

In the ECJ context, the Court itself and a number of observers assume that the Court benefits considerably from its no-dissent rule. This is so for a number of reasons. First, the rule allows the Court to speak as the uniform and

these different jurisdictions." *Id.* at 142. The ECJ's periodic adoption of a particular national approach or standard as an appropriate rule for the European Union as a whole may have a similar impact. Further, awareness of the dynamic by which national law can become European law and then move into other national legal systems may encourage input from a number of national courts desiring to influence the evolution of European law in a direction more favorable to their national traditions. *See* Slaughter, *supra* note 146, at 114 n.46.

230. It is possible, of course, for the states party to the treaty establishing a tribunal to prohibit jurists from filing individual opinions. To that extent, the form of opinions may properly be included as a factor within the control of states. *See supra* Subsection III.B.1. Nevertheless, in the case of the ECJ, the treaty does not prohibit individual opinions; it is the Court itself that has imposed a rule of unanimity. *See* Rules of Procedure of the Court of Justice, Rule 27.5, 1974 O.J. (L 350) 1, *reprinted in* ENCYCLOPEDIA OF EUROPEAN COMMUNITY LAW at B8108 (1992). Similarly, Article 51(2) of the Convention, *supra* note 2, 213 U.N.T.S. at 248, and Article 45(2) of Protocol No. 11, *supra* note 93, expressly permit (but of course do not require) individual opinions, leaving the issue to individual jurists. We have thus included form of opinions as within the power of the tribunals themselves.

quasi-mystical "voice of the law":[231] Judges, originally from six national traditions and now from fifteen, merge their differences and speak as one.[232] Second, unanimous decisions have insulated individual judges from political pressure from their governments.[233] Third, as Judge David Edward observes, the unanimous judgment tradition fosters the relative speed of ECJ decisions, at least in the sense of "avoiding further serious delay."[234] Efforts to streamline the process by excluding dissenting judges from the Court's deliberations after an initial vote on the outcome "would seriously affect, if not destroy, the collegiate character of the Court and its decision-making process."[235]

On the other hand, voices have recently been raised criticizing the impact of the unanimous-decision rule on the reasoning of the Court's decisions. The need to reach a uniform result, these commentators argue, frequently produces strategic ambiguity, awkward transitions, and lowest common denominator statements of the law.[236] These authors thus highlight a tension between uniform authority and the quality of legal reasoning.

Commentary on the ECHR is in greater agreement on the value of multiple opinions. Merrills emphasizes that the ECHR depends on the support of governments, "who must be satisfied that in accepting its obligations . . . they are subscribing to a system whose object and effect are the protection of rights,

231. This view lies at the core of a more general philosophy of legalism, perhaps best summarized in an oft-quoted passage from Martin Shapiro (although he formulates it only as a prelude to a pointed critique):

> [T]he Community [is presented] as a juristic idea; the written constitution as a sacred text; the professional commentary as a legal truth; the case law as the inevitable working out of the correct implications of the constitutional text; and the constitutional court as the disembodied voice of right reason and constitutional teleology.

Martin Shapiro, *Comparative Law and Comparative Politics*, 53 S. CAL. L. REV. 537, 538 (1980). More pragmatically, Derrick Wyatt and Alan Dashwood observe that, "as a young judicial institution, the court needed to build up its authority by presenting a united front to the world." DERRICK WYATT & ALAN DASHWOOD, EUROPEAN COMMUNITY LAW 109 (1993).

232. *See* Everling, *supra* note 188, at 1295. Compare this with the decision of the U.S. Supreme Court to hand down a unanimous opinion against President Nixon in *United States v. Nixon*, 418 U.S. 683 (1974), a decision echoing the Court's earlier choice of a single opinion in *Cooper v. Aaron*, 358 U.S. 1 (1958), which enforced a desegregation ruling issued in the face of strong local resistance. *See* BOB WOODWARD & SCOTT ARMSTRONG, THE BRETHREN: INSIDE THE SUPREME COURT 295-96 (1979).

233. *See* WYATT & DASHWOOD, *supra* note 231, at 109. T.C. Hartley makes the same point: Because of the unanimous opinion, "it is impossible to accuse a judge of being insufficiently sensitive to national interests or of having 'let his government down'; no one outside the Court can ever know whether he vigorously defended the position adopted by his own country or was in the forefront of those advocating a 'Community solution.'" T.C. HARTLEY, THE FOUNDATIONS OF EUROPEAN COMMUNITY LAW 59 (3d ed. 1994).

234. David Edward, *How the Court of Justice Works*, 20 EUR. L. REV. 539, 557 (1995).

235. *Id.*

236. In 1995, the United Kingdom proposed that ECJ judges be permitted to publish dissenting opinions but ultimately withdrew its suggestion. *See* John Palmer, *British Drop Attack on EU Court*, GUARDIAN (Manchester), Oct. 28, 1995, *available in* 1995 WL 9948090; *see also* Frances Gibb, *MPs Urge Major To Restrict Powers of European Court*, TIMES (London), Oct. 20, 1995, *available in* 1995 WL 7705621. Several commentators note that the lack of dissenting opinions makes it difficult to analyze the Court's opinions and to choose those litigation strategies most likely to persuade the ECJ judges. *See, e.g.*, Andrew Watson, *The European Court After* Factortame, 71 INT'L COM. LITIG. 19, 19-21 (1995/1996).

and not national humiliation."[237] In this context, he argues, separate opinions are "especially important" in marshalling government support.[238] Those separate opinions that review issues omitted from the judgment or that reassert a particular government's position "can do much to maintain the correct perspective."[239] Ost concurs, noting the particular value of separate opinions as part of his more general theory that the persuasive value of a judgment "derives from its intrinsic rationality."[240]

It is possible to reconcile these two views if we note that the ECJ talks primarily to national courts, whereas the ECHR depends more directly on the reactions of national bureaucrats and politicians. Addressing an audience of national judges, themselves accustomed to handing down "the law," the ECJ may be right in its calculation that unanimity enhances authority. In addition, this audience was initially relatively small and uniform—judges from six civil law countries at the core of Western Europe. The ECHR, by contrast, has found itself seeking to persuade government officials from fifteen countries, adding the Austrian, British, Irish, Scandinavian, Greek, and Turkish legal systems to the original mix.[241] In this context, evidence that a number of judges could reach the same conclusion, albeit on different grounds, and that contrary arguments had been thoroughly ventilated, as demonstrated by dissenting opinions, could well enhance persuasive power.[242] Indeed, as the number of countries subject to the jurisdiction of the ECJ grows, pressure has mounted on the Court to drop the unanimity rule.[243]

3. *Factors Often Beyond the Control of States or Judges*

The value of a checklist of effective supranational adjudication is not only as an analytical tool, but also as a set of practical recommendations for states and judges. The experiences of the ECJ and the ECHR, however, suggest that not all factors contributing to effective supranational adjudication are within these actors' control. Judges may be presented with disputes that they cannot resolve. The states under their jurisdiction may ultimately be impermeable to supranational penetration due to underlying domestic political conditions. The cultural diversity of both judges and states may be too great to bridge.

Were any of these factors determinative, the rest of the checklist would be futile. It is more likely, however, that while these factors may limit how far

237. MERRILLS, *supra* note 77, at 36.

238. *Id.*

239. *Id.*

240. Ost, *supra* note 194, at 284.

241. *See* ROBERTSON & MERRILLS, *supra* note 81, at 320 n.5.

242. The range of concurrence and dissent in any one case should not be exaggerated, however. The majority of the ECHR's cases are heard in chambers of nine judges. Robertson and Merrills note that only about one case in three is heard by the plenary court. *See* ROBERTSON & MERRILLS, *supra* note 81, at 299.

243. *See The Laws of Canute*, ECONOMIST, Oct. 7, 1995, at 62.

along the spectrum toward fully effective supranational adjudication a particular tribunal is likely to move, there remains considerable room to improve. Moreover, these factors typically receive far less attention from scholars and commentators than those listed above; the causal mechanisms by which they affect supranational adjudication remain relatively uncharted. It is thus also more difficult even to estimate the relative importance of the factors we identify; they are very likely to overlap and even to collapse onto one another. Our ordering reflects analytical convenience as much as relative weight. Finally, we supplement the observations of scholars and commentators on the ECJ and the ECHR with our own analysis based on our earlier definition of supranational adjudication.

a. *Nature of Violations*

A principal factor that has contributed to the success of the European human rights system is the limited nature of complaints brought before the ECHR. Menno Kamminga directly attributes the success of the ECHR to the minor and unintentional nature of most violations found under the Convention, which requires few concessions from the offending state.[244] Practically every case brought to the European Commission of Human Rights concerns either maladministration or the types of conflicts of interests prevalent in any complex society.[245] Indeed, Torkel Opsahl draws a contrast between the kinds of cases typically heard by the ECHR and those often submitted to the U.N. Human Rights Committee by noting the difference in the percentage of cases declared admissible—"almost 50 percent [in the U.N. system] as against less than 3 percent [in the European system]."[246] He attributes much of this difference to the "serious facts of many cases [going to the UNHRC]."[247]

A sad paradox results. At least in the human rights arena, international human rights regimes and the supranational tribunals that enforce them have been most effective in the states that arguably need them least: those whose officials commit relatively few, minor, and discrete human rights violations.[248] As Paul Sieghart points out, the administrative and legislative organs of the states parties in Europe have often made changes in direct response to the "substantial and extensive jurisprudence" of the European

244. *See* Menno T. Kamminga, *Is the European Convention on Human Rights Sufficiently Equipped To Cope with Gross and Systematic Violations?*, 12 NETH. Q. HUM. RTS. 153, 153-54 (1994).

245. *See* A.H. ROBERTSON & J.H. MERRILLS, HUMAN RIGHTS IN THE WORLD 62 (3d ed. 1989). That such cases exist at all demonstrates that human rights are not merely an issue for the nondemocratic world. *See id.*

246. Opsahl, *supra* note 17, at 423.

247. *Id.*

248. *See* Moravcsik, *supra* note 9, at 178-80. These breaches are unquestionably grave from the perspective of their victims and the citizenry of the states involved, but they nevertheless pale in light of the entire spectrum of human rights abuses across states.

Commission of Human Rights and the ECHR.[249] Even within Europe, however, the states most likely to respond to the ECHR are the states with the least to hide. Both the Commission and the ECHR, for example, were relatively powerless in the face of systematic human rights violations in Greece during the military dictatorship in the early 1970s; indeed, Greece ultimately withdrew from the Convention.[250]

A related phenomenon is at work concerning the ECJ, although commentators have not discussed it in precisely the same terms. As policymakers and scholars became increasingly aware of the power of the ECJ in the late 1980s and early 1990s, many gave it credit for devising and implementing the policy of "mutual recognition." Under this policy, European Union member states recognized each other's production standards and other trade-related regulation, thereby providing an alternative to the slow and difficult process of harmonization around a unitary standard.[251] In fact, as two political scientists demonstrate, the ECJ's role was much more modest; although it formulated the concept of mutual recognition in an important decision, large-scale policy change depended on subsequent action by the European Union Commission.[252] This debate over the role of the ECJ is strikingly similar to the debate about the impact of the U.S. Supreme Court's decision in *Brown v. Board of Education*;[253] in both cases, political scientists (and some lawyers) have sought to temper those (mostly lawyers) who are prone to overestimate the power of courts.

For present purposes, however, the story has a different moral. If courts are relatively ineffective at generating the kind of wholesale policy change necessary to respond to systemic problems, it follows that courts faced only with those kinds of problems are likely to be less effective than those charged with policing modest deviations from a generally settled norm or modifying a particular rule or set of rules incrementally. The scope and gravity of the disputes presented to courts is partially within the control of courts themselves and partially within the control of the states that establish them. Doctrines of

249. SIEGHART, *supra* note 159, at 27.

250. Greece signed the Convention in 1953. After the installation of a military dictatorship, the country withdrew from the Convention in 1970. It rejoined the Convention in 1974. *See* ROBERTSON & MERRILLS, *supra* note 81, at 279.

251. *See* DAVID VOGEL, TRADING UP 32-35 (1995); Jacques Pelkmans & Jeanne-May Sun, *Towards a European Community Regulatory Strategy: Lessons from "Learning-by-Doing," in* ORGANIZATION FOR ECON. CO-OPERATION AND DEV., REGULATORY CO-OPERATION FOR AN INTERDEPENDENT WORLD 179, 181 (1995); Michel Waelbroeck, *The Role of the Court of Justice in the Implementation of the Single European Act*, 11 MICH. J. INT'L L. 671, 676 (1990).

252. *See* Karen Alter & Sophie Meunier-Aitsahalia, *Judicial Politics in the European Community: European Integration and the Pathbreaking* Cassis de Dijon *Decision*, 26 COMP. POL. STUD. 535, 541-43, 554-55 (1994) (discussing Case 120/78, Rewe-Zentral v. Bundesmonopolwaltung für Branntwein, 1979 E.C.R. 649); R. Barents, *New Developments in Measures Having Equivalent Effects*, 18 COMMON MKT. L. REV. 271 (1981).

253. 347 U.S. 483 (1954). For a review of this debate and a strong argument that the Supreme Court is incapable of securing social change, see GERALD N. ROSENBERG, THE HOLLOW HOPE: CAN COURTS BRING ABOUT SOCIAL CHANGE? (1991).

standing and justiciability can limit the number and identity of parties permitted to appear before the court and can ensure that a dispute is ready and appropriate for judicial decision. Jurisdictional grants such as the U.S. constitutional requirement that courts hear only "cases or controversies" rather than rendering advisory opinions on pure questions of law[254] can further narrow and shape a particular docket. But in the end, the isolated or systemic nature of the alleged violations of law that a particular court is asked to remedy depends a great deal on the nature of the states themselves that are subject to that court's jurisdiction. As the example of Greece demonstrates, even states who choose their fellow signatories to an international agreement very carefully cannot control for political stability over time. In such circumstances, even a supranational tribunal that has been relatively effective may suddenly find itself adrift and increasingly irrelevant.

b. *Autonomous Domestic Institutions Committed to the Rule of Law and Responsive to Citizen Interests*

The European experience of supranational adjudication is the experience of two supranational tribunals operating within a community of liberal democracies with strong domestic commitments to the rule of law. This dimension of the European experience provides the subtext for much of the analysis of factors discussed in this section, such as the nature of violations or cultural homogeneity. More recently, however, a number of scholars have begun to tackle directly the relationship between liberal democracy and international dispute resolution.

The burgeoning literature on the "democratic peace," seeking to explain why liberal democracies rarely if ever go to war with one another, has spurred scholars to explore other ways in which attributes of a domestic regime-type affect international behavior.[255] Of particular interest here are hypotheses, as yet unproved, concerning the positive impact of liberal democracy on compliance with international commitments, including the judgments of international and supranational tribunals.[256] As defined in this literature, "liberal democracy" combines representative government with a commitment

254. *See* U.S. CONST. art. III, § 2.

255. The relative transparency of democratic politics, for instance, is alleged to have a positive impact on the credibility of commitments entered into by liberal democracies. *See* Lori Fisler Damrosch, *Constitutional Control over War Powers: A Common Core of Accountability in Democratic Societies?*, 50 U. MIAMI L. REV. 181, 183 (1995); Charles Lipson, The Promise of Peace Among Liberal Democracies (1995) (unpublished manuscript, on file with authors).

256. *See* William J. Dixon, *Democracy and the Management of International Conflict*, 37 J. CONFLICT RESOL. 1, 42 (1993) (arguing that democratic states are more likely than others to resolve or ameliorate their international disputes by arrangements secured with the assistance of third parties); Gregory Raymond, *Democracies, Disputes, and Third-Party Intermediaries*, 38 J. CONFLICT RESOL. 1, 24 (1994) (arguing that pairs of democratic states are more likely than dyads including one or more nondemocracies to prefer disagreement to binding third party settlement); Slaughter, *International Law*, *supra* note 55, at 532.

to the rule of law, itself defined to include both an independent judiciary and protection of basic civil and political rights.[257] The specific hypotheses positing a causal connection between liberal democracy and compliance with international obligations generally focus either on a rule-of-law mechanism or on a democratic politics mechanism.[258]

The rule-of-law approaches rest on the basic intuition that states committed to the rule of law domestically will be more law-abiding in the international realm, through the projection or transferral of their domestic habits. Accustomed to self-imposed constitutional constraints at home, constraints enforced by an independent judiciary, they are more likely to accept the constraints of international law as enforced by an international or supranational tribunal.[259] This equation is too simple. On the one hand, states without a domestic tradition of respect for the rule of law and the concomitant recognition of the importance of an independent judiciary are unlikely to respect the judgments of an international tribunal. In many former communist states, law was regarded primarily as a tool of the bourgeoisie; in many former colonies, law has been primarily an instrument of state oppression. On the other hand, states with the strongest traditions of domestic rule of law and independent judiciaries may also conclude that they have no need for international supervision—that, on the contrary, receptivity to international law, including the judgments of a supranational tribunal, might even weaken the domestic system.[260] The frequent hostility of U.S. courts to enforcement of

257. In his pioneering work on the "democratic peace," Michael Doyle actually examines conflict between what he defines as "liberal states": states with some form of representative democracy, a market economy based on private property rights, juridical equality, and constitutional protections of civil and political rights. *See* Doyle, *Foreign Affairs*, *supra* note 6, at 207-08; *see also* Slaughter, *International Law*, *supra* note 55, at 511 ("Liberal democracy . . . denotes some form of representative government secured by the separation of powers, constitutional guarantees of civil and political rights, juridical equality, and a functioning judicial system dedicated to the rule of law.").

258. We borrow this typology from Beth Simmons, who is undertaking an important study of the sources of compliance with the judgments of international and supranational tribunals. The first phase of her project focuses on compliance with the rulings of interstate arbitral tribunals in territorial disputes in Latin America—tribunals that we would identify as international rather than supranational tribunals. *See* Beth Simmons, Capacity, Commitment, and Compliance: International Law and the Settlement of Territorial Disputes (June 1997) (unpublished manuscript, on file with authors). Her work, however, will make a major contribution toward proving or disproving the various hypotheses discussed in this section. A similar distinction between types of explanations in the democratic peace literature more generally can be found in BRUCE RUSSETT, GRASPING THE DEMOCRATIC PEACE: PRINCIPLES FOR A POST-COLD WAR WORLD 11-23 (1993), which contrasts "normative" with "structural" explanations for the democratic peace.

259. *See* ROGER FISHER, IMPROVING COMPLIANCE WITH INTERNATIONAL LAW 30 (1981) (arguing that constraints imposed by international law resemble constitutional constraints in that both are metanorms that rest on shared normative acceptance); Charles A. Kupchan & Clifford A. Kupchan, *Concerts, Collective Security, and the Future of Europe*, 16 INT'L SECURITY 114, 115-16 (1991) ("[S]tates willing to submit to the rule of law and civil society domestically are more likely to submit to their analogues internationally."); Raymond, *supra* note 256, at 24.

260. These attitudes are one explanation for the historic reluctance of U.S. courts to recognize international law. Another explanation notes that the fierce opposition to many international human rights instruments was fueled largely by southern fears that these instruments would be used to advance civil rights for African Americans. In the early 1950s, Senator Howard Bricker led a campaign to amend the Constitution so as to restrain the federal government's treaty-making power. Bricker and his supporters

international law over domestic law can be explained in part on this basis, as can variation in the mode and timing of acceptance of European Community law by European national courts.[261]

The democracy-based hypotheses, by contrast, focus on the power of international legal obligations to mobilize domestic interest groups, who in turn pressure democratic governments to comply.[262] The underlying assumption is that individuals and interest groups will either invoke the rulings of an international tribunal as support for a position they independently espouse or that they will simply hold their governments to account for failure to comply with international law. We make similar arguments about the role of private parties in pressuring government institutions to comply with the rulings of a supranational tribunal. These accounts, however, assume interest group pressure on a unitary state, omitting both the complex interactions of distinct domestic government institutions and the motives of those institutions either to respond to private pressure or independently to push for compliance. Further, they do not distinguish between compliance with international law generally and compliance with international or supranational judgments; thus they cannot take account of the specific dynamics between a supranational tribunal and domestic government institutions.

Drawing on this literature and on our analysis of the experiences of the ECJ and the ECHR, we conclude that the existence (in states subject to the jurisdiction of a supranational tribunal) of domestic government institutions committed to the rule of law, responsive to the claims of individual citizens, and able to formulate and pursue their interests independently from other government institutions, is a strongly favorable precondition for effective

---

feared that the ability of treaties to be self-executing, coupled with Justice Holmes's dictum in *Missouri v. Holland*, 252 U.S. 416, 432 (1920), implying that treaties are not bound by Article I limitations on the scope of lawmaking power, threatened U.S. sovereignty. *See* THOMAS M. FRANCK & MICHAEL J. GLENNON, FOREIGN RELATIONS AND NATIONAL SECURITY LAW 297 (2d ed. 1993). A number of scholars entered the debate on the propriety of such an amendment. *Compare, e.g.*, George Finch, *The Need To Restrain the Treaty-Making Power of the U.S. Within Constitutional Limits*, 48 AM. J. INT'L L. 57 (1954) (arguing for the enactment of the proposed amendment to the Constitution), *with* John B. Whitton & J. Edward Fowler, *Bricker Amendment—Fallacies and Dangers*, 48 AM. J. INT'L L. 23 (1954) (opposing the ratification of the amendment).

261. Europe's highest national courts often fought the hardest against acceptance of European Community law supremacy, in part to defend their institutional prerogatives, but also, particularly in Germany and Italy, to safeguard their role in ensuring a domestic rule of law under their post-war constitutions. *See, e.g.*, KOKOTT, *supra* note 129, at 8-9 (describing the resistance of the German Constitutional Court to the supremacy of European Community law until the ECJ incorporated satisfactory human rights guarantees). French courts resisted accepting European Community law to the extent that they saw it as an invitation to engage in judicial review, thereby undermining a pillar of the French legal system designed to ensure that the law as applied expressed the will of the people rather than the whim of the judges. *See* Karen Alter, The Making of a Rule of Law in Europe: The European Court and the National Judiciaries 191-93 (1996) (unpublished Ph.D. dissertation, Massachusetts Inst. of Tech.) (on file with authors).

262. *See* FISHER, *supra* note 259, at 134; OSCAR SCHACHTER, INTERNATIONAL LAW IN THEORY AND PRACTICE 7 (1991).

supranational adjudication. It may even be a necessary (although not sufficient) condition for maximally effective supranational adjudication.

This precondition is inherent in our definition of effective supranational adjudication as the ability of a supranational tribunal to compel compliance with its judgments by convincing domestic government institutions, either directly or through pressure from private parties, to use their power on the tribunal's behalf. A supranational tribunal can invoke the power of law and the interests of ordinary citizens, but these appeals will be far less persuasive if they do not resonate with domestic political values. Domestic governments that recognize little obligation to protect or represent their citizens will be less subject to popular pressure mobilized, or at least reinforced, by a supranational judgment. Political regimes in which the rule of law is a paper promise will be less likely to produce institutions or individuals willing to privilege supranational legal rules over claims of national interest. And monolithic governments, in which power is effectively exercised only by the executive, simply offer no opportunities for a supranational tribunal to penetrate the state in the first place. Conversely, however, government institutions committed to both the rule of law and separation of powers not only as ends in themselves, but also as bulwarks of individual rights and liberties in systems where the individuals themselves are ultimately sovereign, are primed to be the most receptive to the tools that a supranational tribunal has at its disposal. The presence of those institutions has been an important dimension of the European experience.

Notwithstanding the European experience, however, the link between liberal democracy and effective supranational adjudication is complex and contingent, particularly at the margins. Two further caveats are thus in order. First, as just noted, even if the presence of autonomous domestic institutions committed to the rule of law and responsive to individual citizens is a necessary condition for maximally effective supranational adjudication, it is not sufficient. The story still lacks a motive: a specific incentive for a specific domestic government institution to make common cause with a supranational tribunal against its fellow government institutions. Identifying such incentives requires a detailed understanding of institutional interests and patterns of competition in specific countries.[263] Variation regarding the presence or absence and strength or weakness of these incentives also ensures that the narrative of effective supranational adjudication is not a teleology. To the

263. Karen Alter has made this point persuasively with regard to the incentives facing national courts in European Union member states to forge a partnership with the ECJ. She develops a "judicial competition" model that helps explain the motives of some courts in some countries, which must be modified country by country to take account of the structure and culture of national judicial systems. *See* Alter, *supra* note 261, at 78-93. Other analyses emphasizing the importance of judicial politics in the relationship between the ECJ and European national courts are MARY L. VOLCANSEK, JUDICIAL POLITICS IN EUROPE 245-67 (1986); and J. Golub, *Politics of Judicial Discretion: Rethinking the Relationship Between National Courts and the ECJ*, 9 W. EUR. POL. 360, 377-80 (1996).

contrary, finding and recruiting domestic institutions as partners is likely to be a slow and sticky process.

Second, even in a political system that is otherwise corrupt or oppressive, it is possible that a particular government institution—a court or administrative agency or even a legislative body—will choose to forge a relationship with a supranational tribunal as an ally in a domestic political battle against corruption or oppression. Whether such an alliance would be efficacious depends on the nuances and sensitivities of local politics, but the larger point is that participation in the "community of law" constructed by a supranational tribunal is open not only to countries but also to individual political and legal institutions, regardless of how the state of which they are a part is categorized or labeled. The disaggregation of the state that underlies our distinction between supranational and international adjudication also disaggregates a state's unitary political identity as "democratic" or "undemocratic," "liberal" or "illiberal." Nondemocracies may have democratic impulses, embodied in specific institutions; illiberal states may have strong liberal leanings. The same ability to penetrate the surface of the state that gives supranational tribunals their potential power also creates opportunities for them to operate beyond the club of western liberal democracies.

c. *Relative Cultural and Political Homogeneity of States Subject to a Supranational Tribunal*

Many observers of the ECJ, the ECHR, and the Inter-American system have contrasted the relative homogeneity of the states participating in these systems with the diversity of universal regimes such as the International Covenant on Civil and Political Rights.[264] Merrills, for example, contrasts the ECHR, with members drawn from only one geographic region with common, although not identical, legal traditions, with the International Court of Justice (ICJ), "where the absence of common cultural reference points and the diverse issues for adjudication often makes accommodation extremely difficult."[265] Nisuke Ando ties the competence of both the ECHR and the Inter-American Court of Human Rights to issue binding decisions to the shared strong convictions of all the states party to their founding conventions, convictions "nurtured by a long tradition of common history, religion, culture and human values."[266] He hypothesizes that it is premature to expect states not sharing

264. Covenant, *supra* note 15.

265. MERRILLS, *supra* note 77, at 24. Regarding the ECHR, Merrills notes that the "fact that the [ECHR's] judges share a common outlook and are engaged on a single enterprise does not mean that they will always agree on what to do and how to do it. It does, however, appreciably narrow the scope for disagreement." *Id.* at 23; *see also* SIEGHART, *supra* note 159, at 26-27 (reasoning that states "within the same geographical region, sharing a common history and cultural tradition," will more easily reach agreement on the substance of human rights provisions).

266. Ando, *supra* note 20, at 171-72.

such a common conviction and tradition to authorize an international tribunal to render binding decisions.[267]

In some cases, "cultural and political homogeneity" may be code for liberal democracy in the sense that the commentator does not actually believe that *any* group of culturally and politically homogeneous states would support a supranational tribunal. In other cases, however, commentators appear to be pointing to an additional attribute of the states subject to the jurisdiction of a supranational tribunal that may help or hamper the tribunal's ability to communicate effectively with the subjects of its judgments and to build trust in reaching out to specific government institutions. Cultural and political homogeneity is to some extent within the control of the states choosing to establish a supranational tribunal. Yet homogeneity is not a constant. As the experience of the Council of Europe's expanding membership into Eastern Europe and former Soviet states demonstrates, even nations with very different social and political histories may seek to join a treaty regime with a dynamic and powerful supranational court.[268] Moreover, states seeking to draft "universal" agreements such as the Covenant and other U.N.-based human rights treaties are themselves looking for a common glue to bind many diverse cultures and political systems together.

C. *Reviewing the Checklist*

The foregoing analysis condenses and integrates the extensive writings of judges, lawyers, and commentators, together with our own observations, into a checklist of factors that covary with and are claimed to contribute to effective supranational adjudication in Europe. To review, the factors cluster into three categories: (1) factors within the control of states party to the treaty regime (the composition of the tribunal, the caseload and functional capacity of the court, independent factfinding capacity, and the legal status of treaties and the tribunal's decisions); (2) factors within the control of the supranational tribunal itself (its awareness of audience, neutrality and demonstrated autonomy from political interests, incrementalist style of decisionmaking, the quality of its legal reasoning, its dialogue with other supranational tribunals, and the form of its opinions); and (3) factors often beyond the control of both states and jurists (the nature of the violations to be monitored by the tribunal, autonomous domestic institutions committed to the rule of law, and the cultural and political homogeneity of the states subject to a supranational tribunal).

Generating anything as concrete as a checklist to measure a phenomenon as complex as supranational adjudication inevitably requires making many choices, some of which are bound to invite disagreement. Many will tell the

267. *See id.*
268. *See Two Nations Join Panel for Rights in Europe*, N.Y. TIMES, Nov. 10, 1995, at A10.

story of Europe differently and draw different conclusions. An equally important question is the applicability of the checklist to supranational tribunals outside Europe. The factors in the checklist are not culturally or geographically specific; they require political preconditions that are more concentrated in the West but that are themselves the product of a universalist political ideology and exist in states throughout the world.

Most importantly, the European experience challenges us to transcend the traditional framework of "state versus tribunal," summoning an image of a confrontation between two discrete entities in which the outcome depends upon whether the state defines its (unitary) national interest to include compliance with international law. The ECJ and the ECHR have succeeded in becoming effective supranational tribunals by looking not to states per se but to their component institutions, using the link to private parties granted them as supranational tribunals to penetrate the surface of the state. The decision concerning what effect to accord a supranational judgment is not made by a unitary government, but rather by courts, ministries, and legislative committees competing and cooperating with one another as part of the normal domestic political process. Where states actually live up to the unitary fiction due to a monolithic concentration of power or, conversely, where state institutions do not exercise enough power to establish effective public order, supranational tribunals will be stymied. In all other circumstances, however, many possibilities exist for influencing and coopting domestic institutions.

IV. Applying the Checklist to the United Nations Human Rights Committee

We began with the claim that the ECJ and the ECHR were relatively "effective" supranational tribunals, meaning that their judgments had an impact—not only on the litigants involved, but also on the larger society and on distinct government institutions—comparable to the impact of domestic courts in the states subject to their jurisdiction. The checklist then sought to isolate the specific factors that observers, practitioners, and judges of these courts have identified as contributing to their success. We do not claim that faithful adherence to all the factors on the checklist, by the states party to an agreement establishing a new tribunal and by the tribunal itself, will guarantee the effectiveness of the tribunal. To begin with, a number of important factors on the checklist remain difficult or impossible for either the states or the tribunal to control—other than by sharply limiting the number and identity of participating states. Equally important, however, is the impossibility of generating a script or an algorithm for effective adjudication. Factors such as historical contingency and personality will inevitably claim their due.

Nevertheless, the factors on the checklist highlight common elements in the experience of two important supranational tribunals, experience that may be supplemented by the trajectory of newer tribunals and dispute resolution bodies such as WTO and NAFTA panels, the Inter-American Court of Human Rights, or a new permanent International Criminal Court. Eschewing any magic formula, we argue that bolstering these elements is the most likely prescription for increased effectiveness.

In this part, then, we assess the experience of an international entity that has been evolving from a body that once explicitly understood itself as something other than a court into an increasingly court-like entity—the U.N. Human Rights Committee. Although the UNHRC is by no means a supranational court in the strict sense, it is significant that the Committee's recent efforts to enhance its judicial tendencies and to achieve greater compliance with its decisions have occurred contemporaneously with the emergence, to varying degrees, of numerous other checklist factors. We begin with a brief overview of the history and functions of the Committee. The remainder of this part examines the Committee's performance in light of the specific factors on the checklist from Part III.

A. *An Overview of the Committee*

The UNHRC engages in two principal activities in supervising states parties' compliance with the ICCPR:[269] a reporting procedure and a petition procedure. Although both methods are broadly designed to ensure that states respect their treaty obligations, each procedure requires very different actions on the part of the Committee. These differences highlight the Committee's functions as both an investigative supervisory body and a quasi-judicial monitoring body.[270]

1. *The Reporting Process*

Article 40 of the ICCPR requires all states parties to file reports with the Committee "on the measures they have adopted which give effect to the rights recognized herein and on the progress made in the enjoyment of those rights."[271] Initial reports are due within one year of the treaty's entry into force with the subsequent reports due at five year intervals thereafter.[272] In general, the Committee treats initial reports as a time to establish a

---

269. Covenant, *supra* note 15.

270. *See* MCGOLDRICK, *supra* note 17, at 55 (noting that the Committee's work "includes elements of judicial, quasi-judicial, administrative, investigative, inquisitorial, supervisory and conciliatory functions" and that "its nature may alter in accordance with its exercise of the various functions and roles it performs").

271. Covenant, *supra* note 15, art. 40, 999 U.N.T.S. at 181-82.

272. *See* NOWAK, supra note 15, at 548-49.

constructive dialogue with state representatives and devotes more detailed attention to specific human rights practices in subsequent periodic reports.[273]

Once a state party files its report, the Committee reviews its submission in a public session in New York or Geneva. Government representatives are invited to attend, make brief oral presentations, and respond to the Committee's substantive questions about the report. The scope of the Committee's inquiry is not limited by a state's submission and it is free to use any information available, including documents provided by nongovernmental organizations.[274] After the public hearing, the Committee drafts written comments on the report and on the state party's responses to its questions; these comments are published in its annual report to the General Assembly.[275]

The Committee has adopted guidelines to assist states parties in complying with their reporting obligations. Initial reports are to include two sections: an introduction describing the general legal framework of the state party, followed by an article-by-article presentation of information on (1) the legislative, administrative, or other measures in force in regard to each right; (2) restrictions or limitations imposed on the enjoyment of each right; (3) factors or difficulties affecting the enjoyment of each right; and (4) information on progress made in guaranteeing the right.[276] For periodic reports, the Committee prepares a list of nonexhaustive issues that it intends to cover during the session and forwards them to the state representatives in advance of the meeting. Increasingly, these lists of issues have focused on "factors and difficulties that may be affecting implementation of the Covenant."[277]

The Committee does not conceive of its role in the reporting process as "contentious or inquisitory."[278] Instead, its function "is to assist State parties in fulfilling their obligations under the Covenant, to make available to them the experience the Committee has acquired in its examination of other reports and to discuss with them various issues relating to the enjoyment of the rights enshrined in the Covenant."[279] Because the Committee seeks to understand the applicability of the ICCPR to a very wide field of national laws and

---

273. *See id.* at 562-63; Sandra Coliver, *International Reporting Procedures*, *in* GUIDE TO INTERNATIONAL HUMAN RIGHTS PRACTICE 173, 180-81 (Hurst Hannum ed., 2d ed. 1992).

274. *See* DAVID WEISSBRODT & PENNY PARKER, THE U.N. HUMAN RIGHTS COMMISSION, ITS SUBCOMMISSION AND RELATED PROCEDURES 4 (1993).

275. *See* Fausto Paucar, *The International Covenant on Civil and Political Rights*, *in* UNITED NATIONS, HUMAN RIGHTS COMM., MANUAL ON HUMAN RIGHTS REPORTING at 121-22, U.N. Doc. HR/Pub/91/1 (1991).

276. *See* Coliver, *supra* note 273, at 180.

277. *Work of the Human Rights Committee Under Article 40 of the Covenant on Civil and Political Rights*, U.N. GAOR, Hum. Rts. Comm., 48th Sess., Supp. No. 40, Annex X, at 218, U.N. Doc. A/48/40 (1993) [hereinafter *Human Rights Committee*].

278. *Report of the Human Rights Committee*, U.N. GAOR, Hum. Rts. Comm., 35th Sess., Supp. No. 40, at 85, U.N. Doc. A/35/40 (1980).

279. *Human Rights Committee*, *supra* note 277, at 218.

practices, and because many reports often contain inadequate information,[280] the Committee has generally confined itself to questioning government representatives to obtain additional information or clarification about the implementation of the treaty. It has avoided openly criticizing individual states for failing to comply with their treaty obligations.[281] The Committee, however, has repeatedly expressed its dissatisfaction with the failure of many states parties to submit initial and periodic reports in a timely fashion.[282]

2. *General Comments*

Instead of directly critiquing each report, the Committee addresses common problems collectively by issuing "general comments" to states parties. These comments "summarize the Committee's experience with reports and promote certain obvious goals such as co-operation between states parties, improvement of reporting, and Covenant implementation."[283] Often, the comments express regret at the omission of relevant factual information in state reports or point out issues under the ICCPR that the reports have failed to address in sufficient detail.[284] In addition, they direct states to take account of the Committee's analysis in preparing future reports.[285]

The general comments provide a crucial opportunity for the Committee to articulate its understanding of the treaty's protected rights and freedoms. Although the first two comments concerned procedural aspects of the reporting process,[286] the remainder have addressed the Committee's understanding of the substantive rights enshrined in the treaty. Most of these comments have analyzed individual articles of the ICCPR, such as the right to life protected in Article 6[287] or the prohibition of torture in Article 7.[288] But the

280. *See* Opsahl, *supra* note 17, at 401-02.

281. *See id.* at 407-09.

282. *See Human Rights Committee*, *supra* note 277, at 220-21 (criticizing states for late filings of reports).

283. Opsahl, *supra* note 17, at 412.

284. *See id.* at 414.

285. *See* MCGOLDRICK, *supra* note 17, at 94.

286. *See* General Comment 1/13 (reporting obligation), July 28, 1981, *reprinted in* NOWAK, *supra* note 15, at 848-49; General Comment 2/13 (reporting guidelines), July 28, 1981, *reprinted in* NOWAK, *supra* note 15, at 849.

287. *See* General Comment 14/23, Nov. 2, 1984, *reprinted in* NOWAK, *supra* note 15, at 861; General Comment 6/16, July 27, 1982, *reprinted in* NOWAK, *supra* note 15, at 851-52; *see also* Covenant, *supra* note 15, art. 6, 999 U.N.T.S. at 174-75.

288. *See* General Comment 20/44, Apr. 3, 1992, *reprinted in* NOWAK, *supra* note 15, at 871-73; General Comment 7/16, July 27, 1982, *reprinted in* NOWAK, *supra* note 15, at 852-53; *see also* Covenant, *supra* note 15, art. 7, 999 U.N.T.S. at 175. Other general comments have addressed gender equality, liberty and security of person, freedom of expression, procedural guarantees in civil and criminal trials, prohibition of propaganda for war and advocacy of hatred, the right of self-determination, the rights of the child, the right of nondiscrimination, and rights relating to marriage and the family. *See* NOWAK, *supra* note 15, at 850-75 (reprinting comments).

Committee has also adopted two issue-oriented comments, on the position of aliens[289] and on the rights of detainees.[290]

In developing its analysis, the Committee has relied on the expertise of individual members, information submitted by states parties in their reports, and cases decided under the Optional Protocol.[291] Although adoption of the general comments has "serve[d] rapidly to develop the jurisprudence of the [Committee] under the Covenant,"[292] the statements issued are not scholarly studies. Moreover, "since they are couched in general terms their interpretation may easily create problems of application to specific cases."[293] In assessing the caliber of the Committee's analysis, one commentator states that while some of the comments "have been of a high quality and represent valuable indications of the content of the respective rights," others "have been much less helpful."[294]

3. *The Petition System*

The Committee's other major jurisprudential function is the consideration of written "communications" from individuals under the First Optional Protocol to the ICCPR.[295] The Committee has taken on quasi-judicial functions in interpreting the treaty in these cases.[296] Specifically, it acts as an arbiter of contentious disputes between individuals and states, provides victims of human rights violations with an international forum for relief where domestic remedies

---

289. *See* General Comment 15/27, July 22, 1986, *reprinted in* NOWAK, *supra* note 15, at 861-63.

290. *See* General Comment 21/44, Apr. 6, 1992, *reprinted in* NOWAK, *supra* note 15, at 873-75.

291. *See* Opsahl, *supra* note 17, at 414; *see also* Optional Protocol, *supra* note 15, 999 U.N.T.S. at 302.

292. MCGOLDRICK, *supra* note 17, at 95.

293. Opsahl, *supra* note 17, at 415.

294. MCGOLDRICK, *supra* note 17, at 94; *see also id.* at 471 ("[T]he General Comment on article 19 was both weak and disappointing, being little more than a reiteration of article 19.").

295. *See* Optional Protocol, *supra* note 15, art. 2, 999 U.N.T.S. at 302 ("[I]ndividuals who claim that any of their rights enumerated in the Covenant have been violated . . . may submit a written communication to the Committee for consideration."). Under Article 41 of the ICCPR, states parties may recognize the competence of the Committee to consider a complaint filed by one state party against another alleging a failure to comply with the obligations of the Covenant. *See* Covenant, *supra* note 15, art. 41, 999 U.N.T.S. at 182-83. The Committee then assists the parties in resolving the dispute. *See id.* To date, however, no state has filed a complaint under the Article 41 procedure. *See* NOWAK, *supra* note 15, at 580-603 (discussing the interstate petition procedure).

296. *See, e.g.*, P.R. Ghandhi, *The Human Rights Committee and the Right of Individual Communication*, 57 BRIT. Y.B. INT'L L. 201, 249 (1986) ("Although . . . in no sense a court of law, the Committee has striven to be seen to be acting in a way as nearly as possible similar to that in which a court of law acts."); Opsahl, *supra* note 17, at 426-27 (noting that the Committee "has applied basic principles of a judicial, or quasi-judicial nature concerning, for instance, contradictory proceedings, assessment of evidence, and reasoning in support of its results"); Alfred M. de Zayas, *The Follow-Up Procedure of the UN Human Rights Committee*, 47 REV. INT'L COMM'N JURISTS 28, 30 (1991) ("Admittedly the Human Rights Committee is not . . . a court, but it does exercise analogous responsibilities and it is the only international body to fulfil this need."); Alfred de Zayas et al., *Application of the International Covenant on Civil and Political Rights Under the Optional Protocol by the Human Rights Committee*, 28 F.R.G. Y.B. INT'L L. 9, 11 (1985) ("The Committee applies the provisions of the Covenant and Optional Protocol in a judicial spirit.").

are unavailable or insufficient, and generates a "specific problem-centred jurisprudence."[297]

The Committee cannot perform these functions for all of the states party to the Covenant, however, since it is only authorized to consider complaints against states that have ratified the Optional Protocol.[298] To date, only 86 of the 132 states parties have ratified that agreement.[299] This creates a "double standard of adherence to covenant rights" in which states that have ratified the Optional Protocol are subject to a far greater level of scrutiny of their compliance with the ICCPR than states that have refrained from ratification.[300] For example, in contrast to its reluctance to criticize states parties during the reporting process, the Committee has not hesitated in expressing its displeasure with states that do not respond to an individual's allegations or otherwise decline to take an active role in resolving a case.

Even once a state has ratified the Optional Protocol, the ability to file a petition with the Committee is subject to several restrictions. First, only individuals can bring a complaint before the Committee; a group cannot file a claim on an individual's behalf.[301] Second, if the laws of the state provide domestic remedies for the alleged violations of the ICCPR, those remedies must be exhausted prior to filing a communication with the Committee.[302] Third, the communication must not be an abuse of the right of submission, anonymous, or otherwise "incompatible with the provisions of the Covenant."[303] Fourth, the communication must not be under consideration by another international monitoring body.[304] Finally, the individual must provide sufficient facts to substantiate his or her allegations.[305]

---

297. Matthew Craven, *Towards an Unofficial Petition Procedure: A Review on the Role of the UN Committee on Economic, Social and Cultural Rights*, *in* SOCIAL RIGHTS AS HUMAN RIGHTS: A EUROPEAN CHALLENGE 91, 94 (Krzysztof Drzewicki et al. eds., 1994). A former member of the Committee recently highlighted the interrelationship between the reporting system and the petition system:

> Consideration of states' reports gives the Committee an overall picture of the situation with regard to civil and political rights in a given country. This panorama is indispensable to the evaluation of a state's compliance with international human rights standards. . . .
>
> But frequently details are lost (and I would like to emphasize that in the protection of basic human rights and freedoms all details are very important). Very often, it is only through the consideration of individual communications that complete conformity of national legislation and practice with the requirements of international law can be assessed.

Rein A. Myullerson, *Monitoring Compliance with International Human Rights Standards: Experience of the UN Human Rights Committee*, 1991-1992 CAN. HUM. RTS. Y.B. 105, 107.

298. *See* Optional Protocol, *supra* note 15, art. 1, 999 U.N.T.S. at 302.

299. *See* HUMAN RIGHTS COMMITTEE PRESS RELEASE, *supra* note 15.

300. Anne F. Bayefsky, *Human Rights: The 1966 Covenants Twenty Years Later*, 80 AM. SOC'Y INT'L L. PROC. 408, 409 (1986).

301. *See* NOWAK, *supra* note 15, at 657-59, 681.

302. *See* Optional Protocol, *supra* note 15, art. 2, 999 U.N.T.S. at 302.

303. *Id.* art. 3, 999 U.N.T.S. at 302. Grounds for declaring a communication inadmissible under this clause include incompatibility *ratione temporis*, *personae*, *loci*, and *materiae*. *See* NOWAK, *supra* note 15, at 678-85.

304. *See* Optional Protocol, *supra* note 15, art. 5(2), 999 U.N.T.S. at 303.

305. *See* NOWAK, *supra* note 15, at 666-68.

Assuming an individual overcomes these hurdles, the Committee declares the communication admissible and then receives written submissions by both the aggrieved individual and the state party. The Committee cannot engage in factfinding and it does not take testimony or hear oral arguments from the parties.[306] After reviewing the written submissions, the Committee determines in a private meeting whether the facts presented disclose a violation of the Covenant.

The Committee then authors an opinion, ambiguously referred to in the Optional Protocol as the "views" of the Committee.[307] These views, which "follow a judicial pattern and are effectively decisions on the merits,"[308] set forth the allegations of the author, the responses of the state party, the decision on admissibility, and any interim measures, followed by the facts upon which the Committee bases its decision. The views also list certain "considerations" upon which the Committee has based its decision. These include a state party's degree of cooperation with the Committee in resolving the case, the burden of proof, a reference to one or more general comments or to prior case law, and an interpretation of the substantive requirements of the treaty.[309] Finally, the decisions contain a statement of "the view of the [Committee] on the 'obligation' of the State party in light of [its] findings."[310]

From the inception of the petition procedure in 1977 through October 1996, the Committee had registered 716 communications concerning fifty-one states parties.[311] Of these, 239 had been concluded with the adoption of views on the merits.[312] Of the remaining communications, 224 had been declared inadmissible, 115 had been discontinued or withdrawn by the author, and 96 were pending as of October 1996 at the pre- or post-admissibility stage.[313]

B. *Toward an Increasingly Judicial Approach to the Petition System*

Although the foregoing summary reveals the diverse functions that the Committee exercises in monitoring states parties' compliance with the

306. *See* McGoldrick, *supra* note 17, at 134, 143-45. McGoldrick notes that the Optional Protocol does not preclude the Committee from hearing oral argument. *See id.* at 144-45.

307. *See* Optional Protocol, *supra* note 15, art. 5(4), 999 U.N.T.S. at 303.

308. McGoldrick, *supra* note 17, at 151.

309. *See id.*

310. *Id.* at 152. Once adopted, the Committee forwards its views to both parties and publishes them, along with selected admissibility decisions, in its annual report to the General Assembly. *See* Optional Protocol, *supra* note 15, art. 5(4), 999 U.N.T.S. at 303.

311. *See Consideration of Communications Under the Optional Protocol*, U.N. GAOR, Hum. Rts. Comm., 51st Sess., Supp. No. 40, at 66, U.N. Doc. A/51/40 (1996) [hereinafter *1996 Consideration of Communications*].

312. *See id.* As of October 1995, the Committee had found treaty violations in 154 of the 208 decisions on the merits. *See Follow-Up Activities Under the Optional Protocol*, U.N. GAOR, Hum. Rts. Comm., 50th Sess., Supp. No. 40, at 96, U.N. Doc. A/50/40 (1995) [hereinafter *1995 Follow-Up Activities*].

313. *See 1996 Consideration of Communications*, *supra* note 311, at 66.

Covenant, it is the consideration of communications under the Optional Protocol that has recently brought the most attention to the Committee and its work. In addition, the increasing number of states that have ratified the Optional Protocol over the last decade,[314] together with the widening audience of litigants, attorneys, activists, and scholars who follow the Committee's activities, has made the petition system an ever more important part of its work. With greater visibility has come a concomitant rise in the number of communications filed with the Committee and an increase in their complexity.[315]

The Committee's response to these developments reveals a trend of remarkable importance: In numerous and diverse ways, the Committee is behaving more and more like a judicial arbiter of human rights disputes, even when granted only limited powers by states parties. Although lacking many of the institutional characteristics possessed by supranational tribunals such as the ECHR, the ECJ, and the European Commission of Human Rights, the Committee has, within the limits of its authority and sometimes arguably beyond it, followed an increasingly court-like method of operation. Particularly striking, in light of our analysis of effectiveness in Part I, are the Committee's efforts to improve compliance with its decisions.

Since 1990, the Committee has become quite outspoken in its view that defending states are under an obligation to comply with unfavorable decisions against them.[316] Further, it has taken concrete steps to monitor compliance, appointing one of its members as a special *rapporteur* to record states' responses.[317] As of October 1995, the *rapporteur* had received information

314. As of 1991, only 55 States had ratified the Optional Protocol. *See* Opsahl, *supra* note 17, at 421. As of late 1995, 86 States had done so. *See* UNITED NATIONS, ECONOMIC AND SOCIAL COUNCIL, HUMAN RIGHTS COMMITTEE, PRESS RELEASE: HUMAN RIGHTS COMMITTEE CONCLUDES FIFTY-FIFTH SESSION AT GENEVA, U.N. Doc. HR/CT/448 (1995).

315. Although the Committee's early case law generally concerned gross violations of human rights or situations that required only a cursory legal analysis, more recently the Committee has begun to consider cases that require "more subtle legal reasoning." Opsahl, *supra* note 17, at 428, 429.

316. Although the Committee's early decisions failed to announce whether states were obliged to inform the Committee of their responses to its views, in 1990 the Committee began concluding its decisions with the statement that it "would welcome information on any relevant measures taken by the State party in respect of the Committee's views." *See, e.g.*, Torres v. Finland, No. 291/1988, U.N. GAOR, Hum. Rts. Comm., 44th Sess., Supp. No. 40, Annex IX, at 96, 100, U.N. Doc. A/44/40 (1990). The Committee's current practice is to ask for a response from the defending state within 90 days in each case in which it determines that a violation of the ICCPR has occurred. *See, e.g.*, Linton v. Jamaica, No. 255/1987, U.N. GAOR, Hum. Rts. Comm., 48th Sess., Supp. No. 40, Annex XII, at 12, 16, U.N. Doc. A/48/40 (1993).

317. Prior to 1990, a dispute among the members over the legal basis for initiating any follow-up procedures prevented the Committee from assessing the extent of compliance. *See* de Zayas, *supra* note 296, at 30-31. In that year, however, the Committee resolved this internal debate and appointed the special *rapporteur*. *See Measures Adopted at the Thirty-Ninth Session of the Human Rights Committee To Monitor Compliance with Its Views Under Article 5, Paragraph 4, of the Optional Protocol to the International Covenant on Civil and Political Rights*, U.N. GAOR, Hum. Rts. Comm., 45th Sess., Supp. No. 40, Annex XI, at 205, 205-06, U.N. Doc. A/45/40 (1990). The Committee published an analysis of the information received by the *rapporteur* in its 1993 annual report to the General Assembly, *see Follow-Up on Views Adopted Under Optional Protocol to the International Covenant on Civil and Political Rights*, U.N. GAOR, Hum. Rts. Comm., 48th Sess., Supp. No. 40, Annex X(B), at 222, 223-24, U.N. Doc. A/48/40 (1993)

in 81 of 154 views in which the Committee found a treaty violation.[318] Of the responses received, the Committee considered only about thirty percent to be "satisfactory," meaning "that they display[ed] a willingness on the part of the State party concerned to implement the Committee's Views or to offer the applicant an appropriate remedy."[319] In light of this lukewarm response by states parties, the Committee has taken steps to increase adherence to its decisions. Specifically, it has begun to publish the compliance information it collects and to identify publicly each state that refuses to implement its views.[320]

In view of the Committee's own efforts to improve its performance as an increasingly judicial supranational tribunal, it is appropriate and timely to apply the checklist of factors outlined above to the Committee's review of individual petitions under the Optional Protocol. In the subsections that follow, we review the Committee's performance with respect to each of the checklist factors, noting in each instance whether the current status of that factor favors or hinders the Committee's openly professed desire to achieve more effective supranational review of states parties' human rights practices. Where the current status of a particular checklist factor appears to be less than optimal, we also briefly indicate additional steps that states or the Committee itself might take to achieve greater effectiveness.

1. *Factors Principally Within the Control of States Parties*

a. *Composition of the Tribunal*

Article 28 of the Covenant provides that the Committee "shall be composed of nationals of states party to the present Covenant who shall be of high moral character and recognized competence in the field of human rights, consideration being given to the usefulness of participation of some persons having legal experience."[321] This raises an immediate problem with treating

---

[hereinafter *1993 Follow-Up on Views*], and a similar analysis has been published each year thereafter.

318. *See 1995 Follow-Up Activities, supra* note 312, at 96.

319. *Id.* The remaining responses

> either explicitly challenged the Committee's findings on factual or legal grounds (nine replies), indicated that the State party would not, for one reason or another, give effect to the Committee's recommendations (nine replies), promised an investigation of the matter considered by the Committee or constituted much belated submissions on the merits of the case.

Id. On the whole, the Committee characterized these statistics as "encouraging" but "not fully satisfactory." *Id.* at 98.

320. In 1995, the Committee published what it termed a "separate and highly visible chapter on follow-up activities under the Optional Protocol." *Id.* at 99. This chapter includes a list identifying those states that cooperated with the Committee's follow-up procedures and those that did not. *See id.* at 97-98. The Committee has also resolved to give "[e]very form of publicity" to its follow-up procedures, including issuing separate press communiques "highlighting both positive and negative developments," meeting with government representatives, and urging nongovernmental organizations to submit information on compliance. *Id.* at 99-100.

321. Covenant, *supra* note 15, art. 28(2), 999 U.N.T.S. at 179.

the Committee as analogous to other supranational tribunals; unlike members of the ECHR and the ECJ,[322] its members need not be lawyers or jurists. In practice, however, "nearly all members of the Committee have completed a legal education and are or were employed in the legal field,"[323] a fact which commentators believe has resulted in the "high quality of decisions on individual communications."[324]

Although all of the Committee members are acknowledged experts in human rights, the background and experience of individual members vary considerably. Most have worked as university professors specializing in public international law; others are judges, prosecutors, lawyers, diplomats, public officials, or politicians.[325] Because the Committee works on a part-time basis, generally taking up no more than two months of each year,[326] its members often simultaneously work for regional tribunals such as the ECHR, the European Commission of Human Rights, or the Inter-American Commission on Human Rights, or U.N. treaty or political bodies such as the Committee Against Torture, the United Nations Human Rights Commission, and the General Assembly.[327] Members may also be public servants of their states or occupy government office,[328] a status that raises a potential conflict with the Committee's obligations of independence and impartiality.

Given the broad mix of experience among the Committee members, the present composition of the Committee may well be suitable for achieving its professed goal of encouraging states parties to implement its interpretations of the Covenant. This factor is thus likely to be a net plus in assessing the Committee's performance under the checklist. If the experience with the ECJ and the ECHR is any guide, however, states parties should refrain from nominating active government officials to the Committee. They should also consider increasing the number of Committee members with substantial experience and recognized expertise in national law since these individuals may more effectively bridge the gap perceived by national legislators and judges between international and national law. Finally, states parties should also consider other structural changes to the Covenant and the Optional Protocol in order to increase the quasi-judicial nature of the Committee. Possible reforms include increasing the term of member's service from its current four years and permitting automatic reelection of Committee members without the need for renomination by a state party.[329]

---

322. *See supra* Subsection III.B.1.a.
323. NOWAK, *supra* note 15, at 508.
324. *Id.*
325. *See id.* at 508-09 (listing members of the Committee and their professions as of 1993).
326. *See id.* at 529.
327. *See id.* at 508-09 & n.12.
328. *See id.* at 509. As of 1993, only two of the Committee's 18 members were civil servants. *See id.*
329. *See* Covenant, *supra* note 15, arts. 30, 32, 999 U.N.T.S. at 180 (describing current election and nomination procedures).

b. *Case Load or Functional Capacity of the Tribunal*

The early days under the Optional Protocol brought disappointingly few communications to the Committee.[330] During the 1980s, the Committee reached only five to ten decisions on the merits each year.[331] More recently, however, the Committee's case load has begun to increase "markedly":[332] Between October 1993 and July 1994, the Committee adopted thirty-two "views" on the merits and declared thirty cases to be inadmissible;[333] another fifteen views and thirteen admissibility decisions were reached during the next year.[334] During this period, the number of communications filed with the Committee also increased.[335]

Although the Committee's workload is burgeoning and must be regarded as respectable for a fledgling supranational tribunal in the first twenty years of its existence,[336] it is still quite modest given the large number of states party to the Optional Protocol (at eighty-six more than twice the number of signatories to the European Convention on Human Rights)[337] and the vast number of human rights violations occurring every year around the world. Two related factors help explain the relative paucity of cases: the inadequate resources provided to the Committee and the lack of knowledge on the part of potential plaintiffs of the Optional Protocol's function or existence.[338]

The material and financial support necessary to create the physical and personal infrastructure for rendering decisions is a critical factor in the

---

330. *See* MCGOLDRICK, *supra* note 17, at 500 ("The most disappointing feature of the practice under the Optional Protocol had perhaps been the limited number of communications but there has been a substantial increase in recent years.").

331. *See* ROBERTSON & MERRILLS, *supra* note 81, at 65. This figure does not include published decisions declaring communications inadmissible.

332. *Report of the Human Rights Committee to the General Assembly*, U.N. GAOR, Hum. Rts. Comm., 49th Sess., Supp. No. 40, at 5, U.N. Doc. No. A/49/40 (1994) [hereinafter *1994 Human Rights Committee Report*].

333. *See Consideration of Communications Under the Optional Protocol*, U.N. GAOR, Hum. Rts. Comm., 49th Sess., Supp. No. 40, at 64, U.N. Doc. A/49/40 (1994) [hereinafter *1994 Consideration of Communications*].

334. *See Consideration of Communications Under the Optional Protocol*, U.N. GAOR, Hum. Rts. Comm., 50th Sess., Supp. No. 40, at 83, U.N. Doc. A/50/40 (1995) [hereinafter *1995 Consideration of Communications*].

335. *See id.* at 82.

336. It should be remembered that the number of complaints filed with the European Commission of Human Rights (and, as a result with the ECHR) was extremely low for the first two decades of the tribunals' existence and only increased in the late 1970s and early 1980s after the ECHR decided several landmark judgments against the states party to the European Convention. *See, e.g.*, BEDDARD, *supra* note 86, at 6-7; ROBERTSON & MERRILLS, *supra* note 81, at 310-11.

337. *Compare* text accompanying *supra* note 79, *with supra* note 15.

338. *See* MCGOLDRICK, *supra* note 17, at 500. Commentators have also posited a third factor, the siphoning off of potential claimants by other international adjudicatory procedures. *See id.* The potential for such intersystem competition is limited, however, given that many states party to the Covenant and the Optional Protocol are not also members of the European or American regional human rights regimes. In addition, in the absence of a reservation to the Optional Protocol, a human rights plaintiff may bring a complaint before a regional human rights tribunal and then, if rejected, before the Committee.

Committee's ability to enhance its effectiveness.[339] Members of the Committee are chronically starved for resources. They must follow all proceedings while simultaneously preparing interventions and responding to or commenting on state reports covering complex issues of law and fact.[340] Most observers conclude that members of the Committee do more than can reasonably be expected, making it impossible for the Committee to assume added work or to work between sessions without substantial additional resources.[341] The Committee has repeatedly requested such resources from the United Nations, most recently stressing that it could "no longer examine communications expeditiously" in light of its increasing workload and "highlight[ing] the urgent need to reinforce the Secretariat staff."[342] Our analysis confirms the vital importance of responding to this request.

One way to increase the Committee's caseload without overstraining existing resources would be to streamline its procedures. At present, proceedings under the Optional Protocol are quite drawn out, lasting two to three years.[343] The states party to the ICCPR could revise the procedures to reduce delay and increase access. For example, the states parties could permit the Committee to decide cases in geographically representative panels with en banc review by the Committee reserved for exceptional cases.[344]

The low, albeit rising, public profile of the Committee's mandate and its case law also explains the relatively modest number of views decided to date. The Optional Protocol procedure is not widely known to national lawyers and

339. Pursuant to Article 36 of the Covenant, "[t]he Secretary-General of the United Nations shall provide the necessary staff and resources for the effective performance of the functions of the Committee under the present Covenant." Covenant, *supra* note 15, art. 36, 999 U.N.T.S. at 181.

340. *See* Opsahl, *supra* note 17, at 433-43. Indeed, Committee members often feel overwhelmed by their heavy workload. *See* MERRILLS, *supra* note 77, at 16.

341. *See* Opsahl, *supra* note 17, at 381. To reduce the backlog of pending cases under the Optional Protocol, the Committee met an extra week during its 51st session, adopting 16 views and declaring 11 decisions inadmissible. The U.N. Secretary General's failure to provide more staff for this extended session, however, resulted in an increased backlog in the processing of new communications. *See 1994 Consideration of Communications*, *supra* note 333, at 65.

342. *1995 Consideration of Communications*, *supra* note 334, at 83. The Committee stated further:

> [T]he Committee also notes that an increasing number of communications are being submitted in languages which are not among the working languages of the Secretariat, and expresses its concern about the consequent delays in the examination of such communications. The Human Rights Committee reiterates its request to the Secretary-General to take the necessary steps to ensure a substantial increase in the number of staff, specialized in the various legal systems, assigned to service the Committee, and wishes to record that the work under the Optional Protocol continues to suffer as a result of insufficient Secretariat resources.

Id.

343. *See id.*; *see also* de Zayas et al., *supra* note 296, at 16.

344. In the absence of such formal revisions, the Committee has implemented several procedures to streamline its examination of communications, including appointing a special *rapporteur* to process new communications, authorizing a five-member working group that can declare communications admissible when all five members agree, and joining consideration of the admissibility and merits of a communication when both parties consent and the Committee considers it appropriate. These measures have helped to reduce the backlog of cases, albeit to a limited degree. *See* NOWAK, *supra* note 15, at 688 (noting that the establishment of the *rapporteur* on new communications has reduced the backlog of cases pending at the pre-admissibility stage).

advisors in the states parties.[345] Even though respected for its moral and legal authority as an independent human rights body, the Committee still receives comparatively little interest at either the popular or academic level.[346] The Committee, appreciating the need for greater awareness of its work, has recently taken steps to publicize its activities. In particular, it has authorized the holding of press briefings at each of its sessions, encouraged information exchanges with nongovernmental organizations, urged the media to become more acquainted with its activities, and expedited the issuance of its official publications containing key documents and case law.[347]

In sum, the Committee scores quite low on this measure of effectiveness, both because of the inadequate resources devoted to the Committee's activities and because of the relatively limited use of the petition system by individual claimants.[348] It would be easier to publicize the Committee's work, of course, if its decisions were formally binding. To this extent, publicity is likely to covary with other factors that we have identified. Another possibility for raising the profile of the Committee without necessarily changing the status of its determinations would be to amend the Covenant and the Optional Protocol to create new channels of access between it and national courts. If, for instance, national courts were allowed to submit questions arising under the Covenant to the Committee for determination, even if these courts were not formally bound by the resulting opinions, the Committee's influence would spread. States parties could explore such models of court-to-court communication without necessarily expanding the formal legal authority of the Committee.

c. *Independent Factfinding Capacity*

Unlike other supranational courts, the Committee has no authority to conduct independent factfinding or to require states parties to supply information concerning an alleged treaty violation.[349] Nor may it compel the parties or their representatives to appear before it in person to assess their credibility, query their proof, or evaluate their legal arguments. Instead, the Committee must merely consider the communications it receives "in light of

345. *See* McGoldrick, *supra* note 17, at 500.

346. *See id.* at 102. McGoldrick reports that academic attention to the actual practices of the UNHRC is now increasing. *See id.*

347. *See Report of the Human Rights Committee to the General Assembly*, U.N. GAOR, Hum. Rts. Comm., 50th Sess., Supp. No. 40, at 12, U.N. Doc. A/50/40 (1995).

348. We recognize, of course, that increasing the number of petitions filed with the Committee without a concomitant boost in its resources is a recipe for a backlogged docket and frustrated claimants. Thus, the issue of adequate resources may well be the most critical one facing states parties.

349. Nor, like the ECJ, does the Committee sit above tribunals that possess independent factfinding powers. *See supra* notes 122-123 and accompanying text.

all written information made available to it by the individual and the State Party concerned."[350]

Commentators have uniformly criticized the Committee's limited powers in this regard, noting that the current procedure is "unsatisfactory"[351] and "has considerably restricted the possibilities for adequate taking of evidence" since the Committee is unable to verify "conflicting depictions of the facts," either by "oral examination of parties or witnesses or by on-site inspection."[352] Accordingly, these commentators have urged the Committee, with the consent of the state party concerned, to hold oral hearings and conduct on-site investigations.[353] Alternatively, the Committee may suggest, and states parties may seek, an amendment to the Optional Protocol to provide for such procedures.

Although hobbled by its limited textual mandate, the Committee has attempted to compensate for its limited powers by spelling out in detail what is expected of states parties when it brings a communication to their attention. In particular, the Committee has emphasized that a state "should make available to [it] all the information at its disposal,"[354] including "copies of the relevant decisions of the courts and findings of any investigations which have taken place into the validity of the complaints made."[355] The state must also "investigate in good faith all the allegations of violations of the Covenant against it and its authorities and furnish the Committee with detailed information about the measures, if any, taken to remedy the situation."[356]

Notwithstanding these procedural requirements, in numerous cases the Committee has received either insufficient or no cooperation from the state involved. To prevent the truculent attitude on the part of such states from vitiating the Optional Protocol procedures, the Committee has developed a default judgment jurisprudence under which the author's plausible and substantiated allegations form the basis for its findings of fact and legal conclusion that the Covenant has been violated.[357] Although attractive to individuals seeking to hold such states accountable for human rights abuses, this body of decisions nevertheless may be seen as crediting factual assertions

350. Optional Protocol, *supra* note 15, art. 5(1), 999 U.N.T.S. at 303.

351. MCGOLDRICK, *supra* note 17, at 144.

352. NOWAK, *supra* note 15, at 692.

353. *See* MCGOLDRICK, *supra* note 17, at 144-45; Opsahl, *supra* note 17, at 427. McGoldrick has stressed, however, that the Committee "could not cope with oral hearings without a fundamental restructuring of its work and servicing." MCGOLDRICK, *supra* note 17, at 145.

354. Douglas v. Jamaica, No. 352/1989, U.N. GAOR, Hum. Rts. Comm., 49th Sess., Supp. No. 40, Annex X, at 42, 47, U.N. Doc. A/49/40 (1994).

355. Mojica v. Dominican Republic, No. 499/1991, U.N. GAOR, Hum. Rts. Comm., 49th Sess., Supp. No. 40, Annex IX, at 142, U.N. Doc. A/49/40 (1994); *see also* NOWAK, *supra* note 15, at 694.

356. Minanga v. Zaire, No. 366/1989, U.N. GAOR, Hum. Rts. Comm., 49th Sess., Supp. No. 40, Annex X, at 65, 66, U.N. Doc. A/49/40 (1993).

357. *See* NOWAK, *supra* note 15, at 693.

that have not been fully substantiated[358] or skirting difficult legal issues for want of any meaningful adversarial process.[359] This factor, then, clearly weighs against effectiveness, although the Committee's creativity in attempting to close the Covenant's procedural gaps is commendable.

d. *Formal Authority or Status as Law*

The domestic legal status of the Covenant and Optional Protocol, like that of other multilateral treaties including the Treaty of Rome and the European Convention on Human Rights, is a function not of international law but rather of the domestic constitutional and legislative regimes established by the states party to the treaty. In one major respect, however, the ICCPR differs significantly from the European treaty regimes: The "views" of the Committee are not binding under international law on the parties to the dispute before it.[360] The Committee itself considers this fact "a major shortcoming in the implementation machinery established by the Covenant."[361]

The ultimate power to make the Committee's decisions legally binding rests with the states party to the Covenant. Given that states have thus far refused to bind themselves, the Committee initially scores relatively low on this checklist factor as well. The Committee has not permitted states parties to control this issue entirely, however. To the contrary, the Committee has taken steps toward imbuing its views with a tone that suggests they are de facto legally binding in character. These steps include articulating in its case law and general comments an interpretation of the ICCPR strongly suggesting that its views must be obeyed[362] and urging states parties to amend the Optional

358. For example, commentators have reported that the Committee has had particular difficulty in establishing the truth of allegations that individuals have been subject to arbitrary arrest and detention. *See, e.g.*, de Zayas, *supra* note 296, at 36-37.

359. *Cf.* MCGOLDRICK, *supra* note 17, at 367 (finding the Committee's sparse analysis in early decisions attributable in part to the states parties' failure to participate in the proceeding and to provide counterarguments to the authors' allegations).

360. *See id.* at 151; NOWAK, *supra* note 15, at 710; Opsahl, *supra* note 17, at 431.

361. *1993 Follow-Up on Views*, *supra* note 317, at 222.

362. In *Bradshaw v. Barbados*, No. 489/1992, U.N. GAOR, Hum. Rts. Comm., 49th Sess., Supp. No. 40, Annex X, at 305, 307, U.N. Doc. A/49/40 (1994), the Court of Appeal of Barbados had rejected the argument of a death row inmate that "the provisions enabling written representations to the Human Rights Committee, and the procedural and other provisions thereunder," are part of the law of Barbados. As a result, the defendant had no "legitimate expectation that the State would not carry out the sentence of death before his rights under the Covenant and the Optional Protocol ha[d] been considered by the Committee . . . ." *Id.* The Committee criticized this rejection of its powers in no uncertain terms:

> By ratifying the Covenant and the Optional Protocol, Barbados has undertaken to fulfil its obligations thereunder and has recognized the Committee's competence to receive and consider communications from individuals . . . . While the Covenant is not part of the domestic law of Barbados which can be applied directly by the courts, the State party has nevertheless accepted the legal obligation to make the provisions of the Covenant effective. To this extent, it is an obligation for the State party to adopt appropriate measures to give legal effect to the views of the Committee as to the interpretation and application of the Covenant in particular cases arising under the Optional Protocol. This includes the Committee's views . . . on the desirability of interim measures of protection to avoid irreparable damage to the victim of the alleged

Protocol to make the Committee's views legally binding.[363]

2. *Factors Within the Control of the Tribunal*

a. *Awareness of Audience*

The Committee is highly aware that its audience under the Optional Protocol is comprised principally of individuals who have been aggrieved by a state party's alleged violations of their human rights. Thus the Committee has repeatedly "stressed the fundamental importance of individuals having access to it under the [Optional Protocol]."[364] In terms of admissibility requirements,[365] exhaustion of domestic remedies,[366] and the burden of persuasion, the Committee has interpreted the Optional Protocol in a manner favorable to individuals, thereby encouraging them to bring communications before it. This trend has been extensively documented by commentators.[367]

A second audience for the UNHRC is the lawyers who represent individuals before the Committee. Their participation has increased roughly in proportion to the rise in complaints generally, but at roughly fifty percent it has remained steady as a percentage of total cases filed.[368] Representation by attorneys is particularly common in disputes involving states that are among

---

violation.
Id. at 309.

In its recent general comment on the compatibility of state party reservations to the Covenant and the Optional Protocol, the Committee stated that its role under both treaties "necessarily entails interpreting the provisions of the Covenant and the development of a jurisprudence." *General Comment No. 24(52) on Issues Relating to Reservations Made upon Ratification or Accession to the Covenant or the Optional Protocols Thereto, or in Relation to Declarations Under Article 41 of the Covenant*, U.N. GAOR, Hum. Rts. Comm., 50th Sess., Supp. No. 40, Annex V, at 126, U.N. Doc. A/50/40 (1995). The Committee further stated that "a reservation that rejects the Committee's competence to interpret the requirements of any provisions of the Covenant would also be contrary to the object and purpose of that treaty." *Id.*

363. In 1993, the Committee urged states parties to amend the Optional Protocol to "undertake to comply with the Committee's views." *1993 Follow-Up on Views, supra* note 317, at 225. Given that more than one-third of the states party to the Covenant have thus far refrained from ratifying the existing Optional Protocol, such a move is remarkably bold and forward-looking.

364. MCGOLDRICK, *supra* note 17, at 199.

365. *See* ZWART, *supra* note 17, at 150-52.

366. *See* MCGOLDRICK, *supra* note 17, at 197 (observing that the Committee has adopted "an individual orientated approach, or at least not a State centred approach" to exhaustion of domestic remedies); NOWAK, *supra* note 15, at 703-04 (noting that the Committee has generally interpreted the exhaustion requirement more liberally than has the European Commission of Human Rights).

367. *See, e.g.*, MCGOLDRICK, *supra* note 17, at 198-204; NOWAK, *supra* note 15, at 675-707; ROBERTSON & MERRILLS, *supra* note 81, at 54-69; Ghandhi, *supra* note 296; de Zayas et al., *supra* note 296.

368. A rough comparison of the number of cases in which an individual was represented by counsel (a fact always noted by the Committee on the first page of its decision) in the 37th session as compared to the 49th session illustrates this constancy. During the 37th session (in the early 1980s, when the Committee first began hearing a regular stream of individual complaints), four of seven communications were submitted by counsel. *See Report of the Human Rights Committee to the General Assembly*, U.N. GAOR, Hum. Rts. Comm., 37th Sess., Supp. No. 40, at 141, U.N. Doc. A/37/40 (1982). At the 49th session in 1993-1994, 32 of 60 communications were submitted by counsel. *See 1994 Human Rights Committee Report, supra* note 332, at 64-66.

the most frequent defendants before the tribunal.[369] To the extent that these legal representatives also practice before domestic courts and interact with judges and other legal decisionmakers at the national level, there is increased opportunity for the Committee to disseminate and publicize its views. There is also a greater likelihood that these attorneys will cite the Committee's decisions as a means of influencing the rulings of national courts, thereby leading to enhanced dialogue between the Committee and national courts.

Finally, in recent years, the Committee has targeted its decisions squarely at national courts. In *Sara v. Finland*,[370] for example, the Committee declared a communication inadmissible after finding that the authors, in challenging Finnish law before national courts, had not argued that the law violated the ICCPR. In a move strikingly similar to that taken by the ECJ in *Van Gend & Loos*[371] and its progeny, the Committee praised the Finnish courts for their increasing reliance on international human rights standards[372] and indicated that it would decline to review challenges to Finnish laws where the complainants had failed to raise treaty-based arguments before the Finnish courts.[373] In this way, the Committee simultaneously promised greater deference to those national courts that invoke the standards of the Covenant in domestic law and encouraged individuals to refer communications to it as the final arbiter of the Convention's meaning. The Committee may thus have established the foundation for a relationship similar to that forged by the ECJ with European national courts. For all of these reasons, the Committee scores positively on this checklist factor, following in the footsteps of its regional counterparts.

b. *Neutrality and Demonstrated Autonomy from Political Interests*

Notwithstanding its limited resources and the vast and divergent national legal systems of the states parties it oversees, the UNHRC has shown an increasing willingness to find national governments to have breached their human rights obligations. It has done so, however, only after ensuring that a

369. These states include Jamaica and the Netherlands. At the 49th session, nine out of eleven communications concerning Jamaica, as well as seven out of nine communications concerning the Netherlands, were presented by counsel. See *1994 Human Rights Committee Report*, *supra* note 332, at 64-66.

370. No. 431/1990, U.N. GAOR, Hum. Rts. Comm., 49th Sess., Supp. No. 40, Annex X, at 257, 267, U.N. Doc. A/49/40 (1994).

371. Case 26/62, N.V. Algemene Transp. & Expeditie Onderneming Van Gend & Loos v. Nederlandse administratie der belastingen, 1963 E.C.R. 1.

372. *See Sara*, U.N. GAOR at 267 ("[T]he Finnish judicial authorities have become increasingly aware of the domestic relevance of international human rights standards, including the rights enshrined in the Covenant.").

373. The Committee's practice also parallels that of the ECHR in *Van Oosterwijck v. Belgium*, 40 Eur. Ct. H.R. (ser. A) at 16-17 (1980), in which the court dismissed the case for failure to raise treaty-based arguments before national courts. *See supra* note 163 and accompanying text.

complainant has satisfied important procedural and substantive thresholds of proof that a treaty violation has occurred.

For example, on the one hand, the Committee has refused to permit states to evade their treaty obligations by declining to participate in proceedings under the Optional Protocol. Such a stance results in the finding of a violation by default where the author of a petition can substantiate his or her allegations that such a violation has occurred.[374] And where a state directly flouts the Committee's authority, the Committee has not hesitated to express its condemnation in no uncertain terms.[375] On the other hand, the Committee has required each complainant to demonstrate that his or her communication is admissible—for example, that he or she has exhausted domestic remedies[376]—and to provide credible evidence of a human rights violation, even where the state party refuses to challenge his or her allegations.[377]

Further evidence of the Committee's autonomy from political interests can be found in its increasing willingness to adopt an interpretation of the Covenant that is at odds with the positions espoused by states parties. Indeed, although in several of its early rulings the Committee appeared somewhat reluctant to question states parties' arguments,[378] more recently it has decided

---

374. *See, e.g.*, Mojica v. Dominican Republic, No. 499/1991, U.N. GAOR, Hum. Rts. Comm., 49th Sess., Supp. No. 40, Annex IX, at 142, 144, U.N. Doc. A/49/40 (1994) (explaining that, in the absence of participation by the state party in Optional Protocol proceedings, "due weight must be given to the author's allegations, to the extent they have been substantiated"); *see also* MCGOLDRICK, *supra* note 17, at 149 (noting that "no State party can benefit from its failure to co-operate fully" with the Committee).

375. *See 1994 Consideration of Communications*, *supra* note 333, at 70-71 (expressing "indignation" at Trinidad and Tobago for flouting the Committee's request not to execute a defendant pending consideration of his allegations by the Committee and noting that the State's action "has no precedent in the Committee's practice in capital cases under the Optional Protocol").

376. *See, e.g.*, Amisi v. Zaire, No. 497/1992, U.N. GAOR, Hum. Rts. Comm., 49th Sess., Supp. No. 40, Annex X, at 310, 311, U.N. Doc. A/49/40 (1994) (declaring a communication inadmissible where the author failed to provide information on the exhaustion of domestic remedies). *See generally* MCGOLDRICK, *supra* note 17, at 134-41 (discussing "admissibility conditions" that petitioners must satisfy). It should be noted, however, that the Committee has not adopted an unduly strict reading of its admissibility criteria. Thus, for example, it does not require the exhaustion of available domestic remedies if exhaustion would be futile or would require an extreme delay in the proceedings. *See, e.g.*, Blanco v. Nicaragua, No. 328/1988, U.N. GAOR, Hum. Rts. Comm., 49th Sess., Supp. No. 40, Annex IX, at 12, 17, U.N. Doc. A/49/40 (1994) (holding that the author of a communication need not exhaust domestic remedies that became available after the submission of a petition where "the application of such remedies would entail an unreasonable prolongation of the author's quest to be vindicated for his detention and alleged ill-treatment").

377. *See* Grant v. Jamaica, No. 353/1988, U.N. GAOR, Hum. Rts. Comm., 49th Sess., Supp. No. 40, Annex IX, at 50, 56, U.N. Doc. A/49/40 (1994) (finding no ill-treatment where police were cross-examined on this issue by the author's attorney in national court proceedings and the author failed to provide any supporting medical evidence); *Blanco*, U.N. GAOR at 18 (noting that although the author presented insufficient information to substantiate the allegation of discrimination, the allegations of torture and ill-treatment were substantiated by "very detailed" allegations mentioning the names of officers responsible for, and witnesses to, ill-treatment); *see also* A.R.U. v. Netherlands, No. 509/1992, U.N. GAOR, Hum. Rts. Comm., 49th Sess., Supp. No. 40, Annex X, at 327, 329, U.N. Doc. A/49/40 (1994) (articulating the same principle); Barry v. Trinidad & Tobago, No. 471/1991, U.N. GAOR, Hum. Rts. Comm., 49th Sess., Supp. No. 40, Annex X, at 283, 285, U.N. Doc. A/49/40 (1994) (declaring a communication inadmissible because the author "failed to substantiate" his allegations).

378. *See* Bayefsky, *supra* note 300, at 409-12 (analyzing the early case law).

several controversial cases in favor of individuals over the opposition of national governments and has not shirked from espousing a rights-protective interpretation of the Covenant.[379] Given the rising number of states party to the Optional Protocol and the Committee's increasingly sophisticated legal reasoning, this jurisprudential trend is likely to continue.[380] On balance, therefore, this factor cuts in favor of the Committee's effectiveness.

c. *Incrementalism and Awareness of Political Boundaries*

In its early years, the Committee moved forward cautiously, developing a consensus procedure notable for its absence of politicization and open conflict. This approach allowed the Committee to gain the confidence and respect of states parties.[381] Additional beneficial contacts between the Committee and states parties occur in the Covenant's reporting procedures, through which the Committee strives to maintain a constructive dialogue with government representatives.[382]

The Committee has developed a similar approach under the Optional Protocol, often following the lead of the ECJ and national courts in articulating its most controversial and rights-protective interpretations of the Covenant in decisions giving judgment in favor of states parties.[383] In this way, the

379. *See, e.g.*, Toonen v. Australia, No. 488/1992, U.N. GAOR, Hum. Rts. Comm., 49th Sess., Supp. No. 40, Annex X, at 226, 234, U.N. Doc. A/49/40 (1994) (holding that criminal prohibition of same-sex conduct between consenting adults in private violates the rights of privacy and nondiscrimination); Mukong v. Cameroon, No. 458/1991, U.N. GAOR, Hum. Rts. Comm., 49th Sess., Supp. No. 40, Annex IX, at 171, 181, U.N. Doc. A/49/40 (1994) (holding that the arrest and detention of a candidate of a political opposition party was not "necessary for the safeguard of national security and/or public order" and thus violated the right to free expression); Ng v. Canada, No. 469/1991, U.N. GAOR, Hum. Rts. Comm., 49th Sess., Supp. No. 40, Annex X, at 189, 205, U.N. Doc. A/49/40 (1993) (stating that the extradition of defendant to face death by gas asphyxiation is cruel and inhuman treatment); Ballantyne v. Canada, Nos. 359/1989 & 385/1989, U.N. GAOR, Hum. Rts. Comm., 48th Sess., Supp. No. 40, Annex XII, at 91, 103, U.N. Doc. A/48/40 (1993) (holding that Quebec's French-only sign law violates the right of free expression); *see also* NOWAK, *supra* note 15, at 461 (noting that the Committee's ruling in several cases against the Netherlands that Article 26 of the Covenant provides "substantive equality for women in social law" made headlines and prompted the Netherlands to consider denunciation of the treaty and re-ratification with a reservation to Article 26).

380. *See* Laurence R. Helfer & Alice M. Miller, *Sexual Orientation and Human Rights: Toward a U.S. and Transnational Jurisprudence*, 9 HARV. HUM. RTS. J. 61, 74 (1996) (noting that the Committee's recent practice reflects a willingness to decide cases against states parties).

381. *See* MCGOLDRICK, *supra* note 17, at 503.

382. *See* NOWAK, *supra* note 15, at 562. McGoldrick argues that "[c]ountry specific comments and reports which alienated the States parties, divided the [Committee] and politicized its proceedings would have achieved little in the long term." MCGOLDRICK, *supra* note 17, at 503.

383. *See, e.g.*, Casanovas v. France, No. 441/1990, U.N. GAOR, Hum. Rts. Comm., 49th Sess., Supp. No. 40, Annex IX, at 131, 134-35, U.N. Doc. A/49/40 (1994) (finding that a challenge before an administrative tribunal to dismissal from civil service employment is encompassed within Article 14's requirement that any "suit at law" include a fair hearing, but refusing to find a violation on the facts presented); Santacana v. Spain, No. 417/1990, U.N. GAOR, Hum. Rts. Comm., 49th Sess., Supp. No. 40, Annex IX, at 101, 111-12, U.N. Doc. A/49/40 (1994) (adopting a broad definition of family under Article 23 but finding no violation of the right to found a family on the facts presented); Brinkhof v. Netherlands, No. 402/1990, U.N. GAOR, Hum. Rts. Comm., 48th Sess., Supp. No. 40, Annex XII, at 124, 129, U.N. Doc. A/48/40 (1993) (concluding that "no differentiation shall be made among conscientious objectors on

Committee has succeeded in advancing an interpretation that favors individuals while at the same time diffusing opposition by states parties.[384]

Nevertheless, the Committee is keenly aware of the political limits of its decisions. Thus, for example, both precedent and logic dictate that where a state ratifies the Optional Protocol some years after it has ratified the Covenant, the Committee is competent to consider allegations of human rights violations that occurred during the interim period.[385] In practice, however, the Committee has refused to entertain such petitions,[386] perhaps fearing negative political consequences from the large number of communications that would likely follow such a ruling.[387] On balance, its incremental approach has probably worked in its favor, particularly given the specific political constraints imposed by the Cold War.

d. *Quality of Legal Reasoning*

The importance of the quality of the Committee's legal reasoning to its stature as a quasi-judicial tribunal and to compliance with its decisions has been emphasized by members of the Committee itself and by commentators, all of whom agree that the Committee adheres to the basic requirement that its decisions be "reasoned" in the first instance.[388] In addition, the Committee

---

the basis of the nature of their political beliefs," but declining to find a violation on the facts presented).

384. The Committee can achieve the same result by espousing progressive interpretations of the ICCPR in its general comments, which are intended as nonbinding guideposts for all states parties, and later relying on these interpretations in specific cases decided under the Optional Protocol. In this way, the Committee can introduce more rights-protective interpretations of the treaty without incurring full-scale political resistance by a particular state party. The Committee has followed this interpretive approach in at least one instance. *See Brinkhof*, U.N. GAOR at 129 (relying on an analysis of the state's treatment of conscientious objectors in the general comment on Article 18 in interpreting the obligation of the Netherlands to treat Jehovah's Witnesses and other objectors in the same fashion).

385. The European Commission of Human Rights adopted such a stance for European states that recognized the right of individual petition some years after ratifying the Convention. *See* ZWART, *supra* note 17, at 134-38.

386. *See, e.g.*, E. v. Hungary, No. 520/1992, U.N. GAOR, Hum. Rts. Comm., 49th Sess., Supp. No. 40, Annex X, at 336, 339-40, U.N. Doc. A/49/40 (1994).

387. *See id.* at 341 (separate opinion of Chanet) (criticizing the majority's position declaring a communication inadmissible *ratione temporis* and stressing that the Committee's "decisions should be guided only by the legal principles found in the provisions of the Covenant itself, and *not by political considerations, even of a general nature*, or the fear of a flood of communications from countries that have changed their system of Government" (emphasis added)).

388. As Christian Tomuschat (a former Committee member) states most cogently:

> Legally, the views formulated by the [UNHRC] are not binding on the State Party concerned which remains free to criticize them. Nonetheless, any State Party will find it hard to reject such findings in so far as they are based on orderly proceedings during which the defendant Party had ample opportunity to present its submissions. The views of the [UNHRC] gain their authority from their inner qualities of impartiality, objectivity and soberness. If such requirements are met, the views of the [UNHRC] can have a far-reaching impact . . . .

Christian Tomuschat, *Evolving Procedural Rules: The United Nations Human Rights Committee's First Two Years of Dealing with Individual Communications*, 1 HUM. RTS. L.J. 249, 255 (1980). Erik Mose and Torkel Opsahl suggested as early as 1981 that "[i]f the Committee wishes to contribute to the development of the law of the Covenant through giving reasoned interpretations of its provisions on doubtful points," it must "state more elaborate reasons than in the earliest cases published." Erik Mose & Torkel Opsahl, *The*

has always tried to present the factual and legal positions of both parties as fully as possible before advancing its own analysis.[389] The core of the Committee's legal reasoning, however, occurs in its analysis of the Covenant's obligations and its application of these legal principles to the facts before it.[390] In this domain its reasoning has at times been both truncated and opaque, but it is steadily improving.

The Committee now gives reasons for its decisions in every case and addresses the competing arguments advanced by the parties. For example, the Committee has developed an increasingly sophisticated methodology for analyzing those Covenant rights and freedoms that governments may limit where "necessary" or where "necessary in a democratic society"[391] to protect various vital interests such as public health, morals or the rights of others.[392]

Optional Protocol to the International Covenant on Civil and Political Rights, 21 SANTA CLARA L. REV. 271, 325-26 (1981); *see also* ROBERTSON & MERRILLS, *supra* note 81, at 66 ("[I]f . . . the Human Rights Committee is to be regarded as an effective forum for ventilating complaints, it is essential that it should be proficient.").

389. Each decision of the Committee contains, generally in order, the following elements: the facts alleged by the author of the communication, the parties' positions concerning admissibility, the reasoning behind the decision to declare the communication admissible, a detailed recital of each party's arguments concerning the merits of the case, and lastly, the Committee's own examination of the merits. *See* NOWAK, *supra* note 15, at 708-09. As part of this examination, the Committee often articulates the governing legal principles by referring to the text of relevant Covenant articles, its general comments interpreting those articles, and its prior decisions that provide a gloss on the Covenant's text. It then concludes with a determination that the Covenant has or has not been violated and, in the former case, with the appropriate actions that the state party should take to remedy such a violation. *See id.* at 709.

390. Like other human rights treaties and constitutions, the Covenant does not always specify with precision the scope of a state party's legal obligations; rather, nearly all of its provisions contain equivocal and contextual terms (such as "necessary" or "reasonable") that require interpretation and exposition through the varying fact patterns of individual cases to acquire a settled meaning. Even where the treaty specifies unambiguously what a state party must do or refrain from doing (such as the prohibition against slavery or medical experimentation), the Committee must determine whether the facts alleged fall within the stated legal principle.

391. The "necessary" or "necessary in a democratic society" language appears in the ICCPR as a limitation on the following rights: the right to liberty of movement and freedom to choose residence, *see* Covenant, *supra* note 15, art. 12, 999 U.N.T.S. at 176 ("necessary"); the right to freedom of thought, conscience, and religion, *see id.* art. 18, 999 U.N.T.S. at 178 ("necessary"); the freedom to hold opinions without interference, *see id.* art. 19, 999 U.N.T.S. at 178 ("necessary"); the right of peaceable assembly, *see id.* art. 21, 999 U.N.T.S. at 178 ("necessary in a democratic society"); and the right of freedom of association, *see id.* art. 22, 999 U.N.T.S. at 178 ("necessary in a democratic society"). *See, e.g., id.* art 18(3), 999 U.N.T.S. at 178 ("Freedom to manifest one's religion or beliefs may be subject to only such limitations as are . . . *necessary* to protect public safety, order, health, or morals, or the fundamental rights and freedoms of others." (emphasis added)); *id.* art. 21, 999 U.N.T.S. at 178 ("No restrictions may be placed on [the right to peaceful assembly] other than those which are . . . *necessary in a democratic society* in the interests of national security or public safety, public order (*ordre public*), the protection of public health or morals or the protection of the rights and freedoms of others." (emphasis added)).

392. Developing a workable jurisprudence to balance these competing interests is the hallmark of any successful human rights regime. Sir Robert Jennings writes:

> [A] human rights regime that is indeed working—and not a paper idea—will be normally and mainly concerned not so much with the outrageous, but with highly technical questions, e.g., concerning trade unions and their membership, the right to work, police powers, the minutiae of due process of law, and the like.

Sir Robert Jennings, *Human Rights and Domestic Law and Courts*, *in* PROTECTING HUMAN RIGHTS: THE EUROPEAN DIMENSION 295, 298 (Franz Matscher & Herbert Petzold eds., 1988).

In early decisions, the Committee was reluctant to question the balance struck between individual liberties and other countervailing interests. *See, e.g.*, Hertzberg v. Finland, No. 14/61, U.N. GAOR, Hum.

The same trend is evident in its interpretation of legal obligations not subject to limitation, such as Article 7's categorical prohibition of "torture or cruel, inhuman or degrading treatment or punishment,"[393] and Article 10's unequivocal requirement that "persons deprived of their liberty shall be treated with humanity and with respect for the inherent dignity of the human person."[394] The Committee's initial attempt to give substance to these guarantees has been the subject of much scholarly criticism.[395] More recently, however, the Committee has made significant, albeit less definitive, advances in specifying the scope of these human rights norms in its general comments[396] and in case law.[397]

e. *Judicial Cross-Fertilization and Dialogue*

Although in early decisions the Committee made few references to the

Rts. Comm., 37th Sess., Supp. No. 40, Annex XIV, at 161, 165, U.N. Doc. A/37/40 (1982) ("The Committee finds that it cannot question the decision of the responsible organs of the Finnish Broadcasting Corporation that radio and TV are not the appropriate forums to discuss issues related to homosexuality, as far as a programme could be judged as encouraging homosexual behavior."). As its case law has evolved, however, the Committee has become increasingly likely to scrutinize with care the actions of states parties. *See, e.g.*, Sohn v. Republic of Korea, No. 518/1992, Hum. Rts. Comm., 54th Sess., at 7, U.N. Doc. CCPR/C/54/D/518/1992 (1995) ("While the State party has stated that the restrictions were justified in order to protect national security and public order . . . the Committee must still determine whether the measures taken against the author were necessary for the purpose stated."); Mukong v. Cameroon, No. 458/1991, U.N. GAOR, Hum. Rts. Comm., 49th Sess., Supp. No. 40, Annex IX, at 171, 181, U.N. Doc. A/49/40 (1994) (indicating that the arrest and detention of a political opponent of the governing party was not "necessary for the safeguard of national security and/or public order" and thus violated the right to free expression); Ballantyne v. Canada, No. 359/1989, U.N. GAOR, Hum. Rts. Comm., 48th Sess., Supp. No. 40, Annex XII, at 91, 103, U.N. Doc. A/48/40 (1993) ("The Committee believes that it is not necessary, in order to protect the vulnerable position in Canada of the francophone group, to prohibit commercial advertising in English. This protection may be achieved in other ways that do not preclude the freedom of expression . . . .").

393. Covenant, *supra* note 15, art. 7, 999 U.N.T.S. at 175.

394. *Id.* art. 10, 999 U.N.T.S. at 176.

395. Although the Committee considered numerous issues of ill-treatment under both articles, including incommunicado detention, solitary confinement, denial of medical treatment, and severity of prison conditions, commentators characterize its early opinions as "unhelpful, incomprehensible, or ambiguous" in that they fail "to develop a consistent, intelligible categorization of its views leading to a certain element of arbitrariness in its findings." MCGOLDRICK, *supra* note 17, at 381; *see also* THEODOR MERON, HUMAN RIGHTS LAW-MAKING IN THE UNITED NATIONS 111 (1986) (arguing that, unlike the ECHR and the European Commission of Human Rights, the UNHRC has "failed to elaborate on the concept of the prohibition [on torture] stated in Article 7"); NOWAK, *supra* note 15, at 137 (describing the Committee's unwillingness to address violations of Article 7).

396. *See* General Comment 21/44 (rights of detainees), Apr. 6, 1992, *reprinted in* NOWAK, *supra* note 15, at 873-74; General Comment 20/44 (prohibition of torture), Apr. 3, 1992, *reprinted in* NOWAK, *supra* note 15, at 871-72.

397. *Compare* Vuolanne v. Finland, No. 265/1987, U.N. GAOR, Hum. Rts. Comm., 44th Sess., Supp. No. 40, Annex X, at 249, 256, U.N. Doc. A/44/40 (1989) (discussing what constitutes inhuman or degrading treatment within the meaning of Article 7), *with* Thomas v. Jamaica, No. 321/1988, U.N. GAOR, Hum. Rts. Comm., 49th Sess., Supp. No. 40, Annex IX, at 1, 3, U.N. Doc. A/49/40 (1994) (concluding, in an extremely terse opinion, that the facts presented "disclose a violation of articles 7 and 10, paragraph 1" of the ICCPR). At least in part, the Committee's lack of detailed analysis in these cases can be explained by the fact that the state party refused to cooperate with the Committee or to submit any evidence challenging the authors' allegations. *See* MCGOLDRICK, *supra* note 17, at 367.

rulings of other supranational tribunals, within the last few years it has begun to engage in a dialogue with other such bodies—most notably the ECHR and the European Commission of Human Rights. The emergence of this dialogue provides additional evidence that the Committee understands the importance of communicating with other supranational tribunals concerning interpretive questions applicable to regional and global human rights regimes and of engaging in a common, mutually supportive enterprise.

To date, several different types of interaction between the European and United Nations human rights systems have occurred. Perhaps the most limited form of communication occurs where one of the parties cites to a prior decision of a regional tribunal as precedent in support of its claims before the Committee.[398] Whether arguments influence the Committee is not always clear, because in the majority of decisions the members have not expressed a view as to the soundness of the regional tribunal's decision or reasoning.[399]

A second form of communication occurs when a litigant brings to the Committee a claim that a regional tribunal has already rejected. In such cases we might expect the Committee to explain its departure from regional practice, particularly where the civil and political rights at issue are protected in similar or identical language in the two treaties. In the two instances in which individuals received a favorable decision from the Committee after their claims were rejected by the European Commission of Human Rights, however, the Committee did not attempt to justify its departure from settled European practice.[400]

The last form of interaction occurs in decisions in which the Committee actively considers the reasoning of regional tribunals in prior cases and attempts to harmonize or distinguish them. The most striking example of this phenomenon emerged in a line of cases analyzing whether prolonged detention on death row and its associated physical and psychological disabilities amounts

---

398. *See, e.g.*, Celepi v. Sweden, No. 456/1991, U.N. GAOR, Hum. Rts. Comm., 49th Sess., Supp. No. 40, Annex X, at 165, 167, U.N. Doc. A/49/40 (1994) (reporting a state party's citation of a decision of the European Commission of Human Rights); Howard v. Norway, No. 451/1991, U.N. GAOR, Hum. Rts. Comm., 49th Sess., Supp. No. 40, Annex X, at 146, 151-52, U.N. Doc. A/49/40 (1994) (reporting a state party's citation of a judgment of the ECHR and a decision of the Commission); E.W. v. Netherlands, No. 429/1990, U.N. GAOR, Hum. Rts. Comm., 48th Sess., Supp. No. 40, Annex XIII, at 198, 199-200, U.N. Doc. A/48/40 (1993) (citing to case law of the ECHR and the Commission); Brinkhof v. Netherlands, No. 402/1990, U.N. GAOR, Hum. Rts. Comm., 48th Sess., Supp. No. 40, Annex XII, at 124, 128, U.N. Doc. A/48/40 (1993) (reporting a state party's citation of relevant "case law of the European Commission").

399. In none of the decisions cited *supra* note 398 did the Committee in its examination of the merits refer expressly to the European tribunals' analyses.

400. *See* Coeriel v. Netherlands, No. 453/1991, U.N. GAOR, Hum. Rts. Comm., 49th Sess., Supp. No. 40, Annex X, at 23, U.N. Doc. A/49/40 (1994) (finding a violation of the Covenant after the Commission rejected the same challenge under the European Convention); *Brinkhof*, U.N. GAOR at 124 (same); *see also* Casanovas v. France, No. 441/1990, U.N. GAOR., Hum. Rts. Comm., 49th Sess., Supp. No. 40, Annex X, at 131, 133-34, U.N. Doc. A/49/40 (1994) (concluding, with only cursory analysis, that "rights and obligations in a suit at law" in Article 14 of the Covenant encompass dismissal of civil servants from employment, notwithstanding a contrary conclusion by the European Commission of Human Rights based on identical language in Article 6 of the Convention).

to inhuman or degrading treatment. The ECHR concluded in *Soering v. United Kingdom*[401] that such detention can amount to inhuman or degrading treatment,[402] but the Committee has steadfastly refused to find a violation in similar circumstances. In its first two decisions on this issue, the Committee made no reference to the ECHR's judgment.[403] But in *Kindler v. Canada*,[404] the Committee, while reaffirming its position that death row detention is not a per se violation of the Convention, gave careful consideration to the ECHR's approach, adopting much of its reasoning while distinguishing the unique facts of *Soering* from the case before it:

> In determining whether . . . the imposition of capital punishment could constitute a violation of article 7, the Committee will have regard to the relevant personal factors regarding the author, the specific conditions of detention on death row, and whether the proposed method of execution is particularly abhorrent. In this context the Committee has had careful regard to the judgment given by the European Court of Human Rights in the *Soering v. United Kingdom* case. It notes that important facts leading to the judgment of the European Court are distinguishable on material points from the facts in the present case. In particular, the facts differ as to the age and mental state of the offender, and the conditions on death row in the respective prison systems. . . . The Committee has also noted in the *Soering* case that . . . there was a simultaneous request for extradition by a State where the death penalty would not be imposed.[405]

Such direct transjudicial communication provides further evidence that the Committee is behaving according to the checklist's prescriptions, although the

---

401. 161 Eur. Ct. H.R. (ser. A) at 41 (1989).

402. In *Soering*, the ECHR unanimously concluded that extradition of Jens Soering to face a capital murder charge in Virginia and to await execution on death row would violate the Convention's prohibition of degrading treatment or punishment. In accepting Soering's claim that exposure to the so-called "death row phenomenon" violated the treaty, the court examined several factors, including the six- to eight-year delay prior to execution, the conditions on death row, Soering's age and mental state, the procedures available to challenge his conviction and sentence, and the possibility of extradition to another country where the death penalty had been abolished. *See id.* at 42-44.

403. *See* Barrett v. Jamaica, Nos. 270/1988 & 271/1988, U.N. GAOR, Hum. Rts. Comm., 47th Sess., Supp. No. 40, Annex IX, at 254, U.N. Doc. A/47/40 (1992) (refusing to find a violation in a 14-year stay on death row); Pratt v. Jamaica, Nos. 210/1986 & 225/1987, U.N. GAOR, Hum. Rts. Comm., 44th Sess., Supp. No. 40, Annex X, at 222, U.N. Doc. A/44/40 (1989) (refusing to find a violation in a more than seven-year stay on death row). In *Barrett*, however, Committee member Christine Chanet cited to the *Soering* judgment in support of her conclusion that "[a] very long period on death row . . . cannot exonerate a State party from its obligations under article 7 of the Covenant." *Barrett*, U.N. GAOR at 246 (separate opinion of Chanet).

404. No. 470/1991, U.N. GAOR, Hum. Rts. Comm., 48th Sess., Supp. No. 40, Annex XII, at 138, U.N. Doc. A/48/40 (1993).

405. *Id.* at 151-52 (footnote omitted); *see also* Rodriguez v. Uruguay, No. 322/1988, U.N. GAOR, Hum. Rts. Comm., 49th Sess., Supp. No. 40, Annex X, at 5, 11 n.b, U.N. Doc. A/49/40 (1994) (distinguishing a state party's reliance on a judgment of the Inter-American Court of Human Rights by reference to a later advisory opinion of the Inter-American court and relevant decisions of the Inter-American Commission on Human Rights).

Committee should ensure that it actually addresses the regional precedents cited to it.

f. *Form of Opinions*

Under the ICCPR, the adoption of views by the Committee requires a majority vote of the members present.[406] Responding to a request by Soviet-bloc states, however, the Committee decided in 1977 to resolve cases by consensus rather than by an official vote.[407] Any member of the Committee has the right to call for a vote at any time, but "no formal vote has ever been taken."[408] Although adoption of consensus as a method of work "has made an important contribution to the conciliatory atmosphere in the Committee and to the avoidance of politicization that would impair the efficiency of its work,"[409] it has also "reduce[d] the clarity and precision"[410] of the Committee's views, which often reflect "the lowest common denominator of possible levels of agreement."[411]

In practice, the Committee's rules of procedure, which authorize members to append an "individual opinion" to a consensus decision,[412] have mitigated some of the problems of the consensus approach. Although individual opinions were rarely used in the early years under the Optional Protocol, members have made increasing use of this practice recently, for both decisions on the merits and admissibility decisions.[413] Moreover, Committee members have become far more likely to denominate their individual opinions as dissents rather than merely elaborating on the consensus position or articulating a concurring view.[414]

406. *See* Covenant, *supra* note 15, art. 39(b), 999 U.N.T.S. at 181.

407. *See* NOWAK, *supra* note 15, at 712. Rule 51 of the Rules of Procedure adopts the principle of majority voting but states in a footnote that Committee members should normally attempt to reach decisions by consensus when this does not unduly delay the Committee's work. *See id.* at 541-42.

408. Opsahl, *supra* note 17, at 384.

409. NOWAK, *supra* note 15, at 542.

410. MCGOLDRICK, *supra* note 17, at 199.

411. PAUL R. WILLIAMS, TREATMENT OF DETAINEES: EXAMINATION OF ISSUES RELEVANT TO DETENTION BY THE UNITED NATIONS HUMAN RIGHTS COMMITTEE 90 (1990). Williams continues:

> The opinions of the activist members or members with strong and particular views are not expressed because they are seldom accepted by all the members, whereas the view of the most reticent members are accepted as basic premises for the views of the more active members, and are thus agreed upon and presented in the report.

Id.

412. *See Consideration of Communications Under the Optional Protocol*, U.N. GAOR, Hum. Rts. Comm., 48th Sess., Supp. No. 40, at 162-63, U.N. Doc. A/48/40 (1993).

413. *See* NOWAK, *supra* note 15, at 712; *see also* MCGOLDRICK, *supra* note 17, at 500 ("A number of the more recent views and decisions have occasioned substantial splits within the [Committee] even though this is not evident from the form in which the views appear.").

414. The move to a more juridical style of majority opinion writing is strikingly evident in two 1993 decisions concerning Canada's extradition of two American fugitives to face the death penalty in the United States. In *Kindler v. Canada*, No. 470/1991, U.N. GAOR, Hum. Rts. Comm , 48th Sess., Supp. No. 40, Annex XII, at 138, 154-77, U.N. Doc. A/48/40 (1993), seven members of the 18-member Committee filed dissenting opinions from some aspect of the consensus decision that the extradition did not violate the right

The dubious utility of maintaining a consensus procedure in light of such increasing use of individual opinions, the reduction of political tensions since the end of the Cold War, and the deleterious effect of consensus on the quality of the Committee's reasoning have led commentators to urge the Committee to adopt majority voting for all decisions.[415] Given the heterogeneous array of states party to the Optional Protocol and the direct communication between the Committee and private parties, our analysis under the checklist would support such a reform.

3. *Factors Often Beyond the Control of States or Judges*

One of the essential characteristics of a global human rights regime is that any nation may seek to join and adhere to the regime's substantive obligations and enforcement procedures. The Covenant is precisely such a regime. The states that have ratified the treaty—in contrast to the states party to the Treaty of Rome or the European Convention on Human Rights—are at all stages of political, social, and economic development and have adopted widely divergent approaches to enforcing the rule of law domestically. This diversity of membership presents the Committee with challenges that its European counterparts are less likely to face, challenges that may ultimately circumscribe its potential for becoming fully effective but that it has nevertheless proven itself prepared to meet.

a. *Nature of Violations*

As might be expected from our checklist, the Committee's effectiveness in dealing with gross, systematic human rights abuses is no better than that of any other supranational tribunal. Indeed, the recently published list of states that have failed to provide follow-up information to the Committee includes countries that, as the Committee's views demonstrate, have engaged in gross human rights violations.[416] Whereas the European Commission of Human Rights had to contend with the aftermath of a coup d'état in Greece, the Committee must contend with systematic repression and grave abuses

to life and the right to be free from cruel or inhuman treatment. And in *Ng v. Canada*, No. 469/1991, U.N. GAOR, Hum. Rts. Comm., 49th Sess., Supp. No. 40, Annex X, at 189, U.N. Doc. A/49/40 (1993), eight members filed opinions dissenting in whole or in part from the Committee's conclusion that extradition to face death by gas asphyxiation, while not a violation of the right to life, breached the prohibition against cruel and inhuman treatment.

415. *See, e.g.*, NOWAK, *supra* note 15, at 712 ("Since the East-West conflict has been overcome, the Committee should consider adopting its decisions on individual communications by majority voting."); WILLIAMS, *supra* note 411, at 90-91.

416. *See 1995 Follow-Up Activities*, *supra* note 312, at 97-98 (providing a country-by-country breakdown of replies to the Committee's views and showing that states, such as Cameroon, Equatorial Guinea, Madagascar, Suriname, and Zaire, found to have committed serious human rights violations, had not submitted replies or had submitted inadequate replies).

anywhere in the world. Even here, however, persistence may pay off. For example, after many years of nonaction, the Committee received a statement from Uruguay indicating that, after a change of government, it had released from imprisonment or offered amnesty to several individuals whom the Committee had determined were victims of serious human rights abuses.[417]

b. *Autonomous Domestic Institutions Committed to the Rule of Law and Responsive to Citizen Interests*

The Committee exercises jurisdiction over a number of countries that affirmatively reject democratic government and that seek primarily to ensure the undivided loyalty of all government institutions to the prevailing political power. Likewise the Committee has jurisdiction over a number of other countries that simply fail, for a variety of historical, economic, and geographical factors, to impose any meaningful rule at all. We argued above that such countries are unlikely ever to comply with the judgments of a supranational tribunal; that states unable to maintain a rule of law domestically by institutions responsive to the people would not provide channels or openings by which a supranational tribunal could even make itself heard, much less make its influence felt.[418]

On a macro level, the Committee's individual petition system may have little power to alter the regime type of the states parties or their commitment to the rule of law. But in building from case to case, the Committee can encourage greater compliance by states and the filing of additional claims for relief by targeting its decisions at private parties and disaggregated domestic government institutions seeking to resist either the centralization or the radical fragmentation of power. When the Committee issues a decision against one state, it must thus bear in mind that its views will be observed by government actors, individuals, and nongovernmental organizations in diverse states throughout the world.

Seeking to reach out to this audience, however, the Committee faces a new problem. As Committee member Rosalyn Higgins states: "What may be an appropriate and sensitive interpretation for the Western European democracies is not necessarily so for a global system embracing highly diverse political and economic systems. This is often strongly held by the Western members [of the Committee] themselves."[419] The existence of such a disparate constituency creates a fundamental paradox for the Committee. On the one hand, if it sets substantive standards for the Convention that are too high, it risks an enforcement gap for states with less salutary human rights records. By contrast,

417. *See* MCGOLDRICK, *supra* note 17, at 155 & 223-24 nn.338-41.

418. *See supra* Subsection III.B.3.b. The inverse, however, did not hold: The presence of such institutions committed to the rule of law does not guarantee compliance with supranational judgments.

419. Higgins, *supra* note 8, at 8.

the Committee must weigh the opposing danger that its decisions will fix a global minimum human rights baseline that is too low for many states with both a strong commitment to the rule of law and stringent domestic protection for constitutional liberties.[420]

To date, the Committee has, perhaps understandably, not articulated any overarching methodology for balancing these competing concerns. Instead, it has addressed each alleged violation of the Covenant on the facts before it, whether those facts concern shocking abuses of the right to life, liberty, and physical integrity,[421] or whether they concern nuances of social security and other national welfare legislation that may only exist in industrialized nations.[422] The Committee has indicated, however, that at least in some circumstances it will fix a human rights baseline that requires many states to take remedial measures[423] or will not permit a government to justify a treaty violation by reference to the social, political, or economic conditions prevailing in its territory.[424] The Committee also has not shied away from openly wrestling with and often rejecting the arguments of states parties with comparatively strong human rights records. It thus appears that the Committee is willing to interpret the treaty to provide a level of rights protection more stringent than many states parties would prefer.

We strongly encourage the Committee to continue this course. The logic of the checklist suggests that in many cases "states" or "governments,"

420. *See* Bayefsky, *supra* note 300, at 412-13 (noting that the Committee "has tended to resolve the standard of compliance with international human rights law on a minimum common denominator" and concluding that the Optional Protocol "is in danger of becoming insignificant for individuals from states with generally good human rights records").

421. *See, e.g.*, Kone v. Senegal, No. 386/1989, U.N. GAOR, Hum. Rts. Comm., 50th Sess., Supp. No. 40, Annex X, at 1, U.N. Doc. A/50/40 (1995) (discussing torture and arbitrary detention for four-and-one-half years); Mojica v. Dominican Republic, No. 449/1991, U.N. GAOR, Hum. Rts. Comm., 49th Sess., Supp. No. 40, Annex X, at 142, U.N. Doc. A/49/40 (1994) (discussing disappeared persons and torture); Mika Miha v. Equatorial Guinea, No. 414/1990, U.N. GAOR, Hum. Rts. Comm., 49th Sess., Supp. No. 40, Annex IX, at 96, U.N. Doc. A/49/40 (1994) (discussing arbitrary detention and torture).

422. *See, e.g.*, Pepels v. Netherlands, No. 484/1991, U.N. GAOR, Hum. Rts. Comm., 49th Sess., Supp. No. 40, Annex IX, at 221, U.N. Doc. A/49/40 (1994); Neefs v. Netherlands, No. 484/1991, U.N. GAOR, Hum. Rts. Comm., 49th Sess., Supp. No. 40, Annex IX, at 120, U.N. Doc. A/49/40 (1994).

423. In *Parkanyi v. Hungary*, No. 410/1990, U.N. GAOR, Hum. Rts. Comm., 47th Sess., Supp. No. 40, Annex IX, at 325, 329-30, U.N. Doc. A/47/40 (1992), for example, the Committee held that limiting a prisoner's personal hygiene and outdoor exercise to a total of ten minutes per day violated Article 10 of the Covenant, which states that "[a]ll persons deprived of their liberty shall be treated with humanity and with respect for the inherent dignity of the human person," Covenant, *supra* note 15, art. 10, 999 U.N.T.S. at 176. According to a leading commentator on the Committee's work, "many countries in all regions of the world actually do not comply with this minimum standard." Nowak, *UNHRC Activities*, *supra* note 18, at 18.

424. *See* Mukong v. Cameroon, No. 458/1991, U.N. GAOR, Hum. Rts. Comm., 49th Sess., Supp. No. 40, Annex IX, at 171, 176, U.N. Doc. A/49/40 (1994) (rejecting the state's contention that "the exercise of the right to freedom of expression must take into account the political context and situation prevailing in a country at any point in time"); *id.* at 180 (stating that "certain minimum standards regarding conditions of detention must be observed regardless of a State party's level of development"); *see also* General Comment 21/44, Apr. 6, 1992, *reprinted in* NOWAK, *supra* note 15, at 873-74 (rejecting the claim that compliance with acceptable conditions of detention could be "dependent on the material resources available" in a particular state).

understood monolithically, will disregard the Committee no matter how flexible or contextual it tries to be. Only individuals or institutions who are independently resisting (or thinking of resisting) "government" policies and trying to establish an independent power base are likely to be heard. In such a setting it is vital that the Committee establish a universal baseline that legitimates these forces as part of a global community.

c. *Cultural and Political Homogeneity*

The Committee's ability to improve compliance with its judgments will prove an important test of the cultural and political homogeneity thesis. The Committee and the treaty it superintends are founded on a universalist premise: that basic rights and liberties transcend cultural and political differences by virtue of a shared humanity. Nevertheless, it may be true that institutions such as the Inter-American Court of Human Rights will prove more effective, as the ECHR has been, based in part on their greater legitimacy as the voices of particular geographic regions. Only time, and the emergence of more regional tribunals, will tell.

C. *Summing Up the Committee's Performance Under the Checklist*

Application of the checklist factors to the UNHRC reveals an institution struggling to carry out a wide variety of functions, both quasi-judicial and nonjudicial, with extremely limited resources and a rapidly increasing constituency of states parties, individuals, and nongovernmental actors. Although the Committee's effectiveness is nowhere near that of the ECJ and the ECHR, it is the similarities to, rather than the differences from, its effective European neighbors that we find most striking.

Even given the Committee's vastly broader scope of operations and the necessarily limited attention it can pay to individualized decisionmaking under the Optional Protocol, it is an institution struggling to achieve a distinctively judicial voice and to assert for itself, as have the ECJ and the ECHR, authority as the final arbiter of the meaning of the treaty regime it oversees. What is most noticeable is the Committee's effort, sometimes independently of states parties, to take many of the steps that we identify as likely to improve the effectiveness of its decisions: the improvements in the quality of its reasoning; the wider range of competing arguments aired by its increasing use of concurring and dissenting opinions; its willingness to take a position contrary to that of states parties in high-profile cases; its incremental and cautious advances in interpreting the treaty; its increased efforts to target an audience of individuals and their representatives as well as national courts; and its increasing dialogue with other supranational tribunals. These steps demonstrate a commitment to making the petition system more like a court and as effective a court as possible. Indeed, the Committee has even taken a position with respect to those variables over which it has no formal control, such as the legally binding character of its decisions and compliance with those decisions by states parties.

If the number of states party to the treaty and the number of communications filed with the Committee continue to increase, states parties will soon face a clear choice. If they wish the Committee to continue on its current trajectory, they can seek to alter those checklist factors within their control. Alternatively, they can hobble the Committee's operations by starving it of resources. The Committee itself, however, is likely to continue, within the limits of its abilities and resources, to transform its petition system and to emulate other supranational judicial tribunals in seeking to maximize its effectiveness.

V. A Prescription for Enhancing the Effectiveness of the Human Rights Committee: Converging with the ECHR in a Global Community of Law

Having analyzed the UNHRC's performance in light of our checklist of factors correlated with "effective" supranational adjudication in Europe, the question remains how the Committee and states parties should proceed if they wish to create a more effective supranational regime for redressing human rights abuses. At the most general and perhaps simplistic level of analysis, a prescription is easy to articulate: The Committee and states parties should, within their respective spheres of competence, seek to enhance the Committee's performance with respect to all of the checklist factors. For the Committee, such a prescription would essentially counsel members to continue in the direction that they are already moving, reinforcing those characteristics that tend to make the Committee more "court-like." At its most extreme, such a prescription might include urging states to amend the Covenant and the Optional Protocol to create two supranational institutions: a nonjudicial body charged with monitoring states' obligations under the treaty's reporting process and a separate International Court of Human Rights with investigatory powers and the authority to issue binding decisions as a matter of international law.

Even if, however, such a revolutionary reworking of the Covenant were politically feasible (a dubious proposition at best), the balance of our checklist of factors provides a number of reasons to reject such an ambitious proposal. Although a bifurcated system would maximize many of the factors in the first and second clusters, the supranational judicial body it envisions might well find that compliance with its judgments falters because of shortcomings related to the third cluster of factors, in particular the existence of autonomous domestic institutions responsive to citizen interests, the commitment by states parties to the rule of law within their respective national legal systems, and the grave nature of the violations.

One of the most important lessons of the European experience is that supranational courts and tribunals must move cautiously in their early years, striking a delicate balance between independence and deference, permitting states to adjust and respond to the mechanisms of supranational adjudication. Only after states develop a level of comfort with these mechanisms—and with complying with unfavorable outcomes in specific disputes—will it be feasible to enhance and extend the architecture of the system itself.[425] Accordingly, we believe that for the immediate future a far more modest proposal is in order, one that takes into account the Committee's existing and somewhat limited powers (both quasi-judicial and nonjudicial), the relatively poor record of compliance with the Committee's decisions, and the increasing importance of communication among judicial and quasi-judicial arbiters of individual rights disputes. Our proposal is thus only a first step in a longer-term strategy, the details of which should be reassessed as additional evidence becomes available.

Before elaborating on this proposal, we first describe the core elements of a "community of law" as it has developed in Europe, relating it to the various factors on the checklist. The following section discusses the expansion of this community through transjudicial communication and the emergence of actual transnational judicial institutions. Finally, we spell out the details of our proposal for the UNHRC to engage in a more structured and formal dialogue with the European human rights tribunals as the first step in an effort to build a global community of law.

A. *Elements of a Community of Law*

A community of law emerges alongside effective adjudication, simultaneously contributing to and reflecting the success of a particular tribunal. The ECJ has both drawn on and built a community of law among private parties, lawyers, and courts in the member states of the European Union; the ECHR has benefited from the foundations laid by the ECJ in exploiting and constructing a distinct but overlapping community of law among the same actors in the states party to the Convention. Once a community of law has been constructed, the various factors on the checklist have greater resonance.

---

425. The experience with Protocol No. 11 to the European Convention aptly demonstrates this phenomenon. It was only after more than 30 years of supranational review under the Convention that European nations agreed to make the right of individual petition mandatory, authorizing aggrieved individuals to seek relief from the ECHR (rather than the Commission) in all cases. *See supra* notes 92-98 and accompanying text.

A fully constructed community of law has three attributes. First, it is a web of relations among subnational and supranational legal actors capable of interacting directly with one another. The ECJ used the Article 177 procedure to create links to lower national courts and to litigants, lawyers, and professors with a direct stake in European Community law.[426] Similarly, the ECHR has benefited enormously from the innovation of the Optional Protocol allowing individuals direct access to the court.[427] Checklist factors such as the availability of resources to publicize tribunal decisions, awareness of audience, judicial dialogue, and the limited nature of violations within liberal democracies all contribute to widening and deepening these channels of communication and action.

A second attribute of a community of law is that the interaction between subnational and supranational actors is consistent with the incentives of the individual participants. The ECJ provided incentives for individual litigants, their lawyers, and lower national courts to participate in the construction of the Community legal system. In the process, it enhanced its own power and the professional interests of all parties participating directly or indirectly in its business.[428] Similarly, when the ECHR decides a case against a state, it is deciding for an individual litigant and her lawyer. It is thereby creating incentives for similarly situated litigants and lawyers to consider pursuing a remedy within the ECHR system. As lawyers become more familiar with the jurisprudence of the ECHR, a matter largely of the availability of translation, they become aware of how they can use these decisions to advance their clients' interests.[429] At the same time, public interest groups and nongovernmental organizations with a global human rights agenda can find clients to bring test cases to the court to increase pressure for domestic political reform.[430] Legal academics round out this network, actively pushing

---

426. For a further description of this web of actors, see Burley & Mattli, *supra* note 60, at 58.

427. This description of the Optional Protocol is likely to resonate with political scientists more than with lawyers. From a legal perspective, the Optional Protocol is the instrument that gives substance and impact to the substantive provisions of the European Convention on Human Rights. Robertson and Merrills offer a typical account:

> Under traditional international law the individual has no *locus standi*, on the theory that his rights will be championed by his government. But how can his government be his champion when *ex hypothesi* it is the offender? What is necessary, therefore, is to give the individual access to an international organ which is competent to afford him a remedy even against the government of his national State. The great merit of the European Convention on Human Rights is that it contains just such a procedure.

ROBERTSON & MERRILLS, *supra* note 245, at 109.

428. For further discussion of the role of individual self-interest in the construction of the European Community legal system, see Burley & Mattli, *supra* note 60, at 60.

429. *See* DRZEMCZEWSKI, *supra* note 90, at 305.

430. Kathryn Sikkink describes such groups as forming "principled issue-networks," linked by shared values or principled ideas—beliefs about what is right or wrong. Kathryn Sikkink, *Human Rights, Principled Issue-Networks, and Sovereignty in Latin America*, 47 INT'L ORG. 411, 411-12 (1993). Such a view is not inconsistent with the emphasis on interest in the text; such groups are simply using a supranational tribunal to pursue a different set of (nonmaterial) interests.

domestic courts to take account of ECHR case law.[431]

Many of the same factors on the checklist that help create a web of subnational and supranational actors also appeal to the interests of those actors, including factors such as tribunal resources to publicize activities and awareness of audience. In addition, both casuist reasoning and dissenting opinions can permit a tribunal to speak civilly enough to the losing litigant to encourage her to sue another day. Finally, with respect to our third category of factors, liberal democracies are likely to provide a more hospitable environment for courts and private actors whose interests align with the promotion of a supranational rule of law and who have the freedom to pursue those interests.

A third and final attribute of a community of law is the self-awareness of all participants that they are operating in a nominally apolitical context. They should understand themselves to be linked by a common training and set of basic normative commitments to the autonomy and integrity of the legal process. While it is vital to appreciate the interest-based pillar of a community of law, the normative pillar is equally important. Factors on the checklist such as status as law, capacity for independent factfinding, the quality of legal reasoning, neutrality or autonomy from political interests, and incremental decisionmaking all acknowledge and bolster at least a formal distinction between law and politics that allows the community of law to be an insulated community, shielded from *direct* political interference.

In some sense, this division between the legal and the political is undoubtedly artificial. As just noted, participants in a community of law are aware that they are operating in a *nominally* apolitical context. In another sense, however, the political context is very real—as when the German government was prevented from overturning an ECJ decision contrary to its interests because of a domestic outcry that an action was "inconsistent with the principle of a *Rechststaat*, a state ruled by law."[432] More generally, the ECJ has benefited from both ignorance as to the long-term political significance of many of its legal rulings and the inability of member state governments committed to the domestic rule of law to justify interfering with an international tribunal operating in the same way as, and directly linked to, domestic courts.[433] Equally relevant is the distinction between the treatment of decisions by the ECHR (and to a somewhat lesser extent the European Commission of Human Rights) and the treatment by the Committee of

---

431. *See* Polakiewicz & Jacob-Foltzer, *supra* note 91, at 137 (describing Swiss academics' "fierce criticism" of the constitutional interpretation prohibiting the federal court from judging the conformity of national laws by ECHR standards); *see also* Alter, *supra* note 261, at 111 (discussing the role of academic lawyers in pushing domestic courts to accept European Community law).

432. *See* Alter, *supra* note 261, at 12 (describing the incident in detail).

433. For further elaboration of the significance of a "nominally apolitical context" to the construction of a community of law in the European Community, see Burley & Mattli, *supra* note 60, at 69-70.

Ministers, an explicitly political body charged with handling the more politically sensitive cases. In several states, the public prosecutor is empowered to ask domestic courts to quash decisions found contrary to the Convention by a decision of the ECHR, but not a decision by the Committee of Ministers.[434] More generally, as Andrew Drzemczewski points out in his pioneering study, the courts in a number of countries simply pay less attention to the decisions of the Committee of Ministers, as determined by actual references to Committee versus ECHR decisions.[435] He attributes this discrepancy, in part, to "the political character of the organ itself."[436]

In sum, a community of law is a community of interests and ideals shielded by legal language and practice. It is a community in which the participants—both individuals and institutions—understand themselves to be linked through their participation in, comprehension of, and responsibility for legal discourse. Equally important, participants are perceived by nonparticipants—politicians and other domestic institutions—as engaged in activity that should ordinarily be protected from direct political interference. A community of law thus offers channels through which some parts of the state can circumvent others, or whereby nonstate actors can bypass or at least pressure state actors. The desirability of these channels will depend on preexisting domestic politics—on the extent to which these various state and nonstate actors perceive themselves to be blocked by other state actors and have the freedom and desire to maneuver around them.

B. *Building a Global Community of Law*

Can a community of law be constructed at a global level? As the specific elements of the checklist and the more general attributes discussed above suggest, a true community of law is likely to be limited, at least in the short and medium term, to groups of countries or regions with a strong domestic tradition of the rule of law. Many judges around the world, however, are beginning to conceive of themselves as members of a global community, by virtue of either their role in implementing international norms or a common conception of their role and function within domestic legal systems and a common commitment to the rule of law.

434. *See* Polakiewicz & Jacob-Foltzer, *supra* note 91, at 70 (discussing Belgium); *id.* at 135 (discussing Spain). On the other hand, in Austria, Switzerland, and the Netherlands, decisions of the court and of the Committee of Ministers are granted binding status, while decisions of the Commission are treated as those of an intermediate body. *See id.* at 67 (discussing Austria); *id.* at 128 (discussing the Netherlands); *id.* at 137 (discussing Switzerland). Nevertheless, in countries in which courts are formally instructed to give equal weight to decisions of the court and the Committee of Ministers, in practice they favor the court.

435. *See* DRZEMCZEWSKI, *supra* note 90, at 273, 287, 314, 324.

436. *Id.* at 273.

In this context, an increase in judicial dialogue can reinforce the concept of a global sphere of law that is at least partially protected from direct political interference. As argued above,[437] judges who look to the decisions of their fellow judges in other countries or regions are acknowledging engagement in a common enterprise in which the power of reason and the advantage of prior experience with a particular problem create a presumption of persuasion. In referring to and reinforcing one another, they create a space that is insulated, but not isolated, from politics, economics, and society.

Judges on national and supranational tribunals *are* citing each other, and by no means only in Europe. Commonwealth judges, the judges of national constitutional courts the world over, judges in fledgling democracies looking to their more established counterparts—all are talking to one another. Their conversations are hard to track but are beginning to attract the attention of scholars and litigants.[438]

Perhaps the paradigm case in this regard is a recent decision handed down by the South African Constitutional Court concerning the constitutionality of the death penalty.[439] The decision contains an entire section titled "International and Foreign Comparative Law."[440] This section systematically canvasses decisions relating to the death penalty from international tribunals such as the European Court of Human Rights, the U.N. Human Rights Committee, the Inter-American Court on Human Rights, and the European and Inter-American commissions. In addition, the opinion reviews high-court decisions from the United States, India, Hungary, Canada, Germany, and Tanzania. Finally, the opinion takes account of decisions from two state courts in the United States, California and Massachusetts.

The court's reasons for conducting this survey were twofold. First, it observed that the "international and foreign authorities are of value because they analyze arguments for and against the death sentence and show how courts of other jurisdictions have dealt with [the] vexed issue [of] the death penalty."[441] "*For that reason alone*," the court continued, "they require our

437. *See supra* Subsection III.B.2.e.

438. *See* GLENDON, *supra* note 203, at 158; Glenn, *supra* note 205, at 263 (discussing the use of nonbinding foreign legal sources as "persuasive authority"); Slaughter, *supra* note 146, at 102-12 (discussing a variety of types of transnational judicial notice); *see also* CONSTITUTIONALISM AND RIGHTS: THE INFLUENCE OF THE UNITED STATES CONSTITUTION ABROAD (Louis Henkin & Albert J. Rosenthal eds., 1989); INTERNATIONAL LAW DECISIONS IN NATIONAL COURTS (Thomas M. Franck & Gregory H. Fox eds., 1996); Anthony Lester, *The Overseas Trade in the American Bill of Rights*, 88 COLUM. L. REV. 537, 541 (1988) ("When life or liberty is at stake, the landmark judgments of the Supreme Court of the United States . . . are studied with as much attention in New Delhi or Strasbourg as they are in Washington, D.C., or the State of Washington, or Springfield, Illinois."). The Federal Judicial Center and the American Society of International Law also regularly publish a newsletter on transnational judicial activity titled the *International Judicial Observer.*

439. *See* S. v. Makwanyane, 1995 (3) SA 391 (CC).

440. *Id.* at 17.

441. *Id.* at 18.

attention."[442] Second, these foreign decisions "*may* . . . have to be considered"[443] in light of the provision in the South African constitution that requires South African courts to "'have regard to public international law applicable to the rights entrenched in this Chapter [of the Constitution],'" and that authorizes the courts "'to have regard to comparable foreign case law.'"[444] The court was thus unequivocal as to the value of comparative analysis as an important contribution to the deliberation process. Implicit in this claim, as argued above, is recognition of a community of courts around the world, units engaged in a common endeavor.

Such judicial conversations are not confined to paper. One of the signal developments in the transnational judicial world is the increase in face-to-face meetings among judges. A growing number of both formal and informal fora are dedicated to bringing judges together. The European supreme courts meet every two or three years and publish their proceedings.[445] Following suit, the organization of "Supreme Courts of the Americas" was created in October 1995, at a meeting featuring representatives of the supreme courts of twenty-five countries of the western hemisphere. The delegates to the conference approved a charter with the stated aims of promoting and strengthening "judicial independence and the rule of law among the members, as well as the proper constitutional treatment of the judiciary as a fundamental branch of the state."[446] These objectives are to be achieved through activities such as the provision of "a permanent link" between national judicial systems and various educational and technical assistance systems "designed to promote international judicial cooperation in the hemisphere."[447]

The Washington-based Center for Democracy has also sponsored three conferences to date involving courts of "ultimate appeal" in Central and Eastern Europe and the former Soviet Union.[448] These conferences have also been attended by judges and representatives of the ECHR, the European Commission, the Parliamentary Assembly, the Council of Europe, the U.N. Center for Human Rights, and the countries of Albania, China, Ethiopia, Germany, Italy, Slovakia, and the United States.[449]

Less formal meetings between judges around the world are sponsored by a variety of private organizations. The Mentor Group, based in Boston, has hosted a series of conferences between Justices of the U.S. Supreme Court and justices of the ECJ. New York University Law School also hosted a major

442. *Id.* (emphasis added).
443. *Id.* (emphasis added).
444. *Id.* (quoting S. AFR. CONST. ch. III, art. 35(1)).
445. *See* Slaughter, *supra* note 146, at 103 & n.13.
446. CHARTER OF THE ORGANIZATION OF THE SUPREME COURTS OF THE AMERICAS art. II, § 2.1.
447. *Id.* § 2.2.
448. *European Justices Meet In Washington To Discuss Common Issues, Problems*, INT'L JUD. OBSERVER, Jan. 1996, at 2, 3.
449. *See id.*

conference of judges from both national and international tribunals from around the world in February 1995.[450] The organization InteRights, a nongovernmental organization based in London, has similarly dedicated itself to increasing contacts among judges in commonwealth countries. The aim is to develop awareness of comparative constitutional law, particularly concerning the protection of individual rights. The founder of InteRights reports that judges who have attended its conferences often send each other decisions with cites to both international and other foreign tribunals.[451] Finally, the American Bar Association's Central and Eastern European Law Initiative (CEELI) periodically sends American judges to various Central and Eastern European countries to assist with law reform, codification efforts, and judicial training.[452]

Personal contacts and professional cross-citation may ultimately build a sense of transnational judicial solidarity. Equally important, the resulting decisions can contribute to the development of a genuinely transnational or supranational body of law: a set of principles informed by and building on one another, textually and culturally differentiated as necessary but acknowledging the promise of universality. Such a phenomenon is particularly promising with respect to tribunals charged with interpreting and applying instruments that are themselves avowedly universal (though overlapping with their regional counterparts), such as the Universal Declaration of Human Rights[453] and its progeny.

C. *A Modest Proposal: Dialogue and Convergence Between the European Human Rights Tribunals and the Committee*

1. *Thoughtful Convergence*

Against this backdrop, we offer the following specific proposal for the UNHRC. Although the numerous and diverse variables on our checklist make any single proposal necessarily incomplete in some respects, we believe that the Committee can enhance its effectiveness as a quasi-judicial tribunal by engaging in a dialogue with the ECHR and the European Commission of Human Rights[454] as an important first step toward a broader effort to

450. Papers from the conference were subsequently published in INTERNATIONAL LAW DECISIONS IN NATIONAL COURTS, *supra* note 438.

451. Interview with Lord Lester, Founder, InteRights, in Cambridge, Mass. (January 25, 1995). The international human rights group is also developing a database of commonwealth constitutional jurisprudence. *Id.*

452. *See CEELI Update*, ABA INT'L L. NEWS (ABA, Washington, D.C.), Summer 1991, at 7.

453. G.A. Res. 217, U.N. GAOR, 3d Sess., at 71, U.N. Doc. A/810 (1948) [hereinafter Universal Declaration].

454. As noted above, *see supra* notes 92-98 and accompanying text, although the Commission will be phased out once all states parties have ratified Protocol No. 11 to the Convention, its substantial body of case law will continue to be an important resource for the UNHRC for many years to come.

increase communication with other supranational tribunals and national courts over the interpretation of shared human rights standards. More specifically, we urge the Committee to harmonize its decisions with the case law of the European human rights tribunals.[455] By striving to achieve a policy of thoughtful convergence with European jurisprudence, supplemented by informed divergence where there are justifiable and articulated reasons for doing so, the Committee can link its activities to an established community of law that has nurtured the existence and growth of effective supranational adjudication.

European human rights decisions are a natural point of departure for the Committee in many instances. The ECHR has decided hundreds of cases; the Commission, tens of thousands. "Today there remains hardly any substantive provisions of the Convention that have not been the object of a ruling" by these tribunals.[456] Many of their decisions concern rights and freedoms whose texts are either identical or substantially similar to those protected by the Covenant. It would be a serious omission for the Committee to ignore this relevant body of precedents and the considerable judgment and experience they represent as it confronts similar difficult interpretive questions under the Covenant.

In several cases discussed above,[457] the Committee has recently departed from settled European jurisprudence without any explanation or indication that it was doing so, thereby creating divergent interpretations of parallel treaty texts. Such divergences, particularly those that cannot be justified by arguments grounded upon textual or other differences between the two treaties, create the potential for forum shopping[458] and tend to destabilize the previously harmonious relationship between regional and universal human rights

455. More than 25 years ago, A.H. Robertson anticipated the need to harmonize the workings of the two human rights regimes:

> [I]t should not be beyond the wit of [hu]man[ity]—and more particularly, of lawyers—to work out adequate measures of harmonization of the two systems, the European and the universal, the more so as the fundamental objective of both of them is the same: the better protection of the rights of the common man and of the rule of law throughout the world.

A.H. ROBERTSON, THE INTERNATIONAL PROTECTION OF HUMAN RIGHTS 48 (1970). For years, however, the potential for differing interpretations of the Covenant and the European Convention remained only a theoretical problem. With few decided cases, there was little if any possibility for conflict in specific factual settings. As the preceding discussion demonstrates, however, the increased dialogue between the Committee and the European human rights tribunals has recently resulted in significantly divergent interpretations of parallel rights and freedoms protected by both treaties.

456. Polakiewicz & Jacob-Foltzer, *supra* note 91, at 65.

457. *See supra* Subsection IV.B.2.e.

458. Indeed, in the *Coeriel* and *Brinkhof* cases, individuals received a favorable decision from the Committee after the European Commission of Human Rights dismissed their cases. *See* Coeriel v. Netherlands, No. 453/1991, U.N. GAOR, Hum. Rts. Comm., 49th Sess., Supp. No. 40, Annex X, at 23, U.N. Doc. A/49/40 (1994) (finding a violation of the Covenant after the Commission rejected the same challenge under the European Convention); Brinkhof v. Netherlands, No. 402/1990, U.N. GAOR, Hum. Rts. Comm., 48th Sess., Supp. No. 40, Annex XII, at 124, U.N. Doc. A/48/40 (1993) (same).

regimes.[459] They also create confusing choices for national courts seeking to take international human rights standards into account when construing analogous liberties protected by domestic constitutions.

The quality of the Committee's legal reasoning would also benefit from the Committee's acknowledging the existence of prior relevant European precedents and wrestling with the question of whether to follow or distinguish them. In doing so, the Committee is likely to engage in more rigorous theoretical and conceptual analysis to determine the contours of Covenant rights and freedoms and how they interact with the civil and political liberties protected by overlapping regional and universal human rights regimes. Open dialogue also helps to expose the weaknesses and the strengths of opposing positions and the competing values that undergird them.[460] Finally, dialogue encourages the Committee to participate in a global community of actors in a nominally apolitical process, thereby helping to insulate its rulings from overtly political influences.[461]

Although our proposal for convergence is directed primarily to the European human rights system,[462] we by no means intend to discourage the Committee from consulting the rulings of the Inter-American Court of and

---

459. One example of the danger of divergence can be found in the European Convention for the Prevention of Torture and Inhuman or Degrading Treatment or Punishment, Nov. 24, 1987, Europ. T.S. No. 126, 27 I.L.M. 1152 (1988). That treaty establishes the Committee Against Torture to conduct factfinding investigations within states parties and to issue nonbinding recommendations. *See* Antonio Cassese, *A New Approach to Human Rights: The European Convention for the Prevention of Torture*, 83 AM. J. INT'L L. 128, 129-31 (1989). Although the case law of the ECHR and Commission will provide the Committee Against Torture with a "source of guidance" in making its recommendations, the Committee Against Torture is not precluded from consulting the "case law" developed by other international bodies, including the UNHRC. *Id.* at 138-39. The Committee Against Torture will be able to carry out its responsibilities far more easily if it can draw upon a coherent body of jurisprudence in determining the existence of a treaty violation. *See id.* at 135 (noting, with concern, the possibility that the Committee Against Torture might adopt an interpretation of the Convention "that conflicted with the [ECHR's] jurisprudence on the matter, undermining the authority of the ECHR and creating undesirable confusion").

460. Thus, the Committee's ruling that a long period of detention on death row is not a per se violation of the Covenant was strengthened by its citation to, and open distinguishing of, the ECHR's *Soering* judgment, which found such detention to violate the European Convention only after assessing the particular facts and circumstances of the case before it. *See supra* notes 401-405 and accompanying text.

In a recent decision, six dissenting members of the Committee stated that the majority had retreated from its prior commitment in *Kindler v. Canada*, No. 470/1991, U.N. GAOR, Hum. Rts. Comm., 48th Sess., Supp. No. 40, Annex XII, at 138, U.N. Doc. A/48/40 (1993), to examine the facts of each death row detention case and, as a result, had charted an insufficiently rights-protective course as compared to the European system. *See* Johnson v. Jamaica, No. 588/1994, Hum. Rts. Comm., 56th Sess., at 1, 11-15 U.N. Doc. CCPR/C/56/D/588/1994 (1996) (individual dissenting opinions of Chanet, Bhagwati, Celli, Pocar, Vallejo, and Urbina). Their dissenting views compelled the majority to acknowledge "that its jurisprudence has given rise to controversy" and to "set out its position in detail." *Id.* at 6. We find it significant that the Committee feels compelled to employ more rigorous legal reasoning when analyzing an issue with respect to which it has engaged in an open dialogue with the ECHR.

461. *See supra* Sections V.A-B.

462. The ECJ has developed its own human rights jurisprudence, but the lack of textual overlap between the Treaty of Rome and the Covenant, the defining of ECJ human rights norms principally by reference to the constitutional traditions of the 15 European Union member states, and the aggressively teleological nature of ECJ jurisprudence, suggest that there will be few ECJ cases to which the Committee may profitably refer for guidance.

Commission on Human Rights or the decisions of other treaty bodies charged with reviewing individual complaints concerning human rights abuses.[463] Indeed, as the case law of these courts and quasi-judicial tribunals grows, we encourage the Committee to consult their relevant precedents in addition to European case law. Such consultation could lead to a richer and more nuanced transjudicial communication among all arbiters of civil and political liberties. It bears noting, however, that the Inter-American tribunals have been even less active than the Committee in addressing human rights complaints[464] and that the U.N.-based treaty bodies are still in their infancy.[465] As a result, there are likely to be far fewer bases for comparison.[466]

2. *A Bounded Framework for Divergence*

Our proposal for informed convergence would undoubtedly be opposed by many states, especially those that are not members of any regional human rights regime. These states might argue that in ratifying the Covenant and the Optional Protocol they never intended to be bound by the decisions of the

463. The Committee on the Elimination of Race Discrimination and the Committee Against Torture are authorized to receive complaints from individuals alleging violations of the treaties they oversee. *See* Byrnes & Conners, *supra* note 12, *passim*. The Committee on the Elimination of All Forms of Discrimination Against Women cannot receive such complaints but has recommended that an optional protocol to the Convention on the Elimination of All Forms of Discrimination Against Women be drafted to permit them to be filed. *See id.* at 770-73; *see also id.* at 784-97 (reprinting the proposed optional protocol).

464. *See* SCOTT DAVIDSON, THE INTER-AMERICAN COURT OF HUMAN RIGHTS 195 (1992) ("It is perhaps an abuse of speech to refer to the lack of use of the [Inter-American] Court's contentious jurisdiction. It is possibly more accurate to describe the prevailing situation as one of 'nonuse'."); James F. Smith, *NAFTA and Human Rights: A Necessary Linkage*, 27 U.C. DAVIS L. REV. 793, 839-40 (1994) ("The Inter-American Court's jurisprudence is neither extensive nor impressive but its achievements so far demonstrate that its potential is enormous."); *cf.* Moravcsik, *supra* note 9, at 181-82 (discussing reasons for the relative ineffectiveness of the Inter-American tribunal).

465. *See* Byrnes, *supra* note 12, at 539 (noting that the Committee Against Torture's seven cases during the same time period were all declared inadmissible); Partsch, *supra* note 12, at 363 (noting that the Committee on the Elimination of Race Discrimination decided only two cases at the end of 1991).

466. By directing our proposal to the Committee, we do not mean to imply that the European tribunals should ignore the Committee's views. To the contrary, we believe that a two-way dialogue between the human rights bodies will improve the reasoning and outcomes of both institutions. Indeed, litigants before the ECHR and the European Commission regularly consult the text of the Covenant and the Committee's case law to achieve a more coherent interpretation of the rights and freedoms protected by the Convention. *See, e.g.*, Abdulaziz v. United Kingdom, App. Nos. 9214/80, 9473/81 & 9474/81, 77 Eur. Ct. H.R. (ser. B) at 27 (1990) (Commission report) (citing and following the Committee's views that immigration controls may infringe the right to respect for family life); Silver v. United Kingdom, 51 Eur. Ct. H.R. (ser. B) at 218 (1987) (noting "the clear connection between Article 13 of the Convention and Article 2.3 of the International Covenant; their common intent; and the fact that those concerned in the drafting of the European Convention were dealing with concepts to be found in the United Nations Instruments" (tabulation omitted)); Young v. United Kingdom, App. Nos. 7601/76 & 7806/77, 39 Eur. Ct. H.R. (ser. B) at 55-56 (1984) (Commission report) (Kellberg, J., dissenting) (comparing the scope of freedom of association in the Convention to the scope of the right in other international instruments, including the Covenant).

ECHR and the Commission and that any reliance on European jurisprudence is therefore illegitimate.[467]

We would reject any theory of convergence that recommended such slavish adherence to regional standards as to prevent the Committee from charting its own interpretive course for the Covenant. Our proposal for convergence is not nearly so absolute. To the contrary, we acknowledge that in many instances it will be both legitimate and necessary for the Committee to diverge from settled European case law. If the Committee is to diverge from an established European interpretation, however, it must bear the burden of justifying and explaining its departure. In the sections that follow, we spell out several possible bases for divergence and explore their legitimacy.

a. *Differences in the Rights Protected by the Two Treaties*

The most obvious ground for the Committee to decline to follow European precedent exists when the Covenant guarantees a right that is not found in the Convention. The Committee would have no need to consult regional case law for those civil and political rights that have no European analogue.[468]

467. These states might also claim that a practice that compels the Committee to consult regional sources is itself a violation of the Covenant in that it confers powers on the Committee not expressly specified in the text of the treaty. Several points undermine the force of this argument.

First, although it is the general practice of international monitoring bodies to rely solely on their own constituent treaties and decisional law, that practice has not been universally followed in the human rights context. *See* DAVIDSON, *supra* note 464, at 57, 70, 193-95; MERON, *supra* note 395, at 160-62. European human rights tribunals often refer to the texts of other human rights treaties and case law of other human rights tribunals in determining the scope of the obligations their own treaties impose, and the ECJ has looked for inspiration to the jurisprudence of the ECHR when interpreting fundamental rights under Community law. *See supra* Subsection III.B.2.e.

Second, on numerous occasions, the Committee has already been requested by parties to adopt or diverge from a decision of the European tribunals. *See supra* note 398 and accompanying text. In deciding whether or not to follow Europe's lead, the Committee was compelled to consider arguments based on European case law. Reference to such case law even where the parties have not requested that the Committee do so would provide the Committee with an additional interpretive methodology that would permit it to reach better reasoned decisions, even when it chooses to diverge from a settled European interpretation.

Finally, for many years commentators have used the more developed case law under the Convention to forecast outcomes under the Covenant. There can be little doubt that this body of scholarship has already influenced the Committee's thinking. *See, e.g.*, Higgins, *supra* note 8, at 6 (noting, as a British member of the Committee, that the Covenant "does not exist in isolation and provisions in other instruments can unavoidably intrude upon [the Committee's interpretive] function"); Torkel Opsahl, *The Coexistence Between Geneva and Strasbourg: Inter-Relationship of the International Covenant on Civil and Political Rights and the European Convention on Human Rights and Their Respective Organs of Implementation*, 1991-1992 CAN. HUM. RTS. Y.B. 151, 164 (stating, as a Norwegian member of the Committee, that in interpreting whether individuals will have access to a court in administrative cases, "it is safe to predict that [the issue] will cause many discussions, and many references to the European scene in years to come").

468. The rights and freedoms guaranteed by the Covenant that are absent from the Convention include: the right of all peoples to self-determination, *see* Covenant, *supra* note 15, art. 1, 999 U.N.T.S. at 173; the right of all individuals deprived of their liberty to be treated with humanity and respect, *see id.* art. 10, 999 U.N.T.S. at 176; the right to recognition everywhere as a person before the law, *see id.* art. 16, 999 U.N.T.S. at 177; the prohibition of propaganda for war and of incitement to discrimination, *see id.* art. 20, 999 U.N.T.S. at 178; the rights of the child, including protection from discrimination, registration immediately after birth, the right to a name, and the right to acquire a nationality, *see id.* art. 24, 999

Divergence is also justifiable where both the Convention and the Covenant protect the same right, but the definitions of that right differ in a substantial way. The Committee should consult European precedents when analyzing clauses in the Covenant that are identical or substantially similar to parallel texts in the Convention. But where the language defining the two provisions is not comparable—in other words where the Covenant is either more or less rights-protective than the Convention—the Committee need not defer to European case law.[469] The degree of overlap for this cluster of "definitionally distinct" rights will, of course, necessarily vary with the specific language of each article.

b. *Divergence Where Object and Purpose Differ*

It has long been accepted practice under international law to resolve potentially troublesome questions of textual interpretation by reference to a treaty's "object and purpose."[470] To the extent that the Convention and the Covenant enshrine different substantive goals, those differences may well be relevant to the Committee's analysis and, in certain contexts, can justify a departure from settled European case law. In what follows, we compare the similarities in the object and purpose of both treaties and then consider two ways in which they differ.

Both the European tribunals and the Committee agree that there is something special about human rights conventions that make them unlike many

U.N.T.S. at 179; and the right of ethnic, religious, or linguistic minorities to enjoy their own culture, practice their own religion, or use their own language, *see id.* art. 27, 999 U.N.T.S. at 179.

This catalogue of rights was first identified by A.H. Robertson in 1968. *See* A.H. ROBERTSON, HUMAN RIGHTS IN NATIONAL AND INTERNATIONAL LAW 36-40 (1968). We have omitted from this list the right to equality before the law and the equal protection of the laws protected by Article 26 of the Covenant. *See* Covenant, *supra* note 15, art. 26, 999 U.N.T.S. at 179. While the Covenant guarantees an autonomous right to equality, the Convention protects against discrimination linked to other protected rights and freedoms. *See* NOWAK, *supra* note 15, at 461. The test used by the European tribunals to ferret out invidious discrimination, however, is substantially similar to that applied by the Committee and thus can serve as an important point of consultation for the Committee in determining whether a state party's classification of similarly situated groups violates the Covenant.

We have also omitted from the list those Covenant articles that later were protected in a protocol to the Convention. *See* Protocol No. 4 to the Convention for the Protection of Human Rights and Fundamental Freedoms, Sept. 16, 1963, art. 2, 7 I.L.M. 978, 978 (1986) (protecting liberty of movement and choice of residence within a state); Protocol No. 7 to the Convention for the Protection of Human Rights and Fundamental Freedoms Concerning Civil and Political Rights, art. 1, 24 I.L.M. 535, 535 (1985) [hereinafter Protocol No. 7] (providing procedural safeguards for aliens under threat of expulsion).

469. Robertson identifies four clusters of rights with respect to which there are important definitional differences: (1) the right to life; (2) the right to a fair trial; (3) the right of marriage; and (4) political rights. *See* ROBERSTON, *supra* note 468, at 30-36. With respect to fair trial and marriage rights, several provisions omitted from the Convention were subsequently included in one of its optional protocols. For example, the right to an appeal in criminal cases, the right to compensation for a miscarriage of justice, the principle of double jeopardy (*ne bis in idem*), and equality of rights and responsibilities between spouses "as to marriage, during marriage and in the event of its dissolution" were all included in the seventh optional protocol. *See* Protocol No. 7, *supra* note 468, arts. 2-5, 24 I.L.M. at 535-36.

470. Vienna Convention on the Law of Treaties, art. 31(1), *opened for signature* May 23, 1969, 1155 U.N.T.S. 331, 341 [hereinafter Vienna Convention].

other international agreements. Specifically, these instruments create enforceable rights for individuals, rather than simply obligations of states parties to one another.[471] It follows that a state's surrender of sovereignty is not to be construed strictly,[472] but rather must be given an autonomous international interpretation[473] to make the rights and freedoms guaranteed effective rather than illusory. By construing the treaties in a rights-protective manner, both the tribunals and the Committee ensure that the protections established by the drafters do not become hollow promises honored more in the breach than in the observance. But beyond these important underlying similarities, there are important differences between the two treaties, differences that have become increasingly apparent as each institution's jurisprudence has developed.

i. *Reference to Democratic Principles*

The first difference concerns the European system's emphasis on the principles that prevail in democratic societies. The importance of these principles to the Convention can be gleaned from several sources: the requirement that all states parties must accept "the rule of law and democratic values,"[474] the text of the Convention itself, the preamble and numerous articles that refer to the phrase "democratic society,"[475] and the case law of the ECHR and the Commission, which emphasizes that certain rights and

---

471. *See* Austria v. Italy, App. No. 788/60, 4 Y.B. Eur. Conv. on H.R. 116, 138 (Eur. Comm'n H.R. 1961) (stating that the Convention is not designed to create reciprocal obligations among states but rather to establish a "common public order" for Europe); Cox v. Canada, No. 539/1993, Hum. Rts. Comm., 52nd Sess., at 1, 18 U.N. Doc. CCPR/C/52/D/539 (1994) (Herndl and Sadi, concurring) ("Admittedly, since the primary beneficiaries of human rights treaties are not States but human beings, the protection of human rights calls for a more liberal approach than that normally applicable in the case of ambiguous provisions of multilateral treaties.").

472. *See* J.B. v. Canada, No. 118/1982, U.N. GAOR, Hum. Rts. Comm., 41st Sess., Supp. No. 40, Annex IX, at 151, 162, U.N. Doc. A/41/40 (1986) (individual opinions of Higgins, Lallah, Mavrommatis, Opsahl, and Wako) (stressing that the focus on object and purpose is "especially important in a treaty for the promotion of human rights, where limitation[s] of the exercise of rights . . . are not readily to be presumed"); *see also* NOWAK, *supra* note 15, at xxiv ("[G]enerally recognized rules of interpretation for human rights texts call for a liberal interpretation of rights (*'in dubio pro libertate'*) and a narrow interpretation of restrictions.").

473. *See* Van Dusen v. Canada, No. 12/50, U.N. GAOR, Hum. Rts. Comm., 37th Sess., Supp. No. 40, Annex XII, at 150, 155, U.N. Doc. A/37/40 (1982). The Committee reasoned that the

> interpretation and application of the [Covenant] has to be based on the principle that the terms and concepts of the Covenant are independent of any particular national system of law and of all dictionary definitions. Although the terms of the Covenant are derived from long traditions within many nations, the Committee must now regard them as having an autonomous meaning.

Id.; *see also* NOWAK, *supra* note 15, at xxiv; Higgins, *supra* note 8, at 5-6.

474. Statute of the Council of Europe, May 5, 1949, pmbl., 87 U.N.T.S. 103, 103; *id.* art. 1, 87 U.N.T.S. at 103; *id.* art. 3, 87 U.N.T.S. at 103.

475. Convention, *supra* note 2, pmbl., 213 U.N.T.S. at 222; *id.* art. 8(2), 213 U.N.T.S. at 230; *id.* art. 9(2), 213 U.N.T.S. at 230; *id.* art. 10(2), 213 U.N.T.S. at 230; *id.* art. 11(2), 213 U.N.T.S. at 230.

freedoms and certain kinds of conduct are "hallmarks of democratic societies" that serve as touchstones for interpreting the entire Convention.[476]

The references to democratic societies in the Covenant are less prevalent, although by no means entirely absent. The treaty does not require states parties to adopt any particular political philosophy as a condition precedent to ratification. Nor does the preamble refer to democratic principles, although it does draw inspiration from the Universal Declaration of Human Rights,[477] which itself refers to democratic societies in circumscribing the restrictions that states can impose on protected rights and freedoms.[478] Significantly, however, three articles of the Covenant expressly condition restrictions on rights to those that are "necessary in a democratic society,"[479] mirroring precisely the language of the Convention.[480]

Some commentators have argued that these limited references to democratic societies are sufficient to warrant the conclusion that democratic principles pervade the entire Covenant and should serve as a point of reference for every right it protects.[481] Although civil and political rights have their roots in the liberal democratic tradition, the text of the Covenant belies the argument that democratic principles must inform every clause of the treaty. Indeed, for several articles, the phrase "democratic society" was expressly rejected by the drafters.[482]

The Covenant's limited references to democratic societies have important interpretive consequences. The Committee need not follow the ECHR's practice of using the traditions of democratic liberalism to infuse its interpretation of the entire treaty. Stated another way, there is no single

---

476. Young v. United Kingdom, 44 Eur. Ct. H.R. (ser. A) at 25 (1981). Although the ECHR and the Commission are still in the process of developing these principles, several important guidelines have already emerged. First, the court has placed special emphasis on the rights of minorities, noting that states parties must respect the principles of "pluralism, tolerance and broadmindedness" in their treatment of individuals. *See id.* Certain rights and legal doctrines have also been viewed as especially significant to the maintenance of democratic societies, including respect for the rule of law, freedom of expression and assembly, and the right to political representation. *See* MERRILLS, *supra* note 77, at 125-49.

477. Universal Declaration, *supra* note 453.

478. The Declaration provides:

> In the exercise of his rights and freedoms, everyone shall be subject only to such limitations as are determined by law solely for the purpose of securing due recognition and respect for the rights and freedoms of others and of meeting the just requirements of morality, public order and the general welfare in a democratic society.

Id. art. 29, at 75.

479. *See supra* note 391.

480. *See supra* note 475 and accompanying text.

481. *See, e.g.*, Alexandre Charles Kiss, *Permissible Limitations on Rights*, *in* THE INTERNATIONAL BILL OF RIGHTS, *supra* note 15, at 290, 307 (arguing that "even in the limitations clauses where no explicit mention is made of a democratic framework, the idea of democracy is always underlying").

482. *See* NOWAK, *supra* note 15, at 352 (discussing the drafters' omission of "democratic society" from limitations on freedom of expression and concluding that "[e]ven though this decision . . . in view of the great significance accorded freedom of expression for the functioning of democracy, may not seem understandable, it must nevertheless be taken into account in a system of interpretation of the Covenant"); *see also* Kiss, *supra* note 481, at 306 (noting the drafters' rejection of the phrase from, inter alia, the Covenant's protection of freedom of thought, conscience, and religion).

political vision toward which states party to the Covenant must strive.[483] Indeed, the essential point of a universal human rights treaty is to encourage all states, regardless of their political composition or stage of development, to ratify the agreement. Thus the Committee's reference to democratic principles is likely to be more limited and restricted to particular Covenant rights and freedoms.

Perhaps the most compelling case for the Committee to seek guidance from Europe exists for those Covenant articles in which the phrase "necessary in a democratic society" appears. For these protected rights and freedoms, the Committee should draw inspiration and support for its analysis from the case law of the ECHR and the Commission construing the same phrase in parallel Convention articles. For example, a state party attempting to limit freedom of assembly would have to demonstrate that its restriction of that right is consistent with such democratic principles as "pluralism, tolerance and broadmindedness,"[484] is sensitive to the views of unpopular minority groups,[485] and is narrowly circumscribed to keep the infringement of the

---

483. A telling counterexample to the practice we propose for the Committee is the decision of the Inter-American Court of Human Rights in its advisory opinion in *Compulsory Membership in an Association Prescribed by Law for the Practice of Journalism*, No. OC-5/85, Nov. 13, 1985, *reprinted in* 7 HUM. RTS. L.J. 74 (1986). Like Article 19 of the Covenant, Article 13 of the Inter-American Convention guarantees freedom of expression but authorizes restrictions "necessary" to ensure several competing interests. *See id.* at 82. Unlike Article 10 of the European Convention, however, these restrictions need not be "necessary in a democratic society." Notwithstanding this omission, the Inter-American Court looked to other articles of the Inter-American Convention that reveal the primacy of democratic principles in interpreting the rights guaranteed by the treaty. *See id.* at 83. After citing to European case law, the court used democratic theory to bolster its conclusion that the Inter-American Convention places an extremely high value on free expression:

> Freedom of expression is a cornerstone upon which the very existence of a democratic society rests. It is indispensable for the formation of public opinion. It is also a *conditio sine qua non* for the development of political parties, trade unions, scientific and cultural societies and, in general, those who wish to influence the public. It represents, in short, the means that enable the community, when exercising its options, to be sufficiently informed. Consequently, it can be said that a society is not well informed that is not a society that is truly free.

Id. at 89. Thus, the court effectively read democratic ideals even into those convention articles where the phrase "democratic society" did not appear. *Cf.* DAVIDSON, *supra* note 464, at 195 (claiming that the approach of the Inter-American Court "is clearly within the Western liberal democratic tradition which predicates a certain form of political, social and economic organisation, which in turn has implications for both the interpretation and application of human rights").

484. Young v. United Kingdom, 44 Eur. Ct. H.R. (ser. A) at 25 (1981). As Nowak notes:

> State measures to restrict freedom of assembly must also correspond to a common, *minimum democratic standard*. This standard is lower in a universal international treaty than in a regional one, such as the ECHR. Nevertheless, the criteria of pluralism, tolerance, and broadmindedness mentioned by the European Court of Human Rights in the *Handyside* case may be deemed valid as a general standard for democratic societies. This is accompanied by the principle of people's sovereignty, i.e., popular participation in the political decision-making process, and by the respect for and active protection of human rights, in particular the requirement of democratic equality.

NOWAK, *supra* note 15, at 379 (footnotes omitted) (citing Handyside v. United Kingdom, 24 Eur. Ct. H.R. (ser. A) (1976).

485. *See* Plattform "Ärzte für das Leben" v. Austria, 139 Eur. Ct. H.R. (ser. A) at 12 (1988) (holding that states parties have an affirmative obligation to ensure that demonstrations promoting controversial or unpopular views are protected).

right to an absolute minimum.[486] Although there is less support for applying the same stringent democratic principles to those rights that states may limit where "necessary," the Committee need not dismiss the relevance of any gloss that the European tribunals have placed on these rights. Instead, the overlap of the word "necessary" in both treaties creates a powerful link that can provide the Committee with valuable insight determining the necessity of a restriction.[487]

ii. *Teleological Methods of Interpretation*

The ECHR's determination that the Convention is a "living instrument" to be construed "in light of present day conditions" is one of its most significant and well-documented interpretive tools.[488] Far from being bound by the intent of the treaty's drafters, the court canvasses legal, social, and political developments in Europe as a supplementary means of interpreting open-ended clauses in the treaty and of ensuring that the clauses are relevant to modern-day human rights problems. Where a large majority of European states have, over time, enlarged the scope of a protected right or narrowed the restrictions that may permissibly be imposed on its exercise, the ECHR has often found that a state not keeping pace with these reforms has violated the Convention.[489]

While the European tribunals continue their struggle to develop common European standards, the Committee has focused its attention primarily on defining the application of the Covenant's text to specific factual situations.[490] Although the Committee has never expressly rejected the idea

486. *See* Dudgeon v. United Kingdom, 45 Eur. Ct. H.R. (ser. A) at 21 (1981) (holding that the court makes a final evaluation as to whether a government's arguments for restricting a right are relevant and sufficient and "whether the interference complained of was proportionate to the social need claimed for it").

487. As Nowak explains:

> [T]he requirement of necessity is subject to an *objective minimum standard*, which may be subsequently reviewed by the Committee. The decisive criterion for evaluating whether this standard has been observed is . . . not the principle of democracy but rather that of *proportionality* (Verhältnismäßigkeit) in the given case. Every interference thus requires a precise balancing between the right . . . and those interests to be protected by the interference. Interference is necessary only when its severity and intensity are proportional to a purpose listed in [the text]. . . . The requirement of necessity underscores the principle that restrictions on Covenant rights are always exceptions and may therefore not become the rule. As a result, they are to be interpreted narrowly in cases of doubt.

NOWAK, *supra* note 15, at 211 (footnotes omitted).

488. *E.g.*, Marckx v. Belgium, 31 Eur. Ct. H.R. (ser. A) at 19 (1979); Tyrer v. United Kingdom, 26 Eur. Ct. H.R. (ser. A) at 15 (1978).

489. Textual support for this teleological approach is found in the preamble to the Convention, which states that "the aim of the Council of Europe is the achievement of greater unity between its Members" and that one of the methods by which the aim is to be pursued is the "further realization" of a "common understanding and observance" of human rights in Europe. Convention, *supra* note 2, pmbl., 213 U.N.T.S. at 222; *see also* Cossey v. United Kingdom, 184 Eur. Ct. H.R. (ser. A) at 27 (1990) (Martens, J., dissenting) (citing to the preamble as a basis for the court to develop uniform European standards).

490. *See, e.g.*, Gregory H. Fox, *The Right to Political Participation in International Law*, 17 YALE J. INT'L L. 539, 561 (1992) ("Unlike the U.N. Human Rights Committee, which rarely ventures beyond

of a teleological method of interpretation,[491] several factors militate against its adopting such an approach to the degree practiced by the ECHR and the Commission.

First, with one notable exception,[492] nothing in the language of the Covenant authorizes the Committee to engage in such a practice. Although it is undoubtedly the Committee's function to articulate global human rights standards based on the language of the Covenant and its object and purpose, there is no basis for it aggressively to raise the global baseline in accordance with rights-enhancing law reforms.

Second, practical difficulties counsel the Committee against adopting an aggressively teleological interpretation similar to that employed by the European tribunals. Unlike the European system, which currently comprises 40 states with largely concordant legal systems, the 136 states party to the Covenant span a wide range of legal, political, social, and cultural traditions. Were the Committee to canvass all of these legal systems as a supplementary means of interpreting the rights contained in the Covenant, it would be unlikely to find the high degree of consensus that frequently occurs within the European regional system.

Instead, the Committee will likely adhere to more widely accepted methods of treaty interpretation, construing the Covenant in light of its text, object, and purpose, and where appropriate, the *travaux preparatoires*.[493] Although subsequent practice of states parties is relevant to interpreting the Covenant,[494] the Committee can authoritatively rely on such practice only where a large number of states have adopted it. Given that the pace of legal

---

treaty language in its decisions on participatory rights, European tribunals have adduced extra-textual participatory rights to reflect the common expectations of the parties to the European Convention.").

491. *See* MCGOLDRICK, *supra* note 17, at 159 ("There has as yet been no parallel in the [Committee's] jurisprudence to the 'dynamic approach' to interpretation under the [Convention] . . . ."); *cf.* DAVIDSON, *supra* note 464, at 138 ("[T]he American Court has had little opportunity to engage in the kind of judicial legislation undertaken by its European analogue. This is not to say that elements of teleology are not evident in the jurisprudence of the American Court . . . .").

492. Article 6 of the Covenant, which tolerates application of the death penalty under narrowly limited circumstances, states that "[n]othing in this article shall be invoked to delay or to prevent the abolition of capital punishment by any State Party to the present Covenant." Covenant, *supra* note 15, art. 6(6), 999 U.N.T.S. at 175. In its general comment on the right to life, the Committee suggested that it would be especially vigilant in scrutinizing use of the death penalty and would exhort states parties toward total abolition:

> While it follows from article 6(2) to (6) that States parties are not obliged to abolish the death penalty totally, they are obliged to limit its use and, in particular, to abolish it other than for the "most serious crimes." Accordingly, *they ought to consider reviewing their criminal laws in this light* . . . . The article also refers generally to abolition in terms which strongly suggest (paras. 6(2) and (6)) that abolition is desirable. The Committee concludes that *all measures of abolition should be considered as progress in the enjoyment of the right to life . . . and should be reported to the Committee.* The Committee notes that a number of States have already abolished the death penalty or suspended its application.

General Comment 6/16, *supra* note 287 (emphasis added), *reprinted in* NOWAK, *supra* note 15, at 852.

493. *See* Vienna Convention, *supra* note 470, art. 31(1), 1155 U.N.T.S. at 338; *see also* NOWAK, *supra* note 15, at xxiii-xxiv.

494. *See* Vienna Convention, *supra* note 470, art. 31(3)(b), 1155 U.N.T.S. at 337.

developments on a global scale is slow and that resort to a teleological method of interpretation may reduce Covenant standards to the level of its least rights-protective states parties,[495] the Committee's reliance on an expressly teleological approach is likely to be exceedingly rare.

3. *Divergence from a "European Gloss" on Human Rights*

The differing functions of the teleological method for interpreting the Covenant and the Convention raise one of the most troublesome areas of potential divergence: whether the Committee should follow European jurisprudence where the ECHR and the Commission have relied on uniquely European legal developments to expand the scope of Convention rights and freedoms. Arguably, where the tribunals have breathed new life into the Convention by relying primarily on European law reforms that have no analogue elsewhere on the planet, it would be improper for the Committee to impose the European human rights experience on the entire international community.[496]

It may be possible, however, for the Committee to divorce the "European gloss" on human rights from other beneficial aspects of the tribunals' reasoning

---

495. Andrew Byrnes argues:

> Under a universal human rights treaty . . . to which more than 100 States parties with a wide variety of cultures, legal systems, stages of development are party, *an international body might not so easily identify an actual or evolving international standard or, if it can do so, that standard may be heavily influenced by the least common denominator "drag"*—the feeling that any decision must command a broad level of acceptance within the relevant constituency.

Andrew Byrnes, *Towards More Effective Enforcement of Women's Human Rights Through the Use of International Human Rights Law and Procedures*, *in* HUMAN RIGHTS OF WOMEN: NATIONAL AND INTERNATIONAL PERSPECTIVES 189, 194 (Rebecca J. Cook ed., 1994) (emphasis added).

496. For example, several early rulings of the European Commission of Human Rights permitted European states to criminalize homosexual conduct between consenting adults. *See, e.g.*, X. v. Federal Republic of Germany, 3 Y.B. Eur. Conv. on H.R. 184, 194 (Eur. Comm'n H.R.). In *Dudgeon v. United Kingdom*, 45 Eur. Ct. H.R. (ser. A) at 21 (1981), the European court changed direction and held that such laws violate the right of privacy. An important, although by no means exclusive, basis for this decision was the markedly changed views concerning homosexual conduct in the member states of the Council of Europe. The court reasoned that

> there is now a better understanding, and in consequence an increased tolerance, of homosexual behavior to the extent that in the great majority of the member states of the Council of Europe it is no longer considered to be necessary or appropriate to treat homosexual practices . . . as in themselves a matter to which the sanctions of the criminal law should be applied; the Court cannot overlook the marked changes which have occurred in this regard in the domestic laws of the member States.

Id. at 23-24.

Arguably, such a peculiarly European interpretation of human rights standards should not be persuasive for the Committee. For example, as of 1993, at least 74 countries around the world still criminalized homosexual conduct between consenting adults; moreover, states in Africa, the former communist nations, and other parts of the developing world are those primarily retaining these restrictions. *See* Rob Tielman & Hans Hammelburg, *World Survey on the Social and Legal Position of Gays and Lesbians*, *in* THE THIRD PINK BOOK: A GLOBAL VIEW OF LESBIAN AND GAY LIBERATION AND OPPRESSION 150-51 (Aart Hendriks et al. eds., 1993). If the Committee were to rely unthinkingly on European precedents concerning homosexuality, it could well be accused of imposing a specialized view of human rights throughout the planet.

and analysis. Rather than concentrating on the ECHR's use of European law reforms to interpret the Convention, the Committee might, through careful line-drawing, rely on European case law to assist it in developing an analytical framework for interpreting Covenant rights and freedoms.[497] In addition, the Committee may validly rely on European case law that has expanded the Convention to include a level of rights protection already guaranteed by the Covenant.[498] In this circumstance, the European teleological approach has merely brought the two human rights systems into harmony, thereby permitting the Committee to consult relevant European precedents when interpreting the Covenant.

4. *Divergence Where the Committee Improves on European Precedents*

A final basis for divergence may exist where the Committee has openly acknowledged the existence of relevant regional precedents but has concluded that their reasoning is unpersuasive and that a different interpretation is more consistent with the spirit of the Covenant. In such a situation, the Committee can legitimately depart from a European approach even where the texts of the two treaties are identical.

In determining whether it can improve upon European jurisprudence, the Committee may consider several factors: whether a relevant decision is an isolated case or part of a stable line of precedent that has been applied in a

497. The Committee appears to have followed this approach in its recent decision in *Toonen v. Australia*, No. 488/1992, U.N. GAOR, Hum. Rts. Comm., 49th Sess., Supp. No. 40, Annex IX, at 230, 232 U.N. Doc. CCPR/C/52/D/488 (1994), in which it concluded that criminal sanctions on adult homosexual conduct in Tasmania were an "arbitrary and unlawful interference with . . . privacy" under Article 17 of the Covenant. After construing the term "arbitrary" to require interferences provided by law to be "reasonable in the circumstances," the Committee interpreted the requirement of reasonableness "to imply that any interference with privacy must be proportional to the end sought and be necessary in the circumstances of any given case." *Id.* This analysis is strikingly similar to the ECHR's reasoning in the *Dudgeon* case. *See* 45 Eur. Ct. H.R. (ser. A) at 21-22 (stating that interferences with privacy must be "necessary in a democratic society," satisfy a "pressing social need," and be "proportionate to the legitimate aim pursued"). Significantly, the Committee did not cite to the ECHR's case law, nor did it adopt the ECHR's teleological method of interpretation.

498. For example, although the Convention prohibits discrimination on the grounds of sex in precisely the same language that it prohibits other forms of discrimination, the ECHR has concluded that the "advancement of the equality of the sexes is today a major goal in the member states of the Council of Europe. This means that very weighty reasons would have to be advanced before a difference of treatment on the ground of sex could be regarded as compatible with the Convention." Abdulaziz v. United Kingdom, 94 Eur Ct. H.R. (ser. A) at 38 (1985). Although the Committee has yet to apply a similar heightened level of scrutiny for evaluating gender-based classifications, there is strong textual support for it to do so. In addition to the two nondiscrimination clauses that include a reference to sex, *see* Covenant, *supra* note 15, art. 2(1), 999 U.N.T.S. at 173; *id.* art. 26, 999 U.N.T.S. at 179, the Covenant contains an additional guarantee "ensur[ing] the equal right of men and women to the enjoyment of all civil and political rights set forth in the present Covenant." *Id.* art. 3, 999 U.N.T.S. at 173. It would thus be appropriate for the Committee to view as highly persuasive decisions of the ECHR applying a stringent standard of review to distinctions based on sex, inasmuch as the advancement of sexual equality is as important a goal among the Covenant's signatories as among the Council of Europe's member states.

variety of factual circumstances;[499] whether the case was decided by the Commission or the ECHR;[500] whether the tribunals faithfully applied established doctrinal standards in deciding the case;[501] and, if the same issue has been considered in the Inter-American system, whether its regional tribunals have adopted the European interpretation or diverged from that interpretation.[502] Although divergence on this basis may be rare, the Committee should not be foreclosed from improving upon the tribunals' reasoning. Indeed, the ECHR and the Commission may eventually reconsider their approach in light of the Committee's conclusions, enhancing the two-way dialogue between the United Nations and Europe.

VI. CONCLUSION

The twentieth century opened with a plethora of efforts to encourage peaceful settlement of disputes through judicial or quasi-judicial settlement, leading to the Permanent Court of Arbitration and ultimately the Permanent Court of International Justice.[503] Over the course of the century many other tribunals have been created, both regional and global, general and issue-specific. Many are devoted to the resolution of classic "international" disputes between states. A new generation of tribunals more properly labeled "supranational" addresses disputes between private parties and national governments arising under international agreements. Even as parts of the globe plunge into a new round of conflict and atrocity, new proposals for war crimes tribunals and a permanent international criminal court have quickly followed.[504] Existing mechanisms for international adjudication, such as

499. By applying a judicially created doctrine to a wide range of problems, the European tribunals can test the viability of that doctrine and adapt or modify it to changing circumstances. Prior to such adjudication, there will always be "grey areas" in the tribunals' jurisprudence. *Cf.* O'Boyle, *supra* note 91, at 285 (discussing current open issues in the ECHR's freedom of expression case law).

500. In several instances, the Commission's interpretation of the Convention was later rejected by the ECHR. *See* MERRILLS, *supra* note 77, at 15.

501. *See, e.g.*, Colin Warbrick, *Coherence and the European Court of Human Rights: The Adjudicative Background to the* Soering *Case*, 11 MICH. J. INT'L L. 1073, 1084-85 (1990) (discussing two freedom-of-expression cases in which the court failed to adhere to established doctrine).

502. *See, e.g.*, DAVIDSON, *supra* note 464, at 57, 193-94 (discussing instances in which the Inter-American court relied on reasoning of the European tribunals).

503. *See* JOSEPH MODESTE SWEENEY ET AL., THE INTERNATIONAL LEGAL SYSTEM 44-47 (3d ed. 1988).

504. *See, e.g.*, MICHAEL P. SCHARF, BALKAN JUSTICE: THE STORY BEHIND THE FIRST INTERNATIONAL WAR CRIMES TRIAL SINCE NUREMBERG (1997); M. Cherif Bassiouni, *From Versailles to Rwanda in Seventy-Five Years: The Need To Establish a Permanent International Criminal Court*, 10 HARV. HUM. RTS. J. 11 (1997); M. Cherif Bassiouni & Christopher L. Blakesley, *The Need for an International Criminal Court in the New International World Order*, 25 VAND. J. TRANSNAT'L L. 151 (1992); Cristopher L. Blakesley, *Obstacles to the Creation of a Permanent War Crimes Tribunal*, 18 FLETCHER F. WORLD AFF. 77 (1994); Joel Cavicchia, *The Prospects for an International Criminal Court in the 1990s*, 10 DICK. J. INT'L L. 223 (1992); Timothy C. Evered, *An International Criminal Court: Recent Proposals and American Concerns*, 6 PACE INT'L L. REV. 121 (1994); Michael P. Scharf, *Getting Serious About an International Criminal Court*, 6 PACE INT'L L. REV. 103 (1994).

WTO and NAFTA panels, are adding supranational elements by increasing the access of private parties to the proceedings. Individuals are even being given a right of direct petition against international institutions such as the World Bank.

This renewed millennial faith in the ability of courts to hold states to their international obligations is more likely to be justified than the experience of the intervening decades might suggest. Two tribunals—the European Court of Justice and the European Court of Human Rights—have been strikingly successful. They issue judgments that have a direct impact on the lives of ordinary Europeans, by securing them rights and privileges enshrined in international instruments and by holding their governments—signatories to those instruments—to their word. The two tribunals have compensated for their lack of direct coercive power by convincing domestic government institutions to exercise power on their behalf, through both direct persuasion and pressure from private litigants. We identify this relationship with domestic government institutions as the hallmark of "effective" supranational adjudication.

What lessons can be learned from the European experience? By consulting the analyses of close observers of these tribunals—scholars, lawyers, and the judges themselves—we develop a "checklist" of effective supranational adjudication. We divide it into three sets of factors: those that are within the control of the states party to an agreement establishing a tribunal, those that are within the control of the tribunal itself, and those that are often not subject to the control of either states or jurists. We rank the factors in each category roughly in order of relative impact. Overall, we intend the resulting list to be used both by scholars seeking to evaluate the effectiveness of other tribunals and by judges themselves seeking to improve their own effectiveness.

A striking feature of the checklist is the way in which the judges on the ECJ and the ECHR have exploited the opportunities granted them by the provision of supranational jurisdiction. They have built strong bridges to private litigants, creating a constituency for their judgments that is interested and able to pressure domestic government institutions to take heed and comply with those judgments. They also have forged direct relationships with different domestic institutions: The ECJ deliberately wooed national courts, and the ECHR earned support from courts, administrative agencies, and some national legislators. The majority of the checklist factors within the control of states or judges are linked to this process of constituency-building.

In a growing number of areas of international law, such as human rights law and trade law, individuals have a direct interest in calling their governments to account for violation of international obligations. Individuals also do not face the fears of a reciprocal response or diplomatic ramifications in other issue areas that often deter states from calling one another to account. In this context, the European experience of supranational adjudication augurs well for the prospect of "privatizing" public obligations by translating them into individual rights, creating a potential constituency that an adroit supranational tribunal can bring to life. Ernst-Ulrich Petersmann, for instance, argues that the "rights-based approach [of the ECJ and the ECHR], enabling self-interested individuals to enforce international guarantees of freedom and non-discrimination through the courts, . . . confirms that individuals . . . may be the best guardians and promoters of rule-oriented international cooperation."[505]

Beyond the language of interests, however, lies a deeper point, one that flows from changing conceptions of the state itself and of the sovereignty to which it is entitled. In democracies in which individuals are mobilized in support of the judgment of a supranational tribunal, compliance with that judgment becomes less a question of ceding sovereignty than of responding to constituent pressure. The state is no longer an interlocking set of government institutions in its domestic affairs, with sovereignty lodged in the people, and a unitary entity in its foreign relations, with sovereignty a fundamental attribute of its statehood. Instead, its internal and external face begin to mirror one another, as sovereignty becomes inextricably interwoven with accountability.

The checklist itself and our analysis of the way in which the checklist factors intersect with the unique features of supranational adjudication at least provide the basis for a positive answer to the question posed at the outset of this Article: whether it is possible to expand effective supranational adjudication beyond Europe. In the second half of this Article we apply the checklist to a human rights tribunal that is itself evolving from an explicitly nonjudicial entity into a quasi-judicial one. Over the past decade in particular, the U.N. Human Rights Committee has handed down more and better reasoned opinions, proved itself more willing to stand up to governments accused of human rights violations, and generally moved from a more diplomatic style of dispute resolution emphasizing compromise and avoidance of conflict to a more legal mode of consistent application of general principles. We evaluate this trajectory in terms of each of the factors on the checklist and conclude that the Committee is independently taking many of the steps we enumerate there: improving the quality of its legal reasoning; airing a wider range of competing arguments; being more willing to take a position contrary to that of states parties in high-profile cases; targeting an audience of individuals and their representatives as well as national courts; and increasing dialogue with those courts and with supranational tribunals. From this perspective, the Committee

505. Petersmann, *supra* note 54, at 443. David Wirth reaches a similar conclusion regarding the mechanism of the International Labour Organisation (ILO) allowing workers' and employers' organizations to participate with their governments as formal members of national delegations. *See* David A. Wirth, *Legitimacy, Accountability, and Partnership: A Model for Advocacy on Third World Environmental Issues*, 100 YALE L.J. 2645, 2664 (1991). The ILO gives these substate groups "access to a number of mechanisms to adjudicate nonobservance of binding standards established under ILO auspices." *Id.* These procedures, while far from being universally effective, "have been highly successful in encouraging ILO member states' adherence to binding treaty obligations like those in World Bank loan agreements." *Id.*

is becoming more court-like and is enhancing its effectiveness within the explicit and implicit constraints and resource limitations imposed by the states subject to its jurisdiction.

Those constraints and limitations are very real, however. The universal scope of UNHRC jurisdiction necessarily means that the Committee oversees many different types of political regimes, including a number of governments that are not accountable to their citizens and that are apparently monolithic, with courts, administrative agencies, and legislatures tightly controlled by the reigning political authorities. These states seem relatively immune to a supranational tribunal's efforts to mobilize constituents from below. Notwithstanding these obstacles, however, we argue that the Committee should be able to replicate another dimension of the European experience: the construction of a "community of law." Participation in this community is open not to states per se, but to specific government institutions—particularly courts—that seek to challenge the prevailing political authorities through law.

A community of law has three principal elements: a network of subnational and supranational legal actors (lawyers, judges, and legal scholars) with independent channels of communication; a set of incentives encouraging these actors to interact with one another and to maximize the impact of supranational decisions; and a set of norms distinguishing law from politics in ways that promote an autonomous realm of law protected from direct political interference. Law may be the continuation of politics by other means, but the requirement that political interests be promoted through legal formulations and argument constrains the process. These constraints create a measure of autonomy for legal actors and an internal dynamic that achieves results other than those that would be achieved by direct political jockeying and bargaining.

Communities of law can be created on a national and a supranational basis. They can overlap and reinforce one another. An important mechanism for such reinforcement is judicial dialogue: the cross-citation of decisions by tribunals that have no direct relationship to one another. Invoking the reasoning of another tribunal that has no link to a particular case other than that its previous consideration and pronouncement on an analogous problem acknowledges the power of reason and the value of deliberation over time as well as across cultures. The result does not deny the importance of local legitimacy and cultural diversity; nor does it assume that law can genuinely "float free" of the politics, economics, and cultural traditions of particular peoples. But it assumes the possibility of universal values and professional ideals and seeks to capture and reinforce a concept of transjudicial solidarity.

In this context, we conclude this Article with a specific proposal for linking the UNHRC to the human rights jurisprudence of the ECHR, as a contribution to a genuinely global dialogue among a wider range of supranational and international tribunals and domestic courts. According to this proposal, the UNHRC would actively seek convergence with ECHR reasoning in cases concerning rights and freedoms where the texts at issue are either identical or substantially similar to those protected by the Covenant. At the same time, however, a number of circumstances would prompt divergence from the ECHR's reasoning and results: (1) cases in which the rights protected by the European Convention and the Covenant differ on their face; (2) cases in which the Convention and the Covenant appear to enshrine different substantive goals; (3) cases in which the relevant ECHR precedent reflects a distinctive "European gloss" on the rights under consideration; and (4) cases in which the UNHRC concludes that it can improve on the relevant European precedent.

We advance this proposal in the spirit of the times. Part V begins with a review of a number of ways in which both national and supranational jurists around the world are increasing both formal and informal contacts with one another. The United States has traditionally been the most resistant to such efforts, but a more cosmopolitan outlook is emerging even here. Justice Sandra Day O'Connor, for instance, recently exhorted U.S. judges and lawyers to broaden their intellectual horizons, observing that ample historical precedent exists for "looking beyond American borders in our search for persuasive legal reasoning."[506] She pointed out that while U.S. judges have become "more inward-looking . . . [o]ther legal systems continue to innovate, to experiment, and to find new solutions to the new legal problems that arise each day, from which we can learn and benefit."[507] Vigorous and sustained dialogue between the UNHRC and the ECHR will add a supranational dimension to increasing transnational dialogue among judges. To the extent that these two supranational tribunals themselves draw on national traditions, they will also act as agents of increased cross-fertilization of national laws and judicial decisions. Most importantly, however, such interaction should strengthen both the awareness and the actuality of a common enterprise for all participating judges.

Its length notwithstanding, this Article is only a beginning. Supranational adjudication is a growing phenomenon, both in its pure form and in a number of variations in which private parties play increasingly direct roles in purportedly state-to-state litigation.[508] A full-fledged theory of effective supranational adjudication could use the checklist as a point of departure for assessing the effectiveness of these other tribunals but would inevitably modify

---

506. Sandra Day O'Connor, *Broadening Our Horizons: Why American Judges and Lawyers Must Learn About Foreign Law*, 4 INT'L JUD. OBSERVER 2, 2 (1997).

507. *Id.*

508. Thus, for example, although disputes before ad hoc GATT panels were formally brought by one state against another, it has been observed that "there usually is some kind of a private dispute behind these GATT cases." Andreas F. Lowenfeld, *Transcript of Discussion Following Presentation by Kenneth W. Abbott*, 1992 COLUM. BUS. L. REV. 155, 161. Similarly, the newly adopted Agreement on Trade Related Aspects of Intellectual Property Rights states that intellectual property rights are "private rights," notwithstanding that only states may participate in the treaty's dispute resolution processes. Marrakesh Agreement Establishing the World Trade Organization, Apr. 15, 1994, Annex 1C, pmbl., *reprinted in* 33 I.L.M. 1197, 1198.

it in light of new data confirming or disconfirming our analysis. Commentators analyzing the track record or predicting the future behavior of other supranational and international tribunals and adjudicatory bodies identify many of the same factors that appear in our checklist, but they do not examine the relative impact of these factors within a systematic comparative framework.[509] As such analysis proceeds, theoretical parsimony will be inevitably harder to achieve, giving ground to the nuance and detail of specific case studies. But a more developed theory, useful both for assessing the performance of existing supranational tribunals and generating recommendations on how to improve that performance, is a worthy and attainable goal.

"Effective supranational adjudication" may still seem a pipe dream to many, part of a utopian vision of global governance that is as likely to be realized as the Kantian vision of perpetual peace. Nevertheless, it has been achieved in large measure in at least one region in the world, for many distinctly non-utopian reasons. The search for those reasons and the effort to formulate them as preconditions is as likely to yield pessimistic prognoses for some regions as it is to bolster the prospects for others. Many of the factors on the checklist, even those within the power of the tribunals themselves or of the states that create them, may simply be unattainable. Nevertheless, we hope that the effort to distill such a checklist will help shift the debate over supranational adjudication away from the familiar tropes of realism versus idealism and toward the pragmatics of building regional and, perhaps, ultimately global communities of law.

509. *See, e.g.*, Rochelle Cooper Dreyfuss & Andreas Lowenfeld, *Two Achievements of the Uruguay Round: Putting TRIPs and Dispute Settlement Together*, 37 VA. J. INT'L L. (forthcoming 1997) (creating hypothetical cases to analyze general rules for appropriate resolution of disputes by panels interpreting the Agreement on Trade Related Aspects of Intellectual Property Rights and noting such factors as the quality of legal reasoning, incremental development of jurisprudence, dialogue with the World Intellectual Property Organization, the composition of the panel, and the background of the members); Lopez, *supra* note 12, at 172, 178 (surveying the first two years of dispute resolution under NAFTA and noting that certain decisions were "thorough and well-written" and that panel opinions often contained individual concurring and dissenting opinions); Philip Nichols, *GATT Doctrine*, 36 VA. J. INT'L L. 379, 388 n.40, 396, 399, 425, 431, 455 (1996) (providing a comprehensive analysis of pre-Uruguay Round GATT panel decisions and identifying such factors as the composition of panels and backgrounds of members, unanimity of decisions, the number of complaints filed and cases decided, and the consistency and reasoning of panel decisions); Jeffrey Waincymer, *Reformulated Gasoline Under Reformulated WTO Dispute Settlement Procedures: Pulling Pandora out of a Chapeau?*, 18 MICH. J. INT'L L. 141, 143, 165-66 (1996) (analyzing the first decision by the WTO appellate body and stressing such factors as "approaches to legal reasoning" and "citation of ICJ and other international law cases"); Daniel S. Sullivan, Note, *Effective International Dispute Settlement Mechanisms and the Necessary Condition of Liberal Democracy*, 81 GEO. L.J. 2369 (1993) (linking the effectiveness of supranational dispute settlement to the political regime-type of states parties); *see also* Shell, *supra* note 12, at 911-22 (proposing that private parties be granted standing before WTO panels); Schleyer, *supra* note 12, at 2275 (same).

Part IV
Exceptions

[9]

Legal Differentiation and the Concept of the Human Rights Treaty in International Law

Matthew Craven*

Abstract

The purpose of this article is to explore a question that is commonly posed, but infrequently answered: what is the nature of the relationship between conventional human rights law, and general principles governing treaty law? In its broadest sense the question, as posed, is part of a wider ongoing debate as to the potential 'fragmentation' of international law — a debate which has been encouraged particularly by the development of specific legal regimes with dedicated mechanisms for dispute resolution. More narrowly, the question is concerned with the compatibility of the existing treaty law framework for those legal instruments that purport to protect legal interests other than those of the contracting states. The central point of focus is upon the role and significance of reciprocity in the conceptual structure of human rights 'treaties'. It is argued that, whilst it is possible to maintain that human rights treaties are constructed on the basis of reciprocity, doing so has certain theoretical and practical costs which are not necessarily outweighed by the envisaged harm of understanding them as legal instruments possessing certain distinct characteristics.

1 Introduction

A subtle shift seems to have taken place in the general discourse of international law in recent years. Whereas formerly, international lawyers were concerned with the problem of establishing a credible basis for the systemic character of international law in face of the apparently optional nature of law-creation and dispute-resolution processes,[1] the situation has now been reversed. No longer are we faced with the complaint that insufficient use is made of judicial forms of dispute resolution[2] or that

* Reader in Law, University of London.

1 Cf. Combacau, 'Le droit international: bric-à-brac ou système?', 31 *Archives de Philosophie du Droit* (1986) 85.

2 On the putative 'decline' of the optional clause, see e.g. Gross, 'Compulsory Jurisdiction under the Optional Clause: History and Practice', in L. Damrosch (ed.), *The International Court of Justice at a Crossroads* (1987) 19.

490 EJIL 11 (2000), 489–519

there remain potentially significant lacunae within the law.[3] Rather, the concern is that with the proliferation of international courts and tribunals[4] and the rapid development of certain 'spheres' of international law, the international legal system is poised on the brink of a potentially irreversible process of fragmentation.[5] The apparent variegation of law-creating processes and agencies within the international system and the diffusion of decision-making powers among a wide variety of judicial or quasi-judicial institutions all dealing with largely discrete legal regimes, does suggest that international law may be losing its centre of gravity. If it does, we may face the problem, at some stage in the future, of no longer being able to speak about 'international law' as a singular or unitary phenomenon, but only the law as it applies in certain heteronomous fields (whether that be the law of armed conflict, the law of international trade or environmental law) or as applied by certain courts or tribunals. Whatever one's prognosis of the current situation, it is clear that many of these concerns are by no means new. International lawyers have always struggled with the difficulties of transcending the contractual paradigm of treaty law and of deriving 'general law' from the existence of legal obligation in conventional form, and the current debate only places a new spin on this old problem. The difference today is simply found in the supposition that we already have a coherent 'system' of law and that we are no longer climbing the mountain, so to speak, but poised at its summit looking down.

One particular area in which the potentiality for fragmentation is frequently identified is in the field of human rights. In recent years there has been a growing appreciation that the development of human rights norms and associated processes must necessarily be reflected in the forms and structures of general international law. The concepts of *erga omnes* obligations and *jus cogens* are prime examples of developments in the structure of international law whose recognition has been informed by an overriding concern for human rights.[6] The same may be said for the ILC's work in relation to state responsibility[7] and state succession,[8] and of the recent

[3] Cf. H. Lauterpacht, 'Some Observations on the Prohibition of Non Liquet and the Completeness of the Legal Order', *Symbolae Verzijl* (1958) 196; J. Stone, *Of Law and Nations* (1974) ch. 3.

[4] In the past 10 years, for example, the following bodies *inter alia* have begun work: the International Criminal Tribunal for Former Yugoslavia (1993); the International Criminal Tribunal for Rwanda (1995); the International Tribunal for the Law of the Sea (1996); the UN Compensation Commission (1991); the EFTA Court (1994); and the WTO Dispute Settlement Body and Appellate Body (1995). On the increased use of the ICJ, see e.g. Highet, 'The Peace Palace Hots Up: The World Court in Business Again?, 85 *AJIL* (1991) 646.

[5] See, e.g., Charney, 'The Implications of Expanding International Dispute Settlement Systems: The 1982 Convention on the Law of the Sea', 90 *AJIL* (1996) 69; and Guillaume, 'The Future of International Judicial Institutions', 44 *ICLQ* (1995) 848.

[6] Cf. *Barcelona Traction, Light and Power Case*, ICJ Reports (1970) 32, paras 33–34.

[7] See, e.g., the extension of state responsibility to govern 'authorized' private acts (*Costello-Roberts v. United Kingdom*, 19 EHRR (1998) 112) or for failure to properly protect individuals against abuse (*X and Y v. The Netherlands*, ECHR (1985) Series A, No. 91). See Crawford, 'Revising the Draft Articles on State Responsibility', 10 *EJIL* (1999) 435, at 439–440; and more equivocally Chinkin, 'A Critique of the Public/Private Dimension', 10 *EJIL* (1990) 387, at 393–395.

[8] See, e.g., Draft Articles on State Succession in Relation to Nationality, GAOR, 52nd Sess., Supp. No. 10 (A/52/10), chapter IV, section c.

state practice in the field of recognition[9] and intervention.[10] By the same token, the development of human rights norms through the medium of specific legal regimes has, at times, led to a tension as between the subject-neutral *lex generalis* on the one hand and the particular demands of human rights understood as a subordinate 'subject area' on the other. This may be perceived, most clearly, in the relationship between the general principles of treaty law (encapsulated in the Vienna Convention on the Law of Treaties) and the developing practice and doctrine relating specifically to human rights treaties.

It is often suggested that the general principles governing the application and effect of treaties need to be modified, or perhaps even discarded, when dealing with the specific category of human rights treaties.[11] One example of this tendency may be found in the Human Rights Committee's General Comment No. 24 in which it suggested that the classical rules on reservations embodied in the Vienna Convention were 'inappropriate' and 'inadequate' when dealing with reservations to the International Covenant on Civil and Political Rights, and that the task of determining their compatibility should rest with the Human Rights Committee itself.[12] Another example to the same effect may be found in the separate opinion of Judge Weeramantry in the case concerning the *Application of the Convention on the Prevention and Punishment of the Crime of Genocide*[13] (between Bosnia-Herzegovina and the Federal Republic of Yugoslavia). In that case, Judge Weeramantry pointed out that the question whether or not Bosnia-Herzegovina or Yugoslavia were parties to the Genocide Convention had to be answered, not simply by reference to principles governing ratification or accession, but by reference to what he understood as being the special characteristics of that Convention. He took the view that the Genocide Convention, like any 'humanitarian' treaty, did not represent an exchange of interests or benefits between contracting states, but rather embodied 'a commitment of the participating States to certain norms and values recognized by the international community'.[14] Since the Convention imposed no burdens on the participating states, and since it therefore 'transcended' the concept of state sovereignty, it could be regarded as subject to automatic succession.[15] Yugoslavia and Bosnia-Herzegovina

9 E.g., EC Guidelines on Recognition (1992). See generally Warbrick, 'Recognition of States: Part 2', 42 *ICLQ* (1993) 433.

10 E.g., NATO action in Kosovo. See generally Cassese, '*Ex iniuria ius oritur*: Are We Moving Towards International Legitimation of Forcible Humanitarian Countermeasures in the World Community?', 10 *EJIL* (1999) 23; Simma, 'NATO, the UN and the Use of Force: Legal Aspects', 10 *EJIL* (1999) 1.

11 The argument that certain categories of treaties must be treated in a distinctive way has, of course, been a long-standing point of debate. McNair argued in 1930, for example, that we need to 'free ourselves from the traditional notion that the instrument known as the treaty is governed by a single set of rules, however inadequate, and set ourselves to study the greatly differing legal character of the several kinds of treaties and to frame rules appropriate to the character of each kind'. McNair, 'The Functions and Differing Legal Character of Treaties', 11 *BYIL* (1930) 100, at 106. See also Jenks, 'State Succession in Respect of Law-Making Treaties', 29 *BYIL* (1952) 105.

12 General Comment No. 24 (52), UN Doc. CCPR/C/21/Rev.1/Add.6, para. 17.

13 ICJ Reports (1996) 595, at 645.

14 *Ibid*, at 645–646.

15 *Ibid*, at 649.

could therefore be treated as parties to the Convention whether or not they desired to be so regarded, and irrespective of the steps they may have taken to that end.

Whilst the views of Judge Weeramantry and the Human Rights Committee in each case have certainly attracted criticism,[16] they do partake of a continuing, and very live debate, as to the significance of the development of specific human rights treaty 'regimes' for general international law. At one level, this debate concerns the question whether such regimes can be regarded as creating autonomous, or self-supporting, legal orders that exist independently of general international law. At another level, it is concerned with the question whether human rights treaties may be regarded as being in the nature of a 'special category' within the general corpus of international law, and, if so, how that peculiarity should be given recognition. In either case, there are several underlying issues that inform any response including, for example, the characteristics of what we might choose to call 'legal development', and the nature of our assumptions concerning the general trajectory of legal doctrine.

2 Human Rights Treaties in International Law

In its most general sense, international legal doctrine is characteristically diffident as to the peculiarities of human rights conventions as a specific class of treaties. The international law of human rights, as a subject, is almost universally understood as a distinct subdiscipline of the broader, more general, and apparently subject-neutral, international law. Like other 'subdisciplines' — such as environmental law, economic law or the law of the sea — human rights law may embody certain assumptions and suppositions that demand special recognition. But even whilst affirming the 'peculiarities' of such subdisciplines, legal doctrine traditionally maintains a sense of the similitude of subject areas. This is particularly true in relation to those parts of international law that are regarded as 'structural' in nature: whether that be state responsibility, state succession, custom formation or treaty law. Indeed, for international law to retain an intellectual coherence, and for it to retain the idea that it is an homogeneous 'system', it must at once recognize the diversity of subject matter (and draw fully upon that diversity) but also resist the temptation to conclude thereby that there is no 'general' law.

It has to be recognized, however, that, given its 'decentralized' nature, international law is particularly susceptible to claims of 'special consideration' and that those claims may not always be easy to dismiss. This is particularly evident in the case of human

[16] As to the Human Rights Committee's General Comment, see, e.g., the observations of the UK, the US and France, 3 *IHRR* (1996) 261, at 265, 4 *IHRR* (1997) 6. The UK responded in the following terms: 'The United Kingdom does not ... believe that rules different from those foreshadowed by the International Court and in due course embodied in the Vienna Convention on the Law of Treaties are required to enable the international community to cope with reservations to human rights treaties. The correct approach is rather to apply the general rules relating to reservations laid down in the Vienna Convention in a manner which takes full account of the particular characteristics of the treaty in question.' Observations on General Comment No. 24, 3 *IHRR* (1996) 261, at 261–262, para. 4.

rights treaties and not simply because of the existence of dedicated mechanisms of monitoring or enforcement, but also because in such treaties the two elements of 'form' and 'function' appear to be fundamentally at odds with one another. On the one hand, the form in which the rights are expressed — the treaty — supposes that human rights are merely the incidental subject of a contractual bargain between states. Individual 'right-holders' are therefore simply the fortuitous beneficiaries of a regime that is otherwise concerned with promoting the rights and interests of states. The teleology of the regime on the other hand — focused as it is on individual or group 'human rights' — supposes that the treaties are quasi-constitutional in character. They seem to provide, in other words, a subtle or underlying mode of justification, or validation, for governmental claims to authority and legitimacy in international law.[17] It may be argued, after all, that, in the absence of a general theory of representation in international law,[18] it is only through its commitment to certain basic human rights standards that international law may be rescued from simply being the law of tyrants, slavers or pirates.

Each of these two understandings, however, works against the other: human rights treaties cannot simply be 'constitutional' insofar as they are constructed in the form of agreements between states (they do not in that sense precede those agreements, and exist only in relation to them). Third parties remain third parties, and states are bound only to the extent that they have formally registered their consent. By the same token, human rights treaties cannot simply be 'ordinary treaties', as they seem to be premised upon the idea that the rights pre-exist not only the treaties themselves,[19] but also explain or justify the competence of governments in relation to them. We seem to be faced, then, with a problem of semantics when we speak about this species of 'human rights treaties': are we, at any moment, referring to the fact that they are treaties, or to the fact that they instantiate human rights?[20]

[17] For an explicit defence of this idea, see, e.g., F. Teson, *A Philosophy of International Law* (1998). In brief, Teson argues in favour of a 'Kantian' approach to international law which he understands as entailing, among other things, that 'observance of human rights is a primary requirement to join the community of civilized nations under international law' (at 7).

[18] Allott complains that 'the consciousness-controlling activities of government ... ensured that sovereignty would be externalized into a society which was conceived as being a society containing only sovereigns, a society which would contain no theory of representation, which would leave obscure and unexplained the sense in which the people of the world might be virtually present in international society by reason of the participation of the state-societies'. P. Allott, *Eunomia: New Order for a New World* (1990) 303.

f. also Crawford, 'Democracy and International Law', 64 *BYbIL* (1993) 113.

[19] Human rights treaties characteristically speak of the 'recognition' of rights with the implication that those rights have some prior existence. This idea is made more explicit in the preamble to the International Covenant on Civil and Political Rights (1966) which declares, for example, that 'these rights derive from the inherent dignity of the human person'.

[20] This conflict is one that not only infects how we think of them as treaties, but also how we think of the human rights contained within them. Is, for example, a violation of an individual right to be determined by the extent to which it offends a naturalistic notion of 'human dignity', or by non-compliance with specifically defined legal obligations? Are we, in other words, able to speak about hunger or poverty as a violation of human rights *per se*, or only to the extent that it is linked to a failure to comply with specific conventional obligations? A similar disjunction between rights and obligations is apparent in cases where state obligations appear to exceed the 'naturalistic' content of the right concerned, e.g. in cases of reparation for violation of the right to life.

494 EJIL 11 (2000), 489–519

3 The Vienna Convention on the Law of Treaties

The diffidence of general international law as regards the 'speciality' of human rights treaties is well reflected in the terms of the Vienna Convention on the Law of Treaties. The Convention self-consciously attempts to enunciate principles of treaty law that are applicable to all types of treaty (whether they be bilateral, multilateral, law-making, contractual, dispositive or constitutive) and is concerned primarily with the instrument in which obligation is expressed, rather than with the content of those obligations.[21] It does not, therefore, differentiate in any explicit way between groups of treaties by reference to their subject matter (such as environmental law treaties, treaties of peace, commercial or trade treaties or treaties establishing boundaries or other territorial regimes), nor is any special mention made of the application of treaties to individuals.[22] Instead, 'flexibility' is built into the regime by means of liberal use of the qualification that the principles be applied by reference to 'the object and purpose' of the treaty concerned. In the case of Article 41(1)(b)(ii) concerning the mutual modification of multilateral treaties, or Article 58(1)(b)(ii) concerning the mutual suspension of such treaties, reference to the object and purpose of the treaties seems to be essential. In neither of these cases would it make much sense for two states to agree that they may suspend or modify a human rights treaty (apart from any other form of treaty) in their relations *inter se*, as the general standards of treatment would still pertain with respect to all other states. Mutual modification or suspension, in other words, would essentially be ineffective unless, and to the extent that, all other states parties were in agreement.

The one clear exception identified within the Vienna Convention regime seems to be Article 60(5) which provides that provisions relating to suspension following material breach 'do not apply to provisions relating to the protection of the human person contained in treaties of a humanitarian character'.[23] In practical terms, the rationale for this provision is undoubtedly clear: it would be entirely inappropriate to allow states parties to suspend the operation of a human rights treaty simply because one of their number has materially breached its terms. But whether this is because states would not have any specific legal interest in the default, or for some other reason (such as individuals being the innocent victims of the illegal act,[24] or because the interests of the international community are involved[25]) is less clear.

The one issue that has been recognized as causing problems in the context of treaty

[21] Cf. S. Rosenne, *Breach of Treaty* (1985) 4.

[22] See, e.g., Draft Article 66, Waldock, 'Third Report on the Law of Treaties', *Yearbook of the International Law Commission*, vol. II (1964) 57. See generally Schwelb, 'The Law of Treaties and Human Rights', in M. Reisman and B. Weston (eds), *Towards World Order and Human Dignity* (1976) 263, at 266–272.

[23] See also *Legal Consequences for States of the Continued Presence of South Africa in Namibia (South West Africa) Notwithstanding Security Council 276 (1970)*, Advisory Opinion, ICJ Reports (1971) 16, para. 101. See generally Schwelb, *supra* note 22, at 274–283.

[24] Sir H. Waldock, *Yearbook of the International Law Commission*, vol. I (1966) 63, para. 23.

[25] *Ibid*, at para. 68.

law is the question of reservations.[26] This is a matter that has occupied the International Law Commission for several years[27] and was the subject of an exchange of views between the Human Rights Committee on the one hand[28] and several states including the US, France, the UK and Germany on the other.[29] The full details of this debate are beyond the scope of the present paper, but the central problem is certainly of relevance. Article 20 of the Convention takes the view that there is no automatic requirement of unanimity as to the legitimacy of reservations and, in that regard, follows the position adopted by the ICJ in the *Reservations Case.*[30] Rather, it provides that 'an act expressing a State's consent to be bound by the treaty and containing a reservation, is effective as soon as at least one other contracting State has accepted the reservation'.[31] It states further that the acceptance of a reservation by another state 'constitutes the reserving State a party to the treaty *in relation to that other State*';[32] and that an objecting state may preclude, by express dissent, the entry into force of the treaty as between the objecting and the reserving state.[33] Leaving aside the question whether this scheme governs all reservations, or simply those that are contrary to the object and purpose of the treaty,[34] the picture this paints is one in which a state may be regarded as being party to a treaty in relation to some, but not necessarily all other, states parties. It also suggests that, where a state objects to a reservation, but is prepared to accept the reserving state as party to the treaty, the content of those

26 See, e.g., Higgins, 'Human Rights: Some Questions of Integrity', 52 *MLR* (1989) 1; Redgewell, 'Reservations to Treaties and Human Rights Committee General Comment No. 24 (52)', 46 *ICLQ* (1997) 390; Shelton, 'State Practice on Reservations to Human Rights Treaties', 1 *Canadian Human Rights Yearbook* (1983) 205; Coccia, 'Reservations to Multilateral Treaties on Human Rights', 15 *California Western International Law Journal* (1985) 1; L. Lijnzaad, *Reservations to UN Human Rights Treaties: Ratify and Ruin?* (1995).

27 See, e.g., Reports of Special Rapporteur Pellet, UN Docs A/CN.4/470, and Corr.1 (1995); A/CN.4/477 and Add.1 (1996); and A/CN.4/491 and Corr.1 (1998).

28 General Comment No. 24 (52), *supra* note 12.

29 *Supra* note 16.

30 *Reservations to the Convention on the Prevention and Punishment of the Crime of Genocide*, ICJ Reports (1951), at 23. The main distinction, however, is that the Vienna Convention regime gives states opposing a reservation the choice as to whether or not they wish to be regarded as bound in relation to the reserving state.

31 Article 20(4)(c).

32 Article 20(4)(a).

33 Article 20(4)(b).

34 This turns upon the perceived relationship between Articles 19 and 20 of the Vienna Convention and whether a single-stage or a two-stage test is to be employed. For the view that the latter is to be preferred, see Redgewell, *supra* note 26, at 404–405; Redgewell, 'Universality or Integrity? Some Reflections on Reservations to General Multilateral Treaties', 64 *BYbIL* (1993) 245, at 257; and Bowett, 'Reservations to Non-Restricted Multilateral Treaties', 48 *BYbIL* (1976–1977) 67. The two-stage test, while sound in theory, rests on the assumption that the compatibility of a reservation with the object and purpose of a treaty may be determined without any necessary input from states. The ILC, by contrast, had taken a more realistic view in stating in its commentary that Articles 16 and 17 (later 19 and 20) were to be read together 'because the legal effect of a reservation, when formulated, is dependent on its acceptance or rejection by the other States concerned'. Documents of the Conference, A/CONF.39/11/Add.2, at 23.

obligations may differ as regards different states parties.[35] This situation might be suitable in the context of a treaty providing, for example, for a specific tariff regime to be put in place, and in which one is able to distinguish clearly between obligations owed as regards one party, and those owed as regards another. But it makes remarkably little sense in the context of human rights treaties where, by and large, the content or extent of obligations does not vary according to which states are, or are not, party to the treaty, or indeed as to how many states are party.[36]

It may well be objected that the reservations regime, however incompatible in theory, is nonetheless a practical solution to the problem. Special Rapporteur Pellet, in his Second Report on Reservations to Treaties in 1994, takes exactly this position.[37] The regime of reservations, he asserts, is sufficiently flexible as to effectively cater for all forms of treaties, including, in that regard, human rights treaties, which themselves still seem to contain 'typically contractual clauses'.[38] There is a certain force to this argument. After all, even if a state is bound only with respect to some of the states parties, this will not affect the substance of the obligations assumed which are owed primarily to individuals within the jurisdiction and control of that state. It matters little, therefore, whether a state is party in relation to all other states parties, or simply just one.

This argument, however, only goes halfway: it deals well enough with the position of the reserving state, but does little to ensure the integrity of the treaty concerned.[39] To begin with, it would seem that the whole regime is premised upon the belief that the only relevant legal interests in question are those of the participating states, and that those interests may be effectively protected by either preventing the entry into force of the treaty as between the parties, or by the non-application of the provision to which the reservation applies.[40] If it is accepted, however, that states do not have an *individual* interest in the achievement of the purposes of the regime but only a *common* or *collective* interest (as the ICJ in the *Reservations Case* suggested[41]), it is doubtful whether that interest may be sufficiently preserved where the process is entirely taken up in the actions of individual states. Indeed, since the 'sanctioning effect' of

[35] This turns upon the question of severability. Cf. *Belilos v. Switzerland*, Series A, No. 132. See, Marks, 'Reservations Unhinged: The Belilos Case Before the European Court of Human Rights', 39 *ICLQ* (1990) 300.

[36] As Simma points out: 'In [the] case of human rights conventions, however, there is simply no contractual *quid pro quo* to withhold. There is, sociologically speaking, no interaction between the parties onto which reciprocity could lock. Reciprocal non-application of a reserved provision by another State Party would not only be absurd but also legally inadmissible. . . [S]ince every State Party is bound *vis-à-vis* every other State Party to perform the treaty obligations, a splitting up of such a treaty into pairs of bilateral contractual relations in respect of which the reciprocal alternation of the treaty standard envisaged by the Convention could operate, is impossible.' Simma, 'International Human Rights and General International Law: A Comparative Analysis', 4 *Collected Courses of the Academy of European Law* (1995) 153, at 181–182.

[37] A/CN.4/477/Add.1 (1996).

[38] *Ibid.*

[39] Cf. Higgins, 'The United Nations: Still a Force for Peace', 52 *MLR* (1989) 12.

[40] Article 21(3).

[41] See the text accompanying note 86 below.

opposability has little salience in the context of human rights treaties, this individualization of the process of objection will ensure that the effectiveness of a putatively impermissible reservation remains virtually unassailable unless all other states parties both object and specifically refuse to accept the reserving state as a party to the treaty.[42]

4 The Characteristics of Human Rights Treaties

In light of this apparent disjunction between the terms of general treaty law and the specific characteristics, or demands, of human rights treaties, it may be thought that we are, in reality, dealing with an issue that cannot simply be treated as a question of 'fine tuning' in the way that the ILC is dealing with the matter. Much as the ILC has wished to maintain the 'integrity' of general treaty law, it does seem that the overriding 'contractual' paradigm is largely (if not wholly) inappropriate in the case of human rights treaties. The extent to which that is true, however, depends first of all upon how the apparent 'peculiarity' of human rights treaties is expressed and understood, and what conclusions are to be drawn from it. There are, of course, a number of possibilities.

First, and most obviously, one might make the point that human rights treaties have, as their humanitarian ideal, the protection of the interests of individuals. This, however, is not sufficiently explanatory insofar as it casts the net rather too widely. Numerous treaties can be said to have such an objective including, not merely those treaties commonly regarded as 'human rights treaties', but also treaties such as the ILO conventions on labour rights,[43] 'humanitarian treaties' (the Geneva Conventions[44] and Protocols[45] and the Hague Regulations[46]), and treaties concerned with diplomatic or consular protection,[47] to name but a few. It is undoubtedly possible that

[42] The problem is further exacerbated when the role of supervisory institutions is taken into account. As the Human Rights Committee pointed out in its General Comment No. 24 (52), *supra* note 12, para. 1: 'It is important for States parties to know exactly what obligations they, and other States parties, have in fact undertaken. And the Committee, in the performance of its duties under either article 40 of the Covenant or under the Optional Protocols, must know whether a State is bound by a particular obligation or to what extent.' If a large number of states object to a reservation on the basis that they believe it to be incompatible with the object and purpose of the treaty, whether or not they wish the reserving state to be a party to the agreement *inter se*, the supervisory body will necessarily have to take a view on the question of the effect of that reservation. It is clear, irrespective of the precise legal competence of the supervisory body concerned, that leaving the determination of compatibility solely in the hands of states parties acting in an individual capacity, does little to clarify that process.

[43] E.g., ILO Convention (No. 87) Concerning Freedom of Association and Protection of the Right to Organize (1948); ILO Convention (No. 98) Concerning the Application of the Principles of the Right to Organize and to Bargain Collectively (1949); and ILO Convention (No. 122) Concerning Employment Policy (1964).

[44] Geneva Conventions I to IV (1949).

[45] Protocol I Concerning the Protection of Victims of International Armed Conflicts (1977); Protocol II Concerning the Protection of Victims of Non-International Armed Conflicts (1977).

[46] Hague Regulations of 1899 and 1907.

[47] E.g., Vienna Convention on Consular Relations (1963). See *Case Concerning Consular Rights of Detained Foreign Nationals*, Inter-American Court of Human Rights, Advisory Opinion, OC-16/99.

the category of 'human rights' treaties may be larger or smaller than specific designation might lead to suppose, but it is also apparent that in widening the scope, one is less able to construct an argument for special treatment. The same may be said of the argument that the peculiarity of human rights treaties is found in the fact that they provide for the recognition of individual legal 'rights'. Once again, it is clear that individual 'rights' — and more specifically 'rights of petition' — are recognized in a much wider range of treaties than simply those concerned strictly with 'human rights' (including, for example, Article 87(b) of the UN Charter, and Article 304 of the Peace Treaty of Versailles). Unless arguments as to the specificity of 'human rights treaties' as a category are entirely ill-conceived, it seems clear that neither of these characteristics alone sufficiently explains why 'human rights treaties', in particular, have been regarded as being of a special nature.

Those bodies that have come to recognize the specific characteristics of human rights treaties (included here are the International Court of Justice, the European Commission and Court of Human Rights, the Inter-American Court of Human Rights and the Human Rights Committee) have almost unanimously locked onto a single question: that of 'reciprocity' (or, more specifically, the lack of it).[48] The best, but not necessarily the most well-known, expression of this idea was that provided by the Inter-American Court of Human Rights in the *Effect of Reservations Case*:

> modern human rights treaties in general, and the American Convention in particular, are not multilateral treaties of the traditional type concluded to accomplish the reciprocal exchange of rights for the mutual benefit of the contracting States. Their object and purpose is the protection of the basic rights of individual human beings irrespective of their nationality, both against the State of their nationality and all other contracting States. In concluding these human rights treaties, the States can be deemed to submit themselves to a legal order within which they, for the common good, assume various obligations, not in relation to other States, but towards all individuals within their jurisdiction.[49]

It would be fair to say that the main point which stimulated the Court's approach in this regard was to contrast the Convention regime on the one hand with the standard principles governing diplomatic protection on the other. Whilst the principles of diplomatic protection are premised upon the idea that in seeking to protect its own nationals from the actions of third states, a state is in fact asserting its own rights,[50] the Inter-American Convention regime was quite different. Not only did it dispose of the relevance of nationality for the purpose of protection, but it was no longer concerned

[48] General Comment No. 24 of the Human Rights Committee notes, for example, that human rights treaties 'are not a web of inter-state exchanges of mutual obligations. They concern the endowment of individuals with rights. The principle of inter-state reciprocity has no place save perhaps in the limited context of reservations to declarations on the Committee's competence under Article 41.' General Comment No. 24 (52), *supra* note 12, para. 17. See generally A. Cançado Trinidade, *A Protecao International dos Direitos Humanos — Fundamentos Juridicos e Instrumentos Basicos* (1991) 10–12.

[49] *The Effect of Reservations on the Entry into Force of the American Convention on Human Rights (Arts 74 and 75)*, Advisory Opinion OC-2/82 of 24 September 1982, Inter-American Court of Human Rights (1982), Series A, No. 2, para. 30.

[50] *Mavrommatis Palestine Concessions Case (Jurisdiction)*, 1924 PCIJ Series A, No. 2, at 12.

exclusively with the 'rights of states'. This issue of non-reciprocity, therefore, seems to be the key to unlocking the puzzle of human rights treaties.

Even if the 'peculiarity' of human rights treaties is found in the idea of non-reciprocity, it is immediately apparent that many treaties that putatively fall within this category do not bear that characteristic. Certain treaties, such as the European Social Charter of 1963[51] and the Migrant Workers Convention, specifically premise the enjoyment of certain rights on the possession of nationality of one of the states parties and therefore reinforce the importance of reciprocity. In such cases, the question whether an individual is to enjoy a particular right is contingent upon the state of nationality becoming party to the treaty and therefore the rights of individuals are barely distinguishable from the rights of states. The same can be said for 'humanitarian' treaties — such as the Geneva Conventions of 1949 or their Additional Protocols — which are again premised upon a mutual acceptance of obligations on the part of the states concerned.[52] It would seem then, in speaking about non-reciprocal human rights regimes, we are speaking about a limited category of treaties whose purpose is to recognize and protect individual human rights in a way that is independent of the question of nationality, or of the acceptance of similar obligations by any other particular state party. Treaties that fall within this category presumptively include, among others, the International Covenant on Civil and Political Rights (1966),[53] the International Covenant on Economic, Social and Cultural Rights (1966),[54] the International Convention on the Rights of the Child (1989),[55] the International Convention on the Elimination of All Forms of Racial Discrimination (1965),[56] the Convention on the Elimination of All Forms of Discrimination Against Women (1979),[57] the Convention Against Torture and Other Cruel, Inhuman or Degrading Treatment or Punishment (1984),[58] the European Convention on Human Rights and Fundamental Freedoms (1950)[59] and the Inter-American Convention on Human Rights (1969).[60] Each of these treaties has its own special characteristics, but they do possess sufficient commonality in terms of structure and form to be treated as a relatively discrete category.

51 529 UNTS 89.

52 Common Article 2 of the Geneva Conventions (1949) provides that: 'Although one of the Powers in conflict may not be a party to the present Convention, the Powers who are parties thereto shall remain bound by it in their mutual relations. They shall furthermore be bound by the Convention in relation to said Power, if the latter accepts and applies the provisions thereof.'

53 999 UNTS 171.

54 993 UNTS 3.

55 28 ILM (1989) 1456.

56 660 UNTS 195.

57 19 ILM (1979) 33.

58 24 ILM (1985) 535.

59 213 UNTS 221.

60 9 ILM (1981) 59.

500 EJIL 11 (2000), 489–519

5 The Concept of the Treaty: Consent and Reciprocity

It has to be said that the idea of a non-reciprocal 'treaty' does appear, on the face of it, to be a contradiction in terms. In their simplest form, treaties are conceived primarily in terms of an analogy with contracts in municipal law[61] — that is, as consensual arrangements instituting, through the medium of legal rights and duties, a reciprocal exchange of goods or benefits.[62] If that is the case the claim to non-reciprocity on the part of certain human rights treaties suggests that they are either an entirely novel form of treaty, or perhaps not treaties at all. Such a conclusion, however, is dependent upon the extent to which reciprocity is understood as a critical element of treaty law, and upon how that reciprocity is conceptualized.

If one turns to the Vienna Convention on the Law of Treaties for advice, there is no obvious answer as to the role or importance of reciprocity. The Convention simply defines a treaty (in Article 2) as 'an international agreement concluded between states in written form and governed by international law'. Although one may read much into the idea of an 'agreement',[63] no explicit mention is made either of the notion of reciprocity or that of 'consent' which might otherwise be thought to underlie the idea of a 'treaty'. A reading of the later Articles of the Vienna Convention, however, suggests that both such elements are indeed central to the definition.

First of all, there seems to be no doubt that, according to the Convention, the 'agreement' is constituted in a mutual expression of consent. Articles 11–14 define the means by which the consent of a state to be bound by a treaty may be expressed and 'consent' is deemed central to the putative invalidity of the treaty (Articles 48–51), its termination (Article 54), and for the assumption of rights and obligations on the part of third states (Article 34). What is critical, however, is not simply that that consent is expressed, but that it is expressed in a context of 'mutuality': that, in other words, it takes on a synallagmatic form. Even if one accepts that unilateral declarations may create legally binding obligations (whether or not *erga omnes*),[64] it is clear that the idea of an 'agreement' within the terms of the Convention is not constituted in the acts of individual states. If otherwise, the idea of 'third states' would be literally impossible to conceive, and the notion of mutual modification rendered

[61] See generally H. Lauterpacht, *Private Law Sources and Analogies of International Law* (1927) 155–180; and J. Brierly, *The Law of Nations* (6th ed., 1963) 317–327. R. Jennings and A. Watts, *Oppenheim's International Law*, vol. I (8th ed.) 877, defines treaties as 'agreements, of a contractual character, between States, or organizations of States, creating legal rights and obligations between the parties'.

[62] Bernhardt defines a treaty as 'a consensual agreement between two or more subjects of international law intended to be and considered by the parties as binding and containing rules of conduct under international law for at least one (normally for all) of the parties'. Bernhardt, 'Treaties', in R. Bernhardt (ed.), *Encyclopedia of Public International Law*, vol. VII (1984) 459, at 460.

[63] An 'agreement' would naturally appear to represent a concurrence of opinion or belief as between two or more persons in relation to some fact or course of action.

[64] See, e.g., *Nuclear Tests Case (Australia v. France; New Zealand v. France)*, ICJ Reports (1974), at 253; *Military and Paramilitary Activities in and against Nicaragua*, ICJ Reports (1986), at 131, para. 259; *Frontier Dispute Case*, ICJ Reports (1986) 554, at 573; and *Border and Transborder Armed Actions Case*, ICJ Reports (1988) 105–106, para. 94. See generally Franck, 69 *AJIL* (1975) 612; Rubin, 'The International Legal Effects of Unilateral Declarations', 71 *AJIL* (1977) 1; Macdonald and Hough, 'The Nuclear Tests Case Revisited', 20 *German Yearbook of International Law* (1977) 337.

meaningless. In this context, the principle *pacta sunt servanda* must mean not just that 'promises shall be kept',[65] as is so often assumed, but more specifically and literally that 'agreements shall be followed'. It is, in other words, the multi-party, or relational, dimension of a *pactum* that is central to the assumption of obligations in treaty law.

If treaties can only really be understood as 'agreements' between mutually consenting parties, it does not necessarily follow that they are to be regarded as 'reciprocal'.[66] Indeed, it is apparent that as explanatory mediums the concepts of reciprocity and consent do not necessarily pull in the same direction. As Sandel has pointed out, the morality of any contract or agreement can be understood by reference to 'two related yet distinguishable ideals': one being the ideal of autonomy, which understands its morality in terms of the voluntary character of the transaction, the other being the ideal of reciprocity which understands its morality as being dependent upon the underlying fairness of the exchange.[67] Sandel argues that:

> Each ideal suggests a different basis for contractual obligation. From the standpoint of autonomy, a contract's moral force derives from the fact of its voluntary agreement ... The ideal of reciprocity, on the other hand, derives contractual obligation from the mutual benefits of cooperative arrangements. Where autonomy points to the contract itself as the source of obligation, reciprocity points through the contract to an antecedent moral requirement to abide by fair arrangements, and thus implies an independent moral principle by which the fairness of an exchange may be assessed.[68]

Whilst theoretically distinct, each account of obligation exposes the incompleteness of the other: an emphasis on consent will potentially lead to one being bound by terms that are unfair; and an emphasis on reciprocity will potentially lead to one being bound in ways that one did not choose. Consent, therefore, may on occasion be used as an argument to counter a claim to lack of reciprocity; and reciprocity (fairness) may, on occasion, be used as an argument to counter a claim to a lack of consent. Consent and reciprocity are not, in that sense, mutually reinforcing, and indeed may supplant one another for the purposes of determining the presence of obligation in particular circumstances.

Returning to the Vienna Convention, then, it would appear that the predominance of mutual consent in the construction of a valid treaty necessitates the marginalization of 'material' reciprocity as a condition *sine qua non*. Indeed, it is clear that

[65] Thirlway comments, in relation to the *Nuclear Tests Case*, that: 'The rule of *pacta sunt servanda* is based on a very fundamental idea or principle, and it may be that that fundamental idea can justify attaching legally binding effect to something which, lacking two-sidedness, is not a *pactum*; but "good faith" is perhaps not the best name for it.' Thirlway, 'The Law and Procedure of the International Court of Justice 1960–1989, Part One', 60 *BYIL* (1989) 1, at 9.

[66] It should be noted that there is a difference between two states simply owing obligations to one another within the framework of a legal instrument and those obligations taking on a form of reciprocity that makes the effect of one conditional upon performance of the other.

[67] Schwarzenberger argues, however, that reliance upon reciprocity merely gives a legal system the appearance of being grounded in justice whilst obscuring the powers behind and within the system: Schwarzenberger, 'Jus Pacis ac Belli? Prolegomena to a Sociology of International Law', 37 *AJIL* (1943) 460, at 478.

[68] Sandel, *Liberalism and the Limits of Justice* (1982) 106. See generally C. Fried, *Contract as Promise* (1981); and P. Atiyah, *The Rise and Fall of Freedom of Contract* (1979).

the Convention does not invoke any concept of 'consideration' or 'cause' for the purpose of determining the obligatory effect of treaties. Such an understanding is reflected in general doctrine: it is possible, after all, to conceive of treaties in which one state simply agrees to do something with no substantive or formal *quid pro quo*. The unconditional cession of territory from one state to another by means of treaty might be a good example, as indeed may be the conclusion of a treaty of peace. In such cases, states will assume an obligation to undertake a certain course of action not in a conditional sense — as being dependent upon the actions or omissions of other states parties — but in the sense of a simple promise made in a context of mutuality.[69] That being the case, the constituents of an 'agreement', therefore, do not seem to be contingent upon the content of the instrument which may, or may not, provide for a mutual exchange of goods or benefits. Rather, the constituents are simply formal and found in the expression of a concurrent and mutual act of will. It is noticeable, in that respect, that the Vienna Convention makes no mention of the old category of 'unequal treaties' — treaties that are, in one form or another, 'unfair' or which lack real reciprocity — and provides for no 'escape' from obligations by reason of their content alone.[70] The one exception, here, is of course where the content of the treaty conflicts with a peremptory norm of general international law,[71] but such cases are regarded as exceptional (the content of *jus cogens* itself being unclear). By the same token, reciprocity may enter the equation at the point of determining whether breach by one party of an agreement will entitle the other to suspend the agreement,[72] but that, by definition, is not an issue that goes to the heart of what constitutes a treaty in the first place.

Whilst it may be concluded, therefore, that treaties are not necessarily marked by any form of 'reciprocal exchange' of goods or benefits, the importance placed upon the 'mutuality' of consent suggests that some form of reciprocity might nevertheless be relevant. As we have dealt with the notion thus far, it has been understood in terms of a material exchange of goods or benefits (as, in other words, a form of 'consideration'). Reciprocity, however, can also be understood in other ways. It may, for example, be understood by reference to the political, psychological or sociological interests that underlie the agreement. In this context, it would presumably always be possible to identify mutual interests in the making of a treaty, whether or not the content of the treaty is such as to leave one state in a better position than the other. The importance placed upon consent, after all, assumes that states pursue their interests primarily by means of explicit intentional acts and may, for sundry reasons, accept through consent binding international obligations that restrict their future freedom of action.

69 As the ICJ noted in the *South West Africa Case* (Second Phase), ICJ Reports (1966) 32: 'a legal right or interest need not necessarily relate to anything material or "tangible", and can be infringed even though no prejudice of a material kind has been suffered.'

70 Treaties procured by the threat or use of force may be regarded as 'unfair', but their effect, according to Article 51 of the Vienna Convention, is to nullify the presence of consent. They are not, therefore, treaties rendered null as a result of coercion, but simply not treaties at all.

71 Article 53 of the Vienna Convention on the Law of Treaties (1969).

72 *Ibid*, Article 60.

To say then that states may consent to matters that are not in their own interest (whether in the short, medium or long term) is to say either that they have not properly consented or that they are simply acting irrationally. An emphasis on consent, after all, seems to prioritize a form of purposive rationality, and purposive rationality supposes that treaties are expressive of a mutuality of state interests.

Leaving aside the two understandings of reciprocity outlined above (one concerned with the material fairness of the exchange, the other by the psychological content of 'agreeing') there is a third understanding of reciprocity that corresponds more closely to its ordinary usage in legal doctrine.[73] As Simma points out, 'as a sociological category, motivations prompted by the expectation of reciprocity should clearly be distinguished from reciprocity as an objective aspect of a given legal relationship'.[74] Reciprocity in this third sense represents the logical legal framework of the contract. It is, in that sense, expressive of a mutual, but conditional, exchange of legal obligations in which the possession of rights and obligations of one party are linked to (and perhaps dependent upon) those of the other party.[75] If a state assumes rights or obligations under the terms of a treaty, it is supposed that it must assume them in relation to another legal person, and that other legal person must be a party to the agreement (as otherwise the *pacta tertiis* principle would have little salience). This 'legal reciprocity' assumes, in other words, a dyadic or relational framework of rights and obligations that binds contracting parties only and exclusively as regards other contracting parties (leaving aside the possibility that third states may be assigned and assume rights and obligations in certain limited circumstances).[76]

The relational framework set up by this idea of legal reciprocity can be understood most clearly in bilateral terms according to which one party's rights and obligations are directly linked to those of all other states parties *ut singuli*. It is only by reason of this structure that one is able to speak of the bilateral suspension or modification within the framework of a multilateral treaty,[77] and to the acceptance of reservations by some, but not all, treaty parties. The logic of reciprocity, however, derives not so much from the nature of treaty relations, *per se*, but from the apparent imperatives of a decentralized international system. As Simma has noted:

> As long as the international legal order lacks a centralized enforcement machinery and thus

73 See, e.g., Simma, who points out that '[t]o recognize that in the case of a human rights treaty States parties do not exchange any tangible benefits is one thing. But then to assert that such absence of factual, or "sociological" reciprocity, as it were, leads to the absence of reciprocal legal rights and duties proper is quite another matter. By no means is the second claim a necessary conclusion from the first.' Simma, 'From Bilateralism to Community Interest', *Hague Recueil* (1994) 369.

74 Simma, 'Reciprocity', in R. Bernhardt (ed.), *Encyclopedia of Public International Law*, vol. 7 (1984) 400.

75 Cf. Ago, who makes the more extensive claim that there was always 'a correlation between a legal obligation, on the one hand, and a subjective right, on the other': Ago, Second Report, *Yearbook of the International Law Commission*, vol. II (1970) 192.

76 Simma, *supra* note 73, at 400–401, states that: 'From a purely formal point of view, reciprocity governs every international agreement, independently of its content, and consequently underlies the rules concerning the conclusion and entry into force of treaties, and their application, termination, amendment and modification.'

77 See, e.g., Article 58 of the Vienna Convention on the Law of Treaties (1969).

> has to live with autodetermination and self-help, reciprocity will remain the principle leitmotiv, a constructive, mitigating and stabilizing force, the importance of which can hardly be overestimated.[78]

It is only by reason of reciprocity, therefore, that states will be able to participate in international relations without exposing themselves unduly to the risks involved with non-compliance on the part of other states:[79] it provides the means, in other words, by which states may effectively 'police' those obligations by means of self-help.

In light of the evident importance of reciprocity within general international law, to suggest that certain treaty relations exist which are not premised upon reciprocity appears not only to be a denial of the pertinence of general treaty rules, but also a signal exception to the working suppositions of international law. It would, in particular, be suggestive either of the idea that international law has begun to develop beyond the confines of its own anarchical premises,[80] or that the development of specific regimes has occurred in a partially independent way. In either case, the consequences are significant for the way in which international law as a whole is understood.

6 Reciprocity in the Context of Human Rights Treaties

As has been suggested thus far, the issue of reciprocity seems to present a particular problem when examining the category of human rights treaties. On the one hand, we are presented with a recurrent claim that principles of treaty law should be modified or set aside by reference to the putative non-reciprocal character of human rights treaties, whilst, on the other, we are faced with the idea that legal reciprocity is in reality a constitutive element of treaty relations (or at least the dominant paradigm for those relations). If some sense is to be made of this, therefore, it would seem that there is a need to strategically revisit some of the landmark cases in which the argument as to non-reciprocity began to emerge.

The first, and certainly most influential, case dealing with the application and effect of reservations to 'humanitarian' treaties was the ICJ's Advisory Opinion in the *Reservations Case* of 1951.[81] In that case, the Court placed considerable emphasis upon what it saw to be the 'special nature' of the Genocide Convention:

78 Simma, *supra* note 73, at 400. And further: 'As a horizontal legal system, international law rests upon the logic of reciprocity in its entirety. Reciprocity is at work not only behind the long-established 'traffic rules' of routine international relations but also with equal force behind the legal attempts both to curtail the extremes of power politics and to organize international cooperation for human welfare, irrespective of the political and ideological antagonisms that divide the contemporary world.'

79 As it is put in *The Christina* [1938] AC 485: 'each ... State within the community of nations accepting some subtraction from its full sovereignty in return for similar concessions on the side of others.'

80 For the view that 'reciprocity' marks out a transitional phase in the development of a legal order (from bilateral- to system-level analysis), see E. Decaux, *La Reciprocite en droit international* (1980) 9.

81 *Reservations to the Convention on the Prevention and Punishment of the Crime of Genocide*, ICJ Reports (1951) 23.

> In such a Convention the contracting States do not have any interests of their own; they merely have, one and all, a common interest, namely, the accomplishment of those high purposes which are the *raison d'être* of the convention. Consequently in a convention of this type one cannot speak of individual advantages or disadvantages to States, or of the maintenance of a perfect contractual balance between rights and duties.[82]

In the circumstances, therefore, the Court was led to modify the general rule of unanimity as regards the permissibility of reservations[83] and substitute, in its place, a rule that allowed states to be considered party to the Convention even in cases where another state may have objected to a reservation.[84] The precise rationale for this was, apparently, that:

> The object and purpose of the Genocide Convention imply that it was the intention of the General Assembly and of States which adopted it that as many States as possible should participate. The complete exclusion from the Convention of one or more States would not only restrict the scope of its application, but would detract from the authority of the moral and humanitarian principles which are its basis.[85]

What is immediately apparent from the extracts quoted above is that the implications of the first statement are not entirely borne out in the solution proposed by the Court. If it is to be said that 'one cannot speak of individual advantages or disadvantages', or of the maintenance of a 'perfect contractual balance' in the context of the Genocide Convention, it may seem surprising that a state could be considered party to the treaty in relation to some, but not all, states parties. Surely, if the interest is of a 'common' or 'collective' nature, then the question whether a state is, or is not, a party to the treaty should be for the 'collective' to determine (and not states *ut singuli*). The logical response may be that in employing the characteristic liberal methodology of international law, the only means of determining the content of the 'collective interest' is to seek the views of individual states parties and build up a probabilistic picture from their response. But even then it is hard to justify why one or two objecting states should be able to determine their own position in circumstances in which there is a general presumption that the reserving state should indeed be regarded as a party to the treaty. The 'contractual balance', therefore, seems to have been reintroduced

[82] *Ibid.*

[83] The League of Nations took the view that the validity of a reservation depended upon acceptance by all contracting parties. See, e.g., 'Report of League of Nations Committee of Experts for the Progressive Codification of International Law', 8 LNOJ (1927) 880, at 881.

[84] The Court suggested that the following principles should apply (at 15): 'that a State which has made and maintained a reservation which has been objected to by one or more of the parties to the Convention but not by others, can be regarded as being a party to the Convention if the reservation is compatible with the object and purpose of the Convention; otherwise that State cannot be regarded as being a party to the Convention. [T]hat if a party to the Convention objects to a reservation which it considers to be incompatible with the object and purpose of the Convention, it can in fact consider that the reserving State is not a party to the Convention. [T]hat if, on the other hand, a party accepts the reservation as being compatible with the object and purpose of the Convention, it can in fact consider that the reserving State is a party to the Convention.' The origins of the principles established by the Court are to be found in the policy adopted by the Pan-American Union in 1932, see *Reservations to Multilateral Conventions*, UN Doc. A/1372, 11.

[85] *Ibid.*

into the equation as a result of a palpable lack of epistemic access to 'collective interests' when utilizing a methodology that begins and ends with individual states.[86]

The solution proposed by the ICJ in the *Reservations Case* and, indeed, that assumed later by the ILC in drafting Article 20 of the Vienna Convention, clearly does not sit very easily with its description of the special characteristics of the Genocide Convention itself. In fact, there is a case for saying that the first passage (concerning the absence of 'individual State interests') is largely redundant. After all, the argument that unanimity is no longer a prerequisite for determining the validity of a reservation could simply be achieved by recognizing that the 'object and purpose of the treaty' spoke in favour of universal participation, and that in turn dictated a presumption of conformity. This is not assisted in any material way by denying the fact of reciprocity or indeed by identifying the existence of a 'common' or 'collective' rather than an 'individual interest'. It is simply a particular construction given to the fact of silence.

In light of these points, an alternative explanation for the position of the Court in this case seems to be necessary. The best explanation, in fact, seems to draw less upon the 'special' characteristics of the Genocide Convention and more upon the mechanisms for enforcement found within it. Unlike the other human rights treaties referred to above, the Genocide Convention does not envisage enforcement (or supervision) by means of a dedicated institution. Rather, Article IX of the Genocide Convention explicitly provides that:

> Disputes between the Contracting Parties relating to the interpretation, application or fulfilment of the present Convention, including those relating to the responsibility of a State for genocide . . . shall be submitted to the International Court of Justice at the request of any parties to the dispute.

Since the Convention specifically lays down procedures for 'dispute resolution' (using that idea in its proper sense), and since it is in respect of Article IX that reservations are most frequently attached,[87] it does indeed make sense to suggest that two states may be regarded as parties to the Convention, but not necessarily parties *inter se*. All that would follow from this is that the states parties concerned would not be able to rely upon the Genocide Convention in order to found the jurisdiction of the

86 The consequential relativism inherent in this position is not merely accidental. In fact, it is expressive of the classic paradox of an individualist methodology that infects much of international law: without any authoritative means of determining who is right, we must either assume that everyone is (relativism), or that no one is (scepticism). Since 'law', in a sense, demands an answer, relativism appears the only option. But, as with all relativist positions, the formulation contains a fatal flaw, namely, that we assume that the quality of being 'right' is more than simply an individual preference and that it is tied, in some significant respect, to the views of the relevant community (an 'epistemic community' perhaps). Unfortunately, however, within the framework of a liberal methodology, the voice of that community will virtually always remain inaudible, and we can but only assume that it exists.

87 Reservations to Article IX have been made by Albania, Algeria, Argentina, Bahrain, Bangladesh, China, India, Malaysia, Morocco, the Philippines, Rwanda, Singapore, Spain, the USA, Venezuela, Vietnam and Yemen.

ICJ in case of dispute.[88] If this is the explanation, however, it is explicitly premised upon some idea of reciprocity, at least in the context of dispute resolution.

It would seem, then, that if the issue of non-reciprocity does have salience in relation to 'human rights' or 'humanitarian' treaties, it is not in the manner laid down by the ICJ in the *Reservations Case*, nor is it best demonstrated by a treaty whose only form of 'supervision' is that rendered by the ICJ.[89] The case is of importance, however, insofar as it highlights two further questions that need to be addressed: first, if the logic of non-reciprocity *is* taken at face value, what would this suggest for the question of reservations? And, secondly, to what extent do provisions for 'dispute resolution',[90] and more generally for international supervision and enforcement, serve to deny this pretension of non-reciprocity? Those two issues have themselves been the subject of further deliberation in the context of regional human rights treaties, and the answers provided have been startlingly different from that proposed by the ICJ.

A *Non-Reciprocity and Reservations: The Effect of the* Reservations Case

An answer to the first issue — the issue of reservations — was provided by the Inter-American Court of Human Rights in 1982 when it was called upon to determine the effect of a reservation upon the date of a state's accession to the Inter-American Convention on Human Rights.[91] The approach of the Court to this issue was far more consistent as regards the logic of non-reciprocity than that of the ICJ. But even here, some of its conclusions may be questioned. The Court, taking its cue from the European Commission[92] and the ICJ[93] before it, indicated not only that the treaty did not embody a 'reciprocal exchange of rights for the mutual benefit of the contracting parties', but also that in ratifying the treaty states submitted themselves 'to a legal order within which they, for the common good, assume various obligations, not in

88 As was pointed out by the ICJ in the *Case Concerning the Legality of the Use of Force* (*Yugoslavia v. Canada*), 2 June 1999, para. 19: 'the Court has repeatedly stated "that one of the fundamental principles of its Statute is that it cannot decide a dispute between States without the consent of those States to its jurisdiction" (*East Timor*, Judgment, ICJ Reports (1995) 101, para. 26); and ... the Court can therefore exercise jurisdiction only between States parties to a dispute who not only have access to the Court but also have accepted the jurisdiction of the Court, either in general form or for the individual dispute concerned.' Ironically enough, this would mean that, by objecting to a reservation to Article IX (concerning the jurisdiction of the ICJ), a state would in fact affirm the effectiveness of the reservation.

89 This is particularly important if one is to take seriously the idea that human rights treaties are constitutive of quasi-independent 'legal regimes'. See the text accompanying notes 122–125.

90 A similar provision is found in Article 22 of the International Convention on the Elimination of All Forms of Racial Discrimination (1965). Article 29 of the Convention on the Elimination of All Forms of Discrimination Against Women (1979) and Article 30 of the Convention Against Torture similarly provide for submission of disputes to arbitration.

91 *The Effect of Reservations on the Entry into Force of the American Convention (Arts 74 and 75)*, Advisory Opinion OC–2/82, Inter-American Court of Human Rights (1982), Series A, No. 2.

92 *Austria v. Italy (Pfunders Case)*, 11 January 1961, 4 *Yearbook of the European Convention on Human Rights* (1961) 116.

93 *Reservations to the Convention on the Prevention and Punishment of the Crime of Genocide*, ICJ Reports (1951) 23.

relation to other States, but towards all individuals within their jurisdiction'.[94] The rights involved, therefore, were the rights of individuals, not of other states, and the framework within which they are protected was one of a 'regime' or 'legal order', and not simply a relation in the nature of a bilateral agreement.

As a result of these considerations, the Court concluded, in contrast to the ICJ before it, that it would be 'manifestly unreasonable'[95] to suggest that Article 20(4) of the Vienna Convention applied with the effect of conditioning the entry into force of the American Convention for a particular state upon the acceptance of its reservation by other contracting states.[96] It pointed out that '[a] treaty which attaches such great importance to the protection of the individual ... can hardly be deemed to have intended to delay the treaty's entry into force until at least one other State is prepared to accept the reserving State as a party'.[97] The presumption must, therefore, be one of the conformity of reservations, and the fact of silence interpreted (perhaps) as tacit consent.[98]

The approach ultimately adopted by the Inter-American Court does seem to be far more consistent with the idea of non-reciprocity in the sense that a state's capacity to partake of the regime is not to be conditioned upon its acceptance by other states parties. It is undoubtedly controversial, however, insofar as it seems to suggest that the act of ratification is in the nature of a unilateral act on the part of each 'contracting' state and that other states, therefore, have no legal interest in the nature or quality of that act. It should be pointed out, furthermore, that in denying the relevance of Article 20(4), the Court also seems to deny the relevance of Article 21 concerning the opposability of a reservation. If a state can become party to the Convention entirely independently of the views of other contracting states, it makes little sense then to suggest that the reservation may be opposable. The underlying idea, of course, is that the regime is a strictly non-relational one (or at least only relational as between states and individuals).

The first obvious drawback to the Court's approach in relation to reservations is that the process of acceptance of, or objection to, reservations has a dual function: it

94 *Supra* note 91, para. 30.

95 *Ibid*, at para. 34.

96 Article 20(4)(c) provides that an act expressing a state's consent to be bound by a treaty and containing a reservation 'is effective as soon as at least one other contracting state has accepted the reservation'. Article 20(5) indicates, in addition, that a reservation is automatically considered to have been accepted by a state if it raises no objection by the end of a period of 12 months after notification.

97 *Supra* note 89, para. 34.

98 It is evident that, in reaching this conclusion, the Court was not simply extemporizing loosely on the nature of the American Convention but was, in fact, faced with an apparent textual conflict between two different provisions. On the one hand, Article 75 of the Convention provided that '[t]his Convention shall be subject to reservations only in conformity with the provisions of the Vienna Convention on the Law of Treaties', whilst, on the other hand, Article 74(2) provided that the Convention should enter into force 'on the date of the deposit of [the] instrument of ratification'. In light of Article 20 of the Vienna Convention — which suggests that acceptance of a reservation by at least one state party is necessary for the reserving state to become party to the treaty — the only way of reconciling the two provisions was by qualifying the sense of one or other provision. That the Court chose to qualify Article 75 and to exclude, thereby, the applicability of Article 20 of the Vienna Convention is nonetheless significant.

both preserves the rights and interests of other states parties within the contractual arrangement, whilst simultaneously protecting the integrity of that agreement as a whole. In many treaties these two elements are indivisible in the sense that the agreement is wholly constituted by reference to the legal interests of each individual state party. In human rights treaties, by contrast, these two elements are relatively discrete. The point is, however, that in dispensing with the requirement that reservations be accepted or rejected by other contracting states, the permissibility of a reservation may thereby go entirely unchallenged, and, if so, the integrity of the treaty may ultimately be put at risk. This is reinforced by the fact that the jurisdiction of the Court — which might otherwise concern itself with the compatibility of reservations — is based upon consent.[99] In the absence of a declaration by a reserving state accepting the jurisdiction of the Court, the only body capable of effectively determining the compatibility of a reservation with the object and purpose of the Convention would be the Commission — and the Commission, of course, has no specific competence in relation to the interpretation or application of the Convention.[100]

Much as this drawback is of significance, it should not be overplayed. It is clear, after all, that the 'sanctioning' effect of the Vienna Convention regime itself is barely evident in the case of human rights treaties. If the only consequence of entering a putatively impermissible reservation is that one or two other states refuse to recognize the reserving state as party to the treaty,[101] there is no reason to suppose that a (non-binding) recommendation of the Inter-American Commission would be of any less significance. Indeed, it would be true to say that the Commission is less likely to be concerned with the political fall-out of declaring a reservation incompatible than would be individual states, and, indeed, is more likely to deal with reservations in a more systematic manner. The formal legal incapacity of the Commission, like that of other human rights bodies (including, here, the Human Rights Committee), should not itself be seen as any great impediment to their ability to express views as to the compatibility of reservations.[102] After all, it would be entirely open for reserving states to ignore those views, as indeed it would for them to ignore the views of other individual states parties.

The main problem arising from the Court's approach in this case concerns the question of enforcement or supervision. If states have no 'legal interest' in who may

[99] Article 62 of the Inter-American Convention on Human Rights (1969).

[100] The Inter-American Court has affirmed that 'recommendations' of the Commission do not have 'the character of an obligatory judicial decision for which the failure to comply would generate State responsibility': *Caballero Delgado and Santana Case*, Inter-American Court of Human Rights, 3 IHRR (1996) 548, 17 *HRLJ* 24.

[101] As is pointed out by Hampson ('Working Paper on Reservations to Human Rights Treaties', UN Doc. E/CN.4/Sub.2/1999/28, para. 10): 'When one considers the number of multilateral treaties to which many States are party and the number of potential other parties, it would be surprising if States were meticulous in examining the reservations of other States in order to indicate a view. Silence seems to be a common response. It would seem unlikely to be usually the result of conscious deliberation on the part of other high contracting parties.'

[102] Cf. General Comment No. 24 (52), *supra* note 12.

510 EJIL 11 (2000), 489–519

become a party to the Convention, does it follow that they similarly have no direct legal interest in compliance? The underlying issue, of course, is whether the characterization of the Convention as a non-reciprocal, or an 'objective', regime is simply a generalized appraisal of the Convention, or true in all its facets. The standard answer to the question is, on the face of it, relatively simple. Not only does the phraseology of the Convention make clear that implementation is a matter of concern to all states parties,[103] but, more importantly, Article 45 explicitly provides for an inter-state communication procedure. This would seem to suggest that even if states assume obligations primarily in relation to individuals within their jurisdiction, the performance of those obligations is still a matter of legal concern to other states parties. The fact that Article 45 is an optional procedure does not detract from this argument insofar as Article 45 does not purport to *establish* the rights and duties of states in their relations *inter se*, but rather merely delimits the competence of the Commission in relation to those (pre-existent) rights and duties. It would seem, then, that the legal interest that states parties possess in relation to compliance is not simply an indirect one, in the sense of flowing from a concern to ensure that 'promises are kept'. If that were the case, there would be no overriding reason why states from other regions, and other non-state parties, should not be competent to submit communications. Rather, it is a more direct legal interest that draws upon the fact that this is a treaty regime embodying, in some form or other, rights and obligations that may lead to the legal engagement of one state party by another.[104] Ultimately, therefore, it would seem that the critical point around which the discussion of reciprocity turns is that of 'enforcement' and the characteristics of the 'supervisory' regimes instituted within human rights treaties.

B *Non-Reciprocity and International Supervision: The Case of* Austria v. Italy

Attempting to identify the precise nature of human rights 'supervisory' systems, beyond merely recognizing that they are directed towards the 'protection of the human person', has always been problematic. Various terms are usually employed to describe such systems — including 'implementation', 'monitoring', 'supervision' and 'enforcement' — and all tend to be used interchangeably without any sense that they have distinct connotations for the role of the organ concerned.[105] If there is a common understanding, however, it is that the processes involved are largely indifferent to the rights or interests of other contracting states — they are not, in that sense, concerned

[103] See, e.g., Article 27(3) which requires a state availing itself of the right to suspend the guarantees to inform other states parties of that fact.

[104] Such an idea is doubly reinforced by the fact that the competence of the Commission in relation to inter-state communications is premised upon a mutuality of consent. Article 45(2).

[105] It might be said that, whilst the terms 'monitoring' or 'supervision' suggest that the focus of activity is necessarily upon what happens within each national jurisdiction, 'implementation' and 'enforcement', by contrast, focus on the activities of the supervisory organ. Similarly, whilst 'implementation' suggests something in the nature of a cooperative endeavour, 'enforcement', and to a lesser extent 'monitoring' and 'supervision', are concerned more with taking recalcitrant states to task.

with the vindication of the rights of states party to the treaty concerned, but merely with the fulfilment of the obligations in question. Human rights 'supervision', therefore, seems to be an activity quite distinct from processes of 'dispute resolution' found in other fora. By the same token, it is clear that several human rights treaties, in addition to containing 'quasi-judicial' mechanisms for supervision, also contain provisions that are more explicitly directed towards inter-state dispute resolution. In some such cases, these may involve the submission of such disputes to the ICJ or to arbitration. In others (and particularly where courts are involved) inter-state petitions may be received by the dedicated supervisory body.[106] The question is, therefore, whether such processes necessarily affirm the inherently reciprocal structure of the treaties concerned.

The initial assumption, of course, is that reciprocity is a central *leitmotif* of inter-state dispute resolution and must necessarily play a role in such mechanisms as are found in human rights treaties. A quite different approach to this question, however, was taken by the European Commission of Human Rights in the case of *Austria v. Italy*.[107] In this particular case, Austria had complained to the Commission about criminal proceedings brought against six men of German-speaking origin in the South Tyrol. It argued, among other things, that various aspects of the trial were incompatible with the terms of Article 6 of the Convention. Italy objected to the exercise of jurisdiction on the part of the Commission, however, on the basis that, although Italy was party to the Convention at the date of the proceedings in question, Austria was not and had only subsequently ratified the Convention. The Commission rejected Italy's objections on the grounds that the treaty was not, as such, based upon reciprocity. It explained that:

> the purpose of the High Contracting Parties in concluding the convention was not to concede to each other reciprocal rights and obligations in pursuance of their individual national interests, but to realise the aims and ideals of the Council of Europe, as expressed in its Statute, and to establish a common public order of the free democracies of Europe with the object of safeguarding their common heritage of political traditions, ideals, freedom and the rule of law.[108]

In light of this overriding purpose, the Commission concluded that:

> the obligations undertaken by the High Contracting Parties in the European Convention are essentially of an objective character, being designed rather to protect the fundamental rights of individual human beings from infringements by any of the High Contracting Parties than to create subjective and reciprocal rights for the High Contracting Parties themselves.[109]

The clear purpose of the Commission's remarks in this context was to establish a basis for its own exercise of jurisdiction *ratione temporis* and to avoid the supposition that, although Italy was bound to respect the rights of the men in question, Austria was unable to seize the Commission of the issue simply because at that particular time

[106] E.g., European Convention on Human Rights; Inter-American Convention on Human Rights.

[107] Application No. 788/60, 4 *European Yearbook of Human Rights* (1961) 116.

[108] *Ibid.* at 138.

[109] *Ibid.* at 140.

it was not a party to the Convention itself. It is quite clear that had it been Austria that was brought before the Commission for the acts in question, the Commission would not have been able to exercise jurisdiction. A strict application of the principle of reciprocity, therefore, would mean that Italy could have relied upon the implicit temporal limitation in Austria's instrument of ratification to exclude the jurisdiction of the Commission in this particular case. The fact of non-reciprocity, therefore, was of critical importance not only for the exercise of jurisdiction by the Commission, but also for how the 'regime' as a whole was to be characterized.[110]

Whilst the full implications of the Commission's approach were never made explicit, one may suppose that certain consequences do follow. First of all, it would seem that in denying the applicability of the concept of reciprocity in this case, the Commission was of the view that the inter-state petition mechanism was simply a means of ensuring compliance with obligations, and did not, in that sense, provide for the vindication of individual state 'rights'. Certainly states had a right to petition the Commission under Article 24, but in so doing they were not attempting to secure their own subjective rights, but were serving something in the nature of a 'public' function. The second conclusion seems to follow from this: that the mechanism was essentially one designed to further the ends of the regime as an institution embodying collective values. All states within the regime, therefore, had a legitimate interest in compliance, but the substance of that legal interest did not provide any need for reciprocal engagement. In some senses, therefore, the mechanism would properly be regarded not so much as one designed for 'dispute resolution'[111] but rather as allowing for a form of *actio popularis* for the achievement of certain designated ends.

The approach of the European Commission in *Austria v. Italy* was subsequently both reinforced and qualified by the European Court in the case of *Ireland v. UK*.[112] In that case the Court discussed the implications of Article 1 of the Convention and in doing so, pointed out that the Convention:

> comprises more than mere reciprocal engagements between contracting States. It creates, over and above a network of mutual bilateral undertakings, objective obligations ... which benefit from a 'collective enforcement'.[113]

This mechanism of 'collective enforcement' under Article 24, according to the Court 'allows Contracting States to require the observance of those obligations without having to justify an interest deriving ... from the fact that a measure they complain of has prejudiced one of their own nationals'.[114] Nor was it necessary to show that any particular individual had been harmed by the law or administrative

[110] Article 24, for example, provides that states may refer to the Commission '*any* alleged breach of the provisions of the Convention', and not merely breaches that involve nationals of the complaining state. See also, in that regard, *Application of the Convention* (article *on the Prevention and Punishment of Genocide*), ICJ Reports (1996) para. 34.

[111] It is a curiosity that only one Article of the Convention (Article 55) actually refers to the process as one of 'dispute settlement', and this only by way of excluding recourse to other such processes.

[112] *Ireland v. United Kingdom*, ECHR, Series A, No. 25, Judgment of 18 January 1978, 2 EHRR 25.

[113] *Ibid.*

[114] *Ibid.*

practice, or that domestic remedies had been exhausted. The legal interest of states, it would seem, derived simply from the fact of being participants in the regime, and committed to the furtherance of the regime's object and purpose. What is significant about the Court's statement, however, is that, in affirming the peculiarities of the Convention in this respect, it did not express the idea of non-reciprocity in the same terms as the Commission before it, or indeed the Inter-American Court subsequently. As the above extract makes clear, although in the view of the Court the Convention benefits from a collective enforcement, and although it creates obligations of an 'objective nature', it does, nevertheless, found itself upon a 'network of mutual bilateral undertakings' based on reciprocity. It is, in other words, still a treaty of the usual form, albeit one whose mechanism of enforcement was not premised upon the normal rules of diplomatic protection.[115]

7 Form, Purpose or Cognition? The Alternative Identities of the Human Rights Treaty

Ultimately, there seem to be several different ways of reconciling the issue, the choice among which turns upon several factors including the nature of the values enunciated within the treaty concerned; the understanding of who is, or who is not, a participant in the regime; and finally the relationship between human rights 'regimes' and the perceived structure of international law. The variety of possible approaches to this question may be captured succinctly in three different models that may be identified largely by their dominant paradigm as 'formalist', 'purposive' or 'cognitivist'.

The first approach is largely formalist in orientation, and is one which seems to have prevailed within the ILC at least. Its most coherent exponent is Simma, who explains the nature of human rights treaties in the following way:

> On the normative level, the treaties under consideration set forth reciprocal rights and obligations in precisely the same way as their more traditional counterparts. The difference lies in the fact that, in the case of pure social or humanitarian conventions, the mutual rights of the States parties are not accompanied by any material benefits accruing to them. Whereas in cases of agreements regulating genuine inter-State relations treaty obligations have to be accepted and carried out as the *conditio sine qua non* for the enjoyment of the advantages accruing from the other parties' performance, the standards prescribed by the conventions of the novel type could also be realized unilaterally. That States assume such social or

[115] The UK emphasized precisely this point in its comments on General Comment No. 24, *supra* note 16. Ironically enough, however, in its pleadings before the ICJ in the *Reservations Case*, the UK took the view that 'this type of convention does not provide for reciprocal benefits between the parties of a tangible character. It provides almost exclusively for the assumption by them of obligations ... not dependent on the assumption of a similar obligation by the other parties... In short, we are in the presence here of absolute obligations, not subject to any considerations of reciprocity at all.' *Reservations to the Convention on the Prevention and Punishment of the Crime of Genocide*, ICJ Pleadings (1951) 64 and 387–388.

> humanitarian obligations in treaty form in spite of this fact can be explained by the interest each contracting party has in every other party keeping step by accepting identical obligations. To speak of 'community interest' in this regard instead of common interests pure and simple is both unnecessary and ambiguous.[116]

As far as Simma is concerned, then, human rights treaties can be adequately accommodated within the bilateralist framework of standard treaty law. State interests, here, are ever present and simply 'overlapping', or 'intersecting', rather than divergent. Human rights treaties, accordingly, are still founded upon a series of bilateral relationships between contracting parties subject only to the qualification that compliance is not *necessarily* premised upon that relationship. For Simma, therefore, the claim to non-reciprocity in the case of human rights treaties is largely misconceived: they are only non-reciprocal in the sense that they lack any clear underlying sociological or material exchange, but not insofar as legal reciprocity is concerned.

There is considerable attraction in Simma's analysis from a formal point of view, not least because it negotiates a path between accepting the special characteristics of human rights treaties whilst maintaining the credibility of the existing structures of treaty law. It also explains, quite effectively, the presence within human rights treaties of 'typically contractual' clauses such as those providing for dispute resolution, for 'entry into force' following ratification of a certain number of states, and for unilateral denunciation. That being said, it is not perfect in its capacity to accommodate the variety of textual provisions. It does not explain, for example, why modification by majority decision should be possible,[117] why contracting states should not be able to prevent the entry into force of the Convention as regards states entering impermissible reservations, or why reciprocity may not be a relevant jurisdictional factor in inter-state disputes (as was evident in *Austria v. Italy*). But these, it might be argued, are simply minor and inconsequential exceptions that do not detract from the general presumptive framework.

The second approach centres more upon the teleology of the regimes rather than their form, and takes more seriously the notion of non-reciprocity. On this analysis, human rights treaties are properly understood to be concerned with the protection of the legal interests of individuals or groups rather than those of states themselves. They embody (depending upon one's view) either a series of unilateral commitments on the part of participating states as regards individuals or groups falling within their jurisdiction, or a series of 'internationalized constitutional agreements' that seek to establish enforceable legal relations as between public authorities and the individuals in question.[118] In either case, participating states may be seen to have certain procedural rights in order to effectuate, or protect, the object of that regime, but those rights are not directed towards the pursuit or protection of their own specific legal

[116] Simma, *supra* note 73, at 401.

[117] E.g., Article 50(2) of the Convention on the Rights of the Child (1989).

[118] In other circumstances, the dominant example of an 'internationalized constitutional agreement' would seem to be the Dayton Agreement for Bosnia-Herzegovina, 35 ILM (1996) 75.

interests which are neither present nor relevant.[119] To turn Simma's analysis around, it may be said that the regimes recognize a form of sociological reciprocity (in the sense that states understand the protection of human rights as being conducive to international peace and good order[120]), but do not necessarily invoke or enunciate any notion of legal reciprocity.

This analysis draws largely upon a 'cosmopolitan' or 'liberal' vision of international legal relations[121] that denies the exclusivity (or perhaps the reality) of state corporate personality and the sharp delineation between internal and external spheres of activity. It emphasizes rather the fundamental centrality of individuals as legal actors and concerns itself with the complex interdependence between national and international legal orders. The benefits of this approach are to be found in the way it more closely equates the relevant legal interest with the identity of the 'rights holders' under the agreement (i.e. the individuals or groups in question), and in the way it more faithfully adheres to the logic of the regime (i.e. to effectuate 'domestic change' rather than 'international coordination'). Furthermore, insofar as this model privileges the individual, or group, rights framework, it also provides better justification for automatic succession to human rights treaties: succession to obligations under such treaties would not, if viewed in this way, have any necessary third-party effect, and would, if anything, be necessitated by the international character of the rights in question. Clearly, however, to understand human rights treaties in this way would amount to a significant departure from the general 'contractual' paradigm, and would necessarily entail a re-evaluation of the role of individuals in the law-creative process.

The third approach, and that which draws more obviously upon the constitutive nature of legal 'regimes',[122] is to view human rights treaties as embodying certain 'collective values' (and not simply 'common values' to use Simma's distinction) which both define and transcend individual states' legal interests. Since the treaty, according to this view, is the product of coordinated action by states acting in concert, the substantive values and protected legal interests embodied also partake of this character. In ratifying the treaty, therefore, states assume obligations not in relation to each other state *ut singuli*, but to all other participating states as a collective.[123] Each

[119] Cf. Fitzmaurice, who comments that '[c]ertain kinds of multilateral treaties do not involve direct benefits for any of the participating countries. The benefit is of a general character arising from participation in a common cause for the general good.' Fourth Report on the Law of Treaties, UN Doc. A/CN.4/120, 2 *Yearbook of the International Law Commission* (1959) 54.

[120] This idea was initially propounded by Kant, 'To Perpetual Peace: A Philosophical Sketch' [1795] in *Perpetual Peace and Other Essays* (Humphrey trans. 1983) 107. It has since been endorsed by e.g. F. Teson, *A Philosophy of International Law* (1998) 9–14; Doyle, 'Liberalism and World Politics', 80 *APSR* (1986) 1151; Rummel, 'Libertarianism and International Conflict', 27 *Journal of Conflict Resolution* (1983) 27.

[121] See, e.g., Slaughter, 'International Law in a World of Liberal States', 6 *EJIL* (1995) 503; Teson, *supra* note 120.

[122] On 'regime theory' generally, see A. Hasenclever, P. Mayer and V. Rittberger, *Theories of International Regimes* (1997). See also Simma, 'Self-Contained Regimes', 16 *Netherlands Yearbook of International Law* (1985) 111.

[123] One way of explaining this framework without reference to the idea of a contractual bargain, may be by resort to the notion of *erga omnes* obligations. Cf. Simma, *supra* note 73, at 370.

state, therefore, may be seen to have a legal interest in the performance of the obligations concerned, and it is to that end that inter-state petition mechanisms are directed. This may seem to indicate a return to the type of relational structure that is expressive of the idea of reciprocity,[124] but the important factor is that the legal interest possessed by states is a derivative, and not exclusively personal, one. The regime, in other words, is seen in 'constructivist' terms,[125] as being constitutive of the nature and identity of those state interests rather than simply being a product of a mutual exchange between individual states. Individual state interests, in other words, are entirely bounded by (and constituted within) the interests of the regime as a whole, and exist only insofar as they correspond with that of the collective.

Given the emphasis, in this third approach, upon the nature of the regime as the source of legal interests, it would seem to follow that, whatever the formal position in 'treaty law', it is the regime's institutions that must play the dominant role in determining the treaty's application and effect. The effect of reservations or the question of compliance, in other words, can only be determined by the centralized institutions that are constitutive of the regime, and are not matters on which individual states may (legally speaking) take a different view. The obvious objection, of course, is that when one begins with an individualist methodology that is focused exclusively upon state activities (and particularly state consent), one may always deny the 'reality' of the 'collective'. Such an objection, however, is not one that can easily be deployed without warranting a re-examination, in turn, of the nature of state, or governmental, competence.

Ultimately, each of these three approaches as to the nature and form of human rights treaty regimes draws upon particular facets of those institutions: first, that they are treaties (the formal), secondly, that they embody 'human rights' (the purposive) and, thirdly, that they institute some form of discrete legal regime (the cognitivist). What seems apparent, however, is that an emphasis on any one facet will necessarily prejudice the others. To say that they are 'simply' treaties, is to say that the 'rights' embodied are little more than epiphenomena (conclusions that may be derived from the existence of state obligations), and that their dominant rationale is the protection of pre-existent state interests. Similarly, to say that they are concerned primarily with the protection of human rights, is to say that their legal form is secondary and their correspondence with other legal interests (sovereignty, territorial integrity) largely accidental. Current practice, it seems, attempts to meld these competing conceptions,[126] and the resulting tension is very much evident in the contradictions outlined above. On the issue of reservations, for example, each approach offers a radically

[124] See Kratochwil and Ruggie, 'International Organization: A State of the Art or an Art of the State', 40 *International Organisation* (1986) 753.

[125] For 'constructivism' in general, see, e.g., Wendt and Duvall, 'Institutions and International Order', in E.-O. Czempiel and J. Rosenau (eds), *Global Changes and Theoretical Challenges: Approaches to the World Politics for the 1990s* (1989) 51.

[126] It is characteristic, for example, to suggest that human rights treaties simultaneously embody both state legal interests and individual legal interests: see e.g. H. Lauterpacht, *An International Bill of the Rights of Man* (1945).

different answer. For example, in determining the effect of a putatively 'incompatible' reservation, an emphasis on the instrument's form might suggest that compatibility should be determined by unanimous consent. An emphasis upon its existence as a 'regime', by contrast, might suggest that the matter should be determined by the (presumptively) competent institutions, while an emphasis on teleology might suggest that the benefits of universal ratification outweigh the disadvantages of partial commitment. That no one approach is fully explanatory, however, reflects not only the evident complexity of the treaties themselves, but also the apparent tensions that are maintained within existing conceptions of international law.

8 Conclusions

The purpose of this article has been to explore, through the particular optic of human rights treaties, a generic issue that, in formalist terms, concerns the putative relationship between what is referred to as 'general law' and a *lex specialis*. This relationship is one overtly concerned with a simple question of substance: to what extent can the general framework of treaty law be applied, without exception, to human rights treaties among other forms of treaty? It is, however, also concerned with more fundamental issues that go beyond simply a question of textual exegesis. Whatever model employed to describe the relationship, necessarily invokes a particular understanding as to the nature of the international legal order, and in doing so reflects upon certain divisional suppositions that characterize that understanding: included here are the divisions between 'law' and 'legal obligation', between the 'general' and the 'specific', between 'public' and 'private' law, and between the so-called primary and secondary rules that underlie a common conception of law.[127]

To put the matter starkly, one may ask what is involved in insisting that the framework of general treaty law applies as regards human rights treaties? The answer, it would seem, is not simply an appeal to terminological accuracy (i.e. that conventions, covenants, charters or protocols are indeed 'treaties'), nor a concern to exclude any other status that might be given to their content. Rather, it is an appeal to the apparent integrity of 'general international law' as being a cohesive, unitary and all-embracing phenomenon which is itself dependent upon the implicit delineation between different 'forms of law'. We are asked, it seems, to differentiate in a hierarchical sense between the generality of treaty law and the specifics of particular treaties, and assume thereby the existence of a differentiation between secondary rules of structure and the primary rules of 'behaviour'. We are expected, furthermore, to understand (in nothing more than an intuitive sense it may be said) how the object of our attention falls within the framework of this understanding: the Vienna Convention on the Law of Treaties, after all, is no more than simply a treaty in its form, even if its content is regarded as being something 'other'.

[127] E.g., H. Hart, *The Concept of Law* (1956) 77–96. See also Combacau and Alland, '"Primary" and "Secondary" Rules in the Law of State Responsibility: Categorizing International Obligations', 16 *Netherlands Yearbook of International Law* (1985) 81.

If there is an explanation for this attitude, it is best illustrated by Weber's approach as regards the necessary development of formal rationality and functional specialization in modern bureaucratic societies,[128] in which he views the development of law as being marked by an ever increasing complexity of legal forms and processes. This increased complexity, far from signalling the imminent demise of the system, is actually the hallmark of its maturity: it is part of the process of 'bureaucratic rationalization' that sees the replacement of 'substantive rationality' (concerned with ethical, prudential or aesthetic choices of a non-legal character) by a systemic 'formal rationality' that allows cases to be decided by logical deduction from existing legal rules and concepts constituting a gapless system.[129] The development of law, therefore, is seen primarily in terms of its 'specialization', which itself is a corollary of the system's increasing capacity to control or eliminate arbitrariness and to render more effective the achievement of certain socially desirable ends.[130] Legal development (*qua* specialization), in other words, is a product of the increasingly intensive manner in which the existing general principles are applied and developed in particular contexts.

The vision of international law engendered by this model of 'legal development' is far from perfect. Not only does it entirely gloss over the enduring problem of legitimacy (under what conditions may the 'general structure' come into being?), but it also fails to explain how the law may effectively respond to the changing structures, attitudes and interests of the society within which it operates. If the process is entirely deductive (as is suggested), the general framework would establish the rational boundaries of development of the *lex specialis* which could not be broached without discarding its claim to be formally rational, and without stepping 'outside the law' so to speak. The field of specialism would, therefore, be entirely constrained by existing suppositions as to the 'nature' of international law as a whole and would, itself, be incapable of influencing the general shape or tenor of those suppositions. In the triumph of 'law', in other words, would be found the seeds of its own destruction — law would become effectively moribund and incapable of change.

Even if 'deductive reasoning' has its limits, the answer is not to be found in a resort to inductive reasoning,[131] or indeed to some qualified 'dialectic', but rather in the acceptance that the formal differentiation between such 'forms of law' are largely hypothetical and, in any case, not of critical importance for our commitment to, or understanding of, international law. Indeed, once one accepts that the boundaries of international legal activity are not determined *a priori*, by reference to any particular jurisdiction, power, competence or capacity, and that its utility is not found solely in

[128] M. Weber, *Economy and Society* (1978) 85–86, 225–226, 956–959 and 975.

[129] *Ibid.* at 656–657.

[130] See generally D. Milanovic, *Weberian and Marxian Analysis of Law* (1989) 37–41.

[131] Inductive reasoning follows a similarly flawed pattern: if the 'general law' is simply the product of points of commonality that are found in the various fields of specialism, it would not, in that sense, constrain or control the development of specific norms, principles or processes and would continue to have salience only so long as the fields of specialism were themselves compatible one with the other. Specialization, in other words, would slowly undermine the claim to unity of the law as a whole.

the preservation of the interests of elites, oligarchies or autocracies, it becomes less problematic to accept that legal regimes may come to be created and develop independently of a framework that insists that the 'inter-state' compact is the only legal form worthy of mention. It is certainly true that 'treaty law' has a general utility and that human rights treaty bodies may, from time to time, refer to certain of those 'governing principles' (e.g. *pacta sunt servanda*), but that is a far cry from any supposition that the instruments in question can only be understood within that framework, or indeed that they have no salience otherwise. Importantly, it may be argued that, since human rights treaties not only serve to place certain limits upon the nature and scope of governmental authority but also contribute to the development of a justifiable basis for that authority (albeit in no unproblematic manner), they cannot therefore simply be regarded as the accidental data of an otherwise disinterested legal system. Whatever one's term for them, to say that they are 'only treaties' is merely to place them within a highly contingent set of understandings as to the nature of international legal relations.

[10]

HUMAN RIGHTS TREATIES, INVALID RESERVATIONS, AND STATE CONSENT

By Ryan Goodman[*]

A continuing debate in international human rights law concerns the result of invalid reservations to multilateral treaties. The cardinal rule holds that a reservation cannot be incompatible with the object and purpose of a treaty.[1] Yet a normative puzzle remains: what legal remedy should follow the determination of the invalidity of a reservation? Leading commentators have discussed a limited set of options.[2] Three choices can be identified:

Option 1: The state remains bound to the treaty except for the provision(s) to which the reservation related.

Option 2: The invalidity of a reservation nullifies the instrument of ratification as a whole and thus the state is no longer a party to the agreement.

Option 3: An invalid reservation can be severed from the instrument of ratification such that the state remains bound to the treaty including the provision(s) to which the reservation related.

The third option—holding that an invalid reservation can be severed—has recently encountered strong opposition. According to this view, which I call the anti-severability (AS) position, international law permits only the first or second remedy. That is, the AS position categorically rejects the possibility that an invalid reservation could be severed (leaving the reserving state bound to the treaty without the benefit of the reservation). Proponents of the AS position ground their argument on a foundational precept of international law: the principle of state consent. They argue that a state cannot be bound by treaty terms that it specifically declined to accept. Because its normative foundations are cast in terms of state consent, an AS consensus has quickly begun to emerge.

In this article, I argue that reservations to human rights treaties should be presumed to be severable unless for a specific treaty there is evidence of a ratifying state's intent to the contrary.[3] This argument has two parts: the first part contends that severability should be an

[*] J. Sinclair Armstrong Assistant Professor of International, Foreign, and Comparative Law, Harvard Law School. This article benefited greatly from presentations before the faculties of Boston University School of Law, Harvard Law School, the University of Maryland School of Law, the University of Michigan School of Law, and the University of Pennsylvania Law School. I wish to thank especially the participants of the Faculty Works-in-Progress at the University of Chicago Law School, as well as Douglas Baird, David Barron, Adam Feibelman, Richard Friedman, Jack Goldsmith, James Hathaway, Don Herzog, Derek Jinks, David Kennedy, Harold Hongju Koh, Saul Levmore, Catharine MacKinnon, Eric Posner, David Sloss, Peter Spiro, Henry Steiner, William Stuntz, and Adrian Vermeule for helpful comments and suggestions.

[1] Vienna Convention on the Law of Treaties, *opened for signature* May 23, 1969, Art. 19, 1155 UNTS 331; ANTHONY AUST, MODERN TREATY LAW AND PRACTICE 110–12 (2000).

[2] *E.g.*, Belilos Case: Note of the Public Hearings, Oct. 26, 1987 (morning), Eur. Ct. H.R. Doc. Cour/Misc (87) 237, at 45–47 (statement by Luzius Wildhaber) (on file with author); FRANK HORN, RESERVATIONS AND INTERPRETATIVE DECLARATIONS TO MULTILATERAL TREATIES 219 (1988); Iain Cameron & Frank Horn, *Reservations to the European Convention on Human Rights: The* Belilos *Case*, 1990 GERMAN Y.B. INT'L L. 69, 115–16.

[3] This article concerns human rights treaties exclusively; whether its conclusions extend to other areas of public international law raises important considerations that are not addressed here. Its implications are especially limited, or nonexistent, in areas in which treaty regimes generally do not permit reservations—e.g., arms control. The reasons that some states enter human rights regimes—e.g., to lock in domestic policy choices or to promote obligations in other countries—may have analogues in other areas, such as global environmental regulation or

option for a third-party institution (e.g., a domestic court, a national human rights commission, a regional court, the International Court of Justice (ICJ), a treaty body) to invoke after having found a reservation invalid; the second part contends that severance should be presumed to be the optimal remedy. In application, the severance test that I propose would involve an intent-based inquiry: deciding whether the invalid reservation constituted an essential condition of the state's consent to be bound. A reservation is not essential if the state would have ratified the treaty without it. An inessential reservation would be nullified, and the state would remain bound to the treaty without the benefit of the reservation.

This approach better reflects and protects state consent than the AS position. In part II, I discuss the consent of other state parties: allowing a state to remain a party to a treaty with exemptions that are incompatible with its object and purpose would infringe other state parties' interests. In part III, I discuss the consent of the reserving state: a state's consent to be bound involves a complex balancing of concerns such that denying severance as a remedy in certain circumstances will actually abrogate the reserving state's overriding interests.

If these contentions are correct, they demonstrate a false opposition at the heart of the severability debate. The ongoing dispute has been cast in terms of a choice between protecting state consent and protecting human rights and long-term international agreements. This conceptualization is understandable since earlier debates correctly pitted the very capacity to enter reservations against the interest of state consent, and treaty law often raises concerns about state sovereignty. On closer examination, however, a different impression emerges: a human rights regime that allows for severing invalid reservations maximizes state consent.

I. THE SEVERABILITY CONTROVERSY

According to conventional wisdom, severing invalid reservations tramples on state consent. This understanding has accordingly shaped the terms of the severability debate. Opposition to severability has now been expressed by the governments of France, the United Kingdom, and the United States;[4] members of the International Law Commission;[5] some members of the Human Rights Committee;[6] and prominent international legal scholars.[7] Together, these actors' views form the AS position, whose strength is built on the principle of state consent.

Rather than discuss each of these actors' particular claims, I propose to describe their points of agreement, which essentially define the AS position. That position can be divided into its positive and normative components. The positive component maintains that international law currently provides for only two remedial responses to an invalid reservation: the state remains party to the treaty but is still not bound by those terms that the reservation modified or excluded (option 1), or the state is no longer party to the treaty (option 2).[8]

humanitarian law. However, one would have to study treaty practices and governmental objectives closely before rendering any conclusions on the efficacy or normative appeal of severability in those domains.

[4] Observations by France on General Comment 24, 4 INT'L HUM. RTS. REP. 6 (1997) [hereinafter France Observations]; Observations by the United Kingdom on General Comment 24, 3 INT'L HUM. RTS. REP. 261 (1996) [hereinafter UK Observations]; Observations by the United States on General Comment 24, 3 INT'L HUM. RTS. REP. 265 (1996) [hereinafter U.S. Observations]. For the Human Rights Committee's General Comment No. 24, see UN Doc. CCPR/C/21/Rev.1/Add. 6 (1994), *available at* <http://www.unhchr.ch/tbs/doc.nsf>.

[5] Report of the International Law Commission on the Work of Its Forty-ninth Session, UN GAOR, 52d Sess., Supp. No. 10, at 107, paras. 83, 142, UN Doc. A/52/10 (1997).

[6] Kennedy v. Trinidad and Tobago, Communication No. 845/1999, app., UN Doc. CCPR/C/67/D/845/1999 (dissenting opinion).

[7] *See, e.g.*, Roberto Baratta, *Should Invalid Reservations to Human Rights Treaties Be Disregarded?* 11 EUR. J. INT'L L. 413 (2000); Curtis A. Bradley & Jack L. Goldsmith, *Treaties, Human Rights, and Conditional Consent*, 149 PA. L. REV. 399, 438 (2000); *cf.* P. R. GHANDHI, THE HUMAN RIGHTS COMMITTEE AND THE RIGHT OF INDIVIDUAL COMMUNICATION 376 (1998).

[8] *See, e.g.*, U.S. Observations, *supra* note 4, at 269; Bradley & Goldsmith, *supra* note 7, at 438.

Some AS proponents recognize that the first option effectively leaves the state in the same position as if the reservation were in force.[9] Given the unpersuasive nature of this outcome, AS proponents place emphasis on the second option.

The normative component of the AS view rests on the principle of state consent: AS proponents contend that severability conflicts with a state's having ratified on the condition that it not be bound by certain terms of the agreement. Severing an invalid reservation and thus binding the state to the very provisions it rejected is thought to transgress foundational normative commitments.[10] This argument appears so persuasive that other commentators, including those who favor severing invalid reservations, conceive of severability as in opposition to state consent.[11]

In short, the issue of state consent dominates the severability debate, and participants in that debate generally accept that the principle of state consent undercuts the appeal of a severability regime. Although I reject this common conception, I make no attempt to unsettle the centrality of state consent. Instead, I argue that its relevance and implications have been misunderstood.

II. Consent of Other State Parties

The first remedial option—i.e., that the state remains bound to the treaty except for the obligations to which the incompatible reservation related—would infringe the interest of other state parties. Their interest consists in preserving the bargained-for elements of a multilateral agreement, which incompatible reservations or similar arrangements would defeat. No scholar has offered a sustained defense of the first remedy, and various commentators have referred to it as implausible.[12] Nevertheless, the U.S. government recently suggested that it is a viable option,[13] and some AS proponents have described it as congruent with positive international law.[14] Therefore, the relationship between the incompatibility test and other state parties' consent must be analyzed to show why the first remedial option is not viable in contemporary treaty practice.

The structure of modern reservations law, as set forth in the ICJ's opinion in *Reservations to the Convention on the Prevention and Punishment of the Crime of Genocide* and in the Vienna Convention on the Law of Treaties,[15] is committed to safeguarding these interests of state parties. Prior to the *Reservations* opinion, international practice generally applied a unanimity rule: a state could enter a reservation to a multilateral treaty only if it was accepted by all the other parties.[16] The rule reflected a rigid dedication to maintaining the integrity of all terms of a treaty and to obtaining every state party's consent to any changes in it.[17] As

[9] Bradley & Goldsmith, *supra* note 7, at 438.

[10] *See, e.g.*, France Observations, *supra* note 4, at 8; UK Observations, *supra* note 4, at 264–65; U.S. Observations, *supra* note 4, at 269; GHANDHI, *supra* note 7, at 376; Baratta, *supra* note 7, at 419, 420; Bradley & Goldsmith, *supra* note 7, at 436–37.

[11] *See, e.g.*, Elena A. Baylis, *General Comment 24: Confronting the Problem of Reservations to Human Rights Treaties*, BERKELEY J. INT'L L. 277, 303, 326 (1999); Henry J. Bourguignon, *The* Belilos *Case: New Light on Reservations to Multilateral Treaties*, 29 VA. J. INT'L L. 347, 380, 382 (1989); Richard W. Edwards, Jr., *Reservations to Treaties*, 10 MICH. J. INT'L L. 362, 373 (1989).

[12] *See, e.g.*, Cameron & Horn, *supra* note 2, at 116; William A. Schabas, *Invalid Reservations to the International Covenant on Civil and Political Rights: Is the United States Still a Party?* 21 BROOK. J. INT'L L. 277, 317 (1995); *cf.* AUST, *supra* note 1, at 118–19 (not even entertaining this remedy as an option).

[13] U.S. Observations, *supra* note 4, at 268–69.

[14] *E.g.*, Bradley & Goldsmith, *supra* note 7, at 438.

[15] Vienna Convention, *supra* note 1; Reservations to the Convention on the Prevention and Punishment of the Crime of Genocide, Advisory Opinion, 1951 ICJ REP. 15 (May 28) [hereinafter Reservations].

[16] Jean Kyongun Koh, *Reservations to Multilateral Treaties: How International Legal Doctrine Reflects World Vision*, 23 HARV. INT'L L.J. 71, 80–84 (1982) (describing different approach followed in Latin American regional agreements).

[17] IAN SINCLAIR, THE VIENNA CONVENTION ON THE LAW OF TREATIES 54–56 (2d rev. ed. 1984); G. G. Fitzmaurice, *Reservations to Multilateral Conventions*, 2 INT'L & COMP. L.Q. 1 (1953).

a pragmatic matter, the unanimity rule became increasingly unworkable owing to the rising number of states involved in treaty negotiations and the quest for universal ratification of important treaties. As for the normative foundation of the unanimity rule—its concern for the consent of other state parties—the modern law of reservations largely incorporated, rather than abandoned, it.

The two basic features of the modern approach provide substantial protection for this dimension of state consent. Under the system, (1) states are free to enter reservations that are compatible with the object and purpose of a treaty, and (2) an official objection by a state (state *O*) to a validly entered reservation by another state (state *R*) alters the treaty relationship only between those two parties.[18] The first feature—the prohibition on incompatible reservations—creates an important floor. It protects against infringements of the core aspects of the agreement bargained for by the negotiating states. Allowing a state to remain a party to the treaty with an incompatible reservation—or allowing the equivalent (i.e., the first remedial option)—would undermine the consent of the states that drafted and ratified the treaty. Any reservation that contravenes the object and purpose of the treaty thus requires the unanimous approval of all state parties, because it constitutes a fundamental change to the agreement.[19]

Thus, while the incompatibility test restricts the conditions states can place on their consent to join a treaty, it does so in consideration of the consent of the other state parties. This continuity between unanimity and flexibility was implicitly reflected in the *Reservations* opinion. The Court began its analysis by acknowledging the importance of state consent under the unanimity rule: "It is well established that in its treaty relations a State cannot be bound without its consent. . . . [N]one of the contracting parties is entitled to frustrate or impair, by means of unilateral decisions or particular agreements, the purpose and *raison d'être* of the convention."[20] The incompatibility test functions so that the "purpose and *raison d'être* of [a] convention" could not be subject to reservations, while superficial or minor aspects of the convention could be. Thus, in articulating the new rule, the Court explained that core aspects of the treaty would not be sacrificed to an excessive quest for universal ratification: "[E]ven less could the contracting parties have intended to sacrifice the very object of the Convention in favour of a vain desire to secure as many participants as possible. The object and purpose of the Convention thus limit both the freedom of making reservations and that of objecting to them."[21] The *Reservations* opinion suggested, and the Vienna Convention later confirmed, that the limit on "the freedom of making reservations" involves a direct prohibition on states' ability to formulate reservations.[22]

Concerns to maintain the core of an agreement assume special significance in the case of human rights treaties. In such contexts, the very purpose of the multilateral regime is to codify and maintain a minimum level of global standards. Allowing states to join the treaty with incompatible reservations would repudiate or downgrade its normative, or standard-setting, base. This result, of course, cannot be controlled by individual state objections, because state *O*'s objections apply only to the relationship between itself and state *R*. Accordingly,

[18] Vienna Convention, *supra* note 1, Arts. 19–21; Reservations, 1951 ICJ REP. at 26–27.

[19] Belinda Clark, *The Vienna Convention Reservations Regime and the Convention on Discrimination Against Women*, 85 AJIL 281, 306 (1991).

[20] Reservations, 1951 ICJ REP. at 21.

[21] *Id.* at 24. The majority view among legal scholars is that, under the modern system, individual states cannot "accept" state *R*'s incompatible reservation, unless all state parties consent to such a fundamental change. *See, e.g.*, AUST, *supra* note 1, at 117 (describing contrary view as "most unlikely"); HORN, *supra* note 2, at 121; D.W. Bowett, *Reservations to Non-Restricted Multilateral Treaties*, 1976–77 BRIT. Y.B. INT'L L. 67, 83; Clark, *supra* note 19, at 304; Catherine Redgwell, *Universality or Integrity? Some Reflections on Reservations to General Multilateral Treaties*, 1993 BRIT. Y.B. INT'L L. 245, 257; *cf.* SINCLAIR, *supra* note 17, at 81 n.78. *But see* José M. Ruda, *Reservations to Treaties*, 146 RECUEIL DES COURS 95, 111, 190 (1975 III).

[22] Reservations, 1951 ICJ REP. at 26–27, 24.

state *O* cannot prevent the incompatible reservations from affecting the constitutive elements of the treaty.

In sum, the modern approach should be viewed as harmonizing—rather than choosing between—universality and integrity. A question might be posed: universal accession to what? According to the contemporary approach, the answer is universal accession to the object and purpose of the treaty; for human rights treaties, this means obtaining universal agreement on a set of fundamental normative propositions. Allowing states to accede to the treaty with incompatible amendments would thus negate a central reason for achieving universality. In short, universality and integrity serve a common objective, and the law of reservations reflects state parties' interests by promoting that common pursuit.

The place and importance of state consent within the modern law of reservations demonstrates the main problem with the first remedial option. AS proponents notably do not contest the purpose or virtues of the incompatibility rule. Indeed, it would be difficult, if not impossible, to maintain durable multilateral treaty regimes without it. Yet allowing the first remedial option is functionally equivalent to allowing states to maintain incompatible reservations. Perhaps this result explains AS proponents' reluctance to endorse the first remedial option explicitly. For example, AS proponents Curtis Bradley and Jack Goldsmith suggest that the first remedial option is available as a matter of positive international law.[23] They acknowledge, however, that, in accordance with this remedy, the state would "not [be] a party to the treaty provisions with respect to which it has reserved . . . *which yields the same result as if the [reservation] were enforced.*"[24] Allowing such a result would negate the purpose of having a determination of incompatibility in the first place. Why decide whether the reservation is incompatible if the remedy for incompatibility is to maintain the same result? As the above discussion makes clear, accepting the first remedial option would reject the balance between universality and integrity, which the modern law of reservations is designed to protect. In terms of interstate considerations, the first remedial option would thus contravene the interests of state consent, that is, the interests in preserving the core principles of the treaty.

For these reasons, the reservations controversy has essentially centered on the two other options: sever the reservation or invalidate the act of ratification. The choice between them substantially depends on the implications for the consent of the reserving state.

III. Consent of the Reserving State

The normative appeal of a severability regime can be grounded in its protection of state consent. Specifically, the following analysis advances a theory that conforms the severability inquiry to the functions and motivations of state accession to multilateral treaties. I argue that this approach reflects aspects of the reserving state's consent that an AS regime overlooks. This discussion exclusively considers the internal interests of the reserving state, not those of other state parties.

Admittedly, the AS position is at its strongest in this regard: severing a reservation appears to tread significantly on a reserving state's consent. AS proponents conclude that the better solution would be to find that the state is no longer a party to the treaty; that is, to consider its entire act of accession void. The following discussion evaluates the AS view on its own terms, determining which reservations regime—one that allows for severability or one that does not—would better maximize state consent.

This discussion makes four claims. Some of these claims will initially seem counterintuitive and can be fully evaluated only against the empirical analysis that follows. Indeed, the AS perspective might appear at first blush to be commonsensical. I contend, however, that the

[23] Bradley & Goldsmith, *supra* note 7, at 438.

[24] *Id.* (emphasis added).

AS position rests on questionable assumptions, which if modified or relaxed render the position unpersuasive. For the purpose of clarity, let me sketch the four basic claims at the outset.

The first claim is that, in many cases, AS proponents' second remedial option—considering a state with an invalid reservation no longer a party to a treaty—would produce significant negative impacts for state consent.[25] For instance, as evidenced below, expelling a state might unravel an interconnected arrangement of civil rights guarantees or unlock policy choices that were intended to be sealed shut.[26] The second claim is that, in many cases, states discount, or would not suffer, domestic sovereignty costs that AS proponents suggest result from severing a reservation and keeping the state bound. This may be the case, for instance, in post-totalitarian states that deliberately invest their future in international legal developments out of a marked distrust of domestic institutions.[27] In these cases, the "loss" to domestic sovereignty is a price the domestic polity is more than willing to pay. The third claim involves a balancing of the first two: in many cases, the harm to state consent in voiding its membership in a treaty will outweigh the harm in voiding only the reservation and keeping the state bound.

Finally, in evaluating the competing concerns identified by the first three claims, "critical" reservations must be distinguished from "accessory" reservations. The former involve conditions a state considers essential to its ratification regardless of the benefits of being party to the treaty. The latter involve conditions a state considers ideal, but dispensable in order to obtain the benefits of treaty membership. A severability regime would sort between the costs and benefits (as identified in the first three factors) based on these two types of reservations.[28] Accordingly, the appropriate test for determining whether a reservation is severable turns on an intent-based inquiry: whether the reservation was an essential condition of consent in that the state would not have ratified the treaty without it.[29] The foundation for these claims, however, remains to be shown.

The Structure of Conditional Consent

In consenting to multilateral human rights treaties, states generally try to accomplish two goals: (1) to promote human rights standards (whether domestically or internationally or both); and (2) to minimize the treaty's infringement on aspects of domestic sovereignty that the state does not want to relinquish. Reservations are devices for meeting both goals. By submitting a reservation as a condition of ratification, a state can become a party to a multilateral treaty while limiting aspects of the agreement that contravene domestic interests the state seeks to protect.

[25] A severability regime will also be able to capture benefits of the second remedial option because the system would have the decision between severance and voiding the state's membership determined by an evaluation of state consent in the given circumstance.

[26] *See infra* text at notes 39–65 & 83–100.

[27] *See infra* text at notes 39–65.

[28] Providing a catalogue of these types of reservations is beyond the scope of this article. Depending on the interpretive material used to evaluate whether a reservation is essential, such a catalogue would probably require analyzing the legislative history of a country's ratification and could not be discerned from the face of the reservation alone. Representative examples of inessential reservations might include the Swiss reservation in *Belilos*, Turkey's reservation in *Loizidou*, and the types of "phase out" reservations described below. Some states' reservations on rights to a fair trial—for example, Russia's reservations to the European Convention on Human Rights—might also fit this category. In short, for a significant set of reservations a third-party institution could potentially (even mistakenly) find the condition incompatible with the object and purpose of the treaty, but the state would not have predicated joining the regime on that condition.

[29] This approach resembles approaches taken in American contracts law and statutory construction. *See* Champlin Ref. Co. v. Corp. Comm'n of Okla., 286 U.S. 210, 234 (1932) ("Unless it is evident that the legislature would not have enacted those provisions which are within its power, independently of that which is not, the invalid part may be dropped if what is left is fully operative as a law."); RESTATEMENT (SECOND) OF CONTRACTS §184(1) (1981) ("If less than all of an agreement is unenforceable . . . , a court may nevertheless enforce the rest of the agreement in favor of a party . . . if the performance as to which the agreement is unenforceable is not an essential part of the agreed exchange.").

On its face, this description simply reiterates the standard account that reservations are essential to obtaining the universal ratification of treaties. That is, without the ability to submit a reservation, many states would be unwilling to assent to all terms of a particular treaty and thus would never submit to ratification. The politics of treaty relations, however, adds a complication to this account. For fairly straightforward reasons, a state may include more reservations than required to obtain its consent. Whether counting on other states not to object to its reservations or discounting the cost of such objections, a state may include supererogatory conditions in its package of reservations. Although some reservations are essential—integral to the state's consent to the treaty—others may be described as what Judge Armand-Ugon, in a related context, called "an accessory stipulation."[30]

In various multilateral agreements, especially those without a juridical supervisory organ, states may incur little cost for submitting accessory reservations. Under the Vienna Convention, state *R* generally suffers only bilateral costs if another state objects to its reservation. That is, the effect of state *O*'s objection to state *R*'s reservation is either (1) that the treaty terms to which the reservation relates do not apply between the two states, or (2) that the treaty as a whole does not enter into force between the two states.[31] Primarily owing to diplomatic sensitivities, states avoid choosing the second option, if they are politically willing to enter an objection at all. As for the first option, because the rule of reciprocity produces the exact same result as the reservation,[32] state *R* loses nothing if state *O* selects this alternative. States consequently have little incentive to avoid submitting accessory reservations.

The administrative costs of monitoring and reviewing other states' reservations make states "sluggish in their reaction to reservations.... [I]t is a fact of international life."[33] This feature of treaty practice is even more pronounced in the area of human rights. Human rights treaties do not involve the kind of reciprocal duties between states that directly affect one another's domestic interests. Admittedly, some states, especially leading military powers, may consider grave human rights violations in other countries a threat to their own security interests, and some states may perceive the promotion of universal human rights standards as a constitutive part of their country's political identity.[34] Still, neither of these interests is as direct, or affects domestic constituencies as immediately, as the reciprocal duties imposed in other multilateral contexts such as trade and arms control. A state may find another state's reservations objectionable, or even violative of the basic understanding of the treaty, but unless the former's own domestic interests are directly implicated, monitoring, scrutinizing, and reacting to other states' reservations are simply not priorities.[35]

The political context of human rights agreements is thus conducive to the submission, if not piling on, of accessory reservations. The package of reservations a state submits reflects the ideal relationship it wishes to have in relation to the treaty, not the essential one it requires so as to be bound. Consequently, a severance determination must distinguish between essential and accessory reservations, weighing the dual goals of treaty ratification in that calculation. By taking these factors and the various modalities of state practice into account, we can assess which reservations regime best protects state consent.

[30] Interhandel (Switz. v. U.S.), Preliminary Objections, 1959 ICJ REP. 6, 94 (Mar. 21) (Armand-Ugon, J., dissenting).

[31] Vienna Convention, *supra* note 1, Art. 21(3).

[32] Vienna Convention, *supra* note 1, Art. 21(1); SINCLAIR, *supra* note 17, at 76–77 ("Most commentators accordingly believe that, even in the case of a 'modifying' reservation, the legal effects of an objection to and acceptance of the reservation are identical, when the treaty remains in force between the objecting and reserving States.").

[33] SINCLAIR, *supra* note 17, at 63 (explaining that this phenomenon results "if only for the reason that many administrations are simply not equipped to keep under constant review reservations to multilateral conventions formulated by other States"); *see also* AUST, *supra* note 1, at 115–16 ("Even in the best managed ministries reservations are not always given the attention they deserve.... If one studies any list of reservations it is surprising how few states object even though a clearly objectionable reservation has been made.").

[34] *See* Ryan Goodman, *Norms and National Security: The WTO as a Catalyst for Inquiry*, 2 CHI. J. INT'L L. 101 (2001).

[35] *See, e.g.*, Clark, *supra* note 19, at 281.

The Modalities of Conditional Consent

Situations in which a state would prefer severability to nonseverability are common and can be fairly easily appreciated. They involve cases in which a state submits a reservation when ratifying a treaty but, on balance, would have assented to the treaty without the condition. In these cases, the state gains substantial benefits in terms of the first goal discussed above—promoting human rights (whether domestically or abroad or both)—whereas the second goal—protecting certain domestic interests—is not an essential condition of the state's consent to be bound. If the two goals conflict, achieving the first goal matters more to the state than the protection the reservation affords to the second.

Before analyzing the specific modalities of state practice, I should address two concerns: one related to the appropriateness of the decision whether to sever, and the other related to the appropriate decision maker. With regard to the first, an objection might be raised that considering a state no longer a party to a treaty is more respectful of its consent in these situations because this remedy would allow the state to re-accede to the treaty without the reservation if that is what the state truly desires. The problem with this argument is its failure to consider (1) the potential impact on a state of expelling it from a treaty regime, and (2) the massive transaction costs a government, or domestic polity, might have to deal with to re-accede to the treaty. In the United States, the latter would likely entail exceptional political efforts to obtain the president's and Senate's support for a treaty all over again. Some of those transaction costs can severely delay or, worse, preclude reratification despite the polity's interest in joining the treaty. As for the former concern, in many countries expulsion from treaty membership—without a searching inquiry into whether the state's original consent to be bound accords with this outcome—would release the state from a commitment that the original ratification was mainly meant to lock firmly in place. These circumstances are more clearly demonstrated in the detailed analysis of modalities of state consent presented below. The discussion in part IV of an interpretive presumption in favor of severability also addresses aspects of this first objection.

A separate objection may be raised that the best solution is simply to give the state the choice—to decide between withdrawing the invalid reservation and withdrawing from the treaty as a whole. Before I address this objection, note that the foundation for its claim also repudiates the AS view. The objection suggests leaving the choice up to the state, and thus treats the AS proponents' second remedial option (excluding the state from treaty membership) as equally unacceptable. The objection therefore shares some features with arguments I have raised against the AS view. Nevertheless, if valid, this objection challenges the idea of embracing a severability regime as well.

Several reasons show that the objection is unwarranted, and that the scheme it suggests is a second-best alternative to a regime in which a third-party institution determines the issue of severability. First, as explained in part II, under well-settled international law the interpretation of a state's consent to be bound focuses on the state's expression of intent at the time of ratification (time 1). While a state's concerns at time 2 (when the reservation is called into question) are important, the inquiry turns on the interpretation of the state's intent and the purpose of the reservation at time 1. That initial decision is what all the parties, the adjudicator and state *R* included, are analyzing. Thus, the severance approach and the objection to it may share the commitment to respecting the state's ability to decide. The latter, however, privileges the state's interests at the wrong point in time.

Second, even if we relax this assumption, or feature, of how international law operates, a severability regime adequately protects a state's decisional freedom at time 2. A safeguard of a severability regime is that a state can withdraw from the treaty if the reservation is severed. As I explain below, the costs are much lower for a state in this scenario than in one where a state is ousted from the treaty and seeks reratification.

Third, in many cases giving the state the option, or suspending its treaty status until it decides, would defy the state's consent. Newly established democracies and established democracies with genuinely monist constitutions may prefer severance of an inessential reservation and continuous membership in the treaty. Giving the state the option may invite domestic turmoil, rollbacks of liberal gains, significant costs from having to re-debate fundamental questions of governance, and the indefinite suspension of a wide array of rights guarantees. Third-party severance of an inessential reservation, especially for many newly established democracies, would maintain a central purpose of ratifying the treaty: to guard against significant fluctuations in the status of international law under domestic law.

Fourth, even if we examine state interests only at time 2, the idea that a state should choose between withdrawing the reservation and withdrawing its membership as a whole is not practical in many situations of third-party evaluation. For example, the U.S. government would not make that choice based on a singular decision of the Nevada Supreme Court. Thus, the state court would still have to decide as an interpretive matter whether the reservation should be considered severed or the entire ratification void. As another example, a determination by the Human Rights Committee that a reservation should be considered severed does not bind any state. Certainly, such a determination by the Committee helps open a critical discourse and may be used as persuasive authority by other institutions. Because the decision is nonbinding, however, a government is not legally compelled to decide between the reservation and treaty membership. The effect of the Committee's decision is restricted to its zone of authority, namely, its functions of reviewing states' periodic reports and cases under the First Optional Protocol to the International Covenant on Civil and Political Rights (ICCPR). Since a state is unlikely to withdraw from the Covenant as a whole in response to the Committee's concerns, the Committee must still decide the appropriate—even if somewhat theoretical—outcome.

Finally, even if we consider only state *R*'s interests at time 2, a third-party institution will not be able to escape severance analysis if the state ultimately decides not to choose. Notably, others have contemplated such a scenario. In response to a suggestion that state *R* be given the option whether to remove an invalid reservation or withdraw from a treaty, the Swedish representative, at a meeting of the Sixth Committee, countered: "[O]ther States parties and monitoring bodies [also] have a role to play in bringing about such a desired result. And what happens if the reserving State does not take action?"[36] The Swedish statement reflects the current state of affairs between the Human Rights Committee and the United States. The Committee has informed the United States that it considers two of the government's reservations invalid. The United States, however, has maintained both the reservation and its treaty membership, partly by virtue of the previous factor I discussed (nonenforceability of the Committee's views). In situations such as these, the third-party institution must decide.[37] If a third-party institution with binding authority were to leave the severance question for the state to decide and the state simply did not exercise a choice, the decision whether to sever would fall squarely back on the institution.[38]

[36] Lars Magnuson, *Elements of Nordic Practice 1997: The Nordic Countries in Coordination*, 67 NORDIC J. INT'L L. 345, 350 (1998) (reproducing text of Swedish statement on behalf of Nordic countries before Sixth Committee, Nov. 4, 1997).

[37] Another problem in giving a state the decisional choice is that it does not appropriately address issues of justice in the instant case (e.g., the interest of the defendant in a juvenile death penalty case). With regard to the case at hand, is the state bound to the treaty with the reservation voided or was the state's accession never truly valid? The answer to these questions may affect not only the remedy for the case at hand, but also retrospective relief for cases that proceeded under the treaty when it was considered to be in force.

[38] Antonio Cassese, *A New Reservations Clause*, *in* RECUEIL D'ÉTUDES DE DROIT INTERNATIONAL EN HOMMAGE À PAUL GUGGENHEIM 266, 280 (1986) (suggesting the same problem might arise in a collegiate system in which the collection of state parties decides that state *R*'s reservation is invalid, but state *R* chooses neither to remove the reservation nor to withdraw from the treaty).

With these objections and the answers to them in mind, the following analysis provides a basis for evaluating whether a severability regime or an AS regime most effectively serves state consent.

Newly established democracies. The greatest potential cost of an AS regime would be to newly established democracies. Andrew Moravcsik recently presented "the first systematic empirical test"[39] of international relations theories that try to explain why states establish and bind themselves to international human rights regimes. Moravcsik argues that republican liberal theory best explains the dynamics of the accession by newly democratic states to binding human rights agreements: "[It] is a tactic used by governments to 'lock in' and consolidate democratic institutions, thereby enhancing their credibility and stability vis-à-vis nondemocratic political threats."[40] That is, these regimes attempt to entrench certain political choices in fear, or anticipation, that a future illiberal regime will roll back liberal gains. Treaties, especially if incorporated as higher law, allow governments to perform that task. Regardless of which international relations theory wins out, the empirical record seems clear that this phenomenon of state practice is widespread.

How much success the strategy of solidifying liberal gains achieves is questionable. Nevertheless, it is the policy choice of these governments, one that would be considerably undermined by the instability resulting from an AS regime. Under an AS regime, newly established democracies could not rely on the treaties for the purposes they desire. Without severance as a remedial option, they might more easily lose their membership in human rights treaties at some point in the future. This level of prospective uncertainty is not what these states want, nor is it the ground on which their consent to the treaty was built.

State accession to treaties in the manner described by Moravcsik appears to be useful (1) in reducing the excesses of a future illiberal government (e.g., through the protection of rights of minorities), but also (2) in hedging against illiberal tendencies short of a regime takeover, and (3) in providing guarantees of political rights that can assist in preventing these illiberal developments in the first place (e.g., by protecting freedom of speech and freedom of association). Of course, a treaty alone may not achieve these results, but it is a useful mechanism for supporting the liberal effort to do so. In terms of ascertaining the intent behind a state's ratification, it would accordingly be inappropriate to eliminate the severance option categorically. A system that rigidly precludes severance would potentially invite instability at important stages of consolidating liberal regimes. Therefore, when it comes to state consent to be bound, a superior strategy in the face of an invalid reservation is emplacement of a system that can respect the primacy of the lock-in motive over the competing interests served by the reservation.

Related state interests in consent to be bound should also be taken into account. Newly established democracies, for example, may opt for entrenching particular political decisions through a treaty so as to integrate themselves into the liberal international community. Such initiatives may reflect a desire not only to prevent backsliding, but also to tie the state to the currents of international legal developments. This strategy may thus reflect a pragmatic calculation that the international legal order has more conceptual and material resources than the fledgling domestic liberal order. More important, the interest in fastening the state to international normative and legal developments may emanate directly from a profound distrust of domestic institutions due to recent experience with, and emergence from, a totalitarian past. As a result, the dominant political sentiment in such states may significantly discount the "sovereignty cost" in tying the government's hands to external human rights regimes.[41]

[39] Andrew Moravcsik, *The Origins of Human Rights Regimes: Democratic Delegation in Postwar Europe*, 54 INT'L ORG. 217, 219 (2000).

[40] *Id.* at 220.

[41] Thomas Buergenthal, *Modern Constitutions and Human Rights Treaties*, 36 COLUM. J. TRANSNAT'L L. 211, 214 (1997).

Consistent with this account, and with the predictive aspect of Moravcsik's project, are the constitutional systems of newly established democracies in post-Communist Eastern Europe and the former Soviet republics. Many of these countries' constitutions include provisions incorporating treaties as enforceable domestic law and as superior in constitutional status to statutory and administrative law.[42] In addition, a large number of these states have ratified the major human rights treaties, including the First Optional Protocol to the ICCPR.[43] Some of these states have also enacted a national law on international treaties, which elaborates the constitutional relationship between treaties, the domestic legal system, and foreign relations powers. A remarkable aspect of these national laws is the number of provisions regulating domestic political actors by reference to standards of "international law" or "international norms."[44] Structurally, these systems reflect faith in the international legal order as a tool for organizing and controlling internal politics and juridical practices.

Beneath these formal constitutional arrangements can be found significant evidence of a genuine commitment to using treaties to lock in liberal gains or to advance the domestic system along the path of liberal consolidation. First, international law affords a repository of conceptual resources and juridical analogues to bridge gaps in domestic norms during the passage from one political regime to the next. As Ruti Teitel argues in her comparative project on liberal transitions, international law thus offers one of the tropes in which the new state enfolds and defines itself and through which judges render decisions, even if only in appearance, according to a consistent rule of law.[45] Second, the political history of the drafting and approval of many of these constitutional provisions suggests that such measures are not superficial. They are often the result of hard-fought battles between reformers and conservatives over the structure of the future regime.[46] Third, while the data are still limited, an expanding record of constitutional court cases in various countries indicates the willingness of the judiciary to rely on international law in striking down domestic legislation.[47] These three factors help prove that the monist constitutional provisions of newly established democracies reflect and propel important political commitments with regard to international law. Taken together, these factors also indicate a lack of domestic costs in severing a reservation and keeping a state bound to a treaty regime. In these contexts, severance will be fully consistent with the state's general approach to letting international law govern.

[42] *See, e.g.*, ARM. CONST. Art. 6, cl. 5; BULG. CONST. Art. 5, §4; CZECH REP. CONST. Art. 10; EST. CONST. Art. 123, §2; GEOR. CONST. Art. 6, §2; KAZ. CONST. Art. 4, §3; MOLD. CONST. Art. 4, §2; POL. CONST. Art. 91, §2; ROM. CONST. Art. 20, §2; RUSS. CONST. Art. 15, §4; SLOV. CONST. Art. 11; TAJ. CONST. Art. 10, cls. 3–4. For English translations of the above Constitutions, see CONSTITUTIONS OF THE COUNTRIES OF THE WORLD (Albert P. Blaustein & Gisbert H. Flantz eds., 1971–).

[43] International Covenant on Economic, Social and Cultural Rights, Dec. 16, 1966, 993 UNTS 3 [hereinafter ICESCR]; International Covenant on Civil and Political Rights, Dec. 16, 1966, 999 UNTS 331 [hereinafter ICCPR]; First Optional Protocol to the International Covenant on Civil and Political Rights, Dec. 16, 1966, 999 UNTS 171. Between 1990 and 1999, the following states ratified the ICESCR, the ICCPR, and the Optional Protocol to the ICCPR, respectively: Armenia (1993, 1993, 1993); Bosnia and Herzegovina (1992, 1993, 1995); Croatia (1991, 1992, 1995); the Czech Republic (1993, 1993, 1993); Estonia (1991, 1991, 1991); Georgia (1994, 1994, 1994); Kyrgystan (1994, 1994, 1995); Latvia (1992, 1992, 1994); Lithuania (1991, 1991, 1991); Macedonia (1994, 1994, 1994); Slovakia (1993, 1993, 1993); Slovenia (1992, 1992, 1992); Tajikistan (1999, 1999, 1999); Turkmenistan (1997, 1997, 1997); Uzbekistan (1995, 1995, 1995). Office of the UN High Commissioner for Human Rights, Status of Ratifications of the Principal International Human Rights Treaties (May 13, 2002), *at* <http://www.unhchr.ch/pdf/report.pdf>.

[44] *See, e.g.*, Law on International Treaties, Oct. 16, 1997 (Geor.), *translated in* 4 SUDEBNIK 389 (1999); Law on International Treaties, July 21, 1999 (Kyrg.), *translated in id.* at 410; Edict of the President of the Republic of Kazakhstan Having the Force of a Law on the Procedure for the Conclusion, Performance, and Denunciation of International Treaties, Dec. 12, 1995, *translated in* 1 *id.* at 405 (1996); Federal Law on International Treaties of the Russian Federation, June 16, 1995, *translated in id.* at 456; Law on International Treaties, Dec. 22, 1995 (Uzb.), *translated in id.* at 487.

[45] RUTI TEITEL, TRANSITIONAL JUSTICE 20–21, 33–34 (2000).

[46] *See, e.g., infra* text at notes 50–53.

[47] Vladlen S. Vereshchetin, *New Constitutions and the Old Problem of the Relationship Between International Law and National Law*, 7 EUR. J. INT'L L. 29 (1996) (describing recent constitutional court cases in Hungary, Poland, and Russia).

Such abstract statements should be tested against empirical conditions, and the Russian experience offers a suitable case study in this regard. In terms of national orientation toward the international legal system, Professor Gennady Danilenko, a leading expert on the region, remarked, "In many respects, Russia is an illustration of the Eastern European trend."[48] Danilenko described Russian citizens' and policymakers' confidence and political investment in international institutions over domestic ones:

> The focus on international law was motivated by several politico-legal considerations, some of which retain their validity for Russia today. First, there was a consensus among policy makers and citizens that Soviet internal law lagged behind legal standards that had been developed at the international level. Second, the reliance on international law indicated that international institutions were accorded more trust than national institutions, which had lost much of their legitimacy after the failure of the Communist idea and revelations in the media about the totalitarian state's gross violations of human rights. Third, international standards, in particular human rights standards, enjoyed a high degree of legitimacy.... The legitimacy attributed to international human rights standards was also based on the general perception that they expressed "universal human values" shared by the majority of the international community.[49]

The new Russian Constitution of 1993 reflected these perceptions through a monist approach to international law, a structural decision that took place only after an intense struggle between reformers and conservatives. A driving force behind the reformers' efforts was the country's preoccupation with the question whether Russia would become *pravovoe gosudarstvo* (a law-based state).[50] In 1991 the Russian legislature adopted the Declaration of the Rights and Freedoms of the Individual and Citizen, Article 1 of which proclaimed that "generally recognized international norms concerning human rights have priority over laws of the Russian Federation and directly create rights and obligations for the citizens of the Russian Federation."[51] In 1992 the legislature adopted the declaration, including Article 1, as an amendment to the 1978 Constitution.[52] "By incorporating the whole body of international human rights law into Russian domestic law, the drafters of the 1992 amendment hoped to effect rapid changes in the legal environment."[53]

During the country's transitional period, the Constitutional Court began to rely on international human rights law before these formal constitutional changes occurred. In *The Labor Code Case*, the Court stated:

> It follows from Art. 28 of the [1978] Constitution that Russia ensures good faith fulfillment of obligations arising from the generally recognized principles and norms of international law and from international treaties and agreements signed by Russia. The latter's supremacy over Russian laws is confirmed by the Declaration of the Rights and Freedoms of the Individual and Citizen.[54]

[48] Gennady M. Danilenko, *International Law in the Russian Legal System*, 91 ASIL PROC. 295, 295 (1997).

[49] Gennady M. Danilenko, *The New Russian Constitution and International Law*, 88 AJIL 451, 459 (1994).

[50] ROBERT AHDIEH, RUSSIA'S CONSTITUTIONAL REVOLUTION 13, 18–19 (1997); Alexander N. Domrin, *Issues and Options in the Soviet Transition to the Rule of Law*, COEXISTENCE: A REVIEW OF EAST-WEST AND DEVELOPMENT ISSUES, Mar. 1993, at 1, 5.

[51] *Quoted in* GENNADY M. DANILENKO & WILLIAM BURNHAM, LAW AND LEGAL SYSTEM OF THE RUSSIAN FEDERATION 34 (2d ed. 2000).

[52] Danilenko, *supra* note 49, at 461.

[53] Danilenko, *supra* note 48, at 296; *cf.* Lori Fisler Damrosch, *International Human Rights Law in Soviet and American Courts*, 100 YALE L.J. 2315, 2324 (1991) ("Viewing the linkage from the other direction, Soviet jurists have also emphasized that establishing the primacy of international human rights law could help consolidate the domestic rule of law within the Soviet Union.").

[54] The Labor Code Case, Vestnik Konstitutsionnogo Suda RF [Vestn. Konst. Suda RF], 1993, No. 1, at 29, *reprinted in* DANILENKO & BURNHAM, *supra* note 51, at 30, 32.

The Court's reliance on the 1978 Constitution and the declaration was specious. The former had not yet been amended,[55] and the latter was not binding.[56] The Court's approach, here and in similar decisions during this period, reflected the fact that greater faith was being invested in international human rights than in domestic institutional norms, even to the point of seriously fudging the interpretation of formal domestic enactments.

An internationalist perspective triumphed both in the drafting of the new Russian Constitution and in subsequent judicial decisions. The final text of Article 15 of the 1993 Constitution gives treaties higher status than statutory and administrative law. It states:

> The universally recognized principles and norms of the international law and the international treaties of the Russian Federation are a component part of its legal system. If an international treaty of the Russian Federation stipulates other rules than those established by the law, the rules of the international treaty shall apply.[57]

Article 46 authorizes recourse by citizens to international bodies to appeal adverse domestic judicial and administrative decisions: "Everyone in conformity with the international treaties of the Russian Federation has the right to turn to international organs concerned with the protection of human rights and freedoms if all the means of legal protection available within the state have been exhausted."[58]

As for judicial decisions under the new Constitution, the Constitutional Court has frequently referred to human rights treaties.[59] In 1996 the Court issued a judgment in an especially important case concerning the Criminal Procedure Code and Article 46 of the Constitution. The Court held that decisions by international organs, presumably including the United Nations Human Rights Committee, may lead to domestic reexamination of previously decided criminal cases.[60] In 1995 the Court issued an important "guiding explanation"[61] to lower courts.[62] It instructed the rest of the judiciary that Article 9 of the ICCPR (rights under arrest and detention) has "priority over [the Russian Federation's] domestic legislation" and must be applied so that individuals are guaranteed the ability to petition courts on the lawfulness of their detention.[63] The following year, the Court issued another guiding explanation to lower courts explaining that Article 15(4) meant that self-executing treaties trumped federal law without any need for implementing legislation.[64] Lower courts have now begun to apply treaties in individual cases.[65]

[55] DANILENKO & BURNHAM, *supra* note 51, at 33. Danilenko and Burnham also explain that "this broad clause [Article 28 of the 1978 Constitution] was never interpreted as a general incorporation of international law into the Soviet or Soviet Russian law." *Id.*

[56] *Id.* at 34.

[57] CONST. Art. 15, §4.

[58] *Id.* Art. 46.

[59] Jane Henderson, *Reference to International Law in Decided Cases of the First Russian Constitutional Court, in* CONSTITUTIONAL REFORM AND INTERNATIONAL LAW IN CENTRAL AND EASTERN EUROPE 59, 66–70 (Rein Mullerson et al. eds., 1998) (collecting early cases); *see also* AHDIEH, *supra* note 50, at 154 (describing importance of Court's reliance on international norms in "raising Russia's constitutional standards"); DANILENKO & BURNHAM, *supra* note 51, at 30.

[60] Danilenko, *supra* note 48, at 300.

[61] *Id.* at 298 ("'Guiding explanations' are abstract opinions that are binding on all lower courts.").

[62] Ruling of the Plenary Session of the Supreme Court of the Russian Federation, On the Judicial Practice Concerning Verification of the Legality and Justification of Arrests or the Extension of Periods of Detention, Biulleten' Verkhovnogo Suda RF [Biull. Verkh. Suda RF], 1995, No. 1, at 3, *translated in* DANILENKO & BURNHAM, *supra* note 51, at 43.

[63] *Id.*

[64] Ruling of the Plenary Session of the Supreme Court of the Russian Federation, On Some Questions Concerning the Application of the Constitution of the Russian Federation by Courts, Biull. Verkh. Suda RF, 1996, No. 1, at 3, *translated in* DANILENKO & BURNHAM, *supra* note 51, at 41.

[65] DANILENKO & BURNHAM, *supra* note 51, at 43; *see also In re* Belichenko and Others, Vestn. Konst. Suda RF, 1998, No. 1, at 47, *translated in* DANILENKO & BURNHAM, *supra*, at 44–45 (Moscow Regional Court opinion holding ICCPR prohibition against double jeopardy trumps Russian Criminal Procedure Code).

If the Russian case represents regional trends, as Danilenko suggested, the empirical record amply supports the need for a severability regime. The Russian experience demonstrates the lack of sovereignty costs in transposing international legal decisions onto domestic legal structures. It also shows, beyond formal constitutional arrangements, the depth of political and ideological commitments to tying issues of governance to international developments. Finally, the post-Communist regional experience expands the empirical reach of the lock-in account, as the dynamics of these states closely resemble those in Moravcsik's study of postwar Europe. Based on sheer numbers, if nothing else, the needs of these states should figure prominently in structuring an effective treaty regime and the law of reservations.

Established democracies. In terms of developing a sensible law of reservations, Moravcsik's empirical work is also important in understanding the ambivalent attitude of some established democracies—such as the United States and the United Kingdom—in acceding to international human rights agreements. Moravcsik explains that established democracies perceive little domestic gain in agreeing to such international commitments and a significant sovereignty cost in doing so. The former perception notably corresponds with the first goal identified above, and the latter corresponds with the second. In terms of the lack of domestic benefits, these states operate with a high baseline of strong democratic traditions and civil rights protections. Consider the United Kingdom's postwar ambivalence toward the European Convention on Human Rights: with such a high baseline, a regional human rights regime had substantially less to offer the citizens of the United Kingdom than, for example, the citizens of postwar Austria. Moravcsik concludes that the factor that ultimately encouraged the United Kingdom to ratify the Convention was the perception that a regional human rights regime would help stave off the threat of totalitarianism in Western Europe, a concern well within the security interests of the British government.[66] The United Kingdom, while being pulled in two directions (wanting to promote human rights abroad but resisting infringements on its own domestic sovereignty), ultimately ratified the Convention on the basis of the international component of the first goal.

The United Kingdom's stance is taken by other established democracies, especially the United States. Moravcsik explains that U.S. unwillingness to accept international human rights obligations represents "the norm . . . among established democracies—a norm related to the relatively low level of offsetting domestic benefits in an established, self-confident democracy."[67] He submits that "established democracies can be expected to support rhetorical declarations in favor of human rights and regimes with optional enforcement that bind newly established democracies but exempt themselves."[68] Jack Goldsmith has described the latter phenomenon as the "United States double standard,"[69] and he and Eric Posner have pointed to its manifestation in U.S. reservation practice.[70] I accept the descriptive accuracy of this aspect of Goldsmith and Posner's claim (and Moravcsik's extension of it to some of the other established democracies[71]). As for the normative question, however, a severability regime offers a better reflection of the reality of this double standard than an AS regime.

What these observers of U.S. practice have touched on are the dual goals of treaty accession with reservations. Even though the baseline of a robust democracy and strong domestic

[66] Moravcsik, *supra* note 39, at 242.

[67] *Id.* at 244.

[68] *Id.* at 229; *see also id.* at 243.

[69] Jack Goldsmith, *International Human Rights and the United States Double Standard*, 1 GREEN BAG (n.s.) 365 (1998).

[70] Jack L. Goldsmith & Eric A. Posner, *A Theory of Customary International Law*, 66 U. CHI. L. REV. 1113, 1175 (1999).

[71] *But see infra* text at note 83 (disagreeing with the empirical accuracy of Moravcsik's model for Nordic states, Belgium, the Netherlands, and others). It should be noted that the United Kingdom appears to be moving from this category of state behavior to one more accepting of international human rights obligations. The enactment of the Human Rights Act in 1998 may make it necessary to cabin my account of UK practice as a pre-1998 representation of this modality.

civil rights protections brings it fewer benefits and a significant sovereignty cost, the United States, as well as other established democracies, has substantial interests in promoting human rights internationally and in participating directly in multilateral treaty regimes (if not in fact adopting a leadership role in such forums). Calling this a "double standard" actually helps highlight the strength of the two poles: the U.S. government exerts tremendous efforts to impose international human rights standards on others and, at the same time, strongly resists the imposition of international human rights standards on its own sovereignty.

The U.S. interests regarding the international dimension of the first goal—promoting human rights abroad—are indicated by the administration's efforts to encourage the Senate to ratify the ICCPR. In letters to the chair and the ranking minority member of the Committee on Foreign Relations, President George Bush stated that "U.S. ratification would also strengthen our ability to influence the development of appropriate human rights principles in the international community and provide an additional and effective tool in our efforts to improve respect for fundamental freedoms in many problem countries around the world."[72] During the ratification hearings, Assistant Secretary of State Richard Schifter emphasized the same general point: "We urge consent to ratification of the Covenant in order to further the observance of human rights in other countries of the world community. The promotion of the increased observance of internationally recognized human rights by all countries is a major foreign policy goal of the United States government."[73]

In his prepared statement, Schifter discussed particular ways in which ratification would serve this goal. First, U.S. ratification would provide "additional concrete evidence of our commitment to support respect for human rights everywhere."[74] Second, it would "augment the force of the Covenant as a principal instrument at the international level."[75] Third, by making it possible to participate in the work of the Human Rights Committee, it would give the United States the opportunity to make "a major contribution . . . to enhanc[ing] the effectiveness of the Human Rights Committee as a watchdog body operating to identify and curb human rights violators."[76] Fourth, the optional provision for state-to-state complaint proceedings under Article 41 could provide the United States with "an added recourse for use in bringing pressure to bear upon human rights violators."[77]

At the same time, Schifter took pains to explain that ratification would involve minimal costs to U.S. sovereignty. He focused on two facets of U.S. ratification: the high U.S. baseline and reservations, declarations, and understandings. First, he explained that, in practice, differences between U.S. domestic law and the ICCPR were so insubstantial that "adherence to the Covenant will bring no fundamental changes to the enjoyment of individual human rights by all Americans."[78] Second, in reviewing the proposed reservations, declarations, and understandings, he stressed that the Covenant should be declared a non-self-executing treaty and he assured the Senate that the administration would not propose implementing legislation to counter that effect.[79]

The breadth of U.S. objectives in joining human rights treaties should suggest that in some circumstances those interests would outweigh the interests served by a particular reservation. If the government were faced with the choice of (1) the complete loss of membership in a

[72] *International Covenant on Civil and Political Rights: Hearing Before the Senate Comm. on Foreign Relations*, 102d Cong. 16 (1992) (statement of Richard Schifter, assistant secretary of state for human rights and humanitarian affairs) (quoting letters from Pres. George Bush to Sen. Claiborne Pell and Sen. Jesse Helms, Aug. 8, 1991)).

[73] *Id.* at 17.

[74] *Id.*

[75] *Id.*

[76] *Id.*

[77] *Id.* at 18.

[78] *Id.*

[79] *Id.*

treaty or (2) the loss of the application or effect of a particular reservation, in some circumstances the government would prefer the latter. Certain features of the American political system suggest that the number of times when that choice would prevail is not trivial. In her extended analysis of the subject, Natalie Kaufman discusses institutional relationships between executive agencies, the president, and the Senate that lead to "attachments [that] are unnecessary."[80] According to Kaufman, wounds left by the debates on the Bricker Amendment in the 1950s often lead the executive branch to overcompensate in submitting its package of reservations to the Senate as a means of securing approval. Kaufman explains that this attitude frequently results in reservations that sweep much more broadly than required for passage:

> [T]he drafters of the attachments raised some issues that probably would not otherwise have been raised and reinforced the sense of controversy that the opposition had settled over the treaties in the 1950s. Most of the proposed attachments addressed specifics that had never been a focus of vocal opposition and hardly seem the creation of a sympathetic executive.[81]

Kaufman's work thus suggests additional reasons that a double-standard state's reservations should not, as a categorical matter, be considered essential to the government's ratification.[82]

In determining the legal consequence of an invalid reservation, a severability regime is well equipped to assess which outcome balances the dual aspects of these states' accession. Some reservations embody essential conditions for the United States or the United Kingdom to assent to a human rights agreement. Others might be expendable—conditions the governments would discard if their retention meant being excluded from, or unable to join, the treaty altogether. Accordingly, expelling these states from a treaty, or voiding their initial act of accession without a more searching inquiry, would in some instances contravene an essential aspect of their consent to be bound. The better approach is to weigh the interest served by the particular reservation against the cost of voiding the act of ratification. A severability regime would maintain the flexibility to balance these competing concerns, while an AS regime would automatically choose one (termination of membership) over the other (severance of the reservation).

Although the above discussion relies partly on Moravcsik's empirical work, his findings do not suffice for our purposes. Moravcsik's analysis appears to fit the cases of the United States and the United Kingdom. His model, however, does not deal effectively with established democracies that defy his theoretical predictions. In particular, a set of states possess the same features that Moravcsik and others would use to classify established democracies, but these states do not support—as Moravcsik claims established democracies can be expected to do—"rhetorical declarations in favor of human rights and regimes with optional enforcement that bind newly established democracies but exempt themselves."[83] On the contrary, several established democracies, such as the Netherlands and Belgium, follow a consistent standard with regard to international human rights law. They evince a deep commitment to incorporating human rights treaties in their domestic law and to promoting international human rights abroad: hence, they can be characterized as consistent, rather than double, standard states.

In addition to the Netherlands and Belgium, the five Nordic states (Denmark, Finland, Iceland, Norway, and Sweden) engage in this modality of state practice. In the early 1970s, these states were among the first to ratify the ICCPR and the International Covenant on Economic, Social and Cultural Rights. Upon ratification of the ICCPR, these states also ratified

[80] NATALIE HEVENER KAUFMAN, HUMAN RIGHTS TREATIES AND THE SENATE 173 (1990); *see also id.* at 159, 161, 174.

[81] *Id.* at 151.

[82] *Cf.* David Sloss, *The Domestication of International Human Rights: Non-Self-Executing Declarations and Human Rights Treaties*, 24 YALE J. INT'L L. 129 (1999) (arguing that executive branch and Senate have had different interpretations of self-executing declarations across different treaties).

[83] Moravcsik, *supra* note 39, at 229; *see supra* text at notes 66–68.

the First Optional Protocol. These governments have all dealt with the filing of individual petitions before a treaty body, lost some of those disputes, and implemented the adverse recommendations.

This modality of state practice comprises a significant set of cases. Their governments are important actors within the international political economy, multilateral treaty negotiations, and UN standard-setting procedures. Because their domestic systems are closely tied to international regimes, they also potentially incur significant costs and benefits from developments in the law of treaties. All of these states have submitted reservations to the ICCPR. If a reservation were found invalid—by a domestic court or by another third-party institution—the determination whether the government was still bound to the treaty would have considerable ramifications.

A noteworthy feature of the Nordic states' practice is their official position on the issue of severability itself. They have each begun systematically to review other states' ratifications with a view to opposing invalid reservations.[84] On several occasions, a Nordic state has officially objected to another state's reservation on the ground that the reservation was incompatible with the treaty and that the consequence was one of severance.[85] At a recent annual meeting of the General Assembly's Sixth Committee, the Nordic states made their position clear:

> [T]he reserving state should be regarded as a party to the treaty without the benefit of the reservation.
>
> This is the so called severability doctrine which has been applied in a number of instances by i.a. the Nordic countries during the past few years.
>
> . . . It is our hope that this part of the report will reflect practice adopted lately by among others the Nordic countries especially in connection with human rights treaties.[86]

Notably, on the basis of this modality of state practice—consistency between the promotion of international rules and domestic incorporation—we should expect these states to respect the same principle of severance if applied to their own systems. That is, the objection they have raised against other states' reservations is one they would accept or embrace having applied to themselves.

The case of the Netherlands points to the negative consequences of a strict AS regime for this modality of state practice. As Henry Schermers explains, Dutch negotiators take particular care in multilateral treaty negotiations because of the direct repercussions of treaty law on domestic governance: "Negotiators from other countries may lightheartedly accept all sorts of treaty obligations which are not subsequently incorporated into their domestic legal systems and therefore become dead letters, whilst a Dutch negotiator always has to take into account that treaty obligations may be invoked in court."[87] Article 94 of the Dutch Constitution gives primacy to treaty obligations over preexisting and subsequent domestic law.[88] This provides the judiciary with a form of "human rights review" not otherwise available in the Dutch system. As components of a parliamentary democracy, Dutch courts cannot review the constitutionality of legislative acts.[89] Hence, a Dutch court can invalidate a law on

[84] Jan Klabbers, *Accepting the Unacceptable? A New Nordic Approach to Reservations to Multilateral Treaties*, 69 NORDIC J. INT'L L. 179 (2000); *see also* Laurids Mikaelsen, *Elements of Nordic and International Practice in the Year of 1996: Denmark*, 66 NORDIC J. INT'L L. 319, 322 (1997).

[85] Klabbers, *supra* note 84, at 185–86.

[86] Päivi Kaukoranta & Manta Lehto, *Elements of Nordic Practice 1998: The Nordic Countries in Coordination*, 68 NORDIC J. INT'L L. 205, 209–10 (1999) (reproducing text of Swedish statement on behalf of Nordic countries before Sixth Committee, Oct. 29, 1998); *see also* Magnuson, *supra* note 36, at 350 (reproducing text of Swedish statement on behalf of Nordic countries before Sixth Committee, Nov. 4, 1997).

[87] Henry G. Schermers, *Netherlands*, *in* 7 THE EFFECT OF TREATIES IN DOMESTIC LAW 109, 112 (Francis G. Jacobs & Shelley Roberts eds., 1987).

[88] CONST. Art. 94; *see also* Schermers, *supra* note 87, at 113; H. H. M. Sondaal, *Some Features of Dutch Treaty Practice*, 1988 NETH. Y.B. INT'L L. 179, 240.

[89] CONST. Art. 120 ("The constitutionality of Acts of Parliament and treaties shall not be reviewed by the courts.").

the ground that it violates a right contained in a multilateral treaty, but not on the ground that it violates a right contained in the Constitution.[90] Some commentators have described the Dutch system as assigning treaties primacy over the Constitution itself,[91] suggesting that the Dutch example is an extreme outlier.[92] The main features of the Dutch system, however, are shared by other states (e.g., Belgium, Finland, and others). These states' domestic legal systems not only give human rights treaties primacy over domestic legislation; they do so to the point of dependence on such treaties for substantive civil and political rights protections.

The Dutch record confirms the structural elevation of international treaty obligations over important domestic policy choices. The system ties its fate to international treaty law in a similar fashion to the lock-in dynamics of newly established democracies; though here the government does so out of concern for continued commitments to cosmopolitanism and liberal rights guarantees, not as a hedge against a potential illiberal regime. Dutch practice includes numerous court decisions invalidating legislation on the ground that it violates a treaty.[93] Notably, such decisions do not simply apply purely domestic legal expressions against one another (i.e., the government's enactment of a treaty against the government's enactment of a statute).[94] The courts are willing, if not keen, to rely on international interpretations of the treaty provisions. The courts are also willing to "fill gaps" in domestic legislation by having recourse to treaty obligations.[95] As for reservations in particular, in a significant case a Dutch court explained that a "reservation constitutes a derogation from the regime of the Convention and should, therefore, be so construed as to respect the intention of the reservation, on the one hand, and *to limit this derogation from the Convention's regime to the fullest possible extent, on the other hand.*"[96] In another case, the Supreme Court gave the withdrawal of a reservation retroactive effect so as to produce stability among Dutch international commitments.[97]

[90] Henry G. Schermers, *Some Recent Cases Delaying the Direct Effect of International Treaties in Dutch Law,* 10 MICH. J. INT'L L. 266, 268 (1989).

[91] *See, e.g.,* John H. Jackson, *Status of Treaties in Domestic Legal Systems: A Policy Analysis,* 86 AJIL 310, 320 (1992).

[92] The degree to which the Dutch system is an outlier is questionable. The constitutional provision empowering courts to invalidate domestic law states only that "*[s]tatutory regulations* in force within the Kingdom shall not be applicable if such application is in conflict with provisions of treaties." CONST. Art. 94 (emphasis added). Under Article 91(3), treaties that conflict with the Constitution must receive supermajority approval at the same level as required to amend the Constitution itself. E. A. Alkema, *Foreign Relations in the Netherlands Constitution of 1983,* 31 NETH. INT'L L. REV. 307, 320 (1984) ("Article 91, paragraph 3, requires a qualified majority for the approval of treaties containing provisions which conflict with the Constitution. The two-thirds majority is the same as that required for a constitutional amendment.").

[93] *See, e.g.,* Aalt Willem Heringa, *Judicial Enforcement of Article 26 of the International Covenant on Civil and Political Rights in the Netherlands,* 1993 NETH. Y.B. INT'L L. 139, 178 (describing cases by the Centrale Raad van Beroep, the highest court in public service and social security matters, striking down legislation in violation of ICCPR); *id.* at 174–75 (describing Supreme Court cases holding legislation violated Article 26 of the ICCPR but allowing Parliament to choose remedy); *see also id.* at 145 n.18 ("On a yearly basis hundreds of cases, dealing mainly with human rights treaties, such as the European Convention and the ICCPR, are decided."); *cf.* Schermers, *supra* note 87, at 113–14 (collecting cases invalidating legislation under human rights and other treaties).

[94] *Cf.* L. ERADES, INTERACTIONS BETWEEN INTERNATIONAL AND MUNICIPAL LAW: A COMPARATIVE CASE LAW STUDY 627–34 (Malgosia Fitzmaurice & Cees Flinterman eds., 1993) (collecting cases).

[95] *See, e.g.,* T.S.M. Compagnie d'Assurance Transports A.G. v. Geisseler Transport, 1993 NETH. Y.B. INT'L L. 395 (Sup. Ct. Nov. 16, 1990). The Court held:

> The Dutch legislature has not so far complied with this obligation. It follows that the Dutch courts, which are obliged to interpret and apply Dutch law as far as possible in such a way that the State complies with its treaty obligations, must fill this "gap in the legislation" . . . in a manner that is in keeping with the system of the law and consistent with the cases regulated by law.

Id. at 397 (citation omitted).

[96] Bremi B.V. and Elart-Gunneman B.V. v. Amcor Ltd., 1982 NETH. Y.B. INT'L L. 371, 374 (Ct. App. Arnhem Oct. 1, 1979) (emphasis added); *see also* Schermers, *supra* note 87, at 117 (referring to this case as demonstrating that "[a] reservation should be restrictively interpreted"). *Compare* K. M. v. Netherlands, 1989 NETH. Y.B. INT'L L. 322, 324 (allowing extradition based on narrow interpretation of Dutch reservation to European Convention on Extradition).

[97] X. v. Raad voor de Kinderbescherming te s-Gravenhage [The Hague Child Care and Protection Board], 1989 NETH. Y.B. INT'L L. 341 (Sup. Ct. Jan. 29, 1988) (holding a child maintenance order enforceable despite its having been issued at a time when the reservation—which barred enforcement of such orders—was still in effect).

Some of these court cases generated a political outcry, at times even prompting officials to call for withdrawal from a treaty.[98] The criticism of these decisions is similar to the objections one might expect in response to a decision severing a reservation: the critics contend that the Netherlands is being held to a commitment that was not clearly understood as an obligation at the time of ratification and that does not accord with the country's national interest. Such claims are even more compelling in the context of the courts' reliance on international sources of interpretation exogenous to the Netherlands political order. Nevertheless, the prevailing political sentiment appears to be a steadfast commitment to membership in these treaties and, to a significant degree, to the international interpretive development of the obligations entailed.[99] As H. H. M. Sondaal, a senior official in the Dutch Ministry of Foreign Affairs, explains, when the government decides to join a treaty, it knowingly "places itself in a tight straightjacket."[100]

A strict AS rule would release the government from this self-constraint, and suspend a panoply of civil and political rights protections in a manner the system would have a difficult time withstanding. For systems like that of the Netherlands, the government's reliance on human rights treaties also suggests that its reservations should not categorically be considered essential to accession. The level of reliance also indicates the disruption that could result if the government's membership in an important treaty were interrupted for even a temporary period. That is, even if the government decided to reratify the convention, the interim period would incur substantial costs. While an AS regime would probably involve such costs, a severability regime would be designed to avoid them.

The double- and consistent-standard states analyzed above constitute opposite ends of a spectrum. Between the two lies an intermediate category of established democracies (such as Australia, Canada, Switzerland, and arguably India). In contrast to the double-standard democracies, these states evince genuine interest in incorporating human rights treaties in domestic law and in maintaining membership in them by dint of domestic political interests, not simply external foreign policy goals. However, their domestic systems of governance are not reliant on, or committed to, these treaties for the same ideational and pragmatic purposes as the consistent-standard states. The intermediate states, like all states, have an incentive to enter both essential and accessory reservations when ratifying multilateral agreements. Like the other states, they would face significant transaction costs if forced to consider reratification after being ejected from the treaty. A determination whether to sever an invalid reservation should therefore try to gauge the overriding goals of state consent in relation to the reservation in question.

The treaty practices of intermediate states indicate that some of their reservations may be considered inessential to their consent to be bound. For example, in *Belilos v. Switzerland*, the European Court of Human Rights considered Switzerland's reservation to Article 6 of the European Convention (the right to a fair trial); the Court found the reservation invalid and severed it.[101] Wanting to remain party to the treaty,[102] the Swiss government argued against the possibility that "a State which had made an invalid reservation would simply not

[98] *See, e.g.*, Heringa, *supra* note 93, at 170.

[99] Another indication of prevailing political sentiments is the Dutch minister for foreign affairs' response to interrogatories from Parliament on reservations to the Biological Weapons Convention. The minister stated: "Reservations which are incompatible with the object and purpose of a treaty are not void in international law, though a state which makes such reservations can never invoke them successfully." Reservations to the Biological Weapons Convention, 1982 NETH. Y.B. INT'L L. 216, 216–17. Although a premise of his explanation appears flawed, the minister's statement suggests acceptance of treaty practice in which a reservation may not be available to a state well after ratification because of its incompatibility with the object and purpose of the agreement.

[100] Sondaal, *supra* note 88, at 240.

[101] Belilos v. Switzerland, 132 Eur. Ct. H.R. (ser. A) (1987).

[102] *Id.* at 28; Edwards, *supra* note 11, at 376–77 ("[P]resumably motivated by a desire to remain a party to the treaty, Switzerland argued against this solution [of nullifying its status as a state party] . . .").

be party to the treaty."[103] During oral argument, the Swiss representative made the following plea: "The Swiss Government considers that it would be obviously disproportionate, both in the view of the other Contracting Parties to the Convention and in that of Switzerland, to apply this solution [of annulling its status as a state party] in the Belilos case."[104]

A further indication of intermediate states' accessory reservations is revealed by what might be called tentative or "phase out" reservations. Australia's reservation to Article 4 of the Convention on the Elimination of Racial Discrimination provides a useful example. Article 4(a) requires state parties to criminalize the dissemination of racist hate speech and propaganda.[105] Australia, however, submitted the following reservation:

> Australia is not at present in a position specifically to treat as offences all the matters covered by article 4(a) of the Convention. Acts of the kind there mentioned are punishable only to the extent provided by the existing criminal law dealing with such matters as the maintenance of public order, public mischief, assault, riot, criminal libel, conspiracy and attempts. It is the intention of the Australian Government, at the first suitable moment, to seek from Parliament legislation specifically implementing the terms of article 4(a).[106]

One must wonder whether this reservation can possibly be conceived of as an essential condition of Australia's accession to the treaty. While Australia ratified the treaty in 1975, it has yet to enact legislation of the scope envisioned by Article 4(a).[107] If Australia's reservation were found to be incompatible with the object and purpose of the treaty, it would be highly questionable to consider the reservation a critical component of the state's accession to the treaty and Australia no longer a party.[108]

Of course, this type of analysis can also get a little tricky. For example, in the *Fisheries Jurisdiction* case,[109] the ICJ noted in passing that Canada's reservation was "not only an integral part of the current declaration but also an essential component of it, and hence of the acceptance by Canada of the Court's compulsory jurisdiction."[110] Spain had initiated the proceedings within a year of Canada's submitting the reservation, and the reservation was widely understood to address a particularly time-bound concern of the Canadian government. This understanding was evidenced in a statement by the Canadian minister for foreign affairs before the Canadian Senate: "As you know, to protect the integrity of this legislation, we registered a reservation to the International Court of Justice, explaining that this reservation would of course be temporary. . . ."[111] Admittedly, declarations accepting the Court's compulsory jurisdiction are not treaties, but they are closely analogous. As with Australia's reservation to the Convention on Racial Discrimination, the temporary quality of Canada's reservation is instructive.

[103] Eur. Ct. H.R. Doc. Cour/Misc (87) 237, *supra* note 2, at 45.

[104] *Id.*

[105] International Convention on the Elimination of All Forms of Racial Discrimination, *opened for signature* Mar. 7, 1966, Art. 4, 660 UNTS 195.

[106] International Convention on the Elimination of All Forms of Racial Discrimination, Declarations and Reservations (Feb. 5, 2002), *at* <http://www.unhchr.ch/html/menu3/b/treaty2_asp.htm>.

[107] During a periodic report to the Committee on Racial Discrimination, Australia explained that it had recently introduced civil penalties (and some criminal sanctions) in accordance with Article 4(a). UN Doc. CERD/C/335/Add.2 (1999). Australia acknowledged that because Article 4 envisions criminal sanctions against racial vilification, "[t]he Government . . . is not in a position to remove the reservation." *Id.*, para. 416. Admittedly, one might take this to mean that Australia's reservation is still important to the state's relationship to the treaty. Whether it is, or ever was, *critically* important is the type of question that this article suggests is the relevant one to ask.

[108] Notably, the Italian government adopted a position similar to Australia's, in discussing its reservations to Article 4(a). UN Doc. CERD/C/SR.1077, para. 11 (1995).

[109] Fisheries Jurisdiction (Spain v. Can.), 1998 ICJ REP. 432 (Dec. 4). The case involved a dispute over Canada's alleged seizure of a Spanish vessel in international waters. The Court held that it did not have jurisdiction because Canada's declaration of acceptance of the Court's compulsory jurisdiction included a reservation barring adjudication of matters relating to conservation and management measures.

[110] *Id.* at 457, para. 59.

[111] *Id.* at 457, para. 60 (quoting Canadian minister for foreign affairs, May 12, 1994).

It invites serious reflection as to whether the reservation would be considered essential in the future. If it were deemed invalid in a different dispute, for example, twenty years later, a strong argument could be made that when submitted the reservation was said not to be essential as a long-term or unending condition.

Nondemocratic states. As a descriptive matter, there are strong reasons to believe—based on recent empirical research in international relations scholarship—that a severability regime would capture important nuances in the practices of nondemocratic states.[112] International relations scholars have recently begun to use sociological tools to understand the processes by which states pass from illiberal to liberal regimes. Some of these projects have generated significant insights into the dynamics of nondemocratic states' accession to human rights treaties. For example, Thomas Risse, Stephen Ropp, and Kathryn Sikkink provide a theoretically robust account of how nondemocratic states (1) respond to domestic and international political pressure in ratifying human rights treaties, (2) begin to defend their actions according to international legal rules, and (3) potentially move through a "process of socialization" toward the incorporation of international norms.[113] Their model does not account for all types of nondemocratic states, because extant social and material conditions are not always sufficient to propel the socialization process. However, their systematic analysis of numerous paired case studies (ranging from Tunisia-Morocco to the Philippines-Indonesia to Guatemala-Chile) effectively describes various state practices and forms a strong empirical basis for accepting their theoretical claims.

Most significant for our purposes is the critical step in the socialization process from a phase of "tactical concessions"[114] to one of "prescriptive status."[115] These are the moments when we can expect states to ratify human rights treaties, and thus the political context in which the value the government attaches to a reservation would be indicated. In the "tactical concession" phase, such governments make cosmetic changes to placate domestic and international pressure groups. For example, a government may release some political prisoners, exercise greater permissiveness toward political demonstrations, or pass relatively superficial legislation.[116] These concessions can propel certain causal mechanisms, resulting in further dynamic changes that potentially lead to the phase of "prescriptive status." In this subsequent phase, the state begins to, and then finally does, accept international norms. If successfully completed, the prescriptive status phase will lead to the final phase of rule-consistent behavior.[117]

Whether or not nondemocratic states attach reservations to treaties may indicate their position in this process and, in turn, how to evaluate the nature of their conditioned consent. Commentators have observed that nondemocratic states (such as Iraq, Libya, and the former Soviet Union) have tended to ratify human rights treaties without any reservations. The standard account is that these states so heavily discount international legal obligations that they do not feel the need to specify conditions that would ensure conformity of their domestic legal arrangements with the requirements of the treaty. They ratify for purely symbolic purposes. At first glance, the minimal use of reservations by nondemocratic states might suggest that the concern about where to place such states in a severability model is

[112] I should note at the outset of this section that the following discussion involves a more detailed theoretical analysis of the practice of nondemocratic states than is needed for the descriptive argument. However, I delve into that aspect because the normative questions raised cannot be answered without an appreciation of the theoretical framework.

[113] Thomas Risse, *"Let's Argue!": Communicative Action in World Politics*, 54 INT'L ORG. 1 (2000); Thomas Risse & Stephen C. Ropp, *International Human Rights Norms and Domestic Change*, *in* THE POWER OF HUMAN RIGHTS 234 (Thomas Risse, Stephen C. Ropp, & Kathryn Sikkink eds., 1999); Thomas Risse & Kathryn Sikkink, *The Socialization of International Human Rights Norms into Domestic Practices: Introduction*, *in id.* at 1, 11.

[114] Risse & Sikkink, *supra* note 113, at 25.

[115] *Id.* at 29.

[116] *Id.* at 25.

[117] *Id.* at 31.

marginal. While the small number of reservations does diminish the concern, this phenomenon should also prompt heightened attention when nondemocratic states actually use reservations.

On the basis of variations in the empirical case studies, Risse and Ropp[118] conclude that a nondemocratic state's accession to a human rights treaty may involve features of both "tactical concession" and "prescriptive status."[119] However, the authors do not pay special attention to reservation practices. Yet, because reservations are designed to adjust obligations incurred by a treaty, these scholars' conceptual model suggests that a nondemocratic state that ratifies a treaty with reservations has begun to accept the prescriptive legitimacy of international rules. In these contexts, a state may be genuinely balancing competing goals so that a particular reservation may not be an essential condition of its accession to the treaty.

The dynamic nature of this modality of state practice is illustrated by Chile.[120] According to Ropp and Sikkink, Chile's phase of tactical concessions lasted from 1975 to 1988.[121] The subsequent phase of prescriptive status concluded in 1990—the year Chile elected a new president through a democratic process, ratified the American Convention on Human Rights, and accepted the compulsory jurisdiction of the Inter-American Court.[122] Importantly, Chile ratified the Convention Against Torture near the end of the tactical concessions phase. In 1987 General Pinochet sent a draft act of ratification to Chile's legislative body for approval.[123] Pinochet's accompanying memorandum spoke in terms of the need to comply with international norms in appearance, if not deed.[124] The proposed act of ratification included significant reservations, and in 1988 the junta ratified the Convention with these conditions attached.

The need for a severability regime can be seen in relation to Chile's reservation to Article 2 of the Convention Against Torture. Article 2 mandates that "[e]ach State Party shall take effective legislative, administrative, judicial or other measures to prevent acts of torture," and further specifies that "[a]n order from a superior officer or a public authority may not be invoked as a justification of torture."[125] One of Chile's reservations attempted to carve a hole in that obligation. It stated that if a subordinate initially challenged a superior officer's order to commit torture, Article 2 would not apply in the event the superior re-insisted that the order be followed.[126] When Chile came up for review before the Committee Against Torture, the validity of the reservation was seriously questioned. The committee informed Chile that it considered the reservation "incompatible with the Convention."[127] The committee's views

[118] Risse, Ropp, and Sikkink sometimes write in teams of two and sometimes alone. All three are the editors of THE POWER OF HUMAN RIGHTS, *supra* note 113.

[119] *See, e.g.*, Risse & Ropp, *supra* note 113, at 248.

[120] Stephen C. Ropp & Kathryn Sikkink, *International Norms and Domestic Politics in Chile and Guatemala, in* THE POWER OF HUMAN RIGHTS, *supra* note 113, at 172.

[121] *Id.* at 184.

[122] *Id.* at 190.

[123] Augusto Pinochet Ugarte, President of the Republic, to the Honourable Junta de Gobierno, Communication BOL 913-10 (Nov. 11, 1987), *at* <http://www.remember-chile.org.uk/news/pintcts1.htm> [hereinafter Pinochet Comm. 913-10].

[124] *Id.* The communication stated:

> From the point of view of Chile's international position, the aspiration to become a party to the Convention, reflects its actual decision to recognise in practice the existence of fundamental human rights. In this way, it will be possible to disprove the accusations which have been put forward systematically against our country in international forums on human rights.

[125] Convention Against Torture and Other Cruel, Inhuman, or Degrading Treatment or Punishment, Dec. 10, 1984, Art. 2, 1465 UNTS 85.

[126] Convention Against Torture and Other Cruel, Inhuman or Degrading Treatment or Punishment, Declarations and Reservations, at n.16 (Feb. 5, 2001), *at* <http://www.unhchr.ch/html/menu3/b/treaty12_asp.htm> [hereinafter Torture Declarations and Reservations].

[127] Report of the Committee Against Torture, UN GAOR, 45th Sess., Supp. No. 44, at 64, para. 349, UN Doc. A/45/44 (1990).

were supported by the fact that twenty states had officially objected to Chile's reservation on the ground that it was incompatible with the object and purpose of the treaty.[128] Some of these states notably took the position that the reservation should be considered severed and Article 2 in full effect.[129] The committee, however, commented only on the antecedent question of invalidity.

In response to the committee's criticism, the government defended the reservation, explaining that it "had formulated [the] reservation, in order to reconcile the principle of exoneration of responsibility established in its domestic legislation with the obligations arising from the Convention."[130] Significantly, Chile described its reservations as provisional in nature:

> With regard to all the reservations formulated by Chile to the Convention, the representative pointed out that they had been lodged by the Chilean Government partly for reasons of substance, partly for procedural reasons, and partly also because the present Government of Chile was about to be replaced by another government to which it wished to leave the entire responsibility of deciding whether it agreed to be bound by all the provisions of the Convention and thus to withdraw the reservations.[131]

To be sure, the above explanation is post hoc and invites skepticism. However, it also indicates significant play in the joints in terms of whether a nondemocratic state's reservation to a treaty is necessarily critical to that state's ratification.

In fact, the documentary record preceding ratification supports the Chilean representative's explanation. When Pinochet forwarded the proposed act of ratification to the legislative body, he discussed two of the reservations in his memorandum, but he did not specifically mention the reservation to Article 2.[132] He also stated that those reservations that had already been submitted at the time of signature were "considered necessary" but only for "the primary purpose of not accepting the authority of the Committee against Torture."[133] More important, a Technical Report by the Ministry of Foreign Affairs accompanied the proposed act of ratification. The Technical Report indicated that the reservation was not vital. Specifically, it stated that domestic law was already in conformity with Article 2: "The third paragraph of Article 2 prescribes that superior orders from an official or public authority may not be invoked as justifying torture. This provision is consistent, for example, with the provisions of article 330 of the Military Justice Code."[134]

In sum, Chile's reservation to Article 2 brings a number of severability-related factors into focus, foremost among these that the record of nondemocratic states' accession to human rights treaties is more complex than one might assume. As Risse, Ropp, and Sikkink's empirical case studies show, the act of ratification itself may bridge the divide between phases of the socialization process. As a response to domestic and international pressure, a state's decision to join a human rights agreement may reflect a tactical concession or an expression of prescriptive status or both. Chile's practice with regard to the Convention Against Torture shows that a reservation may not be essential to a nondemocratic state's decision to ratify a treaty. Indeed, a state's very ratification of an agreement necessarily means that some goals are being pursued by that act of accession. If the state is responding to domestic political pressure or beginning the move to prescriptive status, its decision to join the treaty should be credited as a dimension of the first goal identified above: the culmination and expression of political support (though not through the ballot box) for promoting domestic human rights. Chile's

[128] Torture Declarations and Reservations, *supra* note 126, at n.16.

[129] *E.g., id.*, Objections by Australia, Austria, Bulgaria, and Sweden.

[130] Report of the Committee Against Torture, *supra* note 127, at 67, para. 366.

[131] *Id.*, para. 364.

[132] Pinochet Comm. 913-10, *supra* note 123.

[133] *Id.*

[134] Republic of Chile, Ministry of Foreign Affairs, Technical Report (n.d. [1987]), *at* <http://www.rememberchile.org.uk/news/pintcts2.htm> (visited June 5, 2002).

reservation to Article 2 shows that, in some cases, honoring a state's initial act of ratification and the expression of political pressures reflected in that decision may require treating a reservation as dispensable. This result would reflect the nondemocratic state's consent.

A treaty regime that respects the choice of nondemocratic states' consent in the same manner that it respects the consent of other states may raise some normative concerns, which should be addressed. In response to such concerns, it is worth emphasizing two aspects of the impact of a severability regime on the human rights practices of nondemocratic states. First, a severability regime provides a meaningful opportunity to keep a state bound to a human rights treaty despite an invalid reservation. In sharp contrast, an AS regime would consistently nullify a state's ratification without ever inquiring into the severability question. The discussion of Chile presents an especially poignant example of that difference.

The British House of Lords' decision concerning Pinochet's extradition turned on the fact that Chile was a party to the Convention Against Torture between 1988 and 1990. According to the Law Lords, the start date of 1988 was set because domestic extradition rules required Chile, Spain, and the United Kingdom to be contemporaneous parties to the Convention. The end date of 1990 was set because Spain's extradition request involved only claims of torture that had occurred before the new Chilean government was established by democratic elections in 1990. If the severability question had been raised in such a case, an AS regime would have potentially quashed the extradition request (if the reservation were deemed invalid), while a severability regime would probably have maintained it. That is, if the reservation were invalid, under an AS regime Chile's act of ratification would appear to be void. Notably, proponents of Pinochet's extradition would not be helped by the fact that, in 1989, Spain and the United Kingdom had officially asserted that Chile's reservation to Article 2 was incompatible with the object and purpose of the Convention, or an unacceptable condition.[135] Of course, the House of Lords controversy is just one illustration. Similar questions would be raised even more directly by a third-party institution in a case involving subordinate Chilean military officers—whether the case occurred in 1999 or in 1989, and whether it involved an extradition request or not. In such cases, a severability regime would be likely to produce an outcome favorable to human rights protection, while an AS regime would make it difficult, if not impossible, to capture that benefit.

The second important aspect of the impact of a severability regime on nondemocratic states is that it facilitates progressive movement through the phases described by Risse, Ropp, and Sikkink. This understanding helps address perhaps the most serious normative concern regarding the application of a severability regime to such states: the prospect of privileging a nondemocratic state's interests at the time of ratification (time 1) instead of a successor democratic state's interests at the point the reservation comes into question (time 2).[136] Simply put, in those cases where a reservation was essential at the time of ratification, the successor democratic state may be ejected from the treaty despite its being against the democratic state's interest. Although this concern goes beyond the dispute between a severability regime and an AS regime—and, in fact, might be described as fine-tuning the type of severability regime adopted—it is important enough to be treated here, even if briefly.

First, Risse, Ropp, and Sikkink's model explains in a sophisticated manner how nondemocratic states engage in strategic behavior in earlier phases of the socialization process. If the severability regime privileged state interests at time 2, nondemocratic states would rationally be reluctant to ratify the treaty. This is especially true where a government's authoritarian elements expect to retain some political power, but not enough to counter the successor government's overall preference for severing a reservation deemed to be invalid. A severability

[135] Torture Declarations and Reservations, *supra* note 126, at n.16.

[136] Compare *supra* part III, "The Modalities of Conditional Consent" (discussing aspects of this choice in terms of a time 1 (point of ratification) versus a time 2 (point of case or controversy at hand)).

rule that privileges time 1 assures the nondemocratic state of greater control over prospective severance questions than a rule that privileges time 2. Accordingly, this system provides a stronger incentive for such states to ratify the treaty, notably at a time when, for the sake of human rights, the ratification probably matters the most.

Second, a severability regime that privileges time 1 corresponds in important respects with Risse's elaboration of the socialization model. Risse argues that inducing nondemocratic governments to engage openly in the discourse of international legal norms, including juridical justifications to defend their actions, helps to facilitate progressive change.[137] A severability regime—especially one that applies the default rule proposed in part IV[138]—includes an information-forcing mechanism that stimulates discourse by the nondemocratic state in international legal terms. For example, states have an incentive to defend their reservations as essential or to make such a preference clear at the outset. As I explain in the following part, the degree to which a severance presumption potentially misjudges nondemocratic states' preferences will incidentally advance these states' movement along the socialization process. That is, the steps these states take, in order to avoid that outcome, will engage them in the dialogic process Risse identifies as productive.

To recapitulate: the discussion in part III has addressed, and endeavored to settle, the central controversy in the current dispute over invalid reservations—whether, given the principle of state consent, severance should be an option. The widespread and increasing acceptance of the AS position has effectively made this question the stopping point of any further inquiry into severability because of an assumed relationship between treaties and state consent. The record of state practice, however, clearly demonstrates that foreclosing severance as an option would countermand the principle of state consent. Numerous cases drawn from different modalities of state practice lack the "sovereignty costs" that AS proponents contend are entailed by keeping a state bound to a human rights agreement without the benefit of its reservation. State treaty practices may also reflect a strategy to promote human rights abroad or to stave off domestic political pressure, which would be significantly frustrated if the government were ejected from an agreement and forced to reratify. Indeed, across a range of cases, the remedial option of severance is precisely what states would prefer when binding themselves to such agreements. Greater sovereignty costs, in fact, lie on the side of an AS system in such situations. Once this part of the debate is settled, or its terms better understood, we might begin to think about the appropriate way to structure a regime that includes severance as an option.

IV. Toward a Presumption of Severance

The above analysis of state treaty practice not only demonstrates the need for severing invalid reservations in particular circumstances, but also points toward the way to structure a regime that distinguishes between those circumstances and ones in which severance is inappropriate. A central problem in designing or administering such a regime concerns what an adjudicator should do in the face of silence or ambiguity. If a state includes explicit language at the time of ratification stating whether it considers certain reservations essential

[137] Risse, *supra* note 113, at 28–29. A government's interactions with international and domestic audiences can be conceived as a two-level game. *See* DOUBLE-EDGED DIPLOMACY: INTERNATIONAL BARGAINING AND DOMESTIC POLITICS (Peter B. Evans, Harold K. Jacobson, & Robert D. Putnam eds., 1993). In the context of nondemocratic states, this dynamic can help produce democratic change because the internal and external audiences share common, mutually reinforcing, liberal democratic objectives. The same may not be true, however, for treaty practices of democratic states. In those cases, a government's actions at the international level may be used to lock out, or constrain, future democratic choices. In that respect, a severability system may appear to work against democratic norms; but a critical point is that for these states, at time 1, ratification with severable reservations is a legitimate exercise of democratic expression. In terms of implications for time 2, one might view these practices as a form of constitutionalism or self-binding behavior in which democratic polities often engage.

[138] *See infra* text at note 139.

or nonessential conditions of its accession, the adjudicator's task will be simple. When the text is silent or ambiguous, however, a default rule or interpretive presumption is required to determine the outcome. Such a rule will also be required for cases in which states have already acceded to a treaty without knowing to specify their intent at the time; for existing human rights treaties, that retrospective tail will be exceptionally long.

In this part, I sketch the basic outlines of a "severance presumption,"[139] which I conclude is necessitated by the empirics of state treaty practice. The presumption I propose is that adjudicators should assume an invalid reservation is not an essential condition of a state's decision to ratify a treaty unless evidence to the contrary is provided.[140] A significant factor in setting the appropriate presumption involves reducing error costs. For example, if the adjudicator misjudges the state's intent, is it better for the error to fall in the domain of underinclusiveness or overinclusiveness?

The record of state treaty practice strongly suggests that error costs derived from a nonseverance presumption exceed those from a presumption favoring severance. In most of the cases, states have consented to having aspects of their legal system modified by international legal developments. In the strongest cases of this kind—newly established democracies—states often prefer locking as much of their domestic fates as practicable into international structures. An adjudicator's erroneous expulsion of a state from a treaty risks significant costs along two dimensions: international (e.g., a sovereignty impact from the state's expulsion against its will, reputational costs to the state's international standing, loss of a leadership or participatory role in the regime) and domestic (e.g., the unhinging of a wide array of judicially enforceable civil and political rights protections, facilitation of illiberal rollbacks). The result would probably involve significant transaction costs in the process of reratifying the agreement.

On the other hand, erroneous severance by the adjudicator, maintaining the state's membership in the treaty, would also risk significant, but seemingly more limited, costs: international (e.g., a sovereignty impact from the state's being held against its will) and domestic (e.g., the creation of legal obligations the state was not prepared to accept; the potential infringement of "counter-rights," such as limiting freedom of speech in the name of regulating hate speech). In this situation, however, the state has a relatively easy recourse: withdrawal. This back-end solution helps prevent such errors from producing severe impacts. There are potential reputational costs to withdrawal, but these should be balanced against the fact that the state would have preferred expulsion in the first place.

The virtues and vices of the severance presumption can be usefully considered by reference to the choice between majoritarian default rules and penalty (or information-forcing) default rules in the law of contracts.[141] In contracts scholarship, these two default rules are often discussed as the best alternatives in responding to gaps in long-term relational contracts. In the face of silence in an agreement, an adjudicator can adopt either a default rule that mimics what the majority of parties in similar circumstances would have selected (a majoritarian default) or a rule that burdens the party with more information to reveal that information to other parties, as well as to the adjudicator (a penalty, or information-forcing,

[139] Although the presumption concerns a factual determination and severance is a legal conclusion, for the sake of simplicity I will call the presumption a "severance presumption." Logically, a "nonseverance presumption" would have the adjudicator presume a reservation to be an essential condition of a state's consent to ratification unless contrary proof is provided.

[140] Domestic legal scholars may be familiar with this type of presumption, as it arises in jurisprudential questions regarding the severability of invalid provisions of statutes. In the domestic context, American legal scholars have sharpened an analogous doctrinal question to determining which presumption—one favoring severance or one against it—best fits drafters' intent and dynamics of the legislative process. *See, e.g.*, Emily Sherwin, *Rules and Judicial Review*, 6 LEGAL THEORY 299 (2000); Adrian Vermeule, *Saving Constructions*, 85 GEO. L.J. 1945 (1997).

[141] Richard Craswell, *Contract Law: General Theories*, *in* 3 ENCYCLOPEDIA OF LAW AND ECONOMICS 1 (Boudewijn Bouckaert & Gerrit de Geest eds., 2000); Ian Ayres & Robert Gertner, *Filling Gaps in Incomplete Contracts: An Economic Theory of Default Rules*, 99 YALE L.J. 87, 91 (1989).

default). As discussed below, a severance presumption may split the difference by capturing some of the virtues of each of these default rules, while avoiding potential shortcomings.

In the context of reservations to human rights treaties, a strict majoritarian default rule would prove unworkable. Such a rule requires the adjudicator to replicate how the majority of parties would have addressed an issue or resolved a problematic aspect of an agreement. Given the heterogeneity of state treaty practice and the various interests involved in different types of reservations, it would prove practically impossible to set a strict majority default rule.[142] As others have explained, in circumstances of such uncertainty or institutional inability to determine how a majority of parties would act, a better rule is perhaps an information-forcing one.[143]

A penalty default rule also has significant drawbacks when applied in the reservations context but, at the same time, demonstrates certain values the severance presumption would serve. A fundamental problem in applying a device like a penalty default rule to severance of reservations is that it would directly conflict with the principle of state consent. Indeed, "penalty defaults are purposefully set at what the parties would not want—in order to encourage the parties to reveal information to each other or to third parties (especially the courts)."[144]

Nevertheless, the penalty default rule does illuminate other benefits of a severance presumption. Specifically, the potential for error costs implicit in a severance presumption should be understood as information forcing. With this presumption as the governing standard, *R* states—which are in the best position to know whether their own reservation is an essential condition of consent—will be encouraged to reveal that information. That is, the knowledge ex ante that an adjudicator may interpret their intent incorrectly (error costs) gives *R* states an incentive to reveal more information about their preferences.

This effect also has benefits with respect to the treatment of nondemocratic states. Notably, a default rule is inescapable: one has to be set one way or the other. Setting the default rule will also be likely to burden some parties more than others. The information-forcing feature of a severance presumption has the effect of falling disproportionately on nondemocratic states, because the presumption is probably incorrect in most of those cases. As described in the section on such states in part III, this information-forcing effect produces normatively attractive results by encouraging those states to engage openly in international legal discourse.

A primary reason that a severance presumption captures benefits associated with both default rules relates to the error costs. A presumption favoring nonseverance risks more harmful outcomes than the severance presumption. Perhaps most important is the corrective action that states can adopt: reratification (in response to an erroneous decision not to sever) and withdrawal (in response to an erroneous decision to sever). The corrective action is far more difficult in the former case than in the latter. The coalition building required in ratification struggles, for example, will probably prolong this corrective strategy in many countries. During the interim period, illiberal rollbacks in newly established democracies and suspension of rights guarantees in consistent-standard states are possible. In terms of ultimate effectiveness, the transaction costs of ratification are high enough that successful corrective action might not be achieved in many cases. Accordingly, in selecting which interpretive presumption to incorporate into the management of a reservations regime, states should rationally select a severance presumption. On balance, this choice would limit potential encroachments on states' overriding interests in acceding to the treaty regime.

This approach to modeling a reservations regime helps explicate the broader relationship between state consent and the presumption selected. My majoritarian analysis above admittedly avoids inquiring into whether, at a narrow level of abstraction, a majority of states would

[142] *See* Craswell, *supra* note 141, at 4–5 (describing difficulties in adopting majoritarian default rules in highly heterogeneous contexts).

[143] *See, e.g.*, Cass R. Sunstein, *Must Formalism Be Defended Empirically?* 66 U. CHI. L. REV. 636, 647 (1999).

[144] Ayres & Gertner, *supra* note 141, at 91; *see also id.* at 129–30.

have considered a reservation to be an essential condition of consent. (As a practical reality, I believe such an inquiry would be hopeless, given the divergent modalities of state treaty practice and types of reservations.) Instead, the above analysis applies the sensibility of a majoritarian default rule at a broader level of abstraction by asking what presumptive rule the majority of states would prefer in administering the regime.

Considering the application of the default rule at these two levels of abstraction also helps clarify important aspects of the relationship between state consent and those features of a penalty default rule reflected in a severance presumption. While in certain cases a severance presumption will function as a penalty—when a state had actually intended its reservation to be nonseverable—in terms of a systemwide choice, states should still select this presumption because, on balance, it best preserves interests involved in participating in such treaty regimes. Thus, we should not confuse (1) the infringements on the expression of state consent that result from applying the default rule in particular cases with (2) broader questions evaluating the systemwide impact of deploying a severance presumption or determining whether state consent is maximized by a severability regime.

In the final analysis, these default rules, although generated by law and economics scholars in the context of studying contracts and accordingly limited in their application, can help clarify the rationale for selecting one presumptive rule over another. Scholars have discussed applying such default rules, by analogy, to analyzing the constitutionality or statutory construction of legislation.[145] In our context, these conceptual tools can go only so far. The literature on the law of contracts generally assumes such default rules will be applied strictly. Unless the default rule is applied as an irrebuttable or superstrong presumption, information-forcing effects and the purpose behind seeking majoritarian solutions cannot be obtained.

Indeed, the law and economics approach generally takes efficiency as its organizing principle, which does not fit comfortably with the nature of the concerns related to treaty regimes and state consent. For example, under a conventional law and economics approach, efficiency is maximized by setting a majoritarian default rule because this method, first, allows third-party institutions to bypass figuring out the particularities of individual cases and, second, allows parties to avoid transaction costs in their negotiations ex ante. Likewise, a penalty default rule forces the sharing of information, which helps ensure that parties will arrive at the most efficient outcome once preferences and relative capabilities are known.

In the context of our discussion, however, efficiency is not the organizing principle, and greater flexibility in employing a presumption, perhaps even a weak one, is preferable. Thus, reference to default rules should be understood as borrowing by analogy. To achieve its full value, the severance presumption would need to be applied flexibly. In fact, in many cases the presumption is sure to be rebutted by evidence that the state considered the reservation essential to its consent to be bound. Third-party institutions would need to be given the discretion to apply this presumption so that state consent would be respected over the course of administering the regime. The point is not only for third-party institutions to favor the severance option to avoid making costly mistakes, but also for the adjudicator to be provided with the decisional freedom to honor the state's contrary interests (i.e., not severing the reservation) when those interests are sufficiently clear.

A severance presumption can be expected to have the greatest impact in its retrospective application because of the high number of ratifications of human rights treaties. As a prospective matter, however, we might speculate on the behavioral effects that a severance presumption would have on states' ratification practices. Some of these effects may be anticipated, because the severability option and severance presumption are both selected to maximize

[145] *See, e.g.*, Jack L. Goldsmith, *The New Formalism in United States Foreign Relations Law*, 70 U. COL. L. REV. 1395, 1430–36 (1999) (applying these default rules as analogs for evaluating strong presumptions and formalist rules in U.S. foreign relations law); Sunstein, *supra* note 143, at 645–50.

state interests at the time of ratification. Newly established democracies and consistent-standard states, for example, should be more inclined to join human rights regimes that possess these features than regimes without such features. Their governments' future participation in such regimes would be more predictable and stable. States in general would also enjoy greater freedom to attach questionable reservations, because invalid reservations would not automatically jeopardize membership down the line. This freedom should expand the pool of bargaining chips for securing domestic support to enter regimes, and help placate advocates of ratification who disagree with certain proposed reservations. At the same time, third-party institutions (including domestic courts) should feel more empowered to review questionable reservations, because a finding of invalidity would not automatically annul the state's membership. Of course, some states might begin attaching provisos stating that their reservations are essential. The result of such actions for these states would be no different from having an AS regime, but it would be more closely calibrated to reflect state consent. Moreover, as explained, the option of stipulating that some reservations are inessential might enable the government to attach additional reservations to orient its relationship to the treaty regime. Thus, even these states would have an interest in taking advantage of severability.

A final concern is that a severance presumption discourages ratification by reducing ambiguity in the political process. On this view, ambiguity of legislative intent might, in some circumstances, help initiatives pass through the political process and a severance presumption would undermine that dynamic by compelling governmental actors to make clear statements. This concern, however, should also register for an antiseverance presumption and for an AS regime. Both of those would also compel governmental actors to convey clear information if they wanted to counteract the effect of the presumption or rule. Having a loose severance presumption, which can be rebutted both by legislative history and by clear textual statements, should help relieve the concern regarding ambiguity. Such flexibility would allow legislators to draft instruments of ratification against the background of a clearer, but nevertheless modest, presumption.

V. CONCLUSION

The current severability debate has been characterized by an antinomy common to public international law arguments: the imposition of multilateral agreements (especially human rights treaties) versus the interests of sovereignty and state consent. The tendency to think in these terms can be traced to conventional concerns about the penetration of international law into areas of domestic governance and more recent concerns about the erosion of the nation-state's power and autonomy caused by globalization. Some commentators, however, have also started to move away from these categorical oppositions. Recent scholarship has revealed how weaker conceptions of sovereignty existed during and ever since the creation of the Westphalian state.[146] Moreover, other scholars have begun to discuss the need to integrate commitments to international rights and multilateralism with a genuine commitment to sovereignty and state consent.[147] In a sense, much of the international relations scholarship discussed above, by identifying dynamic reasons that states choose to bind themselves to international agreements, points in the same direction.

The argument advanced in this article serves as a practical application of this more recent trend. I have sought to uncover the particular interests that motivate states to bind themselves to multilateral human rights obligations and, on the basis of that empirical record, to determine which reservations regime best reflects state consent. The final result suggests that the

[146] STEPHEN D. KRASNER, SOVEREIGNTY: ORGANIZED HYPOCRISY (1999).

[147] *See, e.g.*, ABRAM CHAYES & ANTONIA HANDLER CHAYES, THE NEW SOVEREIGNTY: COMPLIANCE WITH INTERNATIONAL REGULATORY AGREEMENTS (1995); Kal Raustiala, *Sovereignty and Multilateralism*, 1 CHI. J. INT'L L. 401, 417–18 (2000); Anne-Marie Slaughter, *The Real New World Order*, FOREIGN AFF., Sept.–Oct. 1997, at 183.

debate over the consequence of invalid reservations has been premised on a false opposition. For diverse reasons, which can be catalogued according to particular modalities of state treaty practice, governments bind themselves to international agreements and, at the same time, attach one of two types of reservations: ones that are essential to their consent to be bound and ones that are inessential, or accessory, stipulations. As discussed in part III, a severability regime would best reflect the purpose and interests of states' accession. As discussed in part IV, such a regime should include a rule of decision that favors severing an invalid reservation, that is, considering the reservation supererogatory unless it is established that the state intended otherwise.

Of course, this resolution leaves some questions that proceed from it unanswered. Beyond the scope of this article is a set of questions about what type of evidentiary material constitutes a valid indication of contrary state intent and what burden of proof should be applied for evidence to rebut the severance presumption. A separate set of questions entails determining the optimal treaty regime if we were to suspend the value of state consent or to introduce other normative variables. The first set of questions is derivative of the principal subject of this article and is outside its scope. The second set can be addressed either independently or, better yet, once we first settle how state consent functions and what structural choices best represent those state interests.

Beyond these questions, which are related to the project itself, it is hoped that the type of resolution offered by this article can advance discussions about institutional structure, state consent, and the modalities of divergent governmental practice more broadly. For instance, the conclusions reached here suggest important (though counterintuitive) ways that state consent can be maximized by enhancing third-party institutions' ability to regulate reservations and other state treaty practices. The same conclusions also indicate factors to be taken into account in analyzing and designing international legal arrangements in which various third-party institutions have overlapping or shared institutional authority, some with enforcement power and others with effective control only within their particular spheres of activities.

A general approach is to obtain a better understanding of the empirical dynamics of state consent and to thread those empirical insights through an analysis of the design and functions of international and domestic structures. In that way, we can better address controversies that rest on unexamined empirical assumptions or, at the very least, clarify what is genuinely at stake. In terms of the severability debate, the AS paradigm has gained ascendancy due to its intuitive connection to state consent. A closer examination of treaty practice, however, shows that assumptions underlying that connection are unsustainable. In the end, the antithesis is true. A treaty regime that precludes severing invalid reservations—or, for that matter, a severability regime that considers reservations presumptively essential to a state's ratification—contravenes the normative commitment to state consent.

Part V
Challenges

[11]

Globalization and the Convergence of Values

Alex Y. Seita*

As the twentieth century comes to a close, the circumstances of individual nations–their affairs, news, and problems–have tended increasingly to reach and captivate global audiences. A predominant reason has been the economic importance of foreign countries. Greater numbers of domestic businesses, employees, and consumers have looked to foreign markets, investors, and products for economic prosperity as well as economic competition. While driven primarily by economic factors, the process of globalization–in which international issues become as important as national, state, and local matters–has significant political and other noneconomic content. Democracy and human rights are, for example, as much a part of globalization as are free market principles. While globalization has detrimental effects, they can be minimized through the cooperative efforts of the United States and the other industrialized democracies which share basic economic and political values. America and its democratic allies should strongly promote and carefully manage globalization, for it has significant beneficial implications for humanity. Globalization is causing, and being reinforced by, a worldwide convergence of economic and political values that portend a possible, though distant, future world in which human beings will look upon themselves as part of a single humane civilization comprised of a single human race.

Introduction

Globalization is one of the great forces shaping the world today. It is a multifaceted concept encompassing a wide range of seemingly disparate processes, activities, and conditions–some nebulous, others concrete–that often reinforce as well as clash with each other. They are connected together by one common theme: what is geographically meaningful now transcends national boundaries and is expanding to cover the entire planet. Globalization has led to an awareness that international issues, not just domestic ones, matter.

Globalization means many things. It is foremost an economic process.[1] Economic globalization refers to the world-wide integration of mar-

* B.S., California Institute of Technology; M.B.A., Stanford; J.D., Stanford. Professor of Law, Albany Law School of Union University. E-mail address: ASEIT@MAIL.ALS.EDU. I am grateful to Sheila Shea for her comments, and I appreciate the research assistance of Nandini Nair, Byron Olsen, Lisa Ruoff, Rebecca Slezak, and Bonnie Thomas. This article was supported by a research grant from the Albany Law School.

1. *See infra* notes 38-58 and accompanying text.

30 Cornell Int'l L.J. 429 (1997)

kets.[2] In economic globalization, markets for goods, services, financial capital, and intellectual property take on transnational or global proportions. A paramount consequence of market integration has been increased economic interdependence among nations.

Globalization is also a political event, as evidenced by the spread of democracy and human rights among nations.[3] Although it may be less extensive and have a less immediate impact than economic globalization, political globalization nevertheless has a significant international presence. There are now a greater number of democratically governed countries protective of fundamental human rights—rights that all human beings are entitled to, such as the rights to life and liberty, freedoms of expression and religion, freedom from torture or discrimination, and the right to a fair trial.[4] A majority of the world's population may now live under democratically elected governments affording a measure of basic human rights.[5]

In addition to its all-important economic and political roles, globalization has numerous other dimensions. They reflect the wide range of human activity and thought, from the technological, cultural, legal, philosophical, and environmental, to the criminal and detrimental. The various aspects of globalization often interact with each other. For example, technology not only facilitates economic and political globalization, but together with economic globalization helps to introduce different cultures into local consciousnesses.[6]

Law has been important in managing economic globalization and may become as important with respect to political globalization.[7] The ideology of globalization can be broadly divided into substantive and procedural components. The most important procedural element is the rule of law—the idea that disputes will be settled and agreements negotiated through the observance of established principles rather than the use of force or the intimidation of power.[8] In turn, the substantive principles, what the rule of law seeks to enforce, are those that nations have selected to settle disputes and negotiate agreements. The rule of law can be a way of resolving conflicts effectively, peacefully, and cooperatively.

Furthermore, globalization enhances the perceived importance of distant international problems relative to local problems. Thus, protection of the environment beyond national borders has attracted strong international support, and the conflict between environment protection and economic development created the global issue of sustainable development.[9]

2. *See, e.g.*, C. Fred Bergsten, *Globalizing Free Trade*, FOREIGN AFF., May-June 1996, at 105; Zia Qureshi, *Globalization: New Opportunities, Tough Challenges*, FIN. & DEV., Mar. 1996, at 30; MICHAEL E. PORTER, THE COMPETITIVE ADVANTAGE OF NATIONS 14-15 (1990).
3. *See infra* notes 59-82 and accompanying text.
4. *Cf. infra* notes 37 (listing human rights), 63 (defining democracy).
5. *See infra* note 67.
6. *See infra* notes 77-98 and accompanying text.
7. *See infra* notes 144-60 and accompanying text.
8. *See infra* note 147 and accompanying text.
9. *Cf. infra* note 186.

On the downside, technology together with economic and political globalization can facilitate the movement of criminal and terrorist activities across national boundaries and help criminals and terrorists to operate like efficient international businesses.[10]

Most significantly for this Article, however, globalization is an important source of common economic and political values for humanity. Globalization is simultaneously a cause and a consequence of the convergence of basic economic and political systems among nations. As the activities of globalization help to converge economic and political systems, their existence reciprocally facilitates the expansion of globalization. Momentously, the convergence of these systems is leading to the convergence of fundamental values–deeply held beliefs about what is right and wrong.[11]

There is a widespread, though not universal, acceptance among nations of the basic values of liberal democracy: a market economy (or free markets), a democratic government, and the protection of human rights. Although particular details may differ from country to country, the general nature of these values is the same. The convergence of basic economic and political values among nations is a pivotal event because it is a necessary, though not sufficient, condition for the eventual emergence of a consensus among human beings that there is but one human race.[12]

This Article argues that the United States and the other industrialized democracies (e.g., the members of the European Union, Japan, and Canada), collectively referred to as the "West,"[13] should vigorously support and substantially guide the process of globalization. As it is currently emerging, globalization fosters desirable common national values by advancing *general* forms of market economies, democracy, and human rights.[14] It is precisely those general characteristics of liberal democracy that constitute the foundational pillars and shared values of the United States and the other industrialized democracies.[15]

Because the exact form of globalization is not a fixed certainty, the United States and the other industrialized democracies should aggressively configure globalization to be consistent with and to promote the values of

10. *See infra* notes 91, 132.

11. Value judgments (alternatively, beliefs, views, ideas, and opinions) about what is "good" or "bad" are never statements of *facts*. *See* 8 ENCYCLOPEDIA OF PHILOSOPHY 229-32 (1967). Other characterizations of "good" or "bad" might be "appropriate" or "inappropriate," "correct" or "incorrect," "necessary" or "unnecessary," and "proper" or "improper." The use of value judgments requires a person to base her decision on personal beliefs, whether or not these beliefs are her fundamental beliefs, beliefs widely shared and deeply felt by other members of society, or beliefs supported by objective evidence. *See* EZRA J. MISHAN, INTRODUCTION TO NORMATIVE ECONOMICS 24-26 (1981) (stating that value judgments are the product of, among other things, intellectual fashions, life experience, specific events, and interests). *See also* THE MIT DICTIONARY OF MODERN ECONOMICS 447-48 (David W. Pearce ed., 4th ed. 1992) [hereinafter DICTIONARY OF MODERN ECONOMICS].

12. *See infra* notes 104-17 and accompanying text.

13. *See infra* note 25.

14. *See infra* notes 118-28 and accompanying text.

15. *See infra* note 26.

liberal democracy. The industrialized democracies must also ensure that the path of globalization fairly balances the values of free market economics, democracy, and human rights, while accommodating such vital concerns as the protection of the environment, concerns that do not yet generate as strong a global consensus as the three convergent values.[16]

The mechanism for configuring globalization to conform to and to balance the values of liberal democracy consists of events and policies that, while difficult to achieve, are not unrealistic and have, to a degree, already been occurring.[17] A particularly useful event might be a catharsis that would place the world into the next millennium without the baggage of the past. Perhaps by the year 2001, the representatives of oppressors, victims, victors, losers, and adversaries could assemble on a world stage in a therapeutic ceremony to put the past behind.[18]

Given their economic preeminence in the world, by acting in unison the industrialized democracies should be able to determine the specific content of globalization. Action from the industrialized democracies is needed because a humane globalization will increase human wealth and reduce human suffering.[19] Morally, the promotion of liberal democratic values and the perspective of a single human race would serve to repay the historic debts that the industrialized countries have incurred over the past centuries.[20]

At the same time, the industrialized democracies must be careful to use their influence responsibly and sensitively, for the wisest ideas pursued for the best motives may be rejected when unilaterally imposed upon the rest of the world. Perceived economic and political "imperialism," though much less malevolent than military imperialism, will not be warmly greeted. The primary vehicle for the industrialized democracies should be the "rule of law"–assuming that they have a substantial, if not commanding voice in determining its underlying principles.

An enlightened globalization will not lead to the establishment of a world government. It could, however, create a new attitude among human beings and serve the interests of the United States.[21] More profoundly, advancing globalization will facilitate an event barely begun that holds the great potential of constructing, in the distant future, the perspective that the human race matters more than its component divisions along race, reli-

16. *See infra* notes 170-186 and accompanying text.

17. Some such possibilities are respect for the rule of law through support for multilateral dispute settlement, vigorous financial and political support for countries in transition to liberal democracy, greater regional economic and political integration, and structural changes in the United Nations. *See generally* Alex Y. Seita, *Putting the Past Behind and Humanizing Globalization* (May 1, 1997) (unpublished manuscript, on file with author).

18. Nations, for example, could apologize for their historical debts and for historical tragedies, and pledge reformed behavior in the twenty-first century. The ceremony would not be restricted to nations but could also include governments, organizations, and groups. *See id.*

19. *See id.*

20. *See id.*

21. *See id.*

gion, or ethnicity.[22] The vision of a common humanity is reason enough to embrace globalization.

I. The Background of Globalization

Today, more than ever, the events of foreign lands have important economic and political consequences for local inhabitants. To be sure, foreign events have had significant ramifications in the past. Centuries ago, seminal inventions in China revolutionized the culture, science, and warfare of Europeans; the opening of American borders to European immigrants from the 19th through the mid-20th centuries gave millions a new home; and the conflicts in Europe during World War I eventually brought the United States onto the European battleground.[23]

But these events were of *sporadic* importance. For example, after World War I ended, the United States isolated itself in a number of respects from international politics and trade; America declined membership in the League of Nations and enacted the Smoot-Hawley tariffs in 1931 which drastically reduced imports.[24] By contrast, transnational activities and affairs now have *continuous* importance, repeatedly affecting not just distant countries, but also the entire global community at times. The continuous importance of international events is a defining characteristic of globalization.

Another feature of globalization with potentially profound implications is the convergence of basic economic and political values among nations towards the liberal democratic values of the industrialized democracies, the "West."[25] For the West, the liberal, democratic values of market

---

22. *See infra* notes 104-17 and accompanying text.

23. *See* ROBERT TEMPLE, THE GENIUS OF CHINA: 3,000 YEARS OF SCIENCE, DISCOVERY AND INVENTION 7, 149-51, 81-84, 110-16, 224-29 (1986) (discussing the seminal inventions made by the Chinese, e.g., paper and printing, the magnetic compass, and gunpowder, and later utilized by Europeans); 1 BUREAU OF THE CENSUS, U.S. DEP'T OF COMMERCE, HISTORICAL STATISTICS OF THE UNITED STATES, COLONIAL TIMES TO 1970, at 105 (1975) (showing that the great majority of immigrants to the United States from 1820 to 1950 came from Europe) [hereinafter HISTORICAL STATISTICS OF THE UNITED STATES].

24. *See* UNITED NATIONS, EVERYONE'S UNITED NATIONS: A HANDBOOK ON THE WORK OF THE UNITED NATIONS 5 (10th ed. 1986) [hereinafter UNITED NATIONS]; JOHN H. JACKSON, WORLD TRADE AND THE LAW OF GATT 9 (1969).

25. Identifying the most important industrialized democracies is easy, although compiling a list of all the industrialized democracies may not be. The most important industrialized democracies are members of the group of seven (G-7) nations: the United States, Japan, Germany, Great Britain, France, Italy, and Canada. *See, e.g.*, INTERNATIONAL MONETARY FUND, WORLD ECONOMIC OUTLOOK: OCTOBER 1996, at 155-57 (1996) [hereinafter WORLD ECONOMIC OUTLOOK]. *See generally* C. FRED BERGSTEN & C. RANDALL HENNING, GLOBAL ECONOMIC LEADERSHIP AND THE GROUP OF SEVEN (1996).

A good proxy for the major industrialized democracies is the group of 23 nations that the International Monetary Fund (IMF) calls the "industrialized countries": the United States, Japan, Canada, Australia, Iceland, New Zealand, Norway, Switzerland, and all 15 countries of the European Union. *See* WORLD ECONOMIC OUTLOOK, *supra*, at 155-57. The fifteen nations of the European Union are Austria, Belgium, Denmark, Finland, France, Germany, Greece, Ireland, Italy, Luxembourg, the Netherlands, Portugal, Spain, Sweden, and the United Kingdom. *See What Is the Economic Union?* (visited Apr. 3, 1997) <http://europa.eu.int/en/eu/states.htm>. Although the European Union is not a

economies, democracy, and human rights are fundamental.[26] Given the arguably shallow roots of liberal democratic values in a number of countries and the absence of democracy and human rights in many others, this process may perhaps be too incomplete to be described as a convergence of

---

"country," it possesses international legal personality, speaks for all member nations in most external or international economic matters, and represents one step in a planned path to a future entity with some characteristics of a single country (e.g., common citizenship, a single monetary currency, a common defense policy). *See generally* Treaty Establishing the European Economic Community, Mar. 25, 1957, 298 U.N.T.S. 11; Single European Act, Feb. 17-28, 1986, 25 I.L.M. 506; Treaty on European Union, Feb. 7, 1992, 31 I.L.M. 247, 253 (Maastricht Treaty); *Europa Homepage* (visited Dec. 8, 1996) <http://europa.eu.int> (website for the European Union). While all 23 industrialized countries are democracies that protect human rights, several of these have not been so throughout the entire post-World War II period (i.e., Greece, Portugal, and Spain had military dictatorships for decades).

Another possible proxy for the industrialized democracies is the Organisation for Economic Co-operation and Development (OECD). *See generally OECD Online* (visited Jan. 20, 1997) <http://www.oecd.org> (website for the Organisation for Economic Co-operation and Development). The 29 member nations of the OECD include the Czech Republic, Hungary, Mexico, Poland, South Korea, and Turkey, in addition to the IMF's 23 industrialized nations. *See About OECD: Member Countries* (visited Jan. 20, 1997) <http://www.oecd.org/about/member-countries.html> (from OECD website). The members of the OECD identify themselves as "governments of the industrialised democracies" that seek, among other things, "co-operation among nations essentially on domestic policies where these interact with those of other countries, in particular through trade and investment." *See About OECD: The OECD and its Origins* (visited Jan. 20, 1997) <http://www.oecd.org/about/origins.htm> (from OECD website). This description of "industrialized democracies" is reasonably accurate, although some OECD countries may lack (or for a long time did lack) some democratic features and human rights.

For convenience, this article describes the 23 IMF-designated industrialized nations collectively as the "West," although that term is arguably misleading. Some commentators would reserve the term "West" exclusively for U.S. allies of European heritage or for friendly but neutral European democracies with wealthy economies. They would instead characterize nations like Japan, South Korea, and Turkey as part of the "Free World." *See* Michael Lind, *Pax Atlantica: The Case for Euramerica*, WORLD POL'Y J., Spring 1996, at 1-2. Unlike the other 22 nations, Japan is not predominately a caucasian nation with European roots. It is also a country that has been frequently characterized, inaccurately, as being qualitatively different from the other 22 nations which are supposed to be identical to each other. *See, e.g., A Survey of Tomorrow's Japan*, ECONOMIST, July 13, 1996, at 5. For a discussion of Japan's role in international affairs as well as Japan's more important similarities with the other industrialized countries, see Alex Y. Seita, *Japan's Role in Globalization* (May 1, 1997) (unpublished manuscript, on file with author).

Placing Japan solely in the "Free World," however, seems odd as that phrase also describes an increasingly large number of countries whose economies are nowhere as prosperous as most of the IMF's 23 industrialized countries, let alone Japan's. On the other hand, Japan is an American ally, and the term "West" has often been used to describe the U.S.-led alliance of wealthy industrialized nations. Using the term "West" to describe the IMF's 23 industrialized nations avoids having to refer to "western and Japanese" governments, corporations, etc.

26. For example, the OECD (whose 29 members include all 23 nations of what this article refers to collectively as the "industrialized democracies") states that its "membership is not determined by wealth, but rather by what the Members have in common, which is their commitment to an open market economy, pluralistic democracy and respect for human rights." *See About OECD: Member Countries* (visited Jan. 20, 1997) <http://www.oecd.org/about/member.htm>.

fundamental values. Nevertheless, today there are greater similarities between the economic and political systems of nations than at any other time in the short history of globalization.[27] With careful and generous support from the West, this similarity of systems may evolve into a similarity of fundamental values.

A. Globalization's Beginning

Identifying the birth of globalization is an elusive task, but one possible date is the year 1945, when the United States led the Allied powers in creating the United Nations and its companion international organizations, the International Monetary Fund (IMF) and the International Bank for Reconstruction and Development (World Bank).[28] Later in 1948, the United States and its democratic allies established the General Agreement on Tar-

---

27. The economic conflict between market and command economy paradigms has ended in the former's favor. The classes of imperial powers and colonies that existed at the end of World War II have vanished, and virtually all nations are now politically independent. *See infra* note 65. Democracy, not authoritarianism, is the prevailing form of government among nations. *See infra* note 59. With the end of the Cold War, the protection of human rights has not had to compete with national security concerns, and there has been at least pervasive formal recognition of the importance of human rights. *Cf. infra* note 60.

28. *See* UNITED NATIONS, *supra* note 24, at 3 (United Nations Charter signed on June 26, 1945, in San Francisco, and the United Nations officially came into existence on October 24, 1945); INTERNATIONAL MONETARY FUND, ARTICLES OF AGREEMENT (1968) (IMF Articles of Agreement adopted on July 22, 1944, and entered into force on December 27, 1945) [hereinafter IMF ARTICLES OF AGREEMENT]; SUSAN GEORGE & FABRIZIO SABELLI, FAITH AND CREDIT: THE WORLD BANK'S SECULAR EMPIRE 33-36 (1994) (the Articles of Agreement of the International Bank for Reconstruction and Development were adopted on July 22, 1944, and entered into force on Dec. 27, 1945). The International Bank for Reconstruction and Development (IBRD) and its affiliates–the International Finance Corporation (IFC, established in 1956), the International Development Association (IDA, established in 1960), the International Centre for Settlement of Investment Disputes (ICSID, established in 1966), and the Multilateral Investment Guarantee Agency (MIGA, established in 1988)–are collectively known as the World Bank Group, and the IBRD and the IDA together are collectively known as the World Bank. *See* WORLD BANK, ANNUAL REPORT 1996, at 6-7 [hereinafter WORLD BANK]; WORLD BANK GROUP, THE WORLD BANK GROUP: LEARNING FROM THE PAST, EMBRACING THE FUTURE 3 (1994).

Membership in the IBRD is restricted to members of the IMF. *See* WORLD BANK, INTERNATIONAL BANK FOR RECONSTRUCTION AND DEVELOPMENT: ARTICLES OF AGREEMENT art. II, § 1 (1944) [hereinafter IBRD ARTICLES OF AGREEMENT]. In turn, membership in the IFC, IDA, and MIGA is restricted to members of the IBRD. *See* INTERNATIONAL FINANCE CORPORATION, ARTICLES OF AGREEMENT art. II, § 1 (1956); INTERNATIONAL DEVELOPMENT ASSOCIATION, ARTICLES OF AGREEMENT art. II, § 1 (1960); MULTILATERAL INVESTMENT GUARANTEE AGENCY, CONVENTION ESTABLISHING THE MULTILATERAL INVESTMENT GUARANTEE AGENCY art. 4 (1985). Contracting states that have signed ICSID need not be members of the IBRD. *See* INTERNATIONAL BANK FOR RECONSTRUCTION AND DEVELOPMENT, REPORT OF THE EXECUTIVE DIRECTORS ON THE CONVENTION ON THE SETTLEMENT OF INVESTMENT DISPUTES BETWEEN STATES AND NATIONALS OF OTHER STATES art. 67 (1965).

Both the IMF and the IBRD were products of the United Nations Monetary and Financial Conference held at Bretton Woods, New Hampshire, from July 1-22, 1944, under the leadership of the United States. *See generally* U.S. DEPARTMENT OF STATE, PUB. NO. 2866, PROCEEDINGS AND DOCUMENTS OF THE UNITED NATIONS MONETARY AND FINANCIAL CONFERENCE, BRETTON WOODS, NEW HAMPSHIRE, JULY 1-22, 1944 (1948). Though initially involved in the process of creating the IMF and the IBRD, the Soviet Union later declined to join either institution, choosing instead to exercise its political influence

iffs and Trade (GATT), another important economic institution for globalization along with the IMF and the World Bank.[29] The motivations for creating these international institutions were at once noble and selfish.

After the devastating experience of World War II, the victorious Allies were determined to prevent any reoccurrence of similar world wars. Their motivating hope was that a collegial body of nations would ensure the peaceful resolution of conflicts and provide a collective defense against wrongful aggression.[30] Thus, the United Nations was the focus of political attempts to prevent future acts of aggression. Further, unlike the League of Nations, the United Nations made the promotion of human rights one of its basic purposes.[31] Toward that end, the United Nations created various human rights institutions and generated human rights conventions and

through its position as a permanent member of the U.N. Security Council. *See* Harold James, International Cooperation Since Bretton Woods 48-58 (1996).

29. Originally, the United States and its western allies had planned to establish the International Trade Organization (ITO), an international institution comparable in statute to the IMF and the IBRD, with the responsibility of promoting international trade. The ITO, however, was never established due to the refusal of the United States to approve it. Instead, the General Agreement on Tariffs and Trade (GATT)–the trade treaty that would have been administered by the ITO–became a de facto organization devoted to the expansion of world trade. *See* Jackson, *supra* note 24, at 36-53. *See generally* General Agreement on Tariffs and Trade, Oct. 30, 1947, 61 Stat. A-11, T.I.A.S. 1700, 55 U.N.T.S. 194 [hereinafter GATT]. The GATT was authenticated on October 30, 1947, and entered into force on January 1, 1948, with the United States as one of the original contracting parties (members). Jackson, *supra* note 24, at 45, 899. As with the IMF and the IBRD, the Soviet Union declined to join the GATT. *See id.* at 898-901. Years later, the World Trade Organization (WTO), the modern-day equivalent of the ITO, emerged from the GATT Uruguay Round Agreements and was established on January 1, 1995. *Cf. Open for Business*, WTO Focus (World Trade Org.), Jan.-Feb. 1995, at 4. The agreement establishing the WTO includes a number of agreements that cover specific trade issues. *See* Marrakesh Agreement Establishing the World Trade Organization, Apr. 15, 1994, 33 I.L.M. 13, 15-16 (1994) [hereinafter WTO Agreement]. "Multilateral" agreements apply to all WTO members and "plurilateral" agreements apply only to members that have accepted them. *See* WTO Agreement, *supra*, art. II, paras. 2-3. All references to GATT in this article are to the original GATT treaty of 1947 (GATT 1947), and not to the legally distinct GATT 1994 agreement. The latter is part of the WTO Agreement and contains, among other things, all of the provisions of GATT 1947. *Compare* WTO Agreement, *supra*, art. II, para. 4, *with* General Agreement on Tariffs and Trade 1994, Agreements on Trade in Goods, Apr. 15, 1994, Marrakesh Agreement Establishing the World Trade Organization, Annex 1A, §1, 33 I.L.M. 29 (1994).

30. *See, e.g.*, U.N. Charter pmbl.; Rosemary Righter, Utopia Lost: The United Nations and World Order 311-13 (1995). *See generally* U.N. Charter arts. 33-38 (Chapter VI: Pacific Settlement of Disputes), 39-51 (Chapter VII: Action with Respect to Threats to the Peace, Breaches of the Peace, and Acts of Aggression). For a comprehensive treatment of the pervasive role the United States played in the establishment of the U.N. Charter, see Ruth B. Russell & Jeannette E. Muther, A History of the United Nations Charter: The Role of the United States 1940-1945 (1958).

31. One of the purposes of the United Nations is "[t]o achieve international cooperation in . . . promoting and encouraging respect for human rights and for fundamental freedoms for all without distinction as to race, sex, language or religion." U.N. Charter art. 1, para. 3; *see also id.* arts. 13 para. 1b, 55 para. c, 55, 76 para. c. The covenant of the League of Nations had no comparable purpose or general provisions dealing with human rights. *See* Ruth B. Henig, League of Nations Covenant 179-89 (1973). There were, however, articles that touched on human rights concerns. *See id.* arts. 22 (colonies of defeated nations in World War I to be administered by the victors in a manner consis-

declarations.[32]

At the same time, the Allies thought it critical to lay the foundations for the economic prosperity of the international community.[33] Prosperous countries, it was thought, would be less inclined to wage wars. Thus, the Allies promoted activities that would raise the standard of living among peaceful countries. For example, the Allies established international economic institutions which were in part created to promote international monetary cooperation (the IMF), to foster economic development in less developed countries (the World Bank), and to increase international trade (the GATT).[34]

---

tent with the "well-being and development of [the native] peoples"), 23 ("fair and humane conditions of labour for men, women, and children").

32. For example, the U.N. Commissions on Human Rights and on the Status of Women were established in 1946. *See* FRANK NEWMAN & DAVID WEISSBRODT, INTERNATIONAL HUMAN RIGHTS 5-8 (1990). Also, many human rights conventions and declarations have emerged from the United Nations. *See, e.g.*, Universal Declaration of Human Rights, G.A. Res. 217 III(A), U.N. GAOR, 3d Sess., Supp. No. 127, at 71, U.N. Doc. A/810 (1948); Convention on the Prevention and Punishment of the Crime of Genocide, G.A. Res. 2670, U.N. GAOR, 3d Sess., pt. 1, at 174, 78 U.N.T.S. 277 (1948); International Covenant on Economic, Social and Cultural Rights, G.A. Res. 2200 A(XXI), 21 U.N. GAOR, 21st Sess., Supp. No. 16, at 49, U.N. Doc. A/6316, 993 U.N.T.S. 3 (1966); International Covenant on Civil and Political Rights, G.A. Res. 2200, U.N. GAOR, 21st Sess., Supp. No. 16, at 52, U.N. Doc. A/6316, 999 U.N.T.S. 171 (1966); International Covenant on the Elimination of All Forms of Racial Discrimination, G.A. Res. 2106 A(XX), 660 U.N.T.S. 195 (1965). The full texts of all of these conventions, as well as other human rights instruments, can be found at the United Nations human rights website. *See Welcome to the United Nations Human Rights Website* (visited Dec. 11, 1996) <http://193.135.156.15/welcome.htm> (U.N. website containing information relating to human rights, including "the full texts of over 90 international human rights treaties, declarations and principles, as well as their status of ratification").

33. *See* JAMES, *supra* note 28, at 27-57.

34. *See* IMF ARTICLES OF AGREEMENT, *supra* note 28, art. I (purpose of IMF); IBRD ARTICLES OF AGREEMENT, *supra* note 28, art. I (purpose of IBRD); GATT, *supra* note 24, pmbl. (purpose of GATT). Immediately after the end of World War II, the more pressing priority of these two institutions was to help rebuild countries ravaged by war. *See, e.g.*, IBRD ARTICLES OF AGREEMENT, *supra* note 28, arts. I(i), (v). By initial design,

> [T]he [IMF] is an *adjustment institution* whose short-term loans are directed to financing deficits that are either inherently temporary or intended to be temporary because of the adoption of adjustment policies, [while] the World Bank is a *development institution* whose long-term loans are directed to the promotion of development. . . .
>
> . . . .
>
> This division of labor became blurred after 1974.

John Williamson, *The Lending Policies of the International Monetary Fund*, *in* IMF CONDITIONALITY 605, 617 (John Williamson ed., 1983) (emphasis in original). Over the years, there has been considerable convergence in the activities of the IMF and the World Bank as it has become clear that macroeconomic adjustment and balance of payments problems (IMF areas of expertise) are linked to economic development and microeconomic policies concerning investment in such areas as infrastructure, training, and education (World Bank areas of expertise). Also, the constituencies of the two institutions have converged. Originally concerned with the problems of all countries, the IMF now only provides funds to developing or poor countries (including former communist countries). Thus, its constituencies are the same as those of the World Bank. *See* JAMES, *supra* note 28, at 143-44, 325-27, 527-29. *See generally* INTERNATIONAL MONETARY FUND, ANNUAL REPORT 1996, at 3 (1996) [hereinafter IMF] (the International Monetary Fund provides funds to low-income and heavily indebted poor countries, including

The creation of the United Nations, the IMF, the World Bank, and the GATT were key moments in globalization. These institutions signaled the start of an era of cooperative behavior, however imperfect, among nations. While the number of nations involved was limited, their cooperation required the development and formal recognition of common interests. The GATT and the United Nations, in particular, were critical components in the genesis of globalization.[35] In seeking to reduce barriers to trade of goods, the GATT contained free market principles that favored lower tariffs, banned quotas, and prohibited discrimination against foreign goods.[36] The United Nations, at least on paper, championed the principles of human rights and democratic forms of government.[37] As these principles

countries in transition from command to market economies, to help them cope with balance of payments problems); WORLD BANK, *supra* note 28, at 6 (the central purpose of the World Bank Group is to promote economic and social progress in developing countries by offering them loans, grants, co-investment financing, and investment insurance).

35. Of course, the GATT was not the only factor in economic globalization. The European Community Treaties were instrumental to integrating the markets of western Europe, and the United States opened its huge domestic market to imports from allied and neutral countries. *See, e.g.*, STEPHEN D. COHEN ET AL., FUNDAMENTALS OF U.S. FOREIGN TRADE POLICY: ECONOMICS, POLITICS, LAWS, AND ISSUES 34-38 (1996); Gary Clyde Hufbauer, *An Overview*, *in* EUROPE 1992: AN AMERICAN PERSPECTIVE 1-3 (Gary Clyde Hufbauer ed., 1990). Also, the Marshall Plan and similar aid programs from the United States, along with some support from the World Bank and IMF, helped to rebuild war-shattered economies, whose recovery led to greater international trade. *See, e.g.*, JAMES, *supra* note 28, at 72-84; Alex Y. Seita, *Discussing Japan Rationally*, 25 L. & POL'Y INT'L BUS. 193, 211 n.84 (1993).

36. *See, e.g.*, GATT, *supra* note 24, arts. I, II, III, XI. Articles I and III banned discrimination based on foreign origin and nationality, respectively. Under the most-favored-nation rule of article I, a contracting party to GATT was obligated to treat the imports from or exports to all other contracting parties no less favorably than it treated the imports or exports of any trading partner (whether a GATT contracting party or not). The national treatment rule of article III required a contracting party to treat imported goods, once through customs, no less favorably than domestic goods (subject to a government procurement exception). Under article II, tariffs could be no higher than the maximum tariffs listed by a contracting party in its tariff schedules. A contracting party determined its tariff schedules after negotiating with other contracting parties, and through reciprocity, lowered its maximum tariffs if other contracting parties did likewise. *See* JOHN H. JACKSON, THE WORLD TRADING SYSTEM: LAW AND POLICY OF INTERNATIONAL ECONOMIC RELATIONS 117-26 (1989). *See generally* WILLIAM R. CLINE ET AL., TRADE NEGOTIATIONS IN THE TOKYO ROUND: A QUANTITATIVE ASSESSMENT (1978). Article XI generally forbade quantitative restrictions (quotas). There were, of course, important exceptions to GATT's general efforts to reduce barriers, and GATT did not cover trade in services and did not adequately handle the issue of liberalizing trade in agriculture, or textiles and apparel. *See generally* WORLD AGRICULTURE TRADE: BUILDING A CONSENSUS (William M. Miner & Dale E. Hathaway eds., 1988); DALE E. HATHAWAY, AGRICULTURE AND THE GATT: REWRITING THE RULES (1987); WILLIAM R. CLINE, THE FUTURE OF WORLD TRADE IN TEXTILES AND APPAREL (1987).

37. *See, e.g.*, Universal Declaration of Human Rights, *supra* note 32, arts. 2 (no discrimination on the basis of race, sex, religion, etc.), 3 (right to life, liberty, and personal safety), 4 (freedom from slavery), 5 (freedom from torture), 7 (equal protection under the law), 10 (right to fair and public criminal proceeding), 18 (freedom of religion), 19 (freedom of expression), 20 (freedom of assembly and association), 21 (right to a democratic government), 23 (right to work, to have just conditions of work, and to form unions), 25 (right to a standard of living adequate for the health and well-being, including food and medical care), 26 (right to education). The boundaries of human rights are

gained international acceptance, economic and political norms developed. That is, common values emerged.

B. Economic Globalization

In current usage, the term globalization refers primarily to economic globalization. As barriers to trade, investment, financial flows, and technology transfers have fallen, there has been an expansion of markets for goods, services, financial capital, and intellectual property to transnational, regional, and even global dimensions.[38] There are several hallmarks of economic globalization. First, it increases opportunities for sellers as well as buyers. Second, economic globalization simultaneously creates new competition. Third, it develops interdependency among nations. Finally, economic globalization spreads the ideology of the free market economy model because the industrialized nations, the major promoters of globalization, advocate free market policies.

The enlargement of markets beyond national boundaries means that both sellers and buyers have greater choices. More firms issue equity

---

the matter of some debate. *See, e.g., infra* note 184 and sources cited (whether protection of the environment is a "human right"); Burns H. Weston, *Human Rights, in* HUMAN RIGHTS IN THE WORLD COMMUNITY: ISSUES AND ACTION 14, 17-18 (Richard P. Claude & Burns H. Weston eds., 2d ed. 1992). No single human right is absolute, since rights must eventually conflict and one right would otherwise dominate all other rights. Human rights can be divided into three broad categories: personal security rights (e.g., freedom from torture, slavery, arbitrary arrest), civil and political liberties (e.g., freedom of expression, religion, participation in government), and depending on the affluence of the country, economic or welfare rights (e.g., right to food, shelter, health care, education). *See, e.g.*, Universal Declaration of Human Right, *supra* note 32; HUMAN RIGHTS AND U.S. FOREIGN POLICY: PRINCIPLES AND APPLICATIONS xviii-xxi (Peter G. Brown & Douglas MacLean eds., 1979). Core human rights–those generally recognized as human rights–are sometimes characterized as first and second-generation rights, while emerging or potential human rights are called third-generation rights. *Cf.* Weston, *supra*, at 18-20; *supra* note 184.

38. With the establishment of the World Trade Organization and the North American Free Trade Agreement, the continuing integration of the European Union, and regional declarations of free trade (e.g., the Asia-Pacific Economic Cooperation forum, APEC), the long-term trend clearly points to the globalization of markets, the geographical expansion of markets to include more competitors and consumers. *See* Canada-United States Free Trade Agreement, Dec. 22, 1987-Jan. 2, 1988, U.S.-Can., KAV 270(s), 27 I.L.M. 281 (treaty integrating Canadian and American markets); North American Free Trade Agreement, Dec. 8-Dec. 17, 1992, U.S.-Can.-Mex., KAV 3417(s), 32 I.L.M. 289 (treaty integrating American, Canadian, and Mexican markets); *supra* note 25 (treaties integrating the markets of the various European Union countries); WTO Agreement, *supra* note 29. *See generally* YOICHI FUNABASHI, ASIA PACIFIC FUSION: JAPAN'S ROLE IN APEC (1995); JOHN S. WILSON, STANDARDS AND APEC: AN ACTION AGENDA (1995). More markets will cover a greater number of countries because barriers to those market commodities will continue to fall, whether or not these are tariffs, legal barriers, or cultural barriers. The reduction of market barriers will widen the geographic areas for markets, in some cases, to world-wide dimensions. Markets will become freer for both sellers and buyers. Companies will be able to sell products to customers in more countries. Businesses and individuals will also be able to buy commodities and services from a greater number of countries. More products will have global markets–not just commodities like automobiles, airplanes, computers, and securities.

securities in, or obtain financing from, international markets.[39] They also find it profitable to sell their goods and services in, or buy their raw materials or components from, international markets. Worldwide trade now amounts to an astonishingly large figure, six trillion dollars in 1995, more than 80% the size of the gross domestic product of the United States, the world's largest economy.[40]

The existence of greater choice also extends to investment opportunities. Companies are investing in foreign countries, buying assets such as securities, businesses, facilities, and land, and have shifted production to

39. This is an example of international financial integration. *See, e.g.*, Hal S. Scott & Philip A. Wellons, International Finance: Transactions, Policy, and Regulations (3rd ed. 1996); Richard J. Herring & Robert E. Litan, Financial Regulation in the Global Economy 13-48 (1995).

40. The gross domestic product of the United States was $7,245.8 billion in 1995. *See National Income and Product Accounts*, Survey of Current Business, July 1996, at 5 tbl. 1.1 (Bur. Econ. Anal., U.S. Dep't Com.) [hereinafter Survey of Current Business, July 1996]. The United States has the world's largest economy, accounting for, by one measure, 21.3% of world gross domestic product in 1995. *See, e.g.*, World Economic Outlook, *supra* note 25, at 156.

From 1992 to 1995, total world exports of merchandise and commercial services amounted to the following (in billions of dollars):

	1992	*1993*	*1994*	*1995*
Merchandise	3,655	3,630	4,090	4,875
Commercial Services	1,017	1,000	1,080	1,230

See Overview of World Trade in 1995 and Outlook for 1996, WTO Focus, May 1996, at 2 tbl. 1 (World Trade Org.) (data for 1993-95) [hereinafter WTO Focus, May 1996]; *Overview of World Trade in 1994 and Outlook for 1995*, WTO Focus, Mar.-Apr. 1995, at 5 tbl. 1 (World Trade Org.) (data for 1992) [hereinafter WTO Focus, Mar.-Apr. 1995]. Theoretically, total world exports should equal total world imports. In practice, however, total world exports differ from total world imports because of differences in evaluation, definition, and data collection. *See* WTO Focus, May 1996, *supra*, at 4 tbl. 3 (giving total world imports of merchandise at $5,015 billion for 1995).

Merchandise trade consists of goods–manufactured goods and primary commodities such as minerals or agricultural, fishery, and forestry products. Commercial services fall into broad categories of transportation, travel (tourism), and other private services (insurance, banking, telecommunications, etc.) and income. *Cf. id.* at 3-4; WTO Focus, Mar.-Apr. 1995, *supra* at 5. In 1994, the six leading exporters and importers of commercial services, in billions of dollars (value) and as percentages of total world trade in commercial services (share), were as follows:

	1994 Exports		*1994 Imports*		*Exports & Imports*
	Value	*Share*	*Value*	*Share*	*Combined Value*
United States	178.2	16.5	125.0	12.0	303.2
Japan	57.2	5.3	109.2	10.5	166.4
France	89.1	8.3	69.9	6.7	159.0
Germany	53.1	4.9	98.8	9.5	151.9
Italy	59.1	5.5	58.0	5.6	117.1
United Kingdom	58.6	5.4	50.8	4.9	109.4

See WTO Focus, May 1996, *supra*, at 8 tbl. 7.

In 1995, exports and imports of merchandise trade were as follows for the European Union and the following countries:

foreign factories.[41] Concurrently, sellers of such domestic assets now have

	1995 Exports of Merchandise Trade (in billions of dollars)	1995 Imports of Merchandise Trade (in billions of dollars)
European Union	750.8	736.1
United States	583.9	770.8
Japan	443.0	335.9
China	148.8	132.0
Russia Federation	80.2	55.7

See id. at 6 tbl. 5 (export and import data for Russian Federation; figure includes trade with former republics of the USSR), 7 tbl. 6 (export and import data for all but Russia; European Union figures exclude intra-European Union trade).

41. For example, consider the total foreign direct investment (FDI) positions of the United States and Japan in 1995:

	FDI in Country	FDI Abroad
United States	$560.1 billion	$711.6 billion
Japan	$ 34.1 billion	$463.6 billion

See Survey of Current Business, July 1996, *supra* note 40, at 47 tbl. 3, 50 tbl. 4 (giving total foreign direct investment in the United States and total American foreign direct investment abroad by historical cost at year-end 1995); Jon Choy, *Foreign Direct Investment in Japan Rebounds*, Japan Econ. Inst., July 21, 1995, No. 27B, at 8, 9 (giving foreign direct investment in Japan as of March 31, 1995, based on notifications, not actual transactions, and excluding disinvestments); *Japan's FY 1994 Foreign Direct Investment*, Japan Econ. Inst., July 7, 1995, No. 25B, at 6, 7 (giving Japanese foreign direct investment abroad as of March 31, 1995, based on notifications, not actual transactions, and excluding disinvestments). Foreign direct investment is foreign investment in domestic real estate, businesses, and factories (as contrasted with "portfolio investment," foreign investment in domestic financial assets such as stocks and bonds). A more technical definition is that a foreign resident has ownership or control, directly or indirectly, of 10% or more of the voting securities of a domestic corporation or the equivalent interest in an unincorporated domestic business. *See* Raymond J. Mataloni, Jr., *A Guide to BEA Statistics on U.S. Multinational Companies*, Survey of Current Business, Mar. 1995, at 38 (Bur. Econ. Anal., U.S. Dep't Com.).

As a percentage of all direct investment, the figure for foreign direct investment in Japan is among the lowest for the industrialized countries. In most industrialized countries, foreign direct investment has had a long and substantial presence. Since the 1980s, the United States has experienced a substantial increase in foreign direct investment. *See* Edward M. Graham & Paul R. Krugman, Foreign Direct Investment in the United States 31-33 (3d ed. 1995). The shares of foreign-owned firms for manufacturing sales, value added, and employment in France, the United Kingdom, and the United States were as follows for 1985 and 1990 (in percentages):

	Sales		Value Added		Employment	
	1985	1990	1985	1990	1985	1990
France	26.7	28.4	25.3	27.1	21.1	23.7
United Kingdom	20.3	24.1	18.7	21.1	14.0	14.9
United States	8.0	16.4	8.3	13.4	8.0	10.8

See id. at 33 tbl. 1.9.

The manufacturing companies of most developed countries produce a substantial percentage of their output in foreign countries. *See* Douglas Ostrom, *MITI Looks to United States, Europe for Lessons on Restructuring*, Japan Econ. Inst., June 21, 1996, No. 23B, at 3 (reporting that in 1994 manufacturing companies of Japan, Germany, and the United States produced 7.9%, 17.5%, and 20.1%, respectively, of their output outside of their home country). Even Japanese companies, which have been latecomers in shifting manufacturing production overseas, now produce more in foreign factories than the total

more buyers to choose from. The liberalization of investment opportunities–the removal of barriers–contributes to the liberalization of trade, and vice versa.[42]

Expanding markets simultaneously generates more competition along with more opportunities;[43] domestic firms must compete not only with domestic but also foreign rivals. While benefiting domestic consumers, foreign competition may threaten domestic businesses and employees.[44] Whether the foreign competition comes from imports or the local subsidiaries of foreign corporations, employees of domestic firms may lose their jobs as these firms lay off surplus employees in order to become more competitive.[45] Where local subsidiaries of foreign corporations provide competition, however, these subsidiaries will create new jobs that replace, in

amount of Japanese exports. For example, Japanese manufacturing companies produced ¥41.2 trillion worth of goods in overseas plants in fiscal year 1995 (ending in March 1996), a figure greater than the total amount of exports from Japan, ¥39.6 trillion ($412 billion and $396 billion, respectively, using a $1 = ¥100 exchange rate, *cf. Currency Markets*, N.Y. TIMES, Apr. 2, 1997, at D17 (as of April 1, one dollar was worth about ¥120)). *See* Sumie Kawakami, *Exporting a Surplus [Focus Japan]*, FAR EAST. ECON. REV., July 4, 1996, at 44.

42. *See Globalisation: Creating a Borderless World?*, OECD LETTER, Aug.-Sept. 1996, at 4 (Org. Econ. Co-Op. & Dev.).

43. *See* PORTER, *supra* note 2, at 7-9.

44. Even buyers can face increased competition, in that they may incur higher costs from increased competition. For example, oil from Russia need no longer be sold at subsidized prices to former Soviet allies. *See* Beth Knobel, *Unpaid Energy Bills Split Russia, Neighbors*, L.A. TIMES, Apr. 14, 1994, at D5.

45. Compare, for example, employment and revenues at several of America's largest corporations in 1978 with 1995.

	No. of Employees		*Revenues ($ millions)*	
	1978	*1995*	*1978*	*1995*
General Motors	839,000	709,000	63,221.1	168,828.6
Ford Motors	506,531	346,990	42,784.1	137,131.0
International Business Machines	325,170	252,215	21,076.1	71,940.0
General Electric	401,000	222,000	19,653.8	70,028.0
Chrysler	157,958	126,000	16,340.7	53,195.0

See Fortune's Global 500: The World's Largest Corporations, FORTUNE, Aug. 5, 1996, at 102, F-1, F-11 (data for 1995 fiscal year ending on or before March 31, 1996) [hereinafter *Global 500*]; Peter Dworkin, *The Fortune Directory of the 500 Largest U.S. Industrial Corporations*, FORTUNE, May 7, 1979, at 268, *available in* LEXIS, News Library, Fortun File (data for 1978). Employment went down as sales (adjusted for inflation) went up. From March 1979 (end of fiscal year 1978) to March 1996 (end of fiscal year 1995), the consumer price index changed from 69.8 to 155.7, an increase of about 123%. *See Bureau of Labor Statistics Data* (visited Oct. 15, 1996) <http://stats.bls.gov:80/cgi-bin/surveymost> (website for Bureau of Labor Statistics, providing consumer price index for all urban consumers). The five companies listed above increased their sales by considerably more than 123%, and four out of five increased sales by over 200%.

Downsizing, of course, is not restricted to the United States. For many employees, not just in America but also in Japan and Europe, globalization has been a bane, exposing them to foreign competition and throwing them out of work. *See, e.g.*, Teresa Watanabe & David Holley, *Japanese Jolted by Demands of Future: As Nation Recovers from Brutal Recession, Traditional Business Practices Mean Little, Older Men Lose Guarantees on Pay, Jobs, Respect*, L.A. TIMES, July 14, 1996, at A1; Joan Warner et al., *Clinging to the Safety Net*, BUS. WK., Mar. 11, 1996, at 62 (regarding European workers).

part, jobs lost at domestic firms.[46] One of the major consequences of increased foreign competition and the domestic drive for efficiency is that countries have become more willing to privatize and deregulate.[47]

By making foreign countries important sources of consumers, investors, and suppliers, globalization creates interdependence. When domestic businesses buy from and sell to foreign markets, their financial welfare becomes linked to those markets. More domestic companies have evolved into multinational corporations, firms that have economic interests in several countries. Businesses set up partnerships with foreign firms, to share technology and risk, in order to create new products.[48] Because customers as well as suppliers are foreign, firms in one country become economically dependent upon firms in other countries. When foreign firms likewise become dependent upon domestic markets, interdependence is established as the economic prosperity of one nation becomes connected to that of other countries. For virtually all countries, transnational trade is important, if not vital, to their economic prosperity.[49]

As economic globalization integrates various national markets into regional or world-wide markets, it also promotes general free market prin-

---

46. In 1994, nonbank U.S. affiliates of foreign companies employed 4,867,000 American workers, or 5.0% of the total nonbank employment in the United States. *See* SURVEY OF CURRENT BUSINESS, July 1996, *supra* note 40, at 102, 113 tbl. 13. In many cases, foreign subsidiaries will pay higher wages than local firms. *See* Ned G. Howenstine & Dale P. Shannon, *Differences in Foreign-Owned U.S. Manufacturing Establishments by Country of Owner*, SURVEY OF CURRENT BUSINESS, Mar. 1996, at 43 (Bur. Econ. Anal., U.S. Dep't Com.) (reporting that the "U.S. manufacturing establishments of each of the major investing countries [Canada, France, Germany, Japan, the Netherlands, and the United Kingdom] tend to be much larger, pay higher wages, and be more productive than the U.S.-owned establishments").

47. *See infra* note 52.

48. *See, e.g.*, Brian Bremner et al., *Keiretsu Connections: The Bonds Between the U.S. and Japan's Industry Groups*, BUS. WK., July 22, 1996, at 52 (numerous tie-ups between U.S. and Japanese multinational companies); Darryl Gibson, *A Profitable Window [Focus Japan]*, FAR EAST. ECON. REV., July 4, 1996, at 48 (joint ventures involving U.S. and Japanese firms, Chinese and Japanese firms, and U.S., German, and Japanese firms); *NTT, IBM Japan Tie up in Small Information Device Field*, JAPAN ECON. NEWSWIRE, June 26, 1996, *available in* LEXIS, News Library, Curnws File (Nippon Telegraph and Telephone Corp. of Japan and IBM Japan Ltd. will jointly develop and sell advanced portable information equipment called personal digital assistants, PDAs, which can be linked with mobile phones and computers); *US, Japanese, Korean Chipmakers Join to Create Faster Memory Chips*, COMPUTERGRAM INTERNATIONAL, June 25, 1996, at No. 2941, *available in* LEXIS, News Library, Curnws File (an international consortium of U.S., Japanese and South Korean companies will develop a memory chip with two to five times faster access times and transfer rates by the year 2000—the participants are Texas Instruments, Micron Technology, and Apple Computer of the United States; Fujitsu and Mitsubishi Electric of Japan; and Hyundai Electronics Industry and Samsung Electronics of South Korea); Evelyn Iritani & Karen Kaplan, *NEC to Merge its PC Unit with Packard Bell Computers: The Move by the Big Japanese Firm Is a Financial Boost for the Struggling Sacramento Company*, L.A. TIMES, June 5, 1996, at D1 (NEC of Japan will merge its personal computer division with Packard Bell of the United States to create an $8 billion-a-year company, Packard Bell NEC). Of course, there are numerous purely domestic alliances as well.

49. For example, the United States had the following total exports and imports of merchandise and services, and GDP for 1992-95:

ciples, such as the quintessential concept of the market mechanism to allocate resources,[50] reduce protectionism in international trade,[51] and

Exports and Imports (Billions of Dollars) for Years 1992-95					
		1992	*1993*	*1994*	*1995*
Merchandise	Exports	440.4	456.8	502.5	575.9
	Imports	536.5	589.4	668.6	749.4
Services	Exports	177.3	186.1	195.8	210.6
	Imports	119.5	125.5	134.1	142.2
TOTAL TRADE: Exports & Imports of Merchandise and Services		1273.7	1357.8	1501	1678.1
GDP		6244.4	6550.2	6931.4	7245.8
TOTAL TRADE as % of GDP		20.5%	20.8%	21.8%	23.2%

See Survey of Current Business, July 1996, *supra* note 40, at 5 tbl. 1.1, 68 tbl. 1 (GDP data for 1994-95, and trade data for 1992-95); *National Income and Product Accounts*, Survey of Current Business, Jan.-Feb. 1996, at 36 tbl. 1.1 (Bur. Econ. Anal., U.S. Dep't Com.) (GDP data for 1992-93). The definition of services differs from that of the World Trade Organization for commercial services, e.g., by including certain military goods. *See* Survey of Current Business, July 1996, *supra* note 40, at 68 tbl. 1, 87 n.3. The figure for 1995 merchandise trade also differs by 1%-3% from that of the WTO, primarily due to different methods of calculation. *See generally supra* note 40 (WTO trade figures). Figures from different organizations often differ because of varying definitions and methods of calculations.

50. The industrialized democracies are more accurately described as having mixed economies which utilize markets as well as government bureaucrats to allocate economic resources (and perhaps, a bit of custom as well). These countries are, however, characterized as market economies (or having free markets), to distinguish them from the command (or planned) economies which utilized bureaucrats much more heavily. *See* Paul A. Samuelson & William D. Nordhaus, Economics 25, 38-48 (13th ed. 1989); The New Palgrave: Problems of the Planned Economy at xi-xiii (John Eatwell et al. eds., 1990). An ideal type of market is the microeconomic concept of a perfectly competitive market, that is,

> a market in which perfect competition exists. The traditional conditions for perfect competition are rather stringent: all items sold must be exactly alike in order to avoid product differentiation; there must be numerous buyers and sellers to prevent any one buyer or seller from influencing the market price; entry or exit barriers to the market must be absent to allow resources like labor or raw materials to enter or leave the market quickly; and market participants must have accurate and instantaneous knowledge of important information, such as the market-determined price of the commodity. The virtue of perfect competition is that it efficiently allocates resources and that it maximizes the welfare of society with respect to the particular market commodity being sold.
>
> Two other important conditions are also implicit in the concept of perfect competition. First, market prices must account for all costs and benefits associated with the sale of the market commodity. Second, market commodities must not be "public goods" which are freely available to all. If these two conditions are not met, an efficient allocation of resources does not occur.
>
> Although these conditions indicate that perfect competition exists nowhere in our world, the ideal of a perfectly competitive market yields useful and accurate predictions when applied to markets that closely resemble it. The stock and foreign exchange markets are often cited by economists as examples which approach perfect competition.

privatize and deregulate.[52] Well before the collapse of the Soviet Union or even the end of the Cold War, the market economy (free market) paradigm of the West emerged as the decisive winner in the economic contest with the command (or planned) economy paradigm of the Soviet bloc.[53] Since globalization is being led by the corporations and governments in the capitalist economies of the industrialized democracies, it naturally advocates the ideology of the winners rather than the losers. Thus, the rules underlying globalization seek to expand markets among market economy rather than command economy principles.[54]

For example, the WTO espouses the implementation of free-market ground rules to cover international trade and trade-related aspects of

---

Alex Y. Seita, *Common Myths in the Economic Analysis of Law*, 1989 B.Y.U. L. REV. 993, 1041-43 (footnotes omitted).

51. Free trade among nations, unimpeded by protectionism, follows the theory of comparative advantage, an important economic principle originating from David Ricardo nearly 180 years ago. *See, e.g.*, PAUL R. KRUGMAN & MAURICE OBSTFELD, INTERNATIONAL ECONOMICS: THEORY AND POLICY 13-35 (1988); RUSSELL D. ROBERTS, THE CHOICE: A FABLE OF FREE TRADE AND PROTECTIONISM (1994) (an entertaining discussion of free trade and protectionism). Free trade is consistent with the concept that a market mechanism should make resource allocation decisions, e.g., that a market of buyer and sellers should determine what commodities should be sold and at what prices. When a government erects trade barriers–whether tariffs, nontariff barriers such as quotas, discriminatory standards or regulations, or local content requirements–the government, not the market, is adding an effective price increase to imported goods. *See* KRUGMAN & OBSTFELD, *supra*, at 184-98.

52. Decreasing government ownership (privatization) and control (deregulation) of industries is also consistent with the idea that the market should make production and purchasing decisions. Privatization places state-owned or controlled companies, factories, and facilities in the hands of private ownership. *See* DICTIONARY OF MODERN ECONOMICS, *supra* note 11, at 345. It follows the free market paradigm because the means of production are supposed to be in the hands of private entrepreneurs in a market economy. On a worldwide basis, privatization has accelerated recently, especially in countries where government ownership of productive facilities was formerly pervasive. *See, e.g.*, COSMO GRAHAM & TONY PROSSER, PRIVATIZING PUBLIC ENTERPRISES: CONSTITUTIONS, THE STATE, AND REGULATION IN COMPARATIVE PERSPECTIVE 1 (1991); Ernst & Young, *The Global Sweep of Privatization*, EUROMONEY, July 1990, supp. 1. Government control of an industry, such as by limiting the number of competitors (including foreign competitors) or the areas of competition, creates entry barriers to industry–a clear departure not just from the perfect market paradigm but also from the general notion that in a market economy the number of sellers should not be limited. Deregulation removes such governmentally imposed barriers to entry. *See* DICTIONARY OF MODERN ECONOMICS, *supra* note 11, at 104. To a lesser extent, there has also been increased deregulation. *See, e.g.*, RICHARD H. K. VIETOR, CONTRIVED COMPETITION: REGULATION AND DEREGULATION IN AMERICA (1994); KENNETH BUTTON, AIRLINE DEREGULATION: THE INTERNATIONAL EXPERIENCE (1991).

53. *See generally* Gregory Grossman, *Command Economy*, *in* THE NEW PALGRAVE: PROBLEMS OF THE PLANNED ECONOMY at 58 (John Eatwell et al. eds., 1990).

54. If the command market model had proven superior to free market model in economic performance, globalization today would have a dramatically different appearance. There would be a global system that fosters greater trade and economic cooperation among command economies, and its rules would have underlying Marxist, not capitalist, premises. After all, the Soviet-led Council for Mutual Economic Cooperation tried to promote greater trade among nations with command economies. *See, e.g.*, JOANNE GOWA, ALLIES, ADVERSARIES, AND INTERNATIONAL TRADE 3, 116, 120 (1994).

investment and intellectual property.[55] Its rules go further than those of the GATT, its predecessor in carrying out the free market principle of comparative advantage by stamping out protectionism among nations.[56] When tools of protectionism–such as tariffs, quotas, or domestic subsidies–are reduced, foreign imports can better enter a domestic market, creating more competition for local firms. The presence of increased competition contributes to the development of more efficient local firms as only the fittest firms will survive in a competitive marketplace. The use of a market and consumer choice, rather than a bureaucracy, to determine the survival of firms and products is the essence of a free market.[57] Not surprisingly, the various WTO agreements are expected to substantially

55. The IMF and the World Bank, too, have promoted market economy principles. *See, e.g.*, James *supra* note 28, at 323 (IMF conditionality, the terms on which it will lend, has often required budgetary and domestic credit restraints, as well as trade liberalization); World Bank, The East Asian Miracle: Economic Growth and Public Policy 10 (1993) [hereinafter East Asian Miracle] (advocating a "market friendly" strategy in which "the appropriate role of government is to ensure adequate investments in people, provide a competitive climate for private enterprise, keep the economy open to international trade, and maintain a stable macroeconomy"); Barend A. de Vries, Remaking the World Bank 6, 56-58 (1987) (describing how the World Bank has encouraged decentralized planning rather than command-type central planning, and has made substantial loans to help borrowing nations increase their economies' efficiency and competitiveness, such as by liberalizing trade); *cf.* John Williamson, *Introduction, in* IMF Conditionality, *supra* note 34, at xiii (stating that one complaint of borrowing countries is that the IMF is "ideologically biased in favor of free markets and against socialism"). At this time, however, the WTO is the most important of the international economic institutions in carrying out the implementation of free market principles, primarily the idea of opening markets (liberalizing trade) among countries. The WTO agreements have gone beyond the GATT in covering trade in services as well as trade-related aspects of intellectual property and trade-related investment measures. *See* General Agreement on Trade in Services, Apr. 15, 1994, Marrakesh Agreement Establishing the World Trade Organization, Annex 1B, 33 I.L.M. 44 (1994); Agreement on The Trade-Related Aspects of Intellectual Property, Including Trade in Counterfeit Goods, Apr. 15, 1994, Marrakesh Agreement Establishing the World Trade Organization, Annex 1C, 33 I.L.M. 81 (1994); Agreement on Trade-Related Investment Measures, Agreements on Trade in Goods, Apr. 15, 1994, Marrakesh Agreement Establishing the World Trade Organization, Annex 1A, *available in* <http://itl.irv.uit.no/trade_law/documents/freetrade> (visited Mar. 29, 1997). Further, the WTO agreements address more meaningfully the subjects of agriculture, textiles, and apparel. *See* Agreement on Agriculture, Agreements on Trade in Goods, Apr. 15, 1994, Marrakesh Agreement Establishing the World Trade Organization, Annex 1A, *available in* <http://itl.irv.uit.no/trade_law/documents/freetrade> (visited Mar. 29, 1997); Agreement on Textiles and Clothing, Agreements on Trade in Goods, Apr. 15, 1994, Marrakesh Agreement Establishing the World Trade Organization, Annex 1A, *available in* <http://itl.irv.uit.no/trade_law/documents/freetrade> (visited Mar. 29, 1997).

56. For instance, the WTO makes a member's subsidy to its domestic industry actionable by another member if its effect "is to displace or impede the imports of a like product of another Member into the market of the subsidizing Member." Agreement on Subsidies and Countervailing Measures, Agreements on Trade in Goods, Apr. 15, 1994, Marrakesh Agreement Establishing the World Trade Organization, Annex 1A, art. 6.3(a), *available in* <http://itl.irv.uit.no/trade_law/documents/freetrade> (visited Mar. 29, 1997).

57. *See supra* note 50.

increase global income.[58]

C. Political Globalization

As economic globalization expands, it has been accompanied by a somewhat lesser degree of political globalization in that there are now substantial numbers of elected governments.[59] Also, the rhetoric of human rights has gained universal acceptance, and more nations than ever before have pledged to protect human rights.[60] With political globalization, there is

58. *See WTO to Boost Global Income by $500 Billion*, FOCUS (GATT Newsletter), Oct. 1994, at 1.

59. *See, e.g.*, Judith Matloff, *Democracy, of a Sort, Sweeps Africa*, CHRIST. SCI. MONITOR, Aug. 7, 1996, at 10. The 1995-96 Freedom House survey observes that

> The rise in the number of formal democracies continued in 1995. This year's survey shows that there are now 117 democracies.... This represents just over 61 percent of the world's 191 countries. From the perspective of a decade ago the gain is all the more impressive. Ten years ago, less than 42 percent of the world's countries were formal democracies.
>
> Today, 3.1 billion persons out of a world population of 5.7 billion live under democratically elected governments. While not yet a universal standard, democracy has deepening and widening roots in all parts of the world....
>
> That 61 percent of all countries and nearly 55 percent of the world's population live under governments and legislatures elected in generally free and fair political processes represents a landmark shift. Today it is the expectation of the clear majority of citizens that their governments be accountable to them through regular elections. Such a broadening global consciousness does not guarantee full freedom, but it does create the basis for more free societies and for greater engagement by citizens in public affairs. Widening public democratic consciousness throughout the world, as well as growing expectations by the Western advanced industrial democracies that countries which receive significant aid should respect fundamental human rights and democratic procedures reinforces this trend.

Adrian Karatnycky, *The Comparative Survey of Freedom 1995-1996: Democracy and Despotism: Bipolarism Renewed?*, *in* FREEDOM IN THE WORLD: THE ANNUAL SURVEY OF POLITICAL RIGHTS & CIVIL LIBERTIES 1995-1996, at 3, 4-5 (Roger Kaplan ed., 1996) [hereinafter FREEDOM IN THE WORLD 1995-96] (annual Freedom House survey).

60. At the second World Conference on Human Rights, all 171 participating states adopted the Vienna Declaration and Programme of Action, which declared

> All human rights are universal, indivisible and interdependent and interrelated. The international community must treat human rights globally in a fair and equal manner, on the same footing, and with the same emphasis. While the significance of national and regional particularities and various historical, cultural and religious backgrounds must be borne in mind, it is the duty of States, regardless of their political, economic, and cultural systems, to promote and protect all human rights and fundamental freedoms.

United Nations World Conference on Human Rights: Vienna Declaration and Programme of Action art. 5, U.N. Doc. A/CONF.157/24, pt. 1 (1993), 32 I.L.M. 1661, 1665 (1993). *See generally* HUMAN RIGHTS: AN AGENDA FOR THE NEXT CENTURY (Louis Henkin & John L. Hargrove eds., 1994) [hereinafter HUMAN RIGHTS].

More countries have formally pledged to protect human rights. For example, there have been numerous state parties to the following human rights instruments: Convention on the Prevention and Punishment of the Crime of Genocide, *supra* note 32 (122 parties); International Covenant on Economic, Social and Cultural Rights, *supra* note 32 (135 parties); International Covenant on Civil and Political Rights, *supra* note 32 (135 parties); and International Covenant on the Elimination of All Forms of Racial Discrimination, *supra* note 32 (148 parties). *See Texts of the International Human Rights Instruments* (visited Dec. 11, 1996) <http://193.135.156.15/html/intlinst.htm> (U.N. human

more than just the *existence* of elected governments and the *recognition* of human rights by governments. Political globalization has also tended to cause a convergence in political values, with the *genuine acceptance* of democracy and human rights in a greater number of countries.

Compared to the convergence in economic values, the convergence of political values has had a more difficult path. The growth of economic globalization was championed by countries that realized they would gain economically by increased foreign trade. Even the command-economy communist nations sought trade with the capitalist economies of the West.[61] Well before the end of the Cold War, some communist nations even embraced capitalism to an extent. As events in China have clearly shown, dictatorship and a dismal human rights record have not been incompatible with free market policies.[62]

Unlike economic globalization, the support for political globalization historically has been weak, perhaps because its benefits were not as obvious or immediate. Despite their long history predating free market principles, the political values of democracy and human rights have been more dishonored by breach than honored by observance.[63] Most countries did

rights webpage containing links to the status of ratification of over 90 human rights instruments) [hereinafter *Human Rights Instruments*]. "Parties" to a treaty (whether by ratification, accession, etc.) are states that have "consented to be bound by the treaty and for which the treaty is in force." Vienna Convention on the Law of Treaties art. 2, para. (1)(g), U.N. Doc. A/CONF.39/27 at 289, 1155 U.N.T.S. 331 (1969). However, since some of the parties are countries that lack democratic governments and have a poor human rights record, it is clear that for these countries, the human rights instruments have no real meaning. *See, e.g., Human Rights Instruments, supra* (Cambodia and Rwanda are parties to the Convention on the Prevention and Punishment of the Crime of Genocide; Iraq, to the International Covenant on Civil and Political Rights).

61. For example, from 1986 to 1988, the 12-nation European Community (now the 15-nation European Union, with Austria, Finland, and Sweden as new members) imported 74.245 billion ECU ($85.4 billion) of goods from the 8-nation Soviet Bloc (the USSR, East Germany, Poland, Czechoslovakia, Hungary, Romania, Bulgaria, and Albania), and exported 60.212 billion ECU ($69.2 billion). *See* Office for Official Publications of the European Communities, The European Community and Its Eastern Neighbours 11-13 (1990); European Investment Bank, Annual Report 1990, at 51 (1991) (extrapolating from graph an exchange rate of ECU 1.15 = $1). In 1995, Chinese imports of goods to the United States totaled $45.542 billion, and U.S. exports to China totaled $11.750 billion. *See* Survey of Current Business, July 1996, *supra* note 40, at 76 tbl. 2, 78 tbl. 2. Obviously, since it takes two to trade, the desire of the communist nations to trade had to be matched by a corresponding desire on the part of the West.

62. *See, e.g., Survey of China: A Vacancy Awaits*, Economist, Mar. 18, 1995, at survey 3-4; Orville Schell, Mandate of Heaven: A New Generation of Entrepreneurs, Dissidents, Bohemians, and Technocrats Lays Claim to China's Future 331-406 (1994); Nicholas D. Kristof & Sheryl WuDunn, China Wakes: The Struggle for the Soul of a Rising Power 308-69 (1994). *See generally* Susumu Yabuki, China's New Political Economy: The Giant Awakes (Stephen M. Harner trans., 1995).

63. International commerce and trade have been in existence for millennia. But the intellectual foundations of capitalism are more recent. *See, e.g.,* Adam Smith, An Inquiry into the Nature and Causes of the Wealth of Nations (Edwin Cannan ed., 1937); Samuelson & Nordhaus, *supra* note 50, at 4. By contrast, the ideas of democracy and notions analogous to some human rights were discussed long before. *See, e.g.,* Aristotle, The Politics 145-55, 159-64, 240-44 (trans. T. A. Sinclair, 1962) (defining and

not espouse them, and those that did applied these concepts selectively.[64]

For decades after the end of World War II, the spread of humanitarian political values had to contend with severe obstacles.[65] For much of the

---

classifying democracy); Weston, *supra* note 37, at 14-17 (tracing the origin of human rights, known in earlier forms as "natural rights" or "the rights of Man," to ancient Greece and Rome). This article uses the term "democracy" to mean a society that is ruled indirectly by its citizens through their elected representatives. Such a democracy does not always protect "human rights" because a tyranny of the majority may deny human rights to a disfavored minority.

64. As many are undoubtedly aware, the United States, the world's leading symbol for democracy and human rights, denied democratic representation and basic human rights to African-Americans for at least a century before and a century after the United States was born. Native Americans also suffered greatly.

65. Among them were anti-minority attitudes among majorities in democratic countries, entrenched authoritarian traditions in nondemocratic countries, the attempt of colonial powers to retain their colonies, the indifference of the industrialized countries to conditions in developing countries, internecine internal wars in nondemocratic countries, the subordination of political to economic values, and the Cold War. The complications of the Cold War and rampant colonialism almost immediately made the United Nations–the institution designed to keep the peace and promote democracy and human rights–ineffective in doing any of the three.

Since most of the founding members of the United Nations were participants in the Allied cause which had fought against the Axis Powers, some common agreement on U.N. purpose and action could have been expected. But soon after World War II ended, the Cold War began, crippling the ability of the United Nations to act as an arbitrator or enforcer of peace. *See, e.g.*, RIGHTER, *supra* note 30, at 315. Perhaps even without the Cold War, the United Nations would have been ineffective. It was incapable of handling the new type of warfare that became dominant after World War II: "wars of liberation, civil wars, transfrontier guerrilla operations, and even *jihad*." Id. Further, throughout the Cold War, the promotion of democracy and human rights by the United States was secondary in priority to American national security concerns. To contain communism, the United States allied itself with dictatorships or nondemocracies in Argentina, Brazil, Chile, El Salvador, Greece, Guatemala, Indonesia, Portugal, South Africa, South Korea, South Vietnam, Spain, Taiwan, and numerous other countries. *See, e.g.* Tom J. Farer, *On a Collision Course: The American Campaign for Human Rights and the Antiradical Bias in the Third World*, in HUMAN RIGHTS AND AMERICAN FOREIGN POLICY 263 (Donald P. Kommers and Gilburt D. Loescher eds., 1979).

In the following decades, the United Nations proved itself incapable either in preventing or in resolving, by diplomacy or military force, wars and internal conflicts–a number involving wars of independence. Several conflicts grew out of wars of independence in which colonized peoples sought to liberate themselves from European powers. Anti-colonial revolts, some quite bloody, broke out all over the world, eventually leading to independence for European colonies. *See, e.g.*, RAYMOND K. KENT, FROM MADAGASCAR TO THE MALAGASY REPUBLIC (1962) (French Madagascar); DONALD LANCASTER, THE EMANCIPATION OF FRENCH INDOCHINA (1961) (French Indochina); MAHFOUD BENNOUNE, THE MAKING OF CONTEMPORARY ALGERIA: 1830-1987 (1988) (French Algeria). For other new nations, independence from colonial rule was considerably less violent. *See, e.g.*, BRIAN LAPPING, END OF EMPIRE (1985) (nations emerging from the dismantling of the British Empire after World War II); FEDERAL RESEARCH DIVISION, LIBRARY OF CONGRESS, PHILIPPINES: A COUNTRY STUDY 38-39, 41-43 (Ronald E. Dolan ed., 4th ed. 1993) (independence of the Philippines from America). When the United Nations was born in 1945, about 750 million people, nearly a third of the world's population, lived in dependent territories; today, about 1.5 million do. *See Decolonization*, U.N. CHRON., Sept. 1995, at 10.

While no single war of the magnitude of the World Wars occurred, numerous other conflicts emerged, with lethal results. The list of wars, hostilities, conflicts, and suppressions running from the late 1940s through the 1990s is long and depressing: e.g., the

existence of the United Nations, the most important international organization devoted to the promotion of democracy and human rights, many of its leading members either did not observe democratic values or human rights domestically, or subordinated these values to other priorities in foreign affairs.[66] Despite initial obstacles, however, these political values slowly developed roots in non-western countries.

Even before the end of the Cold War, the past two decades saw the emergence of a greater number of countries with democratic governments and protective of human rights.[67] These countries offer political rights and

---

Communist-Nationalist battle for China; the French Suppression in Madagascar; the French Vietnam War; the Chinese Suppression in Tibet; the Soviet Suppression in Hungary; the Korean War; the French Algerian War; the U.S. Vietnam War; the Soviet Suppression in Czechoslovakia; the three Arab-Israeli Wars; the Cambodian Massacres; the Soviet Afghanistan War; the Argentine-British Falklands War; the Iraq-Iran War; the Gulf War; the Bosnian War; and the Rwandan Massacres. During its first four decades, "the U.N. proved manifestly incapable of preventing close to 150 conflicts, including more than 125 in the Third World, which cost some 22 million lives." RIGHTER, *supra* note 30, at 311.

The absence of major wars on the scale of World War II or World War I is attributable not so much to U.N. influence, but to nuclear deterrence–the horrible prospect that another such war would involve the massive use of nuclear weapons and cause the probable destruction of human civilization. One relatively successful U.N. action to punish aggression was the Persian Gulf War of 1991, in which U.N. forces, comprised primarily of United States military personnel, defeated the Iraqi invaders who had conquered Kuwait. *See* ANTHONY C. AREND & ROBERT J. BECK, INTERNATIONAL LAW AND THE USE OF FORCE: BEYOND THE UN CHARTER PARADIGM 53-55 (1993). In that conflict, American leadership together with military assistance from U.S. European allies and political acquiescence from China and Russia allowed the United Nations to take decisive action against a belligerent nation. Even in that "success" story, the root cause of Iraqi aggression–Iraqi dictator Saddam Hussein–was not removed; he continues to rule Iraq. The U.N.-sanctioned invasion of Haiti by American troops might be considered another successful action. *See, e.g., UN Efforts Give "Exemplary Illustration of Diplomacy of Democratization," Says Secretary-General*, U.N. CHRON., Spring 1996, at 4; Richard D. Lyons, *U.N. Authorizes Invasion of Haiti to Be Led by U.S.*, N.Y. TIMES, Aug. 1, 1994, at A1.

Even with colonialism long disappeared and the end of the Cold War, the United Nations has difficulty dealing with conflicts involving civil wars, guerilla operations of minority or occupied populations, and persecution of particular groups by government authorities. *See, e.g.*, RIGHTER, *supra* note 30, at 315. Many hostilities or acts of violence were purely internal to a country, and thus, more difficult for the U.N. to intervene. *See, e.g.*, Michael R. Gordon, *Chechnya Toll Is Far Higher, 80,000 Dead, Lebed Asserts*, N.Y. TIMES, Sept. 4, 1996, at A3 (Russian presidential security adviser Lebed estimating that, to date, 80,000 people have been killed and 240,000 wounded in the fighting between Chechen separatists and Russia troops in the Russian republic of Chechnya); Clestine Bohlen, *War on Rebel Kurds Puts Turkey's Ideals to Test*, N.Y. TIMES, July 16, 1995, § 1, at 3 (Turkish government war against minority Kurds displacing over 300,000 villagers from their homes and resulting in a death toll approaching 18,000).

66. For example, after World War II ended, France fought to keep her colonies from becoming independent, and neither Communist China nor the Soviet Union placed much value on human life. *See, e.g., supra* note 65 (postwar French colonialism); KRISTOF & WUDUNN, *supra* note 62, at 65 (Chinese communist elimination of potential counter revolutionaries); ROBERT CONQUEST, THE GREAT TERROR: A REASSESSMENT 477-78, 484-86 (1990) (citing millions imprisoned at Soviet labor camps in the 1950s).

67. *See* FREEDOM IN THE WORLD 1995-96, *supra* note 59, at 1. Given the disparity of political freedoms and civil liberties between countries, only a rough assessment of the number of countries with democratic governments and human rights is possible. According to one estimate, at the beginning of 1996, 19.55% of the people in the world

civil liberties that make them different in kind from past authoritarian regimes. With the end of the Cold War, many of the former Soviet-allied countries established popularly elected governments. Earlier, elected governments emerged from dictatorships in Latin America, Asia, and Africa.[68] As the transformation of South Africa–the former bastion of apartheid–into a democratic country shows, the unbelievable can happen.

The outlook today is promising for the values of democracy and, to a lesser extent, human rights. First, with the triumph of liberal democracy over communism in the Cold War,[69] the United States and its allies can now more vigorously pursue humanitarian rather than security objectives. Second, the commonality of democracy and human rights in nations has provided more reason for these nations to cooperate among themselves in trade, humanitarian, and security matters, as well as in trying to nurture the qualities of democracy and human rights in authoritarian countries. The remaining authoritarian strongholds face pressures to democratize, and to recognize some level of human rights.[70]

Democracy has been easier to achieve than the protection of human rights, perhaps because the implementation of democracy is technically more easily accomplished (e.g., a popularly elected government), while there may be disagreement over which rights are basic human rights and how these basic rights are to be protected.[71] Furthermore, elected governments need not necessarily protect human rights, especially in nascent

---

lived in free countries (i.e., with a "broad range of political rights and civil liberties"), 41.49% in partly free countries (where some basic rights are denied), and 38.96% in countries that were not free (basic rights are denied). *See* Karatnycky, *supra* note 59, at 4 (1995-96 Freedom House survey). The number of countries in each category in various years were as follows:

YEAR	FREE COUNTRIES	PARTLY FREE COUNTRIES	NOT FREE COUNTRIES
1986	56	56	55
1993	75	73	38
1994	72	63	55
1995	76	61	54
1996	76	62	53

Id. at 8. Other sources also rate the political rights and civil liberties of individual countries. *See, e.g.* HUMAN RIGHTS WATCH, HUMAN RIGHTS WATCH WORLD REPORT 1996 (1995); COUNTRY REPORTS ON HUMAN RIGHTS PRACTICES FOR 1994, REPORT SUBMITTED TO THE COMMITTEE ON FOREIGN RELATIONS U.S. SENATE AND THE COMMITTEE ON INTERNATIONAL RELATIONS U.S. HOUSE OF REPRESENTATIVES BY THE DEPARTMENT OF STATE, 104th Cong. (1995) [hereinafter HUMAN RIGHTS PRACTICES 1994]. *See generally* Marcus W. Brauchli, *More Nations Embrace Democracy–and Find It Often Can Be Messy*, WALL ST. J., June 25, 1996, at A1.

68. *See* Tina Rosenberg, *Overcoming the Legacies of Dictatorship*, FOREIGN AFF., May-June 1995, at 134, 135.

69. This victory is attributable not just to the United States and its allies, but also to the courage and vision of former communist leaders like Mikhail Gorbachev. *See, e.g., infra* note 134.

70. *See* STEPHAN HAGGARD & ROBERT R. KAUFMAN, THE POLITICAL ECONOMY OF DEMOCRATIC TRANSITIONS 4 (1995).

71. For example, some Asian countries disagree with the West on the need for extensive human rights protection. *See, e.g.*, Charles Graybow, *South and East Asia: A Raw Deal for the Masses*, in FREEDOM IN THE WORLD 1995-96, *supra* note 59, at 68, 69-70.

democracies which may have problems of illiteracy, corruption, authoritarian traditions, ethnic or religious conflicts, and a winner-takes-all political system.[72]

The value of democratic governments is that their actions reflect the desires of a majority of the people rather than the wishes of a tyrant or a select few. Democracy is arguably the most basic human right because it recognizes the sovereignty of the people in that a government pursues policies which the majority of the people support through their freely elected representatives. The preferences of at least a majority of its population, rather than the desires of a select few, influence democratic governments. Democratic governments are much more likely to respect human rights, at least those of the majority, than authoritarian regimes which are unaccountable to an electorate. Of course, democracy is not itself a sufficient condition for a humane society, since a majority may persecute or subjugate a minority in a democratic society.[73] A practical benefit of *mature* democracies, those having democratic governments for a long period of time, is that they substantially protect a wide variety of human rights and are much less likely to use military force to resolve conflicts.[74]

---

72. *See, e.g.*, Matloff, *supra* note 59 (reporting on the fragility of African democracies); Howard W. French, *Can African Democracy Survive Ethnic Voting?*, N.Y. Times, Mar. 17, 1996, § 4 at 4 (stating that voter allegiance to tribe, language, and region is stronger than to policy throughout Africa because countries were artificially created by European powers; democratic elections give winners everything and losers nothing). In its 1994-95 survey, Freedom House reported:

> Many of these democracies, however, remain fragile and often are incapable of providing for the basic rights of their citizens . . . .
>
> Many of these fragile democracies are at risk because of internal division, rampant corruption, overarching influence by militaries and oligarchies, and destabilization from abroad. As a result 37 democracies are only Partly Free.
>
> Inter-ethnic and inter-sectarian strife is a major contributing factor in the erosion of political rights and civil liberties in many formal democracies.

Adrian Karatnycky, *The Comparative Survey of Freedom 1994-1995: Democracies on the Rise, Democracies at Risk*, *in* Freedom in the World: The Annual Survey of Political Rights & Civil Liberties 1994-1995, at 3, 4 (James Finn ed., 1995). As examples of democracies at risk, Freedom House listed countries with inter-ethnic or inter-sectarian conflict (e.g., Bosnia, India, Turkey, Mali, Niger); countries in transition from communist rule (e.g., Albania, Romania, Russia); countries recovering from extended periods of guerrilla insurgencies, terrorism, and civil war (e.g., El Salvador, Nicaragua, Mozambique); and countries where the political process and judicial system are tainted by corruption, such as the influence of drug cartels (e.g., Brazil, Colombia, the Dominican Republic, Guatemala, Honduras, Paraguay, Venezuela). *See id.* at 4-5.

73. To take a historical example, the Confederate States of America was formed on February 8, 1861, by seven states that seceded from the United States of America, and eventually grew to consist of eleven seceding states. *See* Samuel E. Morison, The Oxford History of the American People 607-12, 625 (1965) (the eleven confederate states were Alabama, Arkansas, Florida, Georgia, Louisiana, Mississippi, North Carolina, South Carolina, Tennessee, Texas, and Virginia). The confederacy was a democracy, except that the human rights of a large minority were disregarded. In 1860, on the eve of the Civil War, blacks–the great majority of whom were slaves–comprised 42% of the population in the states that later became the Confederate States of America. *Cf.* Historical Statistics of the United States, *supra* note 23, at 24 tbl. ser. A 195-209 (figure of 42% derived from statistical data).

74. While mature and stable democracies are less likely to go to war, newly democratized countries in transition from authoritarian to democratic governments seem more

Despite disagreement over the extent to which human rights should be protected, some level of human rights protection exists for a substantial percentage, if not the majority, of the world's population.[75] For an increasing number of countries, there seems to be a real, as opposed to a rhetorical, acceptance of *some* form of human rights. While inadequate and imperfect, this is an enormous improvement over the past. While outrageous examples of inhumanity still occur, such as in Rwanda, they are universally condemned.[76]

In an indirect way, the cultural impact of economic globalization stimulates political globalization. Economic globalization has long introduced aspects of foreign cultures–especially American culture–either directly by the sale of merchandise such as movies and musical recordings, or indirectly through exposure to foreigners.[77] More than in the past, the opening of new markets through economic globalization has brought a flood of people and companies into foreign lands.

Personal contact, always so important in understanding other human beings, has made foreigners less inscrutable. More business personnel are assigned to overseas offices, more consumers travel abroad as tourists, and more students study in foreign countries.[78] Local residents are more likely than ever before to work for, do business with, or personally know foreigners. In some cases, this transnational encounter may lead to a personal

likely to fight wars than mature democracies or even autocracies. These newly democratizing countries will fight wars even with democratic states. *See* Edward D. Mansfield & Jack Snyder, *Democratization and War*, 74 FOREIGN AFF., May-June 1995, at 79. For example, a combination of nationalism and incipient democratization led to the start of disastrous wars in late 18th-century France, pre-World War I Germany, and Japan in the 1920s. *Id.* at 85-86.

75. There is not a "complete agreement about the nature of [human] rights or their substantive scope–which is to say, their definition." Weston, *supra* note 37, at 17. Still, it is clear that the protection of human rights is widespread. *See supra* note 67.

76. Unfortunately, this universal condemnation has not been matched by immediate universal action to prevent the inhumanity. Because of this inaction, some have suggested the creation of a standing emergency force under the United Nations which would intervene to prevent lethal conflicts. *See infra* note 156.

77. *See, e.g.*, John Yemma, *The Americanization of the World*, BOSTON GLOBE, July 28, 1996, at F1.

78. For example, international tourism receipts, excluding air travel, are estimated to have been $372 billion in 1995 spent by 567 million tourists. *See* Ron Scherer, *Tourism Booms as World's Middle Class Goes Trekking*, CHRIST. SCI. MONITOR, June 12, 1996, at 1 (citing figures from the World Tourism Organization). Eight of the top twenty destinations for tourism in 1995 were countries that were part of the European Union, and twelve were European countries:

affinity with or an in-depth understanding of foreign cultures.[79]

Top Twenty Countries in 1995	*Tourist Arrivals (millions)*
1. France	60.6
2. Spain	45.1
3. United States	44.7
4. Italy	29.2
5. China	23.4
6. Britain	22.7
7. Hungary	22.1
8. Mexico	19.9
9. Poland	19.2
10. Austria	17.8
11. Canada	16.9
12. Czech Rep.	16.6
13. Germany	14.5
14. Switzerland	11.8
15. Greece	11.1
16. Hong Kong	9.6
17. Portugal	9.5
18. Malaysia	7.9
19. Singapore	6.6
20. Thailand	6.5

Id. Many tourists are likely to come from neighboring countries. For example, in 1994, out of 46.4 million Americans traveling to foreign countries, 28.3 million went to Canada or Mexico, while of 45.5 million foreigners traveling to the United States, 26.3 million came from Canada or Mexico. *See* Bureau of the Census, Dep't of Com., Statistical Abstract of the United States 1995, at 266-67 tbls. 430-31 (115th ed., Sept. 1995)) (estimate) [hereinafter 1995 Statistical Abstract]. As for business-related travelers and students, in 1993 there were approximately 3.5 million nonimmigrants admitted to the United States in connection with a business purpose: 2,962,000 business travelers; 145,000 treaty traders and investors; 224,000 temporary workers and trainees; 21,000 representatives of foreign information media; and 132,000 intracompany transferees. *See id.* at 11 tbl. 7. In fall 1993, there were 449,000 foreign students enrolled in U.S. colleges and universities. *Id.* at 188 tbl. 295.

79. Exposure to foreign businesses, tourists, and products is no guarantee that local residents will achieve an in-depth understanding of a foreign culture. A particular foreign culture may be more difficult to understand if it is little studied by local residents and has different historical roots from the local culture. For example, there are significant Japanese investments, large numbers of Japanese tourists and students, and a widespread presence of Japanese consumer products in the United States. *See, e.g.*, Alex Y. Seita, *The Intractable State of United States-Japan Relations*, 32 Colum. J. Transnat'l L. 467, 469 & n.2, 479 & n.31 (1995); 1995 Statistical Abstract, *supra* note 78, at 188 tbl. 295 (in 1994, Japanese students comprised the single largest group of foreign students in the United States, with 44,000 out of a total of 449,000), 267 tbl. 432 (in 1993, Japanese travelers constituted the single largest group of foreign visitors for pleasure admitted to the United States, nearly 3.2 million out of a total of 16.9 million). Despite that, most Americans are still not very familiar with Japanese culture. Japan is still viewed by most Americans in stereotypical terms that may contain some truth but which lack in-depth analysis based on objective data. *See, e.g.*, Robert D. Deutsch & Arthur J. Alexander, *Americans' Images of Japan*, Japan Econ. Inst., May 17, 1996, No. 19A, at 1, 16. Nevertheless, American perceptions of Japan, as well as Japanese perceptions of America, are undoubtedly more accurate and positive today than during World War II and before. *See, e.g.*, John W. Dower, War without Mercy: Race and Power in the Pacific War 15-32 (1986); Sheila K. Johnson, The Japanese Through American Eyes 1-17, 163-71 (1988).

Further, economic globalization has generated an interest in learning foreign languages, primarily English. Perhaps irreversibly, English has become the international language of business and science, with a broader usage than any other language.[80] At the same time, the ability to speak a foreign language other than English gives one a competitive advantage in doing business in nonEnglish-speaking countries.[81]

Doing business with foreigners, in their country or in one's own, requires that one communicate with them, cooperate with them, and be exposed to their political and business values.[82] The political values of democracy and human rights, as well as aspects of foreign cultures, are often inseparable (though secondary) components of economic globalization. Thus, countries that seek to benefit from economic globalization must frequently tolerate political globalization and exposure to foreign cultures. As people know more about foreign cultures, some familiarity with foreign political values is bound to arise.

II. Technology's Vital Role in Converging Values

The advanced communication technology that links much of the world together continues to be crucial to the convergence of economic and political values. This technology is utilized primarily by business entities to facilitate economic globalization.[83] Modern technology has also tended to promote democracy and human rights by making it easier and cheaper for

80. Even though only 377 million people speak English as a first language, probably 1.8 billion people, one-third of the world's population, are regularly exposed to English in their daily lives. By one estimate, a billion people will be speaking or learning English by the year 2000. English is not only the language of business, but that of science as well, with two-thirds of the world's scientists reading scientific information in English and with four-fifths of all stored electronic information in English. *See, e.g.*, William McGurn, *English in Asia: Money Talks*, FAR EAST. ECON. REV., Mar. 21, 1996, at 40; Alexander MacLeod, *Once-Fussy BBC Begins to Speak with Scottish, Irish, Even American Accents*, CHRIST. SCI. MONITOR, Sept. 4, 1996, at 11; Kim Campbell, *The World Rushes to Speak and Write "American" English*, CHRIST. SCI. MONITOR, Sept. 4, 1996, at 10.

81. Being able to speak the language of the country that you wish to do business in is an obvious advantage. *See, e.g.*, Bernard Wysocki Jr., *Utah's Economy Goes Global, Thanks in Part to Role of Missionaries: Mormons' Overseas Stints Yield Linguistic Skills and Network of Contacts*, WALL ST. J., Mar. 28, 1996, at A1. Understanding a country's language means that one can read its newspapers, watch its television programs, and talk to its ordinary citizens. It is an important way in which one understands and appreciates another country's culture.

82. This might mean, for example, that a foreign-owned subsidiary in the United States must adhere to American laws prohibiting sexual harassment. *See, e.g.*, Leon Jaroff, *Assembly-Line Sexism?: Charges of Abusing Women–and Angry Denials–Rock a Midwestern Mitsubishi Auto Plant*, TIME, Jan. 7, 1992, at 1 (Equal Employment Opportunity Commission files the biggest federal sexual-harassment lawsuit in history against a factory operated by the American subsidiary of a Japanese company); Mark Maremont, *Abuse of Power: The Astonishing Tale of Sexual Harassment at Astra USA*, BUS. WK., May 13, 1996, at 86 (allegations of widespread sexual harassment at the American subsidiary of a Swedish company). On the other hand, foreigners may apply their home country's ethical code of conduct while doing business in another country. *See infra* note 168 (discussing foreign corrupt practices).

83. Technology is only a tool, deftly applied by the skilled and wasted by the incompetent. Since technology can provide tremendous advantages for conducting business,

people to communicate without censorship across national boundaries. Communication technology not only exposes a national population to foreign ideas, but also concurrently exposes domestic conditions to a global audience.

This has occurred because economic globalization involves communication technologies with multiple uses. The same technology that transmits a business proposal may also communicate politically embarrassing or other non-business information. These multiple uses of advanced technology cannot easily be separated from each other, making it difficult to restrict the technology to purely business purposes. A country that wishes to participate in international business cannot isolate itself from all uses of communication technologies unrelated to business dealings.[84]

The internet[85] is a recent communication medium with tremendous potential for linking people across national boundaries, furthering mutual interests of the international community, and a myriad of other uses.[86] The internet will become, or may already be, an important or even critical technological medium for business, as well as for scientific research and consumer enjoyment.[87] The internet is the essential part of the "informa-

---

flexible and cost-efficient private firms—the basic actors in the free market—utilize technology as they do any other productive input.

84. For example, faxes expedite international business transactions by connecting different countries through telephone lines. Exact copies of business documents that would otherwise require delivery by overnight courier service can be faxed in a few minutes. Business people can also transmit computer files by connecting a modem to a telephone line. Within minutes, a subsidiary can dispatch data across the world to a parent company which may need the information to make a quick financial decision. Political dissidents can use the same fax machines or computer modems to send pictures, reports, and other information to supporters in foreign countries. *See, e.g.*, Joyce Barnathan et al., *China: Is Prosperity Creating a Freer Society?*, Bus. Wk., June 6, 1994, at 94.

85. *See generally* Ed Krol, The Whole Internet: User's Guide & Catalog (Bruce C. Klopfenstein adapt., 1996); *It's Only Growing Pains: The Second Annual Roundtable on the State of the Internet*, IEEE Spectrum, Sept. 1996, at 46.

86. Children can come into contact with their peers from other countries. *See, e.g.*, *China, Japan Kids Link Via Net*, Japan Times, June 10-16, 1996, at 15 (weekly edition) (Chinese and Japanese elementary students communicating through the internet). Like-minded political groups can exchange information and publicize news events. For example, the internet has numerous human rights resources. *See, e.g.*, *Welcome to the United Nations Human Rights Website* (visited Dec. 11, 1996) <http://193.135.156.15/welcome.htm> (U.N. website containing information relating to human rights); *AAAS Directory of Human Rights Site on the Internet* (visited Oct. 15, 1996) <http://www.aaas.org/spp/dspp/shr/dhr.htm#general> (from website of the American Association for the Advancement of Science, publisher of the journal *Science*, listing human rights resources on the internet).

87. *See, e.g.*, *Annual Report on Information Technology: The Information Appliance*, Bus. Wk., June 24, 1996, at 71 (articles discussing devices that will utilize the internet); John W. Verity, *Invoice? What's an Invoice?: Electronic Commerce Will Soon Radically Alter the Way Business Buys and Sells*, Bus. Wk., June 10, 1996, at 110 (predicting that once necessary software and security measures are in place, the internet's world wide web will become the global infrastructure for electronic commerce); Joan O'C. Hamilton & Heidi Dawley, *Welcome to the World Wide Lab: By Providing Instant Access to Data, the Web Is Changing How Research Is Done and Shared*, Bus. Wk., Oct. 30, 1995, at 66. There are many publications that explain the functions, benefits, and methods of access to the

tion superhighway," a source of information that promises to change fundamentally human lives.[88]

E-mail and computer file transmission on the internet can potentially provide a more powerful (e.g., faster, cheaper, more convenient) business tool than such conventional devices as the postal service, telephones, and faxes. Internet users can transmit and download data, articles, images, movies, speeches, sound recordings, and other information.[89] By providing a forum for the transfer of such information, the internet will help protect the freedoms of expression and choice for followers of any ideological persuasion.[90] Unfortunately, however, it may shield criminal, obscene,

---

internet, including its most powerful and commercially attractive feature–the world wide web. *See, e.g.*, KROL, *supra* note 85; PC MAG., Oct. 10, 1995 (issue focusing on the world wide web).

88. *See, e.g.*, GENERAL ACCOUNTING OFFICE, INFORMATION SUPERHIGHWAY: AN OVERVIEW OF TECHNOLOGY CHALLENGES (GAO/AIMD-95-23, Jan. 1995); GENERAL ACCOUNTING OFFICE, INFORMATION SUPERHIGHWAY: ISSUES AFFECTING DEVELOPMENT (GAO/RCED-94-285, Sept. 1994). The United States government

> envisions the superhighway as a seamless web of communications networks, computers, databases, and consumer electronics–built, owned, and operated principally by the private section–that will put vast amounts of information at users' fingertips. It believes that the superhighway, if freed from the constraints imposed by rigid regulatory regimes, can fundamentally change the way we work, learn, get health care and public services, shop, communicate, and entertain ourselves.

GENERAL ACCOUNTING OFFICE, INFORMATION SUPERHIGHWAY: AN OVERVIEW OF TECHNOLOGY CHALLENGES, *supra*, at 2.

89. Today, the internet is generally not able to transmit data-intensive information (e.g., movies) in real time (i.e., sending a two-hour movie on the internet will take much longer than two hours). In the future, the internet will be able to transmit real-time, full-motion video images along with audio signals that will allow, for instance, the kind of teleconferencing that now occurs through satellite transmission. *See, e.g.*, Laurent Belsie, *Promise from Cable Guys: Internet 300 Times Faster*, CHRIST. SCI. MONITOR, June 28, 1996, at 8 (stating that future home modems will transmit at speeds of 7 to 10 megabits per second, much faster than the 28.8 kilobit modems commonly used by consumers today). *See generally* Jan Ozer, *Sound Blasts the Web*, PC MAG., Mar. 26, 1996, at 103 (discussing the transmission of sound, whether speech or music, as an example of multimedia on the internet's world wide web); Jan Ozer, *Web TV Tunes in*, PC MAG., Mar. 26, 1996, at 129 (discussing the transmission of video, or moving images, as an example of multimedia on the internet's world wide web).

90. The ideology need not be political. Websites, the most popular and most powerful method of transmitting data on the internet, span the gamut of human interests and cater to a myriad of tastes. *See, e.g.*, *Star Trek* (visited Dec. 8, 1996) <http://startrek.msn.com> (website for news about various Star Trek productions); *Welcome to the White House* (visited Dec. 8, 1996) <http://www.whitehouse.gov/WH/Welcome.html> (website to the White House); *NCR Homepage* (visited Dec. 8, 1996) <http://www.nas.edu> (website for the National Research Council, which is administered by the National Academy of Sciences, National Academy of Engineering, and the Institute of Medicine); *Institute for Christian Leadership* (visited Dec. 8, 1996) <http://www.iclnet.org> (a religious website); *Sydney 2000* (visited Dec. 8, 1996) <http://www.sydney.olympic.org/> (website for the 2000 summer Olympic games in Sydney, Australia); *Albany Law School of Union University Homepage* (visited Dec. 8, 1996) <http://www.als.edu> (website for Albany Law School). Thus, huge amounts of information are available to those who wish to receive or transmit information of any kind.

racist, and terrorist activities as well.[91]

A government might attempt to control the content of information transfers. It could screen large numbers of telephone calls, faxes, or computer data; it could restrict access to or intercept messages on the internet. Total censorship, however, would bring a halt to international business.[92] Firms might object if government surveillance is too pervasive. For example, companies might not want government officials to be privy to proprietary information.[93] A certain amount of freedom of communication is therefore assured if a country wishes to be part of a global economy: international firms will leave a nation if censorship prohibitively increases the cost of doing business. This will remain true even if governments attempt to censor communications using the most advanced and cost-effective surveillance technology available.[94]

91. *See, e.g., World Wide Sex Links* (visited Dec. 8, 1996) <http://web.demon.co.uk/photouk/www/links.html> (website providing links, or connections, to sex-oriented websites); *Club Red Light District* (visited Dec. 8, 1996) <http://fun2.fun.nl> (a sex-oriented website); *Anarchy N Explosives* (visited Aug. 8, 1996) <http://www.netcore.ca/~locutus/ane/ane.htm> (website giving recipes for making explosives); *The World Wide Anarchy Page* (visited Aug. 8, 1996) <http://www.break.com.au/~dah/anarmain.html> (same); *Explosive Solutions* (visited Feb. 22, 1997) <http://www.dra.nl/~funny/terrorin.html> (same). These websites are easily located through world wide web search engines which can be used without charge and which search for any type of website. *See, e.g., All-in-One Search Page* (visited Dec. 8, 1996) <http://www.albany.net/allinone> (website listing numerous search engines); *AltaVista: Main Page* (visited Dec. 8, 1996) <http://www.altavista.digital.com> (search engine provided by the Digital Equipment Corporation).

92. Perhaps, for example, international phone calls might be routed through a switchboard where an operator would inquire about the purpose of the call and retain a record of the parties to the telephone conversation. Copies of faxes might have to be transmitted to the government. A government could restrict internet access to registered users who claim to have only business objectives in utilizing the internet. At some point, however, surveillance would become very cumbersome. Imagine, for instance, screening millions of international calls a day.

93. Proprietary information, such as trade secrets, can be immensely valuable to a company. For example, when the Indian government required the Coca Cola Company to disclose the ingredients for its cola soft drink in order to establish a production subsidiary in India, the Coca Cola Company chose not to invest in India. *See* Michael A. Epstein, *If It's the Real Thing, Guard It Carefully: How Companies Can Protect Trade Secrets*, N.Y.L.J., Nov. 22, 1993, at S1 (special section on intellectual property).

94. The Chinese government, for example, is attempting to control the political content of information on the internet in China. All 50,000 domestic internet users in China are required to register with the police and are prohibited from hindering public order. *See* Sheila Tefft, *China Attempts to Have Its Net and Censor It Too*, CHRIST. SCI. MONITOR, Aug. 5, 1996, at 1. Complete censorship, however, would seem to be impossible, especially if the number of users grow to the extent present in the West. Even the most advanced western technology seems incapable of censoring the internet. *See, e.g.* John Markoff, *Japanese Chips May Scramble U.S. Export Ban*, N.Y. TIMES, June 4, 1996, at D1 (reporting that Nippon Telegraph and Telephone, one of Japan's largest corporations, has been selling data scrambling chips that make it difficult, if not currently impossible, for American intelligence and law enforcement agencies to conduct electronic surveillance on telephone lines and the internet). *See generally* Bruce Schneier, *Applied Cryptography: Protocols, Algorithms, and Source Code in C* (2d ed. 1996) (discussing how encryption maintains the secrecy of electronic messages; a sample source code for encryption is included); PHILIP R. ZIMMERMANN, THE OFFICIAL PGP USER'S GUIDE (1995) (discussing "Pretty Good Privacy," a widely used encryption for e-mail).

Communication technologies not essential to international business transactions also serve to bolster humanitarian political values. International news reporting utilizes communication technologies to broadcast major domestic events of all types on a worldwide screen. There are numerous journalists, broadcasters, and commentators whose professional livelihood depends upon bringing newsworthy stories to a foreign, if not international, audience. While most publicized stories may not involve political events, many do. The competitive members of the news media are unlikely to let stories of outrageous acts completely escape the attention of the international public. Furthermore, these news articles may be read by anyone in the world who has access to the internet.[95]

At the same time, news stories alone would not generate international repercussions against repressive governments if purely theoretical political values were involved. There must be influential constituencies that place high priority on the existence of democracy and human rights, that seek to spread those values, and that are galvanized into action upon news of deplorable political conditions. Neither value would flourish unless there were constituencies, either domestic or abroad, that strongly supported it.

The presence of democratic governments and strong protections for human rights in the industrialized countries means that these values are expressed to some degree in their business transactions with other countries.[96] Sizable populations in the industrialized countries also attempt to support democracy and human rights abroad through private means.[97] Moreover, as the living standards of developing countries improve, the citizenry of these countries seem to expect more democratization (first) and

---

95. For example, each day's edition of the *New York Times* can be read at the *New York Times* website–currently, without charge. *See The New York Times on the Web* (visited Dec. 8, 1996) <http://www.nytimes.com>. Scientific and medical information is also available on the web, sometimes free of charge and in full text (picture, charts, tables, and other graphics are usually not available). *See, e.g., Scientific America* (visited Dec. 8, 1996) <http://www.sciam.com> (free access to the current issue of *Scientific American*); *cf. Science On-Line* (visited Dec. 8, 1996) <http://science-mag.aaas.org/science> (free access to abstracts of current and some past issues of *Science*, published by the American Association for the Advancement of Science); *AMA Home Page* (visited Dec. 8, 1996) <http://www.ama-assn.org> (free access to abstracts of current and some past issues of journals published by the American Medical Association); *New England Journal of Medicine On-Line–Home Page* (visited Dec. 8, 1996) <http://www.nejm.org> (free access to abstracts of current and some past issues of the *New England Journal of Medicine*). While this primarily facilitates scientific and medical research, it can also publicize embarrassing information about the state of science and level of health in a country. *See, e.g., infra* note 167.

96. *See, e.g., infra* note 168 and accompanying text (discussing reform of foreign corrupt business practices).

97. For example, non-governmental organizations such as Human Rights Watch, Amnesty International, and international labor unions are supported by private contributions. *See, e.g., Human Rights Watch* (visited Oct. 15, 1996) <http://www.hrw.org> (Human Rights Watch accepts contributions from private individuals and foundations worldwide, and not from any government, directly or indirectly); *cf. Introduction to GreenPeace* (visited Oct. 15, 1996) <http://www.greenpeace.org:80/gpi.html> (GreenPeace, an environmental protection organization, is supported "by small contributions from 5 million supporters in 158 countries and by sales of merchandise.").

human rights (later).[98]

III. The Importance of Globalization

Because globalization promotes common values across nations and can make foreign problems, conditions, issues, and debates as vivid and captivating as national, state, and local ones, it contributes to a sense of world community.[99] It develops a feeling of empathy for the conditions of people abroad, enlarging the group of human beings that an individual will identify with. Globalization thus helps to bring alive persons in foreign lands, making them fellow human beings who simply live in different parts of the world rather than abstract statistics of deaths, poverty, and suffering.

The convergence of basic political and economic values is thus fundamentally important because it helps to establish a common bond among people in different countries, facilitating understanding and encouraging cooperation. All other things being equal, the commonality among countries–whether in the form of basic values, culture, or language–enhances their attractiveness to each other.[100] In addition, convergence increases

---

98. The high living standards of the industrialized West as well as the improving standards of many developing countries have tended to reinforce the viability of democracy and human rights. For both industrialized countries and newly industrializing countries, this may be a reflection of the belief that altruistic desires can be pursued only after the satisfication of basic needs. *See generally* Abraham H. Maslow, Motivation and Personality (2d ed. 1970).

99. Recall, for example, CNN's broadcast of the single man who stood in the path of a line of tanks and stopped their movement in Tiananmen Square. *See* Thomas Collins, *Footage Worthy of a Time Capsule*, Newsday, June 7, 1989, at 71, *available in* LEXIS, News Library, Arcnws File.

100. For example, Americans have found investment in Western Europe more attractive than in other regions of the world, and in the United Kingdom more than in other European countries. By historical cost, the U.S. direct investment position abroad in 1995 was $711.621 billion, with the investment distributed as follows (in millions of dollars):

Region	*Investment*
Europe	363,527
Asia and Pacific	125,968
Latin America and other and Other Western Hemisphere	122,765
Canada	81,387
Middle East	7,982
Africa	6,516
International	3,476

20 Highest Countries	*Investment*
United Kingdom	119,938
Canada	81,387
Germany	43,001
Japan	39,198
Netherlands	37,421
Switzerland	36,342
France	32,645
Bermuda	27,807
Australia	24,713

the possibility that a transformation of attitude will take place for those who participate in transnational activities.

People will begin to regard foreigners in distant lands with the same concern that they have for their fellow citizens.[101] They will endeavor to help these foreigners obtain basic political rights even though the status of political rights in other countries will have no tangible beneficial impact at home.[102] Convergence does not mean that there is a single model of a market economy, a single type of democracy, or a single platform of human rights. They exist in different forms, and nations may have different combinations of these forms.[103]

Brazil	23,590
Belgium	17,785
Italy	16,718
Panama	15,908
Mexico	14,037
Hong Kong	13,780
Singapore	12,570
Sweden	12,226
Ireland	10,970
Spain	9,689
Argentina	7,962

See SURVEY OF CURRENT BUSINESS, July 1996, *supra* note 40, at 47 tbl. 3. More than half of all U.S. investment is in countries with a European culture (Hong Kong and Bermuda are British colonies). Of the twenty countries in which U.S. direct investment is the highest, fourteen have a European culture. Further, six (including Ireland) have a British cultural heritage and are largely English-speaking. The United Kingdom and Canada are by far the largest recipients of U.S. direct investment. To some extent, the attractiveness of Europe, the United Kingdom, and Canada lies in the common heritage that they have with America. The proximity of Canada and the relatively high standard of living in all three are other factors.

101. It is evident for many that the lives of foreigners lack the same importance as that of one's countrymen. *See, e.g., Bush and Schwartzkopf Oppose Haiti Invasion*, CHI. TRIB., Sept. 16, 1994, at C1 (retired General Norman Schwartzkopf saying that "I don't know of one thing in Haiti that's worth the life of a single American service man or woman").

102. There is little need to promote basic economic rights (in the sense of free market rights) in other countries; even Cuba has instituted market reforms. *See* FREEDOM IN THE WORLD 1995-96, *supra* note 59, at 199, 292.

103. *Cf.* HAGGARD & KAUFMAN, *supra* note 70, at 377-79 (but also noting that a multiplicity of factors could prevent the transition to democracy). There are some commentators who think that democracy exists only in one very specific form and that it protects only particular human rights; any country that deviates from such standards is therefore undemocratic and lacks human rights. *See, e.g.*, PETER J. HERZOG, JAPAN'S PSEUDO-DEMOCRACY (1993) (arguing that Japan is not a true democracy and does not adequately protect human rights); ROBERT HARVEY, THE UNDEFEATED: THE RISE, FALL AND RISE OF GREATER JAPAN 208-26 (1994) (same). This view is much too narrow. In different countries with different cultures and traditions, some variation should be expected in the operation of democracy and the protection of human rights. *See, e.g.*, JOSHUA MURAVCHIK, EXPORTING DEMOCRACY: FULFILLING AMERICA'S DESTINY 91-108 (1991) (stating that Japan must be considered democratic by any realistic standard). In the case of Japan, for example, "[d]emocracy in Japan is no less genuine for having acquired a peculiarly Japanese character than for having been initiated by Americans." *Id.* at 107. Some say that because of its hierarchies and other idiosyncrasies, Japan's system is not a democracy at all. The effective answer was reached some forty years ago:

A. The Perspective of One Human Race

The convergence of fundamental values through globalization has profound consequences because it increases the chance that a new perspective will develop, one which views membership in the *human race* as the most significant societal relationship, except for nationality.[104] A person owes his or her strongest collective loyalties to the various societies with which he or she most intensely identifies. Today, this societal identification can be based on numerous factors, including nationality, race, religion, and ethnic group.[105] While it is unlikely that nationality will be surpassed as the most significant societal relationship, globalization and the convergence of values may eventually convince people in different countries that the second most important social group is the human race, and not a person's racial, religious, or ethnic group.[106]

One of the first steps in the formation of a society is the recognition by prospective members that they have common interests and bonds. An essential commonality is that they share some *fundamental values*. A second is that they *identify* themselves as members belonging to the same community on the basis of a number of common ties, including shared fundamental values. A third commonality is the *universality of rights*–the active application of the "golden rule"–by which members expect that all must be entitled to the same rights as well as charged with the same responsibilities to ensure that these rights are protected.

Globalization promotes these three types of commonalities. Globalization establishes common ground by facilitating the almost universal acceptance of market economies, the widespread emergence of democratic governments, and the extensive approval of human rights. The most visible example is economic. With the end of the Cold War, the free market economy has clearly triumphed over the command economy in the battle of the

> The sovereignty of the people, the supremacy of law, the absolute guarantee of basic rights and liberties, the independence of the courts, the recognition of the individual–these must of necessity be the fundamental requirements. Through what machinery they are provided, how they are to be obtained and assured, presents a problem the solution of which may differ widely among men.

Id. (quoting General MacArthur, *from* Supreme Commander for the Allied Powers, Political Reorientation of Japan, p. 92).

104. On an individual level, family, personal, and work ties will ordinarily dominate a person's life.

105. Ordinarily, the identification would occur on the basis of factors such as geography, history, ethnicity, race, religion, and culture. Other possibilities might be political creed, gender, or sexual orientation. These factors could be reduced to a yet more local level–for example, a particular region, tribe, or sect. Individuals could simultaneously view themselves as belonging to more than one society, identifying more strongly with some than others.

106. In some cases, nationality may be subsumed by a regional identification. Perhaps the identify of being a "European" will replace that of the individual nationalities of the European Union. Whether a nationality or regional identification is involved, its paramount importance will not change. Americans are, for instance, still likely to see themselves first as Americans. A closer identification with the human race, however, may mean that Americans will more quickly and vigorously respond to solve international problems that involve human beings who are not Americans.

economic paradigms. Because some variant of a market economy has taken root in virtually all countries, there has been a convergence of sorts in economic systems.[107]

Further, because it often requires exposure to and pervasive interaction with foreigners–many of whom share the same fundamental values–globalization can enlarge the group that one normally identifies with. Globalization makes many of its participants empathize with the conditions and problems of people who in earlier years would have been ignored as unknown residents of remote locations. This empathy often leads to sympathy and support when these people suffer unfairly.

Finally, the combination of shared values and identification produce the third commonality, universality of rights.[108] Citizens of one country will often expect, and work actively to achieve, the same basic values in other countries. They will treat nationals of other nations as they would wish to be treated. The effects of shared values, identification, and universality of rights in globalization could have a pivotal long-term effect–the possibility that a majority of human beings will begin to believe that they are truly part of a single global society–the human race.

This is not to say that people disbelieve the idea that the human race encompasses all human beings. Of course, they realize that there is only one human species. Rather, the human race does not usually rank high on the hierarchy of societies for most people. Smaller societies, especially those based on nationality, race, religion, or ethnicity, command more loyalty.[109] The idea of the human race, the broadest and all-inclusive category of the human species, is abstract and has little, if any, impact on the lives of human beings. To believe in the singular importance of the human race requires an attitudinal shift in which a person views the human race seriously.

---

107. Given the free market outlook of the major economic powers and international economic organizations, a reversal in the ascendant position of the *general* free market model is unlikely to occur in the near future. What will now occur is the fine tuning of the free market model primarily through the World Trade Organization, bilateral agreements, and increased regional integration. Policies of the International Monetary Fund, World Bank, Organisation for Economic Co-operation and Development, and other international institutions will also be influential. There is already a vigorous debate over the benefits of industrial policy in market economies. *See, e.g.*, Seita, *supra* note 35, at 223-28 & nn.149-69 and sources cited therein (discussing Japan's industrial policy). *See generally* East Asian Miracle, *supra* note 55 (discussing factors, including government policies, that have contributed to the high economic growth rates of East Asian market economies).

108. This is necessary because common values and identification alone are insufficient in themselves to create the attitude that membership in the human race is a profound social relationship. Just sharing fundamental values with the people of other countries and empathizing with them may only mean that one will feel regret but do nothing when these people are deprived of the rights that flow from those values. If a society is of essential importance to its members, they will work to protect it and their fellow members.

109. Sometimes these societies almost totally overlap. *See* Seita, *supra* note 79, at 492 n.72 (listing countries, such as South Korea and Japan, where there is a nearly complete overlap of nationality and ethnicity).

This may occur because the convergence of values does not only mean that the people of different countries will share the same basic values. It may also lead to the greater promotion of these values for the people of *other* countries. Historically and certainly today, America and the other industrial democracies have attempted to foster democracy and human rights in other countries.[110] While some part of this effort has been attributable to "self interest," it has also been due to the empathy that the industrialized democracies have had for other countries.[111] The magnitude of these efforts in the future, as in the past, will depend not solely upon the available financial and human resources of the industrialized democracies. It will also depend upon their national will–a factor undoubtedly influenced by the intensity with which the people of the industrialized democracies identify with people in foreign lands.

The perspective that the human race matters more than its component divisions would accelerate cooperative efforts among nations to attack global problems that adversely affect human rights and the quality of human life.[112] Obviously, there is no shortage of such problems. Great suffering still occurs in so many parts of the world, not just from internal armed conflicts,[113] but also from conditions of poverty.[114] There are severe health problems in much of the world which can be mitigated with relatively little cost.[115] There are the lives lost to the AIDS epidemic, and

110. *See* Karatnycky, *supra* note 59, at 6 (industrialized democracies increasingly insistent that foreign aid recipients respect democracy and human rights); *JPN ODA Program* (visited Oct. 15, 1996) <http://infomofa.nttls.co.jp/infomofa/refer/jpnoda.html> (from website of the Japanese Ministry of Foreign Affairs) (One of the four principles Japan follows in providing foreign aid–official development assistance–is that "Full attention should be paid to efforts for promoting democratization and introduction of a market-oriented economy, and the situation regarding the securing of basic human rights and freedoms in the recipient country.").

111. *See* Muravchik, *supra* note 103, at 8-9.

112. *See generally supra* note 37 (giving examples of human rights).

113. *See, e.g.*, Bill Berkeley, *The Longest War in the World*, N.Y. Times, Mar. 3, 1996, § 6 (magazine) at 59 (reporting on the civil war in Sudan that has occupied 30 of the last 40 years and 13 of the past 17 decades, and that has probably killed 1.5 million people since 1983).

114. There is a problem of growing economic disparity among nations. The world is being divided into rich and poor nations, with the gap between the two groups widening. *See, e.g.*, Zaven N. Davidian, Economic Disparities Among Nations: A Threat to Survival in a Globalized World (1994). Further, among developing countries, while many of the nations of East Asia have enjoyed high rates of economic growth, other countries, especially in Africa, have generally had much lower growth rates. *See* World Economic Outlook, *supra* note 25, at 173-76; East Asian Miracle, *supra* note 55, at 1-3.

115. *See, e.g.*, Warren E. Leary, *Billions Suffering Needlessly, Study Says*, N.Y. Times, May 2, 1995, at C5 (citing the first annual survey of global health conducted by the World Health Organization); Patrick E. Tyler, *China Confronts Retardation of Millions Deficient in Iodine*, N.Y. Times, June 4, 1996, at A1 (reporting that the Chinese Public Health Ministry estimates that iodine deficiency during brain development has resulted in over ten million cases of mental retardation in China). Poverty, and its companion, malnutrition, take an especially heavy toll among children. *See, e.g.*, J. Larry Brown & Ernesto Pollitt, *Malnutrition, Poverty and Intellectual Development*, Sci. Am., Feb. 1996, at 38.

the deaths and disabilities caused by land mines.[116] Russia, a nuclear superpower that could end life on this planet, has severe social, economic, and political problems.[117] Making the human race important would not just promote liberal democratic values but would also reduce human suffering and perhaps eliminate completely the risk of nuclear war.

B. General Convergence of Values

Assuming that the formation of a single human society is a possible outcome, two broad questions should be answered: what kind of human society is being created, and is this society desirable. The answer to the latter question will depend on an evaluator's subjective judgment of the society that is being formed. Undoubtedly, the great majority of human beings would abhor a world society that was being created by the conquests of a totalitarian government. Presumably, most Americans (and many citizens of other countries) would reject even a benevolent, democratic global society in which a world government dominated by other countries dictated laws that governed the lives of all human beings. If either outcome were present, many would call for a halt to globalization. Thus the direction that globalization follows is critical for assessing its appeal.

What globalization has brought is a *general* convergence of fundamental economic and political systems among many nations. These systems are not identical. There are still innumerable differences among countries with market economies, democratic governments, and respectful of human rights.[118] The practices of one country may be intolerable to another coun-

116. *See* John C. Caldwell & Pat Caldwell, *The African AIDS Epidemic*, SCI. AM., Mar. 1996, at 62 (discussing the cause of the epidemic in sub-Saharan Africa); Gordon Fairclough, *A Gathering Storm*, FAR EAST. ECON. REV., Sept. 21, 1995, at 26 (reporting on AIDS in Thailand and other Asian countries); Gino Strada, *The Horror of Land Mines*, SCI. AM., May 1996, at 40 (reporting that for the past two decades, antipersonnel land mines have killed or maimed about 15,000 people a year worldwide, primarily civilians and many of them children; that there are an estimated 100 million land mines planted in 64 countries; and that many of these mines have lifespans of hundreds of years); Kevin Fedarko, *Land Mines: Cheap, Deadly and Cruel*, TIME, May 13, 1996, at 54.

117. The Russian life expectancy for men has declined dramatically and the incidence of alcoholism among Russians has soared. *See* Michael Ryan, *Alcoholism and Rising Mortality in the Russian Federation*, BRIT. MED. J., Mar. 11, 1995, at 646 (reporting a Russian male life expectancy of 59 years in 1993 compared with 64.9 in 1987). In some ways, the state of medical services in Russia resembles that of developing nations which cannot afford to treat preventable afflictions. For example, the lack of sophisticated medical technology has given Russia a high rate of deafness among its population. *See* Genine Babakian, *The Silent Minority*, MOSCOW TIMES, Feb. 24, 1996, *available in* LEXIS, News Library, Curnws File (official statistics listing 12 million deaf people out of a population of 150 million, with deafness caused in many by the administration of excessive amounts of ototoxic antibiotics).

118. Corruption, for example, is much more common in certain new democracies than others. *See* Matt Moffett & Jonathan Friedland, *A New Latin America Faces a Devil of Old: Rampant Corruption*, WALL ST. J., July 1, 1996, at A1 (concluding that the appearance of free markets and democracy in a number of Latin American countries has not removed the prevalence of corruption and has merely changed the corrupt players from bureaucrats and military dictators to entrepreneurs and politicians).

try.[119] Furthermore, it is unlikely and probably undesirable that economic and political systems will ever exactly converge. Nor is it foreseeable that the nations of the world will coalesce into one.

Even among the industrialized democracies, there are enough dissimilarities in market economies, democratic governments, and attitudes towards human rights that make some believe that the differences between these nations outweigh the similarities. For example, Japan is frequently characterized as having a producer-oriented market economy, as compared with the consumer-oriented market economy of the United States.[120] In general, the members of the European Union more extensively regulate their economies than the United States, engaging at times in social engineering that seems contrary to market principles as interpreted by Americans.[121] In the area of criminal justice, the United States is virtually alone in permitting the death penalty and imprisons a much higher percentage

119. For example, while Singapore has a free market economy and is a parliamentary republic, certain drug offenses receive a mandatory death penalty, criminals can be beaten with canes, and political censorship is practiced by the government. *See* FREEDOM IN THE WORLD 1995-96, *supra* note 59, at 416-18; HUMAN RIGHTS PRACTICES 1994, supra note 67, at 679-86; *see also* Henry Kamm, *In Prosperous Singapore, Even the Elite Are Nervous About Speaking Out*, N.Y. TIMES, Aug. 13, 1995, at 10. An environment like Singapore's would probably be unacceptable to most Americans.

120. *See, e.g.*, Seita, *supra* note 107, at 198-99 & nn.21-25 and sources cited therein. Japan is not the only industrialized country to differ significantly from the United States in economic practices. For example, according to a U.S. government report, "[t]he fundamental way in which business operates differs in the United States, Japan, and Germany." UNITED STATES GENERAL ACCOUNTING OFFICE, COMPETITIVENESS ISSUES: THE BUSINESS ENVIRONMENT IN THE UNITED STATES, JAPAN, AND GERMANY 6 (GAO/GGD-93-124, Aug. 1993).

121. For example, the European Union follows the legal rule of comparable worth, that persons performing work of equal value should be paid the same, which is contrary to the American rule of equal pay for equal work. Works of equal value are job performances that are deemed to be the same in "value" even though the jobs might be different (e.g., the job of a secretary might be deemed to be the same in value as the job of a truck driver). *See* Case 61/81, Commission v. U.K., 1982 E.C.R. 2601 (the European Court of Justice holding that Great Britain had failed to implement Directive 75/117 which provided for equal pay for work of equal value); EVELYN ELLIS, EUROPEAN COMMUNITY SEX EQUALITY LAW 95-116 (1991) (discussing the Equal Pay Directive which implements the doctrine of comparable worth in the European Union); ELAINE SORENSEN, COMPARABLE WORTH: IS IT A WORTHY POLICY? 3-19 (1994) (discussing the relative weakness of the doctrine in the United States). Health insurance is more universal in EU countries (and other industrialized democracies like Japan) than in the United States. *See* LAURENE A. GRAIG, HEALTH OF NATIONS: AN INTERNATIONAL PERSPECTIVE ON U.S. HEALTH CARE REFORM (1991) (comparing universal health care in Canada, Germany, Japan, the Netherlands, and Great Britain with the lack of universal health care in the United States); *see also* Craig R. Whitney, *Rising Health Costs Threaten Generous Benefits in Europe*, N.Y. TIMES, Aug. 6, 1996, at A1. In many EU countries, the social safety net gives significantly greater benefits than in the United States. *See, e.g.*, Rebecca Blank, *Does a Larger Social Safety Net Mean Less Economic Flexibility?*, *in* WORKING UNDER DIFFERENT RULES 157 (Richard B. Freeman ed., 1994); *cf.* Nicholas D. Kristof, *Welfare as Japan Knows It: A Family Affair*, N.Y. TIMES, Aug. 10, 1996, at A1 (the qualifications for and attitudes about welfare in Japan have historically been significantly different from those in the United States; very few people qualify for welfare in Japan).

of its population than other industrialized democracies.[122]

Nonetheless, the basic economic and political systems of different countries clearly share more similarities than ever before. When asked to characterize their existing economic and political systems, more people in more countries than ever before will respond that they have a "market" economy, that their government is "democratic," and that they protect "human rights." Importantly, the convergence of *values* seems to be accompanying the convergence of *systems*. Certainly, most people in the industrialized democracies would view their existing economic and political systems as expressing the foundational values of their societies–the values that define their society.[123] The convergence of values along liberal demo-

---

122. Except for Japan (which executes a few criminals annually), no other industrialized democracy inflicts the death penalty. *See* Teruaki Ueno, *Japan Hangs Three Death-Row Convicts*, REUTERS, July 12, 1996, *available in* LEXIS, News Library, Curnws File; *Belgium Abolishes Capital Punishment*, AGENCE FRANCE PRESSE, June 13, 1996, *available in* LEXIS, News Library, Curnws File. The number of executions in the United States, all performed by state authorities, numbered 23 in 1990, 14 in 1991, 31 in 1992, and 38 in 1993, with a backlog of 2,716 prisoners under a sentence of death at yearend 1993. *See* BUREAU OF JUST. STAT., DEP'T OF JUST., SOURCEBOOK OF CRIMINAL JUSTICE STATISTICS–1994, at 591 tbl. 6.76, 597 tbl: 6.81 (Kathleen Maguire & Ann L. Pastore eds., 1995). In developing countries, the death penalty is far more common. *See, e.g.*, Bruce Gilley, *Rough Justice: Executions Surge in Tough Anti-Crime Drive*, FAR EAST. ECON. REV., July 4, 1996, at 22 (stating that there were 2,500 publicly revealed executions in China in 1995, with the actual number of executed persons possibly twice as high).

The total number of inmates (including unconvicted persons) at local, state, and federal institutions in America was approximately 1.37 million in 1993. *See* BUREAU OF JUST. STAT., *supra*, at 534 tbl. 6.13, 548 tbl. 6.26. By contrast, the average daily population of penal institutions in Japan (including unconvicted persons) was 45,057 in 1993 and 45,573 in 1994. *See* GOVERNMENT OF JAPAN, SUMMARY OF THE WHITE PAPER ON CRIME 1995, at 68 tbl. III-1. Although the population of the United States is twice that of Japan's, America incarcerates 30 times as many people. *See* WORLD BANK ATLAS 1996, at 8-9 (1995) (giving 1994 population figures of 260,529,000 for the United States and 124,782,000 for Japan) [hereinafter WORLD BANK ATLAS]. The United States today has the world's highest reported imprisonment rate and has been at the top for some time. *See* Jon Jefferson, *Doing Soft Time*, ABA J., Apr. 1994, at 62. Between 1990 and 1991, incarceration rates per 100,000 population were:

COUNTRY	*RATE*
United States	455
South Africa	311
Venezuela	177
Hungary	117
Canada	111
China	111
Australia	79
Portugal	77
Czechoslovakia	72
Denmark	71
Albania	55
Netherlands	46
Ireland	44
Sweden	44
Japan	42
India	34

Id. at 63 (excluding nations from the former Soviet Union).

123. *Cf. supra* note 26 (listing the ties that bind OECD members).

cratic lines means that nations are better situated to negotiate wealth-maximizing trade agreements and to resolve political disputes peacefully.

But in countries in transition from authoritarian to liberal democracy, many people may not yet fully accept their newly established economic and political systems as reflecting fundamental values of what is correct, proper, or right. Whether these transitional countries continue to establish or possess liberal democracies will depend upon how well the systems of liberal democracy work, an outcome that the industrialized democracies should strive vigorously to achieve. Workable systems can evolve into entrenched values.

Obviously, the implantation of the values of liberal democracy in Russia is of paramount concern.[124] Nurturing a democratic Russia is in the vital national interest of the United States (and the rest of the world) for very practical reasons–only Russia and the United States possess sufficient nuclear weapons to end human civilization.[125] Whether by unilateral or multilateral extensions of financial assistance or political inclusion, the industrialized democracies should do their utmost to make Russia a strong liberal democracy. Economic aid should be generous, and Russia should be incorporated into the activities of the industrialized democracies as much as possible.[126]

Not all basic values are converging and nor, perhaps, should they. Religious values are not converging in the sense that the same general religion, such as Christianity, is taking root in a preponderance of countries.[127] Nevertheless, the convergence of economic and political values means that there is a greater basis for cooperation. For that reason, the

124. As former Secretary of State Kissinger has stated,

> Integrating Russia into the international system is a key task of the emerging international order. It has two components which must be kept in balance: influencing Russian attitudes and affecting Russian calculations. Generous economic assistance and technical advice is necessary to ease the pains of transition, and Russia should be made welcome in institutions which foster economic, cultural, and political cooperation–such as the European Security Conference.

Henry Kissinger, Diplomacy 818 (1994).

125. *See, e.g.*, Sam Nunn, *U.S. Investment in a Peaceful Russia*, Issues in Science and Technology, Summer 1995, at 27 (Senator Sam Nunn stating that American aid to Russia to transport, store, and destroy excess nuclear (and other) weapons is in America's national security interests, and that "[i]t is in our interest that Russia establish a durable democratic political system and a durable market-based economic system," *id.* at 30).

126. *See, e.g.*, John M. Logsdon & Ray A. Williamson, *U.S.-Russian Cooperation in Space: A Good Bet*, Issues in Science and Technology, Summer 1995, at 39 (pointing to the important scientific, economic, and political value of U.S.-Russian cooperation in space exploration, especially in the U.S.-led partnership to build the international space station with Canada, Japan, and Europe).

127. While many of the underlying tenets of different religions may be the same (e.g., forbidding killing), people will identify themselves as members of a particular religion rather than followers of particular tenets. Thus, for example, one may say that she is a Christian, Muslim, Buddhist, Jew, or some other religious adherent, but not that she is a follower of the Golden Rule. Of course, it may be the case that the preeminent belief of one religion is not shared by others (e.g., the Christian belief that Jesus was the son of God, died to save humanity, and was resurrected).

"West"[128]–that is, the United States and the other industrialized democracies–should support the process of value convergence.

Sharing the same values creates similar expectations and a common ground for understanding. The more prevalent reliance upon market forces to direct production and consumption means that nations are more likely to trade with and invest in each other. The relative sameness of political values, for example, the prevelant use of negotiation rather than military force in settling disputes, means that nations can have greater trust in and less to fear from each other. The similarity of basic values also means that the different peoples of humanity are one step closer to viewing themselves primarily as part of one human society–the human race–though represented by different governments.

IV. Shaping the Content of Globalization

Despite its ubiquity, globalization is not a given, the inevitable consequence of the confluence of current human events. It is a highly probable long-term outcome, that should be supported in the face of opposing forces, in order to ensure its survival.[129] Although there is no inevitability that the process of globalization will continue, it seems very likely for economic and technological reasons. Autarky and isolationism are disfavored national policies. Absent major international calamities, globalization will grow as market integration, economic interdependence, and technological advances continue.

Nor is the precise shape of globalization a settled outcome. There is not just one distinct type of globalization. The activities, the principles, and the value-converging features of globalization are variables influenced by the leadership of nations such as the United States and international organizations such as the United Nations and the World Trade Organization. How globalization proceeds, especially in its preeminent economic form, is crucial because globalization can be a double-edged sword. It can create international problems as well as elevate human beings into a better

128. As previously discussed, the use of the term "West" is convenient to describe the industrialized democracies but misleading in that Japan, the industrialized democracy with the second largest economy, is an Asian country with cultural roots in China rather than Europe and with a non-Christian, non-white population. *See supra* note 25.

129. Opposition to economic globalization, and the integration of markets, is a strong, though not dominant, movement in the United States as well as in other industrialized countries. Politicians often blame the global integration of markets for declining wages and increasing unemployment or underemployment. *Cf.* David E. Sanger, *A Flare-Up of Passions on Trade and Jobs*, N.Y. TIMES, Feb. 20, 1996, at A1 (Pat Buchanan, candidate for the Republican presidential nomination, denouncing the World Trade Organization and the North American Free Trade Agreement, and pledging to pull the United States out of both organizations); David LaGesse, *Silence on NAFTA Could Prove Fleeting: Candidates May Have to Face Issue if Perot Runs, Mexico Finances Sink*, DALLAS MORN. NEWS, Apr. 6, 1996, at 1A, *available in* LEXIS, News Library, Curnws File (documenting 1992 presidential candidate Ross Perot's opposition to U.S. participation in the World Trade Organization and the North American Free Trade Agreement).

world.[130]

For example, the basic values that globalization spreads can sometimes be at odds with each other and with other important values. Free market practices can weaken democracy through a race to the bottom in permitting unethical business practices, and democracy can suppress human rights through a tyranny of the majority. All three convergent values can conflict with the desire to protect the environment, a desire that is predominantly a concern of industrialized countries.[131] Also, economic and technological interdependency can facilitate the activities of rogue nations and terrorist groups, and make members of the global community vulnerable to transnational crime.[132] Finally, how globalization copes with the paradoxical trend of diversification (e.g., ethnic, political, or religious differentiation) is important.[133]

---

130. It is well recognized that the effects of globalization are not always economic or beneficial. *See, e.g., It's the Global Economy, Stupid: The Corporatization of the World*, THE NATION, July 15-22, 1996 (series of articles on the harmful consequences of the global economy); DAVID C. KORTEN, WHEN CORPORATIONS RULE THE WORLD (1995); RICHARD J. BARNET & JOHN CAVANAGH, GLOBAL DREAMS: IMPERIAL CORPORATIONS AND THE NEW WORLD ORDER (1994); *cf.* sources cited *infra* note 186 (describing the clash between economic development and protection of the environment); JEREMY RIFKIN, THE END OF WORK: THE DECLINE OF THE GLOBAL LABOR FORCE AND THE DAWN OF THE POST-MARKET ERA (1995) (criticizing automation and, to that end, globalization).

131. For a discussion of environmental concerns, see *infra* notes 179-186 and accompanying text.

132. At one time the Bank for Credit and Commerce International (BCCI) was the seventh-largest private bank in the world, with assets of over $20 billion. BCCI's involvement with widespread international banking fraud eventually led to its collapse in 1991. *See, e.g.*, RAJ K. BHALA, FOREIGN BANK REGULATION AFTER BCCI 3-13 (1994); JOHN KERRY & HANK BROWN, 102D CONG., THE BCCI AFFAIR: A REPORT TO THE COMMITTEE ON FOREIGN RELATIONS, UNITED STATES SENATE (Comm. Print 102-140 1992). According to the report produced by Senators Kerry and Brown, BCCI was involved in more than just bank fraud. It was also engaged in laundering drug money, supporting terrorism and arms trafficking, training drug cartel death squads, and supplying prostitutes. *See id.* at 61-72. "BCCI cannot be taken as an isolated example of a rogue bank, but a case study of the vulnerability of the world to international crime on a global scale that is beyond the current ability of governments to control." *Id.* at 17. International crime, of course, involves more than just bank fraud. From bases in one country and supported financially by another country, terrorists can launch attacks into a third country. *See, e.g.*, WESTERN RESPONSES TO TERRORISM (Alex P. Schmid & Ronald D. Crelinsten eds., 1993). Illegal drugs, especially those consumed in the United States, often have transnational origins. *See, e.g.*, OFFICE OF NATIONAL DRUG CONTROL POLICY, EXECUTIVE OFFICE OF THE PRESIDENT, THE NATIONAL DRUG CONTROL STRATEGY, 1996: PROGRAM, RESOURCES, AND EVALUATION 17-20. Finally, from anywhere in the world, one can access pornography or recipes for homemade bombs through the internet. *See, e.g., supra* note 91.

133. *See* Takeyuki Kumamura, *New World Emerges, Demands Fresh Set of Strategies: Globalization, Diversification Both Occurring*, NIKKEI WKLY., July 22, 1996, at 7; J. P. Kavanagh, *A Time of Crisis, Challenge for U.N.*, JAPAN TIMES, Apr. 8-14, 1996, at 9 (weekly edition); *cf.* KISSINGER, *supra* note 124, at 806-08. The Soviet Union has splintered into fifteen separate nations, and ethnic groups within nations (e.g., Kurdish rebels in Turkey and Iraq, Chechen rebels in Russia, and Tamil rebels in Sri Lanka) have called for national independence. Strong group identification–whether ethnic, political, or religious–has led to fanaticism, hatred, and killings in Rwanda, Burundi, Cambodia, and Bosnia.

Managing globalization will require policies and programs that carefully nurture, accommodate tensions among, and emphasize the universality of convergent values. These values need to be supported because the presence of free markets, democracy, and human rights in some countries may represent currently ascendant economic and political *systems*—existing superficial conditions—rather than fundamental *values*. Citizens of more countries may now describe their economic system as "market" based, their structure of government as "democratic," and their panoply of civil liberties as the protection of "human rights." Yet, for newly formed capitalist democracies, their citizens may not completely *accept* these conditions as fundamental values—deeply felt beliefs of what is right.[134]

Balancing these values, when they conflict with each other or with the protection of the environment, is necessary to avoid, primarily, a race to the bottom in economic practices and the unreasonable dominance of economic activities over political and environmental concerns.[135] The universality of convergent values essentially means that human beings will work to ensure that the same general rights—including the satisfaction of basic needs—are available in all countries.[136] The idea that particular rights should be universally present, without geographic limitation, is important not just to the convergence of fundamental values but also to the belief that all human beings belong to the same society and are entitled to the same rights.

A. Fulfilling Western Responsibilities

The industrialized democracies have an essential, indispensable role in determining the policies and programs for globalization that will promote common values, balance competing values, solidify respect for the rule of law, and increase empathy among nations. This role is given not by the grace of God but by a simple fact of economics and by the deep roots of liberal democratic values in the industrialized democracies. They have the lion's share of world wealth, and by it, the ability to finance and influence heavily the course of globalization. In addition, free markets, democracy, and the protection of human rights are fundamental values, permanent and enduring, in the industrialized democracies.

---

134. The belief of many people in these nations in the values of liberal democracy may be quite fragile. Further, the shift in economic or political systems for nations previously under command economies or authoritarian political regimes has created substantial numbers of losers as well as winners. It would be in the self-interest of the industrialized democracies to support those countries in transition from command and authoritarian systems to market and democratic systems. Russia, in particular, should receive generous financial and political help. Without the bold actions of the former Soviet leadership, the end of the Cold War—and the subsequently reduced threat of nuclear war, freedom for the east European countries from Soviet domination, and reunification of Germany—would not have occurred. *See* PHILIP ZELIKOW & CONDOLEEZZA RICE, GERMANY UNIFIED AND EUROPE TRANSFORMED: A STUDY IN STATECRAFT 4-19, 369-70 (1995).

135. *See infra* notes 170-186 and accompanying text.

136. *Cf. supra* note 108 and accompanying text.

It is undeniable that the industrialized nations dominate the world economically. These nations are bound together by the common values of liberal democracy, and are either allied or on friendly terms with the United States. Table 1, below, provides figures for the population, economy, contributions to the United Nations, foreign aid (official development assistance, or ODA), and numbers of the world's largest corporations from the twenty-three industrialized nations collectively referred to as the "West": the United States, Japan, the fifteen-nation European Union, and six other rich industrialized nations.[137]

TABLE 1

	Population in Thousands (1994)	G.N.P. in Billions of Dollars (1994)	Regular U.N. Budget Assessment Rate (%) (1996)	Foreign Aid (ODA) in Billions of Dollars (1995)	No. of World's 500 Largest Companies (1995)
U.S.A.	260,529	6,737,367	25.0000	7.303	153
Japan	124,782	4,321,136	15.4350	14.484	141
European Union	370,221	7,577,378	35.2825	31.513	154

137. The data in Table 1 is derived from several sources. *See* WORLD BANK ATLAS, *supra* note 122, at 8-9 (population figures), 18-19 (GNP figures), 20 (world population; world GNP calculated by multiplying world population by world per capita GNP); UNITED NATIONS SECRETARIAT, STATUS OF CONTRIBUTIONS AS AT 29 FEBRUARY 1996, Annex II, at 5-9 (ST/ADM/SER.B/487, Mar. 14, 1996) (regular U.N. budget assessment rate); *Financial Flows to Developing Countries in 1995: Sharp Decline in Official Aid; Private Flows Rise*, OECD PRESS RELEASE, June 11, 1996 (Org. Econ. Co-op. & Dev.) (giving preliminary figures for OECD member foreign aid in 1995; differences for "West" total are rounded off) [hereinafter OECD PRESS RELEASE]; *Global 500, supra* note 45, at 102, F-30 to F-40 (ranking corporations by revenues).

The "other [rich nations]" mentioned in Table 1 are Australia, Canada, Iceland, New Zealand, Norway, and Switzerland. They, together with the United States, Japan, and the nations of the EU, are classified by the International Monetary Fund as the twenty-three industrialized nations, and are what this Article refers to as the "West." *Cf.* WORLD ECONOMIC OUTLOOK, *supra* note 25, at 155-57. All of the 23 nations except for Greece and Iceland provide foreign aid to developing countries. *See* OECD PRESS RELEASE, *supra*, at 9. Countries that provide foreign aid but that are not among the 23 industrialized nations are not included in the ODA figure. Such non-ODA foreign aid, however, is small by comparison with ODA foreign aid. *See, e.g., OECF to Close Seoul Office as S. Korea Aid Role Grows*, DAILY YOMIURI, Aug. 17, 1996, at 12, *available in* LEXIS, News Library, Curnws File (reporting that in 1994 South Korea provided $150 million in foreign economic assistance).

The figures for world population and GNP, which were taken from the World Bank, apparently omit data from the Republic of China (i.e., Taiwan), a relatively rich and populous nation. *See* WORLD BANK ATLAS, *supra* note 122, at 8-9, 18-20. In 1995, Taiwan's population of 21.3 million was larger than Australia's, and its GNP, by exchange rate conversion, was $253.82 billion, ranking 18th in the world. *See* Sofia Wu, *ROC Ranks 18th in Terms of GNP*, CENTRAL NEWS AGENCY, May 30, 1996, *available in* LEXIS, News Library, Curnws File; *cf.* WORLD BANK ATLAS, *supra* note 122, at 8 (giving a 1994 population figure of 17.8 million for Australia).

As Table 1 shows, the West, with less than 15% of the world's population, generates over 75% of the world's GNP, and has the financial resources to pay most of the U.N.'s regular budget, provide substantial amounts of foreign aid, and produce nearly all of the world's largest corporations. Just America and Japan together account for over 40% of world GNP.[138]

The hand of the West is also dominant in the major international economic institutions which provide substantial flows of financial capital to developing countries and to countries in economic transition from socialism to capitalism.[139] Table 2, below, shows that the big five and the

138. Recent data give first quarter 1996 Gross Domestic Product (GDP) figures of $7,417.8 billion for the United States and $5,028.7 billion for Japan. *See* SURVEY OF CURRENT BUSINESS, July 1996, *supra* note 40, at 5 tbl. 1.1 (giving U.S. GDP for first quarter of 1996); *Economic Indicators*, NIKKEI WKLY., July 22, 1996, at 13 (giving a nominal, seasonally adjusted, annual GDP of ¥502,873.6 billion for January-March 1996, applying an exchange rate of ¥100 = $1, *cf. Currency Markets*, *supra* note 41, at D17). U.S. GDP and GNP are virtually equivalent. *See, e.g.*, SURVEY OF CURRENT BUSINESS, July 1996, *supra* note 40, at 7 tbl. 1.9 (giving first quarter 1996 GNP of $7,423.1 billion for the United States). GNP equals the GDP of a country plus its net overseas property income. *See infra* note 141 (defining gross domestic product).

139. As of June 30, 1996, the International Bank for Reconstruction and Development (IBRD) had approved loans totaling $164,766,000,000, of which $110,246,000,000 was outstanding. *See* WORLD BANK, *supra* note 28, at 173. Also providing substantial funding to developing countries are the IBRD's two affiliates, the International Development Association (IDA), which provides low-interest rate credits (loans) to the poorer developing countries, and the International Finance Corporation (IFC), which finances private sector ventures and projects primarily in less developed countries. As of June 30, 1996, the IDA approved $97,450,000,000 in development credits, of which $72,821,000,000 was outstanding. *See id.* at 203. As of June 30, 1996, the IFC provided cumulative gross commitments of $30,380,906,000 for 1707 enterprises. *See* INTERNATIONAL FINANCE CORPORATION, ANNUAL REPORT 1996, at 143 (1996) [hereinafter IFC]. As of April 30, 1996, the IMF had total loans outstanding of SDR 42,040,000,000 (approximately $60.961 billion). *See* IMF, *supra* note 34, at ii, 178 (using an exchange rate of one SDR = $1.45006; technically, member countries of the IMF purchase currencies rather than borrow from the IMF). The SDR (special drawing right) is an international reserve asset whose value is a function of other currency values. Effective January 1, 1996, it includes:

CURRENCY	*AMOUNT OF UNITS IN SDR*
U.S. dollars	0.582
Deutsche marks	0.446
Japanese yen	27.2
French francs	0.813
Pounds sterling	0.105

See id. at 143.

Other important multilateral economic institutions include regional development banks such as the Asian Development Bank (ADB) and the European Bank for Reconstruction and Development (EBRD), which provide funding and technical assistance for development in their respective regions. As of December 31, 1995, the ADB had approved loans totaling $31,426,926,000, of which $17,530,101,000 were outstanding, to member countries in the Asian and Pacific region. *See* ASIAN DEVELOPMENT BANK, ANNUAL REPORT 1995, at 154 (1995) [hereinafter ADB]. As of December 31, 1995, the European Bank for Reconstruction and Development provided ECU 7,853,000,000 (approximately $10.072 billion) in financing through loans, equity participation, and guarantees to countries and projects in central and eastern Europe. *See* EUROPEAN BANK FOR RECONSTRUCTION AND DEVELOPMENT, ANNUAL REPORT 1995, at 15-17, 53 n.2 (1995)

other industrialized democracies of the West together have a commanding share of the voting power in such major international economic institutions as the International Bank for Reconstruction and Development (IBRD), International Finance Corporation (IFC), and International Development Association (IDA) of the World Bank Group, the International Monetary Fund (IMF), the Asian Development Bank (ADB), and the European Bank for Reconstruction and Development (EBRD).[140]

(using ECU 1.2826 = $1 exchange rate) [hereinafter EBRD]. The ECU, or European currency unit, is a composite currency and a unit of account used by the European Union. Similar to the SDR, its value is determined through a basket of EU member country currencies, which is composed of the individual currencies of the twelve member nations of the EU prior to the addition of Austria, Finland, and Sweden in 1995. The currency composition of the ECU will be frozen until the Euro, the single European currency, is introduced. *See* EUROPE IN FIGURES 342-43 (4th ed. 1995). The ECU will be replaced by the Euro on January 1, 1999. *See The Road to Economic and Monetary Union* (visited Oct. 15, 1996) <http://europa.eu.int/en/agenda/emu/enscsc.html> (from website of the European Union).

140. *See* WORLD BANK, *supra* note 28, at 178 (voting power in IBRD as of June 30, 1996); IFC, *supra* note 139, at 123-24 (as of June 30, 1996); WORLD BANK, *supra* note 28, at 205 (voting power in IDA as of June 30, 1996); IMF, *supra* note 34, at 209 (as of April 30, 1996); ADB, *supra* note 139, at 158 (as of December 31, 1995); EBRD, *supra* note 139, at 60 & n.* (voting rights in EBRD as of December 31, 1995, calculated from data; the voting rights of the United States are restricted because of non-payment of some capital subscriptions, and are reduced from 10.12%). In the Asian Development Bank, the nations with the largest voting power in addition to Japan and the United States are Pacific Rim countries: China (6.65%), India (6.54%), Australia (6.01%), Canada (5.47%), and South Korea (5.28%). *See* ADB, *supra* note 139, at 158-59. The countries of the "West" are listed in *supra* note 25.

Another important international financial institution is the Bank for International Settlements (BIS), whose objectives are "to promote the cooperation of central banks, to provide additional facilities for international financial operations and to act as trustee or agent for international financial settlements." BANK FOR INTERNATIONAL SETTLEMENTS, 66TH ANNUAL REPORT, Apr. 1, 1995-Mar. 31, 1996, at 186. The members of the BIS are central banks, and its seventeen-member board of directors consists of the governors of the central banks of Belgium, Canada, France, Germany, Italy, Japan, the Netherlands, Sweden, Switzerland, the United Kingdom, and the United States, and appointed directors from Belgium, France, Germany, Italy, the United Kingdom, and the United States. *See id.* at 186, 194. Until recently, there were 32 member central banks; in September 1996, nine central banks were admitted as new members (Brazil, China, Hong Kong, India, Mexico, Russia, Saudi Arabia, Singapore, and South Korea). *See The BIS: Join the Club*, ECONOMIST, Sept. 14, 1996, at 78.

TABLE 2

	Population in Thousands (1994)	G.N.P. in Billions of Dollars (1994)	Regular U.N. Budget Assessment Rate (%) (1996)	Foreign Aid (ODA) in Billions of Dollars (1995)	No. of World's 500 Largest Companies (1995)
Other [Rich Nations]	62,204	1,323,079	5.4125	5.700	28
West: US, EU, Japan & Other	817,736	19,958,960	81.1300	59.002	476
West's Share of World Total	14.59%	77.44%	81.13%	100%	95.20%
World Total	5,603,000	25,773,800	100.0100	59.002	500

While there are different ways of calculating the collective economic power of the West, there is no question of the West's economic importance to the world.[141] As much as possible, the West–principally the economic

141. For example, on the basis of purchasing power parities, the International Monetary Fund calculates that the group of 23 industrial countries account for 53.9% of world gross domestic product (GDP), with developing countries accounting for 41.2%, and countries in transition (e.g., Russia, Hungary, and Poland), 4.9%. *See* WORLD ECONOMIC OUTLOOK, *supra* note 25, at 156. There are two common ways to calculate a nation's economy or productive output: gross national product (GNP) or gross domestic product (GDP). The quantitative difference between the two is not significant for the great majority of countries. Table 1, above, uses GNP figures provided by the World Bank. The GDP, however, is the most commonly used measure of national output by both domestic and international authorities. *See, e.g.*, SURVEY OF CURRENT BUSINESS, July 1996, *supra* note 40, at 1-8; WORLD ECONOMIC OUTLOOK, *supra* note 25, at 167-79. The GDP measures the net value of the goods and services produced in a country from economic activity. *See* DICTIONARY OF MODERN ECONOMICS, *supra* note 11, at 297-298. The GDP of a country is related to its GNP in that GDP plus net property income from abroad equals GNP. *See id.* Net property income from abroad equals the difference between what domestic residents receive in profits, dividends, and interest on foreign assets, and what foreign residents receive in profits, dividends, and interest on domestic assets. *See id.* at 304.

Also, either GNP or GDP can be calculated by the use of foreign exchange rate conversions or by purchasing power parities (PPP). Exchange rate conversion emphasizes the international purchasing power of a currency (e.g., dollar or yen), whereas PPP emphasizes the domestic purchasing power of a currency (e.g., how much of that currency is needed to buy a basket of goods and services in domestic markets). In comparing national economies, whether in terms of GDP or GNP, Table 1 uses data based on foreign exchange rate conversions. In the foreign exchange rate method, actual market rates are used to compare national economies. The foreign exchange rate is what one currency is worth in terms of another. For instance, a visitor to Japan will need yen to buy goods and services, and would receive ¥1,000,000 if she went to a bank to exchange $10,000 for yen (at a foreign exchange rate of $1 = ¥100). The foreign exchange rate method makes possible the comparison of the U.S. economy (which is expressed in dollars) with the Japanese economy (which is expressed in yen). *See* WORLD BANK ATLAS, *supra* note 122, at 33. Thus, for example, the GDP of Japan in yen terms is converted into dollars by using market foreign exchange rates, and the Japanese GDP can be compared with that of the United States.

giants of the United States, Japan, and the European Union–should act collectively to create a humane globalization. These three entities should undertake to cooperate even more extensively than they already do. This will require American acceptance of a greater role for the European Union and Japan in western decision-making, a process that historically has been carried out mostly by American leadership. It will also require a more vigorous and creative Japanese presence in international affairs.

The United States, Japan, and the European Union are singled out, not because their citizenry are inherently wiser and more capable than those of other nations, but because their economic power tempered by the humanitarian constraints of their political systems make them best suited

---

The foreign exchange rate conversion method disregards the domestic purchasing power of dollars and yen–the concept of purchasing power parity. *See* Seita, *supra* note 79, at 483 n.44; *see also McCurrencies: Where's the Beef?*, ECONOMIST, Apr. 27, 1996, at 82 (providing a brief summary description of PPP). A given amount of yen may actually buy much less in Japan than what the market foreign exchange rate for dollars and yen would suggest. For instance, if the same basket of goods and services would cost $100 in America and ¥15,000 yen in Japan, the PPP method would yield a PPP exchange rate of $1 = ¥150. Thus, if the U.S. economy was $6 trillion and the Japanese economy, ¥450 trillion, a PPP exchange rate of $1 = ¥150 would make the U.S. economy twice that of Japan's ($6 trillion to $3 trillion), while a market foreign exchange rate of $1 = ¥100 would make the U.S. economy only one-third larger than Japan's ($6 trillion to $4.5 trillion). There is often a difference between market foreign exchange rates and the exchange rates implied by PPP. Both methods are used in international measurements. *See* WORLD BANK ATLAS, *supra* note 122, at 18-19, 33 (giving GNP by market foreign exchange rates and giving per capita GNP in PPP terms).

Nevertheless, this Article uses data based on foreign exchange rates because this method better measures the international importance of a nation's economy than the PPP method. The international purchasing power of a currency–what it will buy in other countries–is determined by foreign exchange markets, not by PPP. For example, whatever a yen might buy at home, what it can buys overseas determines the international importance of the yen. *See* Seita, *supra* note 79, at 482-84 & nn.43-45.

Also, there is some latitude in determining the financial strength of a nation's corporations. Table 1 uses a ranking based on corporate revenues. Other rankings are possible, such as that based on apparent market value. *See The Business Week Global 1000*, BUS. WK., July 8, 1996, at 46, 49 (ranking the world's 1000 most valuable corporations by their market value on May 31, 1996, using May month-end exchange rates for foreign corporations). Under a market value ranking, the 1000 most valuable corporations would be distributed as follows:

	No. of 1000 Most Valuable Corporations (1996)
United States	422
Japan	227
European Union	263
Other	62
	974

See id. at 49-80. Under this method, the United States has by far the single largest number of companies. It is a method, however, that probably has more variability than a ranking based on revenues. For example, while Japanese companies accounted for 48% of the $5.7 trillion market value of the global 1000 in 1988, they had dropped to just 23% of $11.2 trillion in 1996; U.S. companies went from 30% in 1988 to 46% in 1996. *See* William C. Symonds et al., *The Globetrotters Take Over: Worldwide Champions Outpace Domestic Competitors*, BUS. WK., July 8, 1996, at 46. Regardless of the method, however, the dominance of the West is clear.

to shape a better world if they so choose. There is also the reality that although it is the world's richest country and only superpower, the United States cannot manage or finance globalization on its own. Because the three are so important economically, it would be a mistake, as some have gratuitously suggested, for the United States and the European Union to unite to isolate Japan politically and economically.[142]

When necessary, the West should also use its economic power to flesh out the details of market economies, democratic governments, and human rights in the globalization context. While the devil may lie in details, some

142. For examples of the literature favoring the isolation of Japan, see Charles A. Kupchan, *Reviving the West*, 75 FOREIGN AFF., May-June 1996, at 92 (urging the creation of an Atlantic Union, an economic alliance between Western Europe and North America); Lind, *supra* note 25 (urging creation of a Euramerican bloc, consisting of the United States, Canada, and the European Union, that would "present a united front toward Japan in trade matters and toward China with respect to security matters," *id.* at 5).

A policy of isolating Japan and treating it as a potential enemy would cause problems dwarfing current difficulties and lower Japan's incentive to make international contributions. *See generally* Seita, *supra* note 79 (discussing the frictions between the United States and Japan); Seita, *supra* note 25 (discussing the benefits of fully utilizing Japan's economic and human resources). It creates conflict where none presently exists and would be reminiscent of past colonial days when white, Christian nations dominated or subjugated most of the non-Christian world. Alternatively, it has been argued that a "mixed-race or nonwhite majority in the United States . . . will emerge a few generations hence . . . [and] ensure that a Euramerican bloc, far from being a 'white' alliance, would be the most racially diverse bloc on the planet." Lind, *supra*, at 5.

And yet, today, the Euramerica bloc is predominately white, and political power in the United States is exercised overwhelmingly by its white majority. Currently, there is one senator of Black heritage, two of Asian or Pacific Islander heritage, and none of Hispanic heritage. *See* BUREAU OF THE CENSUS, U.S. DEP'T OF COMMERCE, STATISTICAL ABSTRACT OF THE UNITED STATES 1996, at 279 tbl. 442 (116th ed.) (as of January 3, 1995); Elizabeth A. Palmer, *Women, Blacks Hold Steady*, DAYTON DAILY NEWS, Nov. 8, 1996, at 15A, *available in* LEXIS, News Library, Curnws File (reporting that the November 1996 elections produced no change in the number of minorities in the Senate). The two senators of Asian or Pacific Islander heritage are both from Hawaii. *See* Ed Henry, *Seldom-Heard Ahaka Takes the Floor to Assail the Treatment of Asians*, ROLL CALL, Mar. 24, 1997, *available in* LEXIS, News Library, Curnws File (Senator Daniel Akaka and Senator Daniel Inouye). In addition, Senator Ben Campbell of Colorado states that he is partially of Northern Cheyenne Native American descent. *See* Steve Jackson, *Athlete, Artist, Indian Chief: From Dark Horse to Nighthorse, It's Been One Hell of a Ride for Ben Campbell*, DENVER WESTWORD, Sept. 12, 1996 (Features Section), *available in* LEXIS, News Library, Curnws File. Today, there are Asian-American governors in the states of Washington and Hawaii, but there are no Black governors. *See Turnout Tuesday Hit a Record Low of 49 Percent of Eligible Voters*, AGENCE FRANCE PRESSE, Nov. 6, 1996, *available in* LEXIS, News Library, Curnws File (Washington state elected the first Asian-American governor outside of Hawaii); *Whitman Stands Out Among Her Peers: The Only Woman at Governors Meeting*, BERGEN RECORD, Aug. 1, 1995, at A9, *available in* LEXIS, News Library, Curnws File (Asian-American governor in Hawaii but no Black governor in any state); Louis Sahagun, *American Album: Hawaii Governor Fights an Economic Undertow*, L.A. TIMES, Dec. 21, 1995, at A5 (Governor Ben Cayetano of Hawaii, a Filipino American, eying a re-election bid in 1998). There is also only one nonwhite justice out of nine on the United States Supreme Court. Hawaii is a state where the nonwhite majority has arrived, a factor which no doubt has contributed towards its selection of nonwhites as well as whites to Hawaii's highest political and judicial offices. *See* Nancy Yoshihara, *Benjamin Cayetano: On the Success of Asian American Politicians–or Lack Thereof*, L.A. TIMES, Sept. 17, 1995, at M3.

refinement of principles may be required to create a "level playing field" for business competition and to balance competing values. That may open up the charge that the views of the West are being imposed upon, and not necessarily to the benefit of, the rest of the world.

While such an allegation would have substantial historical validity, it could be deflected by the promulgation of rules based on those internal practices of the industrialized democracies. These rules would be a modification of the "Golden Rule." Nations should do unto others what the nations of the West do unto themselves. That undeniably involves the value judgment that the industrialized democracies are better models for economic and political development. It is a value judgement, however, that seems to be shared by most human beings: the flow of immigration between the West and the rest of the world is decidedly one-sided in the former's favor.[143]

143. For a discussion of migration periods and patterns, see BARNET & CAVANAGH, *supra* note 130, at 296-309. Immigration to the major industrialized nations from each other is relatively low. For example, in 1993, the number of immigrants to the United States from the other G-7 (the largest industrialized) nations was dwarfed by the number from developing nations and former communist nations:

Number of Immigrants to United States in 1993		
G-7 COUNTRIES		
	Canada	17,200
	France	2,900
	Germany	7,300
	Italy	2,500
	Japan	6,900
	United Kingdom	18,800
SELECTED COUNTRIES		
	China	65,600
	Dominican Republic	45,400
	El Salvador	26,800
	India	40,100
	Jamaica	17,200
	Korea	18,000
	Mexico	126,600
	Poland	27,800
	Former Soviet Union	58,600
	Vietnam	59,600

See 1995 STATISTICAL ABSTRACT, *supra* note 78, at 11 tbl. 8. While immigration occurs primarily for economic reasons, this data suggests that democracy and human rights also positively influence immigration.

B. Adhering to the Rule of Law

The process of converging values through the activities of globalization is facilitated by procedural mechanisms and substantive principles. Without them, globalization might eventually consist solely of the intermingling of peoples and the economic interdependence of countries without the sharing of values. Convergence is reinforced by procedural mechanisms that implement substantive principles which are derived from and flesh out the meaning of convergent values. One mechanism might consist of unilateral action in which one nation, particularly the United States, imposes its views of appropriate economic behavior on another country.[144] While an economically dominant nation may get its way, the subordinate country may not accept the substantive principle used to justify the unilateral action. The latter country may simply see the "principle" of "might makes right."

Another mechanism exists in multilateral agreements in which nations collectively determine the international legal rights of individual nations.[145] Multilateral agreements often contain dispute settlement procedures that attempt, in theory, to administer impartially the rule of law in judging national, firm, or individual conduct.[146] The "law" would be made up of substantive principles that reflect or accommodate clashes among convergent values. The use of the rule of law is today one of the most effective means to reinforce common values, especially in the areas connected with international trade. The rule of law also avoids the antagonism generated when one nation imposes its views on other nations.

In a broad sense, the rule of law requires respect for substantive principle, not merely power or chance, to settle disputes.[147] Implicit, too, in the rule of law is that disputes are peacefully settled whenever possible,

144. Unilateral attempts at fostering common values have been successful in the aftermath of war when a victorious nation occupied a vanquished one. For example, according to one commentator, the American-catalyzed creation of a permanent and peaceful democracy in Japan "is one of history's greatest and most constructive feats of social engineering." MURAVCHIK, *supra* note 103, at 107. For less dramatic and effective unilateral actions by the United States, see *infra* note 149.

145. *See supra* notes 25 (European Union), 38 (Canada-United States Free Trade Agreement, North American Free Trade Agreement).

146. The dispute settlement procedure of the World Trade Organization applies to the agreement establishing the WTO as well as the numerous WTO agreements. *See* Understanding on Rules and Procedures Governing the Settlement of Disputes, Apr. 15, 1994, Marrakesh Agreement Establishing the World Trade Organization, Annex 2, 33 I.L.M. 112 (1994) [hereinafter Dispute Settlement Understanding]. Many bilateral agreements do not have dispute resolution procedures. *See, e.g.*, Seita, *supra* note 79, at 513-15 & nn.140-44 (listing 21 bilateral treaties between Japan and the United States and the scarcity of dispute resolution procedures in the treaties).

147. *Cf.* GRANT GILMORE, THE AGES OF AMERICAN LAW 105 (1977) (the rule of law "emphasizes principally the importance of procedural due process, the nice observance of established rules, the right of the accused to confront his accuser in open court before he is sent to jail"). For purposes of this Article, the rule of law is briefly discussed only to show its role in facilitating the convergence of values. What is law, what is international law, and what is the rule of law are questions that compel complicated and lengthy answers. *See generally* H.L.A. HART, THE CONCEPT OF LAW (1961); LON L. FULLER, ANATOMY OF THE LAW (1968); HANS KELSEN, THE PURE THEORY OF LAW (Max Knight

and that negotiations and economic sanctions are utilized before military operations are commenced. In the globalization context, acceptance of the rule of law means that most nations will not only acknowledge the applicability of substantive principles to a transnational problem but also accept a solution recommended by an impartial international body.[148] The absence of either condition precludes the existence of a rule of law, and also militates against the development of convergent values.

First, without the recognition that there are substantive principles which are relevant to analyzing a conflict, there is no rule of law because there are no laws to apply. Without substantive principles, convergent values are less likely to emerge. Second, a nation should respect the decisions of a mediating or adjudicatory international organization. If a nation chooses to settle a dispute unilaterally, there is no rule of law since any principle, even if meritorious, would be enforced unequally. The unilateral actor would be a law enforcer against other nations only, and presumably never the object of enforcement.[149] Such discriminatory enforcement diminishes the validity of substantive principles because they do not apply to all nations, and impedes the acceptance of their values as convergent values.

At the same time, the international tribunal or body that implements the rule of law must be impartial and competent, for nations are more likely to abide by the rule of law when they believe that it can be administered fairly and wisely.[150] Further, before abiding by the rule of law in a

---

trans., 1967); International Law Anthology (Anthony D'Amato ed., 1994); Henry J. Steiner et al., Transnational Legal Problems: Materials and Text (4th ed. 1994).

148. One possible embodiment of the rule of law would be the WTO dispute settlement procedures. *See, e.g.*, Dispute Settlement Understanding art. 22, *supra* note 146; *The WTO Dispute Settlement Mechanism*, General Agreement on Tariffs and Trade, GATT Focus, May 1994, at 12-14.

149. Unilateral measures by one country, even if ostensibly taken to protect desirable principles, may engender ill will among other countries affected by those measures. These countries may react by questioning the justifications of the unilateral actor. Eventually, the validity of the principles may come into question if they are applied only to protect one country's interests. For example, the United States frequently takes a unilateral approach to solving economic problems with its trading partners. *See, e.g.*, Trade Act of 1974, Pub. L. No. 93-618, § 301, 88 Stat. 1978 (1974) (codified as amended at 19 U.S.C. § 2411 (1988)) (authorizing the United States to take unilateral action against unfair, even though not internationally unlawful, economic practices of foreign countries). This has not generated feelings of goodwill among U.S. allies. *See, e.g.*, European Commission, Report on United States Barriers to Trade and Investment 1996, at 9-10 (criticizing section 301); Hiroshi Nakamae, *U.S. Worst Violator of Trade Rules, MITI Says*, Nikkei Wkly., June 6, 1994, at 2 (in its *1994 Report on Unfair Trade Policies by Major Trading Partners*, the Japanese Ministry of International Trade and Industry accuses the United States of pursuing unfair trade practices such as section 301).

150. A nation may reject the jurisdiction of an international tribunal to adjudicate a dispute it has with another country. The rejection may be motivated by a perception that the tribunal is biased, or that the tribunal may judge fairly but contrary to the interests of the rejecting nation. It may be difficult to determine the motivation for such a rejection. For example, in 1986 the International Court of Justice held that the United States violated international law (customary international law as well as treaty obligations) by mining Nicaraguan ports, and stated that the United States and Nicaragua should hold settlement talks to determine the amount of appropriate reparations. *See*

particular area, nations usually must conclude that the substantive principles of law are generally acceptable to them. Of course, some principles may be imprecise in order to accommodate different national views about how detailed these principles should be. Because nations may have varying opinions on the desired details of substantive principles and may make political compromises to arrive at their language, these principles may be vague or incomplete.[151] The tribunal or other body that interprets these principles may have considerable leeway to refine, embellish, or expand the meaning of the substantive law.

While an immediate benefit of the rule of law is that current disputes are resolved, a long-term benefit is that the utilization of reason and rules are substituted for power or force. If powerful and weak nations alike will follow the rule of law, then the law, not military or economic power, will determine rights and resolve conflicts. Recognition of the rule of law also means that the substantive principles used to resolve disputes are automatically enhanced since their selection legitimizes them (they are the "law") and reinforces the values that they represent. While these principles are likely to be popular and respected in order to have been chosen as the substantive bases for conflict resolution, their selection is likely to strengthen and broaden their appeal, enhancing the durability of their val-

Military and Paramilitary Activities (Nicar. v. U.S.), 1986 I.C.J. 4 (June 27). The United States, however, did not comply with the court's opinion, even though the United Nations Charter compels U.N. members to comply with decisions of the International Court of Justice in cases in which the member is a party. *See* U.N. CHARTER art. 94, para. 1. Prior to the date of the decision, the United States notified the United Nations that it would end its thirty-eight year acceptance of the "compulsory jurisdiction" of the International Court of Justice. *Compare* United States Department of State Letter and Statement Concerning Termination of Acceptance of I.C.J. Compulsory Jurisdiction (Oct. 7, 1985), 24 I.L.M. 1742, *with* United States Declaration of Aug. 14, 1946, 61 Stat. 1218, T.I.A.S. No.1598, 1 U.N.T.S. 9 (compulsory jurisdiction effective six months after deposit of the declaration with the United Nations). Under the Statute of the International Court of Justice, a state could recognize the compulsory jurisdiction of the court over cases involving that state, thereby avoiding the need for a special agreement to permit the court to hear each individual case. *See* STATUTE OF THE INTERNATIONAL COURT OF JUSTICE art. 36, para. 2, June 26, 1945, 59 Stat. 1055, 1060 (1945). The United States withdrew its acceptance of compulsory jurisdiction in order to avoid having the court decide Nicaragua's case against the United States. The court, however, held that the attempt to withdraw jurisdiction was ineffective. *See* 1986 I.C.J. at 7. *See generally* THE UNITED STATES AND THE COMPULSORY JURISDICTION OF THE INTERNATIONAL COURT OF JUSTICE (Anthony C. Arend ed. 1986).

151. For example, the term "subsidy" was never defined under GATT, although subsidies were a long recognized problem in international trade. *See* JACKSON, *supra* note 24, at 382-83; JACKSON, *supra* note 36, at 255; GATT, *supra* note 29, arts. VI, XVI. Further, the United States had grandfather rights permitting it to levy countervailing duties upon subsidized goods without finding material injury to domestic industry, otherwise a requirement under GATT art. VI, para. 6(a). *See* JACKSON, *supra* note 24, at 258. In another example, the United Nations defined the international crime of genocide to exclude acts against economic or political classes. Genocide covers acts only against a "national, ethnical, racial or religious group." Convention on the Prevention and Punishment of the Crime of Genocide, *supra* note 32, art. 2. The Convention has never been applied. *See* James Podgers, *The World Cries Out for Justice*, A.B.A. J., Apr. 1996, at 52, 54 (discussing the international criminal tribunals for Rwanda and the former Yugoslavia).

ues. Thus, the choice of interpreters and the selection of substantive principles are important decisions.

At times, the viability of the rule of law may require enforcement to ensure adherence to the rule of law. In economic disputes, there could be collectively authorized sanctions.[152] When there are acts of aggression over territorial disputes and economic sanctions have failed to prevent a breach of the peace, the use of military force could be authorized. For example, in 1990, Iraq invaded Kuwait over alleged disputed property rights and territory; in response, the United Nations authorized the use of force by the United States and its allies against the Iraq in the 1991 Gulf War.[153]

For countries like North Korea and Iraq that are not democracies and do not protect human rights, the industrialized democracies should present a unified front in encouraging change and discouraging political oppression and the use of force. While the ad hoc international criminal tribunals for Bosnia and Rwanda are important, the establishment of a permanent international criminal court will better solidify the idea that war crimes must be condemned and adjudicated by the international community.[154] Although it is late, there ought to be a tribunal for Cambodia. There is still no justice for the atrocities against the Cambodian people that occurred in the mid to late 1970s, in what many have called as the equivalent of genocide.[155] The establishment of a standing emergency peacekeeping force might prevent the future reoccurrence of atrocities that

152. *See, e.g.*, Dispute Settlement Understanding, *supra* note 146, art. 22.

153. The United Nations has rarely sanctioned the collective use of force under Chapter VII of the U.N. Charter. The defense of South Korea in 1950 against an invasion by North Korea, the humanitarian relief operations in Somalia in 1992, and the invasion of Haiti in 1994 are the only other examples. *See* Arend & Beck, *supra* note 65, at 51-56; *Multinational Force Dispatched to Pave Way for Aristide's Return*, U.N. Chron., Dec. 1994, at 20.

154. Established by the United Nations, these ad hoc tribunals may presage the establishment of a permanent international criminal court. *See* Podgers, *supra* note 151, at 52. *See generally* Lawyers Committee for Human Rights, In the National Interest: 1996 Quadrennial Report on Human Rights and U.S. Foreign Policy 1-10 (1996); Paul D. Marquardt, *Law Without Borders: The Constitutionality of an International Criminal Court*, 33 Colum. J. Transnat'l L. 73, 96-101, 136-47 (1995); Leila S. Wexler, *The Proposed Permanent International Criminal Court: An Appraisal*, 29 Cornell Int'l L.J. 665 (1996).

155. *See, e.g.*, Payam Akhavan, *Enforcement of the Genocide Convention: A Challenge to Civilization*, 8 Harv. Hum. Rts. J. 229, 230 n.5 (1995); Barbara Crossette, *Waiting for Justice in Cambodia*, N.Y. Times, Feb. 25, 1996, § 4 at 5. In the late 1970s, Pol Pot's Khmer Rouge was responsible for massive numbers of killings and deaths among the Cambodian people. *See, e.g.*, Cambodia 1975-1978: Rendezvous with Death (Karl D. Jackson ed., 1989) (essays discussing the Khmer Rouge's regime in Cambodia). *But see* David P. Chandler, The Tragedy of Cambodian History: Politics, War, and Revolution since 1945, at 236-72 (1991). The number of people who died under the Khmer Rouge government was enormous:

> More than one million people are dead to begin with. Included are not only the victims of Pol Pot's killing fields, where members of the former ruling elite were cut down, but also, hundreds of thousands of men, women, and children who died from disease and starvation directly resulting from the regime's misguided and draconian policies.

took place in Cambodia, Rwanda, Burundi, Bosnia, and elsewhere.[156]

Also, although there has been a general convergence of economic and political values, the application of these values to specific situations is, in most cases, yet to be determined.[157] When it becomes important to specify how these values will apply to particular cases, the use of a multilateral forum will help to win international acceptance of the principles selected to

---

> Out of 7.3 million Cambodians said to be alive on April 17, 1975, less than 6 million remained to greet the Vietnamese occupiers in the waning days of 1978. Although precise figures may never be known, present calculations suggest that in the Cambodian revolution a greater proportion of the population perished than in any other revolution during the twentieth century.

Karl D. Jackson, *Introduction: The Khmer Rouge in Context*, *in* CAMBODIA 1975-1978: RENDEZVOUS WITH DEATH, *supra*, at 3 (footnote omitted); CHANDLER *supra*, at 1.

156. The United Nations might establish a standing emergency force to prevent armed conflicts (in addition to rescuing victims of natural disasters). *See generally Permanent Peacekeeping: The Theoretical & Practical Feasibility of a United Nations Force*, 28 CORNELL INT'L L.J. 619, 645 (1995) (symposium on *Peacekeeping, Peacemaking, & Peacebuilding: The Role of the United Nations in Global Conflict*). While the U.N. emergency force would not be able to intervene in matters involving major power interests, it might be able to move quickly to prevent reoccurrences of tragedies such as those in Cambodia, Rwanda, Burundi, and Bosnia, where the international community failed to prevent massive numbers of deaths. At some point, internal conflicts become so horrendous that outside nations ought to intervene:

> [A]cts of genocide cannot be tolerated by the community of nations. When people are being exterminated because of their ethnicity, race, or social class, outside powers have not only the right but the compulsion to intervene. Ideally they should do this in concert, whether through the United Nations or simply by joint agreement. It was shameful that the United States did not intervene in Rwanda in 1994 to stop the slaughter of half a million Tutsi by the rival Hutu tribe. France alone, to its credit, sent its troops to end the bloodshed. It was no less shameful that in the 1970s not a single Western nation moved against the Khmer Rouge that killed an estimated two million of their own people in their drive to "purify" Cambodia for communism. Finally, it was neighboring Vietnam that entered the killing fields to stop the genocide.

RONALD STEEL, TEMPTATIONS OF A SUPERPOWER 130 (1995); *see also* NEW REPUBLIC, Aug. 7, 1995, at 7, 10-21 (various articles on *Accomplices to Genocide: The Consequences of Appeasement in Bosnia*). America is often blamed for a burden that it never accepted—the job of policing the world. It might be better to have the United Nations policing the world in conflicts outside of major-power interests. The Security Council of the United Nations has the right to intervene, even in purely national conflicts, to prevent breaches of the peace or acts of aggression that involve massive human rights abuses (e.g., genocide). *See* U.N. CHARTER arts. 39-51. *See generally* Fernando R. Tesón, *Collective Humanitarian Intervention*, 17 MICH. J. INT'L L. 323, 336-42, 369-71 (1996) (discussing Security Council authorized U.N. military intervention in countries to prevent massive human rights abuses). There are still conflicts—particularly in Africa—that can potentially kill, or have killed, tens of thousands, if not hundreds of thousands of human beings. *See, e.g.*, Andrew Purvis, *A Contagion of Genocide: The Civil Wars of Rwanda and Burundi Spread to Eastern Zaïre, in a Bloody Conflict the World Ignores*, TIME, July 8, 1996, at 38.

157. For instance, should market economies be allowed to countenance groups of companies that tend to do business more among themselves than with outsiders? *See* Seita, *supra* note 107, at 217-23 & nn.116-48 (discussing Japanese *keiretsu*). Should democratic governments forbid their citizens to exacerbate health and social problems in other countries? *See, e.g., infra* notes 167 (exports of tobacco), 174 (child prostitution). Does the promotion of human rights require the industrialized democracies to accelerate and widen their efforts to relieve hunger, disease, and suffering abroad? *See, e.g., supra* notes 113-117 and accompanying text.

implement these values. The process of filling out the details of these values, that is, determining their principles, is facilitated because there is agreement over basic values. Once a broad framework has been agreed upon, nations can resolve particular difficulties as necessary.[158]

The most fruitful area of further refinement of values is in the economic realm. There is already a process of greater harmonization of rules and practices that affect trade, investment, and intellectual property.[159] Establishing ground rules for international competition will eliminate the perceived unfair advantages of some nations. At the same time, there should be agreement on the proper conduct of governments, businesses, and individuals in transnational activities. Determining proper behavior will create a level playing field for international competition and will avoid actual or perceived disadvantages for some nations.[160]

C. Setting Global Standards and Balancing Values

A major issue raised by globalization is the harmonization of business practices and the accommodation of competing values. Without common rules to govern business behavior, companies from one country might compete at a disadvantage against those of another because each country could have dissimilar rules for acceptable corporate behavior in international business. Setting up the "rules of the game" in international business is important not just to promote economic competition under fair conditions but also to determine the proper balancing of competing values.

---

158. For example, one value of democracy may be "one person, one vote," giving equal voting weight to each citizen. This principle is not always recognized by democracies. Some variation from the exact equating of voting weight might be expected because it may be difficult in practice to make the number of voters eligible to elect a representative precisely the same. In some cases, federalism concerns might lead to large differences in voting weight. For example, two senators are elected from each state in America. *See* U.S. Const. art. I, § 3, cl. 1, *amended by* U.S. Const. amend. XVII, § 1. Thus the senators from California, the largest state by population, represent over 60 times the number of people as the senators from Wyoming, the least populated state. *See* 1995 Statistical Abstract, *supra* note 78, at 28-29 tbls. 27-28 (in 1990, at the time of the most recent census, California and Wyoming had populations of 29.8 million and 454,000, respectively).

159. The European Union is the outstanding example at an international regional level. *See generally* Klaus-Dieter Borchardt, European Integration: The Origins and Growth of the European Union 31-58 (1995). On a global scale, the WTO is potentially of enormous importance in establishing and refining global trade rules. *See generally* Transmission of Legislation and Related Documents to Implement Agreements Resulting from GATT–Uruguay Round–Message from The President of the United States, H.R. Doc. No. 103-316 (1994).

160. *See infra* notes 161-86 and accompanying text. Some of the details of convergent values can be determined by dispute settlement bodies that try to flesh out the substantive principles governing disputes. Other details can be written into the substantive principles themselves. Through either process, the substantive principles become more defined, and refine the content of convergent values if accepted by the international community. As much as possible, the industrialized democracies should ensure that either process successfully works. The dispute settlement body should be fair, competent, and respected. If written in detailed fashion, the substantive principles should represent rules of behavior followed internally within the industrialized democracies, modified to accommodate international conditions.

As with other policies, the single-minded pursuit of free markets, democracy, or human rights can be destructive when carried to an extreme. Any single principle, right, or value has its limits and becomes constrained before taken too far because it will invariably clash with other principles, rights, or values.[161] Like the conflict between liberty and order, or freedom of the press and a defendant's right to a fair trial, there can be conflicts among the activities of the free market, a democratic government, and protection of human rights. While frictions may always be present, they need to be managed by a balancing of values, to determine how far a particular value should be pursued, to prevent one value from unduly dominating the others.

In particular, the dynamism of economic globalization has produced a number of serious, and often novel problems that involve the clashing of economic objectives with democratic values, human rights, and environmental goals.[162] To be solved effectively, these problems require internationally agreed upon rules of behavior which accommodate competing values. For example, an unfettered capitalism can produce a "race to the bottom" in economic behavior, producing deplorable political and environmental effects. Also, nations might engage in economic activities that have harmful transnational environmental effects—"externalities" or "spillover effects."[163]

The industrialized democracies should therefore have two main, interconnected, priorities. First, they should "harmonize" their economic practices that have a significant international effect. Second, they must harmonize practices in a way that optimally accommodates other competing values when conflicts arise. Some judgment about the desirable balance of competing values is unavoidable. Presumably, it would be undesirable to have a harmonized rule that all western corporations may engage in bribery when doing business overseas because that rule would weaken the integrity of political institutions in foreign, primarily developing nations.

---

161. *Cf.* Hudson County Water Co. v. McCarter, 209 U.S. 349, 355 (1908) (Holmes, J.) ("All rights tend to declare themselves absolute to their logical extreme. Yet all in fact are limited by the neighborhood of principles of policy which are other than those on which the particular right is founded, and which becomes strong enough to hold their own when a certain point is reached.").

162. Economic globalization has been blamed for "generating new and fundamental inequities as regions and nations compete for corporate investment, [and for] lowering wage, environmental and human rights standards." *Incorporating the World*, THE NATION, July 15-22, 1996, at 3.

163. "Externalities" or "spillover effects" are the costs and benefits of market commodities not borne by the parties producing or consuming those commodities. Externalities preclude a competitive market because such a market is supposed to take all relevant costs and benefits into account. When some such costs and benefits are excluded from the calculation of market prices, too much or too little of the market commodity may be produced and sold. *See* Seita, *supra* note 50, at 1042 & sources cited n.175. By analogy, "externalities" in the environmental context are the costs or benefits of domestic activities that are not suffered or enjoyed by domestic residents.

Harmonization has already occurred to a degree. Some important examples of ground rules are found in various GATT and WTO agreements, such as those which prohibit dumped and subsidized goods in international trade.[164] Another is the agreement reached by the industrialized democracies on capital adequacy requirements for international banks.[165] There could be global standards on industrial espionage, a problem that directly afflicts western countries rather than developing countries,[166] and the wisdom of harmful exports such as tobacco products.[167]

The area of foreign corrupt practices is another that could be harmonized. There is now no rule that prevents western multinational corporations from committing corrupt practices overseas. Companies from an industrialized country with lax laws on foreign corrupt practices can steal business away from companies headquartered in a country with stringent laws by offering bribes or engaging in other corrupt practices. Without an agreement, western firms from different countries would not compete on equal terms for business contracts in the developing world.

The industrialized democracies are now in the process of reaching an agreement to prohibit bribes and other corrupt business practices in doing business abroad. All the industrialized countries currently make it illegal for companies to engage in corrupt practices at home.[168] The proposed

164. *See* Agreement on Implementation of Article VI of the General Agreement on Tariffs and Trade 1994, Agreements on Trade in Goods, Apr. 15, 1994, Marrakesh Agreement Establishing the World Trade Organization, Annex 1A, *available in* <http://itl.irv.uit.no/trade_law/documents/freetrade> (visited Mar. 29 1997); Agreement on Subsidies and Countervailing Measures, Agreements on Trade in Goods, Apr. 15, 1994, Marrakesh Agreement Establishing the World Trade Organization, Annex 1A, *available in* <http://itl.irv.uit.no/trade_law/documents/freetrade> (visited Mar. 29 1997).

165. *See* Herring & Litan, *supra* note 39, at 107-113. Known as the Basle (or Basel) Accord, this was an agreement that the U.S. government especially sought because it believed that American banks were at a competitive disadvantage compared with the banks of other countries, particularly those of Japan, which had low bank capital requirements. *See generally* Scott & Wellons, *supra* note 39, at 232-92.

166. *See, e.g.*, Paul Blustein, *France, Israel Alleged to Spy on U.S. Firms*, Wash. Post, Aug. 16, 1996, at A28 (The U.S. Central Intelligence Agency identified France, Israel, China, Russia, Iran, and Cuba as the countries that extensively engaged in "economic espionage" against the United States; the CIA also stated that, contrary to popular belief, Japan's efforts to collect economic data "are mostly legal and involve seeking openly available material or hiring well-placed consultants.").

167. Tobacco exports, cigarette industry advertising, and cigarette industry funding of academic research are economically significant in a number of countries. *See, e.g.*, 1995 Statistical Abstract, *supra* note 78, at 823 tbl. 1342 (describing how the United States exported $4.965 billion of cigarettes and $1.303 billion of unmanufactured tobacco in 1994); Kenneth E. Warner et al., *Cigarette Advertising and Magazine Coverage of the Hazards of Smoking–a Statistical Analysis*, New Eng. J. Med., Jan. 30, 1992, at 305 (finding correlation between cigarette advertising in magazines and reduced magazine coverage of the hazards of smoking); Jon Cohen, *Institutes Find It Hard to Kick the Tobacco Funding Habit*, Sci., Apr. 26, 1996, at 490. Whether the source of tobacco is imported or domestic, tobacco consumption is a worldwide problem. *See, e.g.*, Carl E. Bartecchi et al., *The Global Tobacco Epidemic*, Sci. Am., May 1995, at 44; Richard Peto et al., *Tobacco–the Growing Epidemic in China*, J. Am. Med. Ass'n, June 5, 1996, at 1683.

168. While all member nations of the OECD have criminalized the bribery of, and the acceptance of bribes by, public officials, few members have laws that make the bribing

agreement will simply extend that prohibition to activities abroad, and possibly lead to higher ethical standards in developing countries where corruption is endemic. This agreement would be enforceable against the companies most likely to violate the agreement because the great majority of banks and corporations engaged in international business transactions come from the industrialized democracies.[169]

Setting up the "rules of the game" is important not just to promote competition under fair conditions. Common ground rules also balance competing values. In particular, they avoid an injurious race to the bottom in business practices that elevate economic objectives over all others. There are business activities that need global standards because the practices or the secondary effects of economic globalization can directly conflict with the protection of human rights.[170] For example, there could be restrictions on investments in countries that violate human rights,[171] standards on employment conditions by foreign investors in developing nations, and curbs on the involvement of western tourists in the sex industries of developing nations. Global standards can balance economic globalization with the protection of human rights.

Only an international agreement can effectively address the issue of fair labor conditions in facilities operated or utilized by western corporations in developing countries. Otherwise, there might be a race to obtain the lowest possible costs by western corporations, and developing nations might, for economic gain, condone exploitative activities by foreigners. These companies could profit from cheap labor in developing countries, contributing to or preventing improvement in deplorable labor practices, such as thirteen and fourteen-year-old children working fifteen to twenty-

---

of foreign officials a criminal offense. *See Bribes to Foreign Officials: Tax Deductibility to End*, OECD LETTER, June 1996, at 3 (Org. Econ. Co-op. & Dev.). Some progress, however, is being made. For example, the United States has tried to prohibit the use of bribes by U.S. and other western multinational corporations in less developed nations. *See, e.g.*, Foreign Corrupt Practices Act, Pub. L. No. 95-213, 91 Stat. 1494 (1977) (amended 1988); Marlise Simons, *U.S. Enlists Rich Nations in Move to End Business Bribes*, N.Y. TIMES, Apr. 12, 1996, at A10. Also, the members of the OECD have agreed that it is their intention to disallow the tax deductibility of bribes paid to foreign officials. *See id. See generally* Gregory L. Miles, *Crime, Corruption and Multinational Business*, INT'L BUS., JULY 1995, at 34 (discussing the cost of crime and corruption to U.S. multinational corporations, and estimating minimum annual losses of $260 billion in U.S. markets and $105 to $135 billion in foreign markets due to bribery and corruption, business property theft by non-employees, employee theft of property, and intellectual property theft).

169. If not from the 23 industrialized democracies, such companies are probably from the other member nations of the OECD (e.g., South Korea, which has large multinational companies doing business around the world). *See generally supra* notes 25-26 (discussing the industrialized democracies and member nations of the OECD).

170. *See, e.g.*, KORTEN, *supra* note 130, at 229-37 (citing problems such as the "hiring of child labor, cheating workers on overtime pay, imposing merciless quotas, and operating unsafe facilities," *id.* at 229).

171. Unilateral attempts at stopping foreign investment in countries like Myanmar and Cuba might fail. *See, e.g.*, Adam Zagorin, *Punishing Cuba's Partners*, TIME, June 24, 1996, at 54 (American allies strongly critical of a U.S. law punishing foreign firms that use confiscated American assets in Cuba).

hour workdays under armed guard.[172]

Obviously, however, foreign investment can provide sorely needed jobs, for children as well as adults, in developing nations.[173] The condition of child labor is a complex problem involving the shortages of alternatives for children in developing countries. These nations may lack the educational infrastructure to keep all young teenagers in primary or middle schools, and national governments may not fully realize that educating children, rather than making them work, makes more sense for economic growth in the long run.

There is also the growing problem of child prostitution, mostly in economically poorer countries but also in industrialized countries, with increasing transnational traffic.[174] Teenage children have become trapped in prostitution, exploited by pimps who extract most of the children's

172. *See, e.g.*, Eyal Press, *Kathie Lee's Slip*, NATION, June 17, 1996, at 6 (asserting example of children working 15-hour shifts under armed guard); Stephanie Strom, *A Sweetheart Becomes Suspect: Looking Behind Those Kathie Lee Labels*, N.Y. TIMES, June 27, 1996, at D1 (asserting that these same children work 20 hours each day, with no mention of armed guards).

173. At the same time, the desperation of developing countries and their workers should not allow western companies to use their superior bargaining position to extract unconscionable concessions. A basic human right should be the right to work for an "appropriate" wage under "decent" work conditions. Without global standards, there might be a race to the bottom in providing the lowest wages and the worst working conditions. *See* David Holmstrom, *One Man's Fight Against Sweatshops*, CHRIST. SCI. MONITOR, July 3, 1996, at 12. Western investors might give their domestic employees barely minimal advantages over prevailing miserable foreign wages and employment conditions. The problem of child labor in developing countries, however, is not purely one of western creation. The use of child labor is rampant throughout the developing world. *See, e.g.*, Timothy P. McElduff, Jr. & Jon Veiga, *The Child Labor Deterrence Act of 1995: A Choice Between Hegemony and Hypocrisy*, 11 ST. JOHN'S J. LEGAL COMMENT., 581, 584-88 (1996); Timothy A. Glut, *Changing the Approach to Ending Child Labor: An International Solution to an International Problem*, 28 VAND. J. TRANSNAT'L L. 1203, 1205-10 (1995). *See generally* PRESS RELEASES INDEX (visited Apr. 24, 1997) <http://www.ilo.org/public/english/235press/pr/index.htm> (containing press releases on the problem of child labor, from the website of the International Labor Organization, a specialized agency of the United Nations). If the industrialized nations used their economic power to force developing nations to prohibit the use of child labor, tens of millions of poor children would be out of work and possibly forced into even more dangerous occupations. *See* Gordon Fairclough, *Child Labour: It Isn't Black and White*, FAR EAST. ECON. REV., Mar. 7, 1996, at 54. Also, western corporations may show more social responsibility than they are commonly given credit for. Some, perhaps most, western multinationals apparently carry out policies in developing countries that would meet with approval in the industrialized countries. *See, e.g.*, Matt Moffett, *A Racial "Democracy" Begins Painful Debate on Affirmative Action: Blacks Make up 45% of Brazil But Stay Marginalized*, WALL ST. J., Aug. 6, 1996, at A1 (quoting a Brazilian Justice Ministry official as saying that "The companies that discriminate the most in Brazil [against blacks] are Brazilian companies. The best are multinationals, and when multinationals do discriminate it's usually because the directors are Brazilian.").

174. *See, e.g.*, *The Child Sex Trade: Battling a Scourge (Nine-Part Series)*, CHRIST. SCI. MONITOR, Aug. 22-Sept. 16, 1996, at 1; Nicholas D. Kristof, *Asian Childhoods Sacrificed to Prosperity's Lust*, N.Y. TIMES, Apr. 14, 1996, § 1 at 1 (reporting on tens of thousands of children who are working as enslaved prostitutes in Cambodia, India, China, Thailand, the Philippines, Taiwan, and other countries); Margaret A. Healy, *Prosecuting Child Sex Tourists at Home: Do Laws in Sweden, Australia, and the United States Safeguard the Rights of Children as Mandated by International Law?*, 18 FORDHAM INT'L L.J. 1852 (1995).

"earnings" and use the children as virtual slaves. While the growth of child prostitution in developing countries has been fueled to a certain extent by sex tourists from the industrialized world, most exploiters of children are domestic ones.[175] "Employment" for children and local community standards of morality should never justify the use of child prostitutes to satisfy local and western lust. The trade in child sex is just part of the general problem of prostitution present in every country but especially widespread in the developing world.

The sex "market" in the poorer countries attracts male "buyers" from the industrialized countries–Europeans, Americans, Japanese, Australians, Canadians, New Zealanders, and others–who are able to pay higher prices than local customers and thereby increase the supply of prostitutes.[176] Yet, like child prostitution, adult prostitution in developing nations is not a problem caused by the industrialized countries; domestic patrons outnumber foreign ones.[177] Poverty, the lack of economic and educational opportunities for children and women, cultures that tolerate prostitution, and affluent western sex tourists combine to create thriving sex industries in many developing countries.[178]

Another important conflict is with the principle of environmental protection, a value that is generally more strongly held among the industrialized than the developing countries.[179] There is often a clash between the policies of protecting the environment and encouraging economic development. Domestic activities would not be an international problem if their effects were substantially confined within national boundaries. But local activities can have detrimental spillover effects–harmful externalities that have transnational or global effects: radioactive fallout (from nuclear power plant accidents), acid rain, ozone depletion, global warming, and depletion of tropical rain forests.[180] Other local economic activities, while not directly affecting the welfare of foreigners, can cause environmental concern: the decimation of wild fish stocks in the world's oceans by modern industrial fishing,[181] the destruction of coastal areas by economic activities,[182] and the trade in endangered species.[183]

---

175. *See, e.g.*, sources cited *supra* note 174.

176. *See, e.g.*, *id.*; CLEO ODZER, PATPONG SISTERS: AN AMERICAN WOMAN'S VIEW OF THE BANGKOK SEX WORLD v, 1-22 (1994).

177. *See, e.g.*, ODZER, *supra* note 176 (describing the Thai sex industry).

178. *See, e.g.*, sources cites *supra* note 174.

179. *See, e.g.*, DANIEL C. ESTY, GREENING THE GATT: TRADE, ENVIRONMENT, AND THE FUTURE 24-27, 181-203, 238-39 (1994).

180. *See* RICHARD N. COOPER, ENVIRONMENTAL AND RESOURCE POLICIES FOR THE WORLD ECONOMY xx-xxi, 37-68 (1994).

181. *See* Carl Safina, *The World's Imperiled Fish*, SCI. AM., Nov. 1995, at 46. Countries may simply ignore conservation agreements that they sign, or they may even disregard the United Nations. *See id.* at 50-52. "In 1990 high-seas drift nets tangled 42 million animals that were not targeted, including diving seabirds and marine mammals. Such massive losses prompted the U.N. to enact a global ban on large-scale drift nets (those longer than 2.5 kilometers)–although countries like Italy, France and Ireland, continue to deploy them." *Id.* at 51.

182. *See* Don Hinrichsen, *Coasts in Crisis*, ISS. SCI. & TECH., Summer 1996, at 39.

Thus, there should be a balance between the right of nations to utilize their resources and engage in economic activity, and the right of other nations to be free from harmful externalities. Whether this conflict is characterized as one between protection of the environment and free market principles (or democracy or human rights), there is a clash between the value of protecting the environment and a convergent value.[184] Views regarding environmental protection may eventually converge if global standards are agreed upon.[185] Major steps towards possible future convergence have emerged from the Rio Conference, with its aspirational but nonbinding *Agenda 21* and *Rio Declaration on Environment and Development*, which address, among other issues, the problem of "sustainable development."[186] In time, the protection of the environment may become

183. *See, e.g.*, Donald G. McNeil Jr., *Madagascar Reptile Theft Hits Rarest of Tortoises: Stolen Animals Are Thought to Have Been Taken for the World's Illicit Pet Trade*, N.Y. TIMES, July 2, 1996, at C1.

184. While some commentators have argued that protection of the environment is part of a new generation of human rights, that view has not yet gained widespread acceptance. *See* INTERNATIONAL ENVIRONMENTAL LAW ANTHOLOGY 34-37, 61-69 (Anthony D'Amato & Kirsten Engel eds., 1996); VED P. NANDA, INTERNATIONAL ENVIRONMENTAL LAW & POLICY 61-72 (1995). Since any important right could conceivably be viewed as a "human" right, this Article takes the common position that human rights are distinct from environmental protection. The basic international human rights treaties contain provisions that recognize the "inherent right of all peoples to enjoy and utilize fully and freely their natural wealth and resources" and the right of "[a]ll peoples . . . for their own ends, [to] freely dispose of their natural wealth and resources." International Covenant on Economic, Social and Cultural Rights, *supra* note 32, arts. 1 para. 2, 25; International Covenant on Civil and Political Rights, *supra* note 32, arts. 1 para. 2, 47.

185. *See* John H. Cushman Jr., *In Shift, U.S. Will Seek Binding World Pact to Combat Global Warming*, N.Y. TIMES, July 17, 1996, at A6 (reporting that "[f]or the first time, the United States will seek a binding international agreement to reduce the kinds of air pollution, chiefly from burning fossil fuels, that threaten to warm the global climate").

186. The United Nations Conference on Environment and Development (UNCED) was held in Rio de Janeiro, Brazil, from June 3-14 of 1992. Popularly referred to as the Rio Conference or the Earth Summit, the UNCED was the most widely attended environmental conference in history, with over a hundred heads of state and representatives from over 170 nations. *See* NANDA, *supra* note 184, at 103. At the Rio Conference, all nations in attendance (including the United States) unanimously adopted three nonbinding instruments. *See Report of the United Nations Conference on Environment and Development*, 47th Sess., U.N. Doc. A/CONF.151/26 (1992); AGENDA 21: THE EARTH SUMMIT STRATEGY TO SAVE OUR PLANET 1, 24-26 (Daniel Sitarz ed., 1994). *See generally* THE ENVIRONMENT AFTER RIO (Luigi Campiglio et al. eds., 1994).

The first instrument, the *Rio Declaration on the Environment and Development*, deals with the issues of sustainable economic development and achieving an equitable balance between the sometimes conflicting developmental and environmental needs of current and future generations and of different nations. *See Rio Declaration on the Environment and Development*, U.N. Conference on Environment and Development, 47th Sess., Annex 1, U.N. Doc. A/CONF.151/26, vol. 1, at 8 (1992), *available in* 31 I.L.M. 874. The massive text of *Agenda 21*, the second instrument, is contained in three U.N. volumes. *See Agenda 21*, U.N. Conference on Environment and Development, 47th Sess., Annex 2, U.N. Doc. A/CONF.151/26, vol. 1, at 14 *et seq.* [hereinafter *Agenda 21*]. *Agenda 21* addresses numerous environmental issues, with the following major themes: the quality of life on earth, the efficient use of the earth's natural resources, the protection of the earth's global commons (the atmosphere and oceans), the management of human settlements, chemicals and waste, and sustainable economic growth. *See* AGENDA 21: THE EARTH SUMMIT STRATEGY TO SAVE OUR PLANET, *supra*, at 8-19. *See generally*

another converging value.

Conclusion

Globalization has been primarily an economic process that has expanded markets for international trade and opportunities for international investment. Simultaneously, it has increased economic interdependency among nations and made nations economically vital to each other. But globalization is more than just doing business with foreigners and traveling to foreign lands. Through sophisticated technology and international news reporting, globalization connects persons throughout the world and brings into local homes vast amounts of information about transnational issues. It has placed a human face on people in distant lands, and cultivated a global perspective and a sensitivity to different foreign traditions. More people learn about foreign cultures, become interested in foreign affairs, and speak foreign languages. Travelers or alien residents in foreign lands often expect to receive the same basic rights as they do at home.

Profoundly, globalization has contributed to the convergence of basic values among nations towards the liberal democratic values of market economies, democratic governments, and human rights. The clear triumph of market economies over command economies as well as the liberalization of international trade and investment has converted numerous nations over to general free market principles. For people in different countries, globalization has contributed to an expanding consciousness that prefers democratic governments and human rights over authoritarian regimes that repress freedoms.

As values converge, nationals of one country often care enough to work for the enjoyment of similar political rights in other countries. Ultimately, globalization is important and desirable because it encourages a belief in the primacy of the human race. A world in which liberal democratic values abound and people emphasize their status as human beings will be more humane than the world of the past. We should dream of a common humanity for "[w]e are such stuff [a]s dreams are made on."[187]

Agenda 21, supra; AGENDA 21 & THE UNCED PROCEEDINGS, vols. 1-6 (Nicholas A. Robinson ed., 1992 & 1993). The third instrument covers the treatment of forests. *See Non-Legally Binding Authoritative Statement of Principles for a Global Consensus on the Management, Conservation and Sustainable Development of All Types of Forests*, U.N. Conference on Environment and Development, 47th Sess., Annex 3, U.N. Doc. A/CONF.151/26, vol. 3 at 111 (1992), *available in* 31 I.L.M. 881.

The issue of sustainable development is one that has captured the attention of many commentators. *See, e.g.*, SUSTAINABLE DEVELOPMENT AND INTERNATIONAL LAW (Winfried Land ed., 1995); A SURVEY OF ECOLOGICAL ECONOMICS (Rajaram Krishnan et al. eds., 1995); GREENING INTERNATIONAL LAW (Philippe Sands ed., 1994); INVESTING IN NATURAL CAPITAL: THE ECOLOGICAL ECONOMICS APPROACH TO SUSTAINABILITY (AnnMari Jansson et al. eds., 1994); TOWARD SUSTAINABLE DEVELOPMENT: CONCEPTS, METHODS, AND POLICY (Jeroen C. van den Bergh & Jan van der Straaten eds., 1994).

187. WILLIAM SHAKESPEARE, THE TEMPEST act IV, sc. I, l. 156.

[12]

Globalization and Human Rights*

*Robert McCorquodale*** with *Richard Fairbrother****

I. INTRODUCTION

An advertising campaign by the McDonald's food corporation in the late 1990s showed images of Russian soldiers and American grandfathers, young Mexican women and Australian Aboriginal children, all celebrating the thing they share in common: a love of McDonald's food. According to the advertisement: "everyone around the world is saying 'It's Mac time now.'"

These advertising images are simultaneously symptomatic and symbolic of globalization. The apparent universal market and demand for a product, which is created and presented by the use of new communication technologies and produced by a transnational corporation, could be seen as a manifestation of new opportunities provided by globalization for all people after the end of the Cold War. At the same time, the impacts of the universal market on diverse cultures and on state sovereignty, as well as the pervasiveness of development measured in market terms, could indicate the dangers in this process of globalization. These opportunities and dangers arise because globalization is "an economic, political, social, and ideological phenomenon which carries with it unanticipated, often contradictory, and polarizing consequences."[1] This process of globalization is part of an "ever more interdependent world,"[2] where political, economic, social, and

---

* The authors would like to acknowledge with gratitude the financial support of the Australian Research Council which enabled some of this research to be undertaken. This article represents the personal views of the authors and not those of the Australian government.

** *Robert McCorquodale* is Associate Professor in International and Public Law in the Faculty of Law, The Australian National University.

*** *Richard Fairbrother* was a research assistant to Robert McCorquodale and now works for the Australian Department of the Prime Minister and Cabinet.

1. Claire Turenne Sjolander, *The Rhetoric of Globalization: What's in a Wor(l)d?*, 51 Int'l J. 603, 604 (1996).
2. *Report of the Secretary-General Pursuant to the Statement Adopted by the Summit Meeting of the Security Council on 31 January 1992: An Agenda For Peace: Preventative Diplomacy, Peacemaking, and Peace-Keeping*, U.N. GAOR, 47th Sess., ¶ 17, U.N. Doc. A/47/277-S/24111 (1992) [hereinafter Agenda for Peace].

cultural relationships are not restricted to territorial boundaries or to state actors and no state or entity is unaffected by activities outside its direct control. Developments in technology and communications, the creation of intricate international economic and trade arrangements, increasing activity by international organizations and transnational corporations (such as McDonald's), and the changes to international relations and international law since the end of the Cold War have profoundly affected the context within which each person and community lives as well as the role of the state.

The focus of this article is the effect of globalization on the protection of human rights, particularly the protection of human rights through international human rights law. This effect of globalization must be considered because, as the former Secretary-General of the United Nations noted:

> [t]echnological advances are altering the nature and the expectation of life all over the globe. The revolution in communications has united the world in awareness, in aspiration and in greater solidarity against injustice. But progress also brings new risks for stability: ecological damage, disruption of family and community life, greater intrusion into the lives and rights of individuals.[3]

This article examines the processes of globalization and of international human rights law, as well as the impact of the economic processes of globalization on the protection of some human rights. Examples from Africa are primarily used here because the impact can be seen most clearly there. In this analysis, the consequences of globalization, including both the opportunities and dangers that it creates, are considered not only with regard to the protection of human rights, but also in terms of globalization's effect on the international legal order, of which international human rights law forms a part.

II. GLOBALIZATION

Globalization is a contested term and there is no one accepted definition of it.[4] Robertson provides a definition which captures the contradictory elements of globalization: "we may best consider contemporary globalization in its most general sense as a form of institutionalization of the two-fold process involving the universalization of particularism and the particularization of universalism."[5] This twofold process has many aspects. Clearly, it is

3. *Id.* ¶ 12.
4. "Globalization" could mean whatever the user wants it to mean. *See* Sjolander, *supra* note 1, at 603.
5. Roland Robertson, Globalization: Social Theory and Global Culture 102 (1992).

a political, social, and cultural process, but "[i]t is foremost an economic process."[6] Cerny defines the economic process of globalization in the following way:

> it . . . create[s] permissive conditions for a range of distinct but intertwined structural trends—that is, it expands the playing field within which different market actors and firms interact. It transforms the international economy from one made up of holistic national economies interacting on the basis of *national* 'comparative advantage' into one in which a variety of '*competitive* advantages' are created in ways which are not dependent on the nation-state as social, economic, and/or political unit.[7]

As Cerny's definition suggests, economic globalization is seen in terms of "markets" where the actors in the market have changed, as have the goods and services on offer.

The establishment of globalized economic institutions has been both a symptom of and a stimulus for globalization. The development of the World Bank, the International Monetary Fund (IMF), regional development banks such as the European Bank for Reconstruction and Development (EBRD), and, more recently, multilateral trade institutions such as the World Trade Organization (WTO) indicates the trend away from the dominance of the state as the exclusive unit of analysis in international affairs. Acknowledging this trend, the World Bank has stated that:

> [t]he state still defines the policies and rules for those within its jurisdiction, but global events and international agreements are increasingly affecting its choices. People are now more mobile, more educated, and better informed about conditions elsewhere. And involvement in the global economy tightens constraints on arbitrary state action, reduces the state's ability to tax capital, and brings much closer financial market scrutiny of monetary and fiscal policies.[8]

Globalization has thus been transformative in terms of a reconceptualizing of state sovereignty within both international relations and international law.[9]

Of course, states have never had exclusive control over their economic,

---

6. Alex Y. Seita, *Globalization and the Convergence of Values*, 30 CORNELL INT'L L.J. 429 (1997).
7. Phillip G. Cerny, *Globalization and Other Stories: The Search for a New Paradigm for International Relations*, 51 INT'L J. 617, 626 (1996) (footnote omitted). *See also* Hyug Baeg Im, *Globalisation and Democratisation: Boon Companions or Strange Bedfellows?*, 50 AUSTL. J. INT'L AFF. 279 (1996).
8. THE WORLD BANK, WORLD DEVELOPMENT REPORT 1997, at 12 (1997).
9. *See* Cerny, *supra* note 7, at 624; John Stremlau, *Antidote to Anarchy*, 18 WASH. Q. 29, 42 (1995); W. Michael Reisman, *Sovereignty and Human Rights in Contemporary International Law*, 84 AM. J. INT'L L. 866, 869 (1990); Louis Henkin, *Human Rights and State "Sovereignty,"* 25 GA. J. INT'L & COMP. L. 31 (1996).

legal, political, and security affairs. However, the current trend of globalization differs from past transnational influences on state sovereignty in the scale and speed of its operation. For example, foreign exchange trading volumes had, even by the late 1980s, reached $US 1.2 trillion per day, which is nearly forty times the volume of physical international trade[10] and more than the combined foreign currency reserves of all the states in the world.[11] The speed of these huge transactions is crucial, as Luke notes:

> a 'transnational' flow of goods, capital, people and ideas has existed for centuries; it antedates even the rise of modern nation-states. However, this historical flow . . . tended to move more slowly, move less and more narrowly than the rush of products, ideas, persons and money that develops with jet transportation, electronic telecommunication, massive decolonization and extensive computerization. . . .[12]

While the current globalization is different, it is not analytically detached from its historical origins. Despite some claims to the contrary,[13] the philosophical oppositions which characterized the Cold War remain integral to many of the debates concerning globalization today. For example, there are oppositional constructs between political rights and economic development, and, in international legal theory and practice, between accepting a state-based international legal system or pushing for a change to the international system.[14]

Nonetheless, the end of the Cold War represents a new analytical phase in world history. In today's globalization, the actors involved are not only states but also transnational corporations and inter-governmental institutions. Indeed, of the world's 100 biggest economies, only 49 are states, while the remaining 51 economies are corporations.[15] Thus the heads of states may have much less impact on both individuals and on world events than those in charge of transnational corporations. As Luke explains:

---

10. *See* Sjolander, *supra* note 1, at 608 (citing figures produced by the United Nations Conference on Trade and Development (UNCTAD)).
11. *See* Peter Evans, *The Eclipse of the State?: Reflections on Stateness in an Era of Globalization,* 50 World Pol. 62, 67 (1997).
12. Timothy W. Luke, *New World Order or Neo-world Orders: Power, Politics and Ideology in Informationalizing Glocalities, in* Global Modernities 91, 99–100 (Mike Featherstone et al. eds., 1995). The importance of speed in today's globalization is supported by Richard O'Brien, Global Financial Integration: The End of Geography 8 (1992); James Der Derian, Antidiplomacy: Spies, Terror, Speed, and War 133 (1992).
13. *See* Walter Russell Mead, *Trains, Planes, and Automobiles: The End of the Postmodern Moment,* 12 World Pol'y J. 13, 15 (1996) (referring to the various claims about the "end of history," etc, whereby it was considered that a "contemporary society has overcome the fundamental contradictions whose opposition was the motor of Hegelian history.").
14. *See generally* Martti Koskenniemi, From Apology to Utopia: The Structure of International Legal Argument (1989).
15. R.C. Longworth, *Large Companies Now Economically Bigger Than Some Countries,* Chicago Tribune, 15 Oct. 1996.

> who sets the pace in automobile output, who controls the Earth's computer software production, . . . who leads international money markets or who directs world telecommunication systems is materially far more important to most individuals, households and firms than who holds the state leadership in Guatemala, Germany, Ghana or Greece.[16]

Current globalization operates in diverse ways. Falk offers a bifurcated view of globalization. "[G]lobalization-from-above reflect[s] the collaboration between leading states and the main agents of capital formation . . . [of] the New World Order"[17] and concerns the activities of transnational corporations, international economic organizations, and other similar developments. In contrast, "globalization-from-below," includes popular participation at local levels, the building of civil societies, and the enhancement of non-governmental organizations as part of "the strengthening over time of the institutional forms and activities associated with global civil society."[18] Falk appropriately locates human rights in this latter branch.

III. INTERNATIONAL HUMAN RIGHTS LAW

At one time, governments dealt with those within their jurisdiction as they wished and resisted all criticisms of their actions by claiming that human rights were matters of "domestic jurisdiction" and the responsibility of each state alone.[19] Now human rights are an established part of international law with an institutional structure—including substantive definitions of human rights and mechanisms to enforce these rights—and with universal application.[20]

---

16. Luke, *supra* note 12, at 103. Also, "the secretary general of Amnesty International and the chief executive officer of Royal Dutch Shell cast far longer shadows on the international stage than do the leaders of Moldova, Namibia, or Nauru. The state may not be quite ready to wither away, but it's not what it used to be." Peter J. Spiro, *New Global Communities: Nongovernmental Organizations in International Decision-Making Institutions*, 18 WASH. Q. 45, 46 (1995) (endnote omitted). Nowhere has this been more obviously the case than in Asia, where the continuation of the currency crisis has, at least in part, been a result of international financial markets "punishing" states for poor economic management, crony capitalism, and poorly performing banking sectors. It is the IMF, rather than individual Western states, that receives the most publicity for its rescue attempts. *See generally* Martin Feldstein, *Refocusing the IMF*, 77 FOREIGN AFF., March/April 1998, at 20; Donald K. Emmerson, *Americanising Asia?*, 77 FOREIGN AFF., May/June 1998, at 46.
17. Richard Falk, *The Making of Global Citizenship*, *in* GLOBAL VISIONS: BEYOND THE NEW WORLD ORDER 39 (Jeremy Brecher et al. eds., 1993).
18. *Id.*
19. U.N. CHARTER art. 2, para. 7, *signed* 26 June 1945, 59 Stat. 1031, T.S. No. 933, 3 Bevans 1153 (*entered into force* 24 Oct. 1945). *See also* Leo Gross, *The Peace of Westphalia 1648–1948*, 42 AM. J. INT'L L. 20 (1948); Reisman, *supra* note 9, at 866.
20. *See, e.g.*, A.H. ROBERTSON & J.G. MERRILLS, HUMAN RIGHTS IN THE WORLD: AN INTRODUCTION TO THE STUDY OF THE INTERNATIONAL PROTECTION OF HUMAN RIGHTS 286–303 (3d ed. 1989); MARTIN DIXON & ROBERT MCCORQUODALE, CASES AND MATERIALS ON INTERNATIONAL LAW 191–278 (2d ed. 1995); HENRY STEINER & PHILIP ALSTON, INTERNATIONAL HUMAN RIGHTS IN CONTEXT 118–65 (1996).

Every single state has ratified at least one treaty containing legal obligations to protect human rights. Human rights, as law, are now within the discourse of the international community. Human rights issues are raised in political, economic, social, and cultural interactions across the world. States have acknowledged, in principle at least, that "the promotion and protection of all human rights is a legitimate concern of the international community."[21] While only states are legally obliged to protect human rights, international institutions, especially as they are largely comprised of states, arguably also have obligations to protect human rights.[22]

International human rights are globalized. They operate beyond all borders and all state mechanisms. They have become part of the discourse in almost all societies, speaking to both the elites and the oppressed, to institutions and to communities. Human rights are both a part of globalization and separate from globalization.[23]

However, this globalized characterization of human rights is subject to criticism by those who argue that international human rights law does not reflect universal values, but rather Western, European ones. While a critique of human rights as globalized or universal goes beyond the scope of this article, it is important to realize the context within which human rights have developed and are developing. Human rights (though that term was not originally used) developed in the context of certain historical, social, political, and philosophical situations in Europe. They "are one of the monumental legacies left by the Enlightenment. They are one of those grand narratives . . . that spoke the Truth about the world in order to change it, and that promised a final reconciliation at the end of modernity."[24] Theorists from many perspectives[25] have shown the problems with this assumption of

---

21. Vienna Declaration and Programme of Action, U.N. GAOR, World Conf. on Hum. Rts., 48th Sess., 22d plen. mtg., part I, ¶ 4, U.N. Doc. A/CONF.157/23 (1993), *reprinted in* 32 I.L.M. 1661 (1993) [hereinafter Vienna Declaration]. Similar statements are found in the Concluding Document from the Moscow Conference on Security and Co-Operation in Europe (CSCE) (now OSCE), where states involved "categorically and irrevocably [declared] that the commitments undertaken in the field of the human dimension of the CSCE are matters of direct and legitimate concern of all participating States and do not belong exclusively to the internal affairs of the State concerned." Conference on Security and Co-Operation in Europe: Document of the Moscow Meeting on the Human Dimension, *adopted* 3 Oct. 1991, *reprinted in* 30 I.L.M. 1670, 1672 (1991).
22. *See* Vienna Declaration, *supra* note 21. There was a recommendation "that high-level officials of relevant United Nations bodies and specialized agencies at their annual meeting, besides coordinating their activities, also assess the impact of their strategies and policies on the enjoyment of human rights." *Id.* Part II, ¶ 1.
23. *See* Falk, supra note 17, at 39 (stating that globalization-from-below is "both reactive to [globalization] developments and responsive to different impulses and influences.").
24. Rolando Gaete, *Postmodernism and Human Rights: Some Insidious Questions*, 2 Law & Critique 149 (1991). *See also* John Ralston Saul, Voltaire's Bastards: The Dictatorship of Reason in the West (1992).
25. *See, e.g.*, Peter Gabel & Duncan Kennedy, *Roll Over Beethoven*, 36 Stan. L. Rev. 1, 26 (1984); Hilary Charlesworth, *What are 'Women's International Human Rights'?, in*

what is "the Truth" in human rights, because "in its current form, human rights law naturalises and legitimises the subjugating and disciplinary effects of European, masculinist, heterosexual and capitalist regimes of power."[26] Thus, besides the general problem of the lack of enforcement of international human rights law, there is also a debate about whether an international system for protecting human rights is inappropriate and invasive if human rights are dependent on their cultural context.[27] In addition, international human rights law, despite its concern with the protection of the rights of humans, remains largely contained within a state-based framework where the responsibility for violations of human rights is by states alone and the sovereign powers of states are affirmed.[28]

These criticisms have made some impact on the understanding of human rights. For example, it has been recognized that human rights extend beyond civil and political rights to economic, social, cultural, and group rights.[29] In addition, there has been increasing involvement of non-European based systems in the development of human rights.[30] Thus, while the international legal framework for the protection of human rights is based on a universal approach, some account is now taken of the diversity of

---

HUMAN RIGHTS OF WOMEN: NATIONAL AND INTERNATIONAL PERSPECTIVES 58 (Rebecca Cook ed., 1994); Jane Flax, *The End of Innocence, in* FEMINISTS THEORIZE THE POLITICAL 445 (Judith Butler & Joan W. Scott eds., 1992); R. Pannikar, *Is the Notion of Human Rights a Western Concept?*, 120 DIOGENES 76 (1982); Jim George, *Understanding International Relations after the Cold War: Probing Beyond the Realist Legacy, in* CHALLENGING BOUNDARIES: GLOBAL FLOWS, TERRITORIAL IDENTITIES 33 (Michael Shapiro & Hayward R. Alker eds., 1996); Joseph Slaughter, *The Question of Narration: A Voice in International Human Rights Law*, 19 HUM. RTS. Q. 406 (1997).

26. Diane Otto, *Rethinking Universals: Opening Transformative Possibilities in International Human Rights Law*, 18 AUSTL. Y.B. INT'L L. 1, 35 (1997). Similar arguments can be made with respect to neo-classical economics generally because it emerged from the same philosophical foundations as human rights. *See* STEPHEN TOULMIN, COSMOPOLIS: THE HIDDEN AGENDA OF MODERNITY (1990).

27. For the view that human rights are culturally dependent, see, for example, Pannikar, *supra* note 25; Bilahari Kausikan, *Asia's Different Standard*, 92 FOREIGN POL'Y 24 (1993). Those who argue against this view include Fernando R. Tesón, *International Human Rights and Cultural Relativism*, 25 VA. J. INT'L L. 869, 895 (1985); Abdullahi An-Na'im, *Human Rights in the Muslim World: Socio-Political Conditions and Scriptural Imperatives*, 3 HARV. HUM. RTS. J. 13 (1990); Ann F. Bayefsky, *Cultural Sovereignty, Relativism, and International Human Rights: New Excuses for Old Strategies*, 9 RATIO JURIS 42 (1996). *See also* Michael C. Davis, *Constitutionalism and Political Culture: The Debate over Human Rights and 'Asian Values,'* 11 HARV. HUM. RTS. J. 109 (1998).

28. *See* Martti Koskenniemi, *The Future of Statehood*, 32 HARV. J. INT'L L., Spring 1991, at 397; Robert McCorquodale, *Self-Determination: A Human Rights Approach*, 43 INT'L & COMP. L.Q. 857 (1994).

29. *See* Charles Taylor, *Human Rights: The Legal Culture, in* PHILOSOPHICAL FOUNDATIONS OF HUMAN RIGHTS 49 (UNESCO ed., 1986).

30. The role of non-European-based systems in the acceptance of the right to development is one example. *See* Russel Barsh, *The Right to Development as a Human Right: Results of the Global Consultation*, 13 HUM. RTS. Q. 322 (1991).

cultures; both the international instruments[31] and the international human rights tribunals make allowance for each state's "margin of appreciation."[32] Nevertheless, the globalized aspect of human rights can be seen most clearly in the universal power (albeit one which may put the speaker at risk) of the rhetoric of "human rights." According to Williams:

> [f]or the historically disempowered, the conferring of rights is symbolic of all the denied aspects of their humanity: rights imply a respect that places one in referential range of self and others, that elevates one's status from human body to social being. . . .[33] 'Rights' feels new in the mouths of most black [and other oppressed] people. It is still deliciously empowering to say. It is the magic wand of . . . inclusion and exclusion, of power and no power. The concept of rights, both positive and negative, is the marker of citizenship, our relation to others.[34]

Because this rhetoric is heard worldwide, it is necessary to understand it in terms of the types of rights affected by economic globalization.

IV. ECONOMIC RIGHTS AND ECONOMIC GROWTH

Economic rights include the individual right to an adequate standard of living and the individual and group right to development.[35] The right to an adequate standard of living concerns access to the basic essentials for sustaining life, including food, shelter, clothing, and health care.[36] The right

---

31. See the Vienna Declaration, *supra* note 22, Part I, ¶ 5 which provides:

> All human rights are universal, indivisible and interdependent and interrelated. The international community must treat human rights globally in a fair and equal manner, on the same footing, and with the same emphasis. While the significance of national and regional particularities and various historical, cultural and religious backgrounds must be borne in mind, it is the duty of States, regardless of their political, economic and cultural systems, to promote and protect all human rights and fundamental freedoms.

Id.

32. This phrase has been used by, for example, the European Court of Human Rights in the Handyside Case, 24 Eur. Ct. H.R. (ser. A) at 22 (1976).
33. Patricia J. Williams, The Alchemy of Race and Rights, 153 (1991).
34. *Id.* at 164. Williams is, though, generally wary of the globalization of a human rights discourse. However, Rorty asserts that the human rights phenomenon is a "fact of the world," so that the issue of whether humans really have rights is no longer worth debating. Richard Rorty, *Human Rights, Rationality, and Sentimentality, in* On Human Rights: The Oxford Amnesty Lectures 1993, at 111, 116, 134 (Stephen Shute & Susan Hurley eds., 1993).
35. *See* Matthew Craven, The International Covenant on Economic, Social, and Cultural Rights: A Perspective on its Development (1995); Economic, Social and Cultural Rights: A Textbook (Asbørjn Eide et al. eds., 1995). *See also* Jerry Dohnal, *Structural Adjustment Programs: A Violation of Rights,* 1 Austl. J. Hum. Rts. 57 (1994).
36. *See* International Covenant on Civil and Political Rights, *adopted* 16 Dec. 1966, G.A. Res. 2200 (XXI), U.N. GAOR, 21st Sess., Supp. No. 16, arts. 11 & 12, U.N. Doc. A/6316 (1966), 999 U.N.T.S. 171 (*entered into force* 23 Mar. 1976) [hereinafter ICCPR].

to development, while still contentious as a human right, means that "every human person and all peoples are entitled to participate in, contribute to, and enjoy economic, social, cultural and political development, in which all human rights and fundamental freedoms can be fully realized."[37] Accordingly, it can be argued that economic growth will increase protection of economic rights because economic growth brings increased access to health care, food, and shelter, either directly through employment and increased income or indirectly through the improvement and extension of these facilities to more people. For most developing states, particularly those in Africa, economic growth is often fostered through large-scale external investment. This investment comes from globalized economic institutions, such as inter-governmental institutions, including the World Bank and the IMF, or transnational corporations.[38] This argument, therefore, concludes that economic growth through globalization leads to the protection of economic rights such as the right to an adequate standard of living and the right to development.

However, the reality is somewhat different in most instances. There are at least three reasons for this: the type of investment, the basis for investment decisions, and the type of economic growth. First, a great deal of the investment arising from globalized economic sources for the purposes of "development" is allocated only to certain types of projects, such as the building of dams, roads, and runways, and the creation of large-scale commercial farms. There is little or no investment in primary health care, safe drinking water, and basic education. Furthermore, these globalized investment-based projects "create some risks of (legally cognizable) harm to some categories of project-affected people, and some projects generate many risks of very serious harms to many people."[39] The World Bank itself has recognized the risks involved. With regard to large-scale irrigation projects, the World Bank has recognized that:

> [s]ocial disruption is inevitable in large-scale irrigation projects. . . . Local people often find that they have less access to water, land and vegetation resources as a result of the project. Conflicting demands on water resources and

---

37. Declaration on the Right to Development, G.A. Res. 41/128 (Annex), *adopted* 4 Dec. 1986, U.N. GAOR, 41st Sess., Supp. No. 53, art 1.1, U.N. Doc. A/41/53 (1987), *reprinted in* 3 WESTON III.R.2. The right has been subsequently affirmed by the international community. *See, e.g.*, Vienna Declaration, *supra* note 21, Part I, ¶ 10.
38. *See* Timothy M. Shaw & Clement E. Adibe, *Africa and Global Issues in the Twenty-First Century*, 51 INT'L J. 1, 12 (1996). They point out that most "African economies must rely on the [World Bank and IMF] for external financing since they cannot obtain capital from the world's financial markets." *Id.* (footnote omitted).
39. James C.N. Paul, *The Human Right to Development: Its Meaning & Importance*, 25 J. MARSHALL L. REV. 235, 238 (1992).

> inequalities in distribution can easily occur both in the project area and downstream . . . altering the distribution of wealth.[40]

An example of this occurred when representatives of the Penan people of Malaysia told then Senator and now US Vice-President Gore: "We are not being killed by weapons, but when our lands are taken, it is the same as killing us."[41] Their statements "exemplif[ied] the grave human rights offenses that sometimes occur in the effort [by governments and transnational corporations] to develop national resources."[42] Thus, the type of investment generated by globalized economic institutions tends to infringe upon economic rights rather than protect them.

Second, decisions about investment by these globalized organizations are based almost exclusively on financial concerns, including generating profits for banks in the developed states and for other transnational corporations. As such, these concerns are external to the state in which the investment is made, and subsequently fail to focus on social welfare within the state. A classic example of this decision-making process is seen in an infamous internal World Bank memo:

> [S]houldn't the World Bank be encouraging more migration of the dirty industries to the [less developed countries]? . . . The measurement of the costs of health impairing pollution depends on the foregone earnings from increased morbidity and mortality. From this point of view, a given amount of health-impairing pollution should be done in the country with the lowest wages. I think the economic logic behind dumping a load of toxic waste in the lowest-wage country is impeccable and we should face up to that. . . . I've always thought that under-populated countries in Africa are vastly under-polluted; their air quality is probably vastly inefficiently [high] compared to Los Angeles or Mexico City.[43]

This memo, written by then World Bank Chief Economist and now US Deputy Treasury Secretary (and US Treasury Secretary-designate) Lawrence Summers, makes excellent neo-classical economic logic.[44] But this logic can have disastrous consequences for environmental and human rights protection. For example, research has shown that United States-based

---

40. The World Bank, Technical Paper No. 140, 2 Environmental Assessment Sourcebook 96 (1991).
41. Brian B.A. McAllister, *The United Nations Conference on Environment and Development: An Opportunity to Forge a New Unity in the Work of the World Bank Among Human Rights, the Environment, and Sustainable Development*, 16 Hastings Int'l & Comp. L. Rev. 689, 691 (1993).
42. *Id.* at 691.
43. *See Let Them Eat Pollution*, Economist (London), 8 Feb. 1992, at 66 (quoting a World Bank memo written by Lawrence Summers). *See also, Pollution and the Poor*, Economist (London), 15 Feb. 1992, at 18.
44. *See generally* Paul Ormerod, The Death of Economics (1994) (for a critique of contemporary economics).

chemical companies have been exporting pesticides banned in the US to developing states by altering production techniques and changing production sites to avoid strict US labeling laws.[45] Unlabeled containers of hazardous pesticides then become available for purchase over the counter in, for example, parts of Africa.[46] Often, due to lack of proper information by consumers, the pesticides are improperly used and the containers are reused to carry drinking water.[47]

In a globalized economy, the patience of investors to obtain returns on their investment is considerably reduced. In Africa, where long-term investment in infrastructure is needed, investors from developed states can be harsh in their economic decisions. For example, a French diplomat apparently said that "[e]conomically speaking, if the entire black Africa, with the exception of South Africa, were to disappear in a flood, the global cataclysm will be approximately nonexistent."[48] It should also be realized that many of the economic decisions made by the globalized economic institutions are made on the basis of very dubious information and analysis. The quantity and speed of information today does not always improve decision-making.

In broader human rights terms, globalized economic institutions often implement plans that hurt those whose economic rights are most vulnerable. For example, Howard notes that "[i]n Africa today, schools are closing down as governments retrench in the face of structural adjustment programmes imposed by the International Monetary Fund."[49] Because the government is the largest employer in most African states, "[n]ot only do thousands of people lose their jobs . . . , but often all services are drastically cut, especially those of the already underfunded health sector."[50] Those who

---

45. *See* James H. Colopy, *Poisoning the Developing World: The Exportation of Unregistered and Severely Restricted Pesticides from the United States*, 13 UCLA J. Envtl. L. & Pol'y 167, 171, 181 (1995).
46. *See id.* at 177. This action occurs despite the existence of "Responsible Care" and the industry's self-espoused ability to ethically regulate itself. *See* Robert Gottlieb et al., *Greening or Greenwashing?: The Evolution of Industry Decision Making, in* Reducing Toxics: A New Approach to Policy and Industrial Decisionmaking 170 (Robert Gottlieb ed., 1995); Peter Simmons & Brian Wynne, *Responsible Care: Trust, Credibility, and Environmental Management, in* Environmental Strategies for Industry: International Perspectives on Research Needs and Policy Implications 201 (Kurt Fischer & Johan Schot eds., 1993).
47. *See* Colopy, *supra* note 45, at 177. Also, while developing states use only around twenty percent of all pesticides used in the world, over seventy percent of the world's pesticide-related deaths and fifty percent of acute pesticide poisoning occur in developing states.
48. Victor Chesnault, "Que faire de l'Afrique noire?," *Le Monde*, 28 Feb. 1990, at 2, *quoted in* Michael Chege, *Remembering Africa*, 71 Foreign Aff. [America and the World 1991/92], at 148 (1992).
49. Rhoda E. Howard, *Civil Conflict in Sub-Saharan Africa: Internally Generated Causes*, 51 Int'l J. 26, 32 (1996).
50. Mahmood Monshipouri, Democratization, Liberalization & Human Rights in the Third World 54 (1995) (quoting Fran Hoskin). *See also* Anne Orford, *Locating the International: Military and Monetary Interventions after the Cold War*, 38 Harv. Int'l L.J. 443, 464–75 (1997).

are the worst affected when governments are forced to change their priorities are usually the poor, women, and agricultural workers. For example, Zimbabwe used to provide free education for all until adherence to an IMF structural adjustment program caused this to end.[51] As a result, many Zimbabwean girls are no longer being educated because parents make gender-based financial choices.[52] This occurs despite the clear evidence that the education of girls is an investment that "yield[s] the highest rate of return in a developing country."[53]

Indeed, structural adjustment programs have significant gender impact, and often fail to withstand criticism in the same economic terms that they purport to uphold.[54] The United Nations Special Rapporteur on the Realization of Economic, Social and Cultural Rights reported that:

> [s]tructural adjustment programs continue to have a significant impact upon the overall realization of economic, social and cultural rights, both in terms of the ability of people to exercise them, and of the capability of governments to fulfil and implement them. . . . Human rights concerns continue to be conspicuously underestimated in the adjustment process.[55]

Thus, human rights (in the case of Zimbabwe, the rights to education and freedom from discrimination) are violated as a consequence of the policies of the globalized economic institutions.

Additionally, the fact that the economic decision-making process is being taken away from governments and put in the hands of financial "experts" in globalized economic institutions also means that the people and the governments of developing states are not effectively involved in decisions affecting their lives.[56] This has an impact on both state sovereignty

---

51. *See* Maria Nzomo, *The Political Economy of the African Crisis: Gender Impacts and Responses*, 51 INT'L J. 78 (1996).
52. *See* Bharati Sadasivam, *The Impact of Structural Adjustment on Women: A Governance and Human Rights Agenda*, 19 HUM. RTS. Q. 630, 641 n.36 (1997).
53. JOSETTE L. MURPHY, GENDER ISSUES IN WORLD BANK LENDING 22 (1995) (footnote omitted).
54. *See generally* Dohnal, *supra* note 35 (for a cogent summary of structural adjustment programs and their problems).
55. Danilo Türk, *The Realization of Economic, Social and Cultural Rights: Final Report*, U.N. Doc E/CN.4/Sub.2/1992/16 (1992). The World Bank acknowledges this when it states that "[c]omplicating the picture is the fact that some public consumption—teachers' salaries for example, or purchases of medicine—can affect people's lives for the better, and even raise the efficiency of investment. Cutting consumption indiscriminately to boost equally indiscriminate investment is clearly not the answer." THE WORLD BANK, *supra* note 8, at 32. The World Bank promised to provide extra funding to help Indonesian hospitals affected by the financial crisis in Asia in 1997–1998. *See Asian Melt-down Hits Indonesian Hospitals*, GUARDIAN WEEKLY (Manchester), 22 Feb. 1998, at 19.
56. *See* Lawrence Tshuma, *The Impact of IMF/World Bank Dictated Economic Structural Adjustment Programmes on Human Rights: Erosion of Empowerment Rights*, *in* THE INSTITUTIONALISATION OF HUMAN RIGHTS IN SOUTHERN AFRICA 219, 229 (Pearson Nherere & Marina d'Engelbronner-Kolff eds., 1993).

and human rights. People are not able to exercise their right to development because they are not afforded the opportunity to participate in decisions concerning their development. In addition, governments, as well as minorities within a state, are marginalized as power is transferred to bureaucrats and special interest groups. This impact is compounded with the increasing privatization of public functions and public goods. As a result, the ability of governments to protect human rights, even if guaranteed by a constitution and enforced by an independent judiciary, becomes more restricted.[57] Of course, many governments, even when they are in control of economic decision-making, do not take the interests or economic rights of their people into account. However, globalization can restrict the choices open to governments and people, particularly in the human rights area, and thus make it more difficult to attribute responsibility for violations of human rights.

Ironically, it appears that the World Bank has now become concerned about the decreasing role of the state. It now argues that:

> [a]n effective state is vital for the provision of goods and services—and the rules and institutions—that allow markets to flourish and people to lead healthier, happier lives. Without it, sustainable development, both economic and social, is impossible. . . . [T]he state is central to economic and social development, not as a direct provider of growth but as a partner, catalyst, and facilitator.[58]

According to the World Bank, "globalization is [only] a threat to weak or capriciously governed states"[59] which fail to "set the rules that underpin markets and permit them to function."[60] However, the World Bank's support of a role for the state in the decision-making process of economic globalization is problematic because the state's role is seen purely in terms of allowing markets to "flourish." The state's role in allocating resources, dealing with social goods, and protecting human rights are all sublimated to the "market."[61] Indeed, the World Bank's concern for the role of the state is

---

57. *See* Philip Alston, *The Myopia of Handmaidens: International Lawyers and Globalization*, 8 Eur. J. Int'l L. 435, 443 (1997).
58. The World Bank, *supra* note 8, at 1.
59. *Id.* at 11.
60. *Id.* at 34. Though the World Bank also considers that "a state that ignores the needs of large sections of the population in setting and implementing policy is not a capable state." *Id.* at 110.
61. This position could also be seen in the negotiation for a Multilateral Agreement on Investment which would enable transnational corporations to enforce limitations on governments actions, even if these limitations are contrary to the wishes of the people. *See* David Rowan, *Meet the New World Government*, Guardian Weekly (Manchester), 22 Feb. 1998, at 14. However, the International Labour Organization has recently adopted a declaration which states that "all Members . . . have an obligation . . . to respect, to promote and to realize, in good faith . . . the principles concerning the fundamental [labor] rights": *ILO Declaration on Fundamental Principles and Rights at Work* (June 1998) *available on* <http://www.ilo.org>.

purely self-interested; the World Bank itself has noted that "if the history of development assistance teaches anything . . . it is that external support can achieve little where the domestic will to reform is lacking."[62] In this context, such reform must be in accord with the World Bank's own economic philosophies, rather than in terms of the social welfare or the protection of human rights of the people in the State.

The third and final reason that globalization does not necessarily promote economic rights is because there are different types of economic growth. The United Nations Human Development Report 1995 dealt with the impact of damaging forms of economic growth.[63] It found that damaging economic growth includes:

> that which does not translate into jobs, that which is not matched by the spread of democracy, that which snuffs out separate cultural identities, that which despoils the environment, and growth where most of the benefits are seized by the rich.[64]

An example of damaging economic growth, where growth, as it were, is not growth, is where crops are planted for export to gain foreign exchange revenue while the people are deprived of their staple diet. This has happened in both Zimbabwe and Brazil.[65] This kind of damaging economic growth is contrary to the right of self-determination which provides that "[i]n no case may a people be deprived of its own means of subsistence."[66]

---

62. The World Bank, *supra* note 8, at 15.
63. United Nations Development Programme, Human Development Report 1995 (1995).
64. Larry Elliott, *Bridging the North-South Divide*, Guardian Weekly (Manchester), 11 Aug. 1996, at 14 (describing the conclusions of the UNDP Report). One form of damaging growth can be where governments attempt to attract foreign investment by "improving" the physical appearances of cities, such as the extermination of street children in Latin America and the perfunctory cleaning up of slum housing by eviction of low-income tenants in Atlanta prior to the 1996 Summer Olympics. *See id.*
65. *See* Sadasivam, *supra* note 52, at 641 n.36. Brazil has an estimated 86 million undernourished citizens who could be fed with only a 1.6 percent redistribution of Brazilian food production. *See* Joseph Collins, *World Hunger: A Scarcity of Food or a Scarcity of Democracy?, in* World Security: Challenges for a New Century 356, 358 (Michelle T. Klare & Daniel C. Thomas eds., 2d ed. 1994). There is also an impact on health. *See* Jonathan Mann, *Health and Human Rights*, 312 British Med. J. 924 (1996); Michael Kirby, *Human Rights and the HIV Paradox*, 348 Lancet 1217, 1218 (1996).
66. International Covenant on Economic, Social and Cultural Rights, *adopted* 16 Dec. 1966, G.A. Res. 2200 (XXI), U.N. GAOR, 21st Sess., Supp. No. 16, art. 1(2), U.N. Doc. A/6316 (1966), 993 U.N.T.S. 3 (*entered into force* 3 Jan. 1976) [hereinafter ICESCR]; ICCPR, *supra* note 36, art. 1(2). *See also* Christine Chinkin & Shelley Wright, *The Hunger Trap: Women, Food and Self-Determination*, 14 Mich J. Int'l L. 262 (1993) (calling for a different definition of "peoples" or "self"). "Food, shelter, clean water, a healthy environment, peace and a stable existence must be the first priorities in how we define or 'determine' the 'self' of both individuals and groups, instead of the present definitions, which are based on masculinist goals of political and economic aggrandizement and aggressive territoriality." *Id.* at 294.

Another kind of damaging economic growth in which the benefits of economic growth are seized by the rich was exemplified in South Africa during the apartheid regime. There, economic growth was for many years achieved through the exploitation of a large unskilled, insecure, dispossessed, and dependent work force consisting of oppressed blacks.[67] Thus globalization can have the effect of increasing economic inequality when the economic interests which are protected are those of the rich and economically powerful, who are usually the elite urban males.

Economic growth through globalization processes can even encourage human rights abuses beyond state borders by providing economic incentives for trade in goods injurious to humans, such as land mines and military weapons.[68] For example, in 1997, the South African arms manufacturer, Denel, sought to sell to Syria up to $640 million worth of updated weaponry for that country's fleet of T72 tanks. The deal eventually collapsed, partly because of strong criticism from the United States.[69] The South African government responded to the criticism by saying that South Africa was a sovereign state which would not determine its foreign policy with reference to the wishes of other States.[70] This reaction is ironic considering that the globalization of human rights concerns and the impact of the international legal order was integral to the improvement of human rights and the historic change of government in South Africa.

In sum, economic globalization can lead to improved conditions for those in developing states, but it can also encourage economic exploitation and oppression. Globalization may lead to apparent improvements in economic growth, but at a cost to the economic rights of many within a state. Indeed, "[t]he overwhelming thrust of the evidence would appear to support the claim that World Bank and IMF policies are violating human rights."[71] The influence of the economic philosophies of the globalized economic institutions is such that even the concepts of human rights can be affected. For example, the right to development is now partly defined on the

---

67. *See* Heribert Adam, *Cohesion and Coercion, in* The Elusive Search for Peace: South Africa, Israel and Northern Ireland 227 (Hermann Giliomee & Jannie Gagiano eds., 1990). "The danger for South Africa lies in the temptation to create the semblance of a formal democracy, with a universal franchise and veto powers for entrenched interests that leave the enormous economic inequality basically intact." *Id.* at 241.

68. It has been shown that, over the long-term, economic activity in the form of arms production does not contribute to overall economic growth. *See* William Felice, *Militarism and Human Rights,* 74 Int'l Aff. [London] 30 (1998).

69. *See* Arms Transfer Project of the Stockholm International Peace Research Institute (SIPRI), Frosunda, Sweden, available at <http://www.sipri.se> (as verified by the authors' correspondence with Siemon Wezeman of the Arms Transfer Project of SIPRI, Mar. 1999; copy on file with authors).

70. *See id. See also* Defense News Aug. 11–17, 1997, at 21.

71. Dohnal, *supra* note 35, at 82.

notion that "development" means industrialization, westernization, and economic growth.[72] Only a very few of the globalized economic institutions take human rights issues directly into account in their investment decisions, though this may be changing.[73] If human rights issues are not taken into account in these investment decisions, it is likely that human rights will become more endangered as a consequence of those decisions.

V. POLITICAL RIGHTS AND INTERNATIONAL INVESTMENT

There has been debate concerning the relationship between economic globalization and the protection of political rights, the strengthening of civil society and institution building, and the development of democracy. The World Bank has noted that "researchers have yet to reach a consensus on the precise relationship between growth and democracy: about one-fifth of the studies find a positive relationship, one-fifth a negative relationship, and the rest are inconclusive."[74] The main arguments supporting both a positive and a negative relationship will be canvassed here in turn.

It was argued by a former United Nations Secretary-General that there is a positive relationship between democracy and development:

> Democracy and development are linked in fundamental ways. They are linked because democracy provides the only long-term basis for managing competing ethnic, religious, and cultural interests in a way that minimizes the risk of violent internal conflict. They are linked because democracy is inherently attached to the question of governance, which has an impact on all aspects of development efforts. They are linked because democracy is a fundamental human right, the advancement of which is itself an important measure of development. They are linked because people's participation in the decision-making processes which affect their lives is a basic tenet of development.[75]

There is some research to support this argument. For example, Barro studied the economic development of 100 states between 1960 and 1990 and

---

72. *See* Hilary Charlesworth, *The Public/Private Distinction and the Right to Development in International Law*, 12 Austl. Y.B. Int'l L. 190, 196–97 (1992).
73. *See* David Forsythe, *The United Nations, Human Rights, and Development*, 19 Hum. Rts. Q. 334, 342 (1997) (noting that the treaty creating the European Bank for Reconstruction and Development provides that it must advance democratic development).
74. The World Bank, *supra* note 8, at 149. *See also* Michael Davis, *The Price of Rights: Constitutionalism and East Asian Economic Development*, 20 Hum. Rts. Q. 303 (1998).
75. *Report of the Secretary-General: An Agenda for Development—Development and International Economic Cooperation.* U.N. GAOR, 48th Sess., Agenda Item 91, ¶ 120, U.N. Doc. A/48/935 (1994).

compared it with their political development in terms of "more democracy."[76] His study revealed that

> increases in various measures of the standard of living tend to generate a gradual rise in democracy. In contrast, democracies that arise without prior economic development—sometimes because they are imposed by former colonial powers or international organizations—tend not to last. . . .[77] [I]n the worst dictatorships, an increase in political rights tends to increase growth and investment because the benefit from limitations on governmental power is the key matter. But in places that have already achieved a moderate amount of democracy, a further increase in political rights impairs growth and investment because the dominant effect comes from the intensified concern with income redistribution . . .[78] [and] countries at low levels of economic development typically do not sustain democracy. . . . Conversely, non-democratic places that experience substantial economic development . . . become more democratic.[79]

These conclusions offer powerful support for the view often espoused by the globalized economic institutions, that the priority of the international community should be to press for economic growth rather than the direct promotion of human rights.[80] As Barro himself noted: "one way to view the findings is that political freedom emerges as a sort of luxury good . . . [and] if economic freedom were to be established in a poor country, then growth would be encouraged, and the country would tend eventually to become more democratic on its own."[81]

One consequence of this view espoused by Barro is that, even if there is initially some inequality in terms of economic power or some initial decrease in human rights, those who gain economic power will (eventually) press for political power. In other words, changes towards political rights will come from those who have economic power rather than from the general population or human rights activists. The creation of more democratic political institutions in East Asia after rapid economic growth under authoritarian rule is used to support this view.[82] The conclusion drawn is

---

76. Robert J. Barro, Determinants of Economic Growth: A Cross-Country Empirical Study (1997). Barro sets out in detail his assumptions and measurement standards in his book.
77. *Id.* at 52.
78. *Id.* at 59.
79. *Id.* at 61. Support is also found in the fact that Tanzania, despite democratic elections since 1985, is ranked as the third poorest State in the world. *See Democracy Fails to Boost Tanzania Economy*, Guardian Weekly (Manchester), 4 Jan. 1998, at 3.
80. This view is often taken as human rights are seen as "political" while economic development is not. *See* Forsythe, *supra* note 73, at 339–42.
81. Robert Barro, *Democracy: A Recipe for Growth?*, Wall Street J. (Eur. ed.) 9–10 Dec. 1994.
82. *See Democracy on the March Across East Asia*, Guardian Weekly (Manchester), 11 Jan. 1998, at 15.

that "greater integration into the international community . . . enlarges the role of the private sector, promotes a stable legal environment, and restructures the state's relations with its citizens. International economic participation widens political participation."[83]

Another argument supporting a positive relationship between economic globalization and democracy suggests that globalized economic institutions, including transnational corporations, tend to demand that certain conditions exist in a state before they are willing to invest and that these conditions lead to the protection of political rights.[84] These investment conditions, sometimes called "democratic governance" requirements,[85] can include the acceptance of the rule of law, clear and transparent practices by government and local institutions, and international dispute resolution. Thus, it is argued, these investment conditions ensure that there is a democratic system, including judicial guarantees of human rights and political institutions.[86] The apparent links between setting these conditions and democracy are found in instruments such as the Charter of Paris, where "democracy has as its foundation respect for the human person and the rule of law."[87] Similarly, in the opinion of the Inter-American Court of Human Rights, judicial protection and political institutions are essential to the preservation of democracy and the rule of law.[88] The rule of law is crucial

83. Monshipouri, *supra* note 50, at 57–62. *See also* G. Sheridan, *Why We Lack the Weight to Heavy Asia*, Australian, 7 Aug. 1996, at 13. "[I]n today's global economy, it is almost inconceivable that you can have sustained economic growth without increasing the civic space people enjoy." *Id.*
84. *See* Forsythe, *supra* note 73, at 337–39.
85. *See id.* at 334. There is also some debate about whether democracies go to war. *See* I. Oren & J. Mays, *Democracies May Rarely Fight One Another but Developed Socialist States Rarely Fight At All*, 22 Alternatives: Social Transformation and Human Governance 493 (1997); K. Smits, *International Identity Construction and the Liberal Peace*, 47 Peace, Security and Global Change 49 (1995). It has also been argued that when a state "reaches a certain level of economic development, when it has a middle class big enough to support a McDonald's, it becomes a McDonald's country. And people in McDonald's countries don't like to fight wars. They like to wait in line for burgers." *Quoted in* James Langton, *Peace on Earth and Big Macs to All Men*, Daily Telegraph (London), 21 Dec. 1996. *See also* Clifford D. Shearing & Phillip C. Stenning, *Say Cheese!: The Disney Order that is not so Mickey Mouse*, Private Policing 317 (Clifford D. Shearing & Phillip C. Stenning eds., 1987).
86. *See* Monshipouri, *supra* note 50, at 57–62. The need for such an institutional system, including legislative, judicial, and administrative processes, in order to have effective remedies when rights are violated is set out in Article 2 of the International Covenant on Civil and Political Rights, *supra* note 36.
87. Charter of Paris for a New Europe, adopted by the Conference on Security and Co-operation in Europe at Paris, 21 Nov. 1991, *reprinted in* 30 I.L.M. 190, 193–94 (1991).
88. *See Judicial Guarantees in States of Emergency (Arts. 27(2), 25 and 8 of the American Convention on Human Rights)*, Advisory Opinion OC-9/87 of October 6, 1987, Inter-Am. Ct. H.R. (Ser. A) No. 9, ¶¶ 37–38 (1987), *reprinted in* 9 Hum. Rts. L.J. 204, 211 (1988).

because "in a society governed by law, the legal system can be a means for people to protect themselves from bureaucratic abuse, commercial exploitation, and official lawlessness which are generally the lot of the poor and powerless."[89]

The rule of law, at least in terms of the state providing a settled system of rules in order to allow markets to function,[90] is enhanced, either directly by agreements with globalized economic institutions on investment conditions or indirectly by states changing their systems in order to attract investment by these institutions.[91] With regard to direct changes, most investments by globalized economic institutions are governed by some contractual agreement or treaty. These are usually made subject to international law or international arbitration.[92] For example, an increasing number of states are parties to the Convention on the Settlement of Investment Disputes Between States and Nationals of Other States[93] which restricts the ability of states to change their national laws to the detriment of foreign investors. The controversial Multilateral Agreement on Investment (MAI) is a more recent example of a treaty which, if it becomes part of international law, will have a wide range of impacts on state sovereignty, economic conditions in member states, and possibly also on human rights.[94] Other

---

89. Geoffrey Budlender, *Lawyers and Poverty: Beyond Access to Justice*, in SECOND CARNEGIE INQUIRY INTO POVERTY AND DEVELOPMENT IN SOUTHERN AFRICA 7 (Carnegie Conference Paper No. 91, 1984).
90. *See* THE WORLD BANK, *supra* note 8, at 34.
91. *See* John Mukum Mbaku & Mwangi S. Kimenyi, *Democratization in Africa: The Continuing Struggle*, 32 COEXISTENCE 119 (1995). Mbaku and Kimenyi comment that:

> African countries must find other ways to attract foreign resources for growth and development [other than on the basis of Cold War allegiances]. Until appropriate policy reforms are implemented, foreign entrepreneurs are not likely to consider the continent as an attractive place for investment, especially when one considers emerging investment opportunities in Eastern Europe.

Id. It is also possible that changes to law and institutions can create a general local desire for compliance with laws particularly because such new laws are often drafted by people with some understanding of international human rights law.
92. *See generally* ALAN REDFERN & MARTIN HUNTER, LAW AND PRACTICE OF INTERNATIONAL COMMERCIAL ARBITRATION (2d ed. 1987). The World Bank sees these agreements as positive for states because "[c]ountries with weak domestic commitment mechanisms can strengthen their credibility by binding themselves to pay a penalty should they violate the agreement." THE WORLD BANK, *supra* note 8, at 101.
93. *See* Convention on the Settlement of Investment Disputes Between States and Nationals of Other States, *concluded at* Washington, 18 Mar. 1965 (*entered into force* 14 Oct. 1965), 575 U.N.T.S. 159, *reprinted in* 4 I.L.M. 532 (1965). This treaty sets up procedures for the settlement of investment disputes (and the International Centre for Settlement of Investment Disputes (ICSID)) and there are over 130 State parties to the Convention. *See* 14 NEWS FROM ICSID (1997).
94. The text of the Multilateral Agreement on Investment (MAI) is available on <http://www.oecd.org/daf/cmis/mai/negtext.htm> (visited 1 May 1999). A wide range of Organisation for Economic Co-operation and Development (OECD) papers about the MAI are available on the OECD's website <http://www.oecd.org>.

examples include the IMF agreements entered into with governments in East Asia as a consequence of the currency crisis in 1997 and 1998. These agreements contain strict requirements for the governments concerned to change their national financial institutions and investment laws and procedures.[95]

With regard to indirect effects, it is clear that decisions made about economic investment by the globalized economic institutions give considerable weight to political stability.[96] An example of international action linking economic globalization to democracy can be seen in the decision in 1992 by all of the major donor states to stop investment in Malawi until President Banda dealt with the gross breaches of human rights there.[97] This decision was undoubtedly a catalyst for the move to multi-party elections in Malawi.[98] Decisions such as these are used to support arguments that economic globalization, manifested in the use of the threat of non-investment or disinvestment, can lead to the creation or improvement of political institutions that are responsive to the demands of the people.

In contrast, there are arguments which find a negative relationship between economic globalization and political rights.[99] The record to date of the globalized economic institutions in using their investment to foster democracy has been poor.[100] This may be due in part to the pervasive distrust of outsiders by ruling elites,[101] as well as relatively weak "civil societies" and the fragility of many developing states.[102] Indeed, globaliza-

---

95. For Letters of Intent from states receiving IMF support, as well as their Memoranda of Economic and Financial Policies, see *Member Country Publications* (visited 1 May 1999) <http://www.imf.org/external/np/loi/mempub.htm>. For further details on the IMF's response to the Asian crisis, see *The IMF's Response to the Asian Crisis,* 17 Jan. 1999 (visited 1 May 1999) <http://www.imf.org/external/np/exr/facts/asia.htm>. *See also No Bargains for Korea in This Sale,* Guardian Weekly (Manchester), 11 Jan. 1998, at 12; Dave McIntyre, *IMF Leader Turns 007 to Save Asia Markets,* Australian, 31 Dec. 1997, at 26; Lincoln Wright, *IMF: New Imperialistic Force Threatening to Change the Face of Asia,* Canberra Times, 17 Jan. 1998, at C4.
96. *See* Chege, *supra* note 48, at 154. *See also* Michael Steketee, *Disney's Worldly Ambitions,* Australian, 14 Aug. 1996, at 15 (quoting Julian Disney that "even in many wealthy countries, government decisions as to whether they will devote resources to particular social welfare programs are often crucially affected by fears that international financiers will disapprove and directly or indirectly reduce the supply of international finance to that country.").
97. *See* Forsythe, *supra* note 73, at 346.
98. *See* Kevin Brampton, *Making Constitutions: Raising Public Awareness, in* Human Rights and the Making of Constitutions: Malawi, Kenya, Uganda 56, 57–62 (Joanna Lewis et al. eds., 1995).
99. *See* Shaw & Adibe, *supra* note 38, at 19.
100. *See id.*
101. *See* Barry Buzan, *People, States and Fear: The National Security Problem in the Third World, in* National Security in the Third World: The Management of Internal and External Threats 14 (Edward E. Azar & Chung-in Moon eds., 1988).
102. *See* Im, *supra* note 7.

tion, through the creation of international or regional trade and economic institutions, can lead directly to a feeling of loss of political power by groups within states.[103] Globalization also leads to the fostering of "tribalism and other revived or invented identities and traditions which abound in the wake of the uneven erosion of national identities, national economies, and national state policy capacity."[104] Such developments are consistent with Robertson's idea of globalization, including the process of "universalisation of particularism,"[105] where government is determined according to local narratives.

In addition, many of the funding conditions imposed by the globalized economic institutions, such as economic structural adjustment programs, require strong government action for smooth implementation. Authoritarian and military governments are favored by external investors as the best-suited to implement these policies successfully, thereby putting new democracies at risk.[106] Indeed, the World Bank's 1992 report on *Governance and Development*[107] "stressed management, accountability, rule of law, and information and transparency . . . [but] did not explicitly urge that governments be held accountable to their citizens through [democratic processes]."[108] As such, the World Bank's characterization of a credible legal system is solely market-focused. The legal system must provide legal rules and enforcement mechanisms which "establish and apply the rules of the game, lower transaction costs, increase commercial certainty, create incentives for efficiency, and control crime and corruption so that businesses can focus on productive activities."[109] There is no recognition of other reasons for law, including protection of human rights and maintenance of ordered, settled communities.

Indeed, the investment conditions imposed by the globalized economic institutions can lead to distortion of the energies and resources of governments. Even the instances of apparent links between investment and

---

103. Examples include the Scottish and the Chiapas. *See generally* Jorge A. Vargas, *NAFTA, the Chiapas Rebellion and the Emergence of Mexican Ethnic Law*, 25 CAL. W. INT'L L.J. 1 (1994); A. Macartney, *Autonomy in the British Isles*, 54 NORDISK TIDSSKRIFT FOR INT'L RET 10 (1984); Jack Brand, *Scotland and the Politics of Devolution: A Patchy Past, A Hazy Future*, 46 PARLIAMENTARY AFF. 38 (1993).

104. Cerny, *supra* note 7, at 619 (alteration in original).

105. ROBERTSON, *supra* note 5, at 102.

106. *See generally* JOHN CAVANAGH ET AL., BEYOND BRETTON WOODS: ALTERNATIVES TO THE GLOBAL ECONOMIC ORDER (1994); FIFTY YEARS AFTER BRETTON WOODS: THE NEW CHALLENGE OF EAST-WEST PARTNERSHIP FOR ECONOMIC PROGRESS (Miklós Szabó-Pelsöczi ed., 1996); THE IMF, THE WORLD BANK AND THE AFRICAN DEBT (Bade Onimode ed., 1989).

107. THE WORLD BANK, GOVERNANCE AND DEVELOPMENT (1992).

108. Forsythe, *supra* note 73, at 340.

109. THE WORLD BANK, WORLD DEVELOPMENT REPORT 1996: FROM PLAN TO MARKET 86 (1996). *See also* Ibrahim J. Wani, *The Rule of Law and Economic Development in Africa*, 1 E. AFR. J. PEACE & HUM. RTS. 52 (1993).

democracy, such as in Malawi, have been said to emerge from financial concern over repayment of loans and not from a broader interest in the establishment of democracy.[110] Similarly, a case study of the former Yugoslavia traced some of the causes of the conflict there to actions by the globalized economic institutions which stripped that state of many of its functions and led people to seek other sources of community.[111]

Despite these facts, it is still recognized that

> [i]n the new global order unleashed by the collapse of communism, Africans [and other developing States] will have little choice but to pull their own weight by meeting the most exacting standards in domestic governance and economic competitiveness.[112]

The implications from this quotation, as well as the Yugoslavian case study, are twofold. On the one hand, there is an encouraging move away from the use of developing states as places for political ideological conflict and military bases to an acknowledgment that economic decision-making requires consideration of human rights. On the other hand, the economic philosophies expounded in developed states rarely consider the cultural and social ramifications for developing states. In addition, under the pressure of the globalized economic institutions, governments in developing states often lack any effective sovereign power to make decisions to protect minorities or to preserve important cultural and social elements within communities.

It is only in the last few years that globalized economic institutions have begun to take into account non-economic factors such as human rights, environmental degradation, and cultural fragmentation in their investment decisions.[113] This may be due partly to broader human rights concerns and partly to economic considerations. For example, the World Bank's report on *Sub-Saharan Africa: From Crisis to Sustainable Growth*,[114] concluded that "unless these political conditions improved no economic strategy will succeed in reversing economic decline in Africa."[115]

While transnational corporations can have a powerful influence in reforming political conditions, this is only likely to occur where such reform is in the corporations' own interests. Transnational corporations are primarily subject to control by their major shareholders. Arguably, however, they

---

110. *See* Forsythe, *supra* note 73, at 347.
111. *See* Orford, *supra* note 50, at 457.
112. Chege, *supra* note 48, at 149. *See also* Bård-Anders Andreassen, *Democratisation and Human Rights Beyond Borders: On the Donor-Recipient Connection*, *in* THE INSTITUTIONALISATION OF HUMAN RIGHTS IN SOUTHERN AFRICA 195 (Pearson Nherere & Marina d'Engelbronner-Kolff eds., 1993).
113. *See supra* note 73 and accompanying text.
114. THE WORLD BANK, SUB-SAHARAN AFRICA: FROM CRISIS TO SUSTAINABLE GROWTH (1989).
115. Wani, *supra* note 109, at 52.

are subject to the power of the market in terms of the interests of consumers and can therefore be forced, for example, to consider human rights or environmental issues due to strong consumer boycotts.[116] However, this approach is not uniformly applicable; more heed tends to be taken of consumers in the developed states concerning actions in or near developed states close to corporate headquarters. Less attention is paid to consumers in developing states about activities in their distant states.[117] Nevertheless, this selective reaction is inconsistent with human rights because human rights are applicable worldwide and are not limited to matters that only affect consumer groups.

Further, transnational corporations can greatly assist the effectiveness of international sanctions, such as those previously in force against South Africa, which can lead to improved protection of human rights.[118] However, transnational corporations may also choose to ignore these international actions because they are beyond state control.[119] Thus, while opportunities for enhanced human rights protection can emerge from pressure on globalized economic institutions to take more account of human rights issues, so far this pressure (and the resultant impact) has been piecemeal and inconsistent.

Finally, many of the arguments claiming a positive relationship between economic globalization and political rights confuse democracy with human rights. The terms are not synonymous. Although public participation in the public institutions of the states is a right recognized in Article 25 of the International Covenant on Civil and Political Rights,[120] there is no generally accepted human "right to democracy."[121] Not only is the term "democracy" able to sustain many definitions,[122] but human rights are much more

---

116. *See* Debora L. Spar, *The Spotlight and the Bottom Line: How Multinationals Export Human Rights*, 77 FOREIGN AFF., March/April 1998, at 7. The withdrawals of Texaco, Levi Strauss, *inter alia*, from Burma are examples of this consumer pressure. *See id.* at 10.
117. *See* J. Shestack, *Sisyphus Endures: The International Human Rights NGO*, 24 N.Y.L. SCH. L. REV. 89 (1978).
118. *See* COMMONWEALTH COMMITTEE OF FOREIGN MINISTERS ON SOUTHERN AFRICA, SOUTH AFRICA: THE SANCTIONS REPORT (1989).
119. *See* JOINT STANDING COMMITTEE ON FOREIGN AFFAIRS, DEFENCE AND TRADE, PARLIAMENT OF THE COMMONWEALTH OF AUSTRALIA, REPORT NO. 67, HUMAN RIGHTS AND PROGRESS TOWARDS DEMOCRACY IN BURMA [MYANMAR] (1995).
120. ICCPR, *supra* note 36, art. 25.
121. Some jurists have sought to discern such a right. *See* Reginald Ezetah, *The Right to Democracy: A Qualitative Inquiry*, 22 BROOKLYN J. INT'L L. 495 (1997); W. Michael Reisman, *Humanitarian Intervention and Fledgling Democracies*, 18 FORDHAM INT'L L.J. 794 (1995).
122. *See generally* Christine Sylvester, *The White Paper Trailing*, *in* DISCOURSES OF DANGER & DREAD FRONTIERS: AUSTRALIAN DEFENCE AND SECURITY THINKING AFTER THE COLD WAR 134, 142 (Graeme Cheeseman & Robert Bruce eds., 1996); Susan Marks, *The European Convention on Human Rights and its Democratic Society*, 66 BRIT. Y.B. INT'L L. 209, 235–37 (1995); Orford, *supra* note 50, at 463; Im, *supra* note 7, at 290. *Cf.* Seita, *supra* note 6, at 5.

complex and diverse than simply being about democracy or civil and political rights.

Accordingly, it is possible to argue that there is a positive relationship between economic globalization and the protection of political rights. Certainly, the globalized economic institutions have been seeking to make the relationship a positive one by placing democratic governance conditions on investment and by taking some account of non-economic factors in their decision-making. However, the arguments that the relationship is a negative one are also strong. These arguments raise questions about the legitimacy of the democratic governance conditions and the seriousness with which human rights issues, and the nebulous concept of "democracy," are taken into account by both the global economic institutions and transnational corporations. It would appear that instead of creating order, the rule of law, and the protection of human rights, globalization can create conditions for disorder, authoritarian rule, and the disintegration of the state entity with consequent violations of human rights.

VI. CULTURAL RIGHTS AND GLOBAL COMMUNICATIONS

One of the sectors which has been an integral part of economic globalization is the communications industry. Not only has it become a global industry in and of itself, but also it has been a major factor in the globalization of other industries. The worldwide high-speed communications systems developed in recent years have propelled globalization. Information transmitted almost instantly by satellites and computer networks gives economic and political decision makers a worldwide and real-time view. The Internet particularly operates beyond any real state control and easily transcends territorial boundaries.[123]

As a result, information about human rights abuses is disseminated around the world much more quickly and easily, thereby reducing the effectiveness of state internal security regimes. Indeed, as early as 1976, the European Court of Human Rights recognized that "[f]reedom of expression [is] one of the essential foundations of" a democratic institution,[124] and that the communications industry, by providing information, is a vital part of the

123. *See* Reno v. ACLU, 117 S. Ct. 2329 (1997), where the US Supreme Court, by a majority of 7 to 2, held that an Act which sought to limit "obscene or indecent" communications over the Internet was unconstitutional as it was in breach of the right to freedom of speech in the United States Constitution. The Court did note the dramatic expansion of the Internet as a new market-place of ideas.

124. Handyside Case, *supra* note 32, at 23.

protection of human rights.[125] This globalized communications system can provide human rights groups with information, assistance, and support in their resistance to oppression. Human rights non-governmental organizations, such as Amnesty International, flourish in an information-rich environment. When people know about human rights and are aware of human rights abuses, they are more likely to seek to protect them. In addition, the globalized communications system reduces the ability of governments to hide their activities, including acts which violate human rights, from public scrutiny. This exposure can lead to changes in policy by the state concerned. In addition, information provided by the globalized communications industry can lead to international pressure on, or even action against, that state by other states.[126]

However, the difficulty that arises with the impact of the globalized communications industry on the protection of human rights is that the information that it provides is full of both noises and silences. The globalized communications industry often compresses complex issues and events into thirty second "sound bites" for the evening news. Most conflicts and human rights abuses are never reported by the globalized communications industry media, and even some that are, such as events in Liberia, Nagorno-Karabakh, Tajikstan, or Bougainville, frequently merit only thirty seconds. For example, through its focus on Somalia in 1993–1994, the globalized communications industry masked other areas in the world facing equally severe hardships caused by famine, violence, or civil war. In fact, former Secretary-General of the United Nations, Boutros Boutros-Ghali, referred to CNN as the sixteenth member of the Security Council.[127] He lamented that the "Member States never take action on a problem unless the media takes up the case."[128] Thus, in a globalized world, information and communications technology offer opportunities for better human rights protection. So much information is available so quickly that it is inconceivable that something could happen without someone being aware of it. But there are also dangers. So much information is available so quickly that

---

125. *See Autronic AG v. Switzerland,* 12 Eur. H.R. Rep. 485 (1990).
126. Examples are the reactions of some governments to the public response to the media coverage of the situation in Somalia and with Kurdish refugees in Northern Iraq after the Gulf War. *See* David Scheffer, *Use of Force after the Cold War: Panama, Iraq, and the New World Order, in* RIGHT V MIGHT: INTERNATIONAL LAW AND THE USE OF FORCE 146 (Louis Henkin et al. eds., 2d ed. 1991); Matthew Bryden, *Somalia: The Wages of Failure,* 94 CURRENT HIST. 145, 148 (1995); David Rieff, *The Humanitarian Trap,* 12 WORLD POL'Y J. 1, 4 (1996).
127. *See* Rieff, *supra* note 126, at 7. This remark has also been attributed to the US Secretary of State, and former US Ambassador to the United Nations, Madeleine Albright. *See* Nancy Gibbs, *Voice of America,* TIME (Australia), 16 Dec. 1996, at 45.
128. KEITH D. SUTER, GLOBAL AGENDA: ECONOMICS, THE ENVIRONMENT AND THE NATION-STATE 62 (1995).

events get lost in what Der Derian calls the "signal/noise ratio: information overload."[129]

An additional concern arises from the consequences of the information provided by the globalized communications industry. This is seen in the "CNN effect," where the globalized communications industry shapes what is seen and, in doing so, shapes the bases for the decision-making.[130] This has the potential for skewed decision-making because, in contrast to its apparently large influence, CNN is small in size and, therefore, may be unable to cover world events adequately. For example, in 1997, CNN had 23 foreign bureau and 50 overseas journalists.[131] The three traditional wire services each had between four and seven times the number of bureaux and between 10 and 20 times as many overseas journalists.[132] Decisions based on CNN coverage, as many are, including those made during the Gulf War, may be made on insufficient, or insufficiently objective, information.[133] In addition, certain information may be given greater priority than others for the personal business purposes of media owners. This is of increasing concern in an era when control of the globalized communications industry is held by a few groups, who are largely based in the developed States.[134] As Alleyne has commented:

> Because politics is about power, we say that the global flow of news is political: it reflects and determines the international configuration of power. . . . In the case of global news flows, therefore, those with power are those who can determine the very definition of news. Power also rests with those whose voices and perspectives are heard the most.[135]

---

129. DER DERIAN, *supra* note 12, at 141–69.
130. Bryden, *supra* note 126, at 148. While CNN is the focus here, the reality is that there are other major players in the globalized communications industry. They include the five news agencies: Associated Press (US based), United Press International (US based), Agence France-Presse (French based), Reuters (UK based) and ITAR-TASS (Russian based) as well as the global television networks such as CNN and the BBC. *See* MARK D. ALLEYNE, INTERNATIONAL POWER AND INTERNATIONAL COMMUNICATION (1995). CNN's influence does outrank its size, however. *See* Claude Moisy, *Myths of the Global Information Village*, 107 FOREIGN POL'Y 78, 80 (1997).
131. *See id.*
132. *Id.* In 1997, CNN had 50 foreign correspondents working in 23 foreign bureaux. Meanwhile, AP had 520 foreign correspondents in 93 bureaux, Reuters had 1040 in 139 bureaux, and AFP had 1040 in 176 bureaux. *Id.*
133. The impacts of globalization can themselves be based on perceptions rather than based on real information. *See* Paul Kelly, *IMF Tightens the Screws on Suharto*, AUSTRALIAN, 11 Mar. 1998.
134. *See generally* ALI MOHAMMADI, INTERNATIONAL COMMUNICATIONS AND GLOBALIZATION: A CRITICAL INTRODUCTION (1997); HAMID MOWLANA, GLOBAL COMMUNICATION IN TRANSITION: THE END OF DIVERSITY? (1996); EDWARD S. HERMAN, THE GLOBAL MEDIA: THE NEW MISSIONARIES OF CORPORATE CAPITALISM (1997); CEES J. HAMELINK, THE POLITICS OF WORLD COMMUNICATION: A HUMAN RIGHTS PERSPECTIVE (1994).
135. ALLEYNE, *supra* note 130, at 67–69.

Alleyne's comment applies to all those who control communications, both the globalized communications industry and governments. Governments can and do regulate and control communications, as seen during apartheid South Africa:

> the South African public [was] presented with a one-sided picture of the international community by politicians and the media and, inevitably, this same perspective [was] presented by teachers in schools and other educational institutions. Public opinion [was] not, therefore, equipped to question government action in the international arena, with the result that it serve[d] as no restraining force on violations of international law.[136]

The extent to which governments can continue to regulate communications, and hence maintain sovereignty, within their states may depend upon who gets access to information technology. The speed of developments in communications technology and the expense involved means that many in developed states and most in developing states stand in very real danger of missing most of the advantages of global communications technology. However, the impact on the human rights of those in developing states by the globalized communications industry controlled from developed states may already have been felt. It has been argued that

> [u]nder conditions of very scarce resources [as in many developing States], the emulation of the socio-cultural systems and especially the consumption patterns of [developed States] means first of all that the provision of basic foodstuffs, health services, clothing, housing, drinking water, education, reliable transportation and the like is neglected. It furthermore means that production processes tend to be utilised which actually may increase unemployment and underemployment; and that, in fact, resources are wasted in products subject to planned obsolescence. Moreover, to the extent that the satisfaction of foreign-oriented consumption wants requires inputs from abroad, continuing dependence on [developed] countries and their institutions (especially transnational enterprises) that can provide these inputs remains almost unavoidable.[137]

This view indicates not only the possible consequences on the protection of human rights of a globalized communications industry, but also the way in which industry tends to offer a particular economic and political philosophy, where the primacy of the markets and of certain civil and political rights

---

136. John Dugard, *The Conflict Between International Law and South African Law: Another Divisive Factor in South African Society*, S. Afr. J. Hum. Rts. 1, 26 (1986). Similarly, the Malawi government under President Banda controlled and restricted radio communication and facsimile machines and did not allow television in Malawi. *See* Africa Watch, Where Silence Rules: The Suppression of Dissent in Malawi (1990).

137. Karl P. Sauvant, *From Economic to Socio-Cultural Emancipation: The Historical Context of the New International Economic Order and the New International Socio-Cultural Order*, 3 Third World Q. 48, 58–59 (1981).

(such as the rights of freedom of speech, fair trial, and political participation) are constantly propounded to the detriment of economic rights.

One particular impact of the globalized communication industry is on the protection of cultural rights, especially of minorities.[138] Some cultures are brought to life by this industry by being recorded and transmitted on the international communications network, albeit usually from the perspective of the developed state.[139] A successful transnational corporation must take some account of the local culture, and many cultures may be more tenacious and adaptable over time than had been thought.[140] Furthermore, global communications can enable cross-fertilization of ideas which can nurture and support groups working in apparent isolation in their own state.[141]

However, there is the risk that the diverse voices of women, indigenous groups, refugees, and ethnic minorities may be silenced. A type of homogenized, universal, Americanized culture aided by the globalized communication industry, as seen in the opening quotation to this article, may develop.[142] The extent to which this has already occurred is tabulated in the respected magazine, *The Economist*, which, for more than a decade, has produced a "Big Mac Index" in which the price of a Big Mac produced by McDonald's is used, with an increasing degree of seriousness, as an international currency benchmark.[143] The index uses data from the vast

---

138. *See* ICCPR, *supra* note 36, art. 27. Article 27 protects the rights of ethnic, religious, and lingusitic minorities within a state. *Id.*

139. The term "culture" is problematic, particularly for questions about whose culture is being invoked, what is the status of the interpreter, in whose name the argument is being advanced, and who the primary beneficiaries are. *See* Arati Rao, *The Politics of Gender and Culture in International Human Rights Discourse, in* WOMEN'S RIGHTS, HUMAN RIGHTS 167, 174 (Andrea Wolper & Julie Peters eds., 1995).

140. *See* Gwynne Dyer, *World's "Little Languages" Speak Up*, CANBERRA TIMES, 11 Oct. 1997, at C4 (showing that "there is not a shred of evidence to show that English threatens the position of other languages in their own home market.").

141. For example, the Woman and Law in Southern Africa research project has been assisted by communications in uncovering common problems such as patriarchal interpretation of laws and customs. *See generally* ALICE K. ARMSTRONG, STRUGGLING OVER SCARCE RESOURCES: WOMEN AND MAINTENANCE IN SOUTHERN AFRICA (1992).

142. For example, ROBERT J. FOSTER, NATION MAKING: EMERGENT IDENTITIES IN POSTCOLONIAL MELANESIA 151–81 (Robert J. Foster ed., 1996) has concluded that certain fragments of a national culture contained in individual national advertisements are transferred to the consumer. The consumer then becomes part of an imaginary national community of consumers thereby creating a sense of common, national identity and citizenship. This argument could be transposed to the international level as in the opening quotation about McDonald's. Worryingly, some writers have even suggested that promoting American cultural values as a universal norm is appropriate. *See* Seita, *supra* note 6, at 431–33. David Rothkopf also advocates "Americanizing" the world. He illustrates his argument with a picture of a McDonald's restaurant in China, captioned "unveiling a new global culture." David Rothkopf, *In Praise of Cultural Imperialism?*, 107 FOREIGN POL'Y 38, 46 (1997).

143. *See, e.g.*, *Big MacCurrencies*, ECONOMIST (London), 12 Apr. 1997, at 71.

array of states in which McDonald's foods is sold and is based on the notion of "purchasing power parity" by which an American dollar should buy the same amount of goods in all states. The existence of this index shows the depth of the impact of globalization throughout the world, including the extent to which cultures are subject to external pressures to change.

The globalized communications industry enables globalization and propounds certain market-based philosophies shared by the globalized economic institutions and transnational corporations. It offers opportunities for the protection of human rights through its ability to provide information. However, globalization of the communications industry also presents dangers because its information is not always reliable and it may be silent on many important issues.

VII. CONCLUSIONS

Economic globalization does have an impact on the protection of human rights. It simultaneously creates opportunities and presents challenges for the international legal protection of human rights. While there are understandable concerns about both economic globalization and the international legal protection of human rights in terms of their philosophical bases, both are part of the process of globalization in which political, economic, social, civil, and cultural relationships are not restricted to territorial boundaries and are not solely within the control of any one state. As a result, globalization and the international legal order are opportunities to end the absolute sovereignty of the state,[144] and, hence, to further the realization that how a state deals with those within its territory is no longer a matter exclusively within the domestic jurisdiction of a state. It is now a matter of legitimate international concern.[145] In fact, "[n]o modern state can now turn back the rising tide of expectations among the dispossessed within its boundaries, nor demands for free movement and expression: for these are externally triggered, not necessarily by deliberate pressure but simply by communications and involuntary example."[146]

Nevertheless, international human rights law, caught within its framework of state responsibility for human rights violations, is unable to deal fully with the changes to state sovereignty accelerated by the process of globalization. Where the violator of human rights law is not a state or its agent but is, for example, a globalized economic institution or a transnational

144. *See* Agenda for Peace, *supra* note 2, ¶ 17.
145. *See* Vienna Declaration, *supra* note 21, Part I, ¶ 4.
146. Bernard Crick, *The High Price of Peace, in* THE ELUSIVE SEARCH FOR PEACE: SOUTH AFRICA, ISRAEL AND NORTHERN IRELAND 261, 270 (Hermann Giliomee & Jannie Gagiano eds., 1990).

corporation, international human rights law finds it difficult to provide any redress to the victim. In such cases, international human rights law focuses on the responsibility of a state to adopt constitutional, legislative, judicial, administrative, and other measures to ensure that human rights within its territory are protected, no matter who the perpetrator may be.[147] However, this approach tends to be ineffective where a state is unwilling or unable to take these measures due to the possible effect on investment by globalized economic institutions. Therefore, international human rights law needs to take the opportunities presented by globalization to develop a more flexible framework within which responsibility for human rights violations is not state-based; states must provide appropriate mechanisms for all individuals, groups, and others to have standing to bring claims for any violation of human rights.[148]

The other major opportunity offered by economic globalization for the protection of human rights emerges from the decision-making processes of the globalized economic institutions. As has been indicated, human rights issues are now occasionally taken into account by these institutions. This is occurring for a variety of reasons, including perceptions of increased likelihood of returns on investment, fear of consumer boycotts, pressure from non-governmental organizations, and, possibly, concern for the rights of human beings. Furthermore, a relationship between human rights and economic growth, development, and political institutions is being gradually recognized, so that these issues are no longer seen as separate or discrete from one another.

However, pressure still needs to be exerted to ensure that the globalized economic institutions do take international human rights law explicitly into account in all stages of their decision-making.[149] Decision-making is still primarily driven by economic factors. As has been shown, there are some grounds for arguing that economic factors can improve human rights

---

147. *See* ICCPR, *supra* note 36, art. 2.

148. *See* Robert McCorquodale, *Human Rights and Self-Determination, in* THE NEW WORLD ORDER: SOVEREIGNTY, HUMAN RIGHTS AND THE SELF-DETERMINATION OF PEOPLES 9, 25 (Mortimer Sellers ed., 1996). A human rights

> approach affords flexibility in finding solutions for protecting that right and resolving conflicts without dictating one solution. It could even comprehend flexibility in sovereignty—for example, by giving separate British and Irish nationalities to inhabitants of Northern Ireland as a means of protecting the right of self-determination in that situation.

Id.

149. *See* MICHAEL SINGER, THE FUTURE OF INTERNATIONAL HUMAN RIGHTS LAW 12 (International Rule of Law Ctr. Occasional Papers, 2d ser., No. 2, 1997). Some have argued that there is a need to create new international economic institutions "to lend structure and direction to the global marketplace." Richard N. Haass & Robert E. Litan, *Globalization and Its Discontents: Navigating the Dangers of a Tangled World,* 77 FOREIGN AFF., May/June 1998, at 2, 4.

protection. However, because economic globalization is generated by a philosophy in which markets must be allowed to flourish while states are relegated to the role of assisting this flourishing, any benefits for human rights protection tend to be incidental and fragmentary. The globalized communications industry constantly restates these philosophies. Accordingly, as has been indicated, the dangers of economic globalization for human rights can outweigh these incidental benefits. This is made clear in a report by the United Nations Secretary-General:

> Development strategies which have been oriented merely towards economic growth and financial considerations have failed to a large extent to achieve social justice; human rights have been infringed, directly and through the depersonalization of social relations, the breakdown of families and communities, and of social and economic life.[150]

Furthermore, there is the possibility of the fragmentation of states. This fragmentation is fostered by shifting the decision-making processes away from governments and people to globalized economic institutions and transnational corporations which have a limited interest in the social and cultural welfare or the human rights of people in developing states.

A danger of economic globalization is its impact on the concepts and application of human rights. An example of this was seen in the right to development where only certain types of development, such as the construction of transportation infrastructures, have been included within the concept of this right.[151] Another example is the dominance of globalization's focus on certain rights (civil and political) to the virtual exclusion of other rights.[152] But the greater danger is that the values of the international community, embodied in the international legal order and created to protect human rights, are being challenged by the values of the global economic free market. As Alston observes:

> In the world of globalization, a strong reaction against gender and other forms of discrimination, the suppression of trade unions, or the denial of primary education or health care, can often require not only showing that the relevant practices run counter to human rights standards but also a demonstration that they are offensive to the imperatives of economic efficiency and the functioning of the free market. . . . In some respects the burden of proof has shifted—in

---

150. *Question of the Realization of the Right to Development: Global Consultation on the Realization of the Right to Development as a Human Right, Report Prepared by the Secretary-General Pursuant to Commission on Human Right Resolution 1989/45*, U.N. ESCOR, Comm'n on Hum. Rts., 46th Sess., Agenda Item 8, ¶ 153, U.N. Doc. E/CN.4/1990/9/Rev.1 (1990).
151. *See supra* note 72 and accompanying text.
152. *See supra* notes 118–20 and accompanying text.

> order to be validated, a purported human right must justify its contribution to a broader, market-based 'vision' of a good society.[153]

It is these challenges to the values established by international human rights law that must be countered if the human rights of all are to be protected. These values need to be constantly asserted and given meaning because, as Eleanor Roosevelt said:

> Where after all, do universal human rights begin? In small places, close to home—so close and so small that they cannot be seen on any map of the world. Yet they are the world of the individual person: the neighbourhood he lives in; the school or college he attends; the factory, farms or office where he works. Such are the places where every man, woman, or child seeks equal justice, equal opportunity, equal dignity without discrimination. Unless these rights have meaning there, they have little meaning anywhere.[154]

There are a number of opportunities for human rights to be asserted within the current international community. This includes advocating for the inclusion of human rights in international treaties such as the Multilateral Agreement on Investment (MAI) and the WTO;[155] demanding that human rights be considered in the making of foreign policy and in the IMF's policy of "good governance"; and insisting that the activities of transnational corporations are consistent with international human rights law. It is vital that those who seek to protect human rights, particularly through the international legal system, are aware of the opportunities and dangers of globalization for the protection of human rights. Only then can they seek to ensure that the dangers are diminished and the opportunities are taken.

---

153. Alston, *supra* note 57, at 442.
154. Celina Romany, *State Responsibility Goes Private: A Feminist Critique of the Public/Private Distinction in International Human Rights Law*, *in* Human Rights of Women: National and International Perspectives 90 (Rebecca Cook ed., 1994) (quoting Eleanor Roosevelt).
155. *See supra* note 94; Marrakesh Agreement Establishing the World Trade Organization, *opened for* signature 15 Apr. 1994 (*entered into force* 1 Jan. 1995), *reprinted in* 33 I.L.M. 1125, 1144 (1994).

Name Index